# Dating Shakespeare's Plays

# A CATALOGVE
of the ſeuerall Comedies, Hiſtories, and Tragedies contained in this Volume.

## COMEDIES.

*The Tempeſt.* — Folio 1.
*The two Gentlemen of Verona.* — 20
*The Merry Wiues of Windſor.* — 38
*Meaſure for Meaſure.* — 61
*The Comedy of Errours.* — 85
*Much adoo about Nothing.* — 101
*Loues Labour loſt.* — 122
*Midſommer Nights Dreame.* — 145
*The Merchant of Venice.* — 163
*As you Like it.* — 185
*The Taming of the Shrew.* — 208
*All is well, that Ends well.* — 230
*Twelfe-Night, or what you will.* — 255
*The Winters Tale.* — 304

## HISTORIES.

*The Life and Death of King John.* — Fol. 1.
*The Life & death of Richard the ſecond.* — 23
*The Firſt part of King Henry the fourth.* — 46
*The Second part of K. Henry the fourth.* — 74
*The Life of King Henry the Fift.* — 69
*The Firſt part of King Henry the Sixt.* — 96
*The Second part of King Hen. the Sixt.* — 120
*The Third part of King Henry the Sixt.* — 147
*The Life & Death of Richard the Third.* — 173
*The Life of King Henry the Eight.* — 205

## TRAGEDIES.

*The Tragedy of Coriolanus.* — Fol. 1.
*Titus Andronicus.* — 31
*Romeo and Juliet.* — 53
*Timon of Athens.* — 80
*The Life and death of Julius Ceſar.* — 109
*The Tragedy of Macbeth.* — 131
*The Tragedy of Hamlet.* — 152
*King Lear.* — 283
*Othello, the Moore of Venice.* — 310
*Anthony and Cleopater.* — 346
*Cymbeline King of Britaine.* — 369

1. Catalogue page from the First Folio, 1623.

# Dating Shakespeare's Plays:

## A Critical Review of the Evidence

edited by

Kevin Gilvary

Also published by Parapress:
*Great Oxford: Essays on the Life and Works of Edward de Vere, 17th Earl of Oxford,* ed. Richard Malim, 2004
*Thirty-Odd Feet Below Belgium, An Affair of Letters in the Great War, 1915–1916,* ed. Arthur Stockwin, 2005
*The Knocknobbler* by Bernard Cartwright, 2007



ISBN: 978-1-898594-86-4

First published in the UK by
PARAPRESS
9 Frant Road
Tunbridge Wells
Kent TN2 5SD
www.parapress.co.uk



Typeset in Garamond by Helm Information
amandahelm@helm-information.co.uk
www.helm-information.co.uk

Jacket design by Helm Information

Print management by Sutherland Eve Production
guyeve@theeves.fsnet.co.uk

Jacket Illustration: Mark Rylance as Richard II:
photograph by John Tramper, 2003.
Image provided by The Shakespeare Globe Trust.

Printed and bound in Great Britain by
Jellyfish Solutions Ltd, Swanmore, Hampshire.
www.jellyfishsolutions.co.uk

# Contents

The TRAGEDIES



Other Plays

# List of Illustrations

# Acknowledgements

It has been challenge, outweighed by the consequent pleasure, to take over the editing of these efforts at establishing the date range of Shakespeare's plays. I would like to express gratitude to all the contributors listed below, with special appreciation to:

**Arthur Challoner**, who first issued the challenge to members of the De Vere Society to investigate whether Shakespeare must have inevitably written *The Tempest* in 1610–11 and *Macbeth* in 1606. Arthur felt that these were possible dates among a much wider range of possibilities.

**Christopher Dams**, who invited individual members each to examine a play afresh regarding its date of composition. He laid down the strict guidelines which have been followed in this work and insisted on clear distinctions between contemporary records, inferences from these records and outright speculation.

**Philip Johnson**, who passed on many valuable insights from his editing of the comedies before his untimely death in August 2007.

**Eddi Jolly**, who in reading every chapter, has made many valuable suggestions in addition to her own excellent contributions.

**Aliyah Norrish**, who painstakingly read each chapter and contributed numerous helpful ideas.

**Elizabeth Imlay,** for her thorough copy-editing.

**Dr William Leahy,** for his critical encouragement throughout, and the staff at Brunel University Library for their unfailing help.

Each contributor retains the responsibility for the evaluations presented in each chapter. As editor, I remain responsible for any factual error which may have escaped my attention.

**The De Vere Society** (registered charity No. 297855) has been formed as a result of interest in the works of Shakespeare and the question of their authorship. Members review critically evidence for authorship and are interested in all aspects of composition, performance and publication, and the plays' possible audience. Information about the De Vere Society and its activities can be found on its website, www.deveresociety.co.uk and new members are always welcome

Kevin Gilvary,
Brunel University

# List of Contributors

**Barbara Burris** is an independent American researcher, who shared many of her ideas on the dating of *The Merry Wives of Windsor.*

**Arthur M. Challinor** taught at two universities, including a spell as head of department, and later worked as a government adviser. His various writings include a history of the authorship controversy since 1900. He has suggested many ideas on the dating of *The Tempest.*

**Derran Charlton** has devoted much time to investigating Shakespearean authorship. He has researched many archives and other primary sources at various locations. He contributed to the chapters on *Love's Labour's Lost* and *Titus Andronicus.*

**Robert Detobel** is an independent researcher, based in Germany, who made important contributions about the dating of *Cymbeline.*

**Alisatir Everitt,** an independent researcher based in London, contributed the section on *King Lear.*

**Kevin Gilvary** gained a BA and an MA in Classics from the University of Southampton. He has taught in Vancouver, Canada, in Lima, Peru, and in Hampshire. He is a research student at Brunel University and has contributed chapters in all sections.

**Charlotte ('Sally') Hazelton** combines interests in literature (especially drama) with psychology, making a special study of Freud's Oxfordian view of Shakespeare. She has recently retired from practising psychotherapy in London. She wrote the sections on *The Comedy of Errors* and *Macbeth.*

**Stephanie Hopkins Hughes** was for ten years the editor of *The Oxfordian*, an annual journal of Elizabethan research published by the Shakespeare Oxford Society. She contributed the section on *The Taming of the Shrew.*

**Ramón Jiménez** has published many articles about Shakespearean Authorship. He contributed the chapter on *The Famous Victories of Henry V.*

**Philip Johnson** graduated at London University's Kings College, where his lecturers included Professor Geoffrey Bullough. Before he died in 2007, he had begun to edit the comedies, contributing chapters on *Measure for Measure* and *Much Ado About Nothing.*

**Eddi Jolly** graduated in English Literature at Southampton University. She was a lecturer in English Literature, English Language and Critical Thinking. Her interests have resulted in papers on Burghley's library and *Hamlet.* She is a research student at Brunel University.

**Richard Malim** was a solicitor for many years at a law firm in Poole, Dorset. Since his retirement, he has spent much time researching the Authorship Question. He edited a collection of essays under the title *Great Oxford* (2004).

**Alex McNeil** is a graduate of Yale University and Boston Law School. He has served as a court administrator of the Massachusetts Appeals Court since 1974. An Oxfordian since 1992, he is the author of a reference book on American television: *Total Television: a comprehensive guide to programming*, four editions of which have been published by Penguin Books (USA) since 1980.

**Dott. Noemi Magri** was born in Mantova, Italy, where she still lives. A keen interest in Shakespearean authorship dates back to her school years. Her doctoral thesis involved a new critical edition of Sir Philip Sidney's *Astrophel and Stella* on the basis of the first four editions of his sonnets. She has worked in a legal office, as a teacher and teacher trainer, has published prize-winning short stories, and carried out invaluable research in Italy on the Italian plays.

**Joe Peel** is an independent American scholar who contributed the section on *The Merchant of Venice.*

**Marion Peel** is an English Literature graduate and was an English teacher for twenty years. Her Masters degree is in English in education. She contributed to the section on *Twelfth Night.*

**Dr John Rollett**, a physicist by training, has brought his scientific acumen to authorship questions and is sceptical about Oxfordian claims. He contributed the article on *Antony and Cleopatra.*

**Dr Roger Stritmatter** has made a most important contribution to the Oxfordian case with his doctoral dissertation on 'The Marginalia of Edward de Vere's Geneva Bible: Providential Discovery, Literary Reasoning and Historical Consequence'. He has had many articles published on the dating of Shakespeare's plays, including recently in the *Review of English Studies* and in *Critical Survey* on *The Tempest.* He contributed many ideas to the chapter on *A Midsummer Night's Dream.*

**Lee Tudor Pole** is a history and English graduate and an independent researcher, who contributed ideas to the dating of *Henry VIII.*

# Introduction

# The Dating of Shakespeare's Plays

Kevin Gilvary

## When did Shakespeare write his plays?

There is, apparently, a scholarly consensus about the order in which Shakespeare composed his plays and the dates when they were written. This 'scholarly consensus' or 'accepted orthodoxy' can be found in almost every edition of the Complete Works and in almost every biography.

Yet, close comparison of these dates shows some surprising discrepancies: *King John* has been placed by different scholars in every year of the decade up to 1598; *Love's Labour's Lost* is sometimes taken to be the playwright's earliest attempt at comedy, and sometimes part of his mature period, while *Hamlet* can be dated to 1602 only by ignoring allusions which could date it as early as 1589.

When preparing to date the plays, every commentator announces that the primary evidence is very fragmentary and that any date is conjectural and reliant on speculation. Such announcements, however, are soon forgotten as almost every scholar in turn puts forward a precise date for a play – not so much because there is evidence to support it, merely because there is no evidence to contradict the date proposed.

*The Dating of Shakespeare's Plays* is quite different from previous efforts in this field: in this work, the various contributors have challenged the scholarly consensus by simply identifying the *range* of dates for each play rather than arguing for a particular date. In considering Oxfordian dates, the intention is not to prove that the Earl of Oxford may or may not have written the works: the purpose is to consider whether alternative, often earlier, dates for the plays are tenable.

The findings are necessarily inconclusive: as scholar after scholar has said, the evidence to fix a precise date on any particular play is lacking. What follows is a methodical assessment of the range of possible dates for each of the thirty-six plays in the First Folio and for four other plays which have been attributed to Shakespeare.

## What do we mean by the 'date' of a play?

The 'date' of a play can refer to three possible events: when it was composed, when it was first performed or when it was first published. It is important to make careful distinction within the evidence proposed as to which type of date is indicated. Historically, the tendency among scholars has been to assume that the playwright produced one definitive or archetypal version of each play which was then handed over to the acting companies and eventually found its way to publication, either in a quarto or later in the collection of works known as the First Folio. More recently, there has been acceptance that the playwright may have produced different versions of a play, e.g. *King Lear*, which would all therefore have authorial status.[1] The most recent editors of *Hamlet* for the Arden series accept that the three versions of this play might also have all originated from the playwright himself. So, by the 'date' of a play we could be referring to nine different possibilities.[2]

## Date of Composition

This would be the most important date for many scholars, but there is no evidence for the date of composition of any play by Shakespeare. Any such date offered rests on inferences and arguments that are often dependent on belief and speculation.

## Date of First Performance

The date of first performance would also be very important for scholars but there is no evidence to date any première of any play by Shakespeare. The theatrical records are very fragmentary and only two performances *might* have been recorded as premières: Henslowe's *Diary* applies the prefix "ne" to "harey the vi" on 3 March 1592 (but it is not clear which part) and to *Titus Andronicus* on 23 January 1594. The note "ne" might mean 'newly composed', but could also mean 'newly acquired' or even 'newly revised'.[3]

Some plays are not mentioned in performance (e.g. *Antony and Cleopatra* and *Coriolanus*); for those plays which are mentioned, it is quite common for orthodox scholars to make two assumptions:

(a) that the earliest mentioned performance is the *first* staging, e.g. *Cymbeline* is first mentioned by Forman in 1611, who is taken to have seen one of its first performances;

(b) that the first performance must have occurred soon after composition. Various questions arise: firstly, did Forman witness the first *ever* performance of *Cymbeline* or of *The Winter's Tale*? Secondly, were these plays newly composed? It is usual to assume the answer is 'yes' to both these questions but other possibilities exist. Forman himself notes a performance of *Macbeth* (which he dates 1610 but is usually taken to refer to 1611). This is the earliest reference to the Scottish play, yet no editor proposes that *Macbeth* was newly composed when Forman saw it; most editors opt for a date in 1606 but some have accepted that it could have been earlier (or later).

## Date of First Publication

The date of first publication is normally unproblematic and often rests on a combination of an entry in the Stationers' Register with the bibliographic information on the title page.

However, it is quite common for scholars to assume that publication in quarto followed shortly after composition, e.g. that *Richard II* was composed shortly before its registration in 1597. This assumption is again open to doubt: several plays listed by Meres in 1598 (e.g. *The Two Gentlemen of Verona*) were not published for another 25 years.[4]

## Previous Attempts to Date Shakespeare's Plays

There have been many attempts to establish a chronology of the plays of Shakespeare and four are outlined here as having great influence.[5]

## Edmond Malone (1778)

The earliest attempt to sequence and date the plays of Shakespeare occurred soon after David Garrick had organised the Stratford Jubilee in 1769. In 1778, Edmond Malone (1741–1812) published his essay, *An Attempt to Ascertain the Order in which the Plays of Shakespeare Were Written.* It was a noble undertaking and Malone engaged many great minds, including Thomas Tyrwhitt (1730–1786) and George Steevens (1736–1800), in his search for contemporary evidence. Much of the material known today (e.g. The Stationers' Register, title pages to quartos, and the work of Meres) became available to Malone during the course of his investigations but he concluded his essay with the insight that, to some, his project would appear "a tedious and barren speculation".

Malone proposed various dates, most of which are accepted today; a few have been discarded but remain tenable. He identifies *The Winter's Tale* with the entry in the Stationers' Register for *A Winter night's Pastime* in 1594. He dates *Hamlet* to 1596 on the basis of Harvey's marginalia in a copy of Speght's

Chaucer. (As this edition is now dated to 1598, Harvey's written comments should be placed between 1598 and 1601). Malone subsequently changed his mind, placing *Hamlet* later in the sequence, and suggesting that references in the works of Nashe and others were to a lost play by another playwright. He dated *Cymbeline* to 1604 and placed *Henry VIII* in 1601 despite knowledge of Henry Wooton's letter (1613), in which it is written: "The King's players had a new play, called *All is True*, representing some principal pieces of the reign of Henry VIII". Unlike later commentators, Malone is aware that "new" might have been intended in different ways: as 'newly composed', as 'new to the Company' or perhaps as 'new to the general public': previously the play might have been performed at court or in a private house.

Schoenbaum (169) was very dismissive of Malone's efforts:

> When he can find no evidence, [Malone] throws up his hands in despair and assigns a play to a year simply because that year would otherwise be blank and Shakespeare must have been continuously employed. Such is the case with *Coriolanus* (1609) and *Timon of Athens* (1610) for which objective evidence is depressingly scant. Malone's date for *Coriolanus* is, however, a lucky guess.

Schoenbaum is inconsistent. If the objective evidence for dating *Coriolanus* is "depressingly scant" (there is no mention of *Coriolanus* before 1623), Schoenbaum cannot be sure that a date *c.* 1609 is correct.

In the nineteenth century there were many attempts to sequence and date the plays, which wavered between the confident and the cautious: John Payne Collier (*History of English Dramatic Poetry*, 1831) included a reference to the newly discovered diary of John Manningham; he also added further "evidence" which turned out to be forgeries of his own (see the note in Chapter 34, *Othello*).

## Edward Dowden (1874)

In 1863, a versatile scholar called John Kells Ingram contributed a talk on Shakespeare to a series of lectures in Dublin. Ingram outlined the need to establish the chronological order of Shakespeare's works so as to illustrate Shakespeare's personality and the development of his art. He was particularly enthusiastic about using metrical features, such as lines with feminine endings, to date the plays.[6] Ingram's challenge was taken up by his pupil Edward Dowden who succeeded Ingram as Professor of Oratory and English Literature at Trinity College (Dublin University). It was Dowden who confidently delineated the playwright's development of "intellect and character from youth to full maturity" in *Shakespere: A Critical Study of his Mind and Art* (1874). Dowden extended Ingram's suggestion of three developmental periods into four distinct phases and used the statistical approach to establishing a chronology:

(i) frequency of rhyme (ii) occurrence of rhymed doggerel verse (iii) comparative infrequency of the feminine ending (iv) comparative infrequency of the weak ending (v) comparative infrequency of the unstopped line (vi) regular internal structure of the line. To these he added frequency of classical allusions, puns, conceits, wit and imagery (itemised to the point of exhaustion), treatment of clowns, the presence of termagants or shrewish women, difference in the use of soliloquies and symmetry in the grouping of persons. Much of this followed the work of F. G. Fleay and F. J. Furnivall.

Dowden's four phases were:

> *(a)* *in the workshop*. The works of Shakespeare's youth – experiments in various directions – are all marked by the presence of vivacity, cleverness, delight in beauty, and a quick enjoyment of existence. Shakespeare was an apprentice reworking other people's plays.
>
> *(b)* *in the world*. But now Shakespeare's imagination began to lay hold of real life; he came to understand the world and the men in it; his plays began to deal in an original and powerful way with the matter of history.
>
> *(c)* *out of the depths*. The poet now ceased to care for the tales of mirth and love; for the stir and movement of history, for the pomp of war; he needed to sound, with his imagination, the depths of the human heart; to inquire into the darkest and saddest parts of human life; to study the great mystery of evil.
>
> *(d)* *on the heights*. Whatever the trials and sorrows and errors might have been, he had come forth from them wise, large-hearted, calm-souled.[7]

By the time of the third edition (*c.* 1881), Dowden had expanded his groups into twelve; he states: "I claim no certainty for the order of the plays within the groups; but I offer the arrangement of [twelve] groups with great confidence as to its correctness" (Preface, ix). Dowden's groups proved very influential on subsequent scholars, especially on E. K. Chambers. However, Dowden was perhaps revealing more about himself than about the dramatist. Schoenbaum (490–500) is somewhat dismissive of Dowden for various claims, e.g. that *As You Like It* was written when Shakespeare withdrew to the Warwickshire countryside for relaxation, or that the poet had suffered an internal upheaval when composing *Othello* and *Lear*. Schoenbaum further notes that the [so-called] final plays show Shakespeare not so much "on the heights" as "back in the academy". Gary Taylor notes that Dowden's evolutionary view of literature corresponds to Darwin's vision of life but that "by the middle of the twentieth century Shakespeare's texts had been relieved of any such dependence [as envisaged in phase (a) *in the workshop*] on earlier hands" (*Reinventing Shakespeare,* 1990: 282).

Not all Victorian commentators were as confident as Dowden. James Halliwell-Phillipps (*Outlines of the Life of Shakespeare,* 1887, two volumes amounting to 858 pages) recorded a vast range of contemporary references but remained profoundly aware of the limitations of the evidence:

> [The would-be biographer of Shakespeare] is baffled in every quarter by the want of graphical documents, and little more can be accomplished beyond a very imperfect sketch or outline of the material features of the poet's career (I, xvii).

Nevertheless, Frederick Fleay (*A Chronicle History of the Life and Work of William Shakespeare*, 1886) was more confident in assigning dates to plays. Fleay accumulated statistical evidence[8] to support his claims. Sir Sidney Lee, who had been working on the monumental *Dictionary of National Biography*, produced his *Life of William Shakespeare* in 1898, in which he freely conflated factual detail with his own speculation. He refuses to consider the identity of "The Dark Lady" of the sonnets ("speculation is useless") but whole-heartedly embraces the earl of Southampton as the "young man". Despite the fact that Shakespeare does not mention Southampton after 1594, Lee boldly asserts that he "was mindful to the last of the encouragement that the young peer offered him while he was still on the threshold of the temple of fame" (150).

However, Dowden's division of the plays into four phases and assignment of dates within these phases has remained the definitive chronology, e.g. in E. Cobham Brewer's *Dictionary of Phrase and Fable* (1898 and later reprints). Peter Alexander's *Shakespeare's Life and Art* (1938) reproduces Dowden's four phases but does not offer precise dates within them.

## E. K. Chambers (1930)

In 1930, Sir Edmund Chambers published his two- volume *William Shakespeare: A Study of Facts and Problems* – the "most admired and influential work of its kind in the first half of the twentieth century" according to Taylor (1990: 240). It has remained expressive of the orthodox position in all aspects of dating the plays and includes bibliographic detail from the Stationers' Register and title pages. Chambers broke down larger subjects into discrete topics, before reviewing and evaluating previous attempts to date the plays. In Chapter VIII, he deals with 'The Problem of Chronology' (*WS*, I, 243–275), stating:

> We can only rely upon the dates at which 'sources' became available, in most cases too remote to be helpful, and upon allusions in the plays themselves to datable historical events. These require handling with great care. (I, 245)

He was as aware of the limitations of the evidence as Halliwell-Phillips had been and reacted against the narrative biographies of Shakespeare:

> A full literary and psychological analysis can only follow and not precede the establishment of a chronology. And in the meantime we are bound to a circular process. A preliminary dating sets up impressions of temper and style, and the definition of these helps to elaborate the dating. (I, 252)

Nevertheless, Chambers adopts the "admirable treatment of Professor Dowden" and accepts the four stages of Shakespeare's development. Since Chambers expresses his views in a personal tone, modern commentators have generally been able to see which of his statements are opinions, to be confirmed or challenged as the case may be. Shortly after this passage, he opines: "We can be pretty sure that the references to Scottish kings of England in *Macbeth* are Jacobean." While a number of editors now disagree with this, the comment is clearly marked as opinion. Chambers continues:

> Obviously, the grouping of the plays is only the first stage of the chronological problem. There remain the more difficult tasks of determining an order of succession within the groups and between members of overlapping groups. . . . Here it is legitimate to make some cautious use of minor topical allusions. (I, 253)

In Chapter IX, Chambers then takes each play in turn and, based on his idea of the order in which they were written, assigns a date (usually a winter season) for the composition. Some dates are advanced with extreme caution; nevertheless generally Chambers's chronology has become established as the orthodox view.

Some of Chambers's assumptions are not fully shared today. He asserts that Shakespeare produced a single or archetypal version of each play, e.g. of *Hamlet*, "Q2 substantially represents the original text of the play, as written *once and for all* by Shakespeare", I, 412, (emphasis added). He ignores the possibility that the author might have been responsible for the different versions. He talks of a "lyrical period" (to include *Richard II* and *A Midsummer Night's Dream*) when it is not established that such plays must have been composed in the same period of time. He assumes a "tragic period", covering the great tragedies (*Hamlet, Othello, Lear* and *Macbeth*), to which he adds: "*Timon* clearly belongs to the tragic period" (I, 483). By his reckoning, there appears a previous "tragic period" in the mid 1590s, including *Richard II* and *Romeo and Juliet*. He seems to ignore the possibility that *Timon* might have belonged to this earlier tragic period. Chambers assigns dates according to gaps in the author's life: he rejects the proposed date of 1605 for *Timon* because Shakespeare would have been too busy writing other plays in that year, but places it two years later in 1607–8 (with *Coriolanus*) to fill a gap. According to this view, the playwright only worked on one play at a time. Finally, he follows Fleay's statistical analysis of metre for dating the plays (although he uses his own figures). These metrical tests have generally been superseded by stylistic tests on colloquialisms. The links between style and chronology are considered in the third section of this Introduction. Overall, Chambers is an excellent starting point for examining the possible dates for each play and his chronology is referred to in this study as 'orthodox dating'.[9]

## Wells and Taylor (1987)

The other major review in the twentieth century of the canon and chronology of Shakespeare's plays was conducted by Stanley Wells and Gary Taylor (with John Jowett and William Montgomery) in *A Textual Companion* (1987: 69–144). Like Chambers, they offer a systematic review of the dates of the plays in the order in which (according to their findings) they were written. In general, their findings coincide exactly with Dowden and Chambers for 24 plays, averaging just under two years' difference in the remaining plays (see Table 2, Comparative Dates). Wells and Taylor make use of the same bibliographic data and contemporary allusions but add their own new categories of stylistic development, especially with regard to 'colloquialisms'. In general they appear more confident than Chambers, but there are some admissions of gaps in the record. They differ mostly from Chambers in dating *Two Gentlemen* four years earlier, but accept that this play could be dated anywhere between 1589 and 1598. They reject Honigmann's earlier date (*c.* 1587) for this Italian comedy, because it would leave a gap later in the chronology.[10] Overall, Wells & Taylor provide a coherent approach to the dates of the plays, which can be described as orthodox.

## Types of Evidence – External

External evidence consists of contemporary references outside the plays themselves and may be considered in eight ways:

### (a) Dated manuscripts

Dated manuscripts would provide proof of the date of composition. A few manuscripts survive from other playwrights, e.g. Jonson's *The Masque of Queenes* and Thomas Middleton's *A Game at Chess*. However, there is no manuscript, dated or undated, of any Shakespeare play. The one portion of a manuscript attributed to Shakespeare's hand belongs to the play, *Sir Thomas More*. This play is not included in the First Folio and not attributed to Shakespeare elsewhere. Greg's identification of "Shakespeare's hand" in the portion depends partly on similarity of handwriting to Shakespeare's signature (the six examples of which all post-date 1612), partly on similarity of content with crowd scenes in *Julius Caesar* and in *Coriolanus,* and partly on the perceived quality of the passage. The manuscript of *Sir Thomas More* is not dated, but from external references is thought to have been composed between 1579 and 1607, with preferences for 1592–5 or for 1603–4.[11]

**(b) Correspondence concerning literary matters**

There are no letters either to Shakespeare or by him about any of his plays or any literary matter. Such correspondence, however, does exist for contemporary playwrights. Jonson wrote to the Earl of Salisbury from prison saying the cause of his incarceration was "a play".[12] Thomas Nashe wrote a letter in August / September 1596 to William Cotton, saying that he had refused to accept invitations to the country but preferred to stay in town "had I wist hopes & an after harvest I expected by writing for the stage and for the press". He ends with a request for financial assistance.[13] Similar letters exist, e.g. by John Lyly to Robert Cecil (1574), by Gabriel Harvey to Lord Burghley (in 1585) and by Philip Massinger, Nathan Field and Richard Daborne to Henslowe (*c.* 1613, begging for a five pound advance).[14] No such letter exists for Shakespeare.

**(c) Revels Accounts**

The Revels Accounts list plays performed at court but do not indicate when they were written. The winter season at court 1604–5 included performances of at least six plays by Shakespeare: *The Moor of Venis, Mery Wives of Windsor, Mesur for Mesur, the plaie of Errors, Loues labours Lost* and *Henry the fift*. Clearly, Shakespeare cannot have just finished writing all six plays at the same time. In fact, we know that some plays had been completed earlier, since three are mentioned by Meres in 1598 and two more had been published before the 1604/5 season (*Henry V* in 1600; *Merry Wives* in 1602). Only *Measure for Measure* had not been mentioned previously, but this is no evidence for its date of composition.

**(d) Record of payment for plays**

There are no records of payments for the script of any Shakespearean play. Henslowe includes records of payments to other playwrights, but none to Shakespeare. The usual price for a play-script was six pounds. Some payments were made in advance or in instalments (possibly as advances). John Day received six pounds (in instalments) for *Bristow Tragedy* in May 1602. Later that year, on 17 November, Henslowe paid six pounds to Day, Hathaway and Smith for *Merry as may be*.[15]

**(e) Allusions to Shakespeare writing his plays**

There are no allusions to Shakespeare that can indicate when he composed any play.[16]

Since there is no reference to Shakespeare in Webbe's *Discourse of English Poetry* (1586), Puttenham's *Art of English Poesy* (1589) or Harington's *Apology for Poetry* (1591), it is assumed that he did not begin his career until *c.* 1590. However, playwrights were not well known and most plays were published anonymously. *The Spanish Tragedy* (*c.* 1589) was only attributed to Kid by

Thomas Heywood in 1612.[17] Similarly, *Tamberlaine* was not attributed to Marlowe until 1671.[18] David Ellis (*That Man Shakespeare*: 2005: 273–8) has attempted to demonstrate that biographers should not read too much into the 'argument from absence'.

There are various diarists whose records of plays in performance are often taken to indicate a date for composition: Thomas Platter and John Manningham each describe one performance: Platter saw *Julius Caesar* in June 1599; Manningham enjoyed *Twelfth Night* on 2 February 1602. Simon Forman describes performances of *Macbeth, The Winter's Tale* and *Cymbeline* in 1611. There are various accounts of the Globe's burning down during a performance of *Henry VIII* in 1613. It is usual to assume that these plays were only just written, but such allusions only indicate that a play was in existence, not when it was composed.

Some allusions are to plays on stage. Thomas Nashe, in his pamphlet *Pierce Penniless his Supplication to the Divell* (second impression, SR 8 August 1592), states:

> How it would have joyed brave Talbot (the terror of the French) to thinke that after he had lyne two hundred years in his Tombe, he should triumph againe on the Stage, and have his bones embalmed with the tears of ten thousand spectators at least (at several times)...

Talbot fights and dies heroically in *1 Henry VI*, but is not known to feature in any other play. This indicates that the play was well known by 1592. Other allusions are usually to plays already in print and attributed to Shakespeare: in 1599, John Weever published a sonnet to Shakespeare and mentioned Romeo and Richard, both of whom were title characters of published plays. Again, Weever's allusions indicate that the works were popular, not when they were written.

### (f) Francis Meres, 1598

On 7 September 1598, Francis Meres registered his *Palladis Tamia: Wit's Treasury* – a 'bluffer's guide' to English artists and writers. In this, he mentioned Shakespeare as a playwright, listing twelve plays, consisting of six comedies balanced by six tragedies:

> As *Plautus* and *Seneca* are accounted the best for Comedy and Tragedy among the Latins, so *Shakespeare* among the English is the most excellent in both kinds for the stage; for Comedy, witness his *Gentlemen of Verona,* his *Errors,* his *Love Labours Lost,* his *Love Labours Won, his Midsummer's Night Dream,* & his *Merchant of Venice;* for Tragedy, his *Richard the 2, Richard the 3, Henry the 4, King John, Titus Andronicus,* and his *Romeo* and *Juliet.*

This list indicates plays that were in existence by 1598, but gives no further indication of the date of composition. Of these plays, *Love's Labour's Won*, has not been identified; there have been suggestions that it is the name of a lost play or that it is an alternative name for a play otherwise known. Two of the comedies (*Two Gentlemen of Verona* and *Comedy of Errors*) were not published until 1623. One other title, *King John*, may refer to a play published anonymously in two parts as *The Troublesome Reign of King John* in 1591 but somewhat different from *The Life and Death of King John* in F1.

The list is not exclusive. At least three plays are known to have pre-dated Meres without gaining a mention. The three parts of *Henry VI* are not mentioned, but Parts 2 and 3 had been published and Part 1 had been staged by 1592. Other plays might also pre-date Meres: it is usually argued that *Merry Wives* dates to 1597. There is some dispute as to whether the anonymous play, *The Taming of A Shrew* (published in 1594), was Shakespeare's early version of *The Shrew* which appears in F1. Finally, there are three or four allusions to a play about *Hamlet* which pre-date Meres: the usual interpretation is that these are references to another play by another author. But omission from Meres does not prove that a play had not been written. For further consideration of the significance of Meres, see the next section of the Introduction.

### (g) Stationers' Register (SR)

The Worshipful Company of Stationers was granted a royal charter in 1557 giving the monopoly of all printing licences, outside the universities of Oxford and Cambridge, to the Stationers' Company. The Company had the right to search for and to seize all publications which had not been authorised. Their record, known as the Stationers' Register (SR), lists when a play was registered for publication, thus indicating that a play was in existence but not necessarily demonstrating when it had been composed. The SR was used to establish who owned the licence or copyright.[19]

The Stationers' Register mentions fourteen Shakespeare plays up to the death of Elizabeth in 1603. Four more plays were registered in 1607–8, including *Romeo and Juliet* and *Love's Labour's Lost* (which had already been published in the late 1590s), *Antony and Cleopatra* (which was not published until 1623) and *Pericles* which was published in 1609 but omitted from F1. *Othello* was listed in October 1621 and published in 1622. Finally, eighteen plays were registered on 8 November 1623 as "not having been entred to other men".

Some scholars have assumed that a play was usually printed soon after registration, e.g. *1 Henry IV* (registered and published in 1598, dated by Chambers to 1597–8) or *Henry V* (registered and published in 1600, dated by Chambers to 1598–9). There could, however, have been a delay intervening. In 1598, Meres mentions three comedies which did not find their way into the SR until later: *Love's Labour's Lost* was only listed in 1607 while *The Two Gentlemen of Verona* and *The Comedy of Errors* were not listed until 1623. *As You Like It* is mentioned in a kind of memorandum dated 4 August (probably 1600) but the play was not properly registered or published until 1623. Similarly, *Troilus and Cressida* was registered in 1603 but not published until 1608. *Antony and*

*Cleopatra* was registered in 1608 but not published until 1623. Thus an entry in the SR is no indication as to the date of composition.

### (h) Title-Pages

Nineteen of Shakespeare's plays were published in quarto up to 1622, with some bibliographic details. A title page indicates that a play was in existence, but not when the play was written. Details can vary; some surviving copies of the second quarto of *Hamlet* (Q2) indicate the date 1604 and others 1605. The title page to Q2 also carries the declaration: "Newly imprinted and enlarged to almost as much againe as it was, according to the true and perfect Coppie." In the case of Q2, the declaration appears to be true as it is such a different text from Q1. But, the third quarto of the play (1611) bears the same phrases, even though the text of Q3 is almost exactly the same as Q2, and they can only refer to differences from Q1. The publication dates are not entirely valid either: in 1619, Thomas Pavier, in collaboration with William Jaggard, published ten plays "by Shakespeare" (including *Sir John Oldcastle* and *A Yorkshire Tragedy*). Five bore false dates: *The Merchant of Venice* (1600), *A Midsummer Night's Dream* (1600), *Henry V* (1608), *King Lear* (1608) and *Sir John Oldcastle* (1600).[20]

## Types of Evidence – Internal

Internal evidence comes from within the plays themselves and may be considered in three further ways:

### (i) Sources

A source is a text which has had a major influence upon a play, usually concerning plot, characters and setting. Gilbert Highet points out that many of Shakespeare's sources came from the classics, e.g. Plautus, Seneca and Plutarch, and asserts that Shakespeare felt inspired to emulate and surpass these.[21] Most sources are unequivocal. For *Romeo and Juliet*, Shakespeare probably used only one source, *The Tragicall Historye of Romeus and Juliet*, a narrative poem by Arthur Brooke (1562). In his monumental *Narrative and Dramatic Sources of Shakespeare* (1957–73), Geoffrey Bullough carefully distinguishes between a probable source, a possible source and a similar text (which he calls an analogue). In his thorough introductions, Bullough describes the background to these source texts and explains his estimation of them.

The use of a source generally infers the earliest date for the composition of a play. However, in the case of some sources, there is doubt as to whether Shakespeare needed to have read them before writing his play. One such text is Strachey's letter (published in 1625, but said to have been composed 1610), which commentators no longer accept as a definite source for *The Tempest*. Another discarded source is William Camden's *Remaines of a Greater Worke concerning Britaine* which is no longer thought to have influenced *Coriolanus*.[22]

### (j) Allusions to other texts

Thomas Greene makes an important distinction between allusions and sources, stressing that an allusion is a reference to another text which may have been added at a later stage.[23] Since allusions are not integral to a play, they may reflect when a play was revised or they may even be a later interpolation. This is most evident in classical allusions: Ovid's *Metamorphoses* does not seem to have inspired any particular plot but is alluded to in almost every play.

With some allusions, it can be difficult to trace the direction of influence. Samuel Daniel's *Civil War* (1595) is taken to have influenced Shakespeare's *Richard II–Henry IV–Henry V* tetralogy. Among many similar changes from the sources, both authors treat Prince Hal and Hotspur as of a similar age, whereas Hotspur was actually older than Hal's father, Bolingbroke. Similar doubts about the direction of influence exist concerning Daniel's *Cleopatra* and Shakespeare's *Antony and Cleopatra.* It is possible that Shakespeare's was the earlier work and the direction of influence was reversed, as Joseph Conrad once suggested.[24]

### (k) Allusions to contemporary events and people

There is, apparently, only one allusion to a contemporary event in the works of Shakespeare.[25] The Chorus in *Henry V* states before the final act that the crowds would rush out to welcome home a victorious commander such as "the general of our gracious empress / As in good time he may, from Ireland coming, / Bringing rebellion broached on his sword." (5.0.30) The "general" is consistently taken to refer to Robert Devereux, Earl of Essex, who left London with much pomp in March 1599. The passage is therefore dated to the summer of that year, before Essex returned in September in somewhat unfortunate circumstances. However, Essex is not named and the passage in question did not appear in the 1600 quarto, only in the 1623 Folio text. There is a chance that the playwright was alluding to another commander who had set off with equally high expectations, e.g. Sir John Norris, Charles Blunt (Baron Mountjoy) or even Thomas Butler, Earl of Ormonde.[26]

Various attempts have been made to link the plays with astrological events: most notably, David Wiles makes connections between the calendar and *A Midsummer Night's Dream,* while Steve Sohmer argues for similar references in *Julius Caesar.*[27] An astronomer at Texas State University, Donald Olsen, has studied the star described in Bernardo's early speech in *Hamlet* as west of the Pole Star shortly after midnight. Olsen identifies Bernardo's star as a supernova which appeared in 1572.[28] Juliet's nurse states "'Tis since the earthquake now eleven years", which might refer to the earthquake felt in south-east England in April 1580 (and hence fixing the play's composition to 1591), but it might also refer to an earthquake in Verona in 1570 (which would thus indicate a date of composition *c.* 1581).[29] In *Lear,* Gloucester refers to "these late eclipses in the sun and moon" (1.2.97), a reference usually taken to date the composition of *King Lear* shortly after such co-occurrences in October 1605. However, an eclipse of the sun often accompanies an eclipse of the moon and Gloucester might just as well be referring to similar co-occurrences (eclipses of the sun and moon) in July 1590, February 1598 or Nov/Dec 1601 (or to no specific co-occurrences).[30]

If we were sure of the date of composition, we could be sure of the allusion. Since the plays can only be placed within a range of dates, evidence for allusions to contemporary events and people must be offered cautiously.

## Orthodox Dating

The aim of this study is to consider each play individually regarding its publication and performance data (mainly as reported by E. K. Chambers *William Shakespeare: A Study of Facts and Problems,* 1930) and its sources (mainly as reported by Geoffrey Bullough, *Narrative and Dramatic Sources of Shakespeare's Plays*, 1957–73).

The review of the 'orthodox' date assigned to composition of each play begins with Chambers (1930), continues with Stanley Wells & Gary Taylor, *William Shakespeare: A Textual Companion* (1987) and includes the dates proposed in the editions published by the Arden Shakespeare Second Series (1953 – 1982), the Arden Shakespeare Third Series (1995 – present), the Oxford Shakespeare (1982–present) and the New Cambridge Shakespeare series (1990–present). In some cases, the latest edition in the Arden 3 series or in the New Cambridge Shakespeare has not yet been published. All quotations of Shakespeare are from Wells & Taylor, *William Shakespeare: The Complete Works* (1986).

## Oxfordian Dating

The main challenge to the 'orthodox' dating has been made by Oxfordians, who maintain the hypothesis that the works attributed to William Shakespeare were written by Edward de Vere, Earl of Oxford (1550–1604). J. T. Looney in *Shakespeare Identified* (1920) was the first to propose Oxford as a candidate for authorship of the Shakespeare canon and was well aware that many plays were assumed to have been composed after Oxford died in 1604. Yet upon examination, he noted, documentary evidence for post-1604 composition was lacking. Eva Turner Clark, *Hidden Allusions in Shakespeare's Plays* (1931, rptd 1974) developed Looney's thesis and elaborated an alternative and earlier chronology for the composition of the plays using the detailed records reported by E. K. Chambers, *The Elizabethan Stage* (1923). Clark identified many anonymous plays in the 1570s and 1580s with early work by Oxford. Many of her observations are recorded in this book in the relevant sections for each play. For Oxford's life, reference has been made to Alan Nelson's biography,

*Monstrous Adversary: The Life of Edward de Vere, 17th Earl of Oxford* (2003). The ultimate purpose of this book is not to establish (or reject) Oxford's candidacy for authorship but to examine the range of possible dates for each play.

In the conclusion to each chapter, the narrowest possible date range is given, noting that there is no firm evidence to assign any play to any particular year.[31] We should remember that all dates are conjectural at best and heed the words of David Ellis who states (*That Man Shakespeare,* 2005, 273):

> Since the major impediment to writing a life of Shakespeare is a lack of information, more often than not biographers who set out to investigate a particular aspect of their study find themselves staring into a black hole. This at first seems a crippling disadvantage for who, after all, can make bricks without straw?

In the next section of the Introduction, more careful consideration is given to the uses and limits of Francis Meres's evidence. In the final section, there is some attempt to evaluate the use of style and language features in attempting to establish a chronology.

## Notes

1. The earliest editors to accept this as a possibility were Wells and Taylor in their *Complete Works of William Shakespeare* (Oxford, 1986). They print both the text from the Pied Bull Quarto of 1608 as *The History of King Lear* and the Folio Text as *The Tragedy of King Lear*. Previously, the tendency has been to dismiss those quarto texts which were significantly different from the Folio text as 'bad quartos' but this has been challenged recently, e.g. by Kathleen Irace in *Reforming the "Bad" Quartos: performance and provenance of six Shakespearean first editions* (1994), and by Lukas Erne in *Shakespeare as Literary Dramatist* (2003). Clearly, if Shakespeare did produce both the known quarto texts and the Folio texts, then any collection known as *The Complete Works* would need to report these versions as well.
2. In their Arden 3 edition of *Hamlet* (2006: 44), Ann Thompson & Neil Taylor accept that the three printed versions of the play, Q1 (1603), Q2 (1604) and F1 (1623) might have all come from the author's own hand. They further accept as possible (*pace* Jenkins in his Arden 2 edition) that Nashe (1589), Henslowe (1594), Lodge (1596) and Harvey (*c.* 1598–1601) were referring to Shakespeare's play (or at least to a version of it). Other scholars, e.g. Alexander, *Shakespeare's Life and Art* (1939), have asserted that these were definite references to the Shakespeare play.
3. Winifred Frazer and others (*N&Q*, 236, 1991: 34–5) noted that plays are sometimes marked "ne" twice and so could hardly be 'new' second time around. Foakes and Rickert (*Henslowe's Diary*, 2003, xxxiv, 2nd ed.) have suggested: "One possibility that covers all occurrences of 'ne' is that this refers to the licensing of a play-book for performance by the Master of the Revels" (i.e. does not necessarily mean 'newly composed'). Neil Carson in *A Companion to Henslowe's Diary* (2004: 68) notes that some commentators believe that *Titus* must have been written earlier and that the play performed by Sussex's Men would have been marked as "ne" to indicate a revision. Carson adds: "All such speculation is unverifiable."
4. *The Two Gentlemen of Verona* and *The Comedy of Errors* are not mentioned after Meres until 1623. They are listed in the Stationers' Register on 8 November 1623 among 18

plays not previously published. *The Comedy of Errors* was mentioned in a performance at Grays Inn on 28 December 1594. Meres also mentions *Love's Labours Won* which is taken by some to have been an early name for *The Taming of the Shrew*. A play similar in title, plot and characters, *The Taming of A Shrew* was listed in the SR in 1594 and published in a quarto that year. Opinion is divided as to whether Shakespeare was responsible for the quarto of *A Shrew*.

5. For this brief review of previous attempts to fix the dates and chronology of Shakespeare's plays, I have followed Samuel Schoenbaum's *Shakespeare's Lives*, 1970 and Gary Taylor, *Reinventing Shakespeare: a Cultural History from the Restoration to the Present*, 1990.
6. John Kells Ingram's lecture on Shakespeare was published in *The Afternoon Lectures on English Literature* (1863). For the significance of Ingram's part in the story (overlooked by Schoenbaum and Taylor), I am indebted to research by Andrew Murphy (University of St Andrews). See "A Biographical Sketch of John Keils [*sic*] Ingram" by Gregory Moore in *History of Economics Review* (1995).
7. Quoted by Gary Taylor, *Reinventing Shakespeare*, 174–82 (see note 5).
8. Richard Roderick in 1756 had noted that *Henry VIII* had a high number of verse lines with feminine endings (additional, unstressed syllables). The statistical approach to analysis of style was started in earnest by William Walker in 1854 *Shakespeare's Versification and its apparent Irregularities explained by Examples from Early and Late English Writers*, closely followed by Bathurst's *Shakespeare's Versification at different Periods of his Life* in 1857, promoted by Ingram and established by Dowden.
9. Chambers's work was brought up to date by James G. McManaway, "Recent Studies in Shakespeare's Chronology", *Shakespeare Survey*, 3, 1950, 22–33. A systematic review (in line with Chambers's work) can be found in *The Riverside Shakespeare* (ed. G. Blakemore Evans, 1997: 77–87). A shorter review (which follows Wells and Taylor) is given by Stephen Greenblatt in *The Norton Shakespeare*, 1997: 54–57. Many of Greenblatt's comments (e.g. "Shakespeare began his career, probably in the early 1590s" and "We have no direct personal testimony either to support or undermine" [*sc.* these speculations about a possible crisis in Shakespeare's life]) record the uncertainty of the evidence used to date the plays.
10. E. A. J. Honigmann in *Shakespeare: the 'lost years'* (1985) develops his arguments for Shakespeare as an 'early starter' by dating at least six plays to the 1580s. In their reaction against Honigmann's proposal, Wells and Taylor state (*A Textual Companion* (1987: 97): "The urge to push Shakespeare's first play further back into the 1580s is palpably designed to fill the black hole of our ignorance about those years; but since we must then spread the same number of plays over a larger number of years, by filling one big vacuum in the 1580s, we simply create other vacuums elsewhere." Wells & Taylor demonstrate their method of 'plugging the gaps' when they consider *Two Gentlemen of Verona* (109); after noting "The play could belong to any year in the decade before Meres mentioned it," they then assign a *precise* date of 1590–1. Honigmann shows that earlier dates are tenable. Some editors now suggest a date in the 1580s for *Two Gentlemen*.
11. The manuscript has been studied by W. W. Greg, "Shakespeare's Hand in the Play of *Sir Thomas More*" in his appendix to his edition of *Sir Thomas More* (MSR, Cambridge, 1923). The dates have been taken from Stanley Wells & Gary Taylor, *A Textual Companion*, where on page 124 they date it to 1603–4 but on page 139 they seem to prefer 1593–5. R. C. Bald in "*The Booke of Sir Thomas More* and Its Problems", *Shakespeare Survey* 2 (1949), pp. 44–65 accepts that some arguments are tenuous. Other scholars have cast doubts on Greg's conclusion, e.g. Georgio Melchiori, "Hand D in *Sir Thomas More*: An Essay in Misinterpretation in Shakespeare", *Shakespeare Survey*, 38, 1986.
12. Jonson's letter also refers to another imprisoned playwright George Chapman as "a learned and honest Man", reported in *Ben Jonson* ed. C. H. Herford and Percy Simpson.

13. R. B. McKerrow and F. P. Wilson (eds), *The Complete Works of Thomas Nashe,* 5 vols, Oxford, 1958, vol 5, 194.
14. Quoted by Diana Price in *Shakespeare's Unorthodox Biography* (2001: 306), from W. W. Greg (ed.), *English Literary Autographs 1550 – 1650.*
15. Carson *Henslowe's Diary* (60) notes that these might not be all the payments made to a playwright. At any rate, these payments seem to indicate a date when a play was handed over by the playwright(s) to the acting company and make a more reliable guide to the date of composition than does a record of a performance.
16. In a poetical letter to Ben Jonson, Francis Beaumont (*Norton MS* 1403), recalls the witty banter at the Mermaid Tavern. We only have the later testimony of Thomas Fuller in *Worthies* (1662) that Shakespeare was involved: "Many were the wit-combats betwixt him [Shakespeare] and Ben Jonson." For modern biographers, it would be marvellous to have Jonson mocking Shakespeare for missing a "roister to remember" at the Mermaid Tavern because he was in his attic finishing off his latest play about a mad Danish prince. Sadly, this is "such stuff as dreams are made on".
17. J. R. Mulryne, *The Spanish Tragedy,* The New Mermaids Press, 1970, Introduction, p. xv. Thomas Heywood was writing in *The Apology for Actors.*
18. J. W. Harper, *Tamberlaine,* New Mermaids Press, 1971, Introduction, p. viii: "The first clear attribution of the play to Marlowe was by Francis Kirkman in his edition of *Nicomede* (1671)."
19. Edward Arber (ed.), *A Transcript of the Registers of the Company of Stationers of London, 1554–1640* in five volumes (1875–94). They have been reprinted by W. W. Greg and and E. Boswell (eds), *Records of the Court of the Stationers' Company, 1576 to 1602* (1930). They are described (and reported *ad loc.*) by Chambers in *The English Stage* and in *William Shakespeare: A Study of Facts and Problems.*
20. It is usually assumed that the Pavier Quarto of 1619 used false dates to circumvent copyright. This may have caused the Lord Chamberlain in 1619 to forbid publication of plays which the King's Men intended to produce (ultimately as the First Folio). Lukas Erne in *Shakespeare as a Literary Dramatist* (2003) argues that Hemmings and Condell in their preface to F1 were alluding to Pavier's "stolne, and surreptitious copies". Sonia Massai, *Shakespeare and the Rise of the Editor,* Cambridge, 2007, has reviewed these suggestions and offered an alternative view of Pavier's intentions, giving him credit for a collected works of Shakespeare.
21. Gilbert Highet in *The Classical Tradition: Greek and Roman influences on Western Literature* (1949; rptd 1976) describes how the classics came down to Renaissance writers through the three processes of translation, imitation and emulation. He devotes an entire chapter to Shakespeare, covering the authors mentioned in the text and other writers whose influence was less obvious, e.g. Virgil and Caesar.
22. Stuart Gillespie, *Shakespeare's Books,* 2004, notes that Camden's *Remaines* is only cited very briefly and only for two plays: in *Coriolanus* it is only claimed to have influenced the wording in Menenius' fable of the Belly, where the belly is called "a gulf". Gillespie notes that the Fable was used in the main sources, i.e. Livy and Plutarch, and by many other writers such as Sir Philip Sidney. For *King Lear,* a few verbal reminiscences have also been claimed by some editors but dismissed by Muir in his Arden 2 edition (revised 1952) and ignored by R. A. Foakes (Arden 3, 1997) and by Stanley Wells (Oxford Edition, 2000).
23. Thomas Greene in *The Light in Troy: Imitation and Discovery in Renaissance Poetry* (1982) carefully distinguished a passing allusion from sustained interaction with a source text. Stephen Greenblatt in *Shakespeare Negotiations* (1988) considers how a writer such as Shakespeare conducted a dialogue with another text.
24. H. E. Rollins (New Variorum edition of *The Sonnets,* 1944) quotes Joseph Conrad (*Jahrbuch,* 1882, 196) when considering Daniel's possible influence on Shakespeare's sonnets. L. A. Michel (ed.), *The Civil Wars by Samuel Daniel* (1958), considers Shakespeare as both

a source and as a beneficiary of Daniel. Stuart Gillespie in *Shakespeare's Books* (2004) states that considerable disagreement exists over the direction of borrowing, arising from difficulty in establishing the relative dating of Daniel's work and Shakespeare's tetralogy and whether both relied on source(s) now lost. Daniel's *Cleopatra* (the version published in 1594) is usually taken to be an influence on Shakespeare's *Antony and Cleopatra* (registered in 1608 but not published until 1623) as Daniel had made some small revisions in his 1607 edition.

25 Wells & Taylor, *Complete Works,* 567, call it an "uncharacteristic direct, topical reference". But neither the General nor the Empress is actually named in the passage.

26 See further discussion in the chapters on *Henry V* and on *Famous Victories.* Sir John Norris (or Norreys), died in 1597 and was a highly acclaimed soldier under Elizabeth. As the Queen's General in Ireland, he was responsible for the slaughter of innocent people on the island of Rathlin in 1575. Charles Blount, Baron Mountjoy, served as the Queen's Deputy in Ireland in 1600–01. Thomas Butler, Earl of Ormonde, was Lord Treasurer of Ireland and fought to suppress the Desmond Rebellions in 1569–73.

27 David Wiles in *Shakespeare's Almanac: 'A Midsummer Night's Dream', Marriage and the Elizabethan Calendar* (1993); S. Sohmer, *Shakespeare's Mystery Play: The Opening of the Globe Theatre* (1999).

28 D. W. Olsen *et al., Sky & Telescope*, 96, (1998) 68–73, quoted by Eric Altschuler, House Magazine, Royal Astrononmical Society, October 1999.

29 The 1580 earthquake as the source of the reference was suggested by Tyrwhitt and the 1570 Verona earthquake by Hunter, (quoted by H. H. Furness, Variorum edition of *Romeo and Juliet*). There are various contemporary accounts of the earthquake which struck on 6 April 1580, e.g. by Thomas Churchyard and Anthony Munday. Gabriel Harvey's description was published in Spenser's *Three Familiar Letters*, 1580. Steve Sohmer has considered the 1570 Verona earthquake in "Shakespeare's Time-Riddles in *Romeo and Juliet* Solved", *English Literary Renaissance,* 35, 2005: 407–28.

30 John Harvey predicted these co-occurrences of solar and lunar eclipses in *A Discoursive Probleme Concerning Prophesies* (1588), quoted by H. H. Furness, *Shakespeare: King Lear* New Variorum edition, 1880, p. 379.

31 Just as *Dating Shakespeare's Plays* was going to press, similar conclusions were raised in an edition "Questioning Shakespeare" of *Critical Survey,* (2009). Brian Cummings (Sussex University), who has also advocated caution in assigning dates to the plays, is preparing a study of literary biography and Shakespeare entitled: *Shakespeare in the Underworld.*

# The Uses and Limits of Francis Meres

Eddi Jolly

As *Plautus* and *Seneca* are accounted
the beſt for Comedy and Tragedy among
the Latines: ſo *Shakeſpeare* among ẏ Eng-
liſh is the moſt excellent in both kinds for
the ſtage; for Comedy, witnes his *Gẽtlemẽ
of Verona*, his *Errors*, his *Loue labors loſt*, his
*Loue labours wonne*, his *Midſummers night
dreame*, & his *Merchant of Venice*: for Tragedy his *Richard the 2. Richard the 3. Henry the 4. King Iohn, Titus Andronicus* and
his *Romeo* and *Iuliet.*

Francis Meres's book *Palladis Tamia: Wits Treasury* is informative on the dating of twelve Shakespearean plays: they must have been written by 1598, when *Palladis Tamia* was published. However, careful reading of this work shows that Meres is no authority on which Shakespeare plays had not been written before that date.

*Palladis Tamia: Wits Treasury* was entered in the Stationers' Register on 7th September 1598. After a section entitled 'Poets', and before one called 'Painters', Meres placed 'A comparative discourse of our English poets, with the Greeke, Latine and Italian Poets'.[1] Paragraph 24 of this section reads:

> As *Plautus* and *Seneca* are accounted the best for Comedy and Tragedy among the Latines: so *Shakespeare* among y^e English is the most excellent in both kinds for the stage; for Comedy, witnes his *Gentlemen of Verona*, his *Errors*, his *Loue labors lost*, his *Loue labours wonne*, his *Midsummers night dreame*, & his *Merchant of Venice*: for Tragedy his *Richard the 2. Richard the 3. Henry the 4. King Iohn, Titus Andronicus* and his *Romeo* and *Iuliet*. (Meres: 1973: 282)

Editors frequently use this list to contribute to their propositions for dating Shakespeare's plays, but they do not use it consistently. For example, Brian Morris, editing *The Taming of the Shrew*, comments that "the omission of *The Shrew* from Meres' list is not particularly surprising since he was not aiming for completeness" (Morris: 1981: 63). But Agnes Latham, editing *As You Like*

*It*, concludes that "the date of the play is fixed by the fact that it does not appear in the list Meres gives in the *Palladis Tamia*, in 1598" (Latham: 1975: xxvi). A. R. Humphreys, editing *Much Ado* is puzzled by that play's omission from Meres: "The play is not named in *Palladis Tamia* ... The omission might be accidental, but it creates a strong supposition that the play was not known when he completed his list, and so suggests the middle or latter part of 1598 as the earliest date of composition" (Humphreys: 1981: 3). Mares, another editor of *Much Ado*, is equally surprised: "That *Much Ado* is not named is in no way conclusive that it was not in existence, but the quality of the play makes it likely that had Meres known it he would have named it" (Mares: 2003: 8). Harold Jenkins in his edition of *Hamlet* writes: "It cannot have been known to Francis Meres in the autumn of 1598 when it failed to find mention in his *Palladis Tamis* among the plays there listed in witness of Shakespeare's excellence as a writer" (Jenkins: 1982: 1). Thus editors interpret Meres's chapter in several different ways:

1. Meres was not offering a complete list
2. If a play is not mentioned by Meres Shakespeare has not yet written it
3. Meres may have accidentally omitted a play
4. A play of quality is likely to have been mentioned by Meres
5. If a play is omitted it is not known to Meres.

These editors cannot all be right; collectively they are inconsistent.

Jenkins footnotes his comment on *Hamlet*'s date and Meres with a reference to Chambers's *William Shakespeare*, vol. ii, pp 193-4. Chambers, however, quotes briefly and selectively from Meres, and the context is lost. A return to the original chapter is critical for evaluating Meres's evidence regarding the dates of some of Shakespeare's plays.

## Meres: content and style

Understanding Meres's technique is important. He is not original; most of his content is derived from a selection of texts identified by Don Cameron Allen in 1933. These include J. Ravisius Textor's *Officina* (published 1520, with seven reprints before Meres), with material also from, for example, W. Webbe's *A Discourse of English Poetrie* (1586), George Puttenham's *The Arte of English Poesie* (1589), Petrus Crinitus's *De Poetis Latinis* (1518), Erasmus's *Parabolae sive Similia* (1514) or Mirabellus's *Polyanthea* (1503).

His style is characterised by its euphuistic tendencies – extensive alliteration and assonance – and especially by its sustained comparative approach. The chapter title, "A comparative discourse ...", is to be taken literally. Most prominent is its syntactic and grammatical parallelism, which balances a number of classical authors with modern writers. This appositive method is again derivative, imitative of, for example, Richard Carew or Ortensio Lando.[2] The fifty-nine paragraphs, bar five or six, have a very similar structure. The paragraphs begin with the same lexeme, "As…", usually followed by a Greek, Latin or Italian writer or number of such writers, plus their claims to fame. This half of the sentence is concluded by a colon to mark where the comparison pivots, and the second half is initiated by the continuer "so…", the English writer(s), and his/their claims to fame. Mostly the numbers of classical writers match the numbers of English authors, or the numbers in each national group are the same. The majority of these balanced sentences focus on fame in the literary sense, though not quite all. The exemplar paragraph below, chosen for its typical syntactic parallelism and for its brevity, leans more towards infamy in a non-literary sense (Meres 1973: 286v, para. 56):

| | | | |
|---|---|---|---|
| As | Anacreon | died by the pot | : |
| (begins comparison) | (Greek writer) | ('fame') | (colon/pivot) |
| so | George Peele | by the pox. | |
| (continuer) | (English writer) | ('fame') | |

Again and again identical numbers of writers are cited. Paragraph 1 offers three Greek (Orpheus, Linus and Musaus), three Latin (L. Andronicus, Ennius and Plautus) and three English poets (Chaucer, Gower and Lydgate). On the whole Meres only refers to Greek, Latin and Italian writers, followed by English ones. There are a very few exceptions: paragraph 41 refers to the King of Scots; paragraph 46 to "Georgius Buchananus", i.e. Scotsman George Buchanan and paragraph 58 to "Iodelle, a French tragical poet". Meres's preoccupation with symmetry in his comparisons is evident in paragraph after paragraph, with a very careful balance, as table 1 shows. The first five paragraphs are listed as early and typical examples, setting up the pattern for the rest, and subsequent examples are those in which Shakespeare is mentioned.

| **Para** | **First half of sentence: *As* to colon** | | | **Second half of sentence: *so* to end** | **Link/Claim to fame** |
|---|---|---|---|---|---|
| | **Greek** | **Latin** | **Italian** | **English** | |
| 1 | Orpheus<br>Linus<br>Musaeus | L.Andronicus<br>Ennius<br>Plautus | | Chaucer<br>Gower<br>Lydgate | Poets of antiquity |
| 2 | Homer | | Petrarch | Chaucer | Prince/<br>God of Poets |
| 3 | Homer | | | *Piers Plowman* | Quantity |
| 4 | | Ovid | | Harding | Chroniclers |

| Para | First half of sentence: *As* to colon | | | Second half of sentence: *so* to end | Link/Claim to fame |
|---|---|---|---|---|---|
| | **Greek** | **Latin** | **Italian** | **English** | |
| 5 | Sotades Maronites | | | Skelton | Impure and scurrilous matters |
| 8 | 8 writers | 8 writers | | 8 writers | Ornateness |
| 23 | Euphorbus in Pythagorus | | | Ovid in Shakespeare | Soul |
| 24 | | Plautus Seneca | | Shakespeare | 'Tongue' |
| 32 | 3 writers | 2 writers | | 5 writers (Shakespeare 4th out of 5 writers) | Lyric poets |
| 33 | 10 writers | 4 writers | | 14 writers (11/14) | Tragedy |
| 35 | 10 writers | 6 writers | | 17 writers (9/17) | Comedy |
| 38 | 7 writers | 7 writers | | 15 writers (10/15) | Elegy |

Table 1. Symmetry in Meres

The order in which long lists of authors are presented is not alphabetical. Such lists do tend to begin with any titled authors, like "the Lorde Buckhurst" and "Edward Earle of Oxforde". These are then followed by Oxbridge men, like "Maister Rowley once a rare Scholler of learned Pembroke Hall in Cambridge", followed by an apparently random order for the remaining authors cited. It is not immediately obvious that there is any significance in the placing of Shakespeare's name.

In paragraph 24, the critical paragraph quoted at the top of this chapter, the symmetry is broken; the two Roman playwrights Plautus and Seneca are accounted the best for comedy and tragedy, but just one English playwright, Shakespeare, is mentioned. Meres offers twelve titles for Shakespeare. Predictably, those titles follow the endlessly repetitive pattern Meres has established, so that six comedies are balanced by six 'tragedies'.

Comedy: *Gentlemen of Verona, Errors, Loue labours lost, Loue labours wonne, Midsummers night dreame, Merchant of Venice*
Tragedy: *Richard the 2., Richard the 3., Henry the 4., King Iohn, Titus Andronicus, Romeo and Juliet*

It should be evident by now that Meres is committed to symmetry, and the two sets of six plays are exactly that; two balanced lists, and a continuation of Meres's appositive style. Of these, *Love's Labours Won* has not been identified, although it has sometimes been taken as an alternative title for *Much Ado, As You Like It*, or other plays. *The Two Gentlemen of Verona* is not otherwise mentioned until 1623; *The Comedy of Errors* is mentioned in 1594, but not again until 1604. The reference to *King John* might be to the anonymous *Troublesome Raigne of King John* (1591), often taken to be by another author. The lists are examples; they are not a guaranteed list to include all Shakespeare's plays by 1598. This is easily demonstrated by the Shakespearean plays which are known to have existed by 1598, but which are not mentioned by Meres. These are shown in table 2.

| **Play title** | **Date + Elizabethan source** |
|---|---|
| *1 Henry VI* | 1592, Nashe's pamphlet *Pierce Penniless* |
| *2 Henry VI* | 1594, S.R./Q1 (*Contention*) |
| *3 Henry VI* | 1595, Q1 (*True Tragedie*) |
| *Hamlet* | 1589, Nash, 1594 Henslowe, 1596 Lodge |
| *Taming of the Shrew* | 1594 S.R. (*A Shrew*), 1594 (printed), 1596 (sold) |

Table 2. Plays with Shakespearean titles mentioned before 1598, but not included by Meres

## How comprehensive is Meres?

Meres names many contemporary authors without citing the title of any of their writings. These include: Thomas 'Kid', Benjamin Johnson, Thomas Watson, Anthony Munday, Porter and Heywood. For some, Meres mentions author and text. For example, Philip Sidney and his *Countess of Pembroke's Arcadia* is included, but not his *Lady of May* (1578), *Astrophel and Stella* (1591), or *The Defence of Poesie* (1591).

Table 3 lists only those for whom he gives titles. Far more English writers mentioned do ***not*** have the title of any of their works included than do, approximately six times as many. The last column of titles gives examples of texts he omits for those writers: all titles dated ***earlier*** than 1598.

| **Author** | **No. of times cited** | **Titles cited** | **Examples of pre 1598 titles *not* cited** |
|---|---|---|---|
| Henry Howard Earl of Surrey | 2 | Trans. of Virgil's *Aeneid IV* | *Songs and Sonnets* (in Tottel's *Miscellany*, 1557) |
| Michael Drayton | 12 | *Polyolbion* *England's Heroical Epistles* | *Idea, the Shepherd's Garland* (1593) |

| **Author** | **No. of times cited** | **Titles cited** | **Examples of pre 1598 titles *not* cited** |
|---|---|---|---|
| Shakespeare | 9 | *Venus and Adonis*, *Lucrece*, sonnets, 12 plays | *Henry VI* (1594/95)<br>*Hamlet* (1589/94/96)<br>*Taming of the Shrew* (1594/96) |
| Philip Sidney | 6 | *The Countess of Pembroke's Arcadia* | *Lady of May* (1578)<br>*Astrophel and Stella* (1591)<br>*Defence of Poesie* (1591) |
| Edmund Spenser | 9 | *Faerie Queen*<br>*Shepheardes Calendar* | *Astrophel* (1596)<br>*Colin Clout's come home* (1595)<br>*Amoretti* (1596)<br>*Epithalamium* (1596) |
| Warner | 5 | *Albion's England* | *Pan his Syrinx* (1595)<br>Translation of Plautus's *Menæchmi* (1595) |
| George Buchanan | 1 | *Iephthe* | *De Jure Regni apud Scotos* (1579)<br>*Rerum Scoticarum Historia* (1582) |
| Author of [edited by W. Baldwin and G. Ferrers] | 1 | *A Mirrour for Magistrates* | |
| Author of [J. Marston] | 1 | *Pygmalion's Image* | |
| Author of [E. Guilpin] | 1 | *Skialethia* | |

Table 3. Examples of writers cited, with texts cited

This table should indicate clearly that Meres does not intend to offer a full list of every writer's works in 1598, and that he does not do so.

## The accuracy of Meres

There are a number of anomalies which suggest Meres was at best a competent user of his sources rather than an acclaimed literary critic.

One is pointed out by Allen: Meres makes errors. For example, Meres misspells Porcius Licinius, because he is following Petrus Crinitus, whereas Textor, another source Meres used, spells the name correctly as Portius Licinius. On another occasion Meres follows Textor – wrongly – with the name Lucullus, whereas Crinitus correctly spells the name Lucilius (Allen: 1933: 38).

A second is the question of Meres's literary judgement. Mares might have believed that had Meres known *Much Ado* he would have recognised its quality and listed it. But Meres, on a simple citation count, does not even mention Shakespeare the most frequently. Instead, that claim to fame falls to Michael Drayton. Table 4 below reflects the frequency of mention.

| **Examples of writers** | **Number of mentions in '*A comparative discourse...*'** |
|---|---|
| Daniel | 5 |
| Christopher Marlowe | 6 |
| Sidney | 6 |
| Spenser | 9 |
| Shakespeare | 9 |
| Michael Drayton | 12 |

Table 4. Frequency of mention

It seems clear that this bias towards Drayton is the result of personal acquaintance, since he is praised, for example: "Michael Drayton... among schollers, souldiers, Poets and all sorts of people, is held for a man of virtuous disposition, honest conversation, and wel gouerned carriage...". Shakespeare, by comparison, is not even given his first name.

A third anomaly is that Meres does not appear to know the author's name for a small number of texts, referring to him as simply "author of...". The author of *Skialethia* is E. Guilpin, and *Pygmalion's Image* was written by John Marston.

## Meres and Shakespeare: other points

While Shakespeare is praised for his writing, and given three solo paragraphs, Meres does not reveal any personal acquaintance with the elusive playwright. He uses the Christian names of some of the English writers, but he does not use Shakespeare's or refer to him in personal terms, unlike "my friend master Richard Barnfielde". In all, he lists about seventy contemporary writers and it is unlikely that he can have known all of them, especially as he had lived in London for a few years at most and was still only twenty-three when he published this work. Shortly afterwards, he took up a rectorship in Rutland, apparently leaving London for good. Chambers suggested that the omission of the *Henry VI* plays was due to the fact that they had been performed in London before Meres arrived (Chambers: *WS*, 1930 I: 208).

There are further gaps in our understanding. Tantalisingly, Meres refers in this chapter to Shakespeare's "sugred Sonnets", which appear to have been circulated "among his priuate friends, &c", eleven years before the publication of the collection of Shakespeare's sonnets in 1609. Why do we hear nothing from those "private friends" in other contemporary sources? Does "&c" refer to other acquaintances, or other poems? Can we nevertheless deduce that Shakespeare's was a well-known name for a variety of kinds of writing, and that Meres's readers would have understood this?

## Summary

A true Renaissance man, Meres savours the language and writings of his time. He has a very repetitive style, easily proved to be imitative. While on the whole he keeps to comparisons between classical authors and English ones, his parameters are not entirely rigid; he mentions the occasional French writer, and he passes non-literary comments on some too.

At no point does Meres indicate that he intends to cite *all* writings by each author. He does not mention all the writings published by the writers he cites, as Tables 2 and 3 prove. This could be because he does not value them as much as others, or does not know of them, or simply chooses not to. It does not indicate he did not know that they had authored other writings. Freeman, the editor of the edition of Meres used here, writes:

> In eighteen pages of acritical enthusiasm Meres courses the contemporary literary scene, giving crucial testimony, by citation, to the existence of many works, poetic and dramatic, and to the esteem in which they were popularly held.

Meres does exactly what Freeman says. Meres gives "crucial testimony, by citation, to the existence of many works". Exactly – 'many', but not all. As Thompson and Taylor write in their introduction to *Hamlet*, Meres "was not to know how important his list would be for future scholars" (Thompson et al: 2006: 47).

For anyone trying to mine the text for information about Shakespeare, the pickings are limited, but still useful. Meres *is* testimony to the variety of Shakespeare's writings – sonnets, narrative poems, comedies, tragedies. He *is* testimony to the quality of Shakespeare's writing (e.g. Shakespeare's "fine filed phrase"). He praises the writing qualities of several contemporary authors, and Shakespeare is amongst those. Meres *is* testimony to a number of Shakespeare's writings in 1598.

However, Brian Morris's view that Meres "was not aiming for completeness" is accurate in identifying the limits of Meres's usefulness.

# Notes

1. All quotations are from the 1973 reprint, by Garland Publishing, of the 1598 edition published by P. Short for Cuthbert Burbie in London.
2. Respectively, Carew's *The Excellency of the English Tongue*, 1595-6 – e.g. "Will you haue *Platos* vayne? reede Sir *Thomas Smith*. The Ionike? Sir *Tho. Moor*: *Ciceros? Aschame*", and Lando's *Sette Libri de Cathaloghi a' Varie Cose Appartenenti, Non Solo Antiche, Ma Anche Moderne*, 1552. The latter gives catalogues of ancient figures of note with an equal number of modern worthies (Allen: 1933: 29).

# Other Works Cited

Allen, Don Cameron, *Francis Meres's Treatise 'Poetrie', A Critical Edition*, from *University of Illinois Studies in Language and Literature*, XVI, University of Illinois, 1933

Chambers, W. & R., *Chambers's Dictionary of National Biography*, 1974

Chambers, E. K., *William Shakespeare. A Study of Facts and Problems*, Vols 1 & ll, Oxford: Clarendon Press, 1930

Jenkins, Harold (ed.), *Hamlet*, London: The Arden Shakespeare, Methuen, 1982

Humphreys, A. R. (ed.), *Much Ado About Nothing*, London: The Arden Shakespeare, Methuen, 1981

Latham, Agnes (ed.), *As You Like It*, London: The Arden Shakespeare, Methuen, 1975

Mares, F. H. (ed.), *Much Ado About Nothing*, Cambridge: CUP, 2003

Meres, Francis, *Palladis Tamia: Wit's Treasury*, rptd Garland Publishing, Inc., 1973

Morris, Brian (ed.), *The Taming of the Shrew*, Arden Shakespeare, London: Methuen, 1981

Oliver, H. J. (ed.), *The Merry Wives of Windsor*, London: The Arden Shakespeare, Methuen, 1971

Palmer, Alan and Veronica, *Who's Who in Shakespeare's England*, London: Methuen, 2000

Thompson, Ann, and Taylor, Neil, (eds), *Hamlet*, London: The Arden Shakespeare, Thomson Learning, 2006

# Verse, Style and Chronology[1]

Kevin Gilvary

The study of language features has been used mainly to attempt to establish authorship and has also been used extensively in assigning different parts of plays to different authors. Most recently, this has been done to great advantage by Jonathan Hope (1994) and by Brian Vickers (2002). Hope studied three grammatical features: the auxiliary 'do', relative markers and the use of 'thou' and 'you'. He intended to distinguish the hands of Shakespeare and Fletcher in *Henry VIII* and in *The Two Noble Kinsmen,* and then considered apocryphal plays which were included in the Third Folio of 1664, e.g. *A Yorkshire Tragedy.* Vickers extended this method to a consideration of verse tests, e.g. amount of rhyme or blank verse, parallel passages, distinct vocabulary, linguistic preferences, contractions, expletives and function words. He applied this study to five plays in the First Folio, e.g. *Henry VI, Part 1,* and he thus has confidently assigned various parts of disputed plays to Shakespeare's co-authors.

The study of language features has also been employed in trying to establish the sequence and chronology of composition, most notably by Chambers (1930) and by Wells & Taylor (1987). Vickers (2002: 126), on the other hand, accepts that the main dating tools derive from external evidence:

> . . . entries in the Stationers' Register, its publication date; any historical references it contains; allusions in contemporary letters or other documents to its theatrical performance or existence in manuscript.

He notes that stylistic and linguistic features are of "secondary value" but that they "can play a part in confirming or questioning a date established on other grounds." He then applies stylistic methods to dating Hand D, which he calls "Shakespeare's contributions", in the manuscript play, *Sir Thomas More.*[2]

Malone was the first scholar to study style in an effort to establish chronology. Using the test of frequency of rhyme, he designated *Love's Labour's Lost* the earliest play:

> Whenever of two early pieces it is doubtful which preceded the other, I am disposed to believe, (other proofs being wanting) that play in which the greater number of rhymes is found, to have been first composed.[3]

The first commentator to link metre with chronology was Walker, in 1854, closely followed by Bathurst in 1857. Bathurst allowed some speculation to enter into his discussion, as the following remarks show:

> *The Merchant of Venice* is very natural, sometimes excursive, not ratiocinative. The verse, generally, uniform and flowing. One weak ending. Some breaks. The speeches where speakers change, fit into the verse, but not always. It is remarkably one of those pieces which were written when Shakespeare's mind was at ease, original, and independent. Neither disturbed by the rivalship of others, nor stimulated to take pains to write in a more active and dramatic style than naturally occurred to him in the course of his composition.[4]

This approach was developed and popularised by F. J. Furnivall, who argued that Shakespeare should be approached scientifically and that the use of verse to establish chronology was a prelude to appreciating the growth of Shakespeare's mind. Shakespeare's text must be approached:

> As the geologist treats the earth's crust, as the comparative anatomist treats the animal creation.[5]

Furnivall, however, was also of a speculative and romantic nature:

> . . . and then to use that revised order for the purpose of studying the progress and meaning of Shakespere's mind, the passage of it from the fun and word-play, the lightness, the passion, of the Comedies of Youth, through the patriotism (still with comedy of more meaning) of the Histories of Middle Age, to the great Tragedies dealing with the deepest questions of man in Later Life; and then at last to the poet's peaceful and quiet home-life again in Stratford, where he ends with his Prospero and Miranda, his Leontes finding again his wife and daughter in Hermione and Perdita; in whom we may fancy that the Stratford both of his early and late days lives again.[6]

Furnivall seemed to have made up an outline biography and then used metrical tests to support it. While Furnivall compared end-stopped *vs* run-over lines, ten-syllable lines *vs* lines with an extra syllable (feminine lines) and rhyme *vs* blank verse, his friend, Frederick Fleay, counted syllables and rhymes. Fleay developed this into *A Chronicle History of the Life and Work of William Shakespeare*, 1886. The same approach was largely accepted by Sir Edmund Chambers (1930), who prepared five tables with 32 different features of comparison, mainly on verse, fourteen of which are partly reproduced in Tables 6a and 6b (see Appendix). Chambers's chronology (derived from the work of Furnivall and Fleay) has been extremely influential, e.g. on Feuillerat, but the basis on which many judgments were made has been overlooked. Grady (1994: 45) refers to the "now almost forgotten programme of versification analysis", noting that both Furnivall and Fleay had mathematical and classical training as undergraduates. Grady thinks it unlikely that metrical tests "will ever be revived as a scholarly activity, even though they are still cited in textual and chronological discussions". Vickers (2002: 128) also appears sceptical: "if verse tests from the Victorian era still have any validity".

However, since the advent of corpus analysis in the mid 1970s, the style of many Elizabethan authors has been analysed. The main purpose has been to establish or deny authorship, e.g. Merriam (2002) argues that *Henry V* is sufficiently deviant to suggest a different author. These studies of style have NOT been used to establish the *evolution* of style for any other author's works nor compared against authors whose chronology is already known.

A different approach to the problem of chronology was devised by Wells & Taylor. They compared 27 different linguistic items, which they called "colloquialisms in verse" (sixteen of which are reproduced in Tables 7a and 7b), both in plays of the First Folio and other plays attributed to Shakespeare. Their broad findings confirm the traditional dating of Shakespeare's plays. However, there has been no explanation as to *how* a study of style and/or verse can date an author's works. The assumptions seem to run as follows: there is a discernible, measurable and relatively consistent evolution in an author's use of language across a significant number or works and period of time. For this to be useful in dating otherwise undateable texts, the following aspects need to be established.

## 1. Dating Core Texts

Some kind of framework needs to be established within which problem texts can be subsequently located. If the dates of, for example, ten plays could be established with certainty, then it might be possible to plot other texts along gradients of change and allocate them to a likely year. Such a circumstance does not yet exist for Shakespeare, since there is no consistency in the dating of any play. Most commentators have Shakespeare beginning his writing career in *c.* 1590, but there are some who date it earlier, *c.* 1586. Nor is there consensus on which play is his earliest. Some follow Chambers in citing *2 Henry VI,* others follow Wells & Taylor in suggesting *Two Gentlemen*. If inconsistencies of plot and character make one play early, then *Cymbeline,* where coincidence abounds, should be an early play. If "clumsy staging" suggests earliness through immaturity or lack of experience, then should *The Tempest* perhaps be considered early, as about a quarter of the total lines (approx 505 out of 2062) occur in the second scene? The data itself is contradictory: Palmer (19) notes: "Stylistic considerations, notoriously subjective and unreliable, have suggested both early and late dating for *Troilus*." Wells and Taylor (*TxC* 97) conclude:

> The existing or 'orthodox' chronology for all Shakespeare's plays is conjectural.

## 2. Unrevised Texts

In the case of many authors it is recognised that some works were significantly altered between original composition and their eventual publication. Jane Austen's novel *First Impressions* was completed in 1797, but was rejected. She made extensive changes and the revised novel was published as *Pride and Prejudice* in 1813. Because the manuscript of the original novel does not survive, it is impossible to reconstruct which parts were written pre-1797 and which were written between 1797 and 1813.[7] Similarly with Shakespeare's works: were the plays ever, or even extensively, revised? Chambers rejects this idea and believes in the author's definitive version, with other versions being due to changes made by other people. However, Wells and Taylor accept the idea of revision, for in 1986 they published the complete works with two versions of *King Lear*, one based on the 'Pied Bull' Quarto of 1608 (which they call *The History of King Lear*) and the other version based on the First Folio of 1623, which they take to be an authorial revision and call *The Tragedy of King Lear*.

If the author revised one play, why not others? Such a question calls into doubt the basis for making judgements based on style. To continue to use metrical or other stylistic tests on Shakespeare's plays is to assume that each play was composed within a single period, with no revisions, excluding the possibility of dynamic texts which might have been altered at different periods of composition. So this is the second point: in order to have any validity, every core text used for establishing style must be known to have been composed within one short space of time.

## 3. Metre and Chronology

After various efforts in the nineteenth century to link metre and chronology (Walker, 1854; Bathurst, 1857; Furnivall, 1874; Fleay, 1886), Sir Sidney Lee felt able to assert in his *Life of William Shakespeare* (1898):

> [In Shakespeare] metre undergoes emancipation from the hampering restraints of fixed rule and becomes flexible enough to respond to every phase of human feeling. In the blank verse of the early plays, a pause is closely observed at the close of each line, and rhyming couplets are frequent. Gradually the poet overrides such artificial restrictions; rhyme largely disappears; recourse is made more frequently to prose; the pause is varied indefinitely; extra syllables are, contrary to strict metrical law, introduced at the end of lines, and at times at the middle; the last word of the line is often a weak and unemphatic conjunction or preposition.

Lee's fluent argument seems impressive, but falls down when applied to many individual plays: he identified *Merry Wives* as a late play (whereas the tendency of other critics is to place it as a middle play between 1597 and 1602); he proposed *Henry VIII* as an early play, when it is usually placed as a late, or even the last, play.

According to Lee, such features seem to be "deliberate, predictable and closely indicative of period". He argued: "Metrical characteristics prove [*Coriolanus*] to have been written about the same period as *Antony and Cleopatra*, probably in 1609." Lee is confident in his argument but then adds: "In its austere temper, it [*Coriolanus*] contrasts at all points with its predecessor [*Antony and Cleopatra*]" (246–7). Lee does not see any problem with the contradiction: the plays are close in composition due to similarities of style even though they are very different in temper.

Many readers remain sceptical as to whether these two Roman plays were written in the same period. A comparison of linguistic features in the Roman plays produces some different results. On the proportion of prose, *Julius Caesar* and *Antony* have relatively little (7% and 9%), which would place them among the earlier plays, whereas *Coriolanus* has quite a lot (24%) placing it 22nd out of 38 plays. If we take feminine endings, then *Coriolanus* and *Antony* come out as late plays and *Julius Caesar* as a middle play but *Pericles* emerges as an early play. In lines split between speakers, *Coriolanus* and *Antony* would be considered the final plays. Other results are also puzzling: if we take feminine endings, then *1 Henry IV* would be considered a very early play (3%) whereas it is usually placed as a middle play; according to the same criterion, *Richard III* should be considered a late play (18%) rather than early as is more customary.

Chambers's investigation of style as a dating tool was modified by Karl Wentersdorf (1951). Rather than rely on indicators separately, he took four together in a "metrical index". The four features were: (a) extra syllables, (b) overflows or enjambment (where the sense runs on into the next line), (c) pauses in unsplit lines, i.e. where a speaker has a mark of punctuation, e.g. full stop, colon, question mark or exclamation mark in the middle of one line, and (d) lines split between two speakers. The results seemed to confirm the chronology established by Chambers. There is a strong suggestion, however, that Wentersdorf has selected only those stylistic findings which coincide with Chambers's chronology.

Some of these metrical characteristics are, moreover, capable of different analysis. G. T. Wright (1999: 163) describes how an extra syllable or feminine ending may introduce a note of hesitation, of subtlety, of casualness, or simply of difference. Wright quotes from both *As You Like It* ('middle' period) and an 'early' work, *The Rape of Lucrece*. A double onset, or extra syllable at the beginning of a line, occurs to great effect in another 'middle' period play, *Julius Caesar* (2.1. 166):

> Let's be sac | ri fi | cers but | not but | chers Gai | us,

Similarly, the initial unstressed syllable is omitted not just in late plays but also in so-called early plays such as *Comedy of Errors. ( ^ Jailer, take him to thy custody,* 1.1. 155) Or in the middle of lines in plays such as *Richard II* (*Your grace mistakes* | ^ *Only to be brief Left I his title out* 3.3. 10–11). In short, Wright demonstrates that these deviations in metrical characteristics frequently serve a dramatic function.

## 4. 'Colloquialisms' and Chronology

Wells and Taylor (*TxC*: 106) seem to disparage at the same time both metrical tests and critics who are cautious about the reliability of metrical tests: "That change [in Shakespeare's style] has proven difficult to measure in terms which will satisfy every carping critic", and they affirm that their own stylistic tests are "resolutely consistent" (129). They take 26 different language features which they call "colloquialisms'" They hope to demonstrate a (presumably unconscious) evolution in style, perhaps influenced by changes in the language used by people at large. The notion of colloquialism, "an informal, spoken use of language" is problematic today but is much harder to recover from the Elizabethan era. Most of the colloquial features cited by Wells & Taylor (19 out of 26) involve elisions, e.g. with *it, the, them*. One feature is the use of syllabic –*ed* on verbs although clearly this has important use when an unstressed syllable is required. On the basis of this feature *Henry V* would be placed as early and *Taming* as a late play.

Other "colloquialisms" also give strange results, according to the system:

| | |
|---|---|
| *'t,* | places *Hamlet* late and *Troilus* early (both are usually considered middle plays) |
| *i'th',* | places *Coriolanus* as the last play; *Timon* early (both are usually considered late) |
| *o'th',* | places *Pericles* early (usually considered late) |
| *th',* | places *Richard III* late (usually considered early) |
| *'em,* | places *Two Gentlemen* late (usually considered very early) |
| *'ll,* | places *The Tempest* early (usually considered very late) |
| *does* | places *Hamlet* much later than *Coriolanus* (usually considered earlier) |
| *-eth* | places *Antony* quite early and before *1 Henry VI* and *Titus* |

Other 'colloquialisms' include: *'rt, 're, d/'ld, 'lt/'t, st/'ve, I'm, as, this', 'a'/ha', a', o', 's (us, his), 's (is), has.* Taking all 26 'colloquialisms' together, Wells & Taylor produce a graph where the plays come out in the usual order, with the exception of *The Merry Wives of Windsor* and *Hamlet*, (which would appear to coincide with *Measure for Measure c.* 1604). Like Wentersdorf, Wells and Taylor appear to select findings which coincide with the traditional or orthodox chronology.

What is not explained is *why* these particular colloquialisms should indicate an evolving style. *'Tis, 'twas, 'twere, I'll,* and *here's* are omitted on the grounds that such usage shows no sign of evolution. So why should we rate change in use in some elisions but not in others?

*Coriolanus* has the highest ratio of colloquialisms. Does this make it a late play? Or is the bard using a stylistic feature appropriate to the context in which plebeians have a large number of speeches? Similarly, history plays such as *King John, 1 Henry VI,* and *2 Henry IV* have the lowest ratio of 'colloquialisms'. It is quite possible that a lack of 'colloquialisms' reflects the educated characters of these plays (Falstaff after all is a knight). Thus it is possible, that the use of 'colloquialisms' is to some extent deliberate and not the result of an unconsciously evolving style. Wells and Taylor do not explain why some of the dramatist's elisions are taken to have evolved unconsciously, while others apparently did not.

## 5. Deliberate Changes in Style

Charles Dickens was a prolific novelist, with limited opportunity for revising his works, because his texts moved from pen to press very quickly. It is therefore reasonable to assume that the published texts are unlikely to have been subject to revision. Have linguistic tests been used to demonstrate an unconsciously evolving style in Dickens? A novel such as *Great Expectations* is known to have been composed over a 12-month period from 1860–61 and published in *All the Year Round*. It is not suggested that his style changed in that period. Before Dickens wrote *Great Expectations*, he re-read *David Copperfield* (1850).[8] It is very unlikely that we can distinguish between a sub-conscious evolution of Dickens's style, with his own deliberate control over linguistic preferences. Both Dickens and Shakespeare used language to distinguish their characters. Thus the likelihood of being able to recover any subconscious changes in style seems impossible. If Shakespeare first prepared his plays for the theatre and then later for the printing press (as Lukas Erne has argued[9]), how can we identify a "sub-consciously evolving style" as so many commentators have suggested?

## Conclusion

Shakespeare appears to be the only major writer whose works have been dated according to stylistic tests. One possible explanation is that there is a gaping void in the evidence for dating the plays which scholars are anxious to fill. Metrical and other stylistic tests are interesting, but they are not in themselves a reliable basis for *establishing* a chronology for the composition of the plays: as Vickers says, they can only "play a part in confirming or questioning a date established on other grounds". In the case of Shakespeare's plays, these "other grounds" have yet to be established.

## Notes

1. An earlier version of this chapter appeared in *Great Oxford*, ed. R. Malim, Parapress, 2004.
2. Vickers reviews various attempts to date Hand D in *Sir Thomas More* and concludes that it is late, *c.* 1608, from about the same period as *Coriolanus*. Wells & Taylor, (*Textual Companion)* date the play to 1603–4 (p. 124) or to 1593–5 (p. 139).
3. Edmond Malone, "An Attempt to Ascertain the Order in which the Plays of Shakespeare Were Written" in *The Plays of William Shakespeare* ed. S. Johnson and G. Steevens (London, 1778), vol I, 28 quoted by (among others) Samuel Schoenbaum *Shakespeare's Lives*, Oxford 1970: 168.
4. Bathurst, 1857: 57, quoted by H. H. Furness, *New Variorum Edition of Shakespeare,* 1888, vol. 7, p. 283.
5. F. J. Furnivall, *The Literary World*, 9 July 1887, quoted by Hugh Grady, *The Modernist Shakespeare*, p. 46.
6. Opening address to the New Shakespere Society, London, 1874, quoted by Schoenbaum, *Shakespeare's Lives*, 484.
7. Some of Jane Austen's manuscripts survive: *Lady Susan*, two uncompleted novels (*The Watsons* and *Sanditon*), *Plan of a Novel*, a play, *Sir Charles Grandison,* and Chapters 10 and 11 of *Persuasion*. See Brian Southam's *Jane Austen's Literary Manuscripts: A Study of the Novelist's Development through the surviving papers*, Athlone Press, 2002.
8. Peter Ackroyd, *Dickens: Public Life and Private Passions,* London: BBC, 2002.
9. Lukas Erne, *Shakespeare as a Literary Dramatist,* Cambridge: CUP, 2003.

## Other Works Cited

Bathurst, C., *Shakespeare's Versification at different Periods of his Life,* London, 1857

Chambers, E. K., "The Problem of Chronology" in *William Shakespeare: A Study of Facts and Problems,* Oxford: Clarendon Press, 1930, vol. 1, pages 243–274

Feuillerat, Albert, *The Composition of Shakespeare's Plays: authorship, chronology*, New Haven: Yale UP, 1953

Grady, Hugh, *The Modernist Shakespeare*: *Critical texts in a Material World*. Oxford: Clarendon, 1994

Lee, Sir Sidney, *A Life of William Shakespeare,* London: Smith, Elder & Co, 1898

Hope, Jonathan, *The Authorship of Shakespeare's Plays*, Cambridge: CUP, 1994

Merriam, T., "Intertextual Differences between Shakespeare Plays, with special reference to Henry V", *Journal of Quantitative Linguistics*, 2002: 261–73

Palmer, Kenneth (ed.), *Troilus and Cressida,* London: Arden Methuen, 1982

Vickers, Brian, *Shakespeare, Co-Author,* Oxford: OUP, 2002

Walker, W. S., *Shakespeare's Versification and its apparent Irregularities explained by Examples from Early and Late English Writers*. London: J. R. Smith, 1854

Waller, F. O., 'The Use of Linguistic Criteria in Determining the Copy and Dates of Shakespeare's Plays' *Pacific Coast Studies in Shakespeare,* ed. W. F McNeir and T. N. Greenfield, Eugene: University of Oregon Press, 1960

Wells, Stanley & Gary Taylor, *William Shakespeare: A Textual Companion,* Oxford: OUP, 1987

Wentersdorf, Karl, "Shakespearean Chronology and Metrical Tests", in W. Fischer & K. Wentersdorf (eds), *Shakespeare-Studien,* 1951

Wright, G. T., "Hearing Shakespeare's Dramatic Verse" in Kastan (ed.), *A Companion to Shakespeare,* Oxford: Blackwell, 1999

# The Comedies

# 1

# The Tempest

## Philip Johnson and Kevin Gilvary

There is no contemporary evidence to date the composition of *The Tempest*. The play is usually assumed to have been completed by 1611, when it was performed at court. It can be dated any time after 1580, when all the major sources had become available.

### Publication Date

*The Tempest* was entered in the Stationers' Register on 8 November 1623, one of eighteen plays in the First Folio (F1) which had not been registered previously:

> Mr Blounte Isaak Jaggard. Entred for their Copie vnder the hands of Mr Doctor Worrall and Mr Cole, warden, Mr William Shakspeers Comedyes, Histories, and Tragedyes soe manie of the said Copies are are not formerly entred to other men, vizt. Comedyes. The Tempest. The two gentlemen of Verona. Measure for Measure. The Comedy of Errors. As you Like it, All's well that ends well. Twelft night. The winters tale. Histories. The thirde parte of Henry the sixt. Henry the eight. Tragedies: Coriolanus. Timon of Athens. Julius Caesar. Mackbeth. Anthonie and Cleopatra. Cymbeline.

*The Tempest* occupies first position among the comedies and is therefore the first play in F1. Orgel points out that its place at the start of the Folio might be taken to suggest that it was an early play. Chambers describes the printed text as 'a very fair text with careful punctuation'.

## Performance Dates

The Revels Accounts records a performance of 'a play called the Tempest' presented 'att Whitehall before ye Kings Matie', by the King's Men on 1 November 1611. This is presumed to be the première performance, as there is no earlier record of a play under this name. Another performance by the King's Men at Court was recorded for February 1613, one of fourteen plays by a range of writers, to whom there is no attribution in the record of payment.

There is a separate record of a play performed on 11 February 1604/5, when the Court Revels lists *The Spanish Maze*, an otherwise unattributed play. Malim suggested that this play might be identified with *The Tempest.* He notes that thirteen plays and two masques were performed in a short season from Hallowmas (31 October) to Shrove Tuesday (11 February 1605). Of these, some were by other authors, seven were by Shakespeare and one performed on Shrove Monday was *A Tragidye of the Spanishe Maz*, which remains unattributed. Stritmatter and Kositsky (1) have developed the argument that *The Spanish Maze* was a version of *The Tempest.* They observe that there were variable names for several of Shakespeare's plays (e.g. *Twelfth Night / What you Will*), that the definitions of genres had not been fully developed and that Prospero's misfortunes make the play as 'tragic' as, say, *Troilus and Cressida.* They further note that Spanish dynastic arrangements had left Naples, Sicily and other Italian-speaking areas under Spanish rule. Finally, they suggest that the characters see themselves in a maze, both literally and psychologically, e.g. Alonso says: "This is as strange a maze as e'er men trod" (5.1.245).

## Sources

### (a) Contemporary Accounts of Storms, Shipwrecks and Settlements

Geoffrey Bullough maintains that there are no agreed sources for the main plot. Vaughan and Vaughan (Arden edition) explain what happened when scholars were unable to identify any specific source for *The Tempest*:

> When source-hunting was fashionable, especially during the late nineteenth and early twentieth centuries, frustrated scholars scoured English and continental literature for the play's prototype or, at the very least, for a text that might have inspired its basic structure.

As there was no immediately identifiable literary source, attention turned to historical details.

Bullough considers various accounts of storms, settlements and shipwreck from the voyages to Virginia in 1609–11. These accounts have been cited not so much as sources but as inspirations:

1. *A True and sincere declaration of the purpose and ends of the Plantation begun in Virginia*. (Council of Virginia, 1609)
2. Sylvester Jourdain's *Discovery of the Bermudas* (1610)
3. *A True Declaration of the estate of the Colonie in Virginia* (Council of Virginia, 1610)
4. William Strachey's *A True Repertory of the Wracke and Redemption of Sir Thomas Gates, Knight* (letter dated 1610; published 1625).

The historical events can be summarised as follows: in 1607, the first surviving English settlement in North America was founded at Jamestown, Virginia. Two years later, Sir George Somers led a supply expedition of nine ships bound for Jamestown, but his ship, the *Sea Venture*, was damaged in a storm and blown off course. The rest of the fleet reached their intended destination but the *Sea Venture* was brought to the island of Bermuda on 28 July and deliberately beached on a reef; all 150 people aboard (and one dog) landed safely. Important items from the ship such as the rigging were salvaged in an orderly manner. On the island of Bermuda (despite its name 'Ile of Divils'), there were no magical events. During the winter of 1609–10, the crew built two ships, the *Deliverance* and the *Patience*. On 10 May, the adventurers set sail for Jamestown, where they found that most of the other 500 people on their expedition had died.

Of the four Bermuda pamphlets describing these events, Strachey's letter is the only one now thought to have had any influence on *The Tempest:* both Orgel (Oxford, 209) and Vaughan & Vaughan (Arden, 287) limit their appendix on sources to this letter. Vaughan (*SQ*) summarises Strachey's account:

> the *Sea Venture*'s journey toward Virginia; a dreadful storm; the seemingly miraculous crash on Bermuda; the eventful months there, including the construction of two pinnaces; the final leg to Jamestown; the Virginia Colony's deplorable condition; and Virginia's history from late May to mid-July 1610 – most notably, Lord De la Warre's arrival, barely in time, to prevent the abandonment of the Colony.

Clearly the plot of *The Tempest* only corresponds to the first few items (storm, shipwreck, eventful months) but not to the later parts of the letter (construction of new ships, journey to Jamestown and the conditions there). Furthermore, there is no correspondence between the events of the letter and the situation of the play's protagonist (an exiled and embittered nobleman, who plots his revenge on those who wronged him).

Strachey's letter, dated 1610 but not published until 1625, was "evidently in circulation" before (the evidence being no more than apparent references in the play). Bullough, in line with a majority of commentators from Malone onwards, believes that Shakespeare must "just have read Strachey's letter" and probably the other accounts as well. He states that Shakespeare would have found some "promising features":

> A tempest; a shipwreck; a haunted island of ill repute but beautiful and fertile, though uninhabited and almost inaccessible; a mingling of social classes – nobles, gentlemen, tradesmen, labourers, mariners, natives well- and ill-disposed; dissensions leading to dangerous divisions and conspiracies.

More recent commentators, however, are not convinced that Shakespeare must have read such an account. Vaughan and Vaughan list a mere four references to Strachey's letter: (a) the use of the word 'glut' as a noun describing the sea washing over the ship during storm (at 1.1.57 Shakespeare uses it unusually as a verb); (b) reference to St Elmo's Fire compares with Ariel's poetic reference at 1.2.199 to "flamed amazement" – a frequent phenomenon on ships in storms; (c) Strachey's letter refers to the Bermudas which compares with Ariel's reference to the "still-vexed Bermoothes" (F's spelling is invariably changed to "Bermudas") at 1.2.230, apparently to the Bermuda Sea. Strachey was not the first Englishman to visit Bermuda: James Lancaster after sailing to the East Indies put ashore in a storm there for five or six days in 1593 before returning to England in 1594.[1] Another meaning of Bermuda is mentioned by Vaughan and Vaughan, who note that "Bermudas" was also an area of London, notorious for licentious behaviour, as described by Jonson in *Bartholomew Fair* (*c.* 1614) when the Justice of the Peace declares (2.6. 75–8):

> Looke into any Angle of the towne, (the Streights, or the Bermuda's) where the quarrelling lesson is read, and how do they entertaine the time, but with bottle-ale, and tabacco?

Horsman explains in a footnote (following William Gifford in his 1816 edition) that Jonson was referring to a nest of obscure courts, alleys and avenues between the bottom of St Martin's Lane, Half-moon and Chandos-street, "the receptacle of fraudulent dealers, thieves and prostitutes". Thus it is possible that Ariel is not referring to Strachey's 1609 shipwreck. (d) Strachey's shipwrecked mariners drink water with berries as had Caliban.

Other commentators have noted some other apparent borrowings by Shakespeare in one of his last plays, yet each is paralleled elsewhere in the works as the following three examples indicate: (e) Strachey uses 'ague' once in his letter and Stephano mentions Caliban's 'ague' three times (in 2.2), yet Shakespeare uses 'ague' fifteen times elsewhere, including the fictitious character of Sir Andrew Aguecheek in *Twelfth Night*; (f) Strachey has 'hoodwinked' and *The Tempest* 'hoodwink' (4.1.206), but 'hoodwink' occurs five times elsewhere; (g) 'toad' appears once in Strachey and twenty-three times in Shakespeare. Although the correspondences between Strachey and *The Tempest* appear slight, Vaughan (*SQ*) concludes:

> The abundant thematic and verbal parallels between the play and "True Reportory" have persuaded generations of readers that Shakespeare

> borrowed liberally from Strachey's dramatic narrative in telling his island tale.

Kermode (1954), however, accepts that Shakespeare might have composed *The Tempest* without reading Strachey's letter:

> There is nothing in *The Tempest* fundamental to its structure of ideas which could not have existed had America remained undiscovered, and the Bermuda voyage never taken place.

Muir in *The Sources of Shakespeare's Plays* (1978) expands this doubt:

> The extent of the verbal echoes of [the Bermuda] pamphlets has, I think, been exaggerated. There is hardly a shipwreck in history or fiction which does not mention splitting, in which the ship is not lightened of its cargo, in which the passengers do not give themselves up for lost, in which north winds are not sharp, and in which no one gets to shore by clinging to wreckage. (280)

David Lindley, editor of the *New Cambridge Shakespeare* (2002), agrees:

> There is virtually nothing in these texts [the Bermuda pamphlets] which manifests the kind of unambiguous close verbal affinity we have seen in other sources [Virgil, Ovid and Montaigne] so far considered.

Regarding contemporary events, Shakespeare could have drawn on other tales of expeditions and shipwrecks which were also available to Strachey, including Sir Walter Raleigh's 1596 *Discovery of Guiana*, a widely-available report of his expedition to the West Indies, Hakluyt's *Voyages* (1592) and *The Principal Navigations, Voyages, Traffiques and Discoveries, vol.III* (1600), which contains Henry May's account of the wreck of the *Edward Bonaventure* in the Bermudas in 1594.

More recently, Stritmatter and Kositsky (2007 & 2009) have argued that the major historical source was Peter Martyr's *De Orbe Novo* ('Concerning the New World', published in Latin in 1530). Martyr describes the earliest explorations of the Americas from Columbus's first voyage in 1492. Martyr's work was translated by Richard Eden in 1555 as *The Decades of the New Worlde Or West India,* (augmented by Willes in 1577) and could have influenced the composition of the play. Stritmatter and Kositsky tabulate a large number of correspondences, e.g. Prospero calls Caliban "thou tortoise" (1.2.318), while Trinculo wonders whether he is "a man or a fish" (2.2.24–7), and Stephano repeatedly calls him "moon-calf" (e.g., 2.2.109, 2.2.135). In Eden, there is a description of a manatee, unknown at the time in the Old World:

> Into his neates chanced **a younge fyshe** of the kynde of those huge **monsters of the sea** whiche the Thinhabitours caule Manati ... This

> fyshe is **foure footed, and in shape lyke unto a tortoyse ... and her heade utterly lyke the heade of an oxe. She lyeth both in the water and on the lande:** she is slowe of movynge: of condition meeke, gentell, **assocyable and loving to mankind** and of a marvelous sence or memorie as are the elephant and the delphyn**... A monster of the sea fed with man's hand** (130v–131).

Stritmatter and Kositsky note that this account probably also suggested Stephano's reference to Caliban and Trinculo under the gabardine: "This is some monster of the isle with four legs who hath got as I take it an ague" (2.2.65–6).

## (b) Literary Works

Further literary accounts occur in allusions to famous classical accounts of shipwrecks. Bullough considers, then discards, Virgil's *Aeneid* as an influence. Bullough's decision to discard the *Aeneid* is odd: Book I describes Aeneas's shipwreck at Carthage, his reunion with friends thought lost at sea and magical help from Venus in securing a favourable reception from Dido (events which are all paralleled in *The Tempest*). Moreover, characters in *The Tempest* discuss Dido and Aeneas at 2.1.79–90 and argue over whether to identify Carthage with Tunis:

| | |
|---|---|
| ADRIAN | Tunis was never graced before with such a paragon to their queen. |
| GONZALO | Not since widow Dido's time. |
| ANTONIO | Widow! a pox o' that! How came that widow in? widow Dido! |
| SEBASTIAN | What if he had said 'widower Aeneas' too? Good Lord, how you take it! |
| ADRIAN | 'Widow Dido' said you? you make me study of that: she was of Carthage, not of Tunis. |
| GONZALO | This Tunis, sir, was Carthage. |
| ADRIAN | Carthage? |
| GONZALO | I assure you, Carthage. |

Hamilton has offered (intro, x), an interesting interpretation in which Shakespeare's play is "a formal and rigorous rhetorical imitation of the major narrative kernels of *Aeneid*, 1–6." Kallendorf agrees, seeing the play as not only influenced by *Aeneid I* but as a detailed adaptation of it.

Other accounts of shipwrecks included St Paul's shipwreck on Malta (Acts of the Apostles, 27–28:12) when miraculous events were described. Moore shows how Paul's shipwreck would provide more features for the play than Strachey's letter:

> A voyage to Italy within the Mediterranean; discord among the participants; the crew against the passengers; the ship driven by a 'tempest'; loss of hope; an angel visits the ship (*c.f.* Ariel); desperate manoeuvres to avoid the lee shore of an unknown island; detailed description of nautical techniques; the ship runs aground and splits; passengers and crew swim ashore on loose or broken timbers (*c.f.* Stephano coming ashore on a butt of sack); the island has barbarous inhabitants (*c.f.* Caliban); supernatural involvement (Ariel); a seeming miracle; St. Paul immune to snakebite; a safe trip to Italy after a stay on the island.

The dramatist's further use of classical authors in the play has been demonstrated in the case of Ovid at great length by Jonathan Bate, who analyses Prospero's famous abjuration of magic:

> Ye elves of hills, brooks, standing lakes and groves, And ye that on the sands with printless foot Do chase the ebbing Neptune and do fly him . . . (*Tempest*, 51.33–5)

Bate shows how the dramatist draws both on Ovid's original text of the *Metamorphoses* Book VII, 197–209 and on Golding's 1567 translation.

From more contemporary literary texts, Montaigne's Essay *On Cannibals* is seen as a major influence on Shakespeare for the portrait of Caliban and for Gonzalo's lengthy description of his imaginary commonwealth (2.1.149–70). This was proposed by Kermode but ignored by Bullough. Paster also links Montaigne with the references to Dido. Montaigne's essay was published in French in 1580 and translated into English in 1603 by John Florio.

Stritmatter and Kositsky (2007) also place great emphasis on the literary discourse of Erasmus's *Naufragium* ('The Shipwreck') published in 1523 (and considered by Bullough "a possible source"). Stritmatter and Kositsky juxtapose many correspondences including Ariel's speech:

> I boarded the King's ship; now on the beak,
> Now in the waist, the deck, in every cabin,
> I flam'd amazement. Sometimes I'ld divide,
> And burn in many places; on the topmast,
> The yards and boresprit, would I flame distinctly,
> Then meet and join. Jove's lightning, the precursors
> O' th' dreadful thunder-claps, more momentary
> And sight-outrunning were not. (1.2.197–204)

Erasmus has the following similar description of St Elmo's Fire:

> And in **the top of the mast** stood one of the mariners in the basket... **looking about to see if he could spie any land**: fast by this man began to stand a certain round thing like a **ball of fire**, which (when it appeareth alone) is to the shipmen a most fearful sign of hard success, but when

> two of them appear together, that is a sign of a prosperous voyage. **These apparitions were called in old time Castor and Pollux...** By and by the **fiery globe** sliding down by the ropes, tumbled itself until it came to the master of the ship...it having stayed there a while, it rolled itself along the brimmes of the ship, and falling from thence down into the middle roomes, it vanished away...(G1–G1v).

Bullough, however, does consider a range of other literary texts, which appear to be analogues but need not be considered sources: he compares Ben Johnson's *Hymenaei* (1606) with Prospero's' remarks on the ephemerality of the spectacle. He sees comparison of the father–daughter relationshiop with the *Mirrour of Knighthood* (*The first part* of *El Espejo de Principes y Caballeros*, was begun by Ortúñez de Calahorra in 1562 and translated from Spanish by M[argaret] T[yler], 1578, *The third part* translated by R. Parry in 1586?). This romance deals with Prince Palisteo, a magician, who retires with his son and daughter to an island where he builds a magic castle. He rears the daughter in solitude. When she grows up he shows her pictures of many valiant knights and her father uses his magic to bring her preferred knight. The young man is brought by magic across the sea and out of a shipwreck to be the daughter's lover. Their adventures have more than a little in common with Prospero, Miranda and Ferdinand. Bullough also considers as analogues *John a Kent and John a Cumber* by Anthony Munday (1594), *A Most Pleasant Comedie of Mucedorus* Anon (1598) and *Die schöne Sidea* ('The Fair Sidea'), which was perhaps a translation by Jacob Ayrer (1616) of an English play performed in Germany.

Other commentators have traced possible influence of other works of European Literature. Schmidgall has argued that *Primaleon* (a Spanish Romance published in 1512 and translated into English by Anthony Munday 1595) was used by the dramatist. Bilton has argued that Montemayor's *Diana Enamorada* (published in 1560, translated into English *c.* 1582–98), used for *Two Gentlemen of Verona* was an important source. Stritmatter and Kositsky (2007) also cite Ariosto's *Orlando Furioso* (published in 1532 and adapted by Robert Greene as *The Historie of Orlando Furioso* in 1592). Cantos 41–3 seem to parallel the events of *The Tempest.*

## (c) *Commedia dell'Arte*

Bullough also considers various *scenarii*, or outline plots, from the *commedia dell'arte* as analogues; he does not view them as sources because, "there is no proof that Shakespeare ever saw a *commedia dell'arte* acted." Despite this, it seems likely that the author of *The Tempest* combined various pastoral scenarii used by travelling troupes of players in Italy and later written down in manuscripts *c.* 1620. These were transcribed in 1913 by Fernando Neri and translated by Kathleen Lea in 1934 as part of her detailed study of Italian comedy and English drama.

There has been erratic consideration of the *commedia dell'arte*'s contribution to *The Tempest* since E. K. Chambers, who in 1930 made careful note of the similarities. He thought that *Li Tre Satiri* most resembled *The Tempest* in that foreigners are taken for gods, as Trinculo is by Caliban, and the Pantalone and Zanni steal Mago's book, as Trinculo and Stephano plot to steal Prospero's. Baldwin in 1947 asserted that the scenarios were plot-analogues similar to those found for *The Comedy of Errors* and *Two Gentlemen of Verona.* Frank Kermode in the introduction to his 1954 Arden edition of *The Tempest* conceded that there is "a certain resemblance to the Italian Form" and that the *commedia dell'arte* is "the most interesting reputed source".

More recently, Kathleen Lea's development of Neri's study has been ignored, perhaps because the traditional biography can find no plausible connection between the author and the *commedia dell'arte.* Leo Salingar (1974) refers only briefly to the *commedia dell'arte* in his otherwise excellent study. Stephen Orgel (Oxford, 1987) does not mention Italian Comedy. Vaughan and Vaughan (Arden, 1999) give only small consideration to Lea's work. David Lindley (Cambridge, 2002) allows certain general correspondences with Italian Comedy.

The significance of these scenarii, however, is supported by Rebora, Orsini and other experts in Italian Comedy. In 1980, Ninian Mellamphy asserted that it is "virtually certain that Shakespeare's contemporaries had a more than casual knowledge of the *commedia dell'arte.*" Clubb in 1989 developed the idea of contact between the Italian troupes and Shakespeare. One Shakespeare scholar who turned to Italian Comedy was Allardyce Nicoll (1963: 118–9). Nicholl regarded a scenario from the *commedia dell'arte Arcadia Incantada* ('The Enchanted Arcadia') as the *principal* source for the plot of *The Tempest.* This scenario involves Pulchinella entering from one side of the stage describing a shipwreck and the loss of all his ship's company. Then Coviello enters from the other side and says and does the same. The characters then see each other, making the lazzi of fear. (Lazzi are humorous interruptions along set lines, e.g. comic mimes.) They end by recognising each other. The plot then moves to a magician who controls the island through spirits, which offer and then remove food from the starving companions. Various lovers among the shepherds and nymphs are confused. Eventually, the magician is able to right old wrongs, lead the survivors away from the island and abandon his art.

A strong case may be made for the dramatist's close knowledge of the *commedia dell'arte*, as can be seen from a comparison of the plots in three other scenarii – *La Nave* ('The Ship'), *Il Mago* ('the Magician') and *Tre Satiri* ('The Three Satyrs') – with *The Tempest*:

(**M** = *Il Mago*, **N** = *Il Nave*, **S** = *Tre Satiri*)

| **Events in Pastoral Scenarii** | **M** | **N** | **S** | ***Tempest*** |
|---|---|---|---|---|
| Unities of time, place and action | ✔ | ✔ | ✔ | ✔ |
| Scene set in a remote island | ✔ | ✔ | ✔ | ✔ |
| Magician causes Buffoons to be shipwrecked | | ✔ | | 1.1 |
| Pantalone bemoans the shipwreck & his hunger | ✔ | ✔ | ✔ | 2.1 |
| Characters are trapped inside a tree and a rock | | | ✔ | 1.2.275 |
| Characters dress as / are taken by others as gods | ✔ | ✔ | ✔ | 5.1.190 |
| Food magically appears (or disappears) | | ✔ | ✔ | 3.3.20–51 |
| Magician broods and considers marriages of others | ✔ | ✔ | ✔ | 3.1.74–76 |
| Magician controls spirits, devils and/or satyrs | ✔ | ✔ | ✔ | 1.2 |
| Magic garlands / Clothes appear | | ✔ | | 2.1.66–9 |
| Plot to steal magician's book (and / or kill him) | ✔ | ✔ | ✔ | 3.2.90 |
| Lovers are revealed as children of Pantalone & Gratiano | | ✔ | ✔ | 5.1.192–9 |
| Magician renounces his art | | ✔ | | 5.1.54 |

The case for the dramatist's close knowledge of the *commedia dell'arte* becomes stronger when comparing the stock characters with those in *The Tempest*:

| **Characters in Pastoral Scenarii** | **M** | **N** | **S** | ***Tempest*** |
|---|---|---|---|---|
| Pantalone (vain, prosperous and elderly) | ✔ | ✔ | ✔ | Alonso |
| Fausto / Sireno (lost son) | ✔ | ✔ | ✔ | Ferdinand |
| Coviello, his servant | ✔ | | ✔ | Gonzalo |
| Gratiano (old, wealthy & pretentious) | ✔ | ✔ | ✔ | Antonio |
| Elpino (son of Gratiano) | | ✔ | ✔ | Mentioned 1.2.441 |
| Bertolino (dishonest servant) / Zanni | ✔ | ✔ | ✔ | Stephano, Trinculo |
| Filli / Clori (love-struck daughter) | ✔ | ✔ | ✔ | Miranda |
| Amarilli (love-struck local girl) | ✔ | | | (Miranda) |
| Selvaggio (the wild man) | ✔ | | ✔ | Caliban |

| **Characters in Pastoral Scenarii** | **M** | **N** | **S** | ***Tempest*** |
|---|---|---|---|---|
| Magician | ✔ | ✔ | ✔ | Prospero |
| Demon / spirits | ✔ | ✔ | | Ariel |
| Lion | ✔ | ✔ | | mentioned, 2.1.317 |
| Gods | | Bacchus Jove | Jove Mercury Cupid | Iris, Ceres, Juno |

Because of the strong correspondences, it is very likely that Shakespeare knew these Italian pastoral plays, but he made one important alteration: he gave centre stage to The Magician ('Prospero'), making him the protagonist in the drama, with a desire for revenge for his earlier deposition and to return to his former position of authority.

## (d) Italian Politics

Bullough dismissed as a source William Thomas's *History of Italy* (1549), yet it contains many elements in common with *The Tempest*. Thomas based his *History* on researches conducted over a five year period, included a story about a Duke of Genoa, Prospero Adorno, who had been deposed in 1460. This Prospero returned sixteen years later to rule as deputy for the Duke of Milan. Prospero then made an alliance with Ferdinando, King of Naples and continued ruling for many years. In another account, William Thomas also mentions Alfonso, King of Naples, who married the daughter of the Duke of Milan, and in 1495 renounced his state to his son Ferdinand and sailed into Sicily where he gave himself to study, solitariness and religion.

Bullough's dismissal of Thomas is strange, but he accepts:

> It is of course possible that Shakespeare recalled [in Thomas' *History of Italy*] the banished Duke of Genoa and his difficulties when naming Prospero of Milan; he may even have got Ferdinand from Thomas also; but it is not necessary to think so (250).

To the names 'Prospero' (not used as a character's name elsewhere in Shakespeare) and 'Ferdinand' (used elsewhere only once in *Taming of the Shrew*), we may add the following elements: a ruler who was deposed, but returns to rule many years later; an alliance with the King of Naples, whose heir marries the daughter of the Duke of Milan; and a ruler given to quiet study.

## Orthodox Date

Chambers continued the tradition started by Malone of dating the play to 1610–11, composed between Strachey's letter and its recorded performance in 1611. Most commentators have accepted this date. A few have disagreed: Cairncross proposed "not earlier than 1603". Yates, who saw *The Tempest* as "the corner-stone of the total edifice of the last plays", certainly felt "there is room for an earlier version of the play".

## Internal Orthodox Evidence

Orthodox writers focus strongly on the Strachey letter, with its details of storm and shipwreck as shown in sources (a) above. However, the correspondences are weak and it is even possible that that the borrowing process worked in the opposite direction: the text of Shakespeare's *Tempest* was published in 1623 in F1; Strachey's letter was published in 1625.

Various attempts have been made to correlate the style and language of *The Tempest* with other plays, but the dates of these other plays cannot be fixed with precision. The verse of *The Tempest* may be mature and 'emancipated' by some tests, but some odd correlations emerge: the play shares the same proportion of rhymed lines to unrhymed (4%) as *2 Henry VI* and *Richard III*. Yet these history plays (according to Wells and Taylor) were composed 15–20 years earlier. Using measures derived from the use of 'colloquial' language, *The Tempest* has only one verb ending in *–eth* but then *Titus Andronicus*, an 'early play' only has two. Since we don't know how many transcriptions of the play there were between composition and publication, there can be no certainty over whether such judgements are being applied to the playwright or to the scribes.

It has, somewhat romantically, sometimes been suggested that *The Tempest* is Shakespeare's public announcement of his retirement from writing. The notion is derived from Prospero's abjuration of magic:

> By my so potent art. But this rough magic
> I here abjure, and, when I have required
> Some heavenly music, which even now I do,
> To work mine end upon their senses that
> This airy charm is for, I'll break my staff, (5.1.50–54)

When taken with certain phrases in the epilogue: "Now my charms are all o'erthrown ... Now I want Art to enchant" (Ep, 1–2), Prospero's words are taken as personal, autobiographical statements of the playwright. It is not a procedure that has been seriously applied to the speeches of any other play; and it is not a safe one, not least because careful examination of the Italian pastoral *scenarii* show that the magician eventually renounces his art.

## External Orthodox Evidence

Orthodox commentators have cited the 1611 performance as the première performance as there is no earlier record of a play under this name. Such an inference needs to be made cautiously when the records are so fragmentary.

## Oxfordian Date

Clark proposes 1583/4 as the date of writing. Ogburn proposes 1602, while Hess and colleagues prefer 1600 as the date for the mature play (perhaps with some slight later revision). Much later, it was "revised and presented to King James". Price (not an Oxfordian) argues that *The Tempest* may well have been badly misdated.

## Internal Oxfordian Evidence

*The Tempest* can be considered an early play, *c.* 1583–4, for various reasons: it observes the unities of space and time. Shakespeare's only other play to do so is *The Comedy of Errors,* which is taken to be an early play. Most of Shakespeare's plays have 'dynamic staging' where the scene moves from one time and location to another. Secondly, it has a long, tedious exposition of background material in 1.2 when Prospero speaks with Miranda, Ariel and Caliban, and recounts their biographies for the benefit of the audience. In other plays, there is much less exposition, while background details emerge in more natural dialogue.

An early date for composition is also suggested by the visits of troupes of Italian actors to England. According to Chambers (*ES*, ii 261–5), the only provincial payment to Italian players was at Nottingham in 1573. The following year, Italian players are mentioned in the Revels Accounts as playing before the Queen at Windsor and at Reading. Their props suggest a pastoral rather than purely comic performance. Two years later on 27 February 1576, one troupe performed at court, and another under Drousiano was given dispensation to play during Lent in 1578. There are no further recorded visits of Italian players.

Oxford returned from his visit to Italy in April 1576 (Nelson, 121–157) and, during the next five years, he presented plays at court and patronised his own acting companies, one of men, another of boys (Nelson, 239–248). As he had spent much of his time in the northern cities of Verona, Padua, Venice and Siena, it is likely he would have come across performances of the *commedia dell'arte* both in the main squares and in the palaces. Thus it would be logical for him to adapt Italian plays for the English stage in this period.

## External Oxfordian Evidence

Eva Turner Clark proposes 1583–4 as the date of writing, at the time when Oxford was temporarily out of the Queen's favour due to the denunciations of his one-time friends (Nelson, 249–58; 286–91). Clark identifies Alonso with Philip Howard, Antonio with Henry Howard and Sebastian with Charles Arundel. The good old counsellor, Gonzalo, was Oxford's father-in-law, Burghley. She makes further identifications between the action of the play with Oxford's ill-fated attempt to invest in Frobisher's expedition in search of the north-west passage in 1577 (Nelson, 186–91). Clark's early date *c.* 1583–4, is tenable, as all the major sources were available by this time. The latest of them, Montaigne's *Essays* were published in French in 1580, and Oxford had received two hours' daily instruction in French while a boy (Nelson, 37).

Ogburn proposes a date *c.*1603, shortly after the return of Oxford's relative, Bartholomew Gosnold, who surveyed the coasts of Maine and Massachusetts, drawing maps and naming places such as Martha's Vineyard. Ogburn also points out that Oxford had been a previous owner of a ship, the *Edward Bonaventure,* which had been shipwrecked in the Bermudas in 1594 with the loss of half the ship's company.[2] One of the survivors was Henry May, who eventually returned to England and published his tale in Hakluyt's *Principal Navigations, Voyages, Traffiques and Discoveries,* vol.III (1600). Ogburn's date would anticipate the performance of *The Spanish Maze* shortly afterwards.

A further argument for an early date would follow the identification of John Dee (1527–1609), the astrologer and mathematician, with Prospero, as argued by one of his biographers, Richard Deacon. John Dee had been high in the Queen's favour at the start of her reign, but, by 1590, Dee's career and reputation were in sharp decline. Woolley points out that Dee returned from the continent in December 1589 to find his house at Mortlake ransacked – mainly, it seems, by his pupils and associates – with most of his scientific instruments and five hundred expensive books stolen. "The court was unrecognisable": many of his old friends, such as Leicester, were dead, and Hatton and Walsingham soon followed. Astrologers were being ridiculed, and Dee himself was attacked in a pamphlet of 1592. His remaining influential friends failed to secure a job for him, and he went to Manchester. Presenting John Dee on stage as Prospero would be most apposite in the 1580s when Dee was a celebrity. He was well known to Oxford at this time and both were interested in expeditions to explore the north-west passage (Nelson, 186–9).

Lambin identifies a different historical ruler as the model for Prospero: Francesco-Maria de Medici, second Grand Duke of Florence and Tuscany from 1574–1587. As well as encouraging literature and the arts, he had a secret 'cell', now called the Studiolo di Francesco I, on the first floor of the Palazzo Vecchio in Florence, where he conducted alchemical and necromantic experiments. It is likely that Oxford knew, or knew of, this Duke of Florence, since he visited the city in December 1575 (Nelson, 131).

Some Oxfordians have argued for a strong link between Oxford and Prospero because both had been dispossessed of their hereditary rights. There are also similarities between Miranda and Oxford's daughter, Elizabeth, his only child (until 1583). They further call to witness the extensive legal knowledge and understanding shown in the play (as described by Sokol and Sokol, who list the play in the discussion of over twenty legal concepts, e.g. on plantation at 2.1.149–74 and on pre-contract at 4.1.8). This legal knowledge reflects Oxford's training at Gray's Inn (Nelson, 46) as well as the licence granted in 1584 to his friend, Walter Raleigh, to establish a plantation in Virginia at Roanoke. All of these indicate an early date.

## Conclusion

*The Tempest* can be dated between 1580, by which time most if not all the major sources were available and 1611, when the play was recorded in performance. There is no specific evidence to connect the play with the Bermuda shipwreck of 1609. Instead, *The Tempest* appears to employ allusions from Richard Eden's accounts of 1557 (revised 1577). The play draws on many literary sources including Virgil, Ovid, Erasmus and Montaigne, but there is no definite source (literary or historical) after 1580. It also follows the pastoral scenarii of the *commedia dell'arte*; Italian acting companies visited England in the 1570s. The play also took historical names and events from Thomas's *History of Italy* (1549) for the political background. An early date of composition, *c.* 1583, is strongly suggested by many features of content, language and structure. It is possible that *The Tempest* (or a version of it) was performed in February 1604/5 at court under the title *The Spanish Maze*. The play may have been adapted for presentation at court in 1611.

## Notes

1. Bermuda was first identified in a written account by Peter Martyr in his 1511 *De Orbe Novo* and it found its way onto maps and charts from then onwards. The island group seems to have been named after the Spanish explorer Juan de Bermudez, who visited the island *c.* 1503 and again in 1515. Although there were subsequent visits by Spanish mariners, there was no attempt to colonise the archipelago because of the many dangerous reefs. Lancaster's visit in 1593 is recounted by one of the crew, Henry May, in Hakluyt's *Principal Navigations*, 1600 (reprinted in *The Voyages of Sir James Lancaster, Kt, to the East Indies*, 2005).
2. See *Bartholomew Gosnold, discoverer and planter: New England – 1602, Virginia – 1607* by Warner Foote Gookin, who demonstrates that Oxford and Gosnold were cousins. Nelson (188–9) describes the protracted purchase of the *Edward Bonaventure.*

## Other Cited Works

Bate, Jonathan, *Shakespeare and Ovid*, Oxford: OUP, 1993
Brockbank, Philip, "The Island of *The Tempest*", in *On Shakespeare: Jesus, Shakespeare and Karl Marx, and Other Essays,* Oxford: Basil Blackwell, 1989, 322–40
Bullough, G., *Narrative and Dramatic Sources of Shakespeare,* vol. VII, London: Routledge, 1975
Cairncross, A. S., *The Problem of Hamlet: A Solution*, London, 1936
Chambers, E. K., *The Elizabethan Stage,* 4 vols, Oxford: Clarendon, 1923
—, *William Shakespeare: A Study of Facts and Problems,* 2 vols, Oxford: Clarendon, 1930
Clark, E. T., *Hidden Allusions in Shakespeare's Plays*, New York: Kennikat, 1931, rptd 1974
Clubb, L. G., *Italian Drama in Shakespeare's Time,* New Haven: Yale UP, 1989
Deacon, R., *John Dee: Scientist, Geographer, Astrologer and Secret Agent to Elizabeth I*, London: Frederick Muller, 1968
Hamilton, Donna B., *Virgil and* The Tempest*: the Politics of Imitation,* Columbus: Ohio U. P., 1990
Hess, W. R. *et al.,* "Shakespeare's Dates", *The Oxfordian,* 2, Portland, 1999
Horsman, E. A. (ed.), *Bartholomew Fair* by Ben Jonson, Manchester: Revels Plays, 1960
Kallendorf, Craig, *The Other Virgil: 'Pessimistic' Readings of the* Aeneid *in Early Modern Culture,* Oxford: OUP, 2007
Kermode, F. (ed.), *The Tempest*, London: Methuen Arden, 1954
Lambin, Georges, *Voyages de Shakespeare en France et en Italie*, Geneva: Librairie Droz, 1962
Lea, Kathleen, *Italian Popular Comedy: A Study in the Commedia dell'Arte 1560–1620 with Special Reference to the English Stage*, 2 vols, Oxford: Clarendon, 1934
Lindley, David (ed.), *The Tempest*, Cambridge: New Cambridge Shakespeare, CUP, 2002
Malim, Richard, "*The Spanish Maze*" in *Great Oxford,* ed. R. Malim, Tunbridge Wells: Parapress Ltd, 2004, pp. 284–7
Mellamphy, N., "Pantaloons and zannies: Shakespeare's 'apprenticeship' to Italian professional comedy troupes", in *Shakespearean Comedy,* ed. M. Charney, New York: NY Literary Forum, 1980
Moore, P., "The Abysm of Time: the Chronology of Shakespeare's Plays", *Elizabethan Review,* 5, 2, 1997
Montemayor, Jorge de and Gil Polo Gaspar, *Diana* and *The Enamoured Diana,* ed. Judith M. Kennedy, trans. Bartholomew Yong, Oxford and London: Clarendon Press 1968
Muir, Kenneth, *The Sources of Shakespeare's Plays*, London: Methuen, 1978
Moore, Peter, "*The Tempest* and the Bermuda Shipwreck of 1609", *Shakespeare Oxford Newsletter,* 1996
Nelson, A. H., *Monstrous Adversary*, Liverpool: LUP, 2003
Neri, F., *Scenarii delle Maschere in Arcadia*, Città di Castello: Silapi, 1913
Nicoll, Allardyce, *The World of Harlequin,* Cambridge: CUP, 1963
Ogburn, Charlton, *The Mysterious William Shakespeare*, New York: Dodd Mead 1984.

Orgel, S. (ed.), *The Tempest,* Oxford: OUP, 1987
Orsini, N. "Shakespeare in Italy", *Comparative Literature*, Vol. III, 1951
Pastor, G. K., "Montaigne, Dido and *The Tempest*: How Came That Widow In?", *Shakespeare Quarterly,* 35, 1984: 91–4
Price, D., *Shakespeare's Unorthodox Biography,* Westport, CT: Greenwood, 2001
Rebora, P., "Comprensione e fortuna di Shakespeare in Italia", *Comparative Literature,* I, 1949
Salingar, Leo, *Shakespeare and the Traditions of Comedy,* Cambridge: CUP, 1954
Schmidgall, Gary, "*The Tempest* and *Primaleon*: A New Source", *SQ,* 37, 1989: 423–39
Sokol, B. J. and Mary Sokol, *Shakespeare's Legal Language,* London: Continuum Press, 2004
Stritmatter, Roger and Kositsky, Lynne, "*The Spanish Maze* and the Date of *The Tempest*", *The Oxfordian,* 10, 2007: 9–19
—, "Shakespeare and the Voyagers Revisited", *Review of English Studies,* 58, 2007: 447–472
—, " 'O Brave New World': *The Tempest* and Peter Martyr's *De Orbe Novo*", *Critical Survey,* 21, 2009: 7–42
Vaughan, Virginia Mason and Alden T. Vaughan (eds), *The Tempest,* London: Arden Shakespeare, 1999
Vaughan, Alden T., "William Strachey's 'True Reportory' and Shakespeare: A Closer Look at the Evidence", *SQ,* 59.3, 2008: 245–273
Woolley, B., *The Queen's Conjuror: The Life and Magic of Dr Dee,* London: Flamingo, 2001
Yates, F. A., *Shakespeare's Last Plays: a new approach,* London: Routledge, 1975

The dating of *The Tempest* has been the subject of considerable controversy in papers recently posted on the internet, including:

Bilton, Peter, "Another Island, Another Story: a source for Shakespeare's *The Tempest*", *Renaissance Forum.* 5, 2000. (accessed 21 June 2009). http://www.hull.ac.uk/renforum/v5no1/bilton.htm
Kathman, Dave, *Dating The Tempest,* 1999, http://shakespeareathorship.com/tempest.html (accessed 21 June 2009) includes a list of apparent correspondences between *The Tempest* and the Bermuda pamphlets. Kathman offers ways in which Shakespeare could have known Strachey's Letter through connections with various people such as Dudley Digges and Strachey. Kathman concludes that the True Reportory "pervades the entire play".
Kositsky, Lynne and Roger Stritmatter, "Dating *The Tempest*: A Note on the Undocumented Influence of Erasmus, *Naufragium* and Richard Eden's 1555 *Decades of the New World",* www.shakespearefellowship.org 2005. (accessed 21 June 2009).
Multhopp, Volker, *Undating The Tempest.* Accessed on 12 April 2000 at http://users.erols.com/volker/Shakes/DatgTmpt.htm attempts to answer Kathman's article and shows that many of the correspondances are equally valid between the play and possible literary sources.

2

# The Two Gentlemen of Verona

Noemi Magri

*The Two Gentlemen of Verona* can be dated any time between 1559, the publication of *Diana Enamorada* and 1598, when it was mentioned by Meres.

## Publication Date

*The Two Gentlemen of Verona* is one of eighteen plays in F1 which had not previously been published. It was entered into the Stationers' Register on 8 November 1623 alongside other plays as "not formerly entred to other men":

> Mr Blounte Isaak Jaggard. Entered for their Copie vnder the hands of Mr Doctor Worral and Mr Cole – warden, Mr William Shakspeers Comedyes Histories, and Tragedyes soe manie of the said Copies as are not formerly entered to other men. vizt. Comedyes. The Tempest. The two gentlemen of Verona. Measure for Measure. The Comedy of Errors. As you Like it. All's well that ends well. Twelft night. The winters tale. Histories. The thirde parte of Henry the sixt. Henry the eight. Coriolanus. Timon of Athens. Julius Caesar. Tragedies. Mackbeth. Anthonie & Cleopatra. Cymbeline.

The play is named *The Two Gentlemen of Verona* on the title page and as the running title. It occupies the second position in the comedies, coming after *The Tempest* and before *Merry Wives of Windsor.*

## Performance Date

There is no contemporary performance recorded of a play with this title. However, Francis Meres' mention of this comedy in his *Palladis Tamia* (1598) suggests that it had been performed many times before that date.

## Sources

Bullough notes the three main sources as Boccaccio's original novella in Italian (*c.* 1350), *Tito and Gisippo, (Decameron,* X, 8), Thomas Elyot's adaptation of it in his *Boke named the Governour* (1531), and the Spanish prose romance, *Diana Enamorada* by Jorge de Montemajor (1559), the latest source.

The theme of conflict between love and friendship, which is at the heart of *Two Gentlemen*, was much favoured in literature from the middle ages to the 17th century. Medieval romances and Boccaccio's works are among the major sources to which Middle English and renaissance writers are indebted. Boccaccio's *Teseide*, for example, offered Chaucer the plot for his *Knight's Tale.* The theme of male friendship is, moreover, a frequent occurrence in the works of Shakespeare, e.g. *Hamlet, Much Ado, Romeo and Juliet.*

Boccaccio's novella *Tito and Gisippo* enjoyed great popularity in sixteenth-century England, and various parallels of content and verbal expression are evidence that Shakespeare drew on it as a major source, and was indeed directly indebted to it. Both the Italian story and the play start with an educational boat journey; and the closing line of the play, as Leech points out, is almost a literal translation of the Italian: 'One feast, one house, one mutual happiness'. Numerous other verbal parallels give evidence that Shakespeare knew the Italian original. It was not fully translated into English until 1620.

The other major source for the play was *Diana Enamorada* by Jorge de Montemayor (1559), a prose romance in Spanish of courtly love in a pastoral setting. It has not been possible to establish whether Shakespeare read the story in the Spanish original or in a French version by Nicholas Collin (1578, 1587). An English translation of the *Diana* (by Bartholomew Young or Yonge) was not published until 1598 and it has been suggested that Shakespeare had read this translation in manuscript. Some links between the romance and the play have been outlined by Bullough: the treacherous friend, the maid as go-between, the mistress disguised as a page. Kevin Gilvary has outlined the debt to the three traditions of comedy, pastoral and romance.

Bullough further notes some common techniques used in this play and in comedies and romances by John Lyly. He believes that *Euphues and his Wit* (1579) comes closest to *Two Gentlemen.* Shakespeare's debt appears in the courtly atmosphere of his romance plays; he does not derive his plots from them. Leech notes 'many incidental echoings' of Lyly and one major crib from *Midas* (1592) in the Launce–Speed dialogue in 3.1.295–361. There are a number of pastoral plays on the theme which may have influenced Shakespeare: a Latin play for schoolboys, *De Titi et Gisippi firmissima amicitia*, by Ralph Radcliffe, was acted at Hitchin in 1538. Two English verse redactions of the Titus and Gisippus story are extant, but seem to have had little direct influence on *Two Gentlemen.*[1]

In the 1570s, the story of these two friends was still very popular: on 19

February 1577 the Revels Accounts record '*The Historye of Titus and Gisippus*, shown at Whitehall on Shrove Tuesday at night, enacted by the Children of St Paul's' (Chambers, *ES*, IV, 93). Sargent is of the opinion that the dramatist probably did not know "the Latin schoolboy play; but by date and subject matter the English play may well have been of first-rate importance in the writing of *Two Gentlemen*, or possibly an early version of it" (as suggested below, Oxfordian evidence). At any rate, the Court play seems to have some connection with *Two Gentlemen*.

The Revels Accounts record the performance of *The History of Felix and Philomena* by the Queen's Men at Greenwich on the Sunday after New Year's Day, 1584/5. This lost play was probably based on the *Diana*, where the story of Don Felix and Philomena is told. The title of *Two Gentlemen* is suggestive of Anthony Munday's *Fidelio and Fortunio, the Deceits in Love discoursed in a Comedy of two Italian Gentlemen*, translated which he had translated and adapted from the original Italian play, *Il Fedele* by Pasqualigo in 1584. This is in rhyme, and Hosley has suggested that it may have been acted, at Court before the Queen, by Lord Oxford's Children. Munday called himself 'servant of the Earl of Oxford'. He had dedicated a work to his patron in 1579 and wrote plays for the Earl of Oxford's Company.[2]

## Orthodox Date

The play has been variously dated as between 1587 and 1598. Chambers believed that 1594–5 met all the known evidence (a date accepted by the Riverside Edition) but admitted that "the date can hardly be fixed with precision" (*WS*, I, 330). For Chambers, *Two Gentlemen* would be the dramatist's eighth play, coinciding with other plays from the so-called "lyrical period" e.g. *Love's Labour's Lost* and *Romeo and Juliet.* Wells and Taylor (*Textual Commentary*, 109) agree with the difficulty in dating *Two Gentlemen*: "The play could belong to any year in the decade before Meres mentioned it." However, they put it as the earliest in the canon, *c.* 1590–1. They state: "In terms of basic dramatic technique the play is more naïve than anything else in the canon."

Most other editors have sided with Wells & Taylor, pointing out that the rhetorical style of the text, the clumsy versification, the reliance on monologue and duologue and the inconsistencies in handling the plot rank it among the earliest works. McManaway ascribes it to 1593. Leech is inclined to think that it was Shakespeare's first comedy, and offers 1592, but argues that the play was probably composed in four 'stages'. Honigmann takes the date of the play even earlier to 1587. Warren agrees that a precise date for composition is difficult and suggests that *Two Gentlemen* was written at Stratford in the mid 1580s, before the playwright came to London. Some recent editors, however, e.g. Schlueter and Carroll, seem to offer no date for composition.

## Internal Orthodox Evidence

Bullough believes that a play from the Italian *commedia dell'arte* such as *Flavio Tradito* appears to have prompted the use of clownish characters like Launce and Speed, who have nothing to do with the plot.[3] This has suggested to one commentator (Robertson) that there are several hands at work such as Peele, and Nashe (for Launce and his dog). That suggestion may be partly due to lack of evidence as to how the dramatist could become familiar with Italian contemporary drama in the late 1580s or early 1590s, a time when no Italian companies appear to have been acting in England.

Other Italian plays by Shakespeare are usually dated a few years later than *Two Gentlemen*, a span of time too short to allow the playwright to reach the quality of *Romeo and Juliet*, which is not the work of a novice dramatist. The fact that the aspiring dramatist set his first works in Italy – a country that he had presumably never visited, but which he appears to know very well – has always been such a difficult point for orthodox scholars: commentators have tried to find blunders to belittle his knowledge. However, the historical references and geographical descriptions present in *Two Gentlemen* correspond with facts (Magri, 66–78).

## External Orthodox Evidence.

*Two Gentlemen* is first mentioned and attributed to Shakespeare by Francis Meres in his treatise in defence of the English poetical art, *Palladis Tamia* (1598). Shakespeare's greatness is emphasised, and Meres refers also to 'his sugred *Sonnets* [circulated] among his private friends'. It is clear that by 1598 the dramatist had reached a high place in the literary world, and that his quality was well established. It is not known how Meres knew about this work as there is no record of previous performance (under this title) and it had not been published.

Warren noted the description of the comic actor, Richard Tarlton, entertaining Queen Elizabeth with a dog and, linking this to the scene, 2.5, involving Launce and Speed, argued that the play must have pre-dated Tarlton's death in September 1588 long enough for a performance before the court. Warren also refers to a record at Stratford in 1583 of a local man receiving payment for a performance of a play. Noting that the Queen's Men visited Stratford in 1587, he therefore tentatively suggests that Shakespeare may have written the play before he went to London.[4]

## Oxfordian Date

Orthodox chronology is founded purely on guesses, owing to the lack of any connection between the author and his works and on the assumption that, born in 1564, Shakespeare may have moved to London in about 1586, and, having acquired immense classical knowledge – the origin of which has not been evidenced – he must have started to write around 1590–1. Oxfordians reject such a scheme as highly unlikely and argue that the earl of Oxford was writing the plays anonymously and then under the pseudonym of 'Shakespeare'.

Oxford spent a lot of time in Italy in 1575–6 (Nelson, 121–141), sojourning in Verona and Venice, where he would have had ample opportunity to watch, both the learned Italian plays and the street theatre known as the *Commedia dell'arte*. Oxfordians believe that he began to write his own Italian-style plays soon after his return, when he was known to run acting companies. Clark proposes that an early version of *Two Gentleman* was recorded in the Revels Accounts as *The historye of Titus and Gisippus*, which was played at Whitehall on 19 February 1577.[5] This lost play may be taken as Oxford's early version of *Two Gentlemen*, on the grounds that the story of Titus and Gisippus in Boccaccio is one of the main sources of Shakespeare's play, and on account of verbal parallels between it and the novella. Hess et al. propose 1582, for stylistic reasons, while respecting the wealth of 1570s allusions. Anderson opts for an earlier date in the 1570s and explores Oxford's possible connections with Milan.

## Internal Oxfordian Evidence

Precise historical references and geographical details in *Two Gentlemen* point to the authorship of someone with first-hand knowledge of northern Italy. For example, the writer knows about the network of canals across the Lombardy plain, and that it was possible to suffer shipwreck on the Adige, the river flowing through Verona. The mention of 'Saint Gregory's Well' outside the city of Milan's wall has made Leech suppose 'that a now lost additional source existed'. But no lost literary source was necessary to a traveller who had come down from Germany to Italy 'in transit' through the state of Milan. For such, the 'lazaretto of St Gregory' was a regular stop, and Oxford may have lodged there on his way to Venice from Strasbourg.

One detail in the play seems to provide evidence of revision. In 4.1., the Second Outlaw asks Valentine an odd question, whether he has a knowledge of languages: "Have you the tongues?" (l. 33). It is clear that all three characters in this scene speak the same language, though it would have varied in vocabulary and accent from one Italian town to another. Therefore, the question posed does not seem to have a dramatic purpose. Valentine answers (4.1.33–4):

> My youthful travel therein made me happy,
> Or else I often had been miserable.

Since Valentine is young, and at that point still on a journey from Milan to Verona, his mention of 'youthful' travel is apparently inconsistent with his age.

He seems to be speaking of his past life, and referring to himself as someone no longer young.

The passage becomes relevant if it is explained as a later addition. The dramatist, now older, is recalling a journey taken in his own youth. In the Orazio Cuoco document of the Venetian Inquisition it is reported that Oxford had a very good knowledge of Latin and Italian.[6] The dramatist may be ascribing to Valentine the same misery and frustration that he felt in his youth, before being given permission to leave the country. Another detail in the same scene may also be autobiographical. The Third Outlaw asks Valentine if he has "long sojourned" in Milan – a 'foreign' city for a Veronese (4.1 21). The answer is:

> Some sixteen months, and longer might have stay'd,
> If crooked fortune had not thwarted me (4.1.22–3).

The sixteen months correspond approximately to Oxford's stay on the continent, from early January 1575 to April 1576. The "crooked fortune" that he heard about in Paris – a rumour that his wife had been unfaithful – made him hasten home (Nelson, 141–54).

## External Oxfordian Evidence

The hypothesis that an early version of this play was performed at Court on 19 February 1577 is also suggested by three other entries in the Revels Accounts (in Feuillerat). In the section relating to the expenses incurred between 12 and 17 February 1577 for the staging of Court plays, the following is recorded:

> (a) The Mercer. William Roe for silkes by him delivered . . . Crymsen Taffita . . .
> (b) The Haberdasher. Richard Moorer for the making of vj: Senatours' Cappes of Crymsen Taffita. . .
> (c) Necessaries. ffor two formes for the Senatours in the *historie of Titus and Gisippus* . . .

These entries are relevant for two reasons. Firstly, the mention of the Senators establishes a link between Boccaccio's novella and the Court play. Secondly, the entries give significant clues about the costumes used in the performance. In the Italian source, Gisippo, found in a cave by the guards and unjustly accused of killing a man, is tried for murder in the presence of the judges. The trial scene, with its *dénouement* of the two friends' deep affection and Tito's self-accusation with intent to save his friend, a very effective dramatic point, must have represented the climax of the Court play.

In Boccaccio, the judges are called 'praetori': they were the officers who administered the law in ancient Rome at the time of the setting of the novella. Since Shakespeare/Oxford is not likely to have mistaken praetors for senators

– the latter having no judicial power in ancient Rome – the substitution of senators in the Court play may have been suggested to the dramatist by direct contact with political life in Venice, where members of the judicial and legislative councils had 'senator' rank. This would have been in line with moving the scene of the action to Italy.

The Revels Accounts record the expenses for the Senators' caps of crimson taffeta. The colour and fabric bought from the mercer and used by the haberdasher is significant: it is that worn by the Venetian senators of high rank. It seems reasonable to suggest that the playwright himself might have given instructions for their being specially made.

The number of senators mentioned – six – is significant: it corresponds to the number of 'Consiglieri Ducali' or Doge's counsellors in the 'Signoria', the most powerful governing body in the republic. When in session as high magistrates, they were seated on a high bench next to the Doge: three on each side. According to the Revels Accounts, two 'formes', at the total price of 6 shillings, were provided for the six senators, and it is most likely that they seated three each.

It is known that Oxford wrote drama (Nelson, 385–6), and Oxfordians have suggested that several of the plays listed in the Revels Accounts, from the 1570s onwards, are early versions of Shakespeare's works. One in particular, *Agamemnon and Ulisses*, performed at Greenwich on St John's Day (27 December) 1584, by the Earl of Oxford's Boys, is considered by Feuillerat to have been 'one of Oxford's lost comedies' probably known later as *Troilus & Cressida*. The Accounts record plays (no title given) performed by the Children of St Paul's as early as 1565.

If the argument presented here for an original date of 1576–7 (under the title of *Titus and Gisippus)* is correct, then Shakespeare of Stratford cannot be the author of this play. Oxford may well have dramatised the Italian novella into *Titus and Gisippus*, modifying his play a number of times (as Leech had suggested) to the present version, and being influenced in the process by his Italian journey, adding the exact historical references and historical details. The many incidental echoings of Lyly's work from the late 1570s and 1580s strongly indicate collaboration between Oxford and Lyly in the dramatic enterprise.

## Conclusion

*The Two Gentlemen of Verona* can be dated any time between 1559, the publication of *Diana Enamorada* and 1598, when it was mentioned by Meres. Most commentators date the play 1590–94 as very early or even the earliest play in the canon, due to its ungainly verse and inconsistencies of plot and character. Such a date, however, makes no sense in the light of the mature poetry of the *Venus and Adonis* and *The Rape of Lucrece*, published in 1593 and 1594. It is very unlikely that they were by the same author writing at the same period.

## Notes

1. One of these is derived from Elyot. See H. G. Wright. *Early English Versions of the Tales of Guiscardo and Ghismonda and Titus and Gisippus from the Decameron.* EETS, 1937.
2. See Richard Hosley, "The Authorship of Fedele and Fortunio", *Huntingdon Library Quarterly,* 30:4, (1966–7): 315–330 and "The Date of *Fedele* and *Fortunio*", *MLR*, 57 (1962): 385–6.
3. *Flavio Tradito* was one of the *scenarrii* or outline plots included by Flaminio Scala in 1611.
4. Warren (24) quotes the canine anecdote from the State Papers, Domestic, (*Eliz.* ccxv, 89) in which the Queen "bade them take away the knave [Richard Tarlton] for making her to laugh so excessively as he fought against her little dog Perrico de Faldas with his sword and long staff." This anecdote does not seem to reflect the action of *Two Gentlemen,* as Launce describes his dog as particularly unresponsive. It is part of a wider set of allusions suggesting that Tarlton frequently acted with a dog. Chambers (*ES*, II, 342–3) outlines Tarlton's career with the Queen's Men from their foundation in 1583 until his death in 1588.
5. Clark proposes that a play produced at court two days earlier, *Solitary Knight* (Chambers, *ES,* IV, 93), might also have been an early work of Oxford, later known as *Timon of Athens.*
6. Nelson (53) reports how Oxford bought expensive copies of works in French, Italian and Latin in 1569, when aged 19. Nelson also reports (155–75) the testimony of Orazio Cuoco referring to Oxford's competence in Italian and in Latin.

## Other Cited Works

Anderson, Mark, *Shakespeare by Another Name*, New York: Gotham, 2005
Blakemore Evans, G. (ed.), *Riverside Shakespeare,* New York: Houghton Mifflin, 1997
Bond, W. (ed.), *The Two Gentlemen of Verona,* London: Arden, 1906
Bullough, G., *Narrative and Dramatic Sources of Shakespeare,* vol. 1, London: Routledge, 1957
Carroll, W. C. (ed.), *The Two Gentlemen of Verona,* London: Arden, 2004
Chambers, E. K. *The Elizabethan Stage*, 4 vols, Oxford: Clarendon, 1923
Chambers, E. K. *William Shakespeare: a study of facts and problems*, 2 vols, Oxford: Clarendon, 1930
Clark, E. T., *Hidden Allusions in Shakespeare's Plays*, Port Washington, 1974 edn.
Duncan-Jones, K., ed. *Shakespeare's Sonnets,* London: Arden, 1998
Feuillerat, Albert, *Documents Relating to the Office of the Revels in the Time of Queen Elizabeth*, 1908
Gilvary, Kevin, "*Two Gentlemen of Verona:* Italian literary traditions and the Authorship debate", *The Oxfordian,* 8, Portland, 2005
Hess, W. R. *et al.*, Shakespeare's Dates, *The Oxfordian, 2*, Portland, 1999
Hosley, R., *A Critical Edition of Anthony Munday's 'Fedele and Fortunio',* New York: Garland, 1981

Leech, C. (ed.), *The Two Gentlemen of Verona,* London: Arden, 1972
Honigmann, E. A. J., *Shakespeare the 'lost years',* Manchester: MUP, 1985
Looney, J. T., *Shakespeare Identified,* London, 1920
Magri, N., "No Errors in Shakespeare: Historical Truth and *Two Gentlemen of Verona"*, in R. Malim, R. (ed.), *Great Oxford*, Tunbridge Wells: Parapress, 2004: 66–78
Maranini, G., *La Costituzione de Venezia*, 2 vols, Florence: La Nuova Italia, 1974
McManaway, J. G., "Recent Studies in Shakespeare's Chronology", *Shakespeare Survey* 3, Cambridge, 1949
Kennedy, J. M. (ed.), Montemayor *Diana Enamorada*, Oxford: Clarendon, 1968
Nelson, Alan, H., *Monstrous Adversary*, Liverpool: LUP, 2003
Robertson, J. M., *The Shakespeare Canon,* Vol. 1, Ayer Co Pub, 1923
Sargent, R. M., "Sir Thomas Elyot and the Integrity of *The Two Gentlemen of Verona"*, *PLMA,* 65, December 1950
Schlueter, Karl (ed.), *The Two Gentlemen of Verona,* Cambridge: CUP, 1990
Warren, Roger (ed.), *The Two Gentlemen of Verona,* Oxford, OUP, 2008
Wells, Stanley & Gary Taylor (eds), *The Complete Oxford Shakespeare*, Oxford: OUP, 1986
—, *William Shakespeare: A Textual Companion*, Oxford: OUP, 1987

# 3

# The Merry Wives of Windsor

## Philip Johnson

*The Merry Wives of Windsor* can only be dated between 1558, the publication of Fiorentino's *Il Peccorone* and 1602, when it was recorded in the Stationers' Register.

### Publication Date

The play was entered in the Stationers' Register on 18 January 1602 by John Busby and immediately transferred to Arthur Johnson as:

> [SR, 1602] A booke Called an excellent and pleasant conceyted Comedie of Sir Iohn ffaulstafe and the merye wyves of windsor.

Later that year it was published in quarto:

> [Q1, 1602] A most pleasaunt and excellent conceited comedie, of Syr Iohn Falstaffe, and the merrie wiues of Windsor. Entermixed with sundrie variable and pleasing humors, of Syr Hugh the Welch knight, Iustice Shallow, and his wise cousin M. Slender. With the swaggering vaine of Auncient Pistoll, and Corporall Nym. By William Shakespeare. As it hath bene diuers times acted by the Right Honorable my Lord Chamberlaines seruants. Both before her Maiestie, and else-where. London: printed by T. C. [Thomas Creede] for Arthur Iohnson, and are to be sold at his shop in Powles Church-yard, at the signe of the Flower de Leuse and the Crowne, 1602.

In 1619 this text (with a few very minor changes) was reprinted.

> [Q2, 1602] A most pleasant and excellent conceited comedie, of Sir Iohn Falstaffe, and the merrie wiues of Windsor. With the swaggering vaine of Auncient Pistoll, and Corporall Nym. Written by W. Shakespeare. [London]: Printed [by William Jaggard] for Arthur Iohnson [i.e. Thomas Pavier], 1619.

A

Moſt pleaſaunt and excellent conceited Comedie, of Syr *Iohn Falſtaffe*, and the merrie Wiues of *Windſor*.

Entermixed with ſundrie variable and pleaſing humors, of Syr *Hugh* the Welch Knight, Iuſtice *Shallow*, and his wiſe Couſin M. *Slender*.

With the ſwaggering vaine of Auncient *Piſtoll*, and Corporall *Nym*.

By *William Shakeſpeare*.

As it hath bene diuers times Acted by the right Honorable my Lord Chamberlaines ſeruants. Both before her Maieſtie, and elſe-where.

LONDON
Printed by T. C. for Arthur Iohnſon, and are to be ſold at his ſhop in Powles Church-yard, at the ſigne of the Flower de Leuſe and the Crowne.
1602.

2. Title page to the first quarto of *The Merry Wives of Windsor,* 1602. By permission of Bodleian Library, University of Oxford, shelfmark: Arch. G d.45 (6), title page.

The play appeared in the First Folio (F1) in 1623 as the third comedy, after *Two Gentlemen of Verona* and before *Measure for Measure.* Only *Love's Labour's Lost* in the Shakespeare canon uses the same formula 'pleasant conceited comedy'; the formula had first appeared in 1585 in *Fedele and Fortunio*, sometimes attributed to Oxford's secretary, Anthony Munday.

The version printed in F1 is considerably longer than Q1 – about 2700 lines compared with about 1600 lines in the Quarto(s). which is "obviously a garbled and corrupt text." (Chambers, *WS*, I, 429). The Quarto, although more correct in several details (e.g. 'Brooke' rather than 'Broome'), confuses situations and mangles speeches, loses jokes and destroys humour, and it has some peculiar stage-directions. Bullough comments that neither text 'makes a satisfactory play, but they supplement each other'. Summarising the relationship between the two versions, Oliver (p. xxx) concludes: "Behind the Quarto text … there would seem to be a version of *Merry Wives* that was designed for an audience not aristocratic and not primarily intellectual, whereas the full Folio text has much that would appeal only to the more sophisticated."

## Performance Dates

The 1602 Quarto states that the play 'hath bene diuers times Acted by the Honorable my Lord Chamberlaines seruants. Both before her Maiestie and else-where'. The first documented performance of *The Merry Wives of Windsor* took place on the first Sunday of November 1604, in Whitehall Palace. On 20 May 1613, the King's Men were paid for performing fourteen plays, one called 'Sir John ffalstaffe', usually taken to be *Henry IV Part 2*, but it might be *The Merry Wives of Windsor*, since the very next entry mentions another play called 'the Hotspur'. A Court performance by the King's Men is recorded on 15 November 1638.

## Sources

Bullough identifies (apart from the links with the other Falstaff plays) four main narrative elements: the tricking of Falstaff, the wooing of Anne Page, the horse-stealing episodes, and the 'fairy' scene. This in itself complicates the identification of specific sources. Muir, after noting suggestions current in 1957, abandoned the search as useless. Oliver "in another sense" agrees, because "for nearly every incident and situation in the plot ... an analogue or a vaguely possible source has been found in earlier European fiction and farce or in English stories and translations."

The main narrative strand and is the tricking of Falstaff and the latest definite source for this seems to be the second novella of the first day of *Il Pecorone* by Ser Giovanni Fiorentino, published in 1558. There was no English translation until an abridged version appeared in 1632. The Anne Page story, with Falstaff disguised as a woman, has some elements in common with Plautus's Latin play *Casina*; but "the differences far outweigh the resemblances" according to Oliver. Again, there was no available English translation of this play of Plautus.

There were similar stories in English but not so close as Fiorentino: Barnaby Riche, 'Of Two Brethren and Their Wives', in *Riche His Farewell to Militarie Profession* (1581) and by Tarlton in 'The Tale of the Two Lovers of Pisa' in *Tarltons Newes Out of Purgatorie* (1590). Bullough also sees some resemblances between *The Merry Wives* and some realistic comedies from the end of the sixteenth century, including Dekker's *Shoemaker's Holiday* (1599).

The horse-stealing episodes have been linked by some scholars, through various mentions of a 'German', 'Germans' and 'Germany' (4.3.1; 4.5.65, 67, 72 & 82) and of the 'Duke' for whom they are working, to Frederick Count Mömpelgard, heir to the Duchy of Würtemburg. This theory, in the view of its proponents, is reinforced by Q1's odd phrase 'cosen garmombles' ('cozen-Germans' in F1; 'cozen' could mean 'cousin' and/or 'cheat'): the rest looks like a word-play on the Count's name. The Count visited England unexpectedly in 1592, met the Queen and apparently extorted from her a promise that he would be admitted to the Companionship of the Order of the Garter. He became Duke in August 1593 and continued to badger the Queen through envoys. In 1597 he was elected Knight of the Garter *in absentia* – and finally received the insignia, in Stuttgart, in 1603. The connection between the Duke and horse-stealing is extremely obscure, and many scholars, Oliver included, dismiss the theory. But the Duke will reappear in the later discussion of dates.

The fairies' teasing of Bottom in *A Midsummer Night's Dream*, the story of Actaeon – transformed into a stag – in Ovid's *Metamorphoses,* and an episode in Lyly's *Endimion*, where the soldier Corsites is pinched by fairies, parallel the treatment of Falstaff by the 'fairies' in the final scene. Some influence on Falstaff may have been derived from the character of Captain Crackstone in Anthony Munday's *Fedele and Fortunio* (1585), a translation from Luigi Pasqualigo.

## Orthodox Dates

Most recent commentators (Wells & Taylor, Craik, Crane and Melchiori, have favoured a completion date by 1597, linking the play to the Garter Ceremony on 23 April. The garter ceremony is an annual event. Chambers linked the play with a garter ceremony in 1601.

By contrast, F. G. Fleay in 1886, followed by Quiller-Couch, the New Cambridge editor, argued that *The Merry* Wives is a rewriting of *The Jealous Comedy*, a lost play performed by Lord Strange's Men in 1593, when they were performing other plays of Shakespeare (Chambers, *ES* ii 123); Cairncross also proposes 1592–3.

## Possible Links with *Henry IV* Parts 1 & 2 and *Henry V*

Most commentators see *Merry Wives* as linked in the time of composition by "the weight of probability" (Oliver) with the *Henry IV* and *Henry V* trilogy. Not only does Falstaff feature prominently, but several other characters (or at least their names) from those plays make an appearanc, in *The Merry Wives*. The connection, however, presents some puzzles: when does the action of *The Merry Wives* take place – in the early 1400s or in Elizabethan England? And why does Falstaff not know Mistress Quickly? And why does Fenton, who "kept company with the wild Prince and Poins" (3.5.66–7), not know Falstaff?

Although there is no evidence as to whether *The Merry Wives* was written before, during or after the composition of the *Henry IV* plays, Oliver places the comedy between the two parts of *Henry IV*. He accepts the orthodox scheme, which placed *1 Henry IV* in the winter of 1596–7 and *2 Henry IV* in December 1598. Oliver also allows the possibility that *The Merry Wives* and *2 Henry IV* were being written at the same time. This proposal explains why Shallow does not know Falstaff in *The Merry Wives*, and accounts for a few words and phrases found in these plays but not elsewhere in Shakespeare.

It is also possible that *Merry Wives* was written first and that when Shakespeare hurriedly needed to rename Sir John Oldcastle (and friends), he transferred names of similar characters from the comedy.

## Internal Orthodox Evidence

The 1597 date ties in with the theory proposed by Hotson in 1931 (*Shakespeare versus Shallow)* that the play was performed on St George's Day, 23 April, 1597 for the Garter Feast at Whitehall. The action aptly takes place at Windsor, the normal location of the Garter ceremony. One of the five knights elected that year was George Carey, Lord Hunsdon, patron of the Chamberlain's Men and newly appointed Lord Chamberlain.

Of particular significance is the speech of Mistress Quickly, disguised as the Fairy Queen (5.v.56–74). She instructs the fairies to prepare "Windsor Castle" and specifically St George's Chapel, for the installation ceremony, mentioning "the several chairs of order", "each fair instalment [= chapel stall], coat, and sev'ral crest", "the Garter's compass", and "Honi soit qui mal y pense" (the Garter motto) ... "[b]uckled below fair knighthood's bending knee." As a construct, Hotson's theory is ingenious, but (comments Oliver) "unfortunately it falls short of final proof." Nevertheless, this precise date wins the approval of almost all modern editors.

## External Orthodox Evidence:

The only 'evidence', though well known, is of very doubtful worth. It is the tradition (no more than that – Hibbard calls it "powerful yet dubious") first recorded in 1702 that Queen Elizabeth commanded the play "to be finished in fourteen days". In 1709 Rowe elaborated: "She was so well pleas'd with that admirable [sic!] Character of *Falstaff*, in the two Parts of *Henry* the Fourth ... This is said to be the Occasion of his Writing *The Merry Wives of Windsor*."

Oliver is ambivalent about the tradition: it is "often repeated as if it were fact", he writes. Yet he is prepared to assume, in his discussion of the date of composition, that the Queen could have seen *1 Henry IV* during the winter of 1596–7. "She could then have expressed a wish to see Falstaff in love, and a performance of *The Merry Wives* could have followed most opportunely in April." Oliver ignores Rowe's reference to the "two" parts of *Henry IV* – apparently because it is inconvenient for his argument. Samuel Johnson pointed out 250 years ago that Rowe's "How well she was obey'd, the Play it self is an admirable Proof" is simply wrong: Shakespeare did not comply with the Queen's wishes, since Falstaff is never in love, only in need of immediate carnal satisfaction!

## Oxfordian Date

Most Oxfordians place *Merry Wives* in 1584–5 (Clark, Hess with stylistic analysis, and Brazil) although Ogburn Jr. proposed 1573; Holland preferred 1593.

## Internal Oxfordian Evidence

In proposing 1573, Charlton Ogburn sees the wooing of Anne Page by Slender as a comic representation of the negotiations in 1568–9 for the marriage of Philip Sidney to Anne Cecil. A formal settlement was drawn up on 06 August 1569, its terms somewhat similar in monetary value to those mentioned in Act 3, scene 4. Two years later the Cecil–Sidney contract was deemed to have lapsed and Oxford became Anne's bridegroom; Ogburn regards Fenton as a stage representation of the successful real-life suitor. In addition, Ogburn takes it that Doctor Caius "can hardly have had another source than Dr John Caius of Cambridge University ... That he died in 1573 is another indication of the early composition of *Merry Wives*."

The inclusion in the cast of Doctor Caius has intrigued other Oxfordians, especially Anderson: although ostensibly 'French', he is a physician. His real-life namesake was a medical scholar, who created Gonville and Caius College and became its Master in 1559. He was president of the College of Physicians from 1555–60, again in 1562 and 1563, and finally in 1571. As physician to the Court and the City, he became rich. He seems to have professionally attended Queen Elizabeth in 1564, but his name is not in the royal household accounts. Religiously conservative, with Catholic friends, he clashed with the increasingly puritan and Calvinist fellows of his College. They burned the vestments and mass-books that he hoarded, and he had his colleagues placed in the stocks, showing the same pugnacious attitude that his stage namesake displays towards his rivals for Anne Page's hand. But Doran, author of the chapter on 'Medicine' in *Shakespeare's England* (Vol.1), focussing on John Caius's academic ability and achievements, calls him "a very different man from his namesake in *The Merry Wives of Windsor*."

Most orthodox commentators understandably deny any connection between the two Doctors Caius: when Caius died in July 1573, Shakespeare of Stratford was a boy of nine. All attempts to forge a link through Shakespeare's son-in-law, Dr John Hall, are far-fetched: Hall did not attend Cambridge University until some twenty years after Caius's death, and he did not move to Stratford until about 1600 – at least three years after the date of composition favoured by the orthodox. Oliver writes that there can be no direct connection between the two men, and Quiller-Couch can make nothing of the attempt to identify Dr Caius with John Caius. Oxfordians who think that there is a deliberate caricature of the Cambridge don point to Oxford's connections with Cambridge, where he studied, and to his familiarity with the Queen and Court. This leads them to propose, like Ogburn, a very early date for the writing of the play (or parts of it) – namely, before Caius died in 1573.

However, there are problems. Edward de Vere's name (usually written 'Dominus [Lord] Bulbecke') appears in various Cambridge records, mainly at Queens' College, for a period of only six months – from October 1558 to March 1559; he was merely eight years old! After that he was tutored in Essex under the supervision of Sir Thomas Smith (Nelson, 23–6). So it seems very doubtful whether the young boy had any contact with the real John Caius, not yet Master of his eponymous College nor yet involved in his notorious disputes with the Fellows. One must also question how well known Caius was at Court, and wonder why a supposed caricature topical to the early 1570s survived through various productions to 1623. All the same, those convinced about the caricature have some very recent, incidental support: Nutton, in the 2004 *Oxford Dictionary of National Biography*, describes Caius as a short man with a long beard and a squeaky voice, as autocratic and overbearing, with eccentric personal habits: "his name, his profession and his oddity were immortalised by Shakespeare in *The Merry Wives of Windsor*".

Among the evidence Holland produces for 1593 are (as well as the Mömpelgard visit in 1592) the following words and phrases. "Three Doctor Faustuses" (4.5.65) – Holland misses "Mephostophilus" (1.1.20) – must refer to Marlowe's *Dr Faustus*. Its main English source was printed in 1592, and the play is thought by some to have been performed at Court in January 1593 (see Chambers, *ES*, iii, 422–4 for evidence of productions). 'Cony-catch(ing)' is used twice (1.1.116 and 1.3 .31) and occurs again in the plays, in *The Taming of the Shrew.* Greene's three 'cony-catching' pamphlets (on criminal techniques) and a reply using the same term were published in 1592; so the term was current when the play was written.

For a date of composition in the mid-1580s – with some 1590s references added for a later revival – Brazil presents a more recent case. Slender wishes he had his "book of Songs and Sonnets here" (1.1.179–80). This would have been the *Songes and Sonnets* of Henry Howard, Earl of Surrey (who was Oxford's uncle). Published posthumously in Tottel's *Miscellany* in 1557 (ten years after his execution), the volume was so popular that it was republished "at least eight times in the next thirty years" (Oliver). After a gap of eleven years, the last two reprints came out in 1585 and 1587 (the next edition was 300 years later). The topical allusion to Surrey's poems would have been less meaningful in the next decade (and it is missing from the 1602 Quarto).

Some orthodox writers have suggested that Sir Hugh Evans, the comic Welsh parson, was based on a non-Welsh schoolmaster at Stratford, e.g. John Jenkins from London or Thomas Cottam from Lancashire. But Oxford's theatre-manager in the years 1584–6 was Henry Evans, a Welshman who taught the Children of Paul's troupe, a section of 'Oxford's Boys' who performed regularly at Court and for private audiences, throughout the 1580s (Nelson, 247–8). Brazil's claim that the fairies' song in Act 5, scene 5, with its repeated phrase "pinch him", was itself pinched from the Fairy Song in *Endimion*, the Lyly play from the same 1580s period is debatable: and the borrowing of the pinching could have been in reverse. *Endimion* was probably first performed in 1588; the text was published in 1591, but the words of the 'Fairy Song' ("Pinch him, pinch him, black and blue") were not included until Blount's edition of 1632. Hess's stylistic analysis (adjusting the orthodox chronology to Oxford's life) places the play alongside *1 Henry IV* in 1585; but he and his collaborators accept 1597 as the "latest reasonable date of embedded allusions, assuming [the text] to be a revamp of an earlier version".

## External Oxfordian Evidence

Holland, like orthodox scholars, considers that the play was written for an occasion connected with the Order of the Garter; but prefers 1593 when the Order was celebrating its 250th anniversary. He notes than an "exceptional number of Knights of the Garter were installed this year". Thus Oxford would have been celebrating (or perhaps even satirising) such a conspicuous event.

Oxford's copy of the Geneva Bible, which he bought in 1570 (now in the Folger Shakespeare Library, Washington DC), has this passage (II Samuel 21:19) underlined: "Goliath the Gittite: <u>the staffe of whose speare was like</u>

a weauers beame." In 5.1.21–23, Falstaff reproduces part of this clause and humorously couples it with another part-quotation from the Bible: "I fear not Golia(t)h with a weaver's beam, because I know also life is a shuttle." (Job 7:6 reads: "My days are swifter than a weaver's shuttle, and are spent without hope.") Curiously, 'fear', 'Goliath' and 'weaver's beam' occur together in *Pierce's Supererogation*, published by Gabriel Harvey in 1593: "...I feared the brazen shield, and the brazen boots of Goliah and that same hideous speare, like a weaver's beam ...". Harvey's book is thought by some to be a broadside against Thomas Nashe and Oxford.

Roger Stritmatter underscores the importance of this passage for the chronology of the play:

> The concept of fearing the weaver's beam in *The Merry Wives of Windsor* but not in [any known biblical text] is copied in Harvey's 1593 tract. Barring the discovery of a common antecedent source in which Goliath's weaver's beam is 'feared', the simplest explanation for the known evidence is that Harvey read, or more likely observed, a performance of an early version of *The Merry Wives of Windsor.*

This would make 1593 the latest date for the play's first performance.

## Allusions and References

Those which can be dated later may be regarded as topical additions for subsequent productions. For instance, Oliver is uncomfortable with Q1's 'garmombles' and tries to find linguistic alternatives to the suggestion that it is a joke on Count Mömpelgard's name; there is, also, a reasonable suggestion lurking in his commentary that Shakespeare of Stratford would be unlikely to make fun of a particular German nobleman. Cairncross, another orthodox scholar (though unorthodox regarding the chronology of the plays), also finds it "rather improbable" that the playwright would ridicule a newly elected Knight of the Garter. He thinks it "more probable that the jest should have been made soon after the visit of the Duke in 1592, while the memory of his peculiarities was still fresh in mind, and *before* he was elected." As a courtier, Oxford is very likely to have encountered the amusing German, and he also had a personal motive for making fun of him: like Mömpelgard, he was a persistent applicant for membership of the Order of the Garter (unlike the German, he was never elected). In 1592–3, Oxford may well have inserted into this 'Garter' play unflattering topical references to his foreign rival, so recently well known to the Court, and included the jokes about his absence in Act 4, scenes 3 and 5.

Evans sings (with a few variants) lines (3.1.15–25) from Marlowe's lyric 'Come live with me and be my love'. Oliver states that, although thc words were not published until 1599, they presumably became popular as a song before

Marlowe's death in 1593; Chapman assumes knowledge of the words in a play of 1596. This recent 'hit' may have been included in a 1593 or 1597 revival of *The Merry Wives*, perhaps replacing a previous, less up-to-date song. Similarly, Falstaff's metaphor: "She is a region in Guiana, all gold and bounty" (1.3.64–5) may date from 1595–6, as Oliver suggests, when Ralegh sailed to explore the Orinoco, hoping to find the mythical Eldorado; his report, *The Discoverie of the Large, Rich and Bewtiful Empire of Guiana*, was widely read. Alternatively, Holland suggests 1593, when the legend of Eldorado must have been know, because Raleigh sent Captain Whaddon to find out more about the Orinoco region in the spring of 1594.

## Conclusion

The play can only be dated between 1558, the publication of Fiorentino's *Il Peccorone* and 1602, when it was recorded in the Stationers' Register. All the main sources for the play were available in the 1580s.

Although there is no evidence as to whether *The Merry Wives* was written before, during or after the composition of the *Henry IV* plays, there is obviously a case for linking the writing of this play that composition. The most probable date is 1584–5, shortly before a likely date for the *Henry IV* plays, with revision in 1592–3. There is no contemporary evidence about whether *The Merry Wives* was intended to mark a Garter ceremony.

## Other Cited Works

Anderson, Mark, *Shakespeare by Another Name*, New York: Gotham, 2005
Brazil, R., "Unpacking the Merry Wives", *The Oxfordian*, 2, Portland, 1999
Bullough, G., *Narrative and Dramatic Sources of Shakespeare*, Vol. II, London: Routledge, 1958
Cairncross, A. S., *The Problem of Hamlet: A Solution*, London, 1936
Chambers, E. K., *The Elizabethan Stage*, 4 vols, Oxford: Clarendon, 1923
—, *William Shakespeare: a study of facts and problems*, 2 vols, Oxford: Clarendon, 1930
Clark, E. T., *Hidden Allusions in Shakespeare's Plays*, Port Washington, 1974 edn.
Craik, T. W. (ed.), *The Merry Wives of Windsor*, Oxford: OUP, 1989
Crane, David (ed.), *The Merry Wives of Windsor*, Cambridge: CUP, 1997
Doran, A. H. G., "Medicine", in *Shakespeare's England*, Vol. I, Oxford, 1916
Hess, W. R. *et al.*, "Shakespeare's Dates" *The Oxfordian*, 2, Portland, 1999
Hibbard, G. R. (ed.), *Merry Wives of Windsor*, Harmondsworth: Penguin, 1974
Holland, H. H., *Shakespeare, Oxford and Elizabethan Times*, London, 1933
Honigmann, E. A. J., *Shakespeare the 'lost years'*, Manchester: MUP, 1985
Hotson, L., *Shakespeare versus Shallow*, London, 1931
Melchiori, Girgio (ed.), *The Merry Wives of Windsor*, London: Arden, 2000
Muir, K., *The Sources of Shakespeare's Plays*, London: Methuen, 1977

Nelson, A. H., *Monstrous Adversary*. Liverpool: LUP, 2003
Ogburn, C. Jr, *The Mysterious William Shakespeare*,, New York: Dodd Mead, 1984
Oliver, H. J. (ed.), *The Merry Wives of Windsor*, London: Arden, 1971
*Oxford Dictionary of National Biography*. Oxford, OUP, 2004
Quiller-Couch, A. (ed.), *The Merry Wives of Windsor*, Cambridge: CUP, 1921
Stritmatter, R., *The Marginalia of Edward de Vere's Geneva Bible*, Northhampton: Oxenford Press, 2003
Wells, Stanley & Gary Taylor, eds, *The Complete Oxford Shakespeare*, Oxford: OUP, 1986
—, *William Shakespeare: A Textual Companion*, Oxford: OUP, 1987.

# 4

# Measure for Measure

## Philip Johnson

This play can be dated any time between the early 1580s, when all the main sources were available, and 1604, when it was performed at court.

### Publication Date

*Measure for Measure* is one of eighteen plays in F1 which had not previously been published. It was entered into the Stationers' Register on 8 November 1623 alongside other plays as "not formerly entred to other men":

> Mr Blounte Isaak Jaggard. Entered for their Copie vnder the hands of Mr Doctor Worral and Mr Cole – warden, Mr William Shakspeers Comedyes Histories, and Tragedyes soe manie of the said Copies as are not formerly entered to other men. vizt. Comedyes. The Tempest. The two gentlemen of Verona. Measure for Measure. The Comedy of Errors. As you Like it. All's well that ends well. Twelft night. The winters tale. Histories. The thirde parte of Henry the sixt. Henry the eight. Coriolanus. Timon of Athens. Julius Caesar. Tragedies. Mackbeth. Anthonie & Cleopatra. Cymbeline.

It occupies the fourth position in the Comedies, coming after *Merry Wives of Windsor* and before *The Comedy of Errors*. Chambers states that the F1 text was based on a transcript prepared by Ralph Crane, a reliable scrivener, connected with the King's Men in the 1620s.

### Performance Date

The earliest recorded performance was on 26 December 1604, according to the account book of the Office of the Revels which states:

> On S^t^ Stiuens night in the Hall A play caled Mesur for Mesur Shaxberd.

The hall was the Banqueting Hall in the palace at Whitehall. While Chambers (*WS* II, 330–2) had some doubts about the authenticity of this document, editors tend to accept it as genuine (e.g. Gibbons, 2006:21). Most scholars believe this entry to reflect a newly composed play.[1] Bawcutt, however, points out that during this season, there were fourteen plays presented at court, including *Merry Wives of Windsor* and *Comedy of Errors,* which were written earlier. Bawcutt also believes that the players would have been unlikely to risk a newly composed play at court.

## Sources

Geoffrey Bullough identifies three major sources for the main plot – a variation on the traditional tale of the corrupt magistrate. The principal source was an Italian novella in Giraldi Cinthio's *Hecatommithi* (1565) decade 8, tale 5. This collection of 100 stories was published in Venice in 1565 and again in 1575; The work was published in a French translation by Gabriel Chappuys in 1584, but there was no English version until the eighteenth century; Cinthio's text in both the Italian and the French versions was used for *Othello*. Secondary sources for *Measure for Measure* were Cinthio's *Epitia* (1583), a posthumous play, which introduces the role played by Mariana, and George Whetstone's play, *The Right Excellent and Famous Historye of Promos and Cassandra*, registered and published in 1578 (Chambers, *ES,* III, 512), which added a low-life, comic sub-plot.

Brian Gibbons sees links between the puritan outlook of Angelo and pamphlets such as Philip Stubbes's *Anatomy of Abuses* (1583). Stubbes's pamphlet was answered by Nashe's *Anatomie of Absurditie* (1589).[2]

## Orthodox Date

Most scholars accept a date 1603–05. Chambers suggests 1604–5; Lever and Nosworthy propose the summer of 1604; Wells & Taylor concur with 1604; others, such as Halliday, have argued for 1603. Gibbons is much more circumspect in his consideration of a date and, while suggesting links with the 1580s, tentatively accepts a date 1603–4. Bawcutt does not commit to a specific date.

## Possible Parallels between the Duke and James I

Most scholars suggest that the character, interests, attitudes and actions of the Duke closely resemble those of James I. Schanzer quotes much from previous writers on this topic:

> The character of the Duke is a very accurate delineation of that of King

> James, which Shakespeare appears to have caught, with great felicity, and to have sketched, with much truth. (G. Chalmers, 1799; quoted by Schanzer, 1971: 121).

Schanzer summarises, although he elsewhere disparages, the argument of the doctoral thesis of L. Albrecht:

> The Duke is intended to be recognised as an idealised portrait of James I. (L. Albrecht, 1914; Schanzer, 1971: 121).

Shakespeare's motives are said to range from paying "homage", through "flattery" to "anxiously courting" the new king. Passages relevant to this view are:

> DUKE: We have strict statutes and most biting laws,
> The needful bits and curbs to headstrong weeds,
> Which, for these fourteen years, we have let slip …
> *Measure,* 1.3.19–21.

James confessed in *Basilikon Doron* (1599), his tract on 'the properties of government', that he was over-lax in punishing offenders at the start of his reign in Scotland. In the same document, he denounced the popular desire for novelties; and in 3.2.217–9 the Duke complains: "Novelty is only in request, and it is as dangerous to be aged in any kind of course. . . ." In 1603, a further Scottish edition and two English editions of *Basilikon Doron* were published. Some commentators, such as Schanzer (1971: 122–3), are persuaded that it is "inherently probable" that Shakespeare had read – even "carefully mined" – the tract before writing the play.[3]

In 1.1.67–8, the Duke confesses "I love the people / But do not like to stage me to their eyes." This may reflect James's attitude during his 1603 progress to London, and the incident at the Exchange on or about 15 March 1604, when he attempted a secret visit. The dedicatory epistle to the only extant report was written by a member of Shakespeare's company.[4] The Duke's comment on Lucio: "Back-wounding calumny … slanderous tongue." (3.1.445–7), and his later punishment of him: "Here's one in place I cannot pardon" (5.1.498–9.), are typical of James, who was notoriously sensitive to slander. A Scottish Act of 1585 made slander of the king treasonable, and several people were executed under it – one, in 1596, for calling James "ane bastarde." [5] In 4.2.134–6, the disguised Duke asks about his real self: "How came it that the absent Duke had not either delivered him to his liberty or executed him? I have heard it was ever his manner to do so." On 25 April 1603, at Newark, James had a cutpurse, taken in the act, hanged at once without trial, while at the same time he commanded all prisoners in the castle to be freed. Watts remarks that in the winter of 1603–4 James reprieved condemned conspirators who were already on the scaffold at Winchester.

Not all editors are convinced by Shanzer's arguments but consider the parallels "too commonplace" to prove indebtedness. Bawcutt (6) finds it "inherently implausible that a mere playwright would have the impertinence to act as a schoolmaster to the king."

## Possible Parallels between the Play and Political Events in 1604

Taking the performance on St Stephen's Night as a first performance of a newly finished play, evidence has been gathered from specific phrases in the play to reflect current events and concerns. In 1.2.1–5, Lucio and two gentlemen wonder whether "the Duke, with other dukes" will come to "composition with the King of Hungary", and hope for peace. Lever (intro, xxxi) takes this to refer to King James's negotiations with Spain from autumn 1603 and the Hampton Court conference, 20 May – 19 August 1604. Later in the same scene (1.2 80–2), Mistress Overdone complains about the effects on her business of "war ... sweat ... gallows, and ...poverty". Lever (intro, xxxii) assumes that this reflects events in 1603–4: war with Spain, plague (theatres were closed in 1603, re-opening on 09 April 1604), and treason trials at Winchester. Almost immediately (86–89) Pompey tells her of a proclamation: "All houses in the suburbs of Vienna must be plucked down." Lever identifies this with the proclamation of 16 September 1603, which called for the pulling down of suburban houses in London to limit the spread of the plague; it especially affected brothels and gaming houses. Finally, Lever suggests that "Master Starve-Lackey the rapier and dagger man ... Master Forthright the tilter ... and wild Half-can that stabbed pots", who feature in Pompey's comic catalogue of prisoners (4.3.1–20), are allusions to the Statute of Stabbing, passed by Parliament between March and July 1604 to deal with brawling in the streets of London, not least between feuding Englishmen and Scots! Not all commentators have found these allusions convincing.

## Oxfordian Date

Oxfordians in general do not find the 1604 date very convincing and prefer a date up to twenty years earlier. Clark proposes 1581, a date with which Ogburn agrees; Holland prefers 1588; in Hess's general re-dating, 1592 is favoured. Anderson, however, (341–2) argues that Oxford wrote or at least revised the play as late as 1603–4.

## Internal Oxfordian Evidence

Mistress Overdone's complaint about war, sweat, gallows and poverty (1.2.80–2), used by orthodox scholars to date the writing of the play in 1603–4, can equally apply to 1580–1, when there was a 'Papal invasion' of Ireland, at Smerwick Bay, by Italian troops under a Spanish general (1580), plague in London, and the trials and executions of Edmund Campion and other Jesuits.[6] In 1.3.19–21, the Duke refers to "strict statutes and most biting laws ... which for these fourteen years we have let slip". From 12th January 1582, laws against Catholics were vigorously enforced after a period of leniency: monthly fines for non-attendance at church were raised, and it became a felony to harbour Jesuits. Gibbons (3) similarly shows how the puritan outlook in the play was opposed by the Duke. Oxfordians (such as Anderson) point to events in the play which closely parallel events in Oxford's personal life in the early 1580s.

Claudio is imprisoned for "getting Madam Julietta with child" (1.2.70–1). Oxford was imprisoned in the Tower in March 1581, when Anne Vavasor, his mistress, gave birth to a son, baptized Edward; like Juliet, she too was imprisoned (Nelson, 266–75). Angelo deserted Mariana (before marriage) "five years since", chiefly because "her reputation was disvalued in levity" (5.1.215–20). Oxford was estranged from his wife, Anne, from 1576–83 (Nelson, 141–54). While he was in Paris in March 1576, he heard speculation about his wife's unfaithfulness and the paternity of the baby (Elizabeth, later Countess of Derby) born on 2 July 1575. In a letter to Burghley (27 April 1576), Oxford refers to the situation as "the fable of the world", and to his wife as "disgraced" (Nelson, 145–6).

Angelo is reunited with Mariana by the device of the 'bed-trick': she takes Isabella's place in the sexual assignation devised by Angelo (2.1.250ff.; 4.1.228ff.). Oxford, according to two separate accounts, was the victim of a similar trick: Francis Osborne (1593–1659), writing about Philip Herbert in *Traditional Memoirs of the Reigns of Elizabeth and James I*, refers to "that last great Earl of Oxford, whose lady was brought to his bed under the notion of his mistress and from such a virtuous deceit she, the Countess of Montgomery (i.e. Susan Vere, Herbert's first wife) is said to proceed" (Ogburn, 527–8). Morant and Wright state of Oxford, in *The Histories of Essex* (1836):

> He forsook his lady's bed, [but] the father of Lady Anne by stratagem, contrived that her husband should unknowingly sleep with her, believing her to be another woman, and she bore a son to him in consequence of this meeting.

The research of Georges Lambin give further topical weight in favour of a date in the early 1580s. Lambin (not an Oxfordian) shows that major and minor events in the play, as well as names and characteristics of many persons and places in the text, had their historical counterparts in the Paris of 1582–5. The key events – the arrest and trial of Claude (note the name) Tonart for seduction – occurred in August and September 1582.[7] The French king, Henri III, was even more like the ambiguous Duke of the play than James I, and (in the words of a contemporary) "leads the life of a monk more than he maintains the state of a king."[8]

If the play were originally penned in the early 1580s, it would bring its genesis much closer not only to the dates when its major written sources were newly available, but also to events in Oxford's own life. It is reasonable to suggest that all these factors influenced the author's choice of subject matter, and therefore the writing of *Measure for Measure*, by the mid-1580s.

## Conclusion

The play can be dated any time between the early 1580s, when all the main sources were available and 1604, when it was performed at court. There is no contemporary evidence that the play was newly composed in 1604. While many references can be linked to events in 1604, they can equally well apply to the early 1580s. They might also be topical interpolations in an earlier play-text adapted for the 1604 performance – or, indeed many other performances. The real-life events alluded to – war, plague, law-enforcement – were common enough at any time. One must wonder, also, whether James would feel flattered by the supposed portrait of himself in the questionable Duke.

## Notes

1. Bawcutt (1998: 1) has a reproduction of the entry in the Revels Accounts. For further discussion of the 1604 performance, see Alfred Stamp, *The Disputed Revels Accounts*, London, Shakespeare Association, 1930; Alvin Kernan, 'The King's Prerogative and the Law: *Measure for Measure*, Whitehall, December 26, 1604', *Shakespeare, the King's Playwright: Theater in the Stuart Court, 1603–1613*, New Haven, 1995: 50–70.
2. Gibbons (2006: 3) directs us to the Duke's speech at 1.3.19–31 especially.
3. Schanzer quotes from the influential article by David L. Stevenson (1959). The quotation in full reads: "One is forced to think that Shakespeare carefully mined the *Basilikon Doron* in order to be able to dramatize the intellectual interests of his new patron in his comedy" (1959: 196).
4. Lever (Intro, xxxiv) states that the only report of the incident is contained in a tract called *The Time Triumphant* (published in 1604 and attributed to Gilbert Dugdale). The dedicatory epistle was written by Robert Armin, a member of the King's Men.
5. Shanzer quotes Craigie's note in his edition of *Basilikon Doron* (1950), vol 2, page 208. The guilty speaker was an Englishman, John Dickson. In an anecdote, Dickson was said to have called James "ane bastard king not worthy to be obeyed" after being requested to move his ship by royal officers. He was later hanged in Edinburgh.
6. On the 'Papal' invasion of Smerwick Bay, see Patricia Palmer *Language and Conquest in early modern Ireland* (2001). On the trial of Edmund Campion in 1581, see Donna Hamilton, *Anthony Munday and the Catholics* (2005).
7. Lambin, 126 states: "En septembre 1582, à Paris, Claude (Tonart) est condamné à mort pour mariage clandestin. Il n'échappe à la sentence que grâce à

l'indignation publique."

8. Philip Johnson, "*Measure for Measure* and the French Connection", *Great Oxford,* ed. Richard Malim, Parapress, 2004, pp. 196–200. For further details of Henri III (King of France 1574–89), see Desmond Seward, *The Bourbon Kings of France* (1976), who quotes Pierre L'Estoile (*Registre-Journal du regne de Henri III.* Tome II) about the king's bouts of religious fervour: "One can hardly get the king out of the monk's cell . . . Losing himself every day in new devotions, he leads the life of a monk more than he maintains the state of a king."

## Other Cited Works


Anderson, Mark, *Shakespeare by Another Name,* New York: Gotham, 2005

Bawcutt, N. W. (ed.), *Measure for Measure,* Oxford: OUP, 1998

Bullough, G., *Narrative and Dramatic Sources of Shakespeare,* vol. 2, London: Routledge, 1958

Chambers, E. K., *The Elizabethan Stage,* 4 vols, Oxford: Clarendon, 1923

Chambers, E. K., *William Shakespeare: A Study of Facts and Problems,* Oxford: Clarendon, 1930

Clark, E. T., *Hidden Allusions in Shakespeare's Plays,* Port Washington, 1974

Gibbons, Brian (ed.), *Measure for Measure,* Cambridge: CUP, 2006

Hess, W. R. *et al.,* "Shakespeare's Dates", *The Oxfordian,* 2, Portland, 1999

Halliday, F. E., *A Shakespeare Companion,* London: Duckworth, 1952

Holland, H. H., *Shakespeare, Oxford and Elizabethan Times,* London, 1933

Jenkins, E., *Elizabeth the Great,* London, 1958

Lambin, G., *Voyages de Shakespeare en France et en Italie,* Geneva, 1962

Lever, J. W. (ed.), *Measure for Measure,* London: Arden, 1965

Nelson, Alan, H., *Monstrous Adversary,* Liverpool: LUP, 2003

Nosworthy, J. M. (ed.), *Measure for Measure,* London: New Penguin, 1969

Ogburn, C., *The Mysterious William Shakespeare,* London, 1984

Schanzer, E., *The Problem Plays of Shakespeare,* 1963, rptd Routledge, 2005

Stevenson, D. L., "The Role of James I in Shakespeare's *Measure for Measure*", *ELH,* 26, 1959: 188–208

Watts, C., *Measure for Measure,* London: Penguin Masterstudies, 1986

Wells, Stanley. & Gary Taylor (eds), *The Complete Oxford Shakespeare,* Oxford, 1986

—, *William Shakespeare: A Textual Companion,* Oxford: OUP, 1987

5

# The Comedie of Errors

## Kevin Gilvary

*The Comedy of Errors* can be dated between 1566, the date of its latest source, and 1594 when it was performed at Gray's Inn.

### Publication Date

*The Comedy of Errors* is one of eighteen plays in F1 which had not previously been published. It was entered into the Stationers' Register on 8 November 1623 alongside other plays as "not formerly entred to other men":

> Mr Blounte Isaak Jaggard. Entered for their Copie vnder the hands of Mr Doctor Worral and Mr Cole – warden, Mr William Shakspeers Comedyes Histories, and Tragedyes soe manie of the said Copies as are not formerly entered to other men. vizt. Comedyes. The Tempest. The two gentlemen of Verona. Measure for Measure. The Comedy of Errors. As you Like it. All's well that ends well. Twelft night. The winters tale. Histories. The thirde parte of Henry the sixt. Henry the eight. Coriolanus. Timon of Athens. Julius Caesar. Tragedies. Mackbeth. Anthonie & Cleopatra. Cymbeline.

It occupies the fifth position in the Comedies, coming after *Measure for Measure* and before *Much Ado About Nothing.* It is the shortest play in the canon at about 1700 lines.

### Performance Dates

There is one contemporary record of a sixteenth-century performance of what is taken to be *The Comedy of Errors.* The *Gesta Grayorum* (printed in 1688) contains an account of the revels at Gray's Inn during the 1594 Christmas season; for the finale to a night of entertainment and uproar on 28 December:

> a Comedy of Errors (like to *Plautus* his *Menechmus)* was played by the Players.

In 1604, exactly ten years later to the day, it was played as part of the Christmas festivities at Court, '[b]y his Maiesties plaiers. On Inosents Night The Plaie of Errors. Shaxberd' [Revels]. No other production is known before 1716.

The play is apparently mentioned by Meres in *Palladis Tamia* in 1598:

> As *Plautus* and *Seneca* are accounted the best for Comedy and Tragedy among the Latines: so *Shakespeare* among y' English is the most excellent in both kinds for the stage; for Comedy, witnes his *Ge'tleme' of Verona*, his *Errors*, . . .

As the play had not yet been published, Meres is assumed either to have seen the play in performance or perhaps heard of it through a 'court insider' such as Anthony Munday.

## Sources

Bullough states that the play is largely based on the work of the Roman dramatist, Plautus. His *Menaechmi* was published in numerous editions in the sixteenth century, in its original Latin. The comedy arises from the embarrassment of a man searching for his long-lost twin brother, whose intimate acquaintances mistake each for the other. Shakespeare adds to the confusion and slapstick by giving each twin the same name (Antipholus), and by having as their servants another set of long-lost twins – who also share a name (Dromio). The play seems to have been composed before the publication of the first English translation of the *Menaechmi* in 1595.[1]

One episode in Shakespeare's play (in which the wife of one twin bars him from his own house where she is entertaining his brother, believing him to be her husband) appears to be based on another play by Plautus, *Amphitruo.* As Bullough has also pointed out, two strands of the play seem to be based on the story of Apollonius of Tyre, as told by John Gower in his *Confessio Amantis* (1393)*:* the serious opening scene (where Egeon, father of the Antipholus twins, is under threat of death) and the surprising final resolution.[2] Gower's work had been widely published, e.g. by Caxton in 1483 and by Berthelette in 1532.

Bullough also mentions similarities with incidents in Secchi's *Gl'lnganni* of 1549, an Italian play in the 'commedia erudita tradition', not available in English. *Gl'lnganni* ('The Deceits') was also used for *Twelfth Night).* Foakes (intro xxxii–iv) develops further connections with Gascoigne's *Supposes* of 1566 also performed at Gray's Inn. *The Supposes*, a translation of Ariosto's *I Suppositi* (1509), is the latest source for *The Taming of the Shrew.*

## Orthodox Date

The date assigned to the play ranges from 1584–1594. Chambers places it on stylistic and other grounds as the earliest comedy, 1592–3. Orthodox scholars concur that this short play is one of the writer's earliest, but there is much uncertainty and disagreement over what `early' is. Estimates of the most likely date of writing range from 1584–9 (Alexander), up to 1589 (Cairncross), through 1589 (Baldwin, Honigmann), 1588–92 (Mangan), 1591 (Dorsch), 1591–2 (Quiller-Couch), 1590–93 (Foakes) to 1592–94 (Wells & Taylor). Whitworth, following Wells & Taylor's stylistic tests, prefers 1594. Some scholars think it an apprentice piece, perhaps Shakespeare's first play, but others consider it more competent, therefore later, than *The Two Gentlemen of Verona* and *The Taming of the Shrew.*

## Internal Orthodox Evidence

The interpretation of internal evidence for dating the play is varied. The key passage occurs in 3.2. 125–7:

> SYR. ANTIPHOLUS. Where France?
> SYR. DROMIO In her forehead, armed and reverted, making war against her heir.

This is generally recognised as a reference to the civil war in France between Henri of Navarre and the Catholic League. The war broke out in 1589 on the death of Henri III and ended when Henri IV (as Navarre now was) re-converted to Catholicism in July 1593. These dates appear to define a four-year period within which the reference was topically accurate, and within which, therefore, the play must have been written. Quiller-Couch (1968:xiii) and Dorsch (2004:39) tentatively go further and suggest the precise date of 1591 when two English expeditions were sent to France to support Navarre.

Unfortunately, matters are not so clear-cut. Henri IV himself, writing in 1589, asserts: "This foure yeares space I have beene ... the subject of civile armes." Foakes (intro, page xx) reports that his letter was immediately translated into English. As late as 1597 English writers were referring to the civil war as still in progress (1593 marking no more than a truce) and the Edict of Nantes finally ended forty years of religious conflict in 1598. Foakes concludes (intro, xxi) that the evidence of the quotation is consequently unreliable: "The allusion could have made its point at any time in the decade after 1585."

A similar question very soon afterwards in the dialogue produces in Dromio's answer: "The hot breath of Spain, who sent whole armadoes of carracks" (3.2.139–41). This 'hot breath' was interpreted, by the successive Cambridge editors, as an allusion to the recent – for 1591 – defeat of the Spanish Armada in 1588 (Quiller Couch, intro xiii). Other commentators think it could allude to the Great Carrack, a huge Portuguese galleon captured and brought to England in September 1592 (Foakes, xix). Dromio's answer is similarly vague and capable of various interpretations.

## External Orthodox Evidence

The play must have been written by 1598, when Francis Meres's *Palladis Tamia* was published. It refers to "his Errors" as one of Shakespeare's plays, and as part of the proof of his excellence in comedy. The record in the *Gesta Grayorum* is strong evidence that the play was in existence at least four years earlier.

## Oxfordian Date

Clark proposed 1577. Charlton Ogburn Jr concurs with this date. Moore, however, suggests 1587–8 for the key development of the play as we know it in the 1623 text; Hess et al., following Moore, favour 1587.

## Internal Oxfordian Evidence

Moore adopts a different interpretation of 'heir' in the crucial reference to Henri of Navarre (3.2.127), emphasising that it is highly significant that the word is not 'king'. He points out that Henri of Navarre, though a protestant convert, was technically heir to the French throne from June 1584 when, on the death of the Duc d'Alençon, Henri III acknowledged him as his legal successor, "my sole and only heir". A year later, under pressure from the Guise-led Catholic League, which recognised the Cardinal de Bourbon as heir presumptive, Henri III (illegally) removed Navarre from the succession; soon afterwards the War of the Three Henris (France, Guise and Navarre) broke out. However, by the summer of 1589, Henri III and Navarre were allies. This is the "foure yeares space ... of civile armes" that Navarre mentioned in his 1589 letter.

Leonie Frieda (384–5) describes how, on 1 August, Henri III was seriously wounded by an assailant and lost no time in summoning Navarre to his bedside. Before he died, he appointed Henri of Navarre his successor and made his officers and nobles pledge their allegiance to the man who would soon be their new king. Although the League proclaimed their aged cardinal as Charles X, and it took Henri IV over four years to establish his de facto rule over the whole of France (finally entering Paris in 1594), Navarre had become king of France on 2 August 1589.

Whatever the differing catholic attitudes were to Navarre's status, from the protestant viewpoint, Henri of Navarre was 'heir' from June 1584 to August 1589. Moore argues that this would have been an important matter of detail and principle for a protestant English audience, who had common cause with Henri of Navarre. Further weighty considerations in these circumstances would have been Philip of Spain's support of the ultra-Catholics in both England and France, and papal interference in the politics of both countries. So the dates when the 'heir' of France was at war provide a clearly defined period to corroborate Moore's 1587–8 dating of the play.

Commentators have noted the density of legal terminology in *The Comedy of Errors.* Fripp found 150 examples of legal terms, many highly technical. Dorsch notes about a dozen of them in the first scene – more than dramatically necessary. This language, of course, would appeal to an audience with legal training. Sams, who refers to Fripp's researches, finds such language to be evidence for the speculation that Shakespeare had been a lawyer's clerk – one of the many jobs that have been proposed for him during the 'lost' years up to the early 1590s. Oxford was admitted to Gray's Inn on 1 February 1567 (Nelson, 46) and in 1570 the Inn purchased his coat-of-arms. Although he is not known to have bought legal books – his tastes were literary – Oxford spent most of his life dealing with legal problems and lawyers, so there can be no uncertainty about his familiarity with the law (Nelson, 46).

Another feature of the play, which has a direct bearing on the dating, is the influence of John Lyly. The name Dromio occurs in *Mother Bombie,* registered on 18 June 1594 and printed that year, but acted (probably) in 1590. This play has two pairs of changeling children, four servants, four old men and three pairs of lovers. Foakes (intro, xxxiii) lists seven phrases or images in *Mother Bombie* "which recur or are echoed in Shakespeare's play." Lyly's wider influence is felt, according to Foakes, in the tone of much of the dialogue, particularly that between servant and master. By 1579, Lyly was Oxford's secretary and he was his theatre manager during the 1580s (Nelson, 182–3; 238–9). It is more logical to see the Lyly plays and *The Comedy of Errors* coming from a common source and sharing a 'house style' in the 1580s, than to imagine Shakespeare of Stratford either familiarising himself with unpublished court plays before he arrived in London or imitating an earlier style in the mid-1590s.

## External Oxfordian evidence

Clark found brief entries of eleven plays in the Court records of the late 1570s; the texts have not survived and no authors were named. She surmises that some of these plays were written by Oxford, then in his mid-twenties, for performance at Court, and that they were later rewritten and expanded for public performance, to become plays we know in the Shakespeare canon. The first of these listed plays, *The historie of Error,* was performed at Hampton Court, by the 'Children of Powle's', on the night of 1 January 1577. Clark conjectures that this was the earliest version of *The Comedy of Errors.*[3]

Ogburn Jr accepts Clark's conjecture and thinks, on stylistic grounds (he mentions its 'doggerel verse'), that *The Comedy of Errors* is one of the earliest plays. Hess et al. acknowledge Clark's inferences about the early *Errors* play, but favour Moore's interpretation of the internal evidence and, therefore, his 1587 date.

The main source of the play, Plautus' *Menaechmi,* was available only in Latin editions until 1595. Orthodox scholars have to assume that Shakespeare's grammar-school Latin (another undocumented assumption) made him sufficiently "well-equipped to read in the language" (Foakes). Alternatively, Foakes speculates, "it is possible that Shakespeare had seen the first English translation of *Menaechmi,* made by William Warner [but see note 1] and published in 1595." The timing is rather awkward, considering that the latest orthodox date of writing is 1594, so Foakes conjures up a further assumption: "The translation was entered in the Stationers' Register on 10 June 1594 and presumably had circulated earlier in manuscript." The reader is left to supply yet another assumption: that somehow Shakespeare was one of W.W.'s friends and came across this manuscript version.

Oxford's aristocratic education gave him a very solid grounding in Latin. Indeed, Orazio Cuoco,[4] the Venetian teenage chorister who was Oxford's page from 1575 to early 1577 in both Venice and London, testified to the Venetian Inquisition, when he returned to his native city in August 1577, that Oxford "was a person who spoke Latin and Italian well." So we need make no assumptions about Oxford's ability to read Plautus in the original language, and he had no need to wait for the 1594 translation before writing his own play.

Clark's suggestion of 1577 for the play's origins is possible for Oxford. At the age of 26, he would have been a developing playwright, penning a 'late' early comedy, and (as we have seen) fully at ease with the Latin source material. One can reasonably propose that the end of the 1570s is a likely period for the play's original version, with major expansions and revisions up to ten years later, resulting in a version of the play close to, if not indeed the same as, the one we have now.

## Conclusion

*The Comedy of Errors* can be dated after 1566, the date of its latest source. The play was written, known and attributed to Shakespeare by 1598, but 1594 gives us the date of a performance at Gray's Inn of what is generally supposed to be *The Comedy of Errors*. It by no means follows that this was the first performance, or that the play had only just been composed.

## Notes

Thanks are due to Sally Hazelton for many useful suggestions.

1. Gilbert Highet, *The Classical Tradition: Greek and Roman Influences on Western Literature* (1949: 624–5) states that for *The Comedy of Errors*, Shakespeare must have read Plautus's *Amphytruo* in Latin as there was no available translation. Similarly, the dramatist read Plautus' *Mostellaria* in Latin for *The Taming of the Shrew* so he would probably have read the *Menaechmi* in Latin as well. Highet notes: "The only known translation of the *Menaechmi* was published in 1595 by Thomas Creede and attributed to W. W. who may have been William Warner. The publisher in his forward says that W. W. had translated several plays of Plautus "for the use and delight of his private friends, who in Plautus owne words are not able to understand them' and that he himself had prevailed on W.W. to publish this one." Highet further notes that Shakespeare's play does not appear to echo the wording of W. W.'s translation, which is reprinted in Bullough, I, 12–39.
2. Whitworth (2003: 27–37) has an in-depth account of the plot details which might have derived from various stories about Apollonius available at the time, namely its appearance in Gower's *Confessio Amantis*, but also in a later prose version by Laurence Twine, entitled the *Pattern of Painefull Adventures* (1608). Whitworth proposes that Shakespeare's use of the Apollonius tale is more likely to have derived from Twine's version. There were two parallel paths of transmission for the tale. Gower's *Confession* derives from a twelfth-century version in Godfrey of Viterbo's *Pantheon,* while Twine's *Pattern* includes details from the telling in the Latin *Gesta Romanorum,* a popular fourteenth-century compilation of legends. Certain of these details transmit to *Errors,* see Archibald, 1991. Whitworth makes his selection of Twine partly on the basis of its more recent dating. *Pattern* was registered in the S.R. in 1576 with a first edition possibly published before 1594. However, an edition of *Confessio* was issued much earlier, in 1554, leaving what is for Whitworth an uncomfortable gap of forty years between the publication of the source and the writing of the play. This would be "a departure from [Shakespeare's] normal practice of using very recently published works... as sources" (2003: 28). Again, the difficult interrelation of conflicting hypotheses and those compositional behaviours taken as characteristic of Shakespeare's process and position is apparent at every stage.
3. For *The historie of Error*, see Chambers, *ES*, vol IV, 93. The possible connection between the plays was also noted by Highet (cited in a previous note). From the same period, Clark proposes that *The Solitary Knight* played on 17 Feb. 1577 was an early version of *Timon of Athens* and that *Titus and Gisippus* played on 19 Feb. 1577 was an early version of *The Two Noble Kinsmen.*
4. Nelson gives the detailed testimony, 155–7, but mistakenly transcribes the surname as Coquo.

## Other Cited Works

Alexander. P. (ed.), *William Shakespeare: Complete Works,* London: Collins, 1951

Anderson, Mark, *Shakespeare by Another Name*, New York: Gotham 2005

Archibald, E., *Apollonius of Tyre: Medieval and Renaissance Themes and Variations,* Cambridge: D. S. Brewer, 1991

Baldwin, T. W., *On the Compositional Genetics of 'The Comedy of Errors'*, University of

Illinois, 1965
Bland, David (ed.), *Gesta Grayorum,* (1688), *English Reprints Series 22,* Liverpool University Press, 1968: 29–33
Bullough, G., *Narrative and Dramatic Sources of Shakespeare,* vol. 1, London: Routledge & Keegan Paul, 1957
Cairncross, A. S., *The Problem of Hamlet: A Solution,* London: Macmillan, 1936
Chambers, E. K., *The Elizabethan Stage*, 4 vols, Oxford: Clarendon, 1923
Chambers, E. K., *William Shakespeare, A Study of Facts and Problems,* Oxford: Clarendon, 1930
Clark, E. T., *Hidden Allusions in Shakespeare's Plays,* Port Washington: Minos, 1974
Dorsch, T. S. (ed.), *The Comedy of Errors,* , Cambridge: New Cambridge, 1988
Foakes, R. A. (ed.), *The Comedy of Errors,*, London: Arden, 1962
Freeman, Arthur (ed.), *Palladis Tamia* reprint Garland, New York, 1973.
Frieda, L., *Catherine de Medici,* London: Phoenix, 2003
Fripp, Edgar, *Minutes and Accounts of the Corporation of Stratford-upon-Avon and other records, 1553–1620*, Oxford: OUP, 1924
Hess, W. R. *et al.*, "Shakespeare's Dates", *The Oxfordian,* 2, Portland, 1999
Honigmann, E. A. J., *Shakespeare: the 'lost years',* Manchester University Press, 1985
Mangan, M., *A Preface to Shakespeare's Comedies*, London: Longman, 1996
Matus, I., *Shakespeare, in fact,* , New York: Continuum, 1994
Moore, P., "The Abysm of Time: the Chronology of Shakespeare's Plays", *Elizabethan Review,* 5.2, 1997
Nelson, A. H., *Monstrous Adversary,* Liverpool University Press, 2003
Ogburn, C., *The Mysterious William Shakespeare,* New York: Dodd Mead, 1984
Quiller-Couch, A. and J. D. Wilson (eds), *The Comedy of Errors,* 2nd ed, Cambridge University, 1968
Sams, E., *The Real Shakespeare,* Yale University Press, 1997
Ward, B. M., *The Seventeenth Earl of Oxford,* London: John Murray, 1928 rptd 1979.
Wells, Stanley and Gary Taylor (eds), *The Complete Oxford Shakespeare,* Oxford, 1986
— (eds), *William Shakespeare: a textual companion*, Oxford, 1987
Whitworth, Charles (ed.), *The Comedy of Errors,* Oxford: OUP, 2003

# 6

# Much Ado About Nothing

## Philip Johnson

*Much Ado About Nothing* can be dated between 1583, when all the major sources were available, and 1600, when it was published.

### Publication Date

The play, not mentioned by Meres in 1598, was named twice in the Stationers' Register: the first occasion, dated 4th August, shows the title entered informally, along with *Henry V, As You Like It* and Jonson's *Every Man in His Humour.* Chambers (*WS,* I, 145 and 384) cites the following memoranda, which he tentatively dates to 1600; they were written on a spare page in the Register, and included:

> My lord chambelens mens plays entred . . .
> 4 Augusti
> As you like yt , a booke } to be staied
> Henry the ffift, a booke
> Eevry man in his humour, a booke
> The Commedie of muche A doo about nothing a booke

These four titles do not appear in the normal place or format, and all four plays were "to be staied", that is, either their registration or their printing was to be delayed. *As You Like It* was not registered or published until 1623 in the First Folio (F1) while the three other plays were formally registered in August 1600. This second entry was more formal:

> [SR, 1600] 23 Augusti. Andrew Wyse William Aspley. Entred for their copies vnder the handes of the wardens Two bookes, the one called Muche a Doo about nothinge . . . Wrytten by master Shakespere. xijd

The quarto was printed that year:

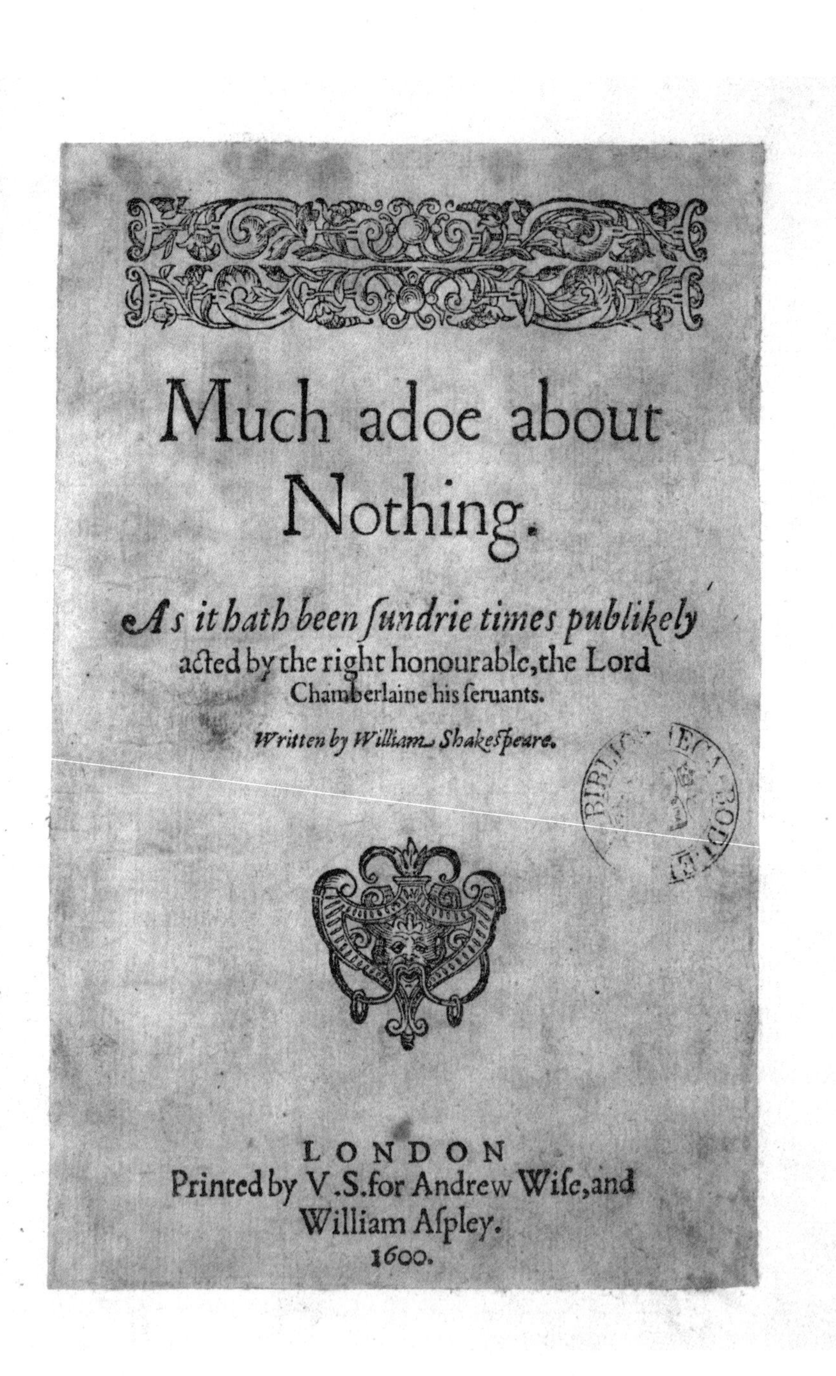

Much adoe about
Nothing.

*As it hath been ſundrie times publikely*
acted by the right honourable, the Lord
Chamberlaine his ſeruants.

*Written by William Shakeſpeare.*

LONDON
Printed by V.S. for Andrew Wiſe, and
William Aſpley.
1600.

3. Title page to the quarto of *Much Ado about Nothing*, 1600.
By permission of Bodleian Library, University of Oxford,
shelfmark Arch. G d. 45 (3), title page.

> [Q, 1600] Much adoe about nothing. As it hath been sundrie times publikely acted by the Right Honourable, the Lord Chamberlaine his seruants. Written by William Shakespeare. London: printed by V[alentine] S[immes] for Andrew Wise, and William Aspley, 1600.

It was not reprinted until the 1623 Folio was published – with only a few minor variations of text and stage directions. It occupies the sixth position among the comedies, after *The Comedy of Errors* and before *Love's Labour's Lost.*

## Performance Date

The quarto title-page states that the play "hath been sundrie times publikely acted" by the Lord Chamberlain's Men but the first recorded performance was on 20th May 1613: John Heminge was paid £93.6s.8d. for presenting fourteen plays, including *Much Adoe abowte Nothinge*; and £60 more for six other performances including *Benedicte and Betteris* (which is usually taken to be an alternative title). These are the only documented performances until after the Restoration.

## Sources

Bullough divided the sources according to three main strands in the play:

**a) Hero and Claudio plot**

The three main sources are Matteo Bandello's *La Prima Parte de le Novelle,* Novella 22 (1554), of which there is no known English translation until the end of the nineteenth century (Mares, 1); François de Belleforest's *Histoires Tragiques,* vol.3, no.8 (1569) – a French translation and expansion of Bandello's story; Ludovico Ariosto's *Orlando Furioso,* Book 5 (1516), translated into heroic couplets by Sir John Harington and published in 1591. Of these, Humphreys cites 'Bandello as the actual source'. Bandello was also used by Shakespeare for *Othello,* and Belleforest was used for *Hamlet.*

F. H. Mares (3–4) states that variants of the episodes and actions of these stories were popular and widely imitated in the latter part of the sixteenth century. They formed the basis of stories such as Whetstone's *The Rocke of Regard* (1576), various poems including Beverley's *The Historie of Ariodante and Ieneura* (*c.*1566) and Spenser's *The Fairie Queene,* Book 2 (1590), and such plays as Munday's (?) *Fedele and Fortunio* (1585).

**b) Beatrice and Benedick plot**

No specific source has been located, but parallels of the 'scorner of love' tradition are found in other Shakespeare plays: *The Merchant of Venice* and, particularly, *The Taming of the Shrew* and *Love's Labour's Lost*. Two writers are cited as the main inspiration for the courtly conversation and comedy of wit in which Beatrice and Benedick engage. First is Baldassare Castiglione, whose *Il Cortegiano* (written 1514, published 1528) was translated into English by Sir Thomas Hoby and published in 1561, with further editions in 1577 and 1588. In addition, Castiglione reports[1] seeing "a most fervent love spring in the heart of a woman" towards a man for whom she had not previously had the least affection, "onely for that she heard say, that the opinion of many was, that they loved together." The second writer is John Lyly, with his euphuistic fiction and dramatic comedies (e.g. *Euphues and his England*, 1580).

**c) The Watch**

Bullough sees some parallels with John Lyly's *Endimion* but no direct influence. *Endimion*, which was published in 1591, but probably written *c.*1587–8, contains a group of incompetent watchmen who argue amongst themselves.

## Orthodox Date

Chambers dates the play to the winter of 1598–9, as do Foakes, and Wells and Taylor; Humphreys, Mares, Zitner and McEachern prefer 1598; Halliday opts for 1599. Peter Alexander suggested an earlier date between 1594–8.

## Internal Orthodox Evidence

In the 1600 quarto, the name 'Kemp' appears instead of 'Dogberry' in the speech-headings of Act 4 Scene 2. Therefore, composition appears to have preceded Will Kemp's departure from the Lord Chamberlain's company, early in 1599.[2] It is also possible that the part was composed with Kemp in mind but that the comic actor did not return to the company as expected.

## External Orthodox Evidence

As *Much Ado* is not mentioned by Francis Meres in his *Palladis Tamia* (1598), Chambers maintains that it must have been written afterwards. He also decides against the possibility that Meres was referring to this play as *Love's Labour's Won* in his list of six comedies (balancing six histories) composed by Shakespeare:

> for Comedy, witness his Gentlemen of Verona, his Errors, his Loue labours lost, his Loue labours wonne, his midsummer night dream, & his Merchant of Venice.

Most editors follow Chambers in rejecting this identification, preferring *Taming of the Shrew* as a more likely candidate. However, Baldwin notes that a book list from 1603 has been found (it had belonged an Elizabethan bookseller called Christopher Hunt) in which several plays were listed, including *Merchant of Venice, Taming of the Shrew,... Loves Labour Lost, Loves Labour Won*. After this, some commentators argued that *Loves Labour Won* should be identified as the main title for *Much Ado,* among them Robert Fleissner, who claimed that 'This is the only title of Shakespeare's which we have without a play to go with it from this period of his career.' Others doubted the identification because a different part of the list included *Much Ado* as a separate play.[3]

## Oxfordian Date

Some Oxfordians have dated the play to 1583 (Eva Turner Clark and Charlton Ogburn, Jnr). Holland favours 1579 for an early version.

## Internal Oxfordian Evidence

The following passages are taken to support the Oxfordian dating and, in some cases, strongly to support Oxford's authorship. Don Pedro's comment, "In time the savage bull doth bear the yoke" (1.1.241–2) reflects both Thomas Kyd's *The Spanish Tragedy* (1587): "In time the sauuage Bull sustaines the yoake" (2.1.3), and Sonnet 47 in Thomas Watson's *Hekatompathia* (1582): "In time the Bull is brought to weare the yoake." The dedicatee of Watson's volume is the Earl of Oxford. Furthermore, Watson's dedication states: "your Honour had willingly vouchsafed the acceptance of this work" [which] "your Lordship with some liking had already perused." The critic Edward Arber has suggested that the "most skilfully written" introductions to the poems may be by Oxford. According to Ogburn, Watson himself hints that Oxford contributed to the volume. Both Holland and Clark suggest that Benedick's: "I look for an earthquake too, then" (1.1.253) alludes to the earthquake felt in England on 6th April 1580.[4]

The metrical form of this dialogue (2.1.88–91):

DON PEDRO My visor is Philemon's roof, within the house is Jove.
HERO Why then, your visor should be thatched.
DON PEDRO Speak low, if you speak love.

matches the fourteen-syllable couplets used by Oxford in his early poetry[5] (and also by Shakespeare in *Cymbeline*[6]). It also recalls Arthur Golding's translation (1567) of Ovid's *Metamorphoses*, in which the incident is related (Humphreys, 70n). Lott (26) comments that Shakespeare probably knew Ovid's poem best from Golding's translation. Since Golding was Oxford's uncle (and possibly his tutor), Oxfordians find this unremarkable. Some suggest that as a teenager

Oxford may have assisted in the translation.

A. R. Humphreys refers to the book of Marco Polo's travels (of which the English translation by John Frampton was published in 1579) as mentioning all the features in Benedick's speech:

> I will fetch you a tooth-picker now from the furthest inch of Asia, bring you the length of Prester John's foot; fetch you a hair off the great Cham's beard; do you any embassage to the pigmies ...' (2.1.248–252).

John Lyly's *Endimion* (published in 1591, but probably written in 1587/8) has, in 4.3, a group of befuddled watchmen given to ludicrous logic. Humphreys notes this and also suggests that, "Shakespeare may half-consciously have recalled [wording] in the earlier play." A close examination of *Endimion* and *Much Ado About Nothing* shows striking similarities in the use of euphuistic style, in proverbial phrases and in imagery, but the direction of influence is not clear. Lyly was associated with Oxford from 1577, worked as his theatre-manager throughout the 1580s and dedicated *Euphues and his England* in 1580 to Oxford (Nelson, 182–3; 247–8; 238). Thus, it would be reasonable to assume that more than "half-conscious" recall was involved in connecting the two similar features of the plays – perhaps even collaboration.

In 3.3.100–2, Borachio tells Conrade: "Stand thee close then under this penthouse, for it drizzles rain, and I will, like a true drunkard, utter all to thee." Humphreys quotes a letter from Lord Burghley to Sir Francis Walsingham (dated 10 August 1586) which refers to the ineffective and ludicrous behaviour of the watchmen in every town he passed through on his journey home from London to Theobalds. The watchmen had been detailed to look out for three conspirators in the Babington plot but they themselves stood around conspicuously in groups of ten or twelve:

> and untill I cam to Enfield I thought no other of them, but that they had stayd for avoyding of the rayne, or to drink at some alehouse, for so they did stand under pentyces at ale houses.

Burghley stopped and interrogated the Enfield watchmen, only to discover how limited was their information about the suspects. Although the situation in the play is not exactly the same (the group of watchmen stay together, but "upon the church bench," while the suspects shelter under the penthouse), the triple parallels of 'rain', 'penthouse' and 'alehouse' / 'drunkard' are intriguing. Humphreys declines to make a direct connection between the Watch of Enfield and that of Messina: the rain / penthouse links are "doubtless sheer coincidence"; but he does venture the observation that "real life may have furnished Shakespeare with inspirations." The ready accessibility of Burghley's experience to his son-in-law – Oxford – is obvious; but how might a young man from Stratford, in his 'lost years,' have chanced upon this particular 'inspiration'? If there is a direct link between the Enfield incident and the play, it would support a mid-1580s date of writing.

Borachio and Conrade's rambling discussion of fashion (3.3.113–137) relates to the key theme of disguise – here, Margaret in Hero's clothes – and reflects Borachio's drunkenness, but it is longer than is dramatically necessary. Holland connects it with the Sumptuary Laws of the spring of 1580, "dealing with certain fashions then in vogue". In 3.4.57–8 Hero, too, is concerned with fashion: "These gloves the count sent me, they are an excellent perfume." In 1576 Oxford gave Queen Elizabeth a pair of perfumed gloves he had brought from Italy (still on view in Hatfield House); "for many years after, it was called the Earl of Oxford's perfume", according to Ogburn. In response to Margaret's "I saw the Duchess of Milan's gown that they praise so"(3.4.14–15), Humphreys quotes Linthicum (1936): "Queen Elizabeth possessed many garments ... Shakespeare probably found at court his inspiration for the Duchess of Milan's gown." While there was no real life Duchess of Milan. A play entitled *The Duke of Milan and Marquis of Mantua* was enacted at Court on 26 December 1579.

## External Oxfordian Evidence

The play is set in Messina, on the north-east corner of Sicily, which was under Spanish rule at the time. Humphreys notes that in 1458, 'A bastard prince of the House of Aragon, named John, assumed the crown of Sicily ... The coincidence of details is doubtless fortuitous.' Humphreys gives this opinion because Messina was a place unfamiliar to contemporary English travellers or "as remote as the moon to the majority of Shakespeare's audience" as McEachern colourfully says. Oxford, however, had travelled extensively in Italy in 1575–76 (Nelson, 121–141) and is known to have impressed the Sicilian Court at Palermo with a famous challenge that went unanswered.[7]

Oxford's own relationship with his wife echoes that of Claudio and Hero. While Oxford was abroad, the Lady Anne gave birth to a daughter, Elizabeth. It was widely rumoured that Oxford was not the father and upon his return to England he refused to see his wife for seven years (Nelson, 141–154). Eventually, they were reunited and Oxford is thought to have expressed his remorse for doubting his wife's faithfulness in a series of plays, including *Much Ado, Othello* and *A Winter's Tale.*

Further evidence in support both of an early date and of Oxfordian composition comes from records of plays performed at court and from the European literary sources. In February 1583, on Shrove Tuesday, *A History of Ariodante and Geneuora* was performed before the Queen at Richmond Palace, by "Mr Mulcaster's children" i.e. the boys of the Merchant Taylors' School (Chambers, *ES* IV, 99). As Ariosto's story of Ariodante and Genevra (in *Orlando Furioso,* Book 5 – see 'Sources', above) is similar to the major plot involving Hero and Claudio, Clark suggests that this is the first presentation at

Court of *Much Ado about Nothing.*

Of the major sources, only Ariosto's *Orlando Furioso* was translated into English before *Much Ado About Nothing* was published in 1600; and, as we saw, Humphreys judges Bandello, translated into French only, to be the actual source. Mares opines: "It seems most likely that Shakespeare was working from the Italian rather than the French – unless he had some other source no longer known to us." Humphreys suggests that it is "against likelihood" that Belleforest's French translation of Bandello "was the version Shakespeare had before him" thus suggesting that the dramatist had read the original in Italian. Oxford displayed abilities in both languages: he was taught French for two hours a day as a boy (Nelson, 37) and he spent ten months in Italy in 1575–6.

There would have been no language problem with Castiglione's *Il Cortegiano*, (translated into English in 1561) for any writer who understood only English. But Humphreys and Mares are silent about two facts concerning the text: firstly, Sir Thomas Hoby, the translator into English, was Burghley's brother-in-law – therefore a member of Oxford's foster-family and later an uncle by marriage; secondly, and more significantly, Oxford wrote the Latin preface to Bartholomew Clerke's 1571 *De Curiali*, a Latin translation of *Il Cortegiano* (Nelson, 237). "My friend" Clerke had been Oxford's tutor at Cambridge. Oxford affirms that his plan to write the preface, as well as to study the translation ('with a mind full of gratitude'), 'seemed to combine a task of delightful industry with an indication of special goodwill".

Finally, Mares notes *Fedele and Fortunio* (1585) by 'M.A.' as a play with a story similar to the Hero–Claudio plot. He identifies 'M.A.' with Anthony Munday, who was Oxford's secretary (Nelson, 238). So, as with Lyly, collaboration and development are a possibility.

## Conclusion

*Much Ado About Nothing* can be dated between 1583, when all the major sources were available, and 1600, when it was published. Three factors, (a) the availability of the major sources and their literary currency between the late 1570s and 1590, (b) the striking linguistic links with texts current in the 1580s, especially with Lyly's *Endimion*, and (c) the contemporary references, strongly support a date of composition in the mid 1580s. There is no reason why a play with such dated roots would be *newly* written in 1598–1600 but it could easily have been *revived* then (as now) due to its enduring qualities.

## Notes

1. The quotations are given by Bullough, vol II page 79, from Book III of Thomas Hoby's translation.

2. Andrew Gurr, *The Shakespeare Company 1594–1642* (2004: 231), describes how Will Kemp left the Lord Chamberlain's Men in 1599 to undertake his famous nine-day dance to Norwich, followed by his dance over the Alps. He returned to England in 1601 and joined Worcester's Men.
3. Lukas Erne in *Shakespeare as Literary Dramatist* (82, note 18) argues that *Love's Labour's Won* might well have been an early title for *Much Ado.* Both T. W. Baldwin (*Shakespeare's Love's Labour's Won: New Evidence from the Account Books of an Elizabethan Bookseller*) and Wells & Taylor (*Textual Companion*, 71–2) see *Love's Labour's Won* as a lost play which Hemmings and Condell excluded from the First Folio due either to its collaborative status, or to its early composition, or both.
4. For further discussion on possible references to the 1580 earthquake and to a serious earthquake in Verona in 1570, see Chapter 28 *Romeo and Juliet*, note 5.
5. Nelson (157–163) refers somewhat dismissively to Oxford's poetry, of which a number of poems are written in this difficult meter. For the text of these poems, see Katherine Chiljan *The Letters and Poems of Edward de Vere.* For those who wish to see if they can distinguish the poetry of Shakespeare from that of Oxford, try the Benezet Test in Richard Whalen, *Shakespeare – who was he? The Oxford Challenge to the Bard* (1994).
6. There has been much discussion about why Shakespeare might have used an old-fashioned metre in an apparently late play. See Maurice Hunt, "Fourteeners in Shakespeare's *Cymbeline*", *Notes & Queries*, 2000, 458–61.
7. In *The Travels of Edward Webbe* (1590), the author states:

> Many things I have omitted to speak of, which I have seen and noted in the time of my troublesome travel. One thing did greatly comfort me which I saw long since in Sicilia, in the city of Palermo, a thing worthy of memory, where the Right Honourable the Earl of Oxenford, a famous man of chivalry, at what time he travelled into foreign countries, being then personally present, made there a challenge against all manner of persons whatsoever, and at all manner of weapons, as Tournaments, barriers with horse and armour, to fight a combat with any whatsoever in the defence of his Prince and Country. For which he was highly commended, and yet no man durst be so hardy to encounter with him so that all Italy over he is acknowledged the only Chevalier and Nobleman of England. This title they give unto him as nobly deserved.

The account is quoted by Nelson (2003: 131), who is doubtful whether Webbe actually saw the event or whether Oxford's challenge was left unmet. Webbe's account has been re-examined by Anderson (89–91). The incident probably happened early in 1576 when Webbe was a galley slave and his Turkish ship put into Palermo.

## Other Cited Works

Alexander, Peter, *Shakespeare's Life and Art,* London: James Nisbet, 1939
Anderson, Mark, *"Shakespeare" by Another Name,* New York: Penguin, 2005

Baldwin, T. W. *Shakespeare's Love's Labour's Won: New Evidence from the Account Books of an Elizabethan Bookseller*, Carbondale, IL: S. Illinois UP, 1957
Bullough, Geoffrey, *Narrative and Dramatic Sources of Shakespeare*, vol. II, London: Routledge and Kegan Paul, 1958
Chambers, E. K., *The Elizabethan Stage,* 4 vols, Oxford: Clarendon, 1923
Chambers, E. K., *William Shakespeare, A Study of Facts and Problems,* 2 vols, Oxford: Clarendon, 1930
Chiljan, Katherine (ed.), *The Letters and Poems of Edward de Vere,* privately printed, 1998
Clark, Eva Turner, *Hidden Allusions in Shakespeare's Plays,* New York: Kennikat, 1931, rptd 1974
Erne, Lukas *Shakespeare as Literary Dramatist,* Cambridge: CUP, 2003
Fleissner, R., "*Love's Labour's Won* and the Occasion of *Much Ado*", *Shakespeare Survey*, 27, 1974
Foakes, R.A. (ed.), *Much Ado About Nothing,* London, Penguin, 1968
Gurr, Andrew, *The Shakespeare Company 1594–1642,* Cambridge: CUP, 2004
Hess, W. R. *et al.*, "Shakespeare's Dates", *The Oxfordian*, 2, Portland, 1999
Halliday, F. E., *A Shakespeare Companion*, London: Duckworth, 1952
Holland, H. H., *Shakespeare, Oxford and Elizabethan Times*, London: D. Archer, 1933
Humphreys, A. R., ed., *Much Ado About Nothing,* London: Arden, 1981
Hunt, Maurice, "Fourteeners in Shakespeare's *Cymbeline*", *Notes & Queries*, 2000
Johnson, P., "John Lyly's *Endimion*" etc., in R. Malim (ed.), *Great Oxford,* Tunbridge Wells: Parapress, 2004: 151–158
Lott, B. (ed.), *Much Ado About Nothing*, London, New Swan, 1977
Mares, F. H. (ed.), *Much Ado About Nothing,* Cambridge: CUP, 1988
McEachern, C. (ed.), *Much Ado About Nothing*, London, Arden Shakespeare, 2006
Nelson, Alan, *Monstrous Adversary,* Liverpool: LUP, 2003
Ogburn, Charlton, *The Mysterious William Shakespeare,* Virginia: EPM, 1984
Wells, Stanley & Gary Taylor Gary (eds), *William Shakespeare: The Complete Works,* Oxford: OUP, 1986
Wells, Stanley & Gary Taylor, *William Shakespeare: A Textual Companion*, Oxford: OUP, 1987
Zitner, S. (ed.), *Much Ado About Nothing*, Oxford: OUP, 1993

7

# Love's Labour's Lost

Derran Charlton and Kevin Gilvary

*Love's Labour's Lost* can be dated between 1578, when all the sources were available and 1598, when it was mentioned three times.

## Publication Date

The earliest surviving text of the play is the quarto edition of 1598.

> [Q1, 1598]: A PLEASANT Conceited Comedie CALLED, Loues Labors lost. As it vvas presented before her Highnes this last Christmas. Newly corrected and augmented *By W.Shakespere.* Imprinted at London by *W. W.* for *Cutbert Burby.* 1598.

This was the first play to be published carrying the name 'Shakespere'. This first known edition shares three features with the 'good' quarto of *Romeo and Juliet* (1599): neither was entered in the Stationers' Register, both were published by Burby, and both claim to be "newly corrected and augmented."Since the 'good' quarto of *Romeo and Juliet* was evidently issued to supplant the 'bad' Quarto of 1597, David argues (intro, xvii) that it is "likely that [Burby's *LLL*] was issued with the same purpose, to replace a 'bad' Quarto of which no copy has survived". This idea has received attention from Felicia Hardison Londré (328), who has suggested that there was an earlier play, the model for *LLL* had been composed by another author.[1] Francis Meres in his *Palladis Tamia* (1598) lists the play among the six comedies (balancing six histories) composed by Shakespeare:

> for Comedy, witness his Gentlemen of Verona, his Errors, his Loue labours lost, his Loue labours wonne, his midsummer night dream, & his Merchant of Venice.

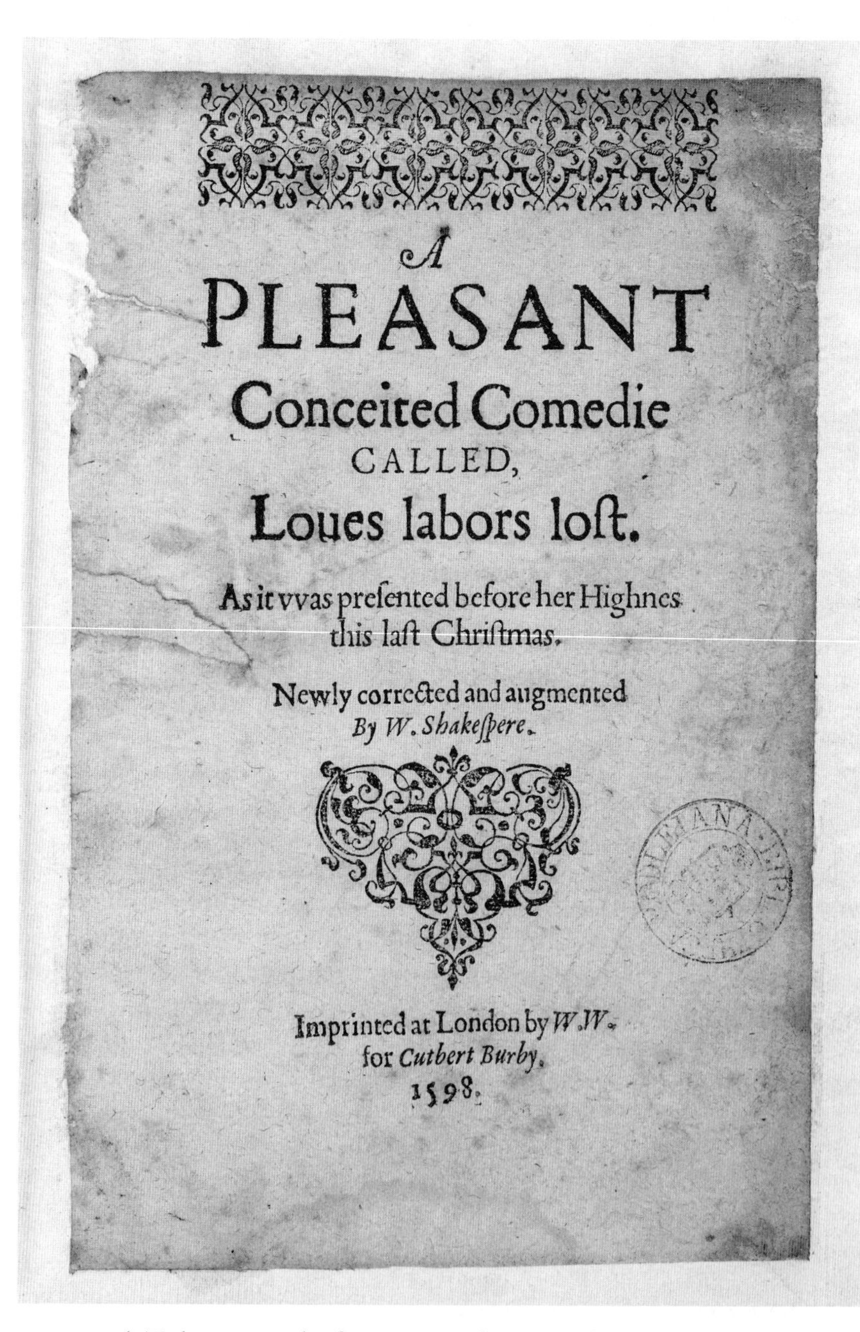

A
PLEASANT
Conceited Comedie
CALLED,
Loues labors loſt.

As it vvas preſented before her Highnes
this laſt Chriſtmas.

Newly corrected and augmented
*By W. Shakeſpere.*

Imprinted at London by *W.W.*
for *Cutbert Burby.*
1598.

4. Title page to the first quarto of *Love's Labour's Lost,* 1598.
By permission of Bodleian Library, University of Oxford,
shelfmark Arch. G d.41 (4), title page.

It is not known if Meres saw *Love's Labour's Lost* in performance or knew of it second hand. Two of the listed plays had not been published by this time, *Two Gentlemen of Verona* and *Comedy of Errors*, while one, *Love's Labour's Won*, has not been identified with any certainty.

The play was not entered in the Stationers' Register until 22 January 1607, when it was transferred from Burby to Nicholas Ling. Later the same year, it was transferred to John Smethwick. The play was published in F1 in 1623 as the seventh comedy, after *Much Ado about Nothing* and before *Midsummer Night's Dream*. A second quarto, based on F1, was printed in 1631:

> [Q2, 1631]: Loues labours lost. A wittie and pleasant comedie, as it was acted by His Maiesties seruants at the Blacke-Friers and the Globe. Written by William Shakespeare.
> London: printed by W. S. [William Stansby] for Iohn Smethwicke, and are to be sold at his shop in Saint Dunstones Churchyard vnder the Diall, 1631.

## Performance Dates

The date of the first performance is unknown. The 1598 title-page indicates a performance at Court the previous Christmas (either 1597 or 1598). If the play was published between 25 March and 24 December 1598, "this last Christmas" began in December 1597 in modern chronology. But in the old style of dating, publication during the next three months, up to what we would call 24 March 1599, would also have counted as 1598 – in which case the previous Christmas was that of 1598. Woudhuysen demonstrates that the assertion of a recent court performance (as, indeed, that of an improved text) is not necessarily reliable: he observes that several plays, reprinted well into the seventeenth century, claimed recent performances before Queen Elizabeth – long after she was dead! The reprint simply copied the title-page of the previous edition.[2]

It is possible that the court performance occurred several Christmases before 1597. Woudhuysen (1998: 61) tentatively suggests that the play might have been written for performance at court by the recently formed Lord Chamberlain's Men, who played on 26 and 27 December 1594.

Specific attention has been called to one of the earliest external references to the play, in the poem *Alba: The Month's Mind of a Melancholy Lover* by the "emphatically minor" poet Richard Tofte (published 1598).[3] Occurring in the third part of the poem, the relevant passage runs:

> *Loves Labor Lost*, I once did see a Play
> Ycleped so, so called to my paine,

David comments on the ambiguity of "once", which suggests "some time long before the time of writing, but it is just possible that it means 'on one occasion only'" (1997: xxiii). Dover Wilson suggests that the play as we have it is a revision of an earlier version acted at the Earl of Southampton's house in the plague year of 1593–4 (1962: 115). This is unlikely, as the Earl of Southampton was a ward at Cecil House under the care of Lord Burghley until he came of age on 6 October 1594.[4]

Halliday suggests that this same earl may be connected with the next recorded performance, in January 1605 (1955: 102). The Revels Account has this entry: "By his Maiesties plaiers. Betwin Newers Day and Twelfe day A play of Loues Labours Lost." This is probably the performance referred to in letters written in January 1605 by Sir Walter Cope and Dudley Carlton. The latter states that the Queen and "a great part of the Court" were feasted at "my Lord of Cranbornes [Robert Cecil's] house," as they had been two nights earlier at "my Lord of Southamptons"; it seems that the play was given a private performance at one of these houses during the week after twelfth night.

The title-page of the second quarto (1631) states that the play was acted publicly "at Blackfriars and the Globe."

## Sources

Bullough finds no single literary source from which the plot might have been derived. He finds that the play is in the tradition of the Italian *commedia dell'arte*, especially in the generic names which occur in the quarto: Braggart for Armado, Pedant for Holophernes, Curate for Nathaniel, Clown for Costard.

Bullough also observes general influence from the courtly plays of John Lyly,

> whose influence is especially potent in the witty, teasing women, the interest in ideas, and the under-plot which parodies high life below stairs. From Lyly spring the scholastic humour of its pedants, the comic use of logic, rhetoric and grammar. . . . the relationship between Armado and Moth recalls that of Sir Tophas and Epiton in [John Lyly's] *Endimion*.

*Endimion* was published in 1591, but had been written by late 1587.[5]

Bullough believes that *Love's Labour's Lost* drew on Pierre de la Primaudaye's *L'Académie française*, published in 1577 (Books 1–2 were translated into English in 1586 by Thomas Bowes). Primaudaye describes how four young nobles withdraw from worldly life to devote themselves to the study of Latin and Greek. Their studies, however, are interrupted by the outbreak of civil war. Primaudaye dedicated his work to Henri III, King of France. Bullough describes the remarkable similarities between the play and events at the court of Navarre at Nérac, in south-west France. Modern knowledge of these events derives mainly from Marguerite de Valois, who died in 1615. Since her *Memoires* were not published until 1628 (and only translated into English in 1658), most scholars are unable to explain remarkable correspondence of the *Memoires* with the play. Margaret had married Henri, King of Navarre (who succeeded his cousin to become Henri IV of France in 1589) in 1572, five days before the St Bartholomew's Day Massacre at Paris. Henri, King of Navarre, received two embassies from France, one in 1578 and the other in 1586, either of which might have served as a model for that in *Love's Labour's Lost*. In 1578–9, the ambassador was indeed a Princess of France (*c.f.* 1.1.133; 2.1.30), Marguerite (Margot) de Valois, estranged wife of Henri, who came to Nérac with her mother, Catherine de Medici. In the earlier visit, an important topic of discussion was Marguerite's dowry, which included Aquitaine (mentioned at 1.1.135; 2.1.8; 2.1.135ff.). On both occasions the royal envoy, reinforcing diplomacy with coquetry, was supported by that bevy of ladies-in-waiting who for their grace and flightiness were known as *'l'escadron volant'*. In the years immediately before her visit, Marguerite had made journeys exactly corresponding to those referred to by the Princess and her ladies in the play: to Alençon (2.1.61) in 1578 and to Liège (Brabant; 2.1.113) in 1577. The other embassy occurred in 1586, when Queen Catherine herself met Henri at Saint Brice, near Cognac. Interestingly, in several places the quarto reads 'Queen' for 'Princess' – Margot, of course, was Queen of Navarre.

The King's 'Academe' is also a reflection of history. In 1583 the English ambassador to the court of France reported to Walsingham that Navarre had "furnished his Court with principal gentlemen of the Religion, and reformed his house". Navarre had in fact followed widespread fashion and become royal patron of an academy, as had his brother-in-law, Henri III of France, who attended his own Palace Academy from 1576–9. The vogue for academies – essentially philosophical debating societies – had started in renaissance Italy. Though the Ducs de Biron and de Longueville were not members of Navarre's academy, they were his political allies from 1589, and the names Boyet, Marcade and de la Mothe appear in contemporary registers of court officials. The King's impetuous riding (4.1.1–2) and his covering the whole sheet, "margin and all," in his letter-writing (5.2.7–8) were actual habits of Henri of Navarre.[6]

Some commentators suggest an echo between *Love's Labour's Lost* and Robert Southwell's *St Peter's Complaint*, published in 1595 (Dover Wilson, 1977: lix). Southwell was in prison from 1592 until his execution in 1595, so it is unlikely that the dramatist could have seen this poem before its publication. The play's possible word-play on 'eyes' and 'stars' is slight and the direction of influence unclear.

## Orthodox Date

Chambers dated the play to 1594 and most commentators follow this dating (Yates, David, Wells & Taylor, Hibbard and Woudhuysen). Richard David argues for a revision before Christmas 1597.

Alexander suggests earlier dates of 1592-94; Honigmann places it in 1592. The OED cites under the head word 'honorificabilitudinitaty': "1588 SHAKES. *L.L.L.* V. i. 44 Thou art not so long by the head as *honorificabilitudinitatibus.*" It is not known how the editors of the OED arrive at so early a date for the play. Athos follows this dating in the Signet Paperback edition.

## Internal Orthodox Evidence

David justifies his dating by historical allusions in the text, such as the matching of several characters in the play, in name at least, with historical French contemporaries of the playwright. Henri IV's period of greatest popularity in England was between 1591 and 1593, before he converted to Catholicism. David observes echoes at 4.2.80–84 of the pamphlet war between Gabriel Harvey and Thomas Nashe (*Pierce Penilesse,* etc.) in 1592–3; of Ralegh's circle of 'atheists,' the 'Schoole of Night' (referred to at 4.3.253 as 'the style of night') and his fall from favour in 1592 on account of his liaison with Elizabeth Throckmorton; and of the appearance of Negro-Tartars (5.2.120–1 ff.) in the Gray's Inn revels at Christmas 1594. He also notes the recurrence of many ideas and images from the Shakespeare poems published in 1593/4, especially *Lucrece.*

Woudhuysen, in his fuller discussion of the dating, notes that 1594–5 is the date generally accepted by scholars, but he acknowledges that "the evidence for it is fairly thin"; he considers attempts to date the play through its French associations or the Gray's Inn revels "unsatisfactory", and finds attempts to use other topical allusions "not convincing" (1998: 59–60).

Woudhuysen's own particular view of the play is that "it draws on a range of [Sir Philip] Sidney's writings and develops some of the literary and artistic problems which exercised him"; its "riches... are bound up with Shakespeare's appreciation of Sidney's achievement as an imaginative writer"; "Shakespeare is showing that he has mastered Sidney's writings, and that he can overgo them" (1998: 6). The play seems to challenge theories which Sidney expounded in *The Defence of Poetry.* Holofernes has a counterpart in the schoolmaster, Rombus, in Sidney's short play, *The Lady of May.* These works did not appear in print until 1595 and 1598 respectively. Woudhuysen suggests that Shakespeare could have read these in manuscript (1998: 3).

Some commentators have cited both the play's structure, and its use of rhyme and its metrical forms as evidence of early composition, though others (including David) recognise that these features could have been deliberately chosen for the highly artificial theme and special purpose of the play (1977: xxiv).

## External Orthodox Evidence

Three references establish that the play was completed by 1598: the title page of Q1, the allusion in Tofte's *Alba* and the list in Meres's *Palladis Tamia*.

## Oxfordian Date

Eva Turner Clark and Charlton Ogburn place the writing of the play before 11 January 1579; Holland seems to allow a few more weeks. Felicia Hardison Londré points to "numerous internal references" indicating 1578 as the original date. More recently Hess, whilst recognising 1578 as the earliest possible date, considers 1583 as the most likely date of writing, on stylistic grounds. Anderson sees strong links between Oxford's situation in 1593 and the events of the play.

## Internal Oxfordian Evidence

The focus of earlier writers has been, of course, the 1578 visit of Marguerite de Valois to her husband, Henri de Navarre. But other allusions reinforce the proposal of 1578. Boyet describes Armado as "a Monarcho" (4.1.98); this was the title assumed by a mad Italian who frequented the English court and died *c.* 1580.[7]

In August 1578 Queen Elizabeth and her court – the Earl of Oxford included – visited Norwich: Oxfordians have suggested that there are two allusions to this visit: firstly, in 4.2.1–2, Nathaniel, a curate, comments: "Very reverend sport, truly, and done in the testimony of a good conscience"; a Norwich minister, Nathaniel Woodes wrote a play called *The Conflict of Conscience*, printed in 1581. Secondly, Holofernes instructs Nathaniel: "Sir, you shall present before her the Nine Worthies" (5.1.111–2); Dovey describes how a pageant of Worthies was presented before the Queen at Norwich, a pageant organised by the poet Thomas Churchyard, of Oxford's household.

Rima Greenhill has demonstrated that various scenes, events and uses of language point to relations between England and Russia in the late 1570s and early 1580s. The pageant of nine worthies seems to recall events from 1584 onwards. She believes that the play is an in-house satire for the court audience of Queen Elizabeth, originally written 1578–9 but updated in the 1580s.

The play contains many features of the euphuistic style made fashionable by the publication of John Lyly's *Euphues, the Anatomy of Wit*, early in 1578. Up until the middle of the twentieth century, it was a commonplace of orthodox criticism that *Love's Labour's Lost* either imitated or satirised Lyly's affected language (his euphuism). But David, writing in 1951, denies any direct connection:

> There is no real similarity between Shakespeare's play and those of Lyly, which belong to an older and more courtly *genre* even than *[Love's Labour's Lost.]*; the ridiculous language of Armado and Holofernes is much nearer to Sidney's *Arcadia* than to Lyly's *Euphues.* (1977: xxxi)

Woudhuysen, writing in the last decade, does not even mention euphuism, though he states:

> The play is in parts reminiscent of the court comedies and the prose romances of John Lyly, especially in the comic use of scholastic knowledge, the advancement of the plot through witty debate rather than through deeds, and the careful ordering and patterning of characters and action. (1998: 62)[8]

This change in approach is understandable. It is difficult for orthodox scholars to explain why a young dramatist, newly arrived in London *c.* 1592, should choose to write a play imitating (or satirising) a literary style which had become unfashionable in the middle of the previous decade. Both Arden editors confirm their difficulty and follow Bullough's observations about the influence of the *commedia dell'arte.* Where did the Warwickshire lad come across that? According to Chambers, Italian players were in England – but not in Stratford-upon-Avon – at various times between 1573–8, when Shakespeare was a youth.

The Harvey–Nashe quarrel has strong implications both for an early date and for Oxfordian authorship. It originated in 1580 after the tennis-court quarrel between Oxford and Sir Philip Sidney: Gabriel Harvey, a member of the Sidney–Leicester team, wrote a lampoon which could be interpreted as an attack on Oxford, and Lyly – by then Oxford's secretary – drew his master's attention to it. At the start of the Marprelate controversy in 1589, Lyly challenged Harvey, whose response was an attack on Nashe. Nashe responded by attacking Harvey in *Pierce Penilesse.* Scholars, orthodox or otherwise, are convinced that, in the play, Moth, called "juvenal" at 1.2.8 and 3.1.64, is taken to satirise Nashe. Fewer are confident about identifying Harvey, but the pedantic Holofernes is a strong traditional candidate and would easily have been identified with Harvey by a courtly audience fully aware of the background. Anderson (260-4) therefore dates the play to 1593-4, identifying Oxford with Berowne and the young William Shakespeare with old Costard. He concludes: "Perhaps the greatest irony in the entire Shake-speare fable in *Love's Labour's Lost* is that de Vere's reputation was already lost." Anderson's dating of the play (or its revision) coincides with the arrival in England of Antonio Pérez (1539-1611), who had been exiled from Spain and was trying to ingratiate himself with nobles at Elizabeth's court. Various commentators have accepted an identification between Pérez and Don Armado.[9]

Although orthodox commentators have tended to focus on the Gray's Inn revels of 1594 as the source of the Muscovite–Russian disguise of the King's party in 5.2, there were earlier stage-representations of Russians: Thomas Lodge, writing in 1579–80, refers to "your Muscovian straungers" having appeared on stage among other exotic creatures. David observes that Muscovy was "much in the news" throughout the 1580s and '90s (1977: 133n).

## External Oxfordian Evidence

Clark and the Ogburns propose that *A Double Maske*, "shewen before her maistie the ffrench Imbassador being present the sonday night after Twelfdaie" – i.e. after 6th January 1579 – was the first version of *Love's Labour's Lost.* [10] On that night, Simier, the envoy of the Duc d'Alençon in the investigation of his possible marriage to Queen Elizabeth, was entertained at court by *A Maske of Amasones* and *A Maske of Knightes*, described as "an entertainment in imitation of a tournament between six ladies and a like number of gentlemen who surrendered to them".

The evidence within the play indicates, firstly, that it must have been written at the latest in the 1580s (it may have been revised later) and, secondly, that it must have been written by an author experienced in courtly and literary matters. Two orthodox scholars make two points for the Oxfordian case most persuasively. First, Alfred Harbage of Harvard University (1962: 27) asked a series of questions:

> Why should a play written for adult professionals in the mid-nineties so much resemble plays written for child professionals in the mid-eighties? The resemblance is not superficial. It is observable in content, form and spirit. It seems highly suggestive that all the basic ingredients of the play became available in a cluster in the ***decade*** [emphasis added] before 1588, and that nothing that became available thereafter was used except incidental phrases.

Secondly, Dover Wilson stated in 1932 (and restated in 1960: 41)

> To credit this amazing piece of virtuosity... to one whose education was nothing more than what a grammar school and residence in a little provincial borough could provide is to invite one either to believe in miracles or to disbelieve in the man from Stratford.

There is considerable evidence linking Oxford to euphuism, and allowing him contact with the *commedia dell'arte*, experience of courtly life and literary debate, and knowledge of affairs in France and with Russia. In 1578 Oxford was twenty-eight years old, a poet and patron of writers, in a position to respond to and adapt the latest literary fashion introduced by Lyly, the man who became his secretary in 1579. Moreover, Oxford was well acquainted with Sir Philip Sidney and was probably familiar with Sidney's literary views in the early 1580s when he was writing *The Defence of Poetry* (he was killed in 1586). Regarding

Sidney's works in manuscript, Oxford would have had considerably easier access than would Shakespeare.

Oxford also had considerable opportunity to see Italian Comedy. In 1575-6, he visited France and Italy, spending much of his time in Venice, so it is more than probable that he had experienced the *commedia dell'arte*. Oxford had also been presented at the court of the French King, Henri III in 1575 and may have visited Henri de Navarre when returning from Italy; he was certainly on good terms with Navarre after he became King Henri IV (Nelson, 121).[11]

## Conclusion

*Love's Labour's Lost* can be dated between 1578 by which time all the sources were available, and 1598 when it was first mentioned. It is likely to have been composed soon after 1578 and revised in 1593.

## Notes

1. "Newly corrected and augmented" refers to a phrase which appears on the title-pages of the respective quartos, which David (1977) discusses severally on pp. xvi, xxviii. Hardison Londré (p. 195–6) supports the argument for a 'bad' quarto, but takes care to point out that the *Romeo and Juliet* quarto of 1599 reads, more specifically, "newly corrected, augmented, and amended". Of course, the point of similarity still stands.
2. Woudhuysen's argument is emphatic: he cites the claim that the anonymous play *Mucedorus* was "Amplified with new additions", a claim which was repeated on the title-pages of editions in 1611, 1613, 1615, 1618, 1619, 1621 and so on. Likewise, *The Shoemakers' Holiday* (1600) continued to claim it had been acted before the Queen on New Year's Day in 1610, 1618, 1624, 1631 and 1657 (1998: 303). Woudhuysen concludes that, considering also the discrepancy between the phraseology of the title-pages, "in these circumstances it would be unwise to try to reconstruct the textual history of *Love's Labour's Lost* on the precedent of *Romeo and Juliet* without further corroborative evidence" (1998: 304). Woudhuysen's edition includes a very detailed discussion of the textual history of the play (Appendix 1, 298–339).
3. The longer passage is available in the first pages of Hibbard's Oxford edition (1990). The description of Tofte is Hibbard's own (1990: 1).
4. See G. P. V. Akrigg, *Shakespeare and the Earl of Southampton*, 1968, pp 23-40 for a description of Southampton's life as a royal ward, brought up by Lord Burghley at Cecil House.
5. The title page in 1591 states that *Endimion* had been performed before the Queen at Greenwich on Candlemass by the Children of Paul's. G. K. Hunter, *John Lyly: the Humanist as Courtier* (187) reports that the only such occasion was in 1588. Chambers cautiously agrees that *Endimion* was performed on this occasion (*ES* iv, 103). Of course, it does not follow that the play had only just been composed, merely that this was its most famous performance.

6. For further discussion of Shakespeare's engagement with the events of Navarre's life, see Hugh M. Richmond, "Shakespeare's Navarre", *Huntington Library Quarterly,* 43 (1978–9), 193–216.
7. For Monarcho, the mad Italian, David (67) gives a very detailed note, based on the description of Thomas Churchyard's *The Phantasticall Monarke,* published in 1580. Monarcho is also mentioned in Nashe's *Saffron Walden* (1596) and in Meres's *Wits Commonwealth* (1598). From 1576–80, Oxford was a leading light at the court of Elizabeth (Nelson, 186–209), and he employed Churchyard at this time as a secretary (Nelson, 223).
8. For further discussion on possible links between these plays, see David Bevington, '"Jack hath not Jill": failed courtship in Lyly and Shakespeare,' *SS,* 42 (1990), 1–13.
9. Gustav Ungerer has identified Don Armado with Pérez (*A Spaniard in Elizabethan England: the Correspondence of Antonio Pérez's exile*), and is followed by many commentators. For a more general account of Antonio Pérez, see the biography by Gregorio Marañón (1947, translated into English by Charles Ley, 1954).
10. Clark (1974: 136), Ogburn (1984: 173). Clark discusses *A Double Maske* in greater detail pp.214–5. Hardison Londré discusses the possibility of an earlier version of the play by another author (1997: 328–9).
11. The English Ambassador wrote that he had presented Oxford to the King and Queen of France on 7 March 1575. In 1576, there was a suggestion that Oxford was in touch with Henri III over the Catholic Question (Nelson, 169). In 1595, Henri IV wrote to Oxford in warm terms:

    > [I write] to inform you of the satisfaction I feel for the good offices you have performed on my behalf in her [i.e. the Queen's] presence, which I beg you to continue and believe that I will always consider it a great pleasure to reciprocate in whatever might bring about your personal satisfaction (Nelson, 349).

    As Oxford did not attend court much in the 1590s, it is not known what he did on behalf of Henri IV. Oxford may have met Henri de Navarre when travelling back to Paris from Italy in April 1576; Oxford passed through Lyon and various military encampments but his exact itinerary is not known (Nelson, 134).

## Other Cited Works

Akrigg, G. P. V., *Shakespeare and the Earl of Southampton*, Cambridge, MA: Harvard UP, 1968

Alexander, Peter, *Shakespeare's Life and Art,* London: James Nisbet, 1939

Anderson, Mark, *"Shakespeare" by Another Name,* New York: Penguin, 2005

Athos, J. (ed.), *Love's Labour's Lost,* New York: Signet Classics, 2004

Bullough, Geoffrey, *Narrative and Dramatic Sources of Shakespeare*, vol. II, London: Routledge and Kegan Paul, 1958

Cairncross, A. S., *The Problem of Hamlet – a Solution*, London: MacMillan, 1936

Carroll, William (ed.), *Love's Labour's Lost,* Cambridge: CUP, 2009

Chambers, E. K., *The Elizabethan Stage,* 4 vols, Oxford: Clarendon, 1923

—, *William Shakespeare, A Study of Facts and Problems,* 2 vols, Oxford: Clarendon, 1930

Clark, Eva Turner, *Hidden Allusions in Shakespeare's Plays,* New York: Kennikat, 1931 (reprinted 1974)

David, R. W. (ed.), *Love's Labour's Lost,* London: Arden 2, 1951

Dovey, Z. M., *An Elizabethan Progress,* Stroud: Alan Sutton, 1996

Fane, Violet, (Mary Margaret Lamb) trans. *Memoires of Marguerite de Valois,* London: J. C. Nimmo, 1892

Greenhill, R., "From Russia with Love: a case of *Love's Labour's Lost*", *The Oxfordian,* 9, 2006: 1–32

Halliday, F. E., *A Shakespeare Companion 1550-1950,* London: Duckworth, 1952

Harbage, A., "*Love's Labour's Lost* and the early Shakespeare", *Philological Quarterly,* XLI, 1, January 1962

Hardison Londré, F., "French Spanish and Russians in *Love's Labour's Lost", Critical Essays,* London: Routledge, 1997

Hess, W. R. *et al.,* "Shakespeare's Dates", *The Oxfordian,* 2, Portland, 1999

Hibbard, G. R. (ed.), *Love's Labour's Lost,* Oxford: OUP, 1990

Holland, H. H., *Shakespeare, Oxford and Elizabethan Times.* London: Denis Archer, 1933

Honigmann, E. A. J., *Shakespeare, the 'Lost Years'.* Manchester: MUP, 1985

Hunter, G. K., *John Lyly: the Humanist as Courtier,* London: Routledge, 1962

Nelson, Alan, *Monstrous Adversary,* Liverpool: LUP, 2003

Ogburn, Charlton, *The Mysterious William Shakespeare,* Virginia: EPM, 1984

Ungerer, G., *Spaniard in Elizabethan England: the Correspondence of Antonio Pérez's exile,* London: Tamesis Books, 1974

Wells, Stanley & Gary Taylor Gary (eds), *William Shakespeare: The Complete Works,* Oxford: OUP, 1986

—, *William Shakespeare: A Textual Companion*, Oxford: OUP, 1987

Wilson, J. Dover (ed.), *Love's Labour's Lost,* Cambridge: CUP, 1962

—, *The Essential Shakespeare*, Cambridge: CUP, 1932, rptd 1960

Woudhuysen, H. R. (ed.), *Love's Labour's Lost,* London: Arden, 1998

Yates, F. A., *A study of 'Love's Labour's Lost',* Cambridge: CUP, 1936

8

# A Midsummer Night's Dream

Kevin Gilvary

A *Midsummer Night's Dream* can be dated between the mid-1580s, when all the major sources were available and 1598, when it was named by Meres.

## Publication Date

This play was entered in the Stationers' Register on 8 October 1600 by Thomas Fisher:

> [SR, 1600] 8 Octubris. Thomas Fyssher. Entred for his copie vnder the handes of master Rodes and the Wardens. A book called A mydsummer nightes Dreame vj[d].

It was published by Fisher shortly afterwards.

> [Q1, 1600] A midsommer nights dreame. As it hath beene sundry times publickely acted, by the Right honourable, the Lord Chamberlaine his seruants. Written by William Shakespeare.
> Imprinted at London,: [By Richard Bradock] for Thomas Fisher, and are to be soulde at his shoppe, at the Signe of the White Hart, in Fleetestreete, 1600.

A Second Quarto, with minor errors but substantially the same, is dated 1600 on the title page but is usually taken to be 1619 as it uses the same printer's device that Jagger was using in that year:

> [Q2, 1619] A midsommer nights dreame. As it hath beene sundry times publikely acted, by the Right honourable, the Lord Chamberlaine his seruants. Written by William Shakespeare. [London]: Printed by Iames Roberts [i.e. William Jaggard for T. Pavier], 1600 [i.e. 1619].

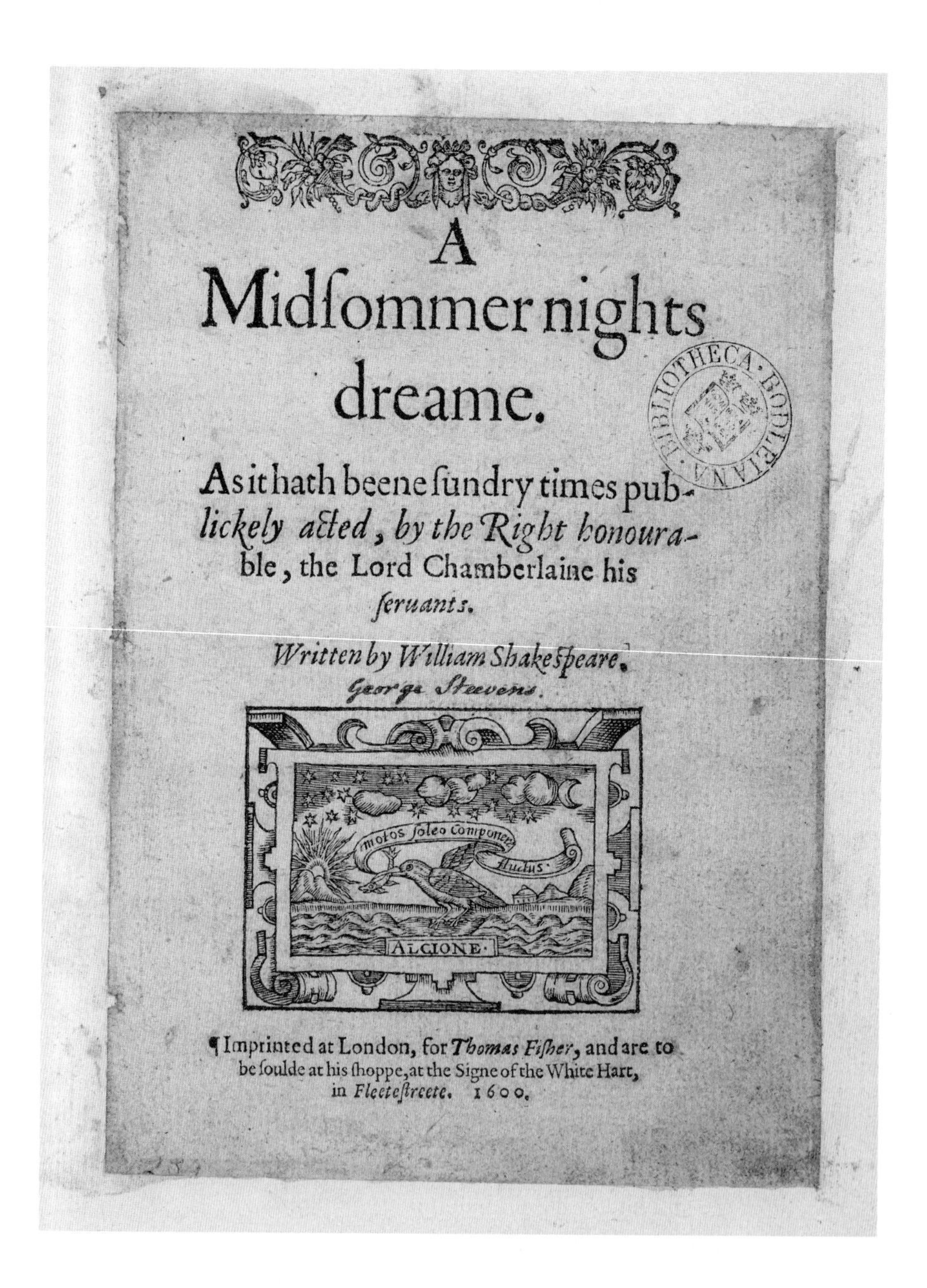
# A
# Midſommer nights
# dreame.

As it hath beene ſundry times pub-
*lickely acted, by the Right honoura-*
ble, the Lord Chamberlaine his
*ſeruants.*

*Written by William Shakeſpeare.*



Imprinted at London, for *Thomas Fiſher*, and are to
be ſoulde at his ſhoppe, at the Signe of the White Hart,
in *Fleeteſtreete.* 1600.



5. Title page to the first quarto of *A Midsummer Night's Dream*, 1600. By permission of Bodleian Library, University of Oxford, shelfmark Arch. G d.45 (1), title page.

Q2 is the basis of the First Folio version of 1623, where it occupies the eighth position, after *Love's Labour's Lost* and before *The Merchant of Venice.*

## Performance Date

The 1600 title-page claims that the play "hath been sundry times publickely acted" by the Lord Chamberlain's Men, and Meres mentions the play in 1598. The only recorded early performance was at Court on 1 January 1604/05: "On New yeares night we had a play of Robin goodefellow", as recorded by Dudley Carleton a fortnight later. However, most scholars believe that the first performance took place at one of two aristocratic weddings attended by Queen Elizabeth – a view reliant on indications in the text rather than on proof. David Wiles has added another wedding as a possible occasion for the play:

(a) Henry Percy, Earl of Northumberland to Dorothy Devereux, Widow of Sir Thomas Perrot and sister of the Earl of Essex, in late 1594;
(b) William Stanley, 6th Earl of Derby, to Elizabeth Vere, daughter of the 17th Earl of Oxford and granddaughter of Lord Burghley on 26 January 1595;
(c) Lord Berkeley's son, Thomas, to Elizabeth Carey, granddaughter of the Queen's Lord Chamberlain, Henry Carey (who was her cousin) on 19 February 1596.

All the brides were goddaughters of the Queen. Chambers thinks both (b) and (c) are possible and leans towards the Stanley–Vere wedding in January 1595. Wiles considers the Percy–Devereux wedding (no actual date is known, but it was probably mid-November, 1594) as there are references to astrological phases and Percy was known to be interested in such matters. Foakes inclines towards the Berkeley–Carey wedding because of the connection with the Lord Chamberlain's Men (named on the title page). Other weddings which have been considered include the Countess of Southampton's with Sir Thomas Heneage on 2 May 1594 and Lady Frances Sidney's with the Earl of Essex in 1590.

Not all editors accept the play as an epithalium. Peter Holland (1995: 112) was very dismissive of this hypothesis:

> The wedding occasion theory appeals to critics who like the concept of a site-specific play with fairies running through the noble house to bless the real wedding of members of the audience, and to those who wish to rescue the play from the clutches of the popular theatre audience. I fail to see the need to want either.

Holland's view remains a minority opinion.

## Sources

Bullough notes that, as with *Love's Labour's Lost*, there are no major literary sources for this play. The dramatist has used his own imaginative skills to draw together a variety of elements linked by the theme of love fulfilled in marriage, including several strands of folklore. Among the identified literary texts which undoubtedly contributed to the play are Chaucer's *The Knight's Tale, The Tale of Sir Topas* and *The Merchant's Tale* (from *The Canterbury Tales*) as well as *The Legend of Good Women* (available in print from the time of Caxton, c 1480); Shakespearean favourites such as Ovid's *Metamorphoses* in Golding's 1567 translation for the story of Pyramus and Thisbe (Book IV) and for Midas's acquisition of the ears of an ass (Book XI); North's translation of *Plutarch's Lives* provided details about Theseus and Hipployta (1579); *Huon of Burdeux* (translated by Lord Berners *c.* 1534) furnished details for Oberon.

Bullough also believes that several works of John Lyly, especially *Galathea,* (written *c.* 1585, printed 1592) and *Endimion* (written *c.* 1588, printed 1591), influenced the play. The metamorphosis of a man into an ass also occurs in Apuleius's *The Golden Ass,* translated by William Adlington in 1566, and in Reginald Scot's *The Discoverie of Witchcraft* (1584). Brooks suggests that Spenser's *Shepheardes Calender* (1579) provided details of weather and flowers, and that Seneca's *Medea* and *Hyppolytus* (translations appeared in an edition by Thomas Newton, 1581) contributed various important details. Brooks notes, with Nevill Coghill, that the play's overall dramatic structure comes from a combination of leading features which appear in Anthony Munday's *John a Kent and John a Cumber.* However, it is not possible to identify the direction of influence, since the date of Munday's play may be either 1590 or 1596.

## Orthodox Date

Chambers dated the play between 1594–96, tending towards a first performance at the Stanley–Vere wedding on 26 January 1595. Most commentators have concurred in placing the writing of the play in the middle years of the 1590s. Enid Welsford sees masque-like elements, supporting the idea of a play for an occasion such as a wedding. Cairncross proposes 1594 (before the month of May); Muir & Schoenbaum, Wells & Taylor and Peter Holland put the play in 1595, Halliday in 1596. Brooks is persuaded by the hypothesis that it was written in the winter of 1595–6 for the Berkeley/Carey wedding; Foakes agrees with Brooks but, like Wells & Taylor, is more cautious about the occasional nature of the play. Wiles is fully convinced that *A Midsummer Night's Dream* was intended as an occasional play and prefers February 1596.

## Internal Orthodox Evidence

Chambers (followed by most commentators) argues for an earliest date of 1594, due to the mechanicals' discussion (3.1. 27–42) of the advisability of bringing a lion on stage for fear of frightening the ladies. It is "highly probable", claims Brooks, that this passage is based on an incident which occurred at the feast for the baptism of Prince Henry of Scotland on 30 August 1594. As King James dined, a chariot was drawn in by a blackamoor; he was a substitute for the real lion which had been intended, "because [the lion's] presence might have brought some feare to the nearest". There was an account of this episode in *A True Reportarie*, registered at the Stationers' Office two months later on 24 October.

C. C. Stopes and A. L. Rowse, however, (among others) ignored the lion episode and argued that the play was written for the wedding of the Lord Treasurer, Sir Thomas Heneage, to the Dowager Countess of Southampton on 2 May 1594, then aged 60 and 41 respectively. There is some evidence to support the theory: Theseus and Hippolyta are a couple whose maturity contrasts with the younger lovers and is also emphasised by the image of the "dowager", a term which appears twice in the first scene of the play:

> THESEUS This old moon wanes! She lingers my desires,
> Like to a step-dame or a dowager
> Long withering out a young man's revenue. (1.1.4–6);

Later in the scene Lysander recalls that he has "a widow aunt, a dowager / Of great revenue" (157–8). 'Dowager' is a rare word in Shakespeare, occurring only five times in the entire canon (the other three are in *Henry VIII).* Although Cairncross reaches his proposed date (before May, 1594) by a very different path, it neatly coincides with the play's production at this wedding. David Wiles has investigated various astrological references in the play, including the phases of the moon and the conjunction of the planets. He too agrees with a date of 1594–5 for one of the three aristocratic weddings at that time, inclining towards the Berkeley–Carey event on 19 February 1596.

Chambers and Brooks consider that the play shares with *Romeo and Juliet*, *Richard II* and *Love's Labour's Lost* a distinctive combination of lyricism and rhetoric, in strongly patterned language, which, for him, both characterises Shakespeare's style in the mid-1590s and is "the decisive test". Although Brooks also involves himself in lengthy discussion of the publication dates of several supposedly relevant texts, of foul weather between 1594 and 1596 (2.2.81–124), and of suggested references to the dead Robert Greene and Christopher Marlowe (who died in 1592 and 1593, respectively), he decides, in the end, that none of these possible parallels or apparently topical references provides specific, decisive evidence which can help to date the play. It is worth noting this further comment: "To recognise the *Dream* as substantially of one date does not involve denying all revision."

## External Evidence

Meres provides a completion date in his reference to the play in *Palladis Tamia* (1598) listing six comedies (to balance six histories) composed by Shakespeare:

> for Comedy, witness his Gentlemen of Verona, his Errors, his Loue labours lost, his Loue labours wonne, his midsummer night dream, & his Merchant of Venice.

## Oxfordian Date

Most Oxfordians consider that *A Midsummer Night's Dream* was composed by the mid 1580s. Clark suggests that its origins lie in a court masque of 1581, followed by a comedy of 1584, with later revision for performance in January 1595; Ogburn Srs propose 1583, identifying *A Pastorall of Phillyda and Choryn*, presented at Court in December 1584, as an early version; Hess *et al.*, on stylistic grounds, place the writing of the play in 1584. The play, according to Oxfordian theory, was revised in the mid-1590s, with contributions from Lyly and Munday, who both worked for Oxford.

## Internal Oxfordian Evidence

Clark argues that the play originated in a masque, first produced in 1581, or in a comedy first produced three years later:

> there can be ... no question of its having been first presented in more or less its present form before the Queen during the Christmas season of 1584 under the title *A Pastorall of Phillyda and Choryn.*

Clark makes the connection with Titania's words to Bottom (2.1.64–8):

> Then I must be thy lady; but I know
> When thou hast stol'n away from fairy land
> And in the shape of Corin, sat all day
> Playing on the pipes of corn, And versing love
> To amorous Phyllida.

Clark was also the first Shakespearean critic to contend that the play includes a parody of the well-known international courtship between Queen Elizabeth and the youngest son of Catherine de Medici, François (formerly Hercules), Duc d'Alençon. Sir Thomas Smith had first recommended the seventeen-year-old Valois prince as a husband for the Queen, in December 1571, and the courtship reached its culmination at the end of 1581. In June 1584, Alençon died of consumption.

According to this theory, Bottom the weaver is a political parody of the Duc d'Alençon, so the episode (3.1.114–193) in which Titania continues her love for Bottom despite his ass's head is a thinly disguised satire on the infamous marriage negotiations between Elizabeth and Alençon. Bottom, in his ass's head, soliloquizes about his situation (3.1.114–7):

> I see their knavery; this is to make an ass of me; to fright me, if they could. But *I will not stir from this place, do what they can*: I will walk up and down here, and I will sing, and they shall hear I am not afraid [emphasis added].

This speech is very reminiscent of Alençon's refusal to leave England at the end of 1581. Although Elizabeth's terms were (as she intended) impossible to accept, Alençon played her at her own game, declaring that he loved her too much to leave her and that he would accept her conditions. Now Elizabeth panicked and by the beginning of February 1582 she had offered him sufficient inducements (funding for his proposed Netherlands campaign as Duke of Brabant) for him to leave England with honour – and to their mutual relief! Clark finds an echo of Bottom's situation in Alençon's:

> [Alençon] put his back to the wall and plainly told the Queen that not only would he refuse to leave England, but he would not even vacate the rooms in her palace until she had given him a definite answer as to whether she would marry him or not.[1]

We find nothing in Hume about Alençon's singing, but there is no denying the aptness of the dramatist's words to the circumstances narrated in Hume.

A mere eighteen lines in a later scene (4.1.7–24) strongly reinforce Clark's theory. Here Bottom uses the French honorific 'monsieur' eleven times, in addressing his attendant fairies; there is a six-fold iteration of the term within one speech of only eight lines. Clark suggests that this can be only for comic effect:

> not only does the frequent use of 'Monsieur' indicate a French original for the character of Bottom, but the request for a 'honey-bag' (16) suggests Alençon's demand for money … of which Elizabeth gave him large sums at different times.

Clark appears to have been unaware of the even more significant fact that 'Monsieur' was also the honorific bestowed upon the younger brother of a king of France, who was heir to the throne; since Alençon was exactly that, we seem to have, in the play, a very precise and pointed reference to him.[2] Brock reminds us that Alençon "came to be known in England by the nickname 'Monsieur', from the Queen's habit of calling him that." It was, of course, a title rather than a nickname; his well-known nickname was 'Frog'.

Marion Taylor concurs with the view that the repetitions of 'monsieur' are significant and, furthermore, cites word-play such as:

> BOTTOM I will discharge it in either your straw-colour beard, your orange-tawny beard, your purple-in-grain beard, or your French-crown-colour beard, your perfect yellow.
>
> QUINCE Some of your French crowns have no hair at all, and then you will play bare-faced. (1.2.86–91)

Marion Taylor suggests that, if Bottom is a parody of Alençon, who was 'heir' presumptive to the French throne, so he could hope to wear the 'French crown' and if Elizabeth was thought to have outwitted him, then he would be left 'bare-faced'. The Alençon references and parodies strongly support the case for a first version of the play in the early 1580s, when a court audience had recently enjoyed first-hand experience of the marriage negotiations. It is true that Spenser parodied the negotiations later in the decade in *The Fairie Queene* (published in 1591), so they must have resonated in the court memory for a while afterwards. But it is difficult to believe that a playwright would freshly revive such topical details, with full comic effect, some fifteen years later in the mid 1590s.

The incident of the 'Scottish lion' by no means precludes a much earlier date of composition for the bulk of the play; this trivial episode happily offered a topical piece of comedy, ideal for later inclusion in the mechanicals' farcical production of 'Pyramus and Thisbe'. Fear of a lion's roar was not new, as in 1584 it was mentioned in Scot's *The Discoverie of Witchcraft*.

Brooks supports C. L. Barber's observation that, like *Love's Labour's Lost*, this play derives its construction in part from Lyly's plan of relating to a central subject a succession of episodes enacted by self-contained groups. Both plays reflect a response to Lyly's court drama which it would be reasonable to describe as "aristocratic rather than popular", he asserts. But there is an alternative explanation: as Lyly's court dramas date from the 1580s, it is, surely, equally reasonable to attribute the similarities to a style popular at the same period of writing. Nelson (238–9) has described how John Lyly was a close associate of Oxford in the 1580s.

It has often been claimed that Oberon's speech to Puck recalls the magnificent pageants staged at Kenilworth in 1575 by the Earl of Leicester, apparently in a last effort to woo Elizabeth:

> My gentle Puck, come hither. Thou rememberest
> Since once I sat upon a promontory,
> And heard a mermaid on a dolphin's back
> Uttering such dulcet and harmonious breath
> That the rude sea grew civil at her song
> And certain stars shot madly from their spheres,
> To hear the sea-maid's music . . . (2.1.148–164)

Although it is very unlikely that the youthful William Shakespeare could actually have witnessed this spectacle (and Oxford was abroad at the time), it is possible that the dramatist could have heard about the events either through hearsay or through the written account of Robert Laneham.[3] If Oberon's speech does recall the Kenilworth spectacle, it would be more likely to support an earlier date in the late 1570s or early 1580s than in the mid 1590s.

## External Oxfordian Evidence

Anderson (287–8) believes that the play was written (or perhaps revised) for the Stanley–Vere wedding in January 1595. Both the father of the bride, the Earl of Oxford, and the groom, the Earl of Derby, were notable courtly playwrights.

## Conclusion

*A Midsummer Night's Dream* can be dated between the mid-1580s, when all the major sources were available, and 1598, when it was named by Meres. There is no direct evidence to date *A Midsummer Night's Dream* and it is most likely that the play originated in the early 1580s as it seems to allude to the Duc d' Alençon. It may have been extensively revised in the mid-1590s as an epithalamium for one of the aristocratic weddings at that time.

## Notes

I would like to thank Dr Roger Stritmatter of the Coppin State University, Baltimore, Maryland, for allowing me to draw extensively in his related article in *The Oxfordian.*

1. Martin Hume, *The Courtships of Queen Elizabeth* (1896, reprinted 2003, page 268), quoted by Charlton and Dorothy Ogburn (1952: 589).
2, The *Encyclopaedia Britannica* reports (under Monsieur): "As an honorific title in the French royal court, it came to be used to refer to or address the eldest living brother of the king. The title Monsieur, without an adjoining proper name, was most notably first applied to Henry III's brother, François, duc d'Alençon, who by the Peace of Chastenoy (1576), popularly called the 'Peace of Monsieur' became the duc d' Anjou." The *Cambridge Modern History*, vol 3 'The Wars of Religion' (1904: 30) also reports: "In 1576, Alençon pressured his brother King Henry III of France into signing the Edict of Beaulieu. The resulting peace became popularly known as the *Peace of Monsieur.*" In *The Merchant of Venic*e, Portia describes (1.2.54–62) the "French monsieur" in very unflattering terms. See chapter 9 for the identification of Portia's French suitor with Alençon.
3. Robert Laneham's [also known as Langham] *A letter whearin part of the entertainment vntoo the Queenz Maiesty at Killinwoorth Castl in Warwik sheer in this summerz progress* (1575, reprinted 1821). There is a modern account by Ronald Binns, *Elizabeth, Shakespeare and the Castle* (2008), mixing history and speculation. Helen Hackett, *Shakespeare and Elizabeth* (2009: 119–124) believes that, while the Kenilworth pageants were recalled by Oberon, it is

more likely that William Shakespeare read about them than that he actually witnessed them.

## Other Cited Works


Alexander, Peter, *Shakespeare's Life and Art,* London: James Nisbet, 1939

Anderson, Mark, *"Shakespeare" by Another Name,* New York: Penguin, 2005

Barber, C. L., *Shakespeare's Festive Comedy,* Princeton: Princeton UP, 1959

Brock, D. H., *A Ben Jonson Companion*, Bloomington: Indiana University Press, 1983

Brooks, H. F. (ed.), *A Midsummer Night's Dream*, London: Arden, 1979

Bullough, Geoffrey, *Narrative and Dramatic Sources of Shakespeare*, vol. II, London: Routledge and Kegan Paul, 1958

Cairncross, A. S., *The Problem of Hamlet – a Solution*, London: MacMillan, 1936

Chambers, E. K., *The Elizabethan Stage,* 4 vols, Oxford: Clarendon, 1923

—, *William Shakespeare, A Study of Facts and Problems,* 2 vols, Oxford: Clarendon, 1930

Clark, Eva Turner, *Hidden Allusions in Shakespeare's Plays,* New York: Kennikat, 1931, rptd 1974

Coghill, Neville, "The Basis of Shakespearian Comedy: a study in medieval affinities", *Essays and Studies,* ed. G. Rostrevor Hamilton, London: John Murray, 1950

Foakes, R. A. (ed.), *A Midsummer Night's Dream,* Cambridge: CUP, 2003.

Frieda, L., *Catherine de Medici,* London: Weidenfeld & Nicolson, 2003

Halliday, F. E., *A Shakespeare Companion 1550–1950*. London, Duckworth,1952

Hess, W. R. *et al.,* "Shakespeare's Dates", *The Oxfordian*, 2, Portland, 1999

Holland, Peter (ed.), *A Midsummer Night's Dream,* Oxford: OUP, 1995

Muir, K. & S. Schoenbaum (eds), *A New Companion to Shakespeare Studies,* Cambridge: CUP, 1971

Nelson, Alan, *Monstrous Adversary,* Liverpool: LUP, 2003

Ogburn, Dorothy and Charlton Sr, *This Star of England*, New York: Coward-McCann, 1952

Ogburn, Charlton Jr, *The Mysterious William Shakespeare,* Virginia: EPM, 1984

Rowse, A, L., *Shakespeare's Southampton: Patron of Virginia*, London: MacMillan, 1965

Stopes, Charlotte, *The Life of Henry, Third Earl of Southampton, Shakespeare's Patron*, Cambridge: CUP, 1922

Taylor, M., *Bottom, Thou Art Translated: political allegory in 'A Midsummer Night's Dream'*, Amsterdam: Rodopi, 1973

Wells, Stanley & Gary Taylor (eds), *William Shakespeare: The Complete Works,* Oxford: OUP, 1986

—, *William Shakespeare: A Textual Companion*, Oxford: OUP, 1987

Welsford, Enid, *The Court Masque: A study in the relationship between poetry and the revels,* Cambridge: CUP, 1927

Wiles, David, *Shakespeare's Almanac: 'A Midsummer Night's Dream', Marriage and the Elizabethan Calendar,* Cambridge: D. S. Brewer, 1993

# 9

# The Merchant of Venice

## Joe Peel (with Noemi Magri)

The *Merchant of Venice* can be dated between 1558, when all the major sources were available and 1598, when it was entered into the Stationers' Register and mentioned by Meres.

### Publication Date

The play was first entered in the Stationers' Register on 22 July 1598, by James Roberts, as

> [SR, 1598] xxij° Julij. James Robertes. Entred for his copie vnder the handes of bothe the wardens, a booke of the Marchaunt of Venyce, or otherwise called the Jewe of Venyce, Prouided, that yt bee not prynted by the said James Robertes or anye other whatsoeuer without lycence first had from the Right honorable the lord Chamberlen vj$^{d}$

It was re-entered on 28 October 1600 by Thomas Hayes, who had acquired the publishing rights:

> [SR, 1600] 28 Octobris. Thomas Haies. Entred for his copie under the handes of the Wardens and by Consent of master Robertes. A booke called the booke of the merchant of Venyce vj$^{d}$.

The First Quarto (Q1) was printed by James Roberts with the date 1600.

> [Q1, 1600] The most excellent Historie of the Merchant of Venice. With the extreame crueltie of Shylocke the Iewe towards the sayd Merchant, in cutting a just pound of his flesh: and the obtayning of Portia by the choyse of three Chests. As it hath beene diuers times acted by the Lord Chamberlaine his Servants. Written by William Shakespeare.
> At London, Printed by I(ames) R(oberts) for Thomas Heyes, and are to be sold in Paules Church-yard, at the signe of the Greene Dragon. 1600. *[Head-title]* The comicall History of the Merchant of Venice. *[Running-title]* The comicall Historie of the Merchant of Venice.

# The moſt excellent Hiſtorie of the *Merchant of Venice*.

VVith the extreame cruelrie of *Shylocke* the Iewe towards the ſayd Merchant, in cutting a iuſt pound of his fleſh: and the obtayning of *Portia* by the choyſe of three cheſts.

*As it hath beene diuers times acted by the Lord Chamberlaine his Seruants.*

Written by William Shakeſpeare.

AT LONDON,
Printed by *I. R.* for Thomas Heyes,
and are to be ſold in Paules Church-yard, at the ſigne of the Greene Dragon.
1600.

6. Title page to the first quarto of *A Merchant of Venice*, 1600. By permission of Bodleian Library, University of Oxford, shelfmark Arch. G d.45 (2), title page.

Chambers describes Q1 as a good text, requiring little emendation. The title-page indicates that the play had been acted at various times by the Lord Chamberlain's Men and that its author was 'William Shakespeare'. The play was transferred in 1619 from Thomas Hayes to his son Lawrence. The Second Quarto (Q2), a reprint of Q1, bears the same date, but it has been demonstrated that it was not, in fact, printed until 1619:

> [Q2, 1619] The Excellent History of the Merchant of Venice. With the extreme cruelty of Shylocke the Iew towards the saide Merchant, in cutting a iust pound of his flesh. And the obtaining of Portia, by the choyse of three Caskets. Written by W. Shakespeare. [device] Printed by J. Roberts, 1600. [i.e. 1619]; *Head-title,* under ornament with royal arms: The Comical History of the Merchant of Venice. *Running-title* The Comicall History of the Merchant of Venice].

The play was published in the First Folio (F1) in 1623, as the ninth comedy, coming after *A Midsummer Night's Dream* and before *As You Like It*. The play remained popular and was published in further quartos in 1637 and 1652.

## Performance Dates

The play had, we are told, been performed several times before 1600, but the first performance of which there is a specific record was given by the King's Men at Court on Shrove Sunday, 10 February 1605, with a repeat presentation two days later.

## Sources

Bullough gives the background on the main sources for the *The Merchant of Venice*. The story of the bond for human flesh is both ancient and widespread, but the version closest to that in the play is found in *Il Pecorone* by Ser Giovanni Fiorentino, (composed *c.* 1380, printed in Italian in Milan, 1558). The first tale of the fourth day shows Gianetto travelling from Venice to the Lady of Belmont. Disguised as a lawyer, the lady delivers Gianetto's godfather from a Jewish usurer. Gianetto gives his ring to the 'lawyer' and back in Belmont, his lady demands the ring of him. No contemporary English version is known, and J. R. Brown suggests in a footnote: "Shakespeare may have been able to read Italian."

Another work, only available in Italian, provides details for the other sub-plot, Jessica's elopement: in the fifteenth-century *Novellino* of Masuccio Salernitano, the fourteenth tale tells of a young cavalier who falls in love with the daughter of a miser. (This text, which was placed on the first Index of Prohibited Books in 1557, also contains the original version of the Romeo and Juliet story, later adapted by Bandello and Brooke.) Bullough shows many coincidences of detail, and notes that there is no known intermediary text for Salernitano's story.

The Trial of the Caskets is known from a variety of sources, such as: the *Gesta Romanorum* (printed in Latin, *c.* 1470, with English translations published *c.* 1515 and by Richard Robinson in 1577):

> And when he had said thus, he commanded to bring forth three vessels, the first was made of pure gold, beset with precious stones without, and within full of dead mens bones, and thereupon was ingraven this posey: Whoso chooseth me shall finde that he deserveth.

The tale also occurs in *Speculum Historiale* by Vincent of Beauvais (composed in Latin *c.* 1244, first printed in 1473 and translated into English in 1483), Boccaccio's *Decameron*, Day 10, Story 1, (composed in Italian *c.* 1353, first printed in 1472, first translated into English in 1620) and the *Confessio Amantis* by John Gower (composed *c.* 1390, published by Caxton in 1483 with later editions, e.g. 1532).

Many scholars (including Chambers, Dover Wilson and Bullough) have speculated that a lost play *The Jew*, referred to in 1579, was "in all probability" the basis of *The Merchant of Venice* – even a first draft of it. There is fuller discussion of this play in the section External Oxfordian Evidence below. *The Jew* was answered by another play, *The Three Ladies of London* by 'R W' (? Robert Wilson), published in 1584. From suggestions in *Three Ladies*, Bullough, following Small, argues that *The Jew* contained both allegorical and realistic characters and dealt with questions of usury and greed.

Another text, *Epitomes de cent histoires* (Paris 1581) by the French writer Alexandre Sylvain, seems closely linked to *The Merchant of Venice*. Bullough believes that the dramatist either knew this text or read it in the 1596 translation by "Lazarus Piot", probably a pseudonym of Anthony Munday as *The Orator*. Each of Sylvain's histories begins with an anecdote, followed by a series of speeches on questions of law, ethics or custom. History no. 95 deals "Of a Jew, who would for his debt have a pound of the flesh of a Christian." Bullough shows various similarities, including his final insistence on his legal right. *Zelauto* by Anthony Munday (published in 1580) is also considered a likely source: in Book III, several details of plot, character and even language are paralleled in the play (including the usurer's daughter and her marriage, and two ladies disguised as attorneys); indeed, Portia's famous speech is especially close to the judge's pleas for mercy in Munday's story.

Marlowe's *The Jew of Malta*, first performed in 1589, is said to have influenced the characterisation of Shylock, as there are several verbal echoes. This view presumes that Marlowe's play came first, but it is possible that Shakespeare's play was earlier. Shaheen analyses the *Merchant*'s large number of references to the Bible (noting that none of Shakespeare's 60 or so biblical allusions in the play are related to Marlowe's 36 allusions). Shakespeare was particularly keen to refer to books from the Old Testament and to Jewish practices and names. It seems that the dramatist used a range of versions of the Bible but for the passage beginning "When Jacob grazed his uncle Laban's sheep . . ." at 1.3.70–89, he especially drew on the Geneva Bible at Genesis 30.37–42 and the accompanying note 'm'. The latest definite source appears to be the edition of *Il Pecorone* published in 1558.

## Orthodox Date

Chambers suggests autumn 1596 as the latest possible date. Wells & Taylor also agree with this date on stylistic grounds, and most editors agree and have accordingly placed composition in the mid 1590s. Brown argues that it was composed between 1596–98. Halio, like the Riverside and Signet editors, opts for 1596–7, Halliday for 1597, Mahood 1597–8. The Clarendon editors and Dover Wilson, finding traces of rewriting, date the original draft from 1594. Cairncross, much more radically, considers that the play could have been written as early as 1589.

## Internal Orthodox Evidence

Various possible allusions from *The Merchant of Venice* to events in the 1590s have been suggested: the play might relate to the 1594 trial and execution of Roderigo López. He had been physician both to the Earl of Leicester and to the Queen, and was accused of attempting to poison them. The passage at 4.1.133–7 has been seen as direct allusion to López, with a translated pun on his name (Portuguese for 'wolf'); Gratiano's attack on Shylock includes: "O, be thou damn'd, inexecrable dog! . . . thy currish spirit Govern'd a wolf . . . ; for thy desires Are wolvish, bloody, starved and ravenous." Malone suggested that 3.2.49–50: "When true subjects bow / To a new-crowned monarch", might allude to the coronation of Henri IV of France at Chartres, on 27 February 1595; Reims, where the ceremony was normally held, was in the hands of rebels, who were thus not "true subjects".

J. R. Brown regards neither reference as significant for dating the play. He also dismisses the suggestion that references to Shylock as a "stranger", and Launcelot's badinage reflecting fears of famine due to the arrival of refugee "strangers" [3.3.27], allude to serious anti-alien riots in London in 1595. Contemporary accounts mention the riots, but do not help date the play, he argues. For Brown, the most satisfactory allusion for dating the play occurs in 1.1.25–29, when Salerio empathises with Antonio:

> I should not see the sandy hour-glass run
> But I should think of shallows and of flats,
> And see my wealthy *Andrew* dock'd in sand
> Vailing her high top lower than her ribs
> To kiss her burial . . . .

*Andrew* is italicised in Q1 as if the name of a vessel. In June 1596, the Spanish warship *San Andrés* was captured by the English in Cadiz harbour, where it had run aground. It was brought back to England, as the *Saint Andrew*, and nearly ran aground on the sandbanks off Chatham. J. R. Brown concludes: "It follows that the allusion could have been written any time after the first news of the Cadiz action reached the Court on 30 July 1596," though not necessarily immediately afterwards. Brown states (with Mahood in agreement) that the play must therefore "have been written in its present form not earlier than August 1596." Brown, however, then allows the obvious possibility that the allusion may have been inserted into the completed play.

Halio is more cautious about the "Andrew" allusion in determining the earliest date of writing. Instead, he justifies his 1596–7 date on the grounds that the theatre proprietors Francis Langley and Philip Henslowe separately imposed "outrageously extortionate" bonds on Shakespeare's company during that period. He supposes that "the negotiations very likely influenced Shakespeare's thinking as he wrote the *Merchant*". Since an outrageously extortionate bond is integral to the original source, Halio's suggestion has significance only for Shakespeare's choice of material, not for his handling of it.

## External Orthodox Evidence

Both the Stationers' Register and Meres (*Palladis Tamia*) confirm that the play was in existence by September 1598. Mahood argues that the entry in the SR indicates that the play was only just written and that the company did not wish anyone else to capitalize on its publication.

## Oxfordian Date

Clark suggests 1579, with which Ogburn concurs; Hess et al. propose 1585 on stylistic grounds.

## Internal Oxfordian Evidence

Oxfordians such as Mark Anderson (133–4) have found a number of allusions in the play which are topical for the late 1570s. In particular, they link Shylock's bond for 3,000 ducats with Oxford's disastrous investment in a failed venture in 1578. Nelson (186–8) describes Oxford's involvement in Martin Frobishier's attempt to find gold. The venture was disguised as a search for the north-west passage:

> Not only was Oxford's offer of £1,000 accepted, but he bought up £2,000 of Michael Lok's investment of £5,000. Unable to raise the cash, Oxford raised credit in the form of a bond.

Frobisher returned on 25 September and hurried to London with samples which turned out to be iron pyrite, the worthless "fool's gold". Nelson continues (187):

> Oxford had not a penny to show for his £3,000 investment, and 29 September [1578], the due-date of his bond, was at hand. Suspicion of fraud lighted upon Michael Lok.

Oxford paid some of the debt but Lok was sent to the Fleet Prison. It is not known if Oxford ever repaid the whole debt. During this period (in fact for about 20 years from 1570), Oxford employed Michael Lok's nephew as one of his secretaries. Because the Jew is not named in the sources and, in the play, is frequently called 'The Jew', Oxfordians believe that the name 'Shylock' is a reference to Michael Lok. Furthermore, Oxford himself had dealings with the Jews in Venice: Nelson (213) quotes a letter from Henry Howard that Oxford claimed: "the Iewes of Italy wold tell another tale, and put both Mathewe, Marke and Iohne to sylenc[e]."

Oxfordians find that further links between Oxford's situation in the late 1570s, and Portia's unflattering descriptions of her suitors (1.2.35–95), present more than mere national stereotypes. Samuel Johnson once commented:

> I am always inclined to believe, that Shakespeare has more allusions to particular facts and persons than his readers generally suppose … Perhaps in this enumeration of Portia's suitors, there may be some covert allusion to those of Elizabeth.

Many details attributed to the suitors reflect characteristics of four international figures, well known to the English Court by reputation, if not personally, in the second half of the 1570s; one was the main suitor of Queen Elizabeth and all of them were involved at a high level in the Netherlands campaigns in and after 1577. The following biographical details derive from Kamen:

**(a) The Neapolitan Prince** (1.2.38–43) has been identified with Don John of Austria by Holland. Don John, half-brother to Philip II of Spain, was also King of Naples; and Naples was Don John's base through the middle of that decade. His courage, inspiring leadership and victory over the Turks at Lepanto in 1571 established his status as a leading figure of the sixteenth century. Both before and after Lepanto Philip, with some justification, had reservations about Don John's youthful lack of judgement. Portia's description of the Neapolitan prince as a "colt indeed" (1.2.39) reflects Don John's impetuosity. As for the next part of her facetious comment: "for he doth nothing but talk of his horse, and he makes it a great appropriation to his own good parts that he can shoe him himself", Holland quotes Motley's *Rise of the Dutch Republic*: "through the country round there was none who could break a lance or ride at the ring like him, and … in taming unmanageable horses he was celebrated for his audacity and skill". Don John became Governor of the Netherlands at the end of 1576 and died in 1578.

**(b) The County Palatine** (1.2..44–51) might be identified with many palatinates – districts with royal privileges – in Europe at this time (including the diocese of Durham in England). Halio argues that this suitor is not the Count Palatine of the Rhine (the Palatinate), since a German is later described satirically. Holland suggests that he alludes to the Archduke Matthias, the son of the Emperor Maximilian, whom the rebel States-General of the Netherlands appointed Governor-General in the autumn of 1577, when he was only twenty. He made a state entry into Brussels on 18 January 1578, but and soon proved to be ineffectual. Portia's describes this suitor: "[h]e doth nothing but frown … hears merry tales and smiles not, (… being so full of unmannerly sadness in his youth)" (1.2.45–49). This accurately fits the personality of Matthias's brother, the Emperor Rudolf II, a "gloomy solitary", "subject to hallucinations and long bouts of melancholy".

**(c) The French Lord, Monsieur Le Bon** (1.2.52–62) can easily be identified with François, Duc d'Alençon, who also nursed ambitions of power in the Netherlands – a goal eventually achieved when in 1582 he became Duke of Brabant and was named 'prince and lord of the Netherlands' by the anti-Spanish rebels. More significantly, however, he was the main candidate for marriage to Queen Elizabeth through most of the 1570s and, as the next brother of the French king, he had the traditional title 'Monsieur'; the term, says Conyers Read, was generally used in England at the time to designate Alençon (see chapter 8, *A Midsummer Night's Dream*, note 2 for a similar identification). Frieda (345–7) describes how Alençon came to England for two weeks in August 1579, and the Queen called him "her frog". His final personal attempt at a marital alliance came in November 1581. In February 1582, Alençon finally parted from Elizabeth and took up his ducal duties in Antwerp.

**(d) Falconbridge, the young baron of England** (ll.63–73) is described as unable to speak foreign languages and "oddly … suited"; in his pick-and-mix of European fashions, he has contemporary parallels. Brown quotes Thomas Nashe in 1594, but there is an earlier analogue; in 1577 William Harrison, in his *Description of England*, wrote: "Today ... the Spanish guise, tomorrow the French toies, [ere] long …the high Alman fashion, by and by the Turkish manner, … otherwise the Morisco gowns, the Barbarian sleeves … you shall not see anie so disguised as are my countriemen of England." There does not seem to have been any contemporary example of that name, but Halio notes that the description is in keeping with his fictional namesake in *King John.*

**(e) The young German, the Duke of Saxony's nephew** (1.2.80–1) is to be identified with Prince John Casimir; he was born in 1543, and became Count Palatine (of the Rhineland-Pfalz) in 1576. Portia plans to make this suitor choose the wrong casket by having Nerissa place on it a glass of Rhenish wine (ll.92–95) – wine from the Palatinate – and the historical Casimir was the Duke of Saxony's son-in-law. As a Calvinist, he was active in the political and religious clashes of mainland Europe. Elizabeth had supplied money since 1567 for Casimir's German mercenaries to support the Huguenots in the French civil wars. Towards the end of 1577, she suggested that Prince Casimir should arrange a Protestant league in Germany. His envoy arrived in England in February 1578, reporting Casimir's desire to help. Elizabeth decided to use him to fight her battles in the Netherlands, where he had already conducted two campaigns. In mid-1578 she sent £40,000 to cover his initial expenses in raising an army, and the export of large quantities of munitions was authorised; in the late summer Casimir duly invaded the Netherlands. Within a year or so, according to one source, he received the Order of the Garter and was banqueted by the City of London.

Noemi Magri's comparison of the play with Venetian legal procedures is given at the end of this chapter. She has also explored (in 'Belmont and Thereabouts') the astonishing knowledge of Venetian topography shown in the play, pointing to early composition and Oxfordian authorship. She demonstrates that Portia's Villa at Belmont should be identified with the Villa Foscari, situated along an inland waterway ten miles from Venice and with a monastery two miles away. This villa also links to a reference by Nerissa about "a Venetian, a scholar and soldier, that came hither in the company of the Marquis of Montferrat" (1.2.109–11). An important visit had been paid to this villa in July 1574 by Henri III, returning to France for his coronation and accompanied by a number of dignitaries, including Guglielmo Gonzaga, Duke of Mantua. This Duke had inherited the title of Marquis of Montferrat from his father in 1550. In 1574, the state of Montferrat was elevated to a Duchy by the then German Emperor Maximilian II. This information again strongly suggests Oxfordian authorship and knowledge of Italian states. Oxford was presented to King Henry III in Paris in January 1575 and would have passed close to the Villa Foscari in November 1575 when travelling from Venice to Padua.

## External Oxfordian Evidence

In 1578 or 1579, a play entitled *The Jew* was in performance at the Bull Inn, London. The evidence for this lost play is in Stephen Gosson's *The School of Abuse*, published in 1579:

> The *Iew* and *Ptolome,* shown at the Bull, and one representing the greedinesse of worldly chusers, and bloody mindes of Usurers; the other very lively describing how seditious estates . . . are overthrown, niether with humrous gesture woulnding the eye, nor with slouenly talke hurting the eares of the chast hearers.

Gosson's summary seems to indicate that the two major plots in *The Merchant* – the choice of caskets and the Shylock bond – were already combined in this early play. While many earlier orthodox commentators, as we have seen, thought this lost play was probably the source; some commentators, e.g. Clark, Holland and Ogburn, propose that *The Jew* was, in fact, the original version of *The Merchant of Venice.*

Ogburn offers two further pieces of evidence for a 1579 date. Firstly, in that year, Edmund Spenser ended a letter to Gabriel Harvey with the words: "He that is fast bound unto thee in more obligations than any merchant in Italy to any Jew there." Ogburn adds the comment of the editor of Harvey's correspondence: "This is an evident allusion to the play *The Jew*, ... the precursor of Shakespeare's *Merchant of Venice.*" Secondly, like Holland, he thinks it "likely" that a play called *The history of Portio and demorantes*, enacted at Whitehall by Sussex's Men on 2 February 1580 (Chambers, *ES*, iv, 97), was *The Jew* under a different title. He suggests that "Porti**o**" is a mistake for "Porti**a**", and "demorantes" a mistranscription of "the merchants". On the other hand, "demorantes" (Latin, 'delaying' or 'those who delay') which in Old French is 'demourants', (modern spelling: demurrant), comes to mean 'those who demur' (OED). *Portio and demorantes* might therefore have been a short comedy played at Court and dealing with Elizabeth's suitors.

The play's sources were available as early as 1558, so a date for the original version in the late 1570s is possible. There are important parallels between *The Merchant* and Munday's *Zelauto*, so the publication of the latter in 1580 seems to be a serious problem for a 1579 dating of the play – but not for Oxfordians. Oxford was employing Munday at that very time (Nelson, 238–9), so Munday's take on the story was presumably accessible to him. In any case, the influence may have been in the reverse direction – we do not have to assume that 'Shakespeare' did all the copying and adapting.

If there is any validity in the suggested matching of the suitors to historical counterparts, it is a notable fact that Oxford had a connexion with each of the four men detailed above. He had letters of introduction to the Holy Roman Emperor Maxillian II for his continental tour in 1575–6 (Nelson, 119); and in 1578 he hoped to serve Don John in some capacity – instead, the Queen wanted him to join Archduke Matthias in the Netherlands (he did neither acoding to Nelson, 181–2). When Oxford was in Germany in 1575, according to the poet George Chapman, Casimir offered a view of his army in the field (Oxford declined; Nelson, 126); and Casimir wrote a letter in autumn 1579 indicating that he knew about the 'tennis-court quarrel' between Oxford and Philip Sidney (whose side he took). Finally, Oxford knew Alençon – probably from his presentation at the French Court in January 1575 and certainly at the English Court in 1579 (Nelson, 202–3).

# The Italian Legal System in *The Merchant of Venice* (by Noemi Magri)

It is widely accepted that Shakespeare "displays a knowledge of Venice and the Venetian dominions deeper than that which he appeared to have possessed about any other Italian state" (H. F. Brown, 160). In *The Merchant of Venice,* the treatment of the Italian and Venetian legal systems has not been given satisfactory explanation from the point of view of either Shakespeare's source of knowledge, or the interpretation of the legal terms themselves and his references to Venetian institutions. Various commentators have mentioned other legal principles which are specific to Italian and Venetian Law but not the English legal system. Thus a deeper inquiry is necessary to establish the level of Shakespeare's accuracy in dealing with this subject matter.

**a) Venetian Criminal Laws**

In the Trial scene (4.1.344-52), Portia, thus definitely dooming Shylock to defeat, refers to the 'laws of Venice' which establish that if an alien attempts the life of 'any citizen, he will be sentenced to the confiscation of his property which will be given part to the offended and part to the State. Such law is present in the Criminal Laws passed by the Senate and other Government Boards from the XVI to the XVIII century. This is a major example of the dramatist's familiarity with crime and punishment in the Venetian Republic.[1]

**b) The single bond**

Throughout the play the word *bond* is used with different meanings:

(i) **obligation, binding agreement**. Shylock says of Antonio, "Let him look to [attend to, take care of] his bond," 3.1.43;

(ii) **what is due** as following previous agreement. Shylock to Antonio who has been declared bankrupt, "I'll have my bond," 3.3.4 ;

(iii) **forfeit** i.e. the thing to be given as a penalty as stipulated by contract. Shylock to Bassanio in Court, "I would have my bond," 4.1.86;

(iv) **deed** (figurative sense), Shylock to Gratiano who is inveighing against the Jew, "Thou canst rail the seal from off my bond", 4.1.138;

(v) **signed agreement, written document**. Portia to Shylock, "I pray you let me look upon the bond." "Here t'is," 4.1.222–3.

However, in the case of the *single bond* only tentative interpretations and unconvincing suggestions have been made. At the beginning of the play after Shylock has complied with Bassanio's request to lend Antonio 3,000 ducats (1.3.1–139), the Jew says to Antonio. "Go with me to a notary, seal me there Your *single bond,* and (in a merry sport) If you repay me not on such a day In such a place, such sum or sums as are Express'd in the condition, let the forfeit Be nominated for an equal pound Of your fair flesh, to be cut off and taken In what part of your body pleaseth me" (1.3.141–50).

That is, Shylock wants their verbal agreement to be ratified and asks Antonio to seal the bond in the presence of a notary; in other words, in order to protect his rights he must obtain a formal written acknowledgement of a verbal agreement. By the Italian Private Right, a deed is void if it is not validated by a signature. Besides, even though a verbal agreement is legally valid, still its execution is very difficult to prove in Court in case the debtor has not met his obligation. Here the dramatist shows himself to be aware that a deed drawn up in the presence of a notary is the most effective evidence of the execution of an agreement.

It appears that the word *single* has been left unexplained. The Arden editor, J. R. Brown (1955: 29) states: "W. L. Rushton *(Shakespeare's Testamentary Language,* 1869: 51) distinguished between a 'single bond' and one with a condition," but this clarifies neither kind of bond. He adds: "It has been suggested that Shylock used the term craftily, to make his condition seem a mere nothing or 'merry sport'." It is true that *single* may mean 'mere' (see O.E.D.) but a 'mere bond' does not mean a 'mere nothing'. Sokol and Sokol (40) state that Shylock has made a mistake since it is clearly a double bond. From all of Act 1 Scene 3, it is clear that Shylock means to take revenge on Antonio who has "rated" him about his "moneys and usances" and has "spit upon his Jewish gaberdine" and "did void his rheum upon his beard". The Jew's words do not show any intent to be merry. The phrase "in a merry sport" better fits the Jew's character if it is interpreted as "in my own sport, to my great joy" and not "just making a joke of it". In Q1, it is printed in brackets as if it were an aside (if it were acted out with a wolfish grin it would certainly express the Jew's mind). Shylock is here thinking that now it is his turn to laugh, he is looking forward to the pleasure he will take in Antonio's downfall; he is sure that Antonio will forfeit, he is well aware of the dangers of the sea (1.3.19–23). Brook also quotes an alternative meaning from the Clarendon edition (1883): "the meaning [of 'a single bond'] is 'a bond with your own signature attached to it, without the names of sureties'." But no sureties were (and are) required to stand for the ratification of a bond at a notary's in Italian Law.

In fact, the term *single* has a precise legal meaning: a *single bond* is (and has been) a particular contractual obligation by which only one of the contracting parties, the 'obliger' (here Antonio), binds himself to the other party, the obligee (Shylock), to fulfil an obligation by contract. Only Antonio is bound to perform a specified action, that is, to return the 3,000 ducats. Once Shylock has lent the 3,000 ducats, he has no obligation to meet towards Antonio and becomes a creditor by right. Under Italian Law (which is derived from Roman Law and has remained unchanged as concerns its fundamental juridical principles),[2] this is called a *contratto unilaterale* 'unilateral contract'.[3] As the word 'unilateral' did not exist in the English language of the time (it is not attested in the OED until 1802), Shakespeare used *single* which, to him, best defined the nature of this particular contract.

**c) The notary**

Under the Italian legal system from the time of the Renaissance, anyone who wants to establish a deed, a will or a written agreement between himself and another party has to submit it to a notary, a public officer appointed by the State. The duties of the notary include drawing up the deed, signing it on behalf of the parties and storing it. Shylock, showing his "kindness"[=willingness, readiness], proposes to go to a notary (1.3.143) where Antonio will sign the bond. 'Notary' is not a term used frequently in English Law, in which the obligations are usually undertaken by solicitors or by commissioners of oaths; Shakespeare does not use the term elsewhere. The reference to a notary in *The Merchant* once more proves the dramatist's familiarity with Italian customs.

**d) The trial (4.1.170–396)**

According to the past and present Italian legal system, a contract between two or more parties has the force of law.[4] A written deed is the most effective means to evidence the contract, especially if the deed is drawn up by a notary. It proves to be so effective that, once the parties have acknowledged that it is not a forgery (Portia to Antonio, "Do you confess the bond?" "I do," 4.1.178), the law establishes that no witnesses need be examined by the judge in Court to prove its validity. Only what is written in the document must be taken into consideration. The narrow legality of Venetian laws (Portia to Shylock: "The Venetian law Cannot impugn you as you do proceed," 4.1.175–6) and Shylock's strict adherence to what is written in the bond ("Is it so nominated in the bond?" 4.1.255) is usually regarded as a negative element in the play and at the same time a counterpoint to Antonio's generosity; in fact, it simply conforms to the relevance of the written document in a legal case.

In dramatising the trial scene, Shakespeare appears to show he was acquainted with the fact that parole evidence (testimonial proof) was (and still is) inadmissible in such a legal case: Portia, as Balthazar Doctor of Law, only examines Antonio and Shylock, i.e. the two contenders ("Which is the merchant here, and which the Jew?" 4.1.171) and does not call anyone to give witness. She only replies to Bassanio, because he has intervened in the hearing to offer to pay "twice the sum". Shakespeare does not make any other character give evidence: Gratiano speaks just to burst out with joy, Nerissa to comment briefly on her husband's wish. Salerio is present but in silence. These are in line with the actual Italian and Venetian legal systems.

**e) The Duke.**

In the list of characters printed in Q3 (1637), the character named "the Duke of Venice" ranks first. He is not one of the main figures in the play, being mentioned only a few times before he appears in the trial scene (4.1). After passing sentence, he leaves the stage. One may even question the reason for his presence at all. His function in the play is to summon the Court of Justice, preside over it, "dismiss" it (4.1.103) if for the moment no agreement can be reached between the two contending parties, summon a "learned doctor" (104–5) who could help to settle the legal dispute, and finally, ratify the judge's statement or use his power to grant the Jew his pardon (4.1.365–9). The Duke in the play thus corresponds to the role of the Doge in Venice. It is a striking parallel which has not been given due consideration.

By the end of the 16th century the authority of the Doge had been limited in order to prevent his assuming absolute power. As the symbol of the State, he was entitled to preside over the meetings of all the Government Boards such as the *Maggior Consiglio* (Major Council, composed of about eight hundred patricians), the Senate, the Council of the Ten, and all the other councils, including the Criminal Courts. Some doges, however, tried to act despotically. Girolamo Priuli wrote in his *Diaries* in the first decade of the 16th century:

> It is common opinion that the prince of Venice is exclusively a symbolic figure and that he cannot do anything without the approval of his Counsellors of the Collegio [the Senate Cabinet] or of the Councils. On the contrary, I wish to affirm that the Venetian prince does what he wants [... ] provided that he does not offend the honour and dignity of the State.[5]

If the Doge opposed a bill, the Maggior Consiglio did not usually pass it. So the proposal would undergo modifications until the Doge's approval was given. Besides, the Doge had the privilege of proposing bills to all the Councils, except the Senate, without any previous discussion or ratification of the bills themselves, on behalf of the Minor Consiglio (the Council formed by the Doge and his six Counsellors).[6] The Venetian aristocrats – members of the various councils or boards – did their best to gain and maintain the favour of the Doge, which implied that they would vote for his proposals trying not to show strong opposition. His presence at the sessions was so essential that in some cases if he was unable to preside over the meetings owing to his bad health – only Dogi in their 70s or 80s were elected, with a few exceptions – the Councils would fall into chaos. In 1567, it was decreed that the Doge should be present at all the sessions of the Maggior Consiglio.[7] The Doge was the first to propose each motion to the Councils and his role in directing Government decisions and affairs was not only exacting but also essential to the order and stability of the Republic.[8] If he did not take part in all the Councils' sessions including those of the Criminal Courts, it would be because they were concomitant.

It may appear strange that a Jew, however rich he might have been, could have appealed to the Duke at night-time over to his daughter's elopement with all his gold and jewels and received his attention. One might think that the Republic's supreme authority had more important concerns than redressing a Jew's wrongs. But history proves that it was the Doge's duty to control the judiciary and administrative offices, and to guarantee the government's honesty and expertise. Doge Marco Barbarigo (d. 1486) established weekly audiences in order to listen to complaints about faulty or bad administration.[9] Leonardo Loredan (Doge from 1501 to his death in 1521) intervened in civil and penal cases resolving matters by his own vote, contrary to what was established by the law.[10] The famous diarist and chronicler of the Republic, Marino Sanuto, reports that Doge Andrea Gritti (1523–1538) summoned the Forty Judges of the Supreme Court of Appeal for penal cases (*Quarantia al Criminal*) in order to pass judgement in a case regarding a nobleman's offensive behaviour.[11] In some cases, the Doge acted as an ombudsman, to whom people appealed for redress and justice.[12] Therefore Shylock's application to the Doge for help corresponds to the reality of Venetian life.

**f) Strangers in Venice**

The dramatist also shows that he was well informed of the privileges which strangers (that is, those who did not belong to Venetian aristocracy or were not native citizens descended from the Romans) enjoyed in Venice. Antonio after his arrest says to Solanio, "The Duke cannot deny the course of law. For the commodity that strangers have With us in Venice, if it be denied, Will much impeach the justice of the state, Since that the trade and profit of the city Consisteth of all nations" (3.3.26–31). Strangers were protected and their rights defended by the laws of Venice because much of the prosperity of the city lay in the welfare of "all nations", that is, of all the different nationalities living and present there. Those who were not citizens of the Venetian Republic were foreigners. They lived in their own areas, e.g. in the *Calle dei Bergamaschi*, 'Street of the people from Bergamo', *Calle dei Tedeschi*, 'Street of the Germans', *Fontego dei Turchi*, 'Warehouse of the Turks'.[13] Shylock was a stranger, "an alien" says Portia (4.1.346) and therefore the Duke would not allow any wrong to be done to him.

With regard to knowledge of Italian and Venetian life and legal procedures, the dramatist must have had direct experience. One such person was Edward de Vere, 17th Earl of Oxford, who spent several months in Venice between January 1575 and March 1576 (Nelson, 121–141).

## Conclusion

*The Merchant of Venice* can be dated between 1558, when all the major sources were available and 1598, when it is mentioned in the Stationers' Register and by Meres.

Claims for its having been written in the mid-1590s have little substance. The sundry allusions championed have no great significance: and none provides a starting-point for the whole play. There are more allusions to events in the late 1570s and early 1580s, making this the most likely time of composition.

## Notes

1. See *Leggi Criminali del Serenissimo Dominio Veneto in un solo Volume raccolte e per pubblico Decreto ristampate, a cura di Angelo Sabini.* Venezia. Pinelli. 1751.
2. Di Marzo, S., *Istituzioni di Diritto Romano,* Milano, 1946: 347–8; *c.f.* Luzzatto, G.I., *Sull'origine e sulla natura dell'obbligazione romana,* Milano, 1934.
3. De Ruggiero, R. – Maroi, F., *Istituzioni di diritto privato,* Milano, Vol. 2 1954: 152–5. A bilateral contract is the one by which the two contracting parties bind themselves to each other to perform an obligation, for example, a buying and selling contract. *C.f.* Grosso, G., *Delle obbligazioni in generale,* Padova, 1935; Grosso, G., *Sistema Romano del Contratti.* Torino, 1945.
4. Ferrara, F., *Teoria dei Contratti,* Napoli, 1940. *C.f.* Ferrara, F, *Trattato di diritto civile italiano,* Roma, 1921; Messineo, F., *Dottrina generale del contratto,* Padova, 1948.
5. Priuli, G., *Diarii,* Vol. 2, p. 394.
6. Maranini, G,. *La Costituzione di Venezia,* Firenze, Vol. 2, 1974: 290.
7. Archivio di Stato, Venezia, Maggior Consiglio, Deliberazioni, Liber Angelus Reg. 29, fol. 29v.
8. Da Mosto, A., *I Dogi di Venezia nella vita pubblica e privata,* Firenze, 1977
9. Malipiero, D., *Annali veneti dall'anno 1457 al 1500,* Firenze, Vol. II, 1843–44: 680.
10. Archivio di Stato, Modena. b.ll, cap. 96, letter of Bartolomeo Carrari to the Duke of Ferrara, dated 10th October 1502.
11. Sanuto, M., *Diari,* 34, 229; 41, 84; 50, 417.
12. Besta, E., *Senato Veneziano,* Venezia, 1899; *c.f.* Besta, E., *Le obbligazioni nella storia del diritto italiano,* Padova, 1937; Finlay, R., *Politics in Renaissance Venice,* New Brunswick, 1978.
13. Tassini, G., *Curiosità veneziane,* Venezia. 1988.

## Other Cited Works

Anderson, Mark, *"Shakespeare" by Another Name*, New York: Penguin, 2005
Barber, C. L., *Shakespeare's Festive Comedy,* Princeton: Princeton UP, 1959
Blakemore Evans, G. (ed.), *Riverside Shakespeare,* New York: Houghton Mifflin, 1997
Brown, H. F., *Studies in the History of Venice*, 2 vols, London: John Murray, 1907
Brown, J. R. (ed.), *The Merchant of Venice,* London: Arden, 1955
Bullough, Geoffrey, *Narrative and Dramatic Sources of Shakespeare*, vol. 1, London: Macmillan, 1957
Cairncross, A. S., *The Problem of Hamlet – A Solution*, London, 1936
Chambers, E. K., *The Elizabethan Stage*, 4 vols, Oxford: Clarendon, 1923
Chambers, E. K., *William Shakespeare, A Study of Facts and Problems*, 2 vols, Oxford: Clarendon, 1930
Clark, Eva Turner, *Hidden Allusions in Shakespeare's Plays*, New York: Kennikat, 1931, rptd 1974
Drakakis, John, *The Merchant of Venice*, London Arden, forthcoming
Farina, William, *De Vere as Shakespeare*, , Jefferson NC: MacFarland, 2005
Frieda, L., *Catherine de Medici*, London, 2003

Halio, J. L. (ed.), *The Merchant of Venice,* Oxford: Oxford, 1993
Hess, W. R. *et al.*, Shakespeare's Dates, *Oxfordian,* 2, Portland, 1999
Holland, H. H., *Shakespeare, Oxford and Elizabethan Times*, London, 1933
Johnson, Samuel, *Notes to Shakespeare's Comedies,* 1765, Bibliobazaar, rptd 2007
Kamen, H. (ed.), *Who's Who in Europe 1450–1750,* London & New York, 2000
Magri, Noemi, "Places in Shakespeare: Belmont and Thereabouts" in *Great Oxford,* R. Malim (ed.), Tunbridge Wells: Parapress, 2004: 91–106
Mahood, M. M., *The Merchant of Venice,* Cambridge: CUP, 2003
Nelson, Alan, *Monstrous Adversary.* Liverpool, LUP, 2003
Ogburn, Charlton, *The Mysterious William Shakespeare,* Virginia: EPM, 1984
Read, C., *Lord Burghley and Queen Elizabeth*, London, 1960
Ross, J. C., "Stephen Gosson and *The Merchant of Venice* Revisited", *Notes & Queries,* 50, 2003: 16–37
Shaheen, Naseeb, *Biblical References in Shakespeare's Plays,* Newark: University of Delaware Press, 1999
Small, S. A., "The Jew", *Modern Langauge Review*, 26, 1931: 281–7
Sokol, B. J. & M. Sokol, *Shakespeare's Legal Language*, London: Continuum, 2004
Wells, Stanley & Gary Taylor (eds), *William Shakespeare: The Complete Works*, Oxford: OUP, 1986
—, *William Shakespeare: A Textual Companion*, Oxford: OUP, 1987
Wilson, J. Dover and A Quiller Couch (eds), *The Merchant of Venice*, Cambridge: CUP, 1953

10

# As You Like It

## Alex McNeil

The play is presumed to date between 1590 (the publication of the main source, Thomas Lodge's *Rosalynde*) and 1600, when it was mentioned in the Stationers' Register. However, *As You Like It* may ante-date Lodge's 1590 romance.

### Publication Date

*As You Like It* did not appear in print until its inclusion in the First Folio of 1623, one of eighteen plays in F1 not previously published. Its title had been entered informally in the Stationers' Register on 4 August in what is usually accepted as 1600, along with *Henry V, Much Ado About Nothing* and Jonson's *Every Man in His Humour.* Chambers observes that various memoranda were written on a spare page of the Register, including the following:

> [SR 1600 ?] My lord chambelens mens plays entred . . .
> 4 Augusti
> As you like yt , a booke } to be staied
> Henry the ffift, a booke
> Eevry man in his humour, a booke
> The Commedie of muche A doo about nothing a booke

These four titles do not appear in the normal place or format, and all four plays were 'to be staied', that is, either their registration or their printing was to be delayed. But the other three plays were formally registered later in August under '1600' and printed within a year; *As You Like It* had to wait until 8 November 1623 to be fully registered among the Folio plays "not formerly entred to other men" – just before its publication in the Folio.

## Performance Dates

The earliest known performance was apparently at the New Theatre Royal in 1669, when Thomas Killingrew was granted a licence for plays which had belonged to the old Blackfriars theatre.[1] A heavily adapted version was played at the Drury Lane Theatre, London, in 1723, but the first known performance of the play "with a text near to what Shakespeare wrote" (Latham, lxxxvii) was at the same theatre in 1740, after which time it was consistently popular. However, there is an oral tradition (recorded in 1865 by the historian William Cory) that in 1603 Mary Herbert, Countess of Pembroke, wrote to her son William, the third earl, asking him to bring James I the three miles from Salisbury to Wilton House, to see a performance of *As You Like It*, as "We have the man Shakespeare with us." Cory did not see the letter – nor has anyone since.[2] Intriguingly, the Chamber Accounts for December 1603 record a payment made to the Chamberlain's Men for presenting at Wilton "before His Maiestie an playe" – a play which is not named (Chambers, *ES*, iv, 168).

## Sources

Bullough lists just two sources for *As You Like It*. The more important was Thomas Lodge's *Rosalynde*, a prose romance written in 1586–7 and published in 1590; further editions followed during the next fifty years, including in 1592, 1596 and 1598. For the ill-treatment of the youngest son by the eldest, Lodge drew on a Middle English poem, *The Tale of Gamelyn*, featuring in several manuscripts of *The Canterbury Tales* (which appeared in print from 1483 onwards). Brissenden states (1994: 10) that Shakespeare takes Lodge's basic story, discards all deaths and most of the physical violence, and introduces more family relationships and extra characters, including the lovers, Touchstone and Audrey; Shakespeare compresses incident and enriches character.

Bullough also considers an anonymous play (composed *c.* 1570 and printed in 1599)[3] a "probable source": *Sir Clyomon and Clamydes* relates the story of two valiant knights. Bullough observes the indirect influence of Montemayor's *Diana* (1559) for the romantic scenes which take place in a pastoral setting. This work was also a source for *The Two Gentlemen of Verona*, which is thought to pre-date Young's 1598 translation (see Chapter 2). Agnes Latham identifies several thematic links with plays put on at court by John Lyly: *Sappho and Phao* (1584), *Galathea* (played in 1586–7) and *The Woman in the Moon* (on the Stationers' Register in 1595).[4]

## Orthodox Dates

Chambers limits the play's composition to 1598–1600, suggesting that 1599 seems reasonable, alongside *Twelfth Night* and *Much Ado*; most scholars (e.g.

Alexander, Hattaway and Marshall) follow. Agnes Latham opts for "a date of composition probably early in 1599" (1975: xxxiv), Wells & Taylor, followed by Brissenden, argue for 1599–1600. Juliet Dusinberre (2003) is much more precise, arguing for the play's completion shortly before its first performance on Shrove Tuesday, 1599.

Some scholars consider an earlier date possible, i.e. pre-Meres. Ward is somewhat ambivalent about dating the play – "in effect somewhere from 1593 to 1599" is the start of his discussion, and he concludes only that "it is impossible to say finally" – but he seems to be persuaded by a date *c.* 1598 (1992: ix, xiii respectively). Ward reasons that the play could have been sketched or drafted earlier, but that in its present form it is too sophisticated for 1593 (1992: ix). Oliver acknowledges internal evidence which has suggested, to some scholars, dates between 1593–9, but firmly opts for the later date, partly because "it is difficult to believe that artistry of this order would have been possible even for Shakespeare as early as 1593". Dover Wilson (as reported by Latham, xxvii–xxvii) accepted that the play was probably performed in 1599 but thought that the present play was a revision of an earlier version of *c.* 1593. He based this conclusion on what he saw as an apparent confusion between verse and prose, the contradictory nature of the time-scheme, and inconsistencies in names and other factual details. Cairncross proposes the period from June 1593–May 1594 for composition.

## Internal Orthodox Evidence

The play's various allusions to Christopher Marlowe would have been topical in 1593–4 around the time that Marlowe was killed (30 May 1593) during an argument about a bill. At 3.3.11, Touchstone states of misunderstood poetry:

> ... it strikes a man more dead than a great reckoning in a little room.

The play includes a direct quotation from Marlowe's poem *Hero and Leander* ("Dead shepherd, now I find thy saw of might: 'Who ever loved that loved not at first sight?'" 3.5.82–3). There is a longer reference to the same pair of lovers in the next scene (4.1.93–101). Ward feels that "[a]ll three, in context, carry a black shadow of death over them ... This would be understandable if Marlowe had just died, less so if it were six years later" (1992: x). However, as indicated above, this feeling is not decisive for Ward. He continues: "but of course Shakespeare didn't quickly forget Marlowe," and suggests that, conceivably, a later point in time might "have seemed a good time to bring to fruition what had long been incubating" (1993: xiii).

Oliver (following Lodge) finds that "great reckoning in a little room" may also be an allusion to "infinite riches in a little room" in Marlowe's *The Jew of Malta* (1.1.37), already well known in 1593, but, overall, Oliver is sceptical about early dating. He argues that a reference to Marlowe's death need not have immediately followed it, and points to the publication of *Hero and Leander* in 1598 as the trigger for the quotation. Although the playwright might have seen that poem in manuscript before 1598, the audience could hardly have in a position to appreciate the quotation.

Latham is ambivalent about possible allusions to Marlowe, claiming that "Marlowe was undoubtedly in Shakespeare's mind as he wrote [the play]" but that by 1599 "it was less likely that an audience would pick up the reference or care particularly to be reminded of the event." She doubts that reference would be made to Marlowe's death by a stage jester, and she suggests that the sentence may have a bawdy significance.[5] Brissenden, sharing these general doubts, ignores any possibility that the play's composition could have occurred before 1599. In a footnote, he identifies Marlowe as the "dead shepherd" of 3.5.82, and cites 1598 as the year when *Hero and Leander* was published (1994: 184n).

Juliet Dusinberre (2003) presents a detailed argument that *As You Like It* was written for performance on Shrove Tuesday, 20 February 1599, mainly because of Touchstone's reference to pancakes: "The pancakes were naught and the mustard was good" (1.2.62–3).[6] There are two further mentions of pancakes in the play, and only one other (*All's Well*) in the rest of the canon. Dusinberre's argument from external evidence is considered in the next section.

Ward finds support for 1599 in Jaques's "All the world's a stage" speech (2.7.139–166): the Globe Theatre opened in 1599 under the motto *Totus mundus agit histrionem*. Latham points out that the thought "is a commonplace of long ancestry", and Oliver believes the speech may or may not have been prompted by the opening of the Globe. Ward also notes that Will Kemp left the Lord Chamberlain's men early in 1599; so Robert Armin, "the more melancholy actor", who joined the company that year, may have played Jaques. Again, Ward notes that it "is impossible to say finally" (1992: xiii). Other commentators, however, have suggested that Armin played the part of Touchstone.[7] Seeking further support for 1599, Ward associates the date of the play with Shakespeare's 1597 purchase of New Place in Stratford, and his being "taken ... back imaginatively" to Warwickshire and the Forest of Arden (1992: xii).

Latham finds those allusions to events in the late nineties "tenuous", and seems more persuaded by allusions in the play which may be related to books published in or around 1598, such as *Hero and Leander* and Lyly's *The Woman in the Moon*, published in 1597 (and entered in the Stationers' Register in 1595). She seems particularly struck by the "curious resemblance" of Act 2 Scene 1 of Greene's play *Orlando Furioso* to its equivalent in *As You Like It*. Latham quotes many parallels – which she then plays down as "poetical commonplaces". The usefulness of *Orlando Furioso* as evidence for dating *As You Like It* also turns out to be uncertain: although an edition of *Orlando Furioso* appeared in 1598, the play may have been performed as early as 1591.

## External Orthodox Evidence

The play does not appear in the list given by Meres in his 1598 *Palladis Tamia.* This is usually taken to indicate that it did not exist at that date and must have been written between Meres's time of writing and 1600, However, the list might be selective: for example, there is also no mention of any play about the reign of Henry VI. Brissenden notes (1994: 4): "Because a play is not in Meres' list is no proof that it did not exist." Similarly, *Merry Wives of Windsor* was not mentioned by Meres but is usually taken to be written in 1597 or earlier. For further discussion of Meres, see the Introduction.

Some commentators (Ormerod 1993, for instance) have suggested that *As You Like It* was named by Meres as *Love's Labour's Won* (which has not otherwise been identified), which would make the play pre-1598. J. H. Walter explained Meres's ignorance – and the inclusion of the wedding masque – by speculating that the play was devised for private performance at the marriage of the Earl of Southampton with Elizabeth Vernon in 1598.

In proposing that *As You Like It* was performed before the court on Shrove Tuesday 1599 due to the reference to pancakes, Dusinberre (2003) also noted an entry in the Accounts of the Treasurer which states that the Chamberlain's Men received £20 for playing before the Queen and Court on that occasion. She finds further support for this in a hand-written poem, which seems to form a fitting epilogue, recorded in Henry Stanford's *Common Place Book* for 1598. If the Chamberlain's Men did perform *As You Like It* on this occasion, she argues that it is possible that the play had only just been completed by then.[8]

Thomas Morley's setting of "It was a lover and his lass" (5.3.15–38) was printed in 1600, which is taken seems to confirm that the play was completed by then. There is, however, no evidence as to whether the song or the play came first, whether the words are Shakespeare's own or, even, whether Morley composed the music. There is, therefore, no necessary connection between the publication date of the song and the composition date of the play.[9]

## Oxfordian Date

Clark suggested 1581–2 with a revision in 1589. Both generations of Ogburn concur. Holland proposed 1589. More recently, Oxfordians Moore and Hess suggest a completion date *c.* 1593. Anderson argues for an original date of composition, *c.* 1578, with a revision date 1599–1600.

## Internal Oxfordian Evidence

Regarding sources, Oxfordians argue that Shakespeare's play was written much earlier and that *Rosalynde* was derivative. They propose that Oxford drew mainly on the medieval poem *The Tale of Gamelyn,* as opposed to later sources. According to this view, Lodge based his prose romance on the earliest version of *As You Like It,* before it was revised to include the additional characters of Jaques, Touchstone, Audrey, William and Martext at the end of the 1580s.

Clark maintains that the main story-line, concerning Orlando and Rosalind, comprised the first version and had been inspired by Queen Elizabeth's open pledge in November 1581 to marry her French suitor, the Duc d'Alençon.[10] Clark draws many parallels between the position of Orlando in the play and the position of Alençon, and between that of Rosalind and Elizabeth.

Many Oxfordians have seen Oxford's self portrait in the melancholic Jaques. Firstly, Jaques is someone who has sold his lands to travel:

> JAQUES: It is a melancholy of mine own, . . . extracted from many objects, and indeed the sundry contemplation of my travels, in which my often rumination wraps me in a most humorous sadness.
>
> ROSALIND: A traveller! By my faith, you have great reason to be sad. I fear you have sold your own lands to see other men's. Then to have seen much and to have nothing is to have rich eyes and poor hands. (4.1.15–23)

This accords well with Oxford, who travelled in Italy in 1575–6 but was frequently threatened with bankruptcy between 1576 and 1591 (Nelson, 121–32; 331). Secondly, Jaques's set speech on the Seven Ages of Man (2.7. 139–166) is not common-place (as has been shown by E. E. Stoll) but the seven stages are depicted in a marble circular mosaic in the floor of the cathedral at Siena, near the crossing, as described by art historian, Samuel C. Chew:

> The Ages are represented thus: Infantia rides upon a hobbyhorse, Pueritia is a schoolboy, Adolescentia is an older scholar garbed in a long cloak, Juventus has a falcon on his wrist, Virilitas is robed in dignified fashion and carries a book, Senectus, leaning upon his staff, holds a rosary, Decrepitas, leaning upon two staves, looks into his tomb.[11]

Oxford stayed in Siena and wrote to his father-in-law, Lord Burghley, from there on 3 January 1576 (Nelson, 132). This letter confirms two separate links between Oxford and Jaques. A further link between Oxford and the play can be observed in the thematic correspondence with plays by Lyly (e.g. *Sappho and Phao,* 1584). Lyly was employed by Oxford during this period and presented his plays at court (Nelson, 238–9).

Clark also suggests that the scene between Touchstone and William (Act 5 Scene 1), and the character Sir Oliver Martext were added in 1589–90. Those Oxfordians who see the fictional William as a reflection of William Shakespeare point out that both were born in the Forest of Arden (5.1.22), and that William says he is "five-and-twenty" (5.1.19), which was Shakespeare's age in 1589. Without accepting such a direct identification, Latham speculates on the possibility of a theatrical in-joke, if Shakespeare acted the part of William. The character of Martext is also relevant to Oxford in the late 1580s. The Marprelate controversy took place in 1588–9 when seven Puritan tracts were published under the pseudonym 'Martin Marprelate' attacking the Anglican Church. To present their responses, the bishops eventually recruited professional writers like Nash, Lyly and Greene; these last two were employed by Oxford (Nelson, 238–9). A reference to the controversy (which at its height also evoked anti-Puritan plays) is relevant in 1589, but not ten years later.

Anderson argues for an earlier date of composition (in the late 1570s) when the three sons of the executed Duke of Norfolk were all married. He believes Oxford revised the play *c.* 1599–1600.

## Conclusion

The play is generally dated between 1590 (the publication of the main source, Thomas Lodge's *Rosalynde*) and 1600 when it was mentioned in the Stationers' Register.

However, if Lodge's *Rosalynde* was based on *As You Like It* rather than being Shakespeare's source, then the play must have been written earlier. There is some evidence for an original version of the play in the 1580s, with revision likely around 1593–4, and a date of completion by 1600.

## Notes

1. Juliet Dusinberre (2003) notes from the document in the PRO (LC 5/12, fols 212–3): "One hundred and eight plays are listed, twenty-one by Shakespeare; *As You Like It* appears between *The Merchant of Venice* and *The Taming of the Shrew.*" Thus *As You Like It* holds the same position as it does in the Folios and the list may have been copied from the contents page. She continues: "The King's Men in 1608–09 reacquired the Blackfriars theater, which the Burbages had leased in 1600 to the Children of the Chapel Royal." The document is reproduced in Dusinberre (2006: 44).
2. E. K. Chambers (WS: vol 2,329) gives an account of the 1865 exchange:

   > In 1865 William Cory, then a master at Eton, was received at Wilton House by Lady Herbert, who told him, 'we have a letter, never printed, from Lady Pembroke to her son, telling him to bring James I from Salisbury to see As You Like It; "we have the man Shakespeare with us." She wanted to cajole the king on Raleigh's behalf – he came.

   Chambers notes that James did visit Salisbury during the time he kept his court at Wilton from 24 October until 12 December, 1603. As the letter has not been verified, many editors remain sceptical about it (see Marshall, 7).
3. Chambers (*ES*, iv, 6) follows previous editors such as Bullen and Greg in dating

*Sir Clyomon and Clamydes* to *c.* 1570.

4. Agnes Latham describes Lyly's apparent influence on the play in detail (1975: lix–lxv). G. K. Hunter, *John Lyly: The Humanist as Courtier* (1962: 342–3) traces similar influence.
5. Latham (1975: xxxiii). J. Bakeless, *The Tragicall History of Christopher Marlowe* (1942), I, pp. 143ff includes a list of references to Marlowe in print between the years 1593–1601.
6. Dusinberre (2003): "Queen and court were eating pancakes in the Great Hall at Richmond for Shrove Tuesday night [1599] when, according to the Declared Accounts, the Chamberlain's Men performed a play. That's why Touchstone's joke is funny. It was pancake day. The Clown in *All's Well That Ends Well* remarks on the fitness of "a pancake for Shrove Tuesday" (2.2.22–23). The Elizabethans ate pancakes stuffed with powdered beef (like a modern fritter) – hence the mustard."
7. Latham discusses Armin (1975: li–lv). See C.S. Felver, "Robert Armin, Shakespeare's source for Touchstone", *Shakespeare Quarterly*, VII (1956), pp.135–7.
8. Dusinberre (2006: 37–41) points to the epilogue in the commonplace book of Henry Stanford, "believed by ... scholars probably to be by Shakespeare," which "fits *As You Like It* better than any other play" (37). The epilogue is addressed "to ye Q. by ye players. 1598" and Dusinberre, following Ringler & May, demonstrates that 1598, according to Old Style dating (in which the new year begins on 25 March), would reinforce February 1599 as a possible date. The epilogue itself mentions "Shrovetide". Dusinberre (2006) reproduces Stanford's entry on p. 38 and in Appendix 1, p. 349.
9. For further discussion, see J. H. Long, "Shakespeare and Thomas Morley", *MLN*, 1950: 17–22.
10. Alison Weir, *Elizabeth the Queen* (1999), quotes a letter from the Spanish Ambassador which describes the "astonishing charade" of Elizabeth's public announcement (339–40).
11. Quoted by Mark Anderson (103) from Samuel C. Chew, *The Pilgrimage of Life*, New Haven, 1962: 150–1.

## Other Cited Works


Alexander, Peter, *Shakespeare's Life and Art*, London: James Nisbet, 1939

Anderson, Mark, *"Shakespeare" by Another Name,* New York: Penguin, 2005

Brissenden, A. (ed.), *As You Like It*, Oxford: OUP, 1994

Bullough, Geoffrey, *Narrative and Dramatic Sources of Shakespeare,* vol. II, London: Routledge and Kegan Paul, 1958

Cairncross, A. S., *The Problem of Hamlet – a Solution,* London: Macmillan, 1936

Campbell, O. J. (ed.), *A Shakespeare Encyclopedia*, London, 1966

Chambers, E. K., *The Elizabethan Stage*, 4 vols, Oxford: Clarendon, 1923

—, William Shakespeare, *A Study of Facts and Problems*, 2 vols, Oxford: Clarendon, 1930

Clark, Eva Turner, *Hidden Allusions in Shakespeare's Plays*, New York: Kennikat, 1931 rptd 1974

Dusinberre Juliet, "Pancakes and a Date for *As You Like It*", *SQ*, 54.4, 2003: 371–

405
Dusinberre, Juliet (ed.), *As You Like It*, London: Arden, 2006
Hattaway, M. (ed.), *As You Like It*, Cambridge: CUP, 2000
Hess, W. R. *et al.*, "Shakespeare's Dates", *The Oxfordian*, 2, Portland, 1999
Holland, H. H., *Shakespeare, Oxford and Elizabethan times*, London: Denis Archer, 1933
Honigmann, E. A. J., *Shakespeare's Impact on his Contemporaries*, London: Macmillan, 1982
Latham, Agnes (ed.), *As You Like It*, London: Arden, 1975
Marshall, C. (ed.), *As You Like It,* Shakespeare in Production, Cambridge: CUP, 2004
Nelson, Alan, *Monstrous Adversary*, Liverpool: LUP, 2003
Ogburn, Dorothy & Charlton Sr, *This Star of England*, New York: Coward-McCann, 1952
Ogburn, Charlton, *The Mysterious William Shakespeare*, Virginia: EPM, 1984
Oliver, H. J. (ed.), *As You Like It*, Harmondsworth: Penguin, 1968
Ormerod, D., "Love's Labour's Lost and Won: the case for As You Like It", *Cahiers élisabéthains,* 44, 1993: 9–21
Stoll, E. E., "Jaques and the Antiquaries", *Modern Language Notes*, liv, 1939: 79–85
Walter, J. H. (ed.), *As You Like It*, London: Heinemann, 1965
Ward, J. P. *Harvester New Critical Introductions to Shakespeare : As You Like It*, London: Harvester-Wheatsheaf, 1992
Weir, Alison, *Elizabeth the Queen,* London: Jonathan Cape, 1998
Wells, Stanley & Gary Taylor (eds), *William Shakespeare: The Complete Works,* Oxford: OUP, 1986
—, *William Shakespeare: A Textual Companion*, Oxford: OUP, 1987

11

# The Taming of the Shrew

Stephanie Hopkins Hughes

This play can be dated after 1579 and any time up to 1598.

## Publication Date

*The Taming of the Shrew* was published for the first time in the First Folio (F1) of Shakespeare's plays in 1623. That version is commonly referred to as *The Shrew* to distinguish it from its supposed 'source', a play called *The Taming of a Shrew* which was published anonymously.

## Publication of the Anonymous '*A Shrew*'

On 2 May 1594 there was entered to Peter Short in the Stationers' Register:

> [SR, 1594, *A Shrew,* anon] Secundo die Maij. Peter Shorte. Entred vnto him for his copie vnder master warden Cawoodes hande, a booke intituled A plesant Conceyted historie called The Tamynge of a Shrowe vj[d]

The play was published later that year:

> [Q1, 1594, *A Shrew*] A Pleasant Conceyted Historie, called The Taminge of a Shrowe ... sundry times acted by the Right honorable the Earle of Pembroke his servants
> Printed at London by Peter Short and are to be sold by Cuthbert Burbie, at his shop at the Royal Exchange. 1594

This version of the play contains about 1480 lines, shorter than most quartos attributed to Shakespeare (see Oliver). A single copy of this edition, held at the Huntingdon Library, survives. It was followed by a reprint in 1596:

A

Pleaſant Conceited

Hiſtorie, called The taming of a Shrew.

As it was ſundry times acted by the *Right honorable the Earle of* Pembrook his ſeruants.

Printed at London by Peter Short and *are to be ſold by Cutbert Burbie, at his* ſhop at the Royall Exchange.

1594.

7. Title page to the anonymous first quarto of *The Taming of a Shrew,* 1594; it has generally been believed that this play was by another author but some scholars have argued that it was an early version by Shakespeare, which he later revised. By permission of Bodleian Library, University of Oxford, shelfmark Facs. e.29, title page.

[Q2, 1596] P.S., sold by Cuthbert Bertie

Two more anonymous editions followed in 1607. The first was entered in the register to Nicholas Ling at the same time as *Romeo and Juliet* and *Love's Labour's Lost*, indicating a clear connection with Shakespeare. The play was published in F1 as *The Taming of the Shrew*, occupying the eleventh position among the comedies, coming after *As You Like It* and before *All's Well That Ends Well*. The 1631 quarto of *The Shrew* derives the text from F1 and attributes the play to Shakespeare.

The relationship between the anonymous *A Shrew* (1594) and Shakespeare's *The Shrew* (1623) has been vigorously debated over the years. Thompson explains the choice of theories:

a) *A Shrew* is the original play, by an unknown writer, and the direct source of the Shakespeare play (as suggested by Chambers);
b) *The Shrew* is the original play and *A Shrew* is a memorial reconstruction by an actor or some other person of the Shakespeare play, i.e. a 'bad quarto' (as argued by Alexander and Dover Wilson, Morris, Miller and Oliver);
c) both *Shrews* derive from a lost original which was Shakespeare's first version of the play (Houk).

Despite the close resemblance in structure between the two plays, the language in *A Shrew* is far less Shakespearean, though not totally without lyrical touches. It has been claimed by some (e.g. Chambers[1]) that the poetic moments sound more like Marlowe or Peele than like Shakespeare. However, Stephen Miller's detailed comparison of the texts leads him to conclude that *The Shrew* is the original play and *A Shrew* is an inferior version of it.

## Performance Dates

On 11 June 1594 a performance of '*the tamyng of A shrowe*' at the Newington Butts theatre is recorded in Philip Henslowe's diary. It is not immediately apparent whether it was performed by the Lord Admiral's Men, the Lord Chamberlain's Men, or a combination of them, when the two companies were 'exiled' there from 3 to 13 June: Henslowe indicates the performance dates of seven plays but not the performers. However, when they returned to the Rose playhouse the following week, the Admiral's Men continued to present three of the Newington plays, but *A Shrew* was not one of them. So Rutter confidently assigns *A Shrew* to the Chamberlain's Men (along with the other three plays, which included *Titus Andronicus* and *Hamlet*). According to Thompson, "it seems clear... that both Pembroke's men and the Lord Chamberlain's Men had *Shrew* plays in their respective repertoires by 1594."

The next recorded performance took place at Court on 26 November 1633.

## Sources

Both *Shrew* plays comprise three elements woven together.

**1) The frame**. A lord discovers a drunken tinker passed out on the ground and, as a jest, has his retainers bring him indoors. When the tinker wakes up, they convince him that he is a great lord, who has just recovered from a spell of madness in which he believed himself to be a lowly tinker. As Thompson points out, such a story is found in many times and places, including the *Arabian Nights*. Close in time to Shakespeare, Heuterus's *De Rebus Burgundicis*, published in 1584, has the Duke of Burgundy playing the trick, including the performance of a comedy. In *A Shrew* the tinker, Slie, is intended to remain on stage throughout; in *The Shrew*, once the play begins, no more is heard from Sly and he can stay on stage or vanish at the director's whim.

**2) The main plot**. A "merry, madcap lord", Petruchio, comes to town to get a wealthy bride, woos and weds the feisty Kate and by various means succeeds in 'taming' her. He prevents her from eating, sleeping, choosing her own clothes or having a say on anything. The techniques described are similar to those used to train hawks. Finally, Kate, realising that it is more important to this man that he have her public allegiance than that his own public image should remain spotless, capitulates in order to bring peace. Uniquely among Shakespeare's works, this plot seems to have been derived more closely from an oral tradition than from any previous written work, ancient or contemporary. Folklore specialist Brunvand amply demonstrates that it is based on an old tale common to all the nations of Europe, and even some in Asia. In his detailed and scientific study, he shows how closely Shakespeare followed the Danish version in all but a few details: Shakespeare softened his version from the folkloric source, in which the abuse of the wife is far greater.

**3) The sub-plot.** Young Lucentio exchanges identities with his servant and disguises himself as a music teacher in order to woo Kate's younger sister, Bianca. This exchange causes a number of comic misunderstandings.

The recognised source of this plot is the play *Supposes*, an English translation, by George Gascoigne, of Ariosto's Italian play *Suppositi*. Gascoigne simultaneously used Ariosto's two versions – the original was in prose, the second in verse. These in turn were based on *Amphytruo*, a Latin comedy by Plautus. *The Supposes* was performed at Gray's Inn in 1566 as part of the winter holiday entertainment of 1566–7, although the translation was not published until 1573; it was republished in 1587. Gascoigne retained all Ariosto's characters and their Italian names.

While both *Shrew* plays take the characters, scenes and plot devices of *The Supposes* for their sub-plot (the wooing of the younger sister), they are used less fully and to less effect in *A Shrew* than in *The Shrew*. In *A Shrew*, some of the characters and their plot elements are eliminated and two individuals are divided into pairs. The author of *A Shrew* gives Kate two sisters, but *The Shrew* gives her only one (neither Ariosto nor his translator gives his girl any).

The female protagonist in both plays is 'Kate'; otherwise there is two different sets of names for most of the characters. Curiously, *The Shrew* went back to *Supposes* for the name of the servant 'Petruchio' (added to Ariosto's play by Gascoigne), and bestows it on his male protagonist in *The Shrew*. Among other sources sometimes proposed are the works of Plautus (providing the names Grumio and Tranio), and writings on falconry by Gervase Markham such as *Country Contentments*, usually dated 1611, but probably earlier; Markham was writing prolifically from *c.* 1590 and was commended by Meres in 1598.

## Orthodox Date

The range of dates proposed for the (Shakespeare) play is 1589 – 94. Chambers fixed on 1593–4 for Shakespeare's play, which is followed by the Riverside and Signet editions. Halliday preferred 1594. Alexander puts the date of writing before 1593, as does Oliver; Wells & Taylor propose 1590–93 and Cairncross places it around 1590. Thompson, also, settles on 1590 as the most likely date. Morris (persuaded by Marco Mincoff's revision of Chambers's chronology) proposes 1589 and most scholars now favour a date *c.* 1590.

## Internal Orthodox Evidence

Morris states simply that there is no internal evidence for dating the play.

## External Orthodox Evidence

Meres does not mention any *Shrew* play. Some commentators have identified it with the mysterious '*Love labours wonne*' in Meres's 1598 list of Shakespearean plays, but Baldwin shows that both *A Shrew* and *Love labours wonne* were to be found in a bookseller's manuscript catalogue of 1603.

Morris supports the view that *The Shrew* is the source of *A Shrew*, and he conjectures that *A Shrew* existed before 21 August 1592, the day when the actor Simon Jewell (of Pembroke's company) was buried. The evidence is somewhat flimsy, but *A Shrew* has the stage direction 'Enter Simon ... '; no better explanation has been put forward than that this is the name of the actor – there is no character of that name. So we have a latest date of early 1592 for *The Shrew*.

Thompson notes the previous detail and mentions verbal parallels between both *Shrew* plays and *A Knack to Know a Knave*, performed at the Rose playhouse on 10 June 1592. She deduces that the anonymous play borrowed from both, indicating an earlier dating of both plays – *The Shrew* being the first to be performed. She affirms *The Shrew*'s affinities with the earliest Shakespearean comedies, *The Comedy of Errors* and *The Two Gentlemen of Verona*, particularly with the former.

Thompson's overall attitude is that Shakespeare originally wrote his play, complete with all the Sly material, for a large company (possibly the Queen's Men) either in the season ended by the closing of the theatres in June 1592 or in the preceding season. During the turbulent years 1592–4, two companies came to possess cut versions of the play, *The Shrew*, which remains close to the original, and *A Shrew*, a memorial reconstruction of the original. It remains possible that *The Shrew* was among the first of Shakespeare's plays and dates back to 1590. Alternatively, some commentators think that *The Shrew*, as it appears in the First Folio, is a substantially later version.

Only three contemporary references have been found to a '*Shrew*' play, the latest – and least relevant – dated 1609. In 1596 Harrington's *Metamorphosis of Ajax* obviously refers to the 1594 printed text of *A Shrew*: "the book of Taming a Shrew". The earliest of the three references is the most significant: a 1593 poem by Antony Chute (*Beawtie Dishonoured*, also called *Shores Wife*) includes the line "He calls his Kate, and she must come and kiss him". Morris and Thompson conclude that this must refer to *The Shrew*, in which Petruchio twice demands a kiss from Katherina (5.1 and 5.2); there are no kissing sequences in *A Shrew*.

## Oxfordian Date

Clark proposes 1579, and Charlton Ogburn Jr. thinks that the 1579 play *A Shrew* "might" be an early version of *The Shrew*. Holland regards *The Shrew* as not by Oxford and dates it to 1598. Hess et al. opt for 1582 and "not later than 1593".

## External Oxfordian Evidence

The many anomalies discerned by scholars in the version published as *A Shrew* suggest that it was not the first or only version of the play from this period. Nor would this be surprising, considering its curious and ambiguous provenance. If (as some scholars suggest) it was in the possession of at least two troupes, that leaves room for alterations of all kinds.

Clark holds that the record in the Court calendar of a holiday play, produced at Richmond Palace by the Children of Paul's in January 1579 (Chambers, *ES*, iv 96, 154), was an early version of *The Taming of the Shrew*. However, the title, *A Morrall of the marryage of Mynde and Measure*, offers no clue, and Clark gives no reasons as to why we should agree. She also suggests that it was written for the marriage of Oxford's sister, Mary Vere, to Lord Willoughby d'Eresby at about this time, on the doubtful basis that Mary had a hot temper.[2]

Oxfordians consider that a number of Shakespeare's best plays were written as wedding entertainments at Court, for families or individuals with whom he had a particular bond. As this play is about a marriage, and, like several others, involves a dénouement in which several couples are united at the end, *Shrew* would seem to have been written for a wedding. Yet, although there is always a measure of satire in the 'wedding' plays, the treatment is far more extreme in *The Shrew*: Katherine's hysterical anguish at her situation, Petruchio's refusal to conform to custom, to dress appropriately or attend the obligatory wedding breakfast, above all his harsh treatment of his wife – modern opinion would call it abuse – go way above the usual level of provocation. Moreover, all does not end happily for everyone: the embarrassment of the other newly-weds and Kate's avowal of submission make this no ordinary wedding play.

This writer proposes that a likely point of origin for *The Shrew* was the Stanley–Spencer wedding of 1579. According to the book by Barry Coward, twenty-year-old Ferdinando Stanley married the wealthy heiress Alice Spencer. Stanley, or Lord Strange as he was known for most of his adult life, became involved in the world of Court theatre. He began by sponsoring tumbling acts for the winter holiday entertainment in 1579–80, and continued to support such Court activities, plus a successful acting company, for most of the '80s and into the '90s. Himself a poet of no mean ability, he was praised by most of the leading poets of the day for his generous patronage of the arts. It was his company, Lord Strange's Men, that made Christopher Marlowe famous in the late 1580s.

Stanley's bride, Alice Spencer, was the youngest of the eight daughters of Sir John Spencer of Althorp in Northamptonshire. He made a fortune both by raising sheep for the wool trade and by marrying an heiress. He was able to marry several daughters into the peerage, espousing them to noblemen in debt. In 1579 Alice topped them all by marrying Lord Strange. Sir John reached the peak of his public prestige when he became Lord Mayor of London in 1594. The prominence of both families as patrons of the arts can be seen from the many works dedicated to them by such writers as Robert Greene, Edmund Spenser and Thomas Nashe.

Alice was far from being a silent, submissive female. She demonstrated intelligence and determination in her long legal battle with Oxford's son-in-law and her own brother-in-law, the sixth Earl of Derby, over property left her in her husband's will. Coward notes that Egerton made frequent complaints about her "biting" tongue.

Lord Strange himself was one of the Leicester faction at Court. This would suggest a motive for Oxford. Strange was a rival both politically and artistically, and his marriage would have given opportunity for Oxford to hurl a theatrical gauntlet before him, demonstrating his skill with what Nashe called his "dudgeon dagger", the wooden sword of the old comic Vice, the weapon of satire, that brings the mighty to their knees by making them look ridiculous.

Strange is recorded as having a particular weakness for finery. Coward informs us that, at his death in 1594 at 36, he left unpaid tailors' and shoemakers' bills of £6000! The comic business between Petruchio and his tailor and haberdasher (4.3) suggest a satire on this weakness. Strange's taste for expensive horses is also recorded by Sir John Harrington, and might have prompted the creation of Petruchio's broken-down old nag. Stone records his enthusiasm for hawking, which could have encouraged the extended metaphor in which methods for taming a hawk are used to tame a wife.

*The Taming of the Shrew* contains significant further names. In the Induction scene, Sly is informed that he must call his wife 'Madam', to which replies "Alice madam or Joan madam?" In 4.1, Petruchio calls for his cousin "Ferdinand ... one, Kate, that you must kiss and be acquainted with"; and there is plentiful use of the word 'strange'. Finally, the character of the formidable Alice, and the fact that everyone was certain the heavily indebted Lord Strange was marrying her for her dowry, fit this scenario very nicely.

If a version of the play was inspired by this particular wedding, it could then have been the one rewritten later for public consumption as *A Shrew*, but it is likely that the version used a full decade earlier for an educated, noble audience would have been different from that of either extant play: *A Shrew*, revised for public performance in 1589–92, or *The Shrew*, the final version as we have it in the First Folio, revised some time in the late 1580s or early 1600s. The language of *A Shrew* is similar in many ways to that of other early anonymous or apocryphal plays that have been pinpointed by scholars with good ears as 'early Shakespeare'. The ornate touches that have confused scholars might not have been an imitation of Marlowe, but purposeful burlesque of a style that was associated with Marlowe. That these flourishes are confined to the two foppish suitors for the hand of Kate's two sisters, suggests that the target audience relished this satirical touch.

The names Shakespeare gives to his characters can be clues to his real-life models. In *A Shrew*, the Petruchio character is called Fernando – too similar to Ferdinand to be disregarded, while one of the two sisters is called Emilia, suggesting a possible connection with Emilia Bassano, the Italian–Jewish court musician whom some commentators (Rowse, Lasocki, Hughes), believe was the Dark Lady of the Sonnets. During the period in question, Emilia Bassano was the mistress of the Lord Chamberlain, Henry Hunsdon, patron of Shakespeare's acting company. His oldest son, Sir George Carey, was married to Elizabeth Spencer, Alice's older sister. These connections would support the idea of the play being a fierce satire on Oxford's peers which, while tolerable to the insulated Court community, would be another matter when it passed into the repertories of public acting companies.

## Conclusion

The play can be dated after 1579 and any time up to 1598 (even though it was not mentioned by Meres) as it is universally taken to be an early comedy. The date of the first version could be as early as 1579 with a date for a revised version 1590–1, when Lord Strange first appears in the Court Calendar. As for the F1 version, its high polish suggests a rewrite in the late 1590s.

This play may have been written originally as a 'roast', to tease two socially powerful young people in the privacy of their family and community circle at the time of their marriage. This would help (in my view) to explain what is often perceived by modern audiences as disturbing misogyny. Although anger had its role in later versions, the origin of *The Taming of the Shrew* may have been no more than an hilarious practical joke.

## Notes

Acknowledgement: some statements above, based on the work of Lawrence Stone and Stephen May, are derived from notes on Lord Strange and the Spencers taken by Mick Clark and generously made available.

1. E. K. Chambers (*ES*, iv, 48) dates the anonymous quarto play *A Shrew* to *c.* 1589. He reports that "its date has been placed in or before 1589, because certain lines of it appear to be parodied both in Greene's *Menaphon* of that year, and in the prefatory epistle to *Menaphon* by Nashe". Chambers *(WS,* i, 322–8 ) is very unsure about the relationship between the plays, Shakespeare's possible authorship of the anonymous quarto and the dates of each play. He gives a balanced discussion, reporting the alternative view of Peter Alexander and J. Dover Wilson.
2. The couple were married between Christmas 1577 and March 1578. For details of the engagement and dowry arrangements, see Nelson, 172–9.

## Other Cited Works

Alexander, Peter, *Shakespeare's Life and Art,* London: James Nisbet, 1939

Anderson, Mark, *"Shakespeare" by Another Name,* New York: Penguin, 2005

Blakemore Evans, G. (ed.), *Riverside Shakespeare,* New York: Houghton Mifflin, 1997

Brunvand, J. H., *The Taming of the Shrew: a comparative study of oral and literary Versions*, New York: Garland, 1991

Bullough, Geoffrey, *Narrative and Dramatic Sources of Shakespeare*, vol. II, London: Routledge and Kegan Paul, 1958

Cairncross, A. S., *The Problem of Hamlet – a Solution*, London: MacMillan, 1936

Chambers, E. K., *The Elizabethan Stage,* 4 vols, Oxford: Clarendon, 1923

Chambers, E. K., *William Shakespeare, A Study of Facts and Problems,* 2 vols, Oxford: Clarendon, 1930

Clark, Eva Turner, *Hidden Allusions in Shakespeare's Plays,* New York: Kennikat, 1931 rptd 1974
Coward, B., *The Stanleys, Lords Stanley and Earls of Derby, 1385–1672,* London: Sidgwick & Jackson, 1985
Halliday, F. E., *A Shakespeare Companion 1550–1951*, London: Duckworth, 1952
Hess, W. R., *et al.* "Shakespeare's Dates", *The Oxfordian*, 2, Portland, 1999
Holland, H. H., *Shakespeare, Oxford and Elizabethan Times*, London: D. Archer, 1933
Houk, Raymond A., "The Evolution of *The Taming of the Shrew*", *PMLA,* 1942: 1009–38
Hughes, S. H., "New Light on the Dark Lady." *Shakespeare Oxford Newsletter* 36.3, 2000
Lasocki, D. and R. Prior, *The Bassanos: Venetian musicians and instrument makers in England, 1531–1665*, Aldershot: Ashgate, 1995
May, S. W., *The Elizabethan Courtier Poets: the poems and their contexts*, Columbia: University of Missouri Press, 1991
Miller, S. R. (ed.), '*The taming of a shrew': the 1594 quarto,* Cambridge: CUP, 1998
Mincoff, M., *Shakespeare, the First Steps*, Sofia: Bulgarian Academy of Sciences, 1976
Morris, B. (ed.), *The Taming of the Shrew,* London: Arden, 1981
Nelson, Alan, *Monstrous Adversary,* Liverpool: LUP, 2003
Ogburn, Charlton, *The Mysterious William Shakespeare,* Virginia: EPM, 1984
Oliver, H. J. (ed.), *The Taming of the Shrew*, Oxford: OUP, 1999
Rowse, A. L. (ed.), *The Poems of Shakespeare's Dark Lady,* New York: Clarkson N. Potter, 1979
Rutter, C. C., *Documents of the Rose Playhouse,* Manchester: MUP, 1999
Stone, L. *The Crisis of the Aristocracy: 1558–1641*, Oxford: Clarendon, 1965
Swan, G. "The Woman's Prize, A Sequal to *The Taming of the Shrew*", *The Oxfordian,* 10, Portland, 2007, 121–141
Thompson, A. (ed.), *The Taming of the Shrew,* Cambridge: CUP, 1984
Wells, Stanley & Gary Taylor (eds), *William Shakespeare: The Complete Works,* Oxford: OUP, 1986
—, *William Shakespeare: A Textual Companion*, Oxford: OUP, 1987
Wilson, J. Dover (ed.), *The Taming of the Shrew*, Cambridge: CUP, 1968

12

# All's Well that Ends Well

Noemi Magri

There is no mention of *All's Well* before 1623. Possible dates of composition range widely between 1567, the publication of William Painter's *Palace of Pleasure,* and the appearance of the play in the First Folio (F1) in 1623.

## Publication Date

*All's Well that Ends Well* was entered in the Stationers' Register on 8 November 1623 as one of eighteen plays which had not been published previously:

> Mr Blounte Isaak Jaggard. Entered for their Copie vnder the hands of Mr Doctor Worral and Mr Cole – warden, Mr William Shakspeers Comedyes Histories, and Tragedyes soe manie of the said Copies as are not formerly entered to other men. vizt. Comedyes. The Tempest. The two gentlemen of Verona. Measure for Measure. The Comedy of Errors. As you Like it. All's well that ends well. Twelft night. The winters tale. Histories. The thirde parte of Henry the sixt. Henry the eight. Coriolanus. Timon of Athens. Julius Caesar. Tragedies. Mackbeth. Anthonie & Cleopatra. Cymbeline.

It occupies the twelfth position in the comedies, after *The Taming of the Shrew* and before *Twelfth Night.* Chambers states that the text is not satisfactory, requiring considerable emendation. There is much variation in the nomenclature, especially for the Countess and for Bertram, which suggests to Chambers that the copy text was close to the author's copy.

## Performance Date

There is no recorded performance of a play entitled *All's Well that Ends Well* before 1741.

## Sources

Bullough states that the main plot – the love story of Helena and Bertram – is derived from the ninth novella of the third day in Boccaccio's *Decameron* (written around 1350, first published in 1470). William Painter's English translation of the Italian story was published in 1566, and again in 1569. The revised third edition (1575) is considered to be Shakespeare's direct source, although some details in the play demonstrate knowledge of the original Italian version as well. Bullough, following the argument of Wright (1955), suggests that Shakespeare must also have read Antoine le Maçon's French version (originally published in 1545 and reprinted many times) of the Italian novella since, according to Bullough, the name Bertram and that of Helena's father (Gerard de Narbon) are closer in form to those given in Maçon than to the ones given in Boccaccio or Painter. Wright even implies that, as Shakespeare must have had Maçon's translation, he did not need to read Painter.[1]

Some allusions to the history of contemporary France (the religious and civil wars), to Italian States and to the relationship between these countries and Austria have not been clarified. But historical details mentioned in the play, though identified only in part, reveal that the playwright had an accurate knowledge of the political affairs of the time.

## Orthodox Date

Chambers and Riverside favour 1602–3; Halliday, more precisely, opts for 1603. Chambers notes that the play is not (apparently) mentioned by Meres in 1598, which he sees as decisive evidence that it had not been written by then (see the Introduction for further discussion). Chambers also identifies the play as part of a group of 'problem comedies' at which no-one laughs, but there appears to be a happy ending. Hunter's "tentative dating" is 1603–4 (1967: xxv). Snyder, "with no reliable guides to further pinpointing", chooses 1604–5 (1998: 24). Wells & Taylor offer 1604–5.[2] Fraser & Leggatt date the play to 1604.

## Internal Orthodox Evidence

Fraser & Leggatt, in line with other scholars, are persuaded – by similarities of theme, characters, tone and versification – to relate the play closely to *Measure for Measure* and *Hamlet*, plays which are traditionally (though without direct evidence) dated to the early 1600s. Fraser & Leggatt also accept the suggestion that the play has many interesting themes in common with *Venus and Adonis* (published in 1593) and with the Sonnets (published in 1609). The date of the sonnets has not been established with any certainty; most editors see them as being either part of the vogue for sonnets in the early 1590s, or as perhaps inspired by them.[3]

## External Orthodox Evidence

Some early commentators thought this to be the play entitled *Love's Labour's Won*, listed as one of Shakespeare's comedies by Francis Meres in 1598 as follows:

> for Comedy, witnes his Gentlemen of Verona, his Errors, his Love Labors lost, his *Loue labours wonne*, his Midsummers night dream & his Merchant of Venice

For modern scholars the idea has become "less compelling" (Hunter, 1967: xx), and Snyder finds "no good grounds for seeing *All's Well* as an early play incompletely revised" (1998: 22).

## Oxfordian Date

Clark's proposal of 1579 is supported by Ogburn Jr. On stylistic grounds, Hess *et al.* suggest 1591 as the likeliest date for the play's composition. Nevertheless, the sources, historical allusions and geographical details of Florence in the 1570s strongly support the case for a date *c.* 1580.

## Internal Oxfordian Evidence

In the play, Bertram is deceived by a 'bed-trick', similar to the one staged in *Measure for Measure.* Anderson (145) points to the fact that Oxford was reportedly reunited with his estranged wife in 1583 by just such a stratagem. There are two separate accounts (given more fully in the chapter on *Measure for Measure*) by Francis Osborne (1593–1659) and in Morant and Wright *The Histories of Essex* (1836).

The playwright's treatment of the source and of the historical background provides evidence for earlier dating of the play than is commonly supposed. Shakespeare transfers Boccaccio's story to his own time and presents historical events which took place up to 1589. Orthodox commentators find no motivation for these historical additions, which serve no dramatic function. Allusions which do not belong to the plot appear to originate in the dramatist's experiences and recollections, which could be easily explained if Oxford were the author. Historical events are telescoped to increase effect, while some allusions may have been added later, during revision. Several points warrant commentary.

**a) Parolles's scarves**. The name of Parolles, not present in the source, is derived from François Rabelais' *Gargantua*, published in France in 1534.[4] Rabelais' satirical work mocks the society of the time, the Church and the educational methods of pedantic grammarians. One section is dedicated to the classification of "*parolles*" (= words). There is a clear connection between the character's name and his speech patterns: "I love not many words" (3.6.84); "You beg more than one word then" (5.2.40).

This strange character has been described as a traitor, coward, braggart, turncoat, opportunist or toady. As his name suggests, he is a man who speaks *à deux paroles*: a double-dealer, not a man of his word. He does not hesitate to betray his lord and friend Bertram. The old French lord Lafeu holds Parolles in contempt and despises his pride in his dress: "if ever thou beest bound in thy scarf and beaten thou shall find what it is to be proud of thy bondage" (2.3.224–6); and, "The soul of this man is in his clothes" (2.5.43–4). Diana, the Florentine lady loved by Bertram, describes Parolles as "that jackanapes with scarves" (3.5.87–8). When he is later exposed, the French soldier dismisses him with these words: "You are undone, captain – all but your scarf; that has a knot on't yet" (4.3.325–6).

Hunter acknowledges that "the latest clothes are Parolles' stock-in-trade" (1967: xlvii), but can offer no explanation for their function in the play. By contrast, Lambin suggests that Parolles's distinctive attire derives its significance from historical events in the late sixteenth century: namely the religious civil wars in France between Catholics and Huguenots, between Holy Leaguers and Royalists, between the powerful Dukes of Guise and any opposing party. Historically, the members of the Catholic League wore a scarf over the shoulder, across the back and breast, and knotted on one side. In the play the French Lord mockingly introduces Parolles to the other lords and soldiers in the Florentine camp as "the 'gallant militarist' ... that had the whole theoric of war in the knot of his scarf" (4.3.145–7). The Leaguers – often at variance with each other – changed the colour of their scarves more than once, as political events changed and with regard to the ensuing advantages to them. At first the scarf was red, like the one worn by the Spaniards; then white, as the Leaguers became supporters of King Henri III; black, after the murder of the Duke of Guise in 1588; and, finally, green, after Henri's assassination in 1589, as a sign of renewal and political stability.

It was the wearing of all these scarves simultaneously that created the comical element of the 'Parolles' scenes. That Parolles did so is evident in Lafeu's comment: "yet the scarves and the bannerets about thee did manifoldly dissuade me from believing thee a vessel of too great a burden" (2.3.204–6). These bannerets would be of regiments from various foreign armies. In the dramatist's mind, Parolles might have been the opportunist who followed any political or religious trend, no matter if honour were lost. By this theatrical means, Shakespeare may have meant to ridicule supporters of the Catholic League, or a particular member of it, who changed sides as easily as they changed scarves.

The whole business of Parolles's scarves suggests that the play was at least revised, if not written, at the time when English audiences would recognise his part in its satirical allusion to contemporary European politics, probably in 1589–90.

**b) Siena and Florence**. "The Florentines and Senois were at war" is all that Boccaccio's novella and Painter's literal translation say of the historical background. In the source there is no further development of the political relationship between France and Florence.

Shakespeare's play, meanwhile, presents historical events of the sixteenth century which are far more complex than the simple piece of information found in Boccaccio. Since the thirteenth century, the two Tuscan cities had been at war, at long intervals. Florence and Siena were fighting in Boccaccio's time and they were again at variance three centuries later. The King of France tells his court: "The Florentines and Senois are by th'ears" (1.2.1). He adds that he has been informed that Florence will ask him for help, but that he intends to refuse. Yet, he is ready to let his gentlemen leave for Tuscany and "stand on either part" (1.2.14): they may choose which city to support.

Shakespeare does not make the king take sides. Yet, in the sixteenth century, France's intervention in the Siena–Florence conflict had become a matter of serious and wide-ranging political implications, involving the most important European states. Shakespeare expands the source, and thus is closer to history. Times had changed: France had become the enemy of Florence and the ally of Siena. In letting the gentlemen support which ever side they wished in the conflict, Shakespeare is faithful both to Boccaccio's text and to history. Historically, it was not Florence but Siena which asked the help of the French king, who sent a small army to defend the town.

The Siena–Florence conflict of 1552–59 was only one of many episodes in the sixteenth-century wars fought between France and Spain over their rights, claimed on the grounds of previous marriages and inheritance, to the Duchy of Naples (which had fallen to Spanish rule in 1504) and to the Duchy of Milan (occupied by the Spaniards in 1535). The Catholic–Protestant conflict was another cause of the hostilities between the European states.

In Shakespeare's version, there seems to be no plausible reason why the French king should at first deny his help to Florence (1.2.12) – in Boccaccio, Beltramo does not hesitate to go to that city. However, from historical details as they are presented in the play, it is evident that the dramatist knew that Florence, an ally of Spain since 1552, had been raised to a dukedom by Emperor Charles V in 1559 and, thus, that it had long been an enemy of France. Interestingly, Oxford stayed in Siena in the winter of 1575–76, writing a letter from there on 3 January 1576, when the conflict between the two Tuscan cities was still a matter of great concern (Nelson, 132). Siena had lost its liberty only a few years before Oxford's visit: it had been occupied by Florentine troops and had fallen under the rule of Cosimo I, Duke of Florence. Such events were still a matter of great relevance to the citizens of Siena in 1575–6, and echoes of those conflicts are present in the play.

## External Oxfordian Evidence

Chambers (*ES*, iv, 96, 154) reports a Court performance "on twelf daie at night" in January 1579 of *The historie of the Rape of the second Helene* by the Lord Chamberlain's Men. Nothing is known about this play, but Clark is of the opinion that it may be a first version of *All's Well*. She bases her hypothesis on some passages containing allusions to classical mythology:

> in 1.3.65–70 Helen of Troy is mentioned; 1.3. 197–9 is an allusion to Tucia the Vestal Virgin who, falsely accused of breaking her vow, thus proved her chastity (the sieve is a symbol of virginity in classical iconography); and 2.1.159–167 is an elaborate image of the horses of the sun and Hesperus, the evening star.

In his 1790 edition of Shakespeare, Malone reproduced Henslowe's inventory (the original is now lost) of properties, costumes and playbooks belonging to the Lord Admiral's men. An entry, dated 13$^{th}$ March 1598, refers to "Perowes sewt, which Wm Sley were". Greg and Foakes & Rickert leave this unexplained, but 'Perowes' is probably Henslowe's spelling of 'Parolles', Bertram's follower and a character whose distinctive clothes (as we have seen) may be a key to historical events and to the identification of historical personages. Chambers (*WS*, ii, 55–78) informs us that Sley belonged to the Lord Admiral's men from 1590–2, after which he was with the Lord Chamberlain's company. Thus Henslowe's indication that Sley wore Parolles's costume, as one of the Lord Admiral's men, is a detail of great relevance in establishing that the play already existed by the early 1590s.

It remains to be explained why Henslowe's *Diary*, an invaluable document for dating Shakespeare's works, records no play entitled either *All's Well* or *The Second Helen*. Helena has been considered the heart of the play: everything develops around her. The medical knowledge she inherited from her father, a renowned doctor, leads her to go to Paris to cure the King's illness and, at the same time, to join Bertram. This skill (also attributed to Helena in the Italian source) may have been considered unusual in a female character by an Elizabethan audience more familiar with love-stricken heroines than with young ladies enlightened by scientific expertise. Helena is French, and Lafeu introduces her to the King as "Doctor She" (2.1.78). On 28 October 1594, Henslowe's *Diary* mentions a play called *The French Doctor*; twelve further performances of this play are recorded by November 1596.[5] This may well be *All's Well*, leaving the Folio editors to take the title that has come down to posterity from Helena's own comment on happy endings (4.4.35). Leggatt (in his introduction to Fraser's New Cambridge Shakespeare edition) asserts that the play does not contain any allusion to other plays after 1604 – the year of Oxford's death.[6]

## Conclusion

There is no ostensible reference to *All's Well* before it appeared in F1 in 1623. Possible dates of composition range widely between 1567, the publication of William Painter's *Palace of Pleasure,* and the appearance of the play in the First Folio (F1) in 1623.

It is possible that the play was presented at court under a different name, perhaps as *The Rape of the Second Helen*, in 1579 and later revised. The play seems to have been on the London stage in 1590–92 when William Sley, the actor playing the part of Parolles, was one of the Lord Admiral's men. Henslowe, as we have seen, mentions Parolles's theatre costume as the property of the Admiral's company in 1598–9.

## Notes

1. Earlier, Wright discussed the relationship of Painter's English translation with the French version in a previous article (1951). With regard to *All's Well*, Wright notes various French names: Helena describes herself as a pilgrim to "St Iaques le grand"; Lafeu bestows on Parolles a "cardecue", i.e. a *quart d'écu* (Onions), a silver coin struck from 1580 and not otherwise known in English before 1704 (*OED*); the names Lavanche and Parolles are also French.
2. In their second edition of *William Shakespeare: The Complete Works* (2005), Wells & Taylor re-date *All's Well* to *c.* 1608 so as to follow *Antony and Cleopatra*, thus demonstrating how difficult it is to fix a date with any certainty.
3. Fraser & Leggatt refer to Roger Warren's article, "Why does it end well? Helena, Bertram and the sonnets", *SS* 22 (1969), 79–92. If the play is close in style to the sonnets, then it would help to know their date. Unfortunately, there is further uncertainty about when these were written: Chambers (*WS*, I, 555–76) has a very detailed discussion on the possible dates of the sonnets without coming to a definite conclusion, intimating that they were composed during the 1590s. Wells & Taylor (1987: 123) place the sonnets only between 1593 and 1603.
4. The first translation of Rabelais' difficult French into English was by Sir Thomas Urquhart in 1653. The name 'Parolles' is spelt with a double -ll- in the Folio. Wells & Taylor (1986) spell 'Paroles' with a single -l- according to modern French orthographic practice, stating (1987: 494) that "Shakespeare clearly intended the French word and there is no justification for disguising it." Shakespeare's use of Rabelais is not confined to this play: Lake Prescott (1998) notes the allusion to "Gargantua's mouth" in *As You Like It*; the debt of Holofernes in *Love's Labour's Lost* to Gargantua's slow scholastic tutor, Holoferne, and the allusions of Mercutio (*Romeo & Juliet*) and Falstaff (*1, 2 Henry IV, Merry Wives*) to Panurge, the wily trickster and companion of Pantagruel.
5. See Foakes & Rickert (1961) for details of the precise dates on which *The French Doctor* was played.
6. See Fraser & Leggatt (2003: 10–11): "We do not have a secure date for *All's Well*; but if we place it in 1603, we may not be far wrong."

# Other Cited Works


Alexander, Peter, *Shakespeare's Life and Art,* London: James Nisbet, 1939

Anderson, Mark, *"Shakespeare" by Another Name,* New York: Penguin, 2005

Blakemore Evans, G. (ed.), *Riverside Shakespeare,* New York: Houghton Mifflin, 1997

Bullough, Geoffrey, *Narrative and Dramatic Sources of Shakespeare,* vol. II, London: Routledge and Kegan Paul, 1958

Chambers, E. K., *The Elizabethan Stage,* 4 vols, Oxford: Clarendon, 1923

—, *William Shakespeare, A Study of Facts and Problems,* 2 vols, Oxford: Clarendon, 1930

Clark, Eva Turner, *Hidden Allusions in Shakespeare's Plays,* New York: Kennikat, 1931 rptd 1974

Foakes, R. A. & R. T. Rickert (eds), *Henslowe's Diary,* Cambridge: CUP, 1961

Fraser, R. & Leggatt, A. (eds), *All's Well that Ends Well,* Cambridge: CUP, 2003

Greg, W. W. (ed.), *Henslowe's Diary.* 2 vols, London: A. H. Bullen, 1904

Halliday, F. E., *A Shakespeare Companion 1550–1950,* London: Duckworth,1952

Hess, W. R. *et al.,* "Shakespeare's Dates", *The Oxfordian,* 2, Portland, 1999

Hunter, G. K. (ed.), *All's Well that Ends Well,* London: Arden, 1959

Lake Prescott, Anne, *Imagining Rabelais in Renaissance England,* New Haven: Yale University Press, 1998

Lambin, Georges, *Voyages de Shakespeare en France et en Italie,* Geneva: E. Droz, 1962

Nelson, Alan, *Monstrous Adversary,* Liverpool: LUP, 2003

Maurois, A., *Histoire de la France,* Paris: Wapler, 1947

Ogburn, Charlton, *The Mysterious William Shakespeare,* Virginia: EPM, 1984

Onions, C. T., *A Shakespeare Glossary* (3rd edition), Oxford: Clarendon, 1995

Snyder, S. (ed.), *All's Well that Ends Well* Oxford: OUP, 1998

Valerio, M., *Detti e Fatti Memorabili,* Torino: UTET, 1971

Wells, Stanley & Gary Taylor (eds), *William Shakespeare: The Complete Works,* Oxford: OUP, 1986

—, *William Shakespeare: A Textual Companion,* Oxford: OUP, 1987

Wright, H. G., "How did Shakespeare come to know *The Decameron?", The Modern Language Review,* 50, 1955: 45–8

Wright, H. G., "The Indebtedness of Painter's Translations from Boccaccio in *The Palace of Pleasure* to the French Version of le Maçon", *The Modern Language Review,* 46, 1951: 431–5

13

# Twelfth Night, or what you will

## Marion Peel

Twelth Night can be dated between 1581, the publication of Barnabe Riche's *Farewell to Militarie Profession*, and 1602, when it was described in performance by John Manningham.

### Publication Date

*Twelfth Night* was entered in the Stationers' Register on 8 November 1623 as one of eighteen plays not previously published:

> Mr Blounte Isaak Jaggard. Entered for their Copie vnder the hands of Mr Doctor Worral and Mr Cole – warden, Mr William Shakspeers Comedyes Histories, and Tragedyes soe manie of the said Copies as are not formerly entered to other men. vizt. Comedyes. The Tempest. The two gentlemen of Verona. Measure for Measure. The Comedy of Errors. As you Like it. All's well that ends well. Twelft night. The winters tale. Histories. The thirde parte of Henry the sixt. Henry the eight. Coriolanus. Timon of Athens. Julius Caesar. Tragedies. Mackbeth. Anthonie & Cleopatra. Cymbeline.

It occupies the thirteenth position in the F1 comedies, coming after *All's Well that Ends Well* and before *The Winter's Tale.*

### Performance Dates

The notebook of John Manningham, a student of law at the Middle Temple, gives a detailed description of a performance there in 1602 of "a play called Twelue night or what you will".

> Feb. 2 At our feast wee had a play called Twelue Night, or what you will, much like the Commedy of Errores, or Menechmi in Plautus, but most like and neere to that in Italian called Inganni a good practise in it to make the Steward beleeve his Lady widdowe was in love with him, by counterfeyting a letter as from his Lady in generall termes, telling him what shee liked best in him, and prescribing his gesture in smiling, his apparaile, &c., and then when he came to practise making him beleeue they tooke him to be mad.

The diary is in the British Museum and Arlidge presents a photocopy of it. Although Race made suggestions that the nineteenth-century writer, John Payne Collier, may have tampered with some entries in Manningham's handwritten diary, the Arden editors, Lothian & Craik, offer four reasons for finding this particular entry genuine:

1. This passage is consistent in lay-out and presentation with other entries in the diary;
2. The mistake that Olivia is in mourning for a lost husband rather than a brother is easier to make when watching the play;
3. The statement that *Gl'Inganni* was the source is not made elsewhere by Collier (who stated Riche as the main source);
4. Collier printed "inscribing his apparell" rather than correctly reading "in smiling, his apparraile".

All editors have accepted the entry as genuine. The King's Men revived the play at Court, under its present title on 6 April 1616, and probably on 2 February 1623 as *Malvolio.*

## Sources

Bullough confirms John Manningham's entry that the ultimate source of the play's story is the Italian play *Gl'Ingannati* ('The Deceived Ones'), written and performed in Siena in 1531, first published in Venice in 1537 and often reprinted. It was translated into French as *Le sacrifice* by Charles Estienne in 1543, republished as *Les Abuséz* in 1549. Most orthodox scholars accept that Shakespeare read the original in Italian. Helen Kaufman argues that two other Italian plays, both by Nicolò Secchi, *Gl'Inganni* ('The Deceived') (composed *c.* 1547, published in Florence, 1562) and *L'interesse* ('Interest' composed *c.* 1547, published in Venice 1581), were probably used by the dramatist; in these a woman, dressed as a man, helps another man woo another woman.

Bullough identifies only one major source in English: the prose story of 'Of Apolonius and Silla' in *Riche his Farewell to Militarie Profession*, published in 1581. While ultimately adapted from Bandello's 1554 Italian play, Barnaby Riche's narrative is derived from Belleforest's 1579 French translation. In writing *Twelfth Night* Shakespeare evidently did use Riche's story, for both include details absent from all previous versions. Firstly, the dramatist used four words found in Riche, (coisterell, garragascoynes, pavion and galliarde) which are not used elsewhere in the canon; secondly, the references to dancing in 1.3 seem to draw on Riche's dedicatory epistle; thirdly, the punishment of Malvolio seems to draw on another of Riche's stories ('Of two brethren and their wives'). There was also a Latin version, *Laelia*, which was produced at Queens' College, Cambridge, possibly as early as 1546–7 (the college accounts show the purchase of costumes for the play) and again in 1595 when the Earl of Essex stayed at the college (Moore Smith, xxvi–xxviii).

## Orthodox Date

Chambers dates the play 1599–1600, immediately preceding *As You Like It* (as does the Signet editor). Most commentators date it 1600–02: Alexander, Lothian & Craik, Warren & Wells and Donno, propose the middle of 1601, Mahood suggests the end of 1601; Wells and Taylor suggest 1601–2, as does the Riverside edition. Halliday has the slightly earlier dating of 1600. Leslie Hotson proposed that the play was written for performance on the twelfth night of Christmas, 6 January 1601, in his full-length study, *The First Night of Twelfth Night.* Arlidge argues that the play was commissioned for performance on 2 February 1602.

Cairncross makes the unusual proposal of 1592.

## Internal Orthodox Evidence

Orthodox commentators have found a few topical allusions to support their 1600–02 dating. Two references to "the Sophy" (the Shah of Persia) (2.5.174; 3.4.271) are generally accepted as references to the journey of Sir Anthony Shurley to the Persian court; it was first known about in the summer of 1598, and two accounts of his travels (he became a roving ambassador for the Shah) were subsequently published, the first in September 1600, the second late in 1601. At 3.2.26. Warren and Wells see an allusion ("like an icicle on a Dutchman's beard") to the Arctic voyage of William Barentz, an account of which was mentioned in the Stationers' Register in 1598.

Further possible allusions from the text concern Will Kemp, a former member of the Lord Chamberlain's Men, who in summer 1601 returned from a continental tour during which he had met Sir Anthony Shirley in Rome. The Clown's comment: "I might say 'element', but the word is overworn" (3.1.57–8) is taken to be an allusion to the triple use of 'out of [one's] element', as a catch-phrase, in Dekker's *Satiromastix*, performed in the second half of 1601 by the Lord Chamberlain's Men and the Children of Paul's. The sung dialogue between Sir Toby and the Clown (2.3.100–8) is closely based on the song 'Farewel dear loue since thou wilt need be gon', first published in Robert Jones's *The First Book of Songes and Ayres* in 1600.

Hood Phillips argues that a celebrated case which went before the Star Chamber in 1602, between Sir Posthumous Hoby and William Eure, involved night-time disturbances and probably inspired the scene between Sir Toby Belch and his friends. Finally, commentators generally agree that Maria's comic image of Malvolio's newly adopted physiognomy – "he does smile his face into more lines than is in the new map with the augmentation of the Indies" (3.2.74–5) – alludes to Edward Wright's 'A Chart of the World on Mercator's Projection', published in Hakluyt's *Voyages in* 1599 and again, with minor corrections, in 1600; the map has radiating rhumb lines, suggesting the wrinkles around Malvolio's eyes. A different interpretation is offered under 'Internal Oxfordian Evidence', below.

Mahood, however, observes that playwrights often revise their script in rehearsal, and adds:

> other changes in a play may be made years later and without the playwright's knowledge. Shakespeare's fellow actors presumably saw no harm in adding the odd topical joke to his plays from time to time.

Thus if the topical allusions are no more than few, it is possible that they were added at a later stage to an existing text.

## External Orthodox Evidence

Manningham's reference to the Middle Temple performance is the only reliable evidence for the existence of the play by 1602. The Arden editors assert there is "no reason to believe that this was the first production of the play". They adduce the following arguments:

a) Manningham did not mention that the play was new;
b) the manuscript shows the word ~~mid~~, crossed out before the title 'twelve' is written, suggesting he had heard of the title *A Midsummer Night's Dream* and momentarily confused the titles;
c) Manningham records similarities with other plays, suggesting that *Twelfth Night* had been on the stage long enough for there to have been talk about its sources.

None of the above arguments seems strong enough to discount the play as newly composed in February 1602. Anthony Arlidge, the Master of Entertainments at the Middle Temple in London, argues that the play was commissioned for performance on 2 February, 1602. He points out that there are a large number of legal phrases, correctly used, which show it was intended for an Inn of Court. These include Sir Andrew's proof upon "the oaths of judgement and reason"

(3.2.13) and his knowledge of the distinction between "battery" and "assault" as well as the right to strike first in self-defence to prevent a threatened attack (4.1.32–5):

> I'll go another way to work with him. I'll have an action of battery against him, if there be any law in Illyria. Though I struck him first, yet it's no matter for that.

Secondly, Arlidge notes some references which he calls 'inn-jokes'. John Shurley, who made the journey to Persia cited above and was Treasurer to the Middle Temple in 1602, is twice the object of ridicule, firstly at 2.5.173–4:

> FABIAN I will not give my part of this sport for a pension of thousands to be paid from the Sophy.

The second reference occurs at 3.4.271–2:

> SIR TOBY They say he has been a fencer to the Sophy.
> SIR ANDREW Pox on't. I'll not meddle with him.

Thirdly, Arlidge links Shakespeare with one of the law students, Thomas Green, who completed his studies at the Middle temple in 1602 and moved to Stratford was where he linked to Shakespeare through legal actions concerning the Welcombe Enclosure (Chambers, *WS*, ii, 141–152).

Leslie Hotson researched contemporary records and argued that the play was especially written for performance on 6 January 1601. In a memorandum, George Carey as the Lord Chamberlain, Lord Hunsdon, gave instructions:

> To confer with my Lord Admirall and the Master of the revells for taking order generally with the players to make choyse of [the] play that shalbe best furnished with rich apparell, have greate variety and change of Musicke and daunces, and of a Subiect that may be most pleasing to her Maiestie

The occasion was when Queen Elizabeth's guest was Don Virginio Orsini, Duke of Bracciano. According to Hotson, the noble Orsini was love-sick for the unattainable Olivia, identified as Queen Elizabeth. In his letters in Italian, this Orsini describes how he sat next to the Queen in the Palace at Whitehall and saw a play performed on 6 January. Hotson describes him as "virtuous, noble, of great estate, of fresh and stainless youth".

Three arguments against Hotson's claim have been advanced:

a) The Lord Chamberlain's memorandum for choosing a suitable play mentions neither title nor author, and it stipulates that it include expensive costumes and a great variety of music and dancing: *Twelfth Night* is not such a play (*Much Ado* is said to be a much better candidate).

This does not appear to be a very strong argument: both Orsino and Olivia are high ranking personages and would be expected to dress in expensive clothing; there is certainly a lot of music in *Twelfth Night* and much scope for dancing.

b) the announcement of the Duke's impending visit left only eleven days, in the busy Christmas period, to write and rehearse a new play; against this it might be said that the play had been planned since the Duke was expected at some point. The coincidence would only be in the title (which appears to have no relation to the action of the play).

c) it is unlikely that the Queen would allow a performance to continue in which she was presented as love-sick for an errand boy or that the visiting Duke would approve the use of his name for the lovesick hero of a comedy.

Hotson's proposal has not found general support among scholars, but certainly raises some interesting connections.

## Oxfordian Date

Clark and Ogburn Jr favour 1580–1; Holland opts for 1587 (or at least finds evidence of revision then). Hess *et al.* find late 1600 the likeliest date, but allow that the present play could have been revised from an earlier version.

## Internal Oxfordian Evidence

We return to the "new map, with the augmentation of the Indies", suggested as evidence that the play was written in 1600–01. Cairncross, not an Oxfordian but prepared to reconsider historical evidence with an open mind, identified the "new map" as "the Molyneux map or globe of 1592". Its forthcoming publication was announced in 1589, and Emery Molyneux engraved his "very large and most exact terrestriall globe" three years later. The newness of this map was emphasised in Blundeville's *Exercises* (1594): "there are found out divers new places towards the North Pole as in the East and West Indies, which were unknown to Mercator". Wright's 1600 map was based on his projection of Molyneux's 1592 globe; indeed, geographers often designate this cartographic landmark the 'Wright–Molyneux Map'. Like the later map which copies it, the globe has the rhumb lines which evoke Maria's unusual simile. Curiously, one of Molyneux's globes stands in the library of the Middle Temple.[1]

Cairncross also states that the Clown's sentence "But indeed, words are very rascals, since bonds disgraced them" (3.1.19–21), was interpreted by some commentators as a reference to the Privy Council's inhibition against the players in 1600 or 1601 – an explanation which he finds unsatisfactory.

> But is it not obvious that some equivocation in the terminology or interpretation of legal bonds is intended? It suggests rather the situation in the sub-plot of Greene's *Looking Glass for London and England* (acted March 8, 1592), where a usurer takes advantage of his debtor's failure to comply with the *literal* conditions of the bond. Such a case seems to be alluded to in *Twelfth Night*. Greene and Shakespeare might well be alluding to the same case. Such an event would confirm the evidence of the map, and fix the date of *Twelfth Night* around 1592. (Cairncross, 132)

Other evidence concerning the acting companies leads Cairncross to conjecture that *Twelfth Night* was written for performance at the Middle Temple by Pembroke's Men on 6 January 1593. Chambers (*ES*, ii, 128) confirms that pembroke's Men performed at Court at that time but the title of the play was not recorded. Two further reasons support Oxfordian authorship and an earlier date: firstly, the sources were in Italian and/or French, which would have been easy enough for the 'Italianate earl' to read. Secondly, Oxford had studied at Gray's Inn and was therefore in a position to have learned much of the legal knowledge evident in this play.[2]

## External Oxfordian Evidence

There is a record from the archives of Abraham Fleming, one-time secretary to Oxford, and his literary protégé, of Oxford writing a play which follows the plot of *Twelfth Night:*

> a pleasant conceit of Vere, earl of Oxford, discontented at the rising of a mean gentleman at the English court, circa 1580

This was mentioned in a list published in 1732 by the antiquarian, Francis Peck, of documents he intended to have printed. Unfortunately, Peck failed to achieve his aim and the document has disappeared. Clark and all the Ogburns base their 1580–1 date on the identification of this "pleasant conceit" with the first draft of *Twelfth Night*. So the play is assumed to allude to the contemporary rivalry for Queen Elizabeth's favour between Oxford and his upstart rival, Sir Christopher Hatton, satirised in Malvolio – "Some are born great … and some have greatness thrust upon 'em" (2.5.140–1). Hatton was a leading Puritan, and Malvolio is termed a "Puritan" three times within seven lines (2.3.140–6); Hatton's nickname was 'Sheep' or 'Mutton', and Malvolio is called a "niggardly rascally sheep-biter" (2.5.5); Hatton's Latin pen-name was 'Felix Infortunatus' (the happy unfortunate one) and this is reversed – "The Fortunate Unhappy" (2.5.154) – in the signature of the prank letter that Malvolio receives. That Hatton was jealous of Oxford has been noted by Alison Weir (289):

> Hatton, who was prone to expressing his resentment in tears or sulks, deeply resented the favour shown by the Queen towards Oxford [i.e. in 1572] because he had recently apparently been given cause to believe that he himself stood higher in her affection than anyone else.

The rivalry between Hatton and Oxford continued over many years. Various identifications have been made between characters in the play and other historical personages. Apart from the clear likeness between Olivia and the Queen, Clark identified Orsino with François, duc d'Alençon (a suitor to Elizabeth at the time) and Sir Andrew Aguecheek with Sir Philip Sidney. Anderson (148–50) has noted the striking parallel between the play and the events in 1579 when Alençon sent ahead of himself an envoy called Jean de Simier. Elizabeth was though to have fallen in love with the envoy instead of with the Duke. As Alison Weir observes (318–21): "Anyone observing them together might have been forgiven for concluding that she meant to marry him rather than his master." Mallin concurs that *Twelfth Night* is based on events some twenty years before its [earliest known] performance concerning the Alençon–Simier wooing of Elizabeth as well as problems with Puritans. A further identification concerns the role of the Fool. Many commentators have noticed the exceptional licence of the Fool to mock Olivia openly (1.5) and Orsino (5.1). They see Oxford as the Fool, who is excused in the words of Olivia (1.5.88):

> There is no slander in *an allowed fool*, though he do nothing but *rail*;

The play may have been linked with an academic performance at Cambridge. On 1 March 1595 an anonymous Latin play, *Laelia,* was performed (or revived; see section 'Sources') at Queens' College, Cambridge to celebrate Essex's visit. The one surviving manuscript (edited by Moore Smith) reveals several similarities to *Twelfth Night*. Sebastian's meeting with Olivia's clown (4.1.1–22) is paralleled in *Laelia*. Both plays have a time discrepancy: in *Twelfth Night,* the elapse of three months is twice mentioned (5.1.92 & 97), yet the stage action lasts three days; in *Laelia* the action lasts two days, while a fortnight is supposed to have elapsed. Viola's readiness to follow Orsino to death (5.1.130–6) parallels *Laelia*. The adjective 'festus' [= festal, celebratory], which occurs twice in the Latin play, suggests the name 'Feste' and "a pang of heart" (2.4.89) matches 'cordolium'. Boas is alone among orthodox commentators in linking *Laelia* with *Twelfth Night*. Oxfordians believe that the author of *Laelia* adopted aspects of the existing Shakespearean play. Interestingly, as a boy, Oxford had studied at Queens' College, Cambridge, where the play was staged.

## Conclusion

This play can be dated between the 1581 publication of Barnaby Riche's *Farewell to Militarie Profession*, and 1602, when it was described in performance by John Manningham. There are a few internal references to support a date *c.* 1601, but these may be no more than topical additions to an existing play. Cairncross's arguments for dating the play, while not designed to support Oxfordian authorship, indicate the likelihood that *Twelfth Night* was largely in its present form by the end of 1592, about nine years before the date conventionally assumed. There are strong indications, from events and people at Court, to suggest an original date of composition *c.* 1580–1.

## Notes

1. For the Molyneux Globe of 1592, see D. B. Quinn, *The Roanoke Voyages, 1584–90* (1955: 850). Mark Monmonier (2004: 11) has described the Wright–Molyneux map. See C. E. A. Bedwell *A Brief History of the Middle Temple* (1909: 83) for the acquisition of the globes.
2 Nelson (23–5) describes how the young earl attended Queens' College, Cambridge and (37) how his daily educational timetable at Cecil House (37) included two hours of French and two hours of Latin. Oxford enrolled at Gray's Inn in 1567 (Nelson, 46) but his purchase of expensive books in French, Italian and Latin showed literary interests. Oxford spent about a year (1575–6) in Italy where an Italian servant testified to the earl's proficiency in Italian and Latin (Nelson, 121–41; 155–7).

## Other Cited Works

Arlidge, Anthony, *Shakespeare and the Prince of Love: The Feast of Misrule in the Middle Temple*, London: Giles de la Mare, 2000
Alexander, Peter, *Shakespeare's Life and Art,* London: James Nisbet, 1939
Anderson, Mark, *"Shakespeare" by Another Name,* New York: Penguin, 2005
Blakemore Evans, G. (ed.), *Riverside Shakespeare*, New York: Houghton Mifflin, 1997
Boas, F. S., *The University Drama in the Tudor Age,* Oxford: Clarendon Press, 1914
Bullough, Geoffrey, *Narrative and Dramatic Sources of Shakespeare*, vol. II, London: Routledge and Kegan Paul, 1958
Cairncross, A. S., *The Problem of Hamlet – a Solution*, London: MacMillan, 1936
Chambers, E. K., *The Elizabethan Stage,* 4 vols, Oxford: Clarendon, 1923
Chambers, E. K., *William Shakespeare, A Study of Facts and Problems,* 2 vols, Oxford: Clarendon, 1930
Clark, Eva Turner, *Hidden Allusions in Shakespeare's Plays,* New York: Kennikat, 1931 (reprinted 1974)
Donno, E. S. (ed.), *Twelfth Night*, Cambridge: CUP, 1985 (updated 2004)
Elam, Kier (ed.), *Twelfth Night, or what you will*, London: Arden, 2008

Halliday, F. E., *A Shakespeare Companion*, London: Duckworth, 1952
Hess, W. R., *et al.*, "Shakespeare's Dates", *The Oxfordian*, 2, Portland, 1999
Holland, H. H., *Shakespeare, Oxford and Elizabethan Times,* London: Denis Archer, 1933
Hood Phillips, Owen, *Shakespeare and the Lawyers*, London: Routledge, 1957 (reprint 2005)
Hotson, Leslie, *The First Night of 'Twelfth Night'* London: Rupert Hart-David, 1954
Kaufman, Helen A., "Nicolò Secchi as a source of *Twelfth Night", SQ*, 5 (1954), 271–80
Lothian, J. M. & T. W. Craik (eds), *Twelfth Night,* London: Arden, 1975
Mahood, M. M. (ed.), *Twelfth Night*, Harmondsworth: Penguin, 1968
Mallin, E. S., *Inscribing the Time: Shakespeare and the End of Elizabethan England,* Berkeley: University of California Press, 1995
Moore Smith, G. C. (ed.), *Laelia*, Cambridge: CUP, 1910
Nelson, Alan, *Monstrous Adversary,* Liverpool: LUP, 2003
Ogburn, Charlton, *The Mysterious William Shakespeare,* Virginia: EPM, 1984
Race, S., "Manningham's Diary: the case for Re-examination" in *N&Q*, 199, 1954, 380–3
Warren, Roger, & Stanley Wells (ed.), *Twelfth Night or what you Will*, Oxford: OUP, 1994
Weir, Alison, *Elizabeth the Queen,* London: Pimlico, 1998
Wells, Stanley & Gary Taylor (eds), *William Shakespeare: The Complete Works,* Oxford: OUP, 1986
Wells, Stanley & Gary Taylor, *William Shakespeare: A Textual Companion*, Oxford: OUP, 1987

14

# The Winter's Tale

## Eddi Jolly

*The Winter's Tale* can be dated between 1588, when all the main sources were available, and 1611, when it was described in performance by Simon Forman. The play may even be earlier if Greene's *Pandosto* is accepted as derived from *The Winter's Tale.*

### Publication Date

*The Winter's Tale* was entered in the Stationers' Register on 8th November 1623, one of eighteen plays in the First Folio (F1) which had not been registered previously:

> Mr Blounte Isaak Jaggard. Entered for their Copie vnder the hands of Mr Doctor Worral and Mr Cole – warden, Mr William Shakspeers Comedyes Histories, and Tragedyes soe manie of the said Copies as are not formerly entered to other men. vizt. Comedyes. The Tempest. The two gentlemen of Verona. Measure for Measure. The Comedy of Errors. As you Like it. All's well that ends well. Twelft night. The winters tale. Histories. The thirde parte of Henry the sixt. Henry the eight. Coriolanus. Timon of Athens. Julius Caesar. Tragedies. Mackbeth. Anthonie & Cleopatra. Cymbeline.

*The Winter's Tale* occupies the fourteenth and final position among the comedies in F1. Chambers describes the printed text as good and believes that the preceding blank page suggests that there was a delay in obtaining a copy for it.

The Stationers' Register has an entry for 22nd May 1594 for an otherwise unknown play:

> *Edward White* Entred for his Copie vnder th[e h]andes of bothe the wardens a booke entituled *a Wynters nightes pastime.* vjd

Some commentators, following Malone, have seen *Wynters Nightes Pastime* as an early attempt to publish *The Winter's Tale*.[1]

## Performance Dates

The most important is Simon Forman's record of a performance of '*the Winters talle*' at the Globe on Wednesday, 15 May 1611. Forman gives a summary of the play's plot, identifying it clearly as *The Winter's Tale* as it is known today:

> Observe there how Leontes, the King of Sicilia, was overcome with jealousy of his wife with the King of Bohemia his friend, that came to see him; and how he contrived his death and would have had his cupbearer to have poisoned, who gave the King of Bohemia warning thereof and fled with him to Bohemia.

Subsequent performances included those at Court on 5 November 1611, in 1612–13 (as one of the seven Shakespeare plays performed at Whitehall before the marriage of King James's daughter, Princess Elizabeth, to Frederick, Elector Palatine), in 1618, around 1619, and another at Court on 18 January 1624 (Chambers: *WS*, I, 288–9).

## Sources

Bullough sees the main source as Greene's *Pandosto or The Triumph of Time*, published in 1588 and reprinted in 1607 as *Dorastus and Fawnia*. This assumption is reasonable according to the recorded performance dates. However, if the date of composition were substantially earlier, Bullough's thesis would need to be reviewed, and the direction of influence would then be reversed. Bullough adds Ovid's *Metamorphoses* (translated by Golding in 1567) which in Book X describes Pygmalion's statue coming to life. Pafford argues that Autolycus's skills could have been drawn from Greene's 'conny-catching' leaflets, published 1591–2.[2]

There is divided opinion as to whether Shakespeare was influenced by the Greek Romances. Samuel Wolff (1912: 432–463) first argued that Shakespeare had used Longus's second-century romance *Daphnis and Chloe*, a story of children abandoned in the countryside and later found to be of high parentage; he also observes that the hunt during a storm (described by the shepherd in 3.3) is present in *Daphnis* but has no parallel in *Pandosto*.

Carol Gesner observes that the visit of the King and Camillo parallels that of the lord of the manor and his train in *Daphnis and Chloe*, perhaps another example of Shakespeare going directly to Longus (1970: 181). *Daphnis and Chloe*, composed originally in Greek, has been attributed to Longus, *c.* 200 AD. Although it did not appear in print until 1598, an Italian translation was published by the humanist Annibale Caro (1507–66) and a French translation from a Greek manuscript by Jacques Amyot (1559) appeared as *Les Amours Pastorales de Daphnis et Chloé.* An English translation was published by Angel Day in 1587. Gesner gives further consideration to Shakespeare's use of the Greek Romances; she proposes a secondary source, that of Heliodorus's *Aethiopica* (translated by Thomas Underdowne in 1569). In *Aethiopica,* the entire moving force is a king's jealousy. She also supports the suggestion that Shakespeare took the deathlike swoon of Hermione and her dramatic return to life from Mateo Bandello's twenty-second tale (1970: 122).[3]

Chambers suggests that some names were taken from Sidney's *Arcadia,* 'Autolycus' from the *Odyssey* (xix. 394) and 'Florizel' from *Amadis de Gaule,* a romance published originally in Spanish in 1524, translated into French in 1551 and eventually into English. *Amadis de Gaule* also describes various statues which come to life. Chambers speculates about whether the statue scene, absent from Greene, was suggested by Lyly's *Woman in the Moon* (1597), or Marston's *Pygmalion's Image* (1598). Sir Sidney Lee proposes that a few lines in Autolycus's speech – "shall be flayed alive; then 'nointed over with honey, set on the head of a wasps' nest" (4.4.784–6) – were drawn from Boccaccio's story of Ginevra.[4]

Bullough notes that many of the names came from Plutarch, such as Camillus, Antigones, Cleomenes and Dion. He is sure that "our rogue" [Autolycus] came from Golding's 1567 translation of Ovid's *Metamorphoses.* Bullough also points out that Vasari's *Lives of the Painters* (1550) gave two epitaphs on Giulio Romano's tomb, one of which claimed that Jupiter envied Romano when he saw his "sculpted and painted statues breathe". Vasari was not translated into English until 1850. These sources indicate Shakespeare's wide reading in both classical and contemporary European literature.

## Orthodox Date

Malone (in his *Variorum* of 1778 and his *Attempt to Ascertain the Order in which the plays attributed to Shakespeare were Written*) suggests 1594, since the Stationers' Register has an entry for 22 May of that year for *a Wynters Nightes Pastime.* Malone was uneasy about the date, however, because Meres did not include *The Winter's Tale* in his list of twelve examples of plays by Shakespeare in *Palladis Tamia* in 1598. Accordingly, Malone wondered whether the date should be 1601 or 1602. Later he suggested 1613, on the grounds that Ben Jonson, in his 1614 *Bartholomew Fair,* alluded to recent plays in his dig at "Tales, Tempests and suchlike Drolleries".

The vast majority of twentieth-century scholars put forward dates which continue to ignore the matter of the Stationers' Register entry of 1594. Like Chambers, who suggests early 1611, scholars often opt for a date of composition close to Simon Forman's recording of a performance: Wells & Taylor, Riverside and Snyder all propose 1610–11; Pafford, early 1611, as does Orgel.

Eric Sams and Janet Spens are exceptions. Sams notes that several of Shakespeare's plays exist in two or more very different versions, which is not true of the plays of his contemporaries. "The simple explanation," he writes, "now universally overlooked, is that the earlier publications were his first versions."

## Internal Orthodox Evidence

Chambers suggests 1611 on the grounds "that the bear and the dance of satyrs were both inspired by those in Jonson's *Masque of Oberon*", first performed on 1 January 1611, though he goes on to speculate that the idea of the bear came from *Mucedorus* (1598). Pafford, too, cites Jonson's masque as "reason to suppose" that the play was written after New Year's Day 1611 (2002: xxii). More generally, Pafford finds that the play's theme, language, style and spirit "all point to a late date", as do "the nature and use of the songs" (2002: xxiii). Again, the direction of influence regarding Jonson is dependent upon the date of *Oberon* being 1611, and would have to be reconsidered if an earlier date was agreed.[5]

Spens is one of the few scholars who take into account the so-called "lost years" and the sudden emergence of the very accomplished *Venus and Adonis* in 1593. She suggests that, previously, Shakespeare had been actively engaged in dramatic work. This leads her to suspect that "all the Romances… were written originally by Shakespeare at the very beginning of his career" (1922: 92).

Walpole, the author of *Historic Doubts on the Life and Reign of King Richard III* (1768), locates the play's composition during the lifetime of Elizabeth I – in other words, before 1603:

> *The Winter's Tale* … was certainly intended (in compliment to Queen Elizabeth) as an indirect apology for her mother, Anne Bolyn. . . . The subject was too delicate to be exhibited on the stage without a veil . . . . The unreasonable nature of Leontes, and his violent conduct in consequence, form a true portrait of Henry VIII. . . . Not only the general plan of the story is most applicable, but several passages . . . touch the real history nearer than the fable. Hermione on her trial says "for honour, 'Tis a derivative from me to mine, And only that I stand for." This seems to be taken from the very letter of Anne Bolyn to the King before her execution, where she pleads for the infant princess, his daughter. Mamillius . . . dies in his infancy; but it confirms the allusion, as Queen Anne, before Elizabeth, bore a still-born son. But the most striking passage . . . [is] where Paulina, describing the new-born princess, and her likeness to her father, says, "She has the very trick of his frown".[6]

Alison Weir, a modern historian and author of *The Six Wives of Henry VIII* (1991), reinforces Walpole's view. She describes how, at her trial, Anne sat in the centre of the court and heard her indictment read in all its detail. Anne refuted each charge firmly, "arguing her case with such clarity that her innocence . . . seemed manifest" (1991: 326). Her old nurse gave way to hysteria when the verdict was announced. Anne apparently received the sentence calmly.

## External Orthodox Evidence

Forman's note is the only evidence that the play had been written by 1611.

## Oxfordian Date

Both Clark and Holland propose that the play was first written in 1584. Clark's argument is based primarily on seeing the play in an historical context. The senior Ogburns favour 1586; Ogburn Jr., 1594 (on the basis of the S.R. entry for '*a Wynters nightes pastime*').

## Internal Oxfordian Evidence

Various points arise. Ideas and lines in *The Winter's Tale* would have contemporary resonance if the play were Elizabethan. Clark begins with a historical note about the Queen commenting on the "smut" on Raleigh's nose, on 27 December 1584. This may be paralleled by Mamillius, whose nose is "smutched" (1.2.123). It could further be argued that the Queen's reluctance to condemn Mary, Queen of Scots, is echoed by Camillo:

> If I could find example
> Of thousands that had struck anointed kings
> And flourish'd after, I'd not do't. (1.2. 358–60)

Thomas Underdown dedicated his translation of Heliodorus's *Aethiopica* to Oxford in 1569, when Oxford was nineteen, with a further edition appearing in 1577 (Nelson, 236–7). This may indicate the young earl's taking an early special interest in the genre. It is possible that the germ of the idea of turning the story into drama might have begun at that time. Angel Day, who published his translation of *Daphnis and Chloe* in 1587, had dedicated *The English Secretarie* to Oxford in the previous year, praising the earl as a man "of learned view and insight", "whose infancy from the beginning was euer sacred to the Muses" (Nelson, 381). Does this establish a link?

Dott. Noemi Magri argues that Oxford, on his travels through Northern Italy in 1575, had seen the remarkable works of Giulio Romano, an artist whose wonderful *trompe l'oeil* murals may still be seen at the Palazzo Te in Mantua. Oxford would also have known that Romano was famed for constructing his statues out of powdered marble (marble proper was a substance hard to obtain in the Mantuan district), and for painting them in an extraordinarily life-like manner. Shakespeare's claim that Hermione's statue was

> a piece many years in doing, and now newly performed by that rare Italian master Giulio Romano, who, had he himself eternity and could put breath into his work, would beguile nature of her custom, so perfectly he is her ape. (5.2.94–9)

would then be not an example of ignorance. It is usually assumed that the claim was an error and that Shakespeare, relatively uneducated as he was, did not know that Romano was a painter, not a sculptor In fact, Romano's ability as a sculptor was described by Giorgio Vasari in 1550 in *Le Vite de Piu Eccellenti Pittori, Scultori e Architettori* (but not translated into English until 1850 when it appeared as *Lives of the Artists*).

A similar point pertains to the criticism of Shakespeare's ignorance of geography which was first mentioned by Jonson in 1619, who said that the dramatist was ignorant that Bohemia was landlocked:

> Thou art perfect then our ship hath touched upon
> The deserts of Bohemia? (3.3. 1–2)

Firstly, it should be noted that Greene's *Pandosto* gives a coastline to Bohemia:

> Egistus King of Sycilia, who in his youth had bene brought up with Pandosto, desirous to shewe that neither tracte of time, nor distance of place could diminish their former friendship, provided a navie of ships, and sayled into Bohemia to visite his old friend and companion. (*Pandosto,* part 1, para. 3)

So Shakespeare may have been following Greene as a source (even though in *Pandosto* the King of Sicily is accused of adultery with the Queen of Bohemia). In addition, the dramatist may have been more knowledgeable than his critics: Pafford (2002: 66) points out that Bohemia under Ottakar II (King of Bohemia 1253–78) had a sizeable coast on the Adriatic from modern-day Trieste to the Istrian peninsula (details in *New Cambridge Medieval History,* V, 395; map p. 757). Bohemia regained this foothold in the early sixteenth century under Vladislas II, the King of Bohemia, Dalmatia and Slavonia. Oxford had spent several months in Venice in 1575–6, and the history of the region would have become known to him. Jonson laughed at the 'error,' but maybe Jonson did not know.[7]

Most of the sources which have been claimed to have been used were available in the 1580s. Certainly Oxford could have read them in Italian or in French (Nelson, 53). These points, along with Walpole's suggested parallels, do begin to root the play in the second half of Elizabeth's reign. Regardless of who the playwright was, such allusions give the play a context it lacks for a 1610–11 date. That sense of context intensifies when aspects of Oxford's personal life are considered. The chief theme of the play is estrangement and then reconciliation between husband, wife and child. Oxford's separation from his wife, Anne, and his refusal to acknowledge paternity of his first child, led to attempts at reconciliation by several outside parties (Nelson, 141–154). In desperation, the Countess of Suffolk proposed in a letter to Mary de Vere dated December 1577, bringing Oxford's daughter to him: ". . . we will have some sport with him . . . and whilst my Lord your brother is with you, I will bring the child as though it were some other child of my friends, and we will see how nature works in him to like it, and tell him it is his own after" (Nelson, 176–7).

## External Oxfordian Evidence

This play is pertinent to the decade of the 1580s, which features travel, voyages, discoveries, shipwrecks and lost hopes, for example of a North West passage. Holland proposes that *Winter's Tale* was first written in 1584. Part of his evidence is that wool prices in England in that year were the same as those quoted in the play (4.3.32–4); his source was Stafford's *A briefe conceipte of English policye.*[8] After his time in the Tower and a period of banishment from Court, Oxford was restored to the Queen's favour in June 1583 (Nelson, 189–90). Thus Walpole's idea that the play was a compliment to Elizabeth is reinforced.

The Stationers' Register, 1594, has an entry for *a Wynters nightes pastime.* That this should refer to a version of *The Winter's Tale* must be considered, because it would not be the only play known from records dated well before actual publication (e.g. *Macbeth*, seen by Simon Forman in 1611, first published 1623), nor the only one to have a change of name (e.g. *The Moor of Venice*, now known as *Othello*).

## Conclusion

*The Winter's Tale* can be dated between *c.* 1585 and 1611. The orthodox dating of this play as *c.*1610–11 depends on several assumptions: that it was written close to the time of the first known performance, that it was a play of the 'mature' playwright, and that the playwright was born in 1564. Bates points out that a 1610–11 date obviously excludes the authorship of Oxford, because he died in 1604 (1998: 66). However, Simon Forman merely records a performance of the play, not the date of its composition.

The date of 1610–11 ignores the similar title of an earlier play in 1594, and further assumes that the author used a number of sources which mainly date from some 20–30 years earlier. This gives the play little or no historical context. A date of composition in the mid to late 1580s, or even just before the entry in the Stationers' Register of 1594, resolves those issues, regardless of who the playwright was.

If Oxford were the author, the topical references, the apparent autobiographical elements, and the closeness to Oxford of the sources and/or their authors, would further support an earlier date for composition, perhaps in the second half of the 1580s.

## Notes

Acknowledgement: thanks are due to Robert Detobel, for providing references regarding doubts about which texts derived from which.

1. Pafford notes that a "booke entituled a Wynters nightes pastime" (Arber, Transcript of the Registers, 1875, ii. 307b; 1877, iv) was entered under Edward White in the Stationers' Register on 22 May 1594 (shortly after two other plays with similar titles to Shakespearean plays: *Famous Victories* and *King Leir*). As Pafford notes (2002: xxv*n*), the word 'night' also appears in the title of the play performed on 5th November 1612 ("The Kings Players: The 5th of nouember A play Called ye winters nightes Tayle"; 2002: xxiii). This concurrence has prompted commentators to suggest "there was an early version which Shakespeare revised in 1611" (2002: xxv). The play was entered into the SR again on 29 June 1624.
2. Pafford (2002: xxx). See also textual notes on pp.81–3, 87–88, 105, 123–4, 127, 134 for Pafford's detailed exposition of these linked features.
3. Stuart Gillespie, *Shakespeare's Books* (2004) gives a detailed discussion. He asserts that Wolff's argument about the influence of *Daphnis and* Chloe is a "now generally discounted suggestion" but that some details in the plays "not anticipated in Shakespeare's immediate sources are present in the [Greek] Romances themselves".
4. Lee (1925: 426). In Boccaccio's story (2nd day, novella ix), the villain Ambrogiuolo, after "being bounden to the stake and anointed with honey," was "to his exceeding torment not only slain but devoured of the flies and wasps and gadflies wherewith that country abounded" (*c.f. Decameron,* translation by John Payne, 1893, i.164). There is another grisly echo at 4.4.791–2, where the clown's son is to be beheld "with flies blown to death."
5. Pafford's concluding paragraph on this point is considerably confused. He writes: "Shakespeare may have begun to write *The Winter's Tale* before the end of 1610 but may not have started it until after the performance of *Oberon* on 1 January 1611: in any case he had certainly finished the play in time for it to be performed on 15 May 1611." (2002: xxiii). Pafford's difficult prose highlights the consequences of the problems which beset the commentator in discussing the solid identification of the direction of influence on any writer.
6. Walpole, *Historic Doubts* (1768: 114–5). This work has recently been digitised by Oxford University and can be freely accessed (in pdf format) online. This suggestion has been pursued by a modern historian, Eric Ives in *The Life and Death of Anne Boleyn* (2004). Ives argues that Hermione's speech closely matches Anne Boleyn's speech in her own defence, that Leontes in his tyrannous jealousy correlates closely to Henry VIII and that one of Henry's friends, Sir

Henry Norreys, was executed for maintaining that the Queen was innocent. According to this view, Perdita corresponds to the banished daughter of Anne & Henry, i.e. Elizabeth herself.

7. In a letter to The Times (of London) on 20 May 1991, Professor Robert Pynsent of the University of London School of Slavonic and East European Studies wrote with reference to Otakar II:

   > At various times before and after that thirteenth century king, Bohemia owned various Adraitic and baltic coastal areas. From 1526 until 1918 (Charles I), with one Stuart hiccup, the Hapsburg kings of Bohemia always had coastal possessions. Bohemia became a mythological kingdom only with Oscar Wilde's Florizel of Bohemia and, a few years later, Mr Chamberlain.

8. *A briefe conceipte of English policye* (STC 23133) was published in 1581 and was attributed to 'W. S.' usually identified as William Stafford (1554–1612), but thought by some have been written by John Hales (d. 1571). See Furnivall's 1876 edition for further discussion.

## Other Cited Works

Abulafia, D. (ed.), *The New Cambridge Medieval History, vol. V, c. 1198– c. 1300,* Cambridge: CUP, 1999

Alexander, Peter, *Shakespeare's Life and Art,* London: James Nisbet, 1939

Anderson, Mark, *"Shakespeare" by Another Name,* New York: Penguin, 2005

Bate, J., *The Genius of Shakespeare,* Oxford: OUP, 1998

Bullough, Geoffrey, *Narrative and Dramatic Sources of Shakespeare*, vol. VIII, London: Routledge and Kegan Paul, 1975

Chambers, E. K., *The Elizabethan Stage,* 4 vols, Oxford: Clarendon, 1923

Chambers, E. K., *William Shakespeare, A Study of Facts and Problems,* 2 vols, Oxford: Clarendon, 1930

Clark, Eva Turner, *Hidden Allusions in Shakespeare's Plays,* New York: Kennikat, 1931 (reprinted 1974)

Furness, H. H., *The Variorum Shakespeare: the Winter's Tale,* Philadelphia: J.B. Lippincott 1898 (reprinted 1926)

Gesner, Carol, *Shakespeare and the Greek Romance*, Lexington: University of Kentucky Press, 1970

Halliday, F. E., *A Shakespeare Companion*, London: Duckworth, 1952

Harvey, P. D. A., *Maps in Tudor England* (joint publication of the Public Record Office and the British Library), London: PRO, 1993

Hess, W. R., *et al.* "Shakespeare's Dates", *The Oxfordian*, 2, Portland, 1999

Holland, H. H., *Shakespeare, Oxford and Elizabethan Times,* London: Denis Archer, 1933

Lee, S., *Shakespeare: a Life*, London: John Murray, 1925

Magri, Noemi, "Italian Renaissance Art in Shakespeare: Giulio Romano and *The Winter's Tale"* in *Great Oxford,* ed. R. Malim, Tunbridge Wells: Parapress, 2004

Moore Smith, G. C., "Lily, Greene and Shakespeare" *Notes and Queries, VIII,* 14 December 1907

Nelson, Alan, *Monstrous Adversary,* Liverpool: LUP, 2003
Ogburn, Dorothy and Charlton Sr, *Shake-Speare: the man behind the Name*, William Morrow and Co, 1962
Ogburn, Charlton, *The Mysterious William Shakespeare,* Virginia: EPM, 1984
Orgel, S., *The Winter's Tale,* Oxford: OUP, 1998
Pafford, J. H. P. (ed.), *The Winter's Tale,* London: Arden, 1963 (2nd edition, 2002)
Sams, E., *The Real Shakespeare: Retrieving the Early Years, 1564–1594*, New Haven: Yale UP, 1995
Snyder, S. & D. Curren Aquino (eds), *The Winter's Tale,* Cambridge: CUP, 2007
Spens, J., *Elizabethan Drama*, London: Methuen, 1922
Ward, B. L., *The Seventeenth Earl of Oxford,* London: John Murray, 1928.
Weir, A., *The Six Wives of Henry VIII*, London: Pimlico, 1991
Wells, Stanley & Gary Taylor (eds), *William Shakespeare: The Complete Works,* Oxford: OUP, 1986
Wells, Stanley & Gary Taylor, *William Shakespeare: A Textual Companion*, Oxford: OUP, 1987
Williamson, H. R., *The Day Shakespeare Died,* London: Michael Joseph, 1962
Wolff, S.L., *The Greek Romances in Elizabethan Prose Fiction*, New York: Columbia University Press, 1912

# The Histories

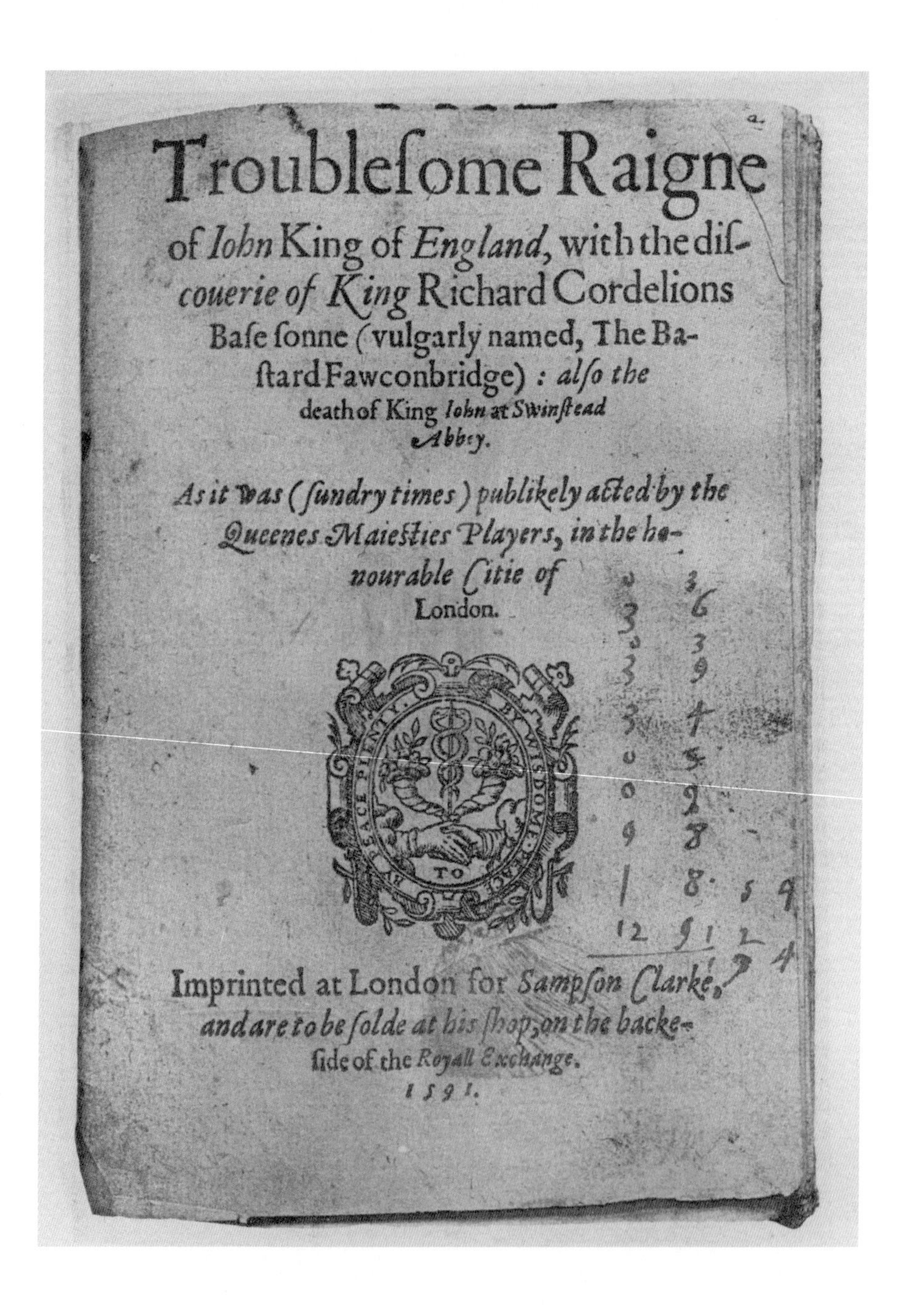
Troubleſome Raigne
of *Iohn* King of *England*, with the diſ-
*couerie of King* Richard Cordelions
Baſe ſonne (vulgarly named, The Ba-
ſtard Fawconbridge) : *alſo the*
death of King *Iohn at Swinſtead*
*Abbey.*

*As it was (ſundry times) publikely acted by the*
*Queenes Maieſties Players, in the ho-*
*nourable Citie of*
London.

Imprinted at London for *Sampſon Clarke,*
*and are to be ſolde at his ſhop, on the backe-*
ſide of the *Royall Exchange.*
*1591.*

8. Title page to the anonymous first quarto of *Troublesome Raigne of King John,* Part I, 1591. It has generally been believed that this play was by another author, but some scholars have argued that it was an early version by Shakespeare which he later revised.

# The Dating of Shakespeare's History Plays

By Kevin Gilvary

The 'scholarly consensus' on the dating of Shakespeare's History plays in general derives from the magisterial work of Sir Edmund Chambers. He gave us a neat scheme of dates for almost forty plays apparently composed between 1590 and 1610, at the rate of two a year, comprising a comedy and either a history or a tragedy. Chambers had proceeded with caution and devoted seventy pages to his discussions of the 'Problem of Authenticity' and 'The Problem of Chronology'. His ordered list of dates is qualified:

> There is much of conjecture, even as regards the order, and still more as regards the ascriptions to particular years. These are partly arranged to provide a fairly even flow of production when plague and other inhibitions did not interrupt it (Chambers, *WS*, I, 269).

Later scholars, however, have not followed such a cautious approach, but have simply accepted his dates as 'fact' rather than 'conjecture'. Wells and Taylor (in *William Shakespeare: A Textual Companion*) follow Chambers in giving a detailed account of the 'Canon and Chronology of Shakespeare's plays' and offer a very similar pattern of dating. Yet a comment in answer to Honigmann's attempt to offer earlier dates implies their own lack of firm evidence about the dates of the plays:

> Curiosity abhors a vacuum, and the urge to push Shakespeare's first play farther and farther back into the 1580s is palpably designed to fill the black hole of our ignorance about those years; but since we must then spread the same number of plays over a larger number of years, by filling one big vacuum in the 1580s, we simply create other vacuums elsewhere (Wells & Taylor, *TxC*, 97).

Wells and Taylor suggest that Shakespeare cannot have written any plays in the 1580s because he would then have had a period in the 1590s when he wrote no plays. Wells and Taylor state the date of composition of *The Life and Death of*

*King John* as 1596, notwithstanding their own admission that the play "could be, and has been, dated in any year in the decade between these two termini" [i.e. between Meres' list in 1598 and Holinshed's *Chronicles* in 1587].

## Date of Composition

There is no direct evidence for the date of *composition* of any of Shakespeare's plays. As Stephen Greenblatt sums up (*Will in the World: How Shakespeare became Shakespeare*, 2004: 13):

> Those springs [of Shakespeare's art] would be difficult enough to glimpse if biographers could draw upon letters and diaries, contemporary memoirs and interviews, books with revealing marginalia, notes and first drafts. Nothing of the kind survives.

In the absence of such direct evidence for the date of *composition* of any of Shakespeare's plays, many assertions and proposals have become gradually accepted as 'fact' in 'scholarly consensus'.

## Stationers' Register

The Stationers' Register (SR) notes the intention of a publisher to *publish* a work, establishing a kind of copyright as well as an 'imprimatur' – an official licence to go to print. Chambers quotes the dates and the entries of Shakespeare's plays in the Stationers' Register and assumes that most of the history plays were composed shortly before their registration, e.g. *Henry V* is said to have been composed in 1599 and published in 1600. This assumption has been followed by later commentators, yet is open to question: some plays, which are thought to have been composed *c.* 1591, e.g. *1 Henry VI* were not recorded in the SR until the publication of the First Folio (1623). Similarly, not all printed plays had been registered in the SR, e.g. there is no entry for *The First Part of the Contention* (*2 Henry VI*). An entry in the SR is probably only useful as a final date (*terminus ante quem*) for the composition of a play, but even then there is doubt: *The Famous Victories of Henry V* was registered in 1594 but, according to the title page, this play was not published until 1598.

## Publications: Quartos (& an Octavo)

The title page of a published play often gives useful information, including the date of publication. Sir Edmund Chambers in *William Shakespeare: A Study of Facts and Problems* quotes the dates for the actual publication of the plays in quarto as mentioned in their title pages.

There were only two publications of history plays in quarto after 1616. A collection of ten plays attributed to Shakespeare was issued in 1619 by Pavier. Only eight of those plays are recognised now as Shakespearean, including three history plays: *Henry V*, *Henry VI Part 2*, *Henry VI Part 3* (these two combined as a single play titled *The Whole Contention between the Two Famous Houses, Lancaster and York*), and two other plays attributed to Shakespeare, *A Yorkshire Tragedy* and *Sir John Oldcastle*. In 1622, sixth quartos appeared of *1 Henry IV* and *Richard III*. The First Folio contained 36 plays by Shakespeare, eighteen of which had not been published before, including three history plays: *King John, 1 Henry VI* and *Henry VIII*.

## Two Tetralogies or an Octology?

Apart from *King John* and *Henry VIII*, the plays fall neatly into two groups of four, and it is generally supposed that they were conceived in two separate groups. Some commentators envisage an original grouping of four plays (*1, 2, 3 Henry VI–Richard III*), which treated events continuously from the funeral of Henry V (1422) to the accession of Henry VII (1485). These four plays are usually referred to as 'The First Tetralogy', although it is not absolutely certain that they were composed before the so-called 'Second Tetralogy', or even whether they were conceived as four plays from the outset. Others see an initial grouping of three plays, *First Part of the Contention–Tragedy of Richard Duke of York–Richard III*, eventually being expanded with a prequel, to emerge as the tetralogy *1, 2, 3 Henry VI–Richard III*.

Similarly, most commentators see the four plays, *Richard II, 1, 2 Henry VI–Henry V*, as conceived at the outset and written later, thus forming the 'Second Tetralogy.' Some commentators envisage another grouping of three plays, *I Henry IV–2 Henry IV–Henry V*, as a trilogy emerging from the anonymous *Famous Victories of Henry V*, eventually being expanded with their own prequel to emerge as the tetralogy *Richard II, 1, 2 Henry VI–Henry V*. Most see these four plays as being conceived as a continuous series from the initial feud between Bolingbroke and Mowbray.

In 2005–08, the Royal Shakespeare Company performed these eight History plays in sequence, which they readily called an octology. While accepting that the tetralogy *1, 2, 3 Henry VI–Richard III* was written before the tetralogy *Richard II, 1, 2 Henry VI–Henry V*, both the director, Michael Boyd, and the company believed that the eight plays were conceived as a continuous sweep of history – an octology. Members of the ensemble have given fascinating accounts of the endeavour in Smallwood's edition *The Players of Shakespeare 6: Essays in the Performance of Shakespeare's History Plays* (Cambridge: CUP, 2007).

## Use of Sources

Geoffrey Bullough in *Narrative and Dramatic Sources of Shakespeare* conducted a very thorough review of the sources used by Shakespeare. In volume III, he dealt with "the earlier history plays" and in volume IV with "the later plays". He concluded that the main sources for the History plays were Hall and Holinshed. Further examination of sources is given in more recent editions of individual plays, e.g. in the Arden, New Cambridge and Oxford Shakespeare editions.

**Edward Hall, *The Union of the Two Noble and Illustre Famelies of Lancastre and Yorke*** (1548–50). Bullough argues that the author began his plan for both the tetralogies by studying Hall's moralising narrative of English History from Henry IV to Henry VIII. Hall (?1498–1547) relied on previous chroniclers, especially Polydore Vergil's account in Latin, *Historia Anglica* (1512–13, later editions, inc. 1545) and, in turn, influenced other writers, e.g. Richard Grafton, *A Chronicle at Large and Meere History of the Affayres of Englande* (1569).

Hall emphasised the providential pattern of history in the coming of the Tudors, which ended the disastrous Civil Wars. Hall's account begins half-way through the reign of Richard II in 1387 with the quarrel between Bolingbroke and Mowbray – exactly where Shakespeare begins *Richard II.* Hall's Chapter Titles anticipate Shakespeare's plays:

| | |
|---|---|
| i | The unquiet time of King Henry the Fourth |
| ii | The victorious acts of King Henry the Fifth |
| iii | The troublous season of King Henry the Sixth |
| iv | The prosperous reign of King Edward the Fourth |
| v | The pitiful life of King Edward the Fifth |
| vi | The tragical doings of King Richard the Third |
| vii | The politic governance of King Henry the Seventh |
| viii | The triumphant reign of King Henry the Eighth |

Tillyard argued (and Bullough agreed) that Hall provided the moral and providential framework for the two tetralogies. While there has been extended criticism of Tillyard's view of the extent of a 'Tudor myth', most commentators editors agree that Hall provides some kind of moral framework for the plays. His work was prohibited and burnt under Mary for giving support to Henry VIII and Protestantism.

**Raphael Holinshed, *The Chronicles of Englande, Scotlande, and Irelande.*** The first edition appeared in two volumes in 1577 and the second was greatly expanded into three volumes in 1587. This second edition, which is often bound together into a single book, comprises some 3½ million words, about four times the length of the First Folio and was thus both valuable and bulky. Holinshed and his co-authors were more like editors, as the work is really a compendium of previous chroniclers and geographers, drawing especially on

Hall, but also on writings by Robert Fabyan, *The New Chronicles of England and France* (1516), parts of Grafton's *Chronicle* (1569) not used by Hall, John Stow's *Chronicles of England*, (1580) and John Foxe's *Actes and Monuments* (1583). Bullough demonstrates how Holinshed is frequently the principal source for the detailed material in the plays. In fact, so close is Shakespeare to Holinshed, e.g. in Canterbury's speech in *Henry V* at 1.2, that Bullough believes the dramatist had the work open in front of him as he composed. Boswell-Stone established that for most readings the second edition was used by Shakespeare, a view supported by Lucille King (see the section on *2 Henry VI*). It is, however, just possible that the playwright used these sources independently of Holinshed.

There was a strong personal link between Oxford and Raphael Holinshed, who prepared the main source for all the History plays. Holinshed was a member of Sir William Cecil's household, where Oxford had been a ward and where his wife Anne Cecil generally resided. Holinshed had dedicated his first edition to Cecil in 1577. In addition, Holinshed had sat as a juror to the enquiry that found Oxford not guilty of manslaughter in 1567. He had also issued a pamphlet in 1573 attacking a man called Brown as the murderer involved in an incident in Shooters Hill, thereby deflecting blame from Oxford (for details see *Monstrous Adversary,* Alan Nelson's unsympathetic biography of Oxford, pp. 48, 90–2). It is possible that Oxford had access to the same material as the editors and contributors to Holinshed's second edition in 1587, which would allow an earlier date than is generally proposed.[1]

Like Hall, ***A Mirrour for Magistrates*** (1559) influenced Shakespeare in providing a tragic framework for his characters in that they often owed their downfall to their own actions. *The Mirror for Magistrates* contained nineteen first person narratives in its first edition (with seven more in its second edition, 1563), in which ghosts from English history, principally from Richard II to Richard III, lament their own downfalls and warn future rulers to moderate their conduct. These narratives were planned in three volumes:

Volume 1: to the end of Edward IV's reign: Tresilian, Mortimer, Gloucester, Mowbray, Richard II, Owen Glendower, Northumberland, Cambridge, Salisbury, James 1 (of Scotland), Suffolk, Cade, York, Clifford, Worcester, Warwick, Henry VI, Clarence, Edward IV; mention is made of three others – those of the duchess Eleanor and duke Humphrey of Gloucester (printed in 1578) and that of Somerset (printed 1563).

Volume 2: to the end of Richard III's reign, contained only eight tragedies: those of Woodville, Hastings, Buckingham, Collingbourne, Richard III, Shore's Wife, Somerset and the Blacksmith.

Volume 3: was planned to cover the period to the end of Mary's reign.

There were over twenty other narratives covering earlier generations printed in later versions. Thus almost all the narratives in the *Mirror for Magistrates* which influenced Shakespeare were to be found in the first edition of 1559.[2]

**Samuel Daniel's epic poem *The First Fowre Bookes of the Civile Wars*** was registered on 11 October 1594 and published twice in 1595 (according to the title page), i.e. two years before the registration and publication of *Richard II*. The first three books deal with the story of Richard II. Most commentators follow Chambers and Bullough in viewing this poem as derivative from the Chronicles (to which it is very much closer) and influential upon the play. Both play and poem make the Richard II's Queen (historically aged ten) a mature woman. Both play and poem make the Prince and Hotspur (historically two years older than Bolingbroke) roughly contemporaries.

The dating of the history plays obviously affects our understanding of the direction of influence; it is usually asserted that Daniel embarked on his epic poem before Shakespeare began his tetralogy, but it is possible that Shakespeare's handling of various themes influenced Daniel. It is not thought that Shakespeare knew Daniel or whether he knew that they were dealing with the same material on a big scale. It is possible however that Daniel's patron, Mary Sidney, brought him into contact with Oxford through her literary salon.

## Obscure Sources

Each of Shakespeare's history plays shows knowledge from at least one obscure source. The great achievement of the dramatist is to integrate arcane details seamlessly into the dramatic narrative. Here is a sample of sources; more details can be found in individual chapters:

| | |
|---|---|
| *King John* | The Wakefield Chronicle (in Manuscript) |
| *Richard II* | French Chronicles *Histoire du Roy d'Angleterre Richard II* |
| *1 Henry IV* | Legal case ivolving Sir John Fastolf of Nacton |
| *2 Henry IV* | anonymous play *Hickscorer* |
| *Henry V* | Latin Chronicle *Gesta Henrici Quinti* |
| *1 Henry VI* | Talbot's epitaph in the Cathedral at Rouen |
| *2 Henry VI* | Grafton's *Chronicles* (for the Simcox miracle) |
| *3 Henry VI* | Ovid's *Heroides* |
| *Richard III* | Dr Legge's *Ricardus Tertius* |
| *Henry VIII* | Margaret of Navarre's Dream |

This is relevant to apportioning Authorship, as Oxford is far more likely to have had access to these unusual sources than Shakespeare of Stratford.

## References to Plays of Shakespeare

Contemporary references to the history plays have been collected by Chambers with occasional additions noted in the Arden and Oxford Shakespeare editions.

Some references seem to be to printed texts attributed to Meres, who praises Shakespeare's *Richard II, Richard III* and *Henry IV*, but does not mention the *Henry VI* plays, which were not attributed to Shakespeare until 1619. If some references, e.g. Henslowe's 1598 mention of a gown for the character of Henry VIII, actually refer to costumes used in Shakespeare's play, then much earlier dates are entailed.

## References in the Plays to External Events

Some commentators, e.g. David Bevington in *Tudor Drama and Politics* (1968), believe that the plays only reflect matters of contemporary concern without alluding to specific events. Others, e.g. Christopher Highley in *Shakespeare, Spenser and the Crisis in Ireland* (1997), argue for precise references. Further consideration of this can be found in the sections on *Richard II, 2 Henry VI* and *Henry V*.

## Shakespeare's Use of Existing Plays

Shakespeare appears to have used a number of plays published anonymously in the 1590s:

| | |
|---|---|
| *Thomas of Woodstock* (?1 *Richard II*) | manuscript |
| *Troublesome Reign of King John* | 1591 (quarto) |
| *True Tragedie of Richard the Third* | 1594 (SR & quarto) |
| *Famous Victories of Henry V* | 1594 (SR); 1598 (quarto) |
| *Arden of Faversham* | 1594 (SR); 1598 (quarto) |
| *Edward III* | 1595 (SR); 1596 (quarto) |

Some commentators, including Oxfordians, view these as early versions of plays by Shakespeare.

## Early Starter?

Most scholars agree that *I Henry VI* is among Shakespeare's earliest plays. In *Pierce Penniless* (1592), Nashe had defended the idea of plays, especially those derived from the *Chronicles*:

> First, for the subject of them, (for the most part) it is borrowed out of our English chronicles, wherein our forefathers' valiant acts (that have lain long buried in rusty brass and worm-eaten books) are revived, and they themselves raised from the grave of oblivion, and brought to plead their aged honors in open presence; than which, what can be a sharper reproof to these degenerate effeminate days of ours?

Ribner believes that few history plays (none of which was Shakespeare's) had been performed on stage by the time of *Pierce Penniless*; from Ribner's list, only a small number were derived from the Chronicles: Legge's *Ricardius Tertius* (a play in Latin, which is only known to have been performed in Cambridge in 1579), Peele's *Jack Straw* (1587–90), the anonymous *True Tragedy of Richard the Third* (1588–90), Peele's *Edward I* (1590–1) Marlowe's *Edward II* (1591) and the anonymous *Famous Victories of Henry the Fifth* (1588) and *1, 2 Troublesome Raigne of King John* (1588–89).

Both J. Dover Wilson (*The Fortunes of Falstaff*) and E. M. W. Tillyard (*Shakespeare's History Plays*) proposed that Shakespeare had begun composing his plays before 1590. E. A. J. Honigmann in *Shakespeare: the 'lost years'*(1985) has developed an alternative chronology, in particular for the history plays, thus suggesting that Nashe was referring to various plays by Shakespeare in 1592. Honigmann proposed the following dates:

| | | |
|---|---|---|
| 1586 | *Titus Andronicus* | |
| 1587 | *Two Gentlemen of Verona* | |
| 1588 | *1 Henry VI* | *Taming of The Shrew* |
| 1589 | *2 Henry VI* | *Comedy of Errors* |
| 1590 | *3 Henry VI;* | *Richard III* |
| 1591 | *King John* | *Romeo & Juliet* |

Although his premise that Shakespeare had a Catholic connection with Lancashire is doubted by many, this does not disqualify Honigmann from showing that the existing evidence can support earlier dates than is usually proposed.

Wells & Taylor, however, reject the idea that Shakespeare was an early starter: 'We have little reason to suppose that Shakespeare began writing in 1586.' They list five arguments against earlier dates:

(1) Honigmann supposes that *The Troublesome Reign of John, King of England* was written in 1590–1, then published in 1591 because the Queen's Men were in financial difficulties. Wells & Taylor do not accept this.

(2) Honigmann's chronology, by pushing back the traditional dating of the early histories, creates a large gap between *King John* (early 1591) and *Richard II* (1595), in which Shakespeare purportedly wrote no history plays at all – a genre which, on Honigmann's account, he had created almost single-handed, and which had been the staple of his early success.

(3) Likewise, after resounding and early successes in tragedy (*Titus* 1586?, *Romeo* 1591?), we are to suppose that Shakespeare did not write another tragedy for eight years.

(4) All of Shakespeare's histories, with the possible exception of *Contention*, must post date publication of Holinshed's *Chronicle*, second edition (1587: STC 13569), and most scholars have

believed that the sudden popularity of the genre owes something to the swell of nationalism associated with the defeat of the Spanish Armada (August 1588).

(5) Finally, Honigmann's early dating asks us to believe that Shakespeare was not mentioned by name in any surviving document for the first seven years of his playwriting career—years in which he allegedly dominated theatrical life, writing a series of plays so successful that they were busily echoed and pillaged by all his elders and contemporaries.

These arguments suggest that dating some plays to the 1580s is unlikely, but it remains a possibility that the history plays were written earlier than has been generally supposed.

## Oxfordian Hypothesis: History Plays as Tudor Propaganda

When ascribing the works of Shakespeare to Edward de Vere, Oxfordians tend to date the plays earlier. The following points apply to the history plays:

(1) Oxford wrote history plays as instruments of Tudor Orthodoxy, mainly from the mid 1580s when the Spanish threat was at its highest. The plays graphically represent the futility of dissension and disloyalty.

(2) Oxford had connections with the authors of both the main sources used for the History plays. Edward Hall attended Grays Inn, as did Oxford at a later date.

(3) Oxford had closer connections with Raphael Holinshed. The first edition of *The Chronicles* had been dedicated to Oxford's father-in-law, William Cecil, Lord Burghley in 1577. Holinshed seems to have been a member of the Cecil household, as he had sat as a juror on the enquiry that found Oxford not guilty of manslaughter in 1567. Holinshed had also issued a pamphlet in 1573 attacking a man called Brown as the perpetrator of a murder in Shooters Hill, thereby deflecting blame from Oxford. The incident is very reminiscent of Prince Hal's antics in *Famous Victories* and in *1 Henry IV.* It is possible that Oxford was composing his plays and consulting the same sources at the same time and in the same place (Cecil House) as Holinshed was preparing his Chronicles. Thus Oxford had the opportunity to consult the same sources as Holinshed before the results appeared in the 1587 edition.

## Conclusion

We do not know the date of composition of any of Shakespeare's history plays. All we can propose for sure is the range of dates within which they were composed.

## Notes

1. Holinshed's *Chronicles* is now the subject of careful scrutiny. See page 287, note 2.
2. For *A Mirrour for Magistrates*, Stuart Gillespie (*Shakespeare's Books*, 2004) gives a brief review of Lily Campbell's 1960 edition.

## Other Cited Works

Anderson, Mark, *"Shakespeare" by Another Name.* New York: Gothem, 2005
Bevington, David, *Tudor Drama and Politics*, Cambridge, MA: Harvard UP, 1968
Boswell-Stone, W. G., *Shakespeare's Holinshed: The Chronicle and The Historical Plays Compared*, London: Longwell's, 1896
Bullough, Geoffrey, *Narrative and Dramatic Sources of Shakespeare*, vol. III ('The Early Histories') vol. IV ('The Later Histories'), London: Routledge and Kegan Paul, 1960 & 1962
Chambers, E. K., *William Shakespeare A Study of Facts and Problems*, 2 vols, Oxford: Clarendon, 1930
Clark, Eva Turner, *Hidden Allusions in Shakespeare's Plays.* New York: Kennikat, rptd 1974
Farina, William, *De Vere as Shakespeare: An Oxfordian Reading of the Canon,* Jefferson, NC: McFarland, 2006
Greenblatt, Stephen, *Will in the World: How Shakespeare became Shakespeare,* London: Jonathan Cape, 2004
Highley, Christopher, *Shakespeare, Spenser and the Crisis in Ireland*, Cambridge: CUP, 1997
Honigmann, E. A. J., *Shakespeare, the "lost years"*, Manchester: MUP, 2005
King, Lucille, "2 and 3 Henry VI – Which Holinshed?", *PMLA*, 1935: 745–52
Nelson, Alan, *Monstrous Adversary,* Liverpool: LUP, 2003
Ogburn, Charlton, *The Mysterious Mr Shakespeare,* Virginia: EPM, 1984
Ribner, Irving, *The English History Play in the Age of Shakespeare*, Princeton, NJ: Princeton UP, 1957
Tillyard, E. M. W., *Shakespeare's History Plays,* London: Chatto & Windus, 1944
Vickers, Sir Brian, *Shakespeare, co-author,* Oxford: OUP, 2002
Wells, Stanley & Taylor Gary, *William Shakespeare: A Textual Companion*, Oxford: OUP, 1987
— (eds), *William Shakespeare: The Complete Works,* Oxford: OUP, 1988
Wilson, J. Dover, *The Fortunes of Falstaff,* Cambridge, CUP, 1943

15

# The life and death of King Iohn

Kevin Gilvary

The earliest date for the known versions of *The Life and Death of King John* (*KJ*) is probably the year of the second edition of Holinshed (1587). The latest possible date is the publication of the First Folio in 1623.

## Publication of *The Troublesome Raigne* (*TR*)

*The Life and Death of King John* (*KJ*) did not appear until the First Folio in 1623. But a very similar play called *The Troublesome Raigne of Iohn King of England*, (*TR*) had been published anonymously in two parts in 1591. The title pages of subsequent editions of *TR* in 1611 and 1622 attributed the play to 'W Sh' and to 'W Shakespeare' respectively. Meres in 1598 mentions a play by Shakespeare called *King John*. The relationship between the two plays has been the subject of much debate.

The general consensus is that *Troublesome Raigne* was not by Shakespeare but by another playwright and that Shakespeare, using this as a source play, composed his own version of *King John* in 1595–96. It has been suggested that the reprints of *TR* were deliberately misattributed so as to boost sales in the same way as was done with *Sir John Oldcastle* or *The London Prodigal*. There have been some, e.g. Honigmann, who have not accepted this version and see *KJ* as the original play, thus pre-dating the publication of *TR* in 1591. Others, e.g. Beaurline, see both *KJ* and *TR* as derived from the same pre-1591 outline plot (scenario), whether or not such an outline had been prepared by Shakespeare.

*The Troublesome Raigne* was published anonymously in two parts, without being recorded in the Stationers' Register:

THE
Second part of the
troubleſome Raigne of King
*Iohn, conteining the death*
of Arthur Plantaginet,
the landing of Lewes, and
the poyſning of King
Iohn at Swinſtead
*Abbey.*
*As it was (ſundry times) publikely acted by the Queenes Maieſties Players, in the honourable Citie of*
London.

Imprinted at London for *Sampſon Clarke,*
*and are to be ſolde at his ſhop, on the backe-*
ſide of the *Royall Exchange.*
*1591.*

9. Title page to the anonymous first quarto of *Troublesome Raigne of King John, Part 2,* 1591; It has generally been believed that this play was by another author but some scholars have argued that it was an early version by Shakespeare, which he later revised.
By permission of the Folger Shakespeare Library.

[Q1 1591] The Troublesome Raigne of Iohn King of England, with the discouerie of King Richard Cordelions Base sonne (vulgarly named The Bastard Fawconbridge): also the death of King Iohn at Swinstead Abbey. As it was (sundry times) publikely acted by the Queenes Maiesties Players, in the honourable Citie of London. . . . .

[Q1 1591] The Second part of the troublesome Raigne of King Iohn, conteining the death of Arthur Plantaginet, the landing of Lewes, and the poysning of King Iohn at Swinstead Abbey. As it was (sundry times) publikely acted by the Queenes Maiesties Players, in the honourable Citie of London. . . . The Second part of the troublesome Raigne of King Iohn, containing the en-traunce of Lewes the French Kings sonne: with the poysoning of King Iohn by a Monke.

The mention of the Queen's Men would suggest a performance date *c.* 1584–9 when they were particularly active (according to Scott McMillin and Sally-Beth MacLean, *The Queen's Men and their Plays,* 1999).

The two parts of *TR* were published together in 1611 and attributed to 'W. Sh', which is usually taken to indicate William Shakespeare:

[Q2 1611] The First and second Part of the troublesome Raigne of John King of England. . . . As they were (sundry times) lately acted by the Queenes Maiesties Players. Written by W. Sh. . . . Valentine Simmes for Iohn Helme . . . 1611.

The two parts were published again in 1622, this time attributed to 'W. Shakespeare':

[Q3 1622] The First and second Part of the troublesome Raigne of John King of England. . . . As they were (sundry times) lately acted. Written by W. Shakespeare. . . . Aug. Mathewes for Thomas Dewe . . . 1622

The bibliographical entries up to 1622 relate only to *The Troublesome Raigne of King John,* which Chambers calls the source-play.

## Publication of *The Life and Death of King John* (*KJ*)

The absence of *The Life and Death of King John* (*KJ*) from the entries for F1 in the Stationers' Register suggests that *KJ* (like *Taming of the Shrew*) was regarded as 'commercially identical with its predecessor' i.e. that *KJ* is a revision by the same author of *TR*:

[F1 1623] [Catalogue] The Life and Death of King John

According to Chambers, *KJ* in F1 is fairly well printed, with normal, slight stage-directions. There are some variations in the speech prefixes. Beaurline suggests that the misreadings and inconsistencies derive from two different scribes using the author's foul papers. One problem concerns the fact that in F1, Actus Secundus has only 74 lines. Modern editors have found various ways to address this.

## Relationship of *Troublesome Raigne* to *King John*

From the publication of Q2 in 1611 through later publications until 1764 at least, *Troublesome Raigne* has been attributed to Shakespeare. Eric Sams notes that *TR* (*John King of England, both parts*) was so attributed in 'an exact and perfect Catalogue of all the Plaies that were ever printed' appended to Edward Archer's 1656 edition of *The Old Law* by Massinger and others. *TR* was again attributed to Shakespeare in Francis Kirkman's catalogues of 1661 and 1671, Gerard Langbaine's catalogue of 1691, Charles Gildon's list in 1699, the W. Mears catalogues of 1713, 1719 and 1726, and an edition of 1764 published by Robert Horsefield. Most modern commentators, however, have not accepted this attribution, and treat *TR* as another playwright's – concentrating on the direction of influence.[1]

Since the two plays treat the same events very closely with only minor differences, a close relationship has been assumed between them. The two parts of *TR* amount to 3,081 lines, whereas there are only 2715 in *KJ*. The first part of *TR* consists of 1,840 lines (corresponding to 1,987 lines in *KJ*); the second part consists of 1196 lines, (corresponding to only 728 lines in *KJ*). The clearest point of comparison lies in the unhistorical Robert Falconbridge, who plays a major part in both plays. There are also some very close verbal parallels between the plays, e.g.

> Then I demand Volquesson, Torain, Main,
> Poitiers and Anjou, these five provinces
> (*TR* 1 827–8; *c.f. KJ* 2.1.528–9)

Brian Boyd has explained various theories as to the relationship between *TR* and *KJ*:

> Is Shakespeare's *King John* a source or a derivative of the anonymous *The Troublesome Raigne of King John* (1591)? In 1989 "the 'orthodox' opinion that *The Troublesome Raigne* precedes *King John*" seemed to one critic 'now . . . so strong as to need no further elaboration or support.' (Hamel). A year later, another made the best case yet for the 'unorthodox' position that *King John* spawned rather than sprang from *The Troublesome Raigne*. (Beaurline).
>
> Everyone concurs that *The Troublesome Raigne* is intimately related to and manifestly inferior to *King John*, but there agreement ends. To some, a writer with the merest fraction of Shakespeare's talent could

> not have followed *King John* almost scene for scene and often speech for speech and yet have repeatedly substituted his own awkward limp for the forceful stride Shakespeare's language has throughout this play. To others, a writer with so little talent would never have been able to reshape Holinshed and other historical sources so well that Shakespeare could work from it, again, almost scene for scene and often speech for speech. . . All participants in the debate agree that 'the author who worked first from the chronicles undertook a massive reorganization of historical material' (Smallwood, 367).

Boyd argues that *TR* was not the source for *KJ*, which is considered in section (c) below.[2]

### (a) Another playwright wrote *Troublesome Raigne*, which Shakespeare revised as King John.

Chambers believes that another playwright wrote *TR*, which Shakespeare "kept open in front of him" when revising it into *KJ*. The reprints of *TR* were in this view deliberately misattributed so as to boost sales in much the same way as *Sir John Oldcastle* or *The London Prodigal*. Most commentators follow Chambers. J. L. Simmons expanded this view by showing that Shakespeare corrects the moral confusion of its predecessor while confirming its theme of the evils of usurpation and rebellion. Guy Hamel argues that the claim for the priority of *TR* is "so strong that it needs no further support". The further support which he gives includes the development of imagery in *KJ*. Beatrice Groves also developed this argument but discounted the claim that Shakespeare was working from an open text because the number of linguistic parallels is small. Sir Brian Vickers has asserted that Robert Peele wrote *TR*.

### (b) Shakespeare wrote both *The Troublesome Raigne* (Q1, 1591) and *King John* (F1)

The straightforward interpretation of the contemporary evidence is that the playwright composed *TR* and then revised it as *KJ*. E. M. W. Tillyard suggested that *TR* might turn out to be a 'bad quarto' of an early version of Shakespeare's play, i.e. that *TR* is early Shakespeare and presumably the author toned down the anti-Catholic bias in *TR* when revising it as *KJ*. Thus Meres was possibly alluding to *TR* when he mentioned a play by Shakespeare entitled *King John*.[3]

This view is now somewhat old-fashioned, having been advanced (according to Sams) by "Sims, Helme, Matthews, Dew, Archer, Kirkman, Langbaine, Gildon, Mears, Horsefield, Pope, Theobald, Warburton, Capell, Steevens, Coleridge, Tieck, Schlegel, Ulrici. . . ." This position has more recently been advocated by Everitt.

**(c) Shakespeare wrote *King John* – *Troublesome Raigne* is derivative**

A few commentators have asserted that *TR* was derived from *KJ*. Honigmann, following Alexander, asserts that *King John* is a good text, while *TR* has the untidy characteristics of a 'bad quarto', with structural inconsistencies, summarising and descriptive directions. He notes that *TR* belongs to the Queen's Men, who also passed off other derivative texts, e.g. *Taming of the Shrew*. The author of *KJ* uses Paris in the right context, whereas *TR* paraphrases Paris imperfectly. Thus, Shakespeare's *KJ* would have to pre-date the publication of *TR* in 1591.

**(d) *King John* and *Troublesome Raigne* derive from the same source**

Suzanne Gary (in an unpublished Ph.D. dissertation)[4] and L. A. Beaurline argue that both plays derive from a scenario or outline plot, which ignored Robin Hood and the signing of Magna Carta (for which King John was most famous) and concentrated on events surrounding the legitimacy of John's accession. Thus an inexperienced and inferior author, with access to Shakespeare's outline plot but without access to his script, composed *TR* with a more hostile anti-Papist line. According to this view, Shakespeare's *KJ* pre-dates the publication of *TR* in 1591, at least in its plot outline.

## Performance Date

There is no recorded performance before 1737. A document from 1669 suggests that *KJ* may have been acted at Blackfriars some time between 1608 and 1642.[5]

## Sources

The problem in deciding sources depends on the view taken of the relationship between the plays *TR* and *KJ*. Boswell-Stone argued that the author of *KJ* relied solely on *TR* without consulting Holinshed independently. J. Dover Wilson went further and argued that Shakespeare used no independent sources for *KJ*. The modern scholarly consensus is that Shakespeare studied the life of John in minute detail from a wide variety of sources, also reading up on Richard I and Henry II in Holinshed. Hall does not appear to have been used, since his account begins *c.* 1397.

**Raphael Holinshed, *The Chronicles of Englande, Scotlande, and Irelande*** (1st ed. 1577 & 2nd ed. 1587) Both Honigmann and Bullough agree that Holinshed was used as the primary source for both plays and report many passages in *KJ* which are based on Holinshed but not found in *TR*, e.g. in reporting at 5.4.37–8 that Melun crossed the Channel before Lewis to encourage the English nobles. Bullough argues that Shakespeare relied mainly on Holinshed, using the expanded second edition. **John Foxe's Actes and Monumments of Martyrs** (1583) is seen by Honigmann and Bullough as a secondary source at many points, e.g. for John's speech in giving up the Crown and receiving it back at 5.1.1–4.

**John Bale's *Kyng Johan*,** was a morality play written *c.* 1540 and revised in 1561. It was probably performed at Ipswich in 1561 and remained unpublished until 1838. The tone of the play is very anti-Catholic, more like *TR* than *KJ*; it draws parallels between John and Henry VIII in their conflicts with Rome. *Kyng Johan* was probably used by the author of *TR* mainly for its tone and purpose, but also by the author of *KJ* for some details, e.g. in elevating Pandulph to a Cardinal. A. J. Piesse believes it was very influential on *KJ*.

Honigmann shows how Shakespeare seems to have used various Latin chronicles, including **Matthew Paris's *Historia Maior***, published in 1571, for details of the loss of the treasure in the Wash, the ***Wakefield Chronicle*** (manuscript) and ***The English Chronicle of Randulph of Coggershall***, for incidental details. Honigmann finally suggests that Shakespeare drew on medieval poems in French about Richard I, such as ***Kynge Rycharde Cuer du Lyon***.

Shaheen discusses biblical references in *TR*, finding few allusions in the two parts, some of which occur in the many biblical references in *KJ*. He thus concludes that *TR* was by another writer. Shaheen's remaining discussion of biblical references in *KJ* is shorter than for other plays (only 16 pages), but at 2.1.87 demonstrates knowledge of Romans 13, where the doctrine of secular rulers as God's agents is expounded.

Braunmuller sees some classical influence, especially of Seneca at 2.1.452 (Hubert's defiance) and at 5.7.28–48 (John's speeches upon being poisoned). Similarly, Ovid is recalled at these points as well. Allusions to specific English literary works are rare, but may include Kyd's *Spanish Tragedy* (1589) echoed at 2.1.137 with reference to a dead lion's beard. Another contemporary play, *Soliman and Perseda* (? 1589–92), may be echoed in a reference to Basilisco at 1.1.244. However, we cannot be sure of the direction of influence.

## Orthodox Dating – Internal Evidence

Chambers announced that there is "no external evidence to fix the date before the mention by Meres", and indeed every year between 1591 and 1598 has had its adherents. If Meres is referring to *Troublesome Raigne*, even the date of 1598 as the *terminus ante* is in doubt.

| | |
|---|---|
| 1590 | J. D. Wilson; Honigmann, Beaurline. |
| 1592–3 | Ribner[6] |
| 1595–6 | Bullough (somewhat uncertainly), Wells & Taylor, Braunmuller |
| 1596–7 | Chambers (cautiously) |

Beaurline suggests that the declamatory style of *KJ* fits well with the style of the *Henry VI* trilogy and thus accords with 1590. Braunmuller sees two major similarities between *KJ* and *Richard II*: both are composed almost exclusively in verse and neither one contains a secondary plot to parallel the royal political action. Braunmuller thus dates both plays to the mid 1590s.

## Metrical and Linguistic Tests

Various metrical tests have placed *KJ* as among the earlier plays in the canon, but such tests remain unreliable. There is a very high number of feminine endings (20%), a low incidence of open-ended (i.e. run-on) lines at 13% and mid-line speech endings at 3%. In these respects, *KJ* is closest to *Romeo and Juliet* and to *Richard II,* which are usually dated to 1595–6. Like *Richard II,* it is composed entirely in verse.

## Orthodox Dating – External Evidence

Honigmann argued strongly for a date *c.* 1590, giving many reasons for the early date: (a) the influence of *KJ* on Daniel's *Complaint of Rosamund*, (1592); (b) an apparent joke at 1.i.140–6 about the thin-man roles assigned to an actor called John Sincko, who was active in 1590; one of the roles has been identified as Falconbridge; (c) correspondences with other early books, e.g. Peele's *Descensus Astraeae* (1591); (d) correspondences with topical events, especially the defeat of the Spanish Armada in 1588, but also the murder of Henri III of France in 1589, and the attempts to forward the promotion of secretary Davidson after Walsingham's death (*c.f.* John's repudiation of Hubert); (e) about seven fictitious 'additions' to the *KJ* play, which appear to resonate with the litigation in 1590 between James Burbage and Widow Brayne over income at the Theatre. Honigmann accepts the implication that seven or eight plays must have already been written by this time and therefore advances the 'early starter' theory for the dating of Shakespeare's plays.

Bullough considers all of these points and then answers them in turn, thinking that the political allusions accord more with a date of 1595/6. He notes that a date after 1593 would have been topical when Henri IV of France converted to Catholicism and he suggests that the passage at 2.i.56–75 may refer obliquely to Essex's setting off for Cadiz on 3 June 1596. Strong parallels have been seen between the play and events under Queen Elizabeth, who had been excommunicated by the Pope in 1570 and resisted foreign intervention. Other parallels, however, between the murderous, usurping John and Elizabeth would not have been very politic.

Some critics, e.g. Bevington, have argued that there is only a loose connection between Shakespeare's history plays and contemporary issues[7] but Braunmuller finds the treatment of inheritance, wills and primogeniture as intensely relevant to Elizabeth's legitimacy as Queen. Pugliatti, following Smallwood among others, views *KJ* in the light of Elizabeth's reign as a commentary on the political crisis in England.[8]

## Oxfordian Dating

Eva Turner Clark, followed by most Oxfordians such as Ogburn, believed that *TR* was an early play by Oxford written *c.* 1579–80 and then revised in the 1590s as *KJ*.

## Internal Evidence

It is possible that Oxford was influenced by John Bale's *King Johan,* which was performed in Ipswich in 1561 and may have been performed at nearby Castle Hedingham, Oxford's ancestral home, when Elizabeth visited that same year. Oxford would have written *TR* in his youth for his own players, who continued to play it when they transferred to the Queens' Men.[9] The hero of *KJ* is Robert Falconbridge, whose descent from Richard I ensures his heroic qualities despite the frequent mention of his bastardy. Similarly, Oxford had cause to ponder issues of legitimacy: his half-sister had tried to declare him illegitimate and the lengthy case was decided in his favour; he fathered an illegitimate son, Sir Edward Vere, his sole male child for many years, and there had been many rumours about the paternity of his eldest daughter, Elizabeth, born in 1575 when he himself was travelling in Italy.[10]

## Oxfordian Dating – External Evidence

Honigmann points out that, in the Armada Period 1583–96, there were frequent patriotic pamphlets, exhorting Englishmen to defend their country, citing many famous English exploits of the past, including a pamphlet by Anthony Munday in 1584. Oxfordians believe that Shakespeare's history plays date to the 1580s and served as an exhortation mainly to the nobles, who would have seen them produced (anonymously) at court. *KJ* deals with the rebellion of the nobles, John's surrender of the crown and John's poisoning – far more apt in the 1580s than in the 1590s. At 1.1.40, Queen Eleanor tells John that he holds the Crown through 'strong possession' not through 'right', another link with political debate in the 1580s rather than the 1590s. There is a will which bars Arthur's right to succeed to the throne – almost exactly as Henry VIII had barred the right of Mary Queen of Scots, especially topical during the 1580s up until Mary's execution in 1587.[11]

Another possible link with Oxford's court experience is the marriage negotiations between an English princess, Blanche, and a French prince Lewis, which take place in Act 2 at the walls of Angiers, the capital of Anjou. These negotiations would have been particularly resonant in 1581 when Elizabeth was courted by Alençon.

## Conclusion

The earliest date for the Folio versions of the play *KJ* is probably the second edition of Holinshed in 1587. They may have been completed by the time of Meres (1598) and the latest possible date is the publication of the First Folio in 1623.

## Notes

1. Eric Sams, "The Troublesome Wrangle Over *King John*", *Notes and Queries*, ccxxxiiii, 1988.
2. Brian Boyd, '*King John* and *The Troublesome Raigne:* Sources, Structure, Sequence,' *Philological Quarterly,* Vol. 74, No. 1, Winter, 1995, 37–56.
3. E. M. W. Tillyard, *Shakespeare's English History Plays,* original edition 1944 (rptd 1980, 215–233).
4. Suzanne Gary, 'The Relationship between *The Troublesome Raigne of King John* King of England and Shakespeare's *King John',* University of Arizona, 1971.
5. Quoted by Beaurline, p. 3, from Irwin Smith, *Shakespeare's Blackfriars Playhouse,* 1966.
6. Irving Ribner, *The English History Play in the Age of Shakespeare*, 1957.
7. David Bevington, *Tudor Drama and Politics*, 1968, and *Shakespeare's Histories*, 2006.
8. Paola Pugliatti, *Shakespeare the Historian*, 1996.
9. Oxford took over his own players in 1580 and some of them went over to the newly formed Queen's Men in 1583 (Nelson, 239–248).
10. Katherine Vere, Lady Windsor, stood to inherit their father's lands (Nelson, 40–1); Edward Vere was born illegitimately to the Queen's lady-in-waiting, Anne Vavasour, in 1581 (Nelson, 266) and Oxford refused to recognise his daughter for about six years (Nelson, 141–155).
11. The Third Succession Act of 1543 barred the Scottish line desended from his elder sister Margaret and allowed for the succession to pass after his own children to the descendants of his younger sister, Mary (Michael Graves, *Henry VIII, A Study in Kingship*, 2003: 140)

## Other Cited Works

Alexander, Peter, *Shakespeare's Life and Art*, London: James Nisbet, 1939
Beaurline, Lester A. (ed.), *King John by William Shakespeare,* Cambridge: CUP, 1990
Braunmuller, A. R. (ed.). *King John*. Oxford: OUP, 1989

Bullough, G., *Narrative and Dramatic Sources of Shakespeare,* vol. IV, London: Routledge, 1962

Chambers, E. K., *William Shakespeare: a study of facts and problems*, 2 vols, Oxford: Clarendon Press, 1930

—, *The Elizabethan Stage*, 4 vols, Oxford: Clarendon, 1923

Clark, Eva Turner, *Hidden Allusions in Shakespeare's Plays*, New York: Kennikat, 1931 rptd 1974

Everitt, E.B., *The Young Shakespeare*, Copenhagen: Rosenkilde and Bagger, 1954

Groves, Beatrice, *Texts and Traditions: Religion in Shakespeare, 1592–1604.*Oxford, Clarendon 2006.

Hamel, Guy, "King John and The Troublesome Raigne: A Re-examination", in *King John: New Perspectives,* ed. D. T. Curren-Aquino, Cranbury, N.J.: Associated University Presses, 1989, pp. 41–61

Honigmann, E. A. J. (ed.), *King John*, Arden², London: Methuen, 1954

Nelson, Alan H., *Monstrous Adversary: The Life of Edward de Vere, 17th Earl of Oxford,* Liverpool: LUP, 2003

Ogburn, Charlton Jr., *The Mysterious William Shakespeare*, Virginia: EPM, 1984

Piesse, Amanda J, 'King John: changing perspectives' in *Cambridge Comapnion to Shakespeare's History Plays*, ed. M. J. Hattaway, Cambridge: CUP, 2002, pp 126–140

Shaheen, Naseeb, *Biblical References in Shakespeare's Plays*, Delaware: University of Delaware Press, 1999

Simmons, J. L., 'Shakespeare's King John and its sources; coherence, pattern and Vision', *Tulane Studies in English,* 17, 1969, 53–72

Smallwood, R. L. (ed.), *King John,* Penguin, Harmondsworth, 1974

Vickers, Sir Brian, *Shakespeare, co-author*, Oxford: OUP, 2002

Wilson, J. Dover (ed.), *King John,* Cambridge: CUP, 1936

Wells, S. & G. Taylor, *William Shakespeare: a textual companion,* Oxford: OUP, 1987

# Richard II, Henry IV Parts 1, 2 and Henry V

Kevin Gilvary

## 'The Second Tetralogy'

The First Folio presents *Richard II, Henry IV Parts 1, 2* and *Henry V* in their historical sequence, after *King John* and before *King Henry VI, Part 1.* There is no evidence for their sequence of composition and no direct evidence as to whether they were conceived as a tetralogy, a trilogy, or piecemeal. All the plays appeared in quarto in sequence between 1597–1600. The general consensus amongst editors is that they were conceived as Shakespeare's 'Second Tetralogy' and composed in sequence between 1595 and 1600,

A grid is helpful to show the relevant publication dates clearly:

| | ***R2*** | ***1H4*** | ***2H4*** | ***H5*** |
|---|---|---|---|---|
| **1595–99** | Q1 1597<br>Q2, Q3 1598 | Q1 1598<br>Q2 1599 | | |
| **1600–04** | | Q3 1604 | Q 1600 | Q1 1600<br>Q2 1602 |
| **1605–09** | Q4 1608 | Q4 1608 | | |
| **1610–14** | | Q5 1613 | | |
| **1615–19** | Q5 1615 | | | Q3 1619 |
| **1620–24** | F1 1623 | Q6 1622<br>F1 1623 | F1 1623 | F1 1623 |

It is thought that the tetralogy had been inspired mainly by Hall's *The Union of the Two Noble and Illustre Famelies of Lancastre and Yorke* (1548–50), which begins with the challenge between Bolingbroke and Mowbray, just as does *Richard II.* Most of the detail seems to derive from Holinshed, with some reference to *The Mirror for Magistrates.*

16

# The life and death of King Richard the second

Kevin Gilvary

The composition of the play *Richard II* in its Quarto form can be assigned anywhere between 1587 (the second edition of Holinshed) and 1597, the publication of the first quarto.

## Publication Date

*The Tragedy of Richard II* was first published in quarto in 1597 and seems to have sold very well. It appeared twice in 1598, with two further quartos before the First Folio.

> [SR 1597] 29° Augusti. Andrew Wise. Entred for his Copie by appoyntment from master Warden Man, The Tragedye of Richard the Second vj$^{d}$.
>
> [Q1 1597] The Tragedie of King Richard the second. As it hath beene publikely acted by the right Honourable the Lorde Chamberlaine his Seruants. London Printed by Valentine Simmes for Andrew Wise, and are to be sold at his shop in Paules church yard at the signe of the Angel. 1597.
>
> [Q2 1598] The Tragedie of King Richard the second. As it hath beene publikely acted by the Right Honourable the Lord Chamberlaine his seruants. By William Shake-speare. London Printed by Valentine Simmes for Andrew Wise, and are to be sold at his shop in Paules churchyard at the signe of the Angel. 1598.

Both Q1 and Q2 have a frontispiece depicting a man with one arm weighed down and his right arm (with wings) reaching towards heaven, with God in the background beckoning. This would appear to anticipate Richard's final words: 'Mount, mount, my soul! Thy seat is up on high / Whilst my gross flesh sinks

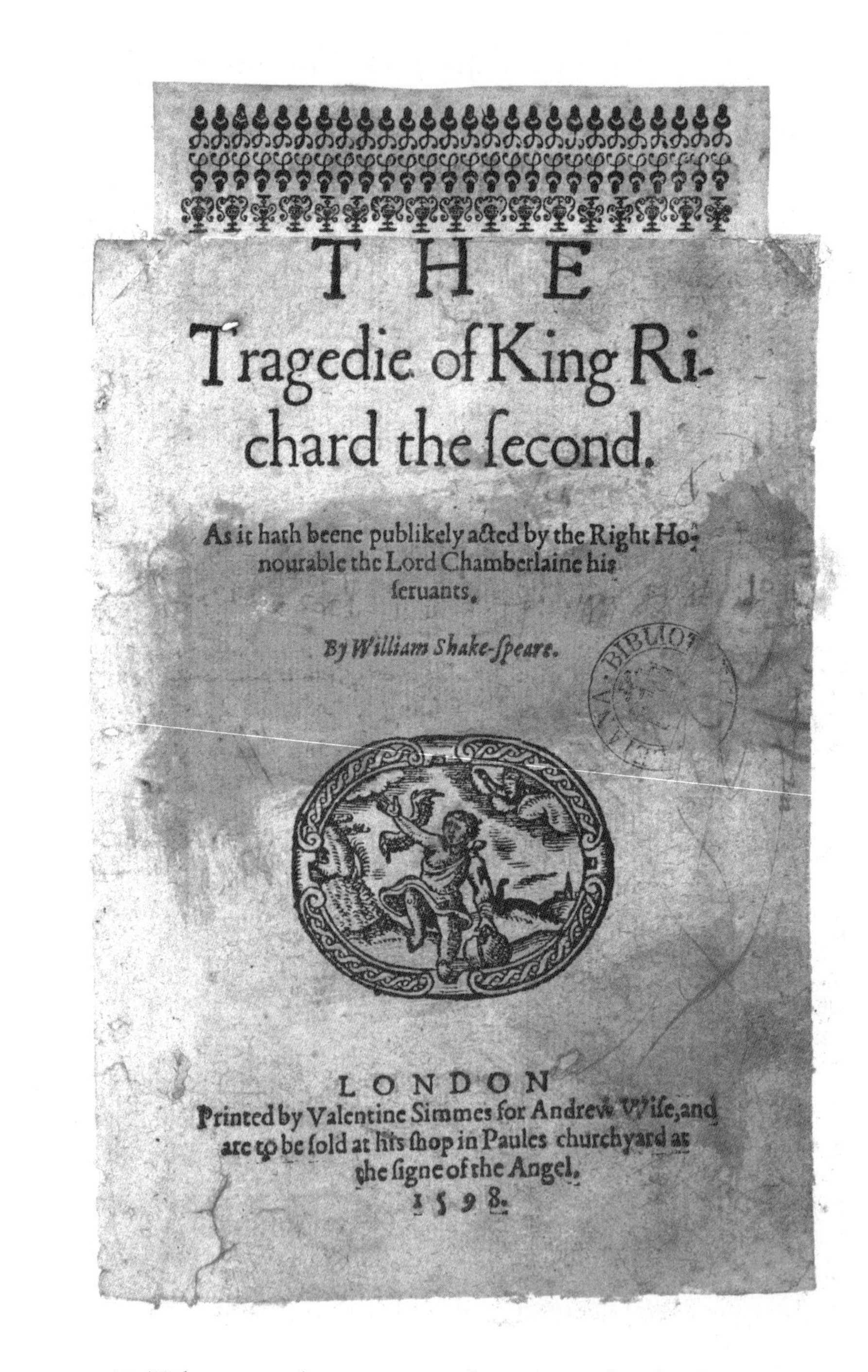

THE

Tragedie of King Ri-
chard the ſecond.

As it hath beene publikely acted by the Right Honourable the Lord Chamberlaine his
ſeruants.

*By William Shake-ſpeare.*

LONDON
Printed by Valentine Simmes for Andrew Wiſe, and
are to be ſold at his ſhop in Paules churchyard at
the ſigne of the Angel.
1598.

10. Title page to the anonymous first quarto of *Richard II*, 1597.
By permission of Bodleian Library, University of Oxford,
shelfmark Arch. G d.45 (4) title page.

downward here to die.' (5.v.111–2). While Q1's author was anonymous, Q2 attributed the play to Shakespeare.

Q3 appeared in the same year but without the frontispiece:

> [Q3 1598] The Tragedie of King Richard the second. As it hath beene publikely acted by the Right Honourable the Lord Chamberlaine his seruants. By William Shake-speare. London Printed by Valentine Simmes, for Andrew Wise, and are to be solde at his shop in Paules churchyard, at the signe of the Angel. 1598.

In 1603, the play was tranferred to Matthew Law:

> [SR 1603] 25 Junij. Mathew Lawe. Entred for his copies in full courte Holden this Day. These ffyve copies folowinge . . . viz iij enterludes or playes . . . The second of Richard the 2. ... all kinges ... all whiche by consent of the Company are sett over to him from Andrew Wyse.
>
> [Q4 1608] The Tragedie of King Richard the second. As it hath been publikely acted by the Right Honourable the Lord Chamberlaine his seruantes. By William Shake-speare. London, Printed by W[illiam] W[hite] for Matthew Law, and are to be sold at his shop in Paules Church-yard, at the signe of the Foxe. 1608.
>
> *[in some copies.]* The Tragedie of King Richard the Second: With new additions of the Parliament Sceane, and the deposing of King Richard, As it hath been lately acted by the Kinges Majesties seruantes, at the Globe. By William Shake-speare. At London, Printed by W. W. for Mathew Law, and are to be sold at his shop in Paules Church-yard, at the signe of the Foxe. 1608.

Q4 contains the first printed example of the deposition scene (as "lately acted", but how lately is not known). Mention is made only in some title pages of Q4. It is thought that this scene was composed at the same time as the rest of the play, but censored.[1] The Q1 text moves from Northumberland's order that the Abbot of Westminster guard the Bishop of Carlisle to the abbot's comment "A woeful pageant have we here beheld." This makes little sense unless the deposition scene intervenes. Similarly, Bolingbroke's command "Convey him to the Tower" at the end of the cut portion neatly anticipates Richard's next appearance en route (5.1.7). It has been accepted that the Deposition Scene was too politically sensitive for publication in 1598–1603, as the suggestion of abdication might have been treasonably applied to Elizabeth.

> [Q5 1615] The Tragedie of King Richard the Second: With new additions of the Parliament Sceane, and the deposing of King Richard. As it hath been lately acted by the Kinges Maiesties seruants, at the Globe. By William Shake-speare At London, Printed for Mathew Law, and are to be sold at his shop in Paules Church-yard, at the signe of the Foxe. 1615

> [F1 1623] The Life & death of Richard the second. *[Histories,* 23–45, sign.b6–d5.

Chambers says that Q1 is a good text, possibly showing the author's supervision. Later quartos were thought to have been set successively from each other. The Folio is thought to have been set from Q5. The play was published anonymously in the first quarto and then attributed to William Shake-speare in 1598 in Q2, and in later quartos.

Tillyard argued that Shakespeare wrote an earlier version of *Richard II* and that the extant version is a revision.[2] J. Dover Wilson expanded this idea of revision, noting various inconsistencies, e.g. Bagot leaves for Ireland (2.3.140), then is executed at Bristol (3.2.122) but is still alive to be tried at 4.1; Bolingbroke refers obliquely to his marriage without further reference (2.1.168–9); Bolingroke's suggestion that Bushy and Green had had homosexual relations with Richard (3.1.11–15). Egan examines the allusive treatment to Gloucester's suspicious death, an event which precedes the events in the play.

## Performance Dates

While there are as a number of references to play performances in the late Elizabethan period, there are only two possible references to *Richard II* in performance before the First Folio was published in 1623. The earliest possible reference is in a letter dated 7 December 1595 in which Sir Edward Hoby invited Sir Robert Cecil to his house in Canon Row, Westminster, for what may have been a performance of *Richard II*:

> Sir, findinge that you wer not convenientlie to be at London to morrow night I am bold to send to knowe whether Teusdaie [9 Dec] may be anie more in your grace to visit poore Channon rowe where as late as it shal please you a gate for your supper shal be open: & K Richard present him selfe to your vewe. . . .

It is not certain whether the sentence 'K Richard present him selfe to your vewe' refers to a performance of a play, or even if this play was Shakespeare's *Richard II.* Although Hoby sent his letter two years before the publication of *Richard II* and *Richard III,* it is thought unlikely that Hoby would greet an important guest with a performance of a cruel tyrant such as Richard III. If a play was intended, it might have been *Thomas of Woodstock* or another play dealing with similar events. It has also been suggested that Hoby might have had a portrait of Richard II to show off.

The play is mentioned by Meres in 1598. At Essex's trial on 5 June 1600 for his mishandling of events in Ireland, concern was expressed at "he Erle himself being so often present at the playing thereof, and with great applause, giving countenance and lyking to the same". Most commentators (e.g. Chambers,

Bullough, Wilson, Gurr and especially Forker) believe that it was Shakespeare's play which was performed on 7 February, 1601, the night before the Essex rebellion. Against this majority view, Peter Ure argued that the work presented at the Globe was Hayward's prose account *The Life and Reigne of Henry IIII*, which had been registered in 1599 and published in 1600. Ure's arguments were expanded by Jon L. Manning and Leeds Barroll, who noted that Hayward's account of the deposition was much more detailed than Shakespeare's, making explicit links between Essex and Bolingbroke.[3] The play was very popular, as Queen Elizabeth herself knew when she remarked shortly after the Essex Rebellion to the Keeper of the Tower of London: "I am Richard. Know ye not that? . . . this tragedy was played 40[tie] times in open streets and houses." (Chambers, *WS*, I, 354)

A performance in a more exotic location is mentioned by a Captain Keeling in his Journal (30 September 1607), that while off Sierra Leone "Captain Hawkins dined with me, wher my companions acted Kinge Richard the Second." Simon Forman describes a performance of "Richard the 2 At the Glob" on 30 April 1611 but the play does not seem to have been Shakespeare's since it involves characters handled very differently, including a treacherous John of Gaunt who actively plotted his son's accession (Chambers, *WS*, I, 354–6).

## Did Shakespeare write a *Richard II Part 1* now lost?

Because our version of *Richard II* starts *in medias res*, there have been various commentators who have suggested that Shakespeare had written the extant play as *Part 2* and that *Part 1* was either lost or could be identified in the anonymous *Thomas of Woodstock*. The characters in *Richard II* assume considerable knowledge of preceding events involving King Richard, his uncle (Thomas of Woodstock, Duke of Gloucester), Mowbray and Bolingbroke. Gloucester had died mysteriously while in custody in Calais, with Mowbray implicated as the King's agent, denounced by Bolingbroke. These events are not explained in *Richard II*, but are covered in *Thomas of Woodstock*. In *Richard II*, Mowbray and Bolingbroke only briefly account for their accusations of treason against each other, yet their banishment has enormous consequences for Richard.[4]

Bullough and later Forker disagreed, noting that Shakespeare's version of *Richard II* does not link to *Thomas of Woodstock* for various reasons: in *Woodstock*, John of Gaunt is eager to overthrow the king and replace him with his son, whereas the John of Gaunt in *Richard II* retains total respect for the position of king. Gaunt refuses the demands of his sister-in-law, the Countess of Gloucester, to seek vengeance for her husband's murder and he sadly accepts the sentence of banishment for his son. In *Woodstock*, Lapoole, not Mowbray, had organised Gloucester's murder. By the end of *Woodstock*, Bushy, Bagot & Green are dead but in *Richard II* they are alive for a while. Against the need for a *Part 1* is the fact that Hall's account begins with the Bolingbroke–Mowbray quarrel. See below for discussion of *Thomas of Woodstock* as a possible source for *Richard II.*

## Sources

Bullough believes that Shakespeare did more research for *Richard II* (and *Hamlet*) than for any other play. He cites Hall & Holinshed as the same two principal historical sources for 'The Second Tetralogy' but adds a wide range of other sources.

**Edward Hall, *The Union of the Two Noble and Illustre Famelies of Lancastre and Yorke*** (1548–50). Bullough believes that the author began his plan for *Richard II* by studying Hall. This moralising narrative begins with Richard's failure to deal competently with the quarrel between Mowbray and Bolingbroke (1397) and shows continuity between the reigns of Richard II, Henry IV (1400–13) and Henry V (1413–22). Bullough also notes some small details which derive from Hall rather than later Chroniclers, e.g. King Richard's stay at Conway Castle; Northumberland's treachery in getting him out.

**Raphael Holinshed, *The Chronicles of Englande, Scotlande, and Irelande*** (1st edn 1577 & 2nd edn 1587). Bullough believes that Holinshed provided most of the detailed material for the play, including details from the Mowbray–Bolingbroke quarrel, most of the names, events and sequence. Shakespeare also used details from Holinshed of a jousting tournament in 1389. It seems that the second edition was used for the line at 2.4.8: "The bay trees in our country are well-withered." The reference was not in the first edition. Shakespeare changed certain elements, e.g. in making Richard's excursion to Ireland both later and less successful than it in fact had been. Hall had omitted the Irish War. Most importantly, Holinshed included details about the abdication and the 33 articles of deposition, which are used in the play.

**The anonymous *Thomas of Woodstock*** is thought by many to have preceded and influenced *Richard II* (although Ure argued that it was not necessary to postulate that Shakespeare knew *Woodstock*). Bullough, following Chambers, dates *Woodstock* tentatively to 1594 and suggests that it slightly affected Shakespeare's handling of the play. William Long concurred in dating *Woodstock* to 1594 according to analysis of handwriting, and decided it had influenced *Richard II,* which would have been composed shortly afterwards in 1595. Long argued that *Woodstock* must ante-date *Richard II* because it conflates the various favorites of Richard who are dealt with severally by Shakespeare, as Bullough had argued.[5] Corbin and Sedge refer to the play as anonymous (but with Shakespearean features) and they make a case for Rowley as author (perhaps dating the play to 1591–5). In the most recent Arden edition, Forker argues that, when composing *Richard II,* Shakespeare may have had in mind another play dealing differently with earlier events in Richard's reign, or he was offering a radically different interpretation of events and characters.

Forker believes that *Woodstock,* like *Edward II,* was a dramatic forerunner of *Richard II.* A thorough study completed more recently by Egan concludes that *Woodstock* was written by Shakespeare in 1592–3 for a touring company (possibly Pembroke's Men) and intended to bridge the historical gap between *Edward III* and *Richard II.* Egan thus refers to *Woodstock* as *Richard II Part 1.* Egan dates the extant manuscript to *c.* 1608, and assigns it the status of a copy made for use in the theatre.

**Marlowe's *Edward II*** is said to have influenced *Richard II.* Marlowe's play was registered in 1593 and published in 1594. Because it concentrates on the character of the king, it is taken to be a development from the *Henry VI* trilogy (where the emphasis is on events and characters in the reign) and thus *Edward II* seems to have influenced both *Richard III* and *Richard II.* Further thematic links exist between the portrayal of Edward II as a weak king fatally overcome by his choice of favorites and *Richard II.* The direction of influence has not, however, been firmly established; it is possible that *Richard II* was earlier and therefore an influence on Marlowe's play.

**Samuel Daniel's epic poem *The First Fowre Bookes of the Civile Wars*** was registered on 11 October 1594 and published twice in 1595 (according to the title page), i.e. two years before the registration and publication of *Richard II.* The first three books deal with the story of Richard II. Bullough follows Chambers in viewing Daniel's poem as derivative from the *Chronicles* (to which it is very much closer) and therefore influential upon the play. Both play and poem make the Queen (historically aged 10) a mature woman and lover of Richard, with special resonance at 5.1. Both play and poem make Prince Hal and Hotspur (the latter historically two years older than Bolingbroke) roughly contemporaries. It is not thought that Shakespeare knew Daniel personally or that they realised that they were dealing with the same material on a big scale. The problem is knowing whether Daniel embarked on his epic poem before Shakespeare began his tetralogy, or whether Shakespeare's handling of various themes influenced Daniel.

***A Mirrour for Magistrates*** (1559, 1563, 1578), like Hall, begins with the reign of *Richard II,* and provides material for many characters featured in the play: Richard himself in the play laments the "sad stories of the death of kings"; Tresilian, an earlier favorite of Richard; Mortimer, his designated heir; Gloucester, his uncle; on Mowbray (especially the speech on his impending exile); and Salisbury and Northumberland, whose deaths featured in later plays (*1H6* and *2H4*). It is even claimed that Richard's playing with the mirror (4.1.266–81) is a deliberate allusion to *A Mirrour for Magistrates.*

**French Chronicles** are also thought to have been used in the composition of *Richard II.* Firstly, *The Chronicle of Froissart* (translated by Berners 1523–25) gives an eye-witness account of Richard's last years as king, probably helping in the composition of the following episodes: John of Gaunt's warning to Richard (2.1); the emphasis on Northumberland's help for Bolingroke; Bolingbroke's general popularity; sympathy for the queen and ultimately for Richard himself. Another French chronicle is less accepted as a direct source because it was only known in a French manuscript: both Hall and Holinshed consulted *La Chronique de la Traïson et mort de Richart Deux Roy Dengleterre* (ed. & trans. by Benjamin Williams, 1846), which deals very sympathetically with the last few years of Richard's reign. Apart from the pathos for Richard, it deals with the 'Masking' conspiracy against Henry, York's loyalty to the king with the execution of the chief participants and it tells of the murder of Richard by Sir Peter Exton. A manuscript of the *Traïson* Chronicle was owned by John Stow. A third French chronicle, *Histoire du Roy d'Angleterre Richard II*, was a metrical poem, composed by Jean Créton, who had been present at Richard's Court. Créton's account is also very sympathetic to Richard. It was available in manuscripts owned by John Stow and John Dee.

Shaheen discusses the large number of Biblical references in *Richard II*. He notes that, while all the sources tend to be moralistic and religious in tone, there are very few actual references to the Bible in the originals. Thus, according to Shaheen, Shakespeare introduced his own religious references. At 1.1.174–5 Shakespeare has the following sharp interchange: "*Richard* . . . Lions make leopards tame. *Mow* Yea, but not change his spots." The author clearly adopts the wording of the Geneva Bible from Jeremiah 13.23 "Can the blacke More change his skin? Or the leopard his spottes?" All other versions have "catte of the mountaine" instead of "leopard". Similarly at 1.2.20, the Duchess laments Gloucester's death: "His summer leaves all faded". The Geneva Bible reads at Ps 1.13 "whose leafe shall not fade" where other versions have "wither".

Although the author rarely refers to classical works in *Richard II*, Richard's self-pitying comparison to Phaëton, which is developed at length at 3.3.176–182, is clearly reminiscent of Ovid's account in *Metamorphoses* I. This image deserves close study as it is central to Richard's character: he will "come down" as a result of his own reckless actions.

## Conventional Dating

Almost all commentators (e.g. Bullough, Gurr, Forker) agree with Chambers who assigned a composition date of 1595, two years before the publication of Q1.

## Internal Evidence

Chambers sees 1595 as possible since "the style and lyrical tone of the scenes in which Richard figures would fit well enough with 1595" but adds that "there is much poor and bombastic matter" which would fit with the *Henry VI* trilogy and *Richard III*, which he puts at 1590–1 in his dating scheme.

## External Evidence

Christopher Highley traces how Ireland is depicted in various history plays, often with the manipulation of the chronicles, to reflect the contemporary situation. Thus Richard in the chronicles simply raises taxes because he is greedy. In the play, however, he seizes John of Gaunt's property to finance his Irish Wars. He returns less successfully in the play than he had done in history. According to Highley, this reflects the tense situation in the mid 1590s when Elizabeth was raising taxes to finance the wars in Ireland but with little success.[6]

## Oxfordian Dating

Oxfordians believe that Shakespeare's history plays date from the 1580s and served as an exhortation mainly to the nobles who would have seen them produced (anonymously) at court. A date of 1595 accords well enough with the Oxfordian assmption of later revision. One performance of *Richard II* in 1595 may have occurred at Hoby's house in Canon Row, Westminster, close to where Oxford was living at the time with his daughter, Elizabeth, and her husband, William Stanley, Earl of Derby. The invited guest, Robert Cecil, was also Oxford's brother-in-law (Nelson, 349–53).

*Richard II* has always been recognised as a ceremonial play, especially in the jousting scene with the balanced speeches and courteous addresses. Oxford was victorious in various tilts held before the Queen (in 1571 and 1581) and one of his addresses to the Queen survives. Oxford also held the title Lord Great Chamberlain, whose role was to supervise ceremonies including coronations. We also find Mowbray's lament over his fall from grace and exile to Venice has parallels with Oxford's own fall from grace and his earlier sojourn in Venice. [7]

Another major suggestion that Oxford was the author lies in Richard's final words at 5.5.5111–12: "Mount, mount, my soul! Thy seat is up on high / Whilst my gross flesh sinks downward here to die." These are reminiscent of words written by Oxford in 1573: "Virtue yet will ever abide with us, and when our bodies fall into the bowels of the earth, yet that shall mount with our minds into the highest heavens." This quotation comes from Oxford's introduction to Bedingfield's translation of *Cardanus Comfort* (STC: 4608).

Significantly, Raphael Holinshed, author of the *Chronicles*, was a member of Lord Burghley's household, where Oxford was a ward (1562–71) and where his wife Anne Cecil generally resided (1571–1588). Holinshed had dedicated his first edition to William Cecil, Lord Burghley, in 1577. In addition, Holinshed had sat as a juror to the enquiry that found Oxford not guilty of manslaughter in 1567. Furthermore, he had deflected blame from Oxford by issuing a pamphlet in 1573 attacking a man called Brown as the perpetrator of a murder in Shooters Hill.[8] Oxford was a fervent Lancastrian, consistent with the portrayal of John of Gaunt, against the interpretation offered in *Woodstock*. His ancestor, Robert de Vere, Duke of Ireland, (1362–92) had been a favorite of Richard, and was portrayed, along with Mowbray in *Leicester's Commonwealth* (1584), as far worse than Bushy, Bagot or Green; curiously Robert de Vere is not mentioned in either *Woodstock* or *Richard II*.[9]

There are further connections with the source writers: Samuel Daniel, author of *The Civile Wars,* was a member of Mary Sidney's literary circle. Oxford had close links with Mary Sidney. It is likely that Oxford and Daniel consulted each other on their grand works, which they developed in different genres. The French Chronicle *Richard II,* which was sympathetic to Richard, was available in a manuscript owned by John Dee. Dee was an associate of Oxford, whose letters as a child in French showed his linguistic virtuosity. The author's use of the Geneva Bible also link with the Earl of Oxford, who bought a copy in 1569. Finally, Ovid's *Metamorphoses* had been translated into English by Oxford's maternal uncle, Arthur Golding, who like Holinshed had been a member of Cecil's household while Oxford was a ward there in the 1560s.[10]

One further anomaly in the dating of the play concerns John of Gaunt's paean to England. Dillian Gordon has suggested that the line at 2.1.46: "This precious stone set in the silver sea" might have been inspired by a tiny detail in the famous Wilton Diptych. This wooden panel, which has been dated *c.* 1395, portrays a holy King Richard accompanied by various angels and saints. At the top of a pole is an orb which depicts a small island in green, surrounded by a sea originally in silver leaf. Gordon is unable to explain how a precious and intimate royal heirloom could have been seen by Shakespeare, but it is quite possible that Oxford, who for a long time was one of Elizabeth's favorite courtiers, might well have observed the diptych closely.[11]

11. Detail of Wilton Diptych

## External Oxfordian Evidence

Both Tillyard (149) and Dover Wilson argued that Shakespeare wrote earlier versions of the *Richard II–Henry V* tetralogy, which he later revised into the extant versions. This accords with Oxfordian dating to 1587–88 in which the play deals with the topical issue of the deposition of a monarch but militates against this as an acceptable course of action. As such, the play was written as a warning against nobles who might have been tempted to plot against Elizabeth.

Eva Turner Clark, however, argued for an even earlier date *c.* 1582, when the Earl of Oxford was languishing in the Queen's displeasure. She notes that the most memorable speech in the play is John of Gaunt's complaint about England being leased out, and she sees Oxford as the author trying to warn the Queen about courtiers such as Henry Howard and Charles Arundel. This would also explain why the Chamberlain's Men in 1601 would have complained about it being an old play. One apparent oversight was the failure of the Privy Council to call to witness the author of the play when investigating the performance the night before the Essex Rebellion. Other authors were punished quite severely for writing plays which did not meet official approval: Hayward was imprisoned from 1600 for publishing *The Life and Reigne of Henry IIII* (Manning, 29–31); Jonson was imprisoned from July–October 1597 for his part authorship of *Isle of Dogs* (Chambers, *ES*, III, 353). Yet no author was seriously interrogated in 1601 for writing a play about the deposition of King Richard II. The reason may have been that *Richard II* was a quasi-official enactment of a historical fact, demonstrating ultimately how wrong it was to seize the crown.

## Conclusion

The composition of the play *Richard II* in its Quarto form can be assigned to any time between 1587 (the second edition of Holinshed) and 1597, the publication of the first quarto.

## Notes

1. David Bergeron, "The Deposition Scene in *Richard II*", *Renaissance Papers* 1974, 31–7 and J. Clare, "The Censorship of the Deposition Scene in *Richard II*" in *Review of English Studies*, 1990, XLI: 89–94. The various interpretations have been reviewed by David Bergeron, "*Richard II* and Carnival Politics" in *SQ*, 42, 1991, 33–43.
2. E. M. W. Tillyard's *Shakespeare's English History Plays,* 1944 rptd 1980, 244–263.
3. John L. Manning (ed.) *Thomas Heywood's Henry IIII,* (introduction); J. Leeds Barroll, "A New History for Shakespeare and his Time" in *SQ*, 29, 1988, 441–

464.

4. Chambers, *W. S.*, I, 352, believes *Woodstock* might have been a source for Shakespeare; Egan refers to *Woodstock* as Shakespeare's *Richard II Part 1.*
5. William B. Long, " 'A bed / for Woodstock' a warning for the unwary", *Medieval and Renaissance Drama in England*, 2, 1985, 91–118.
6. Christopher Highley, *Shakespeare, Spenser and the Crisis in Ireland,* 1997.
7. Nelson describes Oxford's role at the Coronation of James (422–3), his success in the Tilts as the Knight of the Tree of the Sun (261–6) and his visit to Venice (121–32).
8. Nelson on Oxford's acquittal (47–9) and on Holisnhed's pamphlet (89–91).
9. Nigel Saul in *Richard II and the Crisis of Authority,* 1997.
10. Details in Nelson re Dee (186–7), Golding (39–41), Mary Sidney (171–2), Holinshed (90–2).
11. Dillian Gordon *et al.*, *Making and Meaning: The Wilton Diptych.* 1994.

## Other Cited Works

Bullough, G., *Narrative and Dramatic Sources of Shakespeare*, vol. III. London: Routledge, 1960

Chambers, E. K., *William Shakespeare: a study of facts and problems*, 2 vols. Oxford: Clarendon Press, 1930

Corbin, Peter, and Douglas Sedge (eds), *Thomas of Woodstock:* or, *Richard II, Part One* Manchester: MUP, 2002

Egan, Michael (ed.), *The Tragedy of Richard II, Part One: a newly authenticated play by William Shakespeare,* New York: Edwin Mellen Press 2006

Forker, C. R. (ed.), *Richard II*, London: Arden, 2002

Gordon, Dillian et al., *Making and Meaning, The Wilton Diptych*, London: National Gallery Publications, 2004

Gurr, Andrew (ed.), *Richard II*, Cambridge: CUP, 1984

Nelson, Alan H, *Monstrous Adversary: The Life of Edward de Vere, 17th Earl of Oxford,* Liverpool: LUP, 2003

Shaheen, Naseeb, *Biblical References in Shakespeare's Plays,* Delaware: UDP, 1999

Ure, Peter (ed.), *Richard II*, London: Arden, 1956

Wells, S. & G. Taylor, *William Shakespeare: a textual companion*, Oxford: OUP, 1987

Wilson, J. Dover (ed.), *Richard II*, Cambridge: CUP, 1951

17

# The Firſt Part of Henry the Fourth, with the Life and Death of HENRY sirnamed HOT-SPVRRE

Kevin Gilvary

The extant *1 Henry IV* can be dated at any time between the publication of the second edition of Holinshed in 1587, and 1598, when *1 Henry IV* first appeared in print.

## Publication Date

*King Henry IV Part 1* was registered and published in 1598, the year after *Richard II* was published:

> [SR 1598] xxv[to] die Februarij. Andrew Wyse. Entred for his copie vnder thandes of Master DIX: and master Warden Man a booke intituled The histrye of Henry iiij[th] with his battaile of Shrewsburye against Henry Hottspurre of the Northe with the conceipted mirthe of Sir John Ffalstoff vj[d]
>
> [Q1 1598] The History of Henrie the Fourth; With the battell at Shrewsburie, betweene the King and Lord Henry Percy, surnamed Henrie Hotspur of the North. With the humorous conceits of Sir Iohn Falstalffe. At London, Printed by P(eter) S(hort) for Andrew Wise, dwelling in Paules Church-yard, at the signe of the Angell 1598.

It is possible that there were two quartos printed in 1598, the earlier of which now (Qo) only exists in four leaves, covering 1.1.119 to 2.2.106. These leaves, which were used as binding for another book, are more widely spaced and would

THE
HISTORY OF
HENRIE THE
FOVRTH;

With the battell at Shrewsburie,
*betweene the King and Lord* Henry
Percy, *surnamed* Henry Hotspur of the North.

*VVith the humorous conceits of Sir*
Iohn Falstalffe.

Newly corrected by *W. Shake-speare.*

AT LONDON,
Printed by *S. S.* for *Andrew VVise*, dwelling
in Paules Churchyard, at the signe of
the Angell. 1599.

12. Title page to the anonymous first quarto of *Henry IV Part 1*, 1598.
By permission of Bodleian Library, University of Oxford,
shelfmark Arch. G d.45 (5) title page.

have required more sheets for the entire quarto. It is therefore thought that they were quickly revised and probably offer an earlier and superior reading to Q1. Otherwise, the uniformity of speech prefixes and the quality of the readings suggest that Q1 was set from the author's so-called 'fair papers' (Chambers, *WS*, I, 375–384).

In his list of 12 plays by Shakespeare in 1598, Meres mentions *Henry IV* but does not distinguish parts 1 or 2. Like *Richard II, Henry IV* was soon reprinted, and attributed to W. Shake-Speare:

> [Q2 1599] The History of Henrie the Fourth; With the battell at Shrewsburie, betweene the King and Lord Henry Percy, surnamed Henry Hotspur of the North. With the humorous conceits of Sir Iohn Falstaffe. Newly corrected by W. Shake-speare. At London, Printed by S(imon) S(taf-ford) for Andrew Wise, dwelling in Paules Church-yard, at the signe of the Angell. 1599.

The rights to publication were soon transferred from Andrew Wise to Matthew Lawe, which distinguishes the two parts:

> [SR 1603] 25 Junij. Mathew Lawe. Entred for his copie in full courte Holden this Day. These ffyve copies followinge . . . viz iii enterludes or playes . . . The Third of Henry the 4 the first parte. all kinges ... all whiche by consent of the Company are sett ouer to him from Andrew Wyse.

Despite the publication of *Henry IV Part 2* in 1600, subsequent editions of this play are simply called *The History of Henrie the fourth* without any further distinction:

> [Q3 1604] The History of Henrie the fourth, With the battell at Shrewsburie, betweene the King, and Lord Henry Percy, surnamed Henry Hotspur of the North. With the humorous conceits of Sir Iohn Falstaffe. Newly corrected by W. Shake-speare. London Printed by Valentine Simmes, for Mathew Law, and are to be solde at his shop in Paules Churchyard, at the signe of the Fox. 1604.
>
> [Q4 1608] The History of Henry the Fourth, With the battell at Shrewesburie, betweene the King, and Lord Henry Percy, surnamed Henry Hotspur of the North. With the humorous conceites of Sir Iohn Falstalffe. Newly corrected by W. Shake-speare. London, Printed for Mathew Law, and are to be sold at his shop in Paules Churchyard, neere vnto S. Augustines gate, at the signe of the Foxe. 1608.
>
> [Q5 1613] The History of Henrie the fourth, With the Battell at Shrewseburie, betweene the King, and Lord Henrie Percy, surnamed Henrie Hotspur of the North. With the humorous conceites of Sir Iohn Falstaffe. Newly corrected by W. Shake-speare. London, Printed by W(illiam) W(hite) for Mathew Law, and are to be sold at his shop in

Paules Church-yard, neere vnto S. Augustines Gate, at the signe of the Foxe. 1613.

The Dering Manuscript (owned by Sir Edward Dering, 1598–1644, of Surrenden in Kent) interestingly conflates both parts of *Henry IV.* It is usually considered a copy from 1622–3 of a redaction made after 1613. It is based on Q5 of *1 Henry IV* and the 1600 Q of *2 Henry IV.* The Dering MS may have been prepared for amateur theatrics, as many readings anticipate modern interpretations. It covers about 90% of *1 Henry IV* and about 30% of *2 Henry IV.* It has also been suggested that the Dering MS preserves Shakespeare's originally single play *Henry IV,* which the poet later expanded into two parts to capitalize on the popularity of the Falstaff character. The Dering MS is now in the Folger Shakespeare Library, Washington.[1]

[Q6 1622] The History of Henrie the fourth, With the Battell at Shrewseburie, betweene the King, and Lord Henrie Percy, surnamed Henrie Hotspur of the North. With the humorous conceites of Sir Iohn Falstaffe. Newly corrected by W. Shake-speare. London, Printed by T(homas) P(urfoot) for Mathew Law, dwelling in Paules Church-yard, at the signe of the Foxe neere S. Augustines. 1622.

When published in the First Folio, the two parts are distinguished:

[F1 1623] The First part of King Henry the fourth, [*Head-title*] The First Part of Henry the Fourth, with the Life and Death of Henry Sirnamed Hotspur.

Chambers believed that later quartos and the folio derived in sequence from Q1 and that "newly corrected", which occurs from Q2 onwards, is merely a sales pitch. There are about 168 lines in F1, not reported in Q1, which are taken to be cuts as Q1 is left with awkward transitions.

It is widely believed that the character of Falstaff was originally named Sir John Oldcastle (as in the anonymous *Famous Victories of Henry V,* discussed below and in Chapter 40), e.g. he is addressed as "my old man of the castle" (1.2.47) and there is a speech prefix 'Old' in *2 Henry IV* at 1.2.137 where one might expect 'Fal'. In the epilogue to *2 Henry IV,* a pointed reference is made to the fact that he is NOT Oldcastle but Falstaff.

Falstaff shall die of a sweat [*sc.* in France], unless already a be killed by your hard opinions. For Oldcastle died martyr and this is not the man.

Chambers notes that the character was referred to as Oldcastle as late as 1639. Gary Taylor has developed the argument[2] that after a performance of the play in 1596–7 (for which there is no direct evidence), the author bowed to pressure from Sir John Oldcastle's descendant, Sir William Brooke. Brooke, who was the tenth Baron Cobham, held the post of Lord Chamberlain from August 1596 briefly until his death on 5 March 1597. In this capacity, he was responsible for the Office of the Master of Revels and for licensing plays. It is also possible that the pressure to change the name of the braggard soldier from Oldcastle to Falstaff came from Sir William's son, Sir Henry Brooke, eleventh Baron Cobham. Taylor (and others) have further argued that the play called *Sir John Oldcastle, Part 1* (for which Henslowe paid Drayton, Hathaway, Munday and Wilson in October 1599) was an attempt to restore the reputation of the historical Oldcastle, as can be seen in the prologue:

> It is no pampered glutten we present
> Nor aged Councellour to youthfull sinne.

There is further discussion in the edition of Bevington, but there is no definitive evidence as to which person, if any, made the dramatist change the name of the character. It is also possible that Henry Carey, first Baron Hunsdon, had required the change. Hunsdon had succeeded Thomas Radclyffe, Earl of Sussex and served as Lord Chamberlain from 1585–1596, presiding over the Lord Chamberlain's Men from their formation in 1594.

## Relations to *Richard II, Henry IV Part 2* and *The Merry Wives of Windsor*

Most commentators follow Chambers and agree that *Richard II* was composed with *Henry IV* in mind. The theme of father and son appears strongly in the earlier play (Gaunt–Bolingbroke; York–Aumerle; Northumberland–Hotspur) and is developed in the second play. At the end of *Richard II*, Bolingbroke, now Henry IV, compares his own son unfavourably to Hotspur, a rivalry that reaches its climax in *Henry IV Part 1*. Bolingbroke's relationship with the Percys is also developed across the plays. Various prophecies and promises are recalled in *Henry IV*, while Henry IV often alludes to the "crooked ways" in which he had gained the crown.

Similarly, most commentators believe that *Henry IV Part 1* was composed with *Henry IV Part 2* in mind. *Part 1* ends with the dispatch of Henry's princes to deal with the Archbishop of York's Rebellion, which begins *Part* 2. Tillyard[3] and Dover Wilson agree on the idea of a ten-act play. Jenkins and Melchiori believe that Shakespeare envisaged a single five-act play (covering the main action in both parts) but expanded it into two plays as he progressed. Against this, Law has emphasised the differences in the two parts, especially with the reduplication of material, but this is a minority view.

Finally, most commentators agree that *Henry IV Parts 1 & 2* were composed before *Merry Wives of Windsor*, because the comedy assumes knowledge of characters from the history plays. A few believe that Shakespeare broke off his history plays (before or during the composition of *Henry IV Part 2*) so as to write *Merry Wives of Windsor*. This suggestion is considered in the chapter on *Henry IV Part 2*.

## Relation to the anonymous *Famous Victories of Henry the Fifth* (1594 ?)

There is no evidence about the relationship between the anonymously published *The Famous Victories of Henry the Fifth* (*FV*) and Shakespeare's plays. Although *FV* was registered on 14 May 1594 and the earliest extant edition dates from 1598, there are various reasons to think that it was played earlier. The title page of *FV* records that it had been played by the Queen's Men, who were mainly active in the 1580s (according to Scott McMillin and Sally-Beth MacLean, *The Queen's Men and their Plays,* 1999. Richard Tarlton, who died in 1588, is recorded as performing in a Prince Hal play (in *Tarlton's Jests*):

> At the [Red] Bull at Bishops-gate, was a play of Henry the fift, where in the judge was to take a box on the eare; and because he was absent that should take the blow, Tarlton himself, ever forward to please, took upon him to play the same judge, besides his owne part of the clowne.

Since the anecdote suggests events in a single play, *FV,* which are spread across *Henry IV* and *Henry V,* it seems likely that Tarlton appeared in a version of *Famous Victories,* which would mean that it must have been written before 1588.

There is a reference in Nashe's *Pierce Pennilesse* (1592), which recalls a scene similar to the ending in *Famous Victories*:

> What a glorious thing it is to have Henrie the fifth represented on the stage leading the French king prisoner and forcing both him and the Dolphin to swear fealty.

Ribner notes that *FV* only covers the events concerning Prince Hal (or Henry V as he is called) with Oldcastle in the three plays *1, 2 Henry IV* and *Henry V*; *Famous Victories* does not cover Henry IV's dealings with his rebellions.

The following suggestions have been made about *Famous Victories* in its relation to *Henry IV*:

- *FV* is a memorial reconstruction of a longer play by another author, in which Oldcastle featured more prominently (Chambers, Ribner);
- Shakespeare wrote *FV* (although the extant version is a shortened, corrupt version). Shakespeare later adapted and expanded *Famous Victories* into the *Henry IV – Henry V* trilogy (Tillyard, Bullough and especially Pitcher[4]);
- *FV* was an original play by the Earl of Oxford, later adapted and expanded by him (Clark, Jimenez).

It is very clear that there is a close relationship between *Famous Victories of Henry V* and the *Henry IV–Henry V* plays. See Ramon Jimenez, Chapter 40, for further consideration.

## Performance Date

There are no contemporary records of actual performances of *Henry IV Part 1* or *Part 2*. However, judging by the many mentions of Falstaff, it would appear that *Part 1* was performed frequently. The Chamber Accounts of 1612-13 record performances of plays called *Hotspur* (which is presumed to be *1 Henry IV*) and Sir Iohn Falstaffe, which Weis believes was *2 Henry IV*.[5]

## Sources

Bullough cites similar historical sources for *Henry IV Parts 1 & 2* as for *Richard II*.

**Edward Hall, *The Union of the Two Noble and Illustre Famelies of Lancastre and Yorke*** (1548–50). Bullough argues that the author began his plan for the tetralogy by studying Hall but concedes that Hall might not have been used for any details in the *Henry IV* plays. It is thought likely, however, that the dramatist would have read Hall, where the sense of nemesis felt by Henry IV is particularly strong.

**Raphael Holinshed, *The Chronicles of Englande, Scotlande, and Irelande*** (1st ed. 1577 & 2nd ed. 1587). Bullough demonstrates how Holinshed provided most of the detailed material for the play, including Worcester's dismissal from court, Percy's rebellion, Mortimer's capture and the Battle of Shrewsbury. It seems the wording for the second edition was used, e.g. "by smiling *pickthanks* and base newsmongers" (3.ii.25) which is not in the first edition.

**Samuel Daniel's epic poem *The First Fowre Bookes of the Civile Wars*** was registered on 11 October 1594 and published twice in 1595 (according to the title page), i.e. two years before the registration and publication of *Richard II*. Both play and poem make Prince Hal (historical date of birth 1387) and Hotspur (historical birth in 1364, and thus older than Hal's father) roughly contemporaries. Both play and poem make Hal save the King's life from Douglas and kill Hotspur. The problem is knowing whether Daniel embarked on his epic poem before Shakespeare began his tetralogy, or whether Shakespeare's handling of various themes influenced Daniel.

The anonymous ***Famous Victories of Henry the Fifth*** (*c.* 1594 ?) provides the theme of the madcap prince developing into a fine king. While Hal's antics were previously recorded, they were given prominence in this play. *1 Henry IV* takes up the highway robbery; the riotous tavern scenes; the anticipations of mis-rule; the parody of authority; and the reconciliation of the Prince with the King. The companions include Oldcastle (much less developed in *FV* compared to Falstaff in *1H4*), Ned (Poins) and Gadshill. Bullough believes that the extant text of *Famous Victories* is a debased, shortened form of an original play by Shakespeare, which may have been in the repertoire before 1588. See Chapter 40 for further consideration.

Bullough believes that **John Stow's *Chronicles of England*** (1580) and ***Annals of England*** (1592) (or previous chronicles) was an indirect source, as it was almost certainly used by the author of *Famous Victories* for Hal's adventures and for a legal report about Sir John Fastolf of Nacton.

***A Mirrour for Magistrates*** (1559, 1563, 1578), like Hall, begins with the reign of Richard II, and provided material for many characters featured in *I Henry IV*: Bullough believes that the author might have used *The Mirror for Magistrates* (1559) for material on Owen Glendower and Henry Percy, Earl of Northumberland, rather than Hall.

Similarities with *Thomas of Woodstock* (almost certainly used for *Richard II*) have also been noted in the references to misrule (Henry IV anxious that his son will not repeat the mistakes of Richard II), an energetic Chief Justice and the portrayal and intermingling of different social classes.

Shaheen discusses the large number of biblical references in *Henry IV Part 1*. He notes that while all the sources tend to be moralistic and religious in tone, there are very few actual references to the Bible in the original chronicles and only three in *Famous Victories*. Thus, according to Shaheen, Shakespeare introduced his own religious references, especially for Falstaff (who utters 23 out of 55 references). References to classical works are rare, but are evident in some of Falstaff's disquisitions on honour, (e.g. from Plautus' *Miles Gloriosus*, 'the Braggart Soldier') and in Vernon's comparison of Hal to Mercury at 4.1.107, which recalls Ovid's *Metamorphoses IV*. Allusions to specific English literary works are also rare, but include the anonymous *New Enterlude called Thersytes* (1537) for the braggart soldier (Falstaff) and John Lyly's *Endimion* (1591), which seem to have influenced Falstaff's speech at 2.4 368. The direction of influence, however, is not absolutely established.

## Orthodox Date – Internal Evidence

*King Henry IV Part 1* is uniformly dated to 1596 or 1597, soon after the (apparent) composition of *Richard II* and shortly before its own publication in quarto in 1598. Events and themes in *Henry IV Part 1* follow closely on from *Richard II*.

## Orthodox Date – External Evidence

Christopher Highley has argued that there is a close correspondence between *Henry IV Part 1* and events in Ireland in the 1590s. In particular, he sees parallels between Tyrone's rebellion against the rule of Elizabeth and Shakespeare's portrayal of Glendower. Bullough has suggested that the levying of soldiers unfit for service (by Falstaff at 4.i in *1H4* and at 3.ii in *2H4*) resonates with events in the 1590s. Sir John Smithe had published *Instructions, Observations and Orders Militarie* in which he gave advice on the recruitment of soldiers. In September 1596, the Council ordered that a hundred "serviceable" men, not "the baser sort", be levied in Northamptonshire for campaigns in Ireland.[6]

## Oxfordian Dating

There are many links between the behaviour of Hal and the life of the young Oxford. The Boar's Head was the emblem of the de Vere family and the Earl himself had been unfavorably compared to a boar's head by Sir Christopher Hatton. In 1602, the Earl's own players were granted permission to play at the Boar's Head Inn in Eastcheap. Another parallel lies in the depiction of Falstaff committing highway robbery on the King's Receivers at Gad's Hill (between Rochester and Gravesend) only to be robbed by the disguised prince in turn. This is reminiscent of a robbery in May 1573 of two of Lord Burghley's servants by Oxford and some friends. Indeed, Burghley often complained of the low life company kept by his son-in-law.[7] A further comparison lies in the very sympathetic portrait of Henry IV, for whom the Earls of Oxford had fought.[8]

Oxfordians generally agree that the play was intended for performance at court, and that it is possible the Falstaff scenes were developed for popular appeal when the play transferred to the public stage. Clark dates the early revision of *1 Henry IV* shortly after 1583–4 and she cites many details in the play which correspond to the 'Throckmorton Plot' in 1582 to assassinate Queen Elizabeth, with Hal's errant behaviour based on Oxford's own life. The rebellion of the Percys in *1 Henry IV* appears to coincide closely with the Northern Rebellion against Elizabeth in 1569.

Clark argues that *Famous Victories* was written by Oxford in the early 1570s to explain and excuse his behaviour in absconding to the Low Countries without the permission of the Queen. It has been variously described as "crude", "primitive", "almost imbecilic", a "decrepit pot-boiler", and "a medley of nonsense and ribaldry", which seems to mark it out as a youthful endeavour. If Oxford presented his story of a 'truant prince who begs forgiveness of the King', as Clark suggests, before the Queen at Christmas 1574, then it worked: Elizabeth granted Oxford the next week a licence to travel. It may have been the "device" praised and credited specifically to Oxford by the French Ambassador on 3 March 1579 (Chambers, *ES*, IV, 96). Jimenez, however, argues for an even earlier date in the late 1560s, before Oxford attended Gray's Inn. For more details, see Chapter 40.

For the revised version of *Henry IV Part 1*, close connections to early 1587 have been suggested. Firstly, more than one plot against Elizabeth's own life had been made lately, including that of William Parry, member of Parliament and employee of the trustworthy Sir Francis Walsingham. Secondly, the author's words about "fearful muster and prepared defense" apply closely to England in January 1587, with the Spanish armies had not yet been engaged. The change from Oldcastle to Falstaff would thus have been required by Henry Carey as Lord Chamberlain.

## Conclusion

The extant *1 Henry IV* can be dated to any time between the 1587 publication of the second edition of Holinshed, and 1598, when *1 Henry IV* first appeared in print.

## Notes

1. See Kastan's edition, Appendix C, 349–53.
2. Gary Taylor (ed.), *Henry V*, Oxford edition, 1982.
3. E. M. W. *Tillyard's Shakespeare's English History Plays,* original edition 1944 (rptd 1980).
4. Irvine Ribner, *The English History Play in the Age of Shakespeare* (1957). Seymour Pitcher, *The Case for Shakespeare's Authorship of 'The Famous Victories of Henry V'*, 1966. See Jimenez, Chapter 40, for further discussion.
5. Rene Weis (ed.), *King Henry IV Part 2*, 1987. The second part of the text includes mention of many plays:

   > Item paid to the said John Heminges vppon the lyke warrant, dated att Whitehall xx° die Maij 1613, for presentinge sixe severall playes, viz: one playe called A badd begininninge makes a good endinge, One other called the Capteyne, One other the Alcumist, One other Cardenno, One other The Hotspur, And one other called Benedicte and Betteris, All played within the tyme of this Accompte viz: paid Fortie powndes, And by waye of his Majesties rewarde twentie powndes, In all lx$^{n}$.

6. Christopher Highley, *Shakespeare, Spenser and the Crisis in Ireland.* 1997.
7. Nelson describes the robbery (89–93) and the licence for the Boar's Head (390–1).
8. See Verily Anderson, *The De Veres of Castle Hedingham,* 89–92, who describes the support of Richard, 11th Earl of Oxford, for Henry IV and Henry V.

## Other Cited Works

Bevington, David (ed.), *King Henry IV Part 1* Oxford: OUP, 1987

Bullough, G., *Narrative and Dramatic Sources of Shakespeare,* vol. IV, London: Routledge, 1962

Chambers, E. K., *William Shakespeare: a study of facts and problems,* 2 vols, Oxford:

Clarendon Press, 1930
Clark, E. T., *Hidden Allusions in Shakespeare's Plays,* New York: Kennikat, rptd 1974
Farina, William, *De Vere as Shakespeare,* Jeffferson NC: MacFarland, 2006
Hodgdon, Barbara (ed.), *The First Part of King Henry the Fourth,* New York: Bedford Books, 1997
Humphreys, A. R. (ed.), *King Henry IV Part 1,* London: Arden 2, 1960
Humphreys, A. R. (ed.), *King Henry IV Part 2,* London: Arden 2, 1966
Kastan, David Scott (ed.), *King Henry IV Part 1,* Arden 3, London: Arden Shakespeare, 2002
Jenkins, Harold, *The Structural Problem in Shakespeare's 'Henry IV'*, London: Methuen, 1956
Law, R. A., 'Structural Unity in the two parts of Henry IV', *SP* 24, 1927: 223–242
Melchiori, Giorgio (ed.), *The Second Part of Henry IV,* Cambridge: CUP, 1989
Nelson, A. H., *Monstrous Adversary,* Liverpool: LUP, 2003
Shaheen, Naseeb, *Biblical References in Shakespeare's Plays,* Delaware: UDP, 1999
Tillyard, E. M. W., *Shakespeare's History Plays,* London: Chatto & Windus, 1944
Weis, Rene (ed.), *King Henry IV Part 2,* Oxford: OUP, 1987
Wells, S. & G. Taylor, *William Shakespeare: a textual companion,* Oxford: OUP, 1987
Wilson, J. Dover (ed.), *King Henry IV Part 1, Part 2*, Cambridge: CUP, 1946

THE

Second part of Henrie the fourth, continuing to his death, *and coronation of Henrie* the fift.

With the humours of ſir Iohn Fal- *ſtaffe, and ſwaggering* Piſtoll.

*As it hath been ſundrie times publikely* acted by the right honourable, the Lord Chamberlaine his ſeruants.

*Written by William Shakeſpeare.*

LONDON
Printed by V.S.for Andrew Wiſe,and William Aſpley.
1600.

13. Title page to the first quarto of *Henry IV Part 2*, 1598. By permission of Bodleian Library, University of Oxford, shelfmark Arch. G d.43 (3) title page.

18

# The Second Part of Henry the Fourth, containing his Death : and the Coronation of King Henry the Fift

Kevin Gilvary

The extant *2 Henry IV* can be dated to any time between 1587 (the publication of the second edition of Holinshed) and 1600, when *2 Henry IV* appeared in print.

## Publication Date

*Henry IV, Part 2* was registered and published in 1600, two years after *Part 1* and shortly after *Henry V.*

> [SR 1600] 23 Augusti. Andrew Wyse William Aspley. Entred for their copies vnder the handes of the wardens Two bookes, the one called . . . Thother the second parte of the history of Kinge Henry the iiij[th] with the humours of Sir John Falstaff: Wrytten by master Shakespere. xij[d].
>
> [Q 1600] The Second part of Henrie the fourth, continuing to his death, and coronation of Henrie the fift. With the humours of sir Iohn Fal-staffe, and swaggering Pistoll. As it hath been sundrie times publikely acted by the right honourable, the Lord Chamberlaine his seruants. Written by William Shakespeare. London Printed by V[alentine] S[immes] for Andrew Wise, and William Aspley. 1600.

Act 3 Scene 1 was omitted from Q and included in F1. Dover Wilson believes that the scene was omitted because of fear that references to the deposition of Richard II would be censored. Melchiori maintains that this scene does not affect the action (the only new information is that Glendower has died). He believes that this scene was probably added later. About 30% of the play appears in the Dering manuscript (see Kastan, *1 Henry IV,* Arden 3, Appendix C.)

The play entitled *Henry IV* (known to us as *Part 1*) appeared in six quartos but was distinguished from *Part 2* only in an entry in the SR in 1603 and in F1. Meres mentions *Henry IV* (no distinction of parts) among Shakespeare's plays, listing it somewhat puzzlingly among the tragedies. *Part 2,* however, was published only in this quarto before the publication of the First Folio:

> [F1 1623] The Second part of Henry the Fourth, containing his death: and coronation of King Henry the Fift.

Weis believes that the Quarto of 1600 was printed from the foul papers, in which cuts had been made to satisfy the licensers of printed matter; he opines that the Quarto and a promptbook (the latter revised in 1606 to purge it of profanities) were collated to make a transcript for a private person's reading. Finally he suggests that the Folio text of 1623 was printed from this transcript.

## Performance Date

There are no records of early performances of *Henry IV Part 1* or *Part 2*. Because of contemporary references to Falstaff, it has been suggested that *Part 2* was performed alongside *Part 1* during the winter seasons 1596/7 and 1597/8. The Chamber Accounts of 1612–13 record a performance of a play called *Sir Iohn Falstaffe.* Weis believes that this must have been *Part 2,* since the accounts also refer to a play called *Hotspur.*[1]

## Relation to Other Plays

Chambers and most commentators agree on the original plan of a tetralogy and that *Richard II* and *Henry IV Part 1* was composed with both *Henry IV Part 2* and *Henry V* in mind; Weis calls it the "most sequel-esque of Shakespeare's plays". There is frequent reference back to events in previous plays in the tetralogy, e.g. to Richard's deposition. While some commentators believe that *Henry IV* was originally planned as one five-act play and developed into ten acts, most commentators believe that two plays covering the reign of Henry IV were envisaged at the outset. The anonymously printed *Famous Victories of Henry the Fifth* (*FV*) seems to provide the basis for many scenes in *1, 2 Henry IV* & *Henry V.* See Chapter 40 for further consideration of possible relationships.

It appears that Oldcastle was the original name for Falstaff in *Part 2* as well as in *Part 1* from the use of the speech prefix 'Old' at *Part 2* 1.2.117 where one might expect 'Fal'.[2] Weis discusses whether the character of Falstaff in *Part 2* is conceived separately from the character of Falstaff in *Part 1* and concludes that it was not, merely observing different treatment and a dramatic development.

There is divided opinion on whether Shakespeare had completed the tetralogy or not before composing *Merry Wives of Windsor.* Weis tentatively favours the idea that Shakespeare completed *Part 2* by the end of 1596 and then wrote *Merry Wives* in time for performance at the Garter ceremony on 23 April 1597.

## Sources

Bullough cites similar historical sources for *Henry IV Part 2* as for *Part 1* and for *Richard II.*

**Edward Hall, *The Union of the Two Noble and Illustre Famelies of Lancastre and Yorke*** (1548–50). Bullough argues that the author began his plan for the tetralogy by studying Hall. However, Hall does not appear to have been used for many details in the *Henry IV* plays.

**Raphael Holinshed, *The Chronicles of Englande, Scotlande, and Irelande*** (1st ed. 1577 & 2nd ed. 1587). Bullough demonstrates how Holinshed provided most of the detailed political material for *Part 2,* especially Scrope's rebellion. Shakespeare follows both Hall and Holinshed in depicting Henry IV's troubles as the result of his deposition and murder of Richard II. It seems the wording of the second edition was used, e.g. "in this year . . . to be seene" (4.iv 125) which is not in the first edition.

**Samuel Daniel's epic poem *The First Fowre Bookes of the Civile Wars*** was registered on 11 October 1594 and published twice in 1595 (according to the title page), i.e. three years before the registration and publication of *2 Henry IV.* Like Shakespeare, Daniel emphasises Henry IV as sad and conscience-stricken, minimising events after the Battle of Shrewsbury to concentrate on the King's sickness, the Prince's taking the crown and their final reconciliation. The problem is knowing whether Daniel embarked on his epic poem before Shakespeare began his tetralogy, or whether Shakespeare's handling of various themes influenced Daniel.

It is widely agreed that the relevant scenes in the anonymous ***Famous Victories of Henry The Fifth*** (*c.* 1594?) were consciously expanded by Shakespeare into *Henry IV Part 2,* especially in the theme of the wayward prince who develops into a fine king. While Hal's unruly behavour was previously mentioned, it is given prominence in this play, as well as Hal begging forgiveness from his dying father and Henry IV's virtual admission to usurping the crown. Bullough believes that the extant text of *Famous Victories* is a debased, shortened form of the original, which may have been in repertoire before 1588. See a more detailed consideration in Chapter 40.

Bullough believes that **John Stow's *Chronicles of England*** (1580) and ***Annals of England*** (1592) (or previous chronicles) were indirect sources for *Henry IV Part 2.* The Chronicles were almost certainly used by the author of *FV* for Hal's character and behaviour, so whether this is a direct or an indirect source depends on the view taken concerning the authorship of *FV.*

Bullough believes that the author probably used Sir Thomas Elyot's ***The Governour*** (1531) for the conception of justice in the speech by the Chief Justice in 5.2. The anonymous play *Hickscorner* (published in 1510) may have provided material for the character of Falstaff.

Shaheen discusses the number of Biblical allusions in *Henry IV Part 2.* He notes 65 references (compared to 55 in *Part 1*) distributed more evenly through the play; Falstaff only utters 17 (compared to 23 in *Part* 1). Many of the references come from books of the Old Testament, e.g. Job 21.26, which is echoed at 4.3.244–5:

> Only compound me with forgotten dust;
> Give that which gave thee life unto the worms.

Shaheen further notes that Shakespeare often uses the wording of the Geneva Bible (1560), e.g. 4.3.312–314:

> God knows, my son,
> By what by-paths and indirect crook'd ways
> I met this crown.

The Geneva Bible at Psalms 125.5 reads: "These that turn aside by their crooked wayes."

References to classical works are rare; Falstaff quotes the famous dictum: "I came, saw and overcame" (4.2.40). Allusions to specific English literary works are even rarer, perhaps including John Eliot's *Ortho-epia* (1593) and George Peele's play *The Battle of Alcazar* (1594) for Pistol's bragging speech in 2.4.

## Orthodox Date – Internal Evidence

There is no evidence for the date of composition. It is usually suggested that *King Henry IV Part 2* was composed in 1598–9, soon after the assumed date of composition for *Richard II* and *Henry IV Part 2* and shortly before its own publication in quarto in 1600. Events and themes in this play follow on closely from the preceding plays.

## Orthodox Date – External Evidence

It has been suggested that the levying of soldiers unfit for service (by Falstaff at 4.1 in *1H4* and at 3.ii in *2H4*) resonates with events in the 1590s. In 1595, Sir John Smithe had published *Instructions, Observations and Orders Militarie* in which he gave advice on the recruitment of soldiers. In June 1596, Smithe was up before the Star Chamber (according to Bullough) for inciting Essex's men to mutiny. In September of that year, the Council ordered that a hundred "serviceable" men not "the baser sort" be levied in Northamptonshire for campaigns in Ireland.

There seems to be a very topical reference at 5.2.46–9, when Hal offers reassurance:

> Brothers, you mix your sadness with some fear.
> This is the English, not the Turkish, court.
> Not Amurath an Amurath succeeds
> But Harry Harry.

This appears to be a reference to the accession of Mohammed III to the Turkish Sultanate in January 1596 on the death of his father, Murad (Amurath) III: Mohammed III had his brothers strangled. If the dramatist is referring to this event, it is not clear how such information could have been known, as Richard Knolles' *Generall Historie of the Turkes* was not published until 1603. Humphreys notes that his father Amurath had done the same on his accession in 1574, so it is more likely that the dramatist was using Francis Billerbeg's *Most Rare and Strange Discourses of Amurathe the Turkish Emperor* (1584).

Both Taylor and Weis have proposed that *Part 2* was completed in time for performance at court, with *1 Henry IV*, at Christmas 1596, when the Lord Chamberlain forced the removal of the name 'Oldcastle' from both plays; that at the same time Falstaff was substituted, and that the second and third paragraphs of the Epilogue were added later.

## Oxfordian Date

Oxfordians generally agree that Oxford wrote *Famous Victories* in the 1570s and expanded this into the *Henry IV–Henry V* trilogy in the 1580s. All four plays, according to this view, were intended for performance at court. Clark dates the early revision of *1 Henry IV* shortly after 1583–4 and she cites many details in the play which correspond to the 'Throckmorton Plot' of 1582 to assassinate Queen Elizabeth. The play would also be topical shortly afterwards, with possible allusions to the campaign in the Low Countries and the 'Babington Plot' of 1586. Shallow may partly be Sir Henry Wallop, Justice of the Peace for Hampshire (Ogburn).

The opening scene of *2 Henry IV* features Rumour, which recalls Elizabeth's proclamation against rumour on 6 February 1587 (16 February N.S.), two days before the execution of Mary, Queen of Scots. It is at least likely that when 'Rumour' noises it about that "the king [Henry IV] before the Douglas' rage / Stooped his anointed head as low as death" (31–32), the dramatist was in fact alluding to the execution of Mary.

## Conclusion

The extant *2 Henry IV* can be dated to any time between 1587 (the publication of the second edition of Holinshed) and 1600, when *2 Henry IV* appeared in print.

## Notes

1. The first part of the text includes mention of many plays:

> Item paid to John Heminges upon the Cowncells warrant dated att Whitehall xx° die Maij 1613, for presentinge before the Princes Highnes the Lady Elizabeth and the Prince Pallatyne Elector fowerteene severall playes, viz: one playe called Pilaster, One other called the Knott of Fooles, One other Much Adoe abowte Nothinge, The Mayeds Tragedy, The Merye Dyvell of Edmonton, The Tempest, A Kinge and no Kinge, The Twins Tragedie, The Winters Tale, Sir John Falstaffe, The Moore of Venice, The Nobleman, Caesars Tragedye, And one other called Love lyes a bleedinge.

2. As argued by Gary Taylor, ed., *Henry V*, Oxford edition, 1982.

## Other Cited Works


Bevington, David (ed.), *King Henry IV Part 1,* Oxford: OUP 1987

Bullough, G., *Narrative and Dramatic Sources of Shakespeare,* vol. III. London: Routledge, 1960

Chambers, E. K., *William Shakespeare: a study of facts and problems,* 2 vols, Oxford: Clarendon Press, 1930

—, *The Elizabethan Stage*, 4 vols, Oxford: Clarendon, 1923

Clark, Eva Turner, *Hidden Allusions in Shakespeare's Plays.* New York: Kennikat, rptd 1974

Hodgdon, Barbara, *The First Part of King Henry the Fourth,* New York: Bedford Books, 1997

Humphreys, A. R. (ed.), *King Henry IV Part 1,* London: Arden 2, 1960; *Part 2,* London: Arden 2, 1966

Melchiori, Giorgio (ed.), *The Second Part of Henry IV,* Cambridge: CUP, 1989

Nelson, Alan H, *Monstrous Adversary: The Life of Edward de Vere, 17th Earl of Oxford,* Liverpool: LUP, 2003

Ogburn, Charlton, *The Mysterious Mr Shakespeare*, Virginia: EPM, 1984

Shaheen, Naseeb, *Biblical References in Shakespeare's Plays,* Delaware: UDP, 1999

Weis, Rene (ed.), *King Henry IV Part 2,* Oxford: OUP, 1987

Wells, S. & G. Taylor, *William Shakespeare: a textual companion,* Oxford: OUP, 1987

Wilson, J. Dover, *The Fortunes of Falstaff,* Cambridge: CUP, 1943

Wilson, J. Dover (ed.), *King Henry IV Part 1; Part 2,* Cambridge: CUP, 1946

19

# The Life of King Henry the Fift

Kevin Gilvary

The extant *Henry V* can be dated to any time between 1587 (the publication of the second edition of Holinshed) and 1600, when *Henry V* [Q1] appeared in print.

## Publication Date

*Henry V* was registered and published anonymously in 1600, two years after *Henry IV Part 1* and a few weeks before *Henry IV Part 2*. Absent from Meres, it was first mentioned in the Stationers' Register in 1600 along with two other Shakespeare plays (*Much Ado About Nothing* and *As You Like It*) as well as Jonson's *Every Man in his Humour*:

> [SR 1600 ?] 4 Augusti. Henry the ffift, a book to be staied
>
> [SR 1600] 14 Augusti. Thomas Pavyer. Entred for his Copyes by Direction of master White warden vnder his hand wrytinge. These Copyes followinge beinge thinges formerlye printed and sett over to the sayd Thomas Pavyer. viz. . . . The historye of Henry the V[th] with the battell of Agencourt vj[d] .
>
> [Q1 1600] the Chronicle History of Henry the fift, With his battel fought at Agin Court in France. Togither with Auntient Pistoll. As it hath bene sundry times playd by the Right honorable the Lord Chamberlaine his seruants. [Creede's device] London Printed by Thomas Creede, for Tho. Millington, and Iohn Busby. And are to be sold at his house in Carter Lane, next the Powle head. 1600.

Q1 contains only 1,622 lines, compared to 3,381 in F1. Q1 has no Chorus speeches, nor is there a prologue or epilogue, and two complete scenes are omitted:

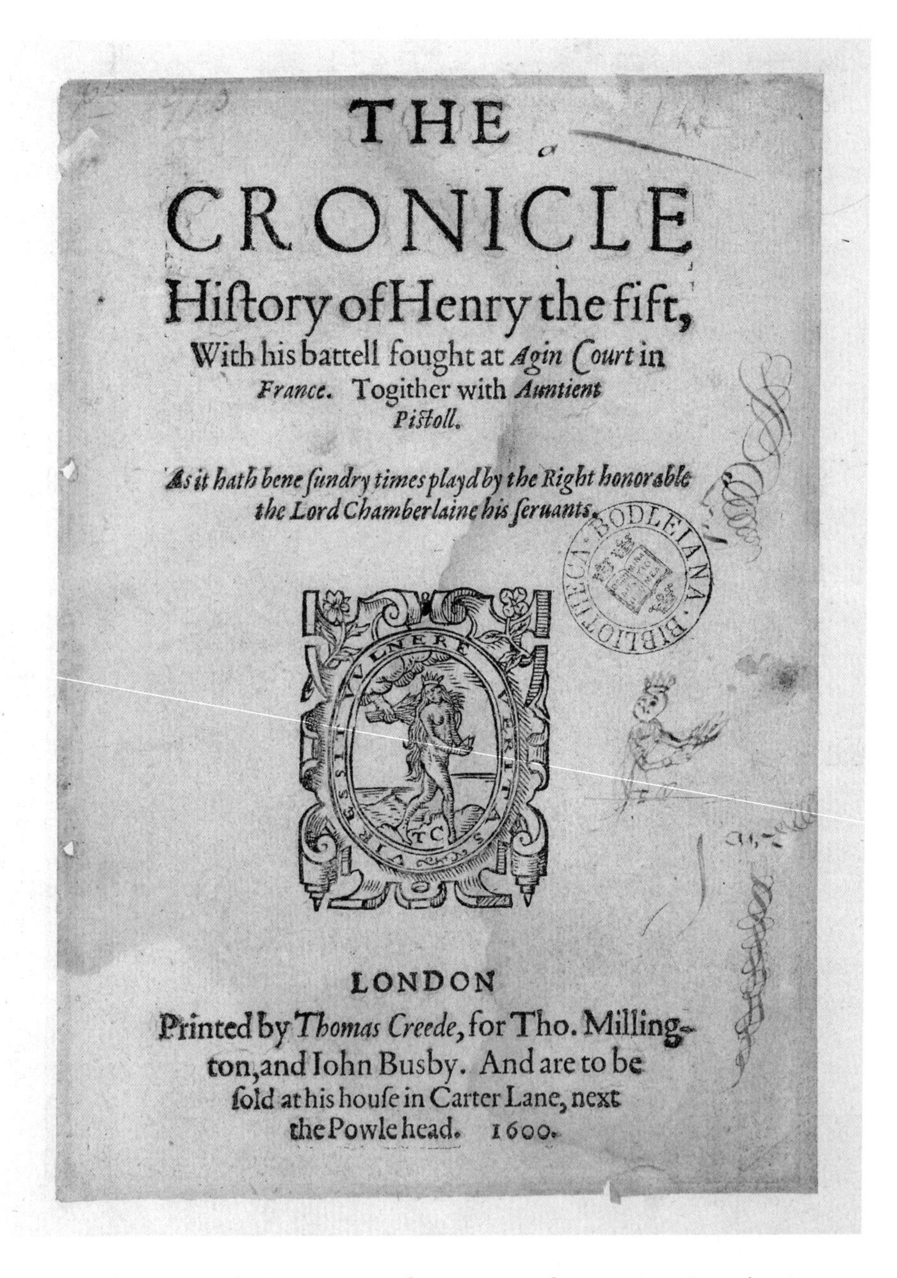

THE
CRONICLE
Hiſtory of Henry the fift,
With his battell ſought at *Agin Court* in
*France*. Togither with *Auntient*
*Piſtoll*.

*As it hath bene ſundry times playd by the Right honorable*
*the Lord Chamberlaine his ſeruants.*





LONDON
Printed by *Thomas Creede*, for Tho. Millington, and Iohn Busby. And are to be
ſold at his houſe in Carter Lane, next
the Powle head. 1600.

14. Title page to the anonymous first quarto of *Henry V*, 1600; this is a particularly short quarto of about 1,600 lines. It does not contain the speeches by the Chorus, not the puzzling reference to "the general of our gracious Empress". By permission of Bodleian Library, University of Oxford, shelfmark Arch. G d.39 (3) title page.

3.1 (Harry's speech at Harfleur) and 4.2 (French arming before Agincourt). That part of scene 3.2 which involves the Scots Captain Jamy and the Irish Captain MacMorris (65–140) is omitted from Q1, possibly, it has been said, to avoid offending James, who was Elizabeth's likeliest successor. Chambers (393), however, sees it as a later addition, "motivated by the Jacobean policy of a union of kingdoms". Chambers also sees Q1 as a "perversion", possibly a version cut for performance. Taylor refers to its gross fluctuation in standards. Pollard[1] and Wilson saw Q1 as one of a group of old plays, partly revised by the author and then transcribed in an abridged form for provincial use in 1593.

*Henry V*, like *Richard II* and *1Henry IV*, was soon reprinted:

> [Q2 1602] The Chronicle History of Henry the fift, With his battell fought at Agin Court in France. Together with Auntient Pistoll. As it hath bene sundry times playd by the Right honorable the Lord Chamberlaine his seruants. [Creede's device] London Printed by Thomas Creede, for Thomas Pauier, and are to be sold at his shop in Cornhill, at the signe of the Cat and Parrets neare the Exchange. 1602.

The play was not reprinted until 1619 (falsely dated 1608), as part of the Pavier Collection:

> [Q3 1619] The Chronicle History of Henry the fift, with his battell fought at Agin Court in France. Together with ancient Pistoll. As it hath bene sundry times playd by the Right Honourable the Lord Chamberlaine his Seruants. [William Jaggard's device] Printed for T[homas] P[avier] 1608.

Chambers believes Q2 was set independently from Q1 and he views Q3 as a conflation.

The play was printed in the First Folio in its historical position after the *Henry IV* plays and before the *Henry VI* plays:

> [F1 1623] The Life of Henry the Fift.

Chambers asserts that F1 was set from the author's own papers and that the shorter Qq were cut versions. Craik agrees, stating that the Chorus passages seem an "integral part of the design." They dismiss the suggestion that the Chorus speeches and other material not found in the Qq were part of a post 1600 revision.

## Performance Date

Apart from the mention on the title page of Q1 of its performance by the Lord Chamberlain's Men some time before 1600, there is only one record of an actual performance. The Revels Accounts record that *Henry V* was performed at court on 7 January 1605 soon after *Love's Labour's Lost* and shortly before

*Every Man out of His Humour* on 8 January and *Every Man in his Humour* on 2 February. Taylor is surprised that there are not more records of performances or more quartos. Similarly, there is only one (possible) allusion to *Henry V* before the First Folio: Jonson sneered at the use of a Chorus in *Every Man in his Humour* (revised text dated 1612–3). The frequent appearance of the Chorus to exhort the audience to use their imagination may have originated as a riposte to Philip Sidney, who in his *Defence of Poesy*, (*c.* 1581–3) had complained about the inadequacy of a theatre stage to represent grand events.

> By and by, we heare newes of a shipwracke in the same place, and then we are to blame if we accept it not for a Rock. Upon the backe of that, comes out a hidious Monster, with fire and smoke, and then the miserable beholders are bound to take it for a Cave. While in the meantime two Armies flye in, represented with foure swords and bucklers, and then what harde heart will not receive it for a pitched fielde? Now, of time they are much more liberall, for ordinary it is that two young Princes fall in love. After many traverses, she is got with childe, delivered of a faire boy; he is lost, groweth a man, falls in love, and is ready to get another child, and all this in two hours space.[2]

There seem to have been various plays about the reign of Henry V in the late 1580s and 1590s. Richard Tarlton is recorded as performing in a Prince Hal play (in *Tarlton's Jests*):

> At the [Red] Bull at Bishops-gate, was a play of Henry the fift, where in the judge was to take a box on the eare; and because he was absent that should take the blow, Tarlton himself, ever forward to please, took upon him to play the same judge, besides his owne part of the clowne.

This must have preceded 1588 when Tarlton died. Since this play appears to have contained events which are found together in *FV* but which are spread across *Henry IV* and *Henry V*, it seems likely that Tarlton appeared in an early version of *Famous Victories*. For Jiménez' argument that *Famous Victories* was written by Oxford and expanded by him into *Henry IV* and *Henry V*, see Chapter 40.

In 1592, Thomas Nashe wrote in *Piers Penniless:*

> What a glorious thing it is to have Henry V represented on the stage, leading the French king prisoner and forcing both him and the Dauphin to swear fealty.

Since this does not correspond to a scene either in the extant versions of *Famous Victories* or *Henry V*, Nashe's comment is taken to refer to a different play altogether. The anonymous *Famous Victories of Henry the Fifth* was registered in 1594 and published in 1598. Because the text is taken to be greatly debased from a longer original, it is possible that Nashe was have been referring to a longer, original version of *Famous Victories,* or to an early version of *Henry* V.

From 1595 to 1596, Henslowe's account book records 13 performances by the Admiral's Men of a 'ne' play he calls 'harey the v'. It is not clear whether 'ne' refers to a new play or to a play already known.[3] An inventory in 1598 of the company's apparel includes "harye the v, velvet gowne". Taylor believes these references are to a third, otherwise lost, play about Henry V.

## Relation to *Richard II, 1, 2 Henry IV* and *Merry Wives of Windsor*

Most commentators agree on the original plan being a tetralogy and that *Richard II* and *1, 2 Henry IV* were composed with *Henry V* in mind. Bolingbroke mentions his concerns over his wayward son in *Richard II* (5.3) where Hotspur attempts to reassure him. Shortly afterwards (at 5.6.42), Henry IV laments the murder of Richard and promises to go on a pilgrimage in expiation. Both these concerns remain with him through both parts of *Henry IV.* In *Henry V,* Hal, now King, throws off his lowly companions, behaves with regal authority and announces that he has built two chantries for prayer for Richard's soul (4.1.290). There is divided opinion on whether Shakespeare had completed the tetralogy or not before composing *Merry Wives of Windsor.*

The epilogue to *2 Henry IV* clearly anticipates events in *Henry V,* but there is an inconsistency:

> our humble author will continue the story with Sir John in it, and make you merry with fair Katherine of France; where (for anything I know) Falstaff shall die of a sweat, unless already a' be killed with your hard opinions; for Oldcastle died martyr, and this is not the man.

Falstaff does not appear in *Henry V* and instead his death is reported at 2.3 There has been much speculation as to why the author changed his mind and 'killed off' so popular a character: possibly it was due to the departure of the actor, Will Kemp, from the Lord Chamberlain's Men: it is argued that he may have been closely associated with the part; or possibly it was because of objections to Falstaff's presence by the Brooke family (as argued independently by Wilson and by Walter). Shakespeare may have had to rewrite some of the scenes and reassign Falstaff's tricks to Pistol. In so doing, Shaheen suggests some biblical references may have been lost, since Pistol only has five allusions, compared to over 40 by Falstaff in the two parts of *Henry IV.*

## Sources

Bullough cites Hall and Holinshed as the major historical sources for *Henry V,* as they had been for other history plays, but he also gives prominence to *Famous*

*Victories.* Shaheen claims that Shakespeare must have had each of these three sources open in front of him when writing this play.

**Edward Hall, *The Union of the Two Noble and Illustre Famelies of Lancastre and Yorke*** (1548–50). Bullough argues that the author began his plan for the tetralogy by studying Hall's moralising narrative of English History from Henry IV to Henry VIII. Hall emphasises the providential pattern of history in the coming of the Tudors, which ended the disastrous Civil Wars. The author follows Hall in placing the tennis-balls incident later (as in *Famous Victories*) and in mentioning Henry's wilder days. The exhortations of Canterbury, Ely and Exeter appear to derive from Hall.

**Raphael Holinshed, *The Chronicles of Englande, Scotlande, and Irelande*** (1st ed. 1577 & 2nd ed. 1587). Bullough demonstrates how Holinshed provided most of the detailed material for the play, including the French countermines at Harfleur, the wish for ten thousand more men and the Constable's taking a ribbon for use as a banner (not in Hall). It seems the second edition was used from the close following of the wording, e.g. 'for some *dishonest* manners of their life' (1.2 49), as in the second edition, where the first edition has 'unhonest'; and 'you have sold . . . his whole kingdom into *desolation*' (2.2 173), as in the second edition, where the first edition has 'destruction'.

The anonymous ***Famous Victories of Henry the Fifth*** (registered in 1594 and published in 1598) demonstrates the theme of the wayward prince developing into a fine king. Bullough shows how *Famous Victories* contributed slightly more to events in *Henry V* than it had to *1,* and *2 Henry IV* combined. It is generally agreed that the author consciously expanded the anonymous *Famous Victories* into *1, 2 Henry IV* and *Henry V.* See Chapter 40 for a detailed consideration of the relationship between the plays.

**Samuel Daniel's epic poem *The First Fowre Bookes of the Civile Wars*** was registered on 11 October 1594 and published twice in 1595 (according to the title page). The sixth and seventh books were published in 1601–02, and the complete poem in eight books was first issued in 1609. It is a poetical account of the struggle between the House of Lancaster and the House of York from the reign of Richard II to that of Edward IV. There is overlap in the material with Shakespeare, but less for Henry V than for Richard II or Henry IV. Daniel expresses a wish for a poet to do justice to Henry V and Bullough believes that Shakespeare might have risen to the challenge.

Among the Chronicles, the dramatist seems to have used **Fabyan's *Chronicle*** (first edition 1516; later editions up to 1559) for the reference at 4.i.289–99 to the chantries built to pray for the soul of Richard II. This detail is most significant, as Henry V is atoning at a key moment for his father's usurpation of the Crown and complicity in Richard's murder. The playwright may also have used Stowe's *Chronicles of England* (1580) and *Annals of England* (1592). The details of the stolen pyx/pax might derive from a Latin chronicle *Gesta Henrici Quinti*. Another Latin source, *Vita Henrici Quinti*, may have been used for the

Frenchmen's boasts about their horses and armour and for the King's habit of inspecting the army. The author may also have consulted the anonymous poem (1530) *Batall of Egyngecourt*.

The scene (3.4) showing the French Princess's language lesson appears to derive from medieval French farces, as Radoff has argued. He draws various and many close parallels from the *Farce Nouvelle très bonne* and other works.[4] The author is knowledgeable enough to finish the scene with a French vulgarism, although how far the audience would have appreciated this is unclear. Bullough has indicated that the language lesson may also derive from the Italian *commedia erudita*: in Secchi's *Interesse,* (published in Florence, 1552) the teacher discusses points of grammar in terms which have sexual overtones.

Shaheen devotes over 20 pages to discussion of the large number of biblical references in *Henry V.* He notes that while all the sources tend to be moralistic and religious in tone, there are few actual references to the Bible in the original chronicles: there are seven in Holinshed, of which Shakespeare uses three. The speech in 1.2 when the Archbishop of Canterbury quotes scripture (Shakespeare's only mention of a book in the Bible by name) he is following both Hall and Holinshed. Thus, according to Shaheen, Shakespeare also introduced many of his own religious references, e.g. Henry's soliloquy before Agincourt (4.1.267–70) appears to owe something to Ecclesiastes 5.12: "The sleeps of him that traueilth is sweete, whether he eate litle or much: but the sacietie (satiety) of the riche will not suffer him to sleepe." Unlike with the allusions in other plays, Shakespeare seems not to have consulted the Geneva Bible (1560) for *Henry V.* One puzzling reference occurs in 3.7.64–5:

> Le chien est retourné à son propre vomissement, et la truie lavée au bourbier.

The Dauphin's insult to the Constable is remarkably apt in context and alludes to 2 Peter 2.22. ("The dogge is returned to his own vomit:, and the sow that was washed to the wallowing in the myre.") The wording in French is found in the older Olivetan Bible, which first appeared in 1535 and remained the standard French Protestant Bible until 1560. It was re-published in editions of 1538, 1539, 1544 and 1544. Later editions, and the new version in 1560, have different wording here. It is astonishing that the dramatist quoted so accurately and appositely from French versions of the Bible and that he could employ the verbal humour in the language lesson involving Katherine; it is not clear how he could have obtained his knowledge, how many of his audience would have appreciated the French, or how many would have appreciated the biblical allusion.

References to classical works are rare, but are evident in some of comic scenes of cowardice (e.g. from Plautus' *Miles Gloriosus,* 'the Braggart Soldier'). Bullough cites Tacitus's *Annals* as the source for the Chorus's description of the English camp at Act 4 and for the King's exhortations to his soldiers. A translation of the *Annals* was published in 1598. Taylor, however, believes that another classical translation, Chapman's *Homer* (also published in 1598), was the source of these passages. Anne Barton pointed out that, in the *Annals,* Germanicus is merely an eavesdropper and does not converse with his subjects, let alone confront them in disguise. She notes that other history plays show a King in disguise meeting ordinary people, e.g. *Edward I* (*c.* 1591) and *1 Edward IV* (pre-1599).[5] Similarly, Craik is not convinced that either Tacitus or Homer was necessarily a source.

Allusions to specific English literary works are also rare. Henry's speech before Harfleur may be echoing Marlowe's *1 Tamberlaine* 4.1, although similar sentiments are expressed in Deuteronomy 20 10–14. Henry's unlikely victory against the odds reflects similar events at the Battle of Crécy, depicted in *Edward III* (printed 1595). In both cases, however, the unexpected English victory was celebrated in the *Chronicles.* The swaggering soldier as depicted in Falstaff and his companions in *1, 2 Henry IV* may also derive indirectly from an *Enterlude called Thersytes* (1537).

## Orthodox Dating – Internal Evidence

*King Henry V* is almost uniformly dated to 1599 or 1600, soon after the assumed composition of *Henry IV Part 2.* Events and themes follow closely on *Henry IV Part 2* in sequence from *Richard II.* Some commentators have, however, placed an earlier date on the play: Pollard and Wilson saw Q1 as one of a group of old plays, partly revised by the author and then transcribed in an abridged form for provincial use in 1593. Jiménez quotes Gurr's suggestion that the Quarto was deliberately cut for performance by its owners, and its immediate printing is a mark of its authority as an official version.[6] This scenario, however, would require Shakespeare writing a three-hour play that was then cut almost immediately for performance in two hours by his Lord Chamberlain's Men, and the cut version to be then printed. Jiménez thinks that it is very unlikely that the play can have been thus composed, cut, staged and printed in just a sixteen-month period.

## Orthodox Dating – External Evidence

Orthodox scholars are agreed that the play dates to 1599–1600, shortly before its publication and they cite a number of external events which correlate to scenes in the play. Almost every commentator is persuaded that the Chorus at 5.0 (in a passage which is not in Q1 and first appears in F1) is referring to Essex, who was sent from London on 27 March 1599 as the Queen's Lieutenant-General and General Governor of Ireland:

> But now behold,
> In the quick forge and working-house of thought,
> How London doth pour out her citizens . . .
> Were now the General of our gracious Empress –
> As in good time he may – from Ireland coming
> Bringing rebellion broached on his sword,
> How many would the peaceful city quit
> To welcome him! (5.0.22–24; 30–34)

Essex was sent to quell the mutiny of Tyrone. As Essex returned to London unsuccessful and in some disgrace on 28 September 1599, this passage at least (if not the whole play) would appear to have been composed during the spring or summer of 1599.

Gary Taylor calls it the only "explicit, extra-dramatic incontestable reference to a contemporary event anywhere in the canon." Taylor, however, is not absolutely sure that the reference is to Essex and considers whether the poet might be referring to a later general, Charles Blount, Lord Mountjoy, who was serving in Ireland 1600–3. Craik suggests that the reference is undoubtedly to Essex and points out that Mountjoy was not as popular as Essex and did not gain a victory until the Battle of Kinsale in December 1601 – too late for his new reputation to be included by the assumed date of the play (and the Chorus speeches are taken to have been cut from the version used for Q1).

Craik adds a further argument for 1599, since the Lord Chamberlain's Men had just opened their new playhouse, the Globe. He suggests that *Henry V* may have premièred at the older and smaller Curtain playhouse. Craik also notes that the Chorus's speech asks the audience to recall the triumphal returns to Rome of Caesar, which may anticipate Shakespeare's composition of *Julius Caesar* (usually dated 1599). It may be noted in passing that that play begins with Caesar's triumphal entry and there are also references to other such entries both by Caesar and Pompey the Great.

Annabel Patterson argues that the play represents an attempt by Shakespeare to reconcile Essex and Elizabeth. Following Essex's imprisonment in 1600, the play was heavily cut so as to pass the scrutiny of the Censor. She compares the suppression of Hayward's *History of Henry IV* in 1599, which had been dedicated to Essex.[7] In a chapter entitled ' "If the cause be not good": *Henry V* and Essex's Irish campaign', Highley makes further links between the play and events during Essex's lieutenancy of Ireland.[8]

Against this identification of the General with Robert Devereux, Earl of Essex, it is worth noting that no name, only the rank, is mentioned and that no event is described – merely hopes for the rebellion to be put down and for the General to receive a victorious welcome on his return to London. There were other generals sent by Elizabeth to Ireland before Essex and these are considered by Jiménez in his Oxfordian dating of the play (see below and Chapter 40).

## Oxfordian Date – Internal Evidence

Oxfordians generally agree that the play was intended for performance at court, as suggested by the highly aristocratic outlook, the depiction of lower-class characters in a poor light and by the use of arcane French references. Oxford was using French very proficiently by the age of twelve as a letter from Paris in his hand demonstrates. He also visited France and was presented at the French Court in 1575. It is possible the comic scenes were added later for popular appeal when the play transferred to the public stage. That the author drew on Holinshed is clear, but whether he needed to have used the second edition of 1587 is not established as there is only one dependent reference.

In considering the relationship of Q1 to F1, Jiménez points out:

> the longer Folio version was written, and probably performed, at some earlier date [than 1599–1600], perhaps for a private audience. When that version proved to be too long for popular consumption – and to have too many characters for the ordinary playing company – it was cut by a third for performance in the late 1590s, and then printed [as Q1]. The earlier and longer version [F1] survived in the author's cupboard, and then in the library of the Grand Possessors. As with many of Shakespeare's manuscripts, it only reached print in the First Folio, where it was attributed to him for the first time.

## Oxfordian Date – External Evidence

Eva Turner Clark argues that Oxford wrote *Famous Victories* at some time in the 1570s and that in the mid 1580s he revised and expanded this early effort into *1, 2 Henry IV* and *Henry V.* Clark draws close parallels between the scene (2.2) involving the exposure of Cambridge, Scroop and Grey as traitors (with a brief reference to Mortimer's right to the Crown) and the discovery of the Babington Plot which incriminated Mary, Queen of Scots. Clark considers that the Chorus' reference to the General at 5.0 also fits 1586 and the anticipated return of the Earl of Leicester from Holland.

Ramon Jiménez argues strongly for *Famous Victories* as an early work of Oxford (*c.* 1570), which he later expanded into the *Henry IV–Henry V* trilogy by 1583/4. Firstly, he identifies the "General of our gracious Empress" as Sir Thomas Butler, Earl of Ormond, a boyhood friend of Oxford, who served the Queen in Ireland in 1583 and sent back the head of the Earl of Desmond to Elizabeth. Jiménez explains the allusion:

> In mid-December of 1583 she had it mounted on a pole and placed on London Bridge (Stow 1176). As we know, the heads of criminals on London Bridge were nothing unusual, but this rebel's head was sent from Ireland to London by a general who had been dispatched there to

> put down a rebellion. What more striking metaphor could Oxford have used for this grisly incident than 'Rebellion broachèd on his sword'? (The *Oxford English Dictionary* cites the use of the verb 'broach' in this specific passage to support the definition 'To stick (something) on a spit or pointed weapon'.)

Secondly, Jiménez believes that Oxford's revised *Henry V* shows a conscious reaction to Philip Sidney's *An Apology for Poetry* (*c.* 1579–83). Near the end of this piece of literary criticism, Sidney attacks his country's playwrights:

> . . . all their plays be neither right tragedies, nor right comedies, mingling kings and clowns not because the matter so carrieth it, but thrust in clowns by head and shoulders, to play a part in majestical matters, with neither decency nor discretion, so as neither the admiration and commiseration, nor the right sportfulness, is by their mongrel tragi-comedy obtained.

Only a few extant plays from this period depict both a king and a clown, and the are never in the same scene. Jiménez shows that *The Famous Victories* "is so riddled with clowns that it might rightly be called a comedy punctuated by historical relief."

Furthermore, Jiménez believes that Shakespeare (puzzlingly, for one of his last history plays) resorts to the use of a Chorus to exhort the audience to imagine the scenes ranging far and wide in time and space. Shakespeare used such dynamic staging in his other history plays, which according to the orthodox dates pre-date *Henry V.* As mentioned on p. 244, Sidney had complained that playwrights expect too much of their audiences:

> Now ye shall have three ladies walk to gather flowers, and then we must believe the stage to be a garden. By and by we hear news of shipwreck in the same place, and then we are to blame if we accept it not for a rock.

To counter this, the author Oxford deliberately makes the Chorus call upon the audience's imagination, not just at the beginning of the play but at the start oF each act. It has always been a problem for conventional dating to explain why, apparently halfway through his career and after writing eight or nine other English history plays, the dramatist suddenly needed to tell people exactly how to behave as a theatre audience.

Like other Oxfordians, Jiménez believes that propagandistic features would have been particularly timely when war with Spain was on the horizon for England, and Oxford's 1586 annuity can be accounted for, as well as his anonymity. A month after Oxford's annuity was granted, the Venetian Ambassador in Spain reported:

> But what has enraged him [King Philip II] more than anything else and

> has caused him to show a resentment such as he never displayed in all his life, is the account of the masquerades and comedies which the Queen of England orders to be acted at his expense (quoted by Ogburn, 692).

Another possible argument in favour of an earlier date and Oxfordian Authorship is mentioned by Craik and concerns the name of the Irish captain, MacMorris (in 3.2). Holinshed reported that an Irish contingent fought under Henry V at Rouen in 1418, but he did not name their leader. In the 1580s, Gabriel Harvey noted some anonymous satirical songs against the 'wild Irish, in particular 'Macke Morrise'.[9]

Henry's famous order to kill every French prisoner (4.4.37) may have derived from either Hall or Holinshed (or both). It would have been topical soon after 1580, as Taylor points out, when 600 Irish, Spanish and Italian soldiers from the Irish uprising were massacred by the English.

Another connection with Oxford, suggestive of an earlier date, concerns Fluellen. Various commentators, e.g. Dover Wilson and Bullough, following Barrell, believe that the character of Fluellen was modelled after the Welsh soldier of fortune Sir Roger Williams (?1540–1595). Fluellen's argumentative speeches resemble William's arguments in *The Actions of the Lowe Countries*, which was not published until 1618. Sir Roger was a follower of Oxford, and served with 'the fighting Veres' (Oxford's cousins, Francis and Horatio) in the Dutch Republic in the 1570s and 1580s. He had no known connection to Shakespeare of Stratford.

## Conclusion

The extant *Henry V* can be dated any time between 1587 (the publication of the second edition of Holinshed) and 1600, when *Henry V* appeared in print.

## Notes

1. Alfred W. Pollard, *Shakespeare Folios and Quartos*, 1909.
2. Sidney's criticisms come towards the end of his work (Richard Dutton, ed, *Sir Philip Sidney: Selected Writings*, 1987: 140; Elizabeth Watson, ed, *Defence of Poesie,* 1997: 120). See the later chapters on *Henry V* and *The Famous Victories of Henry V* for possible answers to other criticisms of theatre by Sidney.
3. Winifred Frazer, "Henslowe's 'ne'", *N&Q*, 1991, 236, 1, 34–5 notes that plays are sometimes marked "ne" twice, and so could hardly be 'new' second time around.
4. M. L. Radoff, "The Influence of French Farce in *Henry V* and *The Merry Wives of Windsor*", *MLN,* 48, 1933, 427–33. Karen Newman, *Fashioning Femininity and Renaissance Drama* (1991: 169) is skeptical about these claims.
5. Anne Barton, "The King Disguised: Shakespeare's *Henry V* and the comical history", in Joseph G. Price, (ed.), *The Triple Bond: Plays, mainly Shakespearean,*

*in Performance,* 1975.

6. Andrew Gurr (ed.), *The First Quarto of King Henry V.* Cambridge: Cambridge University Press, 2000
7. Annabel Patterson, "Back by Popular Demand: the two versions of *Henry V*", *Renaissance Drama*, 1988, 19, 29–62
8. Christopher Highley, *Shakespeare, Spenser and the Crisis in Ireland,* 1997
9. See J. Le Gay Brereton, *MLR*, 1917, 12, for more details.

## Other Cited Works

Bullough, G., *Narrative and Dramatic Sources of Shakespeare,* vol. III, London: Routledge, 1960

Chambers, E. K., *William Shakespeare: a study of facts and problems*, 2 vols, Oxford: Clarendon Press, 1930

Craik, T. W. (ed.), *King Henry V*, London: Arden 3, 1994

Jiménez, Ramon, "Shakespeare's Prince Hal Plays as Keys to the Authorship Question", an internet essay available at www.shakespearefellowship.org (accessed on 11.10.09)

Nelson, Alan H., *Monstrous Adversary: The Life of Edward de Vere, 17th Earl of Oxford*, Liverpool: LUP, 2003

Shaheen, Naseeb, *Biblical References in Shakespeare's Plays,* Delaware: UDP, 1999

Taylor, Gary (ed.), *Henry V,* Oxford: OUP, 1982

Walter, J. H. (ed.), *Henry V.* London: Arden 2, 1954

Wells, S. & G. Taylor, *William Shakespeare: a textual companion,* Oxford: OUP, 1987

Wilson, J. Dover, *The Fortunes of Falstaff,* Cambridge: CUP, 1943

Wilson, J. Dover (ed.), *King Henry V,* Cambridge: CUP, 1947

# I, II, III Henry VI and Richard III

Kevin Gilvary

## 'The First Tetralogy'

## Preface to *1, 2, 3 Henry VI & Richard III*

The First Folio presents *King Henry the Sixt* in three parts, (i.e. as three plays) in their historical sequence after *The Life of King Henry V* and before *The Life and Death of King Richard III.*

## The First Tetralogy

It is usual to refer to the *Henry VI–Richard III* plays as the 'First Tetralogy' on the hypothesis that these four plays were composed before *Richard II–1, 2 Henry IV–Henry V* the 'Second Tetralogy': the Epilogue to *Henry V* suggests that Henry VI's loss of France was already familiar material on the Elizabethan stage:

> Thus far, with rough and all-unable pen,
> Our bending author hath pursued the story,
> In little room confining mighty men,
> Mangling by starts the full course of their glory.
> Small time, but in that small most greatly lived
> This star of England: Fortune made his sword;
> By which the world's best garden be achieved,
> And of it left his son imperial lord.
> Henry the Sixth, in infant bands crown'd King
> Of France and England, did this king succeed;
> Whose state so many had the managing,
> That they lost France and made his England bleed:
> Which oft our stage hath shown; and, for their sake,
> In your fair minds let this acceptance take. *Henry V.* 5.2.1–14

Since there are no other plays which are know to deal with these events, it is assumed that Shakespeare is referring to his own *Henry VI* plays, which must therefore have been composed before the *Henry IV* & *Henry V* plays. On the other hand, the Epilogue to *Henry V* may be a later addition, since it is not included in Q1 (1600). Thus it is possible that *Henry V* (as reported in Q1) was originally composed before the *Henry VI* plays, and that the Chorus speeches were only added to *Henry V* after the *Henry VI* plays were composed.

## Sequence of Composition

There is neither contemporary evidence nor scholarly consensus for the sequence of composition of the *Henry VI* plays. Since the time of Malone, there has been much discussion on the sequence: Cairncross (Arden 2 editor of the *Henry VI* trilogy) and Hammond (Arden[2] editor of *Richard III*) argued for a plain sequence, believing that the four plays were planned and composed as a coherent tetralogy to work through a grand scheme of history, in line with Edward Hall, *The Union of the Two Noble and Illustre Famelies of Lancastre and Yorke* (1548–50). Hall depicted the weaknesses of the reigns of Henry VI and Richard III up to their resolution with the accession of Henry Tudor as Henry VII.

Chambers, *WS*, believes that Parts 2 & 3 were conceived as a two-part play, written before Part 1. He also considered Parts 2 & 3 to be the earliest individual plays in the canon. Others follow Wells & Taylor, Burns and Knowles, who have argued that Parts 2 & 3 were closely followed by *Richard III* with *1 Henry VI* composed a while later (as a 'prequel'). Further complications arise for those who believe that at least one of the plays (*1 Henry VI*) was written collaboratively with the help of another author. The main studies are mentioned under Attribution in the section on *1 Henry VI* which follows.

### Dates for registration and publication of plays in The First Tetralogy

| | *1 H 6* | *2 H 6* | *3 H 6* | *R III* |
|---|---|---|---|---|
| **1590–94** | | SR / Q1 1594 | | |
| **1595–99** | | | O1 1595 | SR / Q1 1597<br>Q2 1598 |
| **1600–04** | | Q2 1600 | SR / Q2 1600 | Q3 1602<br>Q4 1605 |
| **1605–09** | | | | |
| **1610–14** | | | | Q5 1605 |
| **1615–19** | | Q3 1619 | Q3 1619 | |
| **1620–24** | SR / F1 1623 | F1 1623 | F1 1623 | Q6 1622<br>F1 1623 |

20

# The firſt Part of Henry the Sixt.

Kevin Gilvary

*The First Part of King Henry the Sixth* (*1 Henry VI*), as printed in the First Folio, can be dated any time between 1577, the publication date of the first edition of Holinshed and 1592, when Nashe mentions in *Pierce Penniless* that Talbot's fighting prowess has been depicted on stage.

## Registration & Publication Date

There are no entries in the Stationers' Register for any play called 'Henry VI' until the publication of the First Folio in 1623, when eighteen plays appeared in print for the first time. Sixteen of these plays were enter entered in the Stationers' Register on 8 November, 1623:

> Mr Blounte Isaak Jaggard. Entered for their Copie vnder the hands of Mr Doctor Worral and Mr Cole – warden, Mr William Shakspeers Comedyes Histories, and Tragedyes soe manie of the said Copies as are not formerly entered to other men. vizt. Comedyes. The Tempest. The two gentlemen of Verona. Measure for Measure. The Comedy of Errors. As you Like it. All's well that ends well. Twelft night. The winters tale. Histories. The thirde parte of Henry the sixt. Henry the eight. Coriolanus. Timon of Athens. Julius Caesar. Tragedies. Mackbeth. Anthonie & Cleopatra. Cymbeline.

Chambers has argued, with every editor following, that the "thirde parte of Henry the sixt" refers in fact to *The First Part of King Henry the Sixth* as there had previously been entries for *The First Part of the Contention of the Famous Houses of Yorke and Lancaster* (*2 Henry VI*) in 1594, and for *The True Tragedy of Richard Duke of Yorke* (*3 Henry VI* published in Octavo 1595) in 1600. These earlier entries, it is usually suggested, made it unnecessary to enter the 'first' or 'second' parts for the Folio when the three plays were brought together as *Henry VI* plays.

The earliest text of *1 Henry VI* occurs in the First Folio of 1623.

## Performance Date

Hanspeter Born argues that both the following references to performances of a *Henry VI* play in 1592 refer to Shakespeare's *1 Henry VI.* Philip Henslowe made an entry in his diary, "Harey the vj as performed by Lord Stranges Men on 3rd March 1592". The play was marked "ne" and drew enough audience to have it repeated on fourteen occasions to June 19th, and twice in January of 1593. It is thought that this entry refers to one of Shakespeare's three *Henry VI* play(s) as there is no record of any other play about Henry VI. The annotation "ne" is often thought to refer to a new play, but whether "ne" means newly composed, newly acquired, newly licensed, performed at Newington Butts or something else, is not known.[1]

Another likely reference to *1 Henry VI* occurs in Thomas Nashe's pamphlet *Pierce Penniless his Supplication to the Divell* (dedicated to Lord Strange, first impression 1589; the quotation which follows is from the second impression, SR 8 August 1592):

> How it would have joyed brave Talbot (the terror of the French) to thinke that after he had lyne two hundred years in his Tombe, he should triumph againe on the Stage, and have his bones embalmed with the tears of ten thousand spectators at least (at several times) who, in the Tragedian that represents his person, imagine they behold him fresh from bleeding.

Since Talbot fights and dies heroically in *1 Henry VI,* but is not known to feature in any other play, it has been argued that Henslowe and Nashe are referring to *1 Henry VI.* The phrase "Terror of the French" appears to echo the Shakespeare play at 1.4. 42, while at 3.3.5, Joan allows: "Let Talbot triumph for a while." Although King Henry has a small role in *I Henry VI,* the play encompasses only the first twenty years of his reign. Since it follows the historian Edward Hall closely, the author would follow Hall by including the name of the king somewhere in the title.

If the *Henry VI* plays were written in their historical sequence, *Part 1* would therefore pre-date the reference in *Greene's Groats-worth of Witte* (SR, September 1592), where the author asserts:

> for there is an up-start Crow, beautified with our feathers, that with his *Tygers hart wrapt in a Players hyde,* supposes he is as well able to bombast out a blanke verse as the best of you: and beeing an absolute *Johannes fac totum,* is in his owne conceit the onely Shake-scene in a countrey.

The reference to "tiger's heart" appears to parody a line which occurs in *Richard Duke of Yorke* (and *3 Henry VI).*

O tiger's heart wrapped in a woman's hide *3H6 1.4.137*

The reference in *Groatsworth* appears to confirm the suggestion that *3 Henry VI* had been performed by 1592 (although Born suggests that Greene may be quoting from a play that had not yet been performed). Bullough argues that the plays may have been written in sequence, in which case, *1 Henry VI* would therefore have been completed by late 1591. Gary Taylor develops an elaborate argument for the first performance by Lord Strange's Men at the Rose Theatre on 3 March 1592. Harlow has argued that the play must have been written by 1593 as Nashe includes a number of words and phrases from the play in his *Terrors of the Night.*

None of the *Henry VI* plays is mentioned by Meres in 1598. It is possible that the attribution was unknown, or that the plays were thought inferior, or that Meres simply omitted them from his balanced list of six comedies and six tragedies, or perhaps, as Chambers suggests (245), because it was performed before Meres came to London.

## Sequence of Composition

It is not known in what order the *Henry VI* plays were composed. Bullough, Tillyard, Cairncross and Born have argued that *I Henry VI* was planned and written as the first in the sequence in early 1592, closely followed by *Parts 2 & 3.*

Counter arguments advanced by Chambers, J. Dover Wilson and especially Greer have persuaded a majority of commentators that *2, 3 Henry VI* were composed before *1 Henry VI.* Firstly, in *1 Henry VI,* Sir John Talbot has the most lines spoken by any character in the play (407); second place is held by Joan (255). Talbot plays a very important and heroic role as commander of the English forces in France. He is ennobled (3.4) before dying in battle with his son (4.7). However, he is not mentioned in *2 Henry VI* when Gloucester recounts the glorious feats of two dead warriors ("my brother Henry" and "my brother Bedford", whose death is dramatised in *1H6* 3.2), and praises five present nobles:

Have you yourselves, Somerset, Buckingham
Brave York, Salisbury and victorious Warwick,
Received deep scars in France and Normandy?
*2 Henry VI*, 1.1.75–83

A second reason for seeing *I Henry VI* as written later lies in the discrepancy in the dowry arrangements for Margaret of Anjou: there is no mention in *1*

*Henry VI* of the surrender of Anjou and Maine, but this is raised at the outset of *2 Henry VI* and is bitterly resented throughout the play. Greer deploys further arguments on the basis that events spanning thirty years are 'telescoped down' with historical discrepancies being glossed over, e.g. that Joan (d. 1429) and Talbot (d. 1453) did not confront each other in battle.

Another reason for supposing that *I Henry VI* was written at a later stage as a prequel is the apparent inconsistency in the character of Gloucester ("ruffian in the first and almost statesmanlike in the second", Knowles, 114) although not all commentators have noticed any disparity; the actor, Richard Cordery, who played Gloucester in the RSC productions in both 2001–2 and 2007–8, did not notice any such. Indeed, he and the ensemble saw the eight plays from *Richard II* to *Richard III* as a coherent set of eight plays, ' an octology' (reported in Smallwood).

## Attribution and Collaboration

A major complication in dating this play has been the question of authorship and the possibility of collaboration. There remains divided opinion on whether Shakespeare was entirely responsible for the *Henry VI* plays, with special doubts over *1 Henry VI*. This can be seen in recent editions by Hattaway ("Shakespearean" in his Cambridge Edition) and Burns ("co-authored" in his Arden Edition) E.K. Chambers wrote that his doubts on the authorship and sequencing of *1 Henry VI* as a trilogy were dispelled when he had the good fortune to see the three plays enacted on the stage. He was not persuaded by the stylistic tests (see below) but thought "weight must be given to the numerous similes and metaphors from natural history and country life, some of them literary, but others testifying to direct observation" (287). Bullough prefers a sole author, Shakespeare, who planned the *Henry VI* trilogy as a whole:

> My own view is that *Part 1* was probably written first, but was revised after the other parts had been composed and that they must have been written before Easter 1592.

Andrew Cairncross argued for the aesthetic and artistic accomplishments of *I Henry VI* in its own right. He also followed E.M. Tillyard in arguing for Shakespeare's sole authorship of all three plays in the same order as the Folio, basing this on the thematic structure, and unity of the plays. Tillyard had promulgated the so-called Tudor Myth and seen a grand process of history culminating in the accession of the Tudors enacted in the *1, 2, 3 Henry VI–Richard III* tetralogy as part of God's plan. However, this view has lost favour, with more emphasis on individual actions causing civil dissension, and weak central authority with consequent losses of territory. Despite reservations about Tillyard's view of the 'Tudor Myth', Hattaway argued for single authorship.

Edmund Malone was the first to question Shakespeare's authorship of *I Henry*

*VI.* J. Dover Wilson argued for multiple authorship involving Nashe (1567–1601) and Greene (1558–92). Greg accepted the possibity of co-authorship but asserted his belief in revision: "Most likely the play was originally an independent piece, and was altered to form an introduction to the *Contention* plays (parts 2 and 3)." The theory of for collaboration has been extensively expanded by Gary Taylor (1993), who argues for collaboration with Nashe and two other authors, a view cautiously accepted by Burns.

Burns (2000: 73) points out that those who see merit in the plays tend to argue for Shakespeare's sole authorship and those who see no merit, tend to argue for group authorship.

> To make a broad distinction, editors and critics who have valued the play have tended to present it as by Shakespeare, those who haven't see it as by a group of writers who may or may not have included him. Further, scholars of the first persuasion tend to see the plays as a planned three or four part sequence.

Sir Brian Vickers has applied his thorough approach in the analysis of style to the case of *I Henry VI.* In reviewing previous studies of attribution, he notes that in Act 1 there are a large number of stylistic features which suggest Nashe wrote the opening act, e.g. the grammatical inversion of subject and object as:

> Wounds will I lend the French, in stead of Eyes (1.1.87)
> Here by the Cheekes Ile drag thee up and downe (1.3.51)

With reference to a wide variety of features, Vickers concludes that this play was collaborative, with Nashe writing Act 1 *c.* 1592 and Shakespeare revising Nashe's play *c.* 1594.

## Sources

Bullough (followed by Burns) cites the chief historical sources of *I Henry VI* as Hall, whose history was more 'official', rather than Holinshed:

**Edward Hall, *The Union of the Two Noble and Illustre Famelies of Lancastre and Yorke*** (1548–50). Hall's account, which is much longer than Holinshed's, occurs in the chapter 'The troublous season of King Henry the Sixth'. The play does not follow historical events but "darts about the period in a bewildering way" from the accession of Henry VI in 1422 to his marriage to Margaret in 1445 (with the death of Talbot in 1453). Talbot and Joan of Arc are ranged in bitter rivalry although they never met in battle and Joan was executed in 1429.

**Raphael Holinshed, *The Chronicles of Englande, Scotlande, and Irelande*** (first edition, 1577; second edition, 1588). Boswell-Stone writes that for most of the chronicle material used in *I Henry VI*, Holinshed paraphrases from Hall so closely, that it is "impossible to determine which of the authorities were used". It is possible that the dramatist could have consulted the first edition as the following details, found only in the second edition, are few and small: (a) Joan's sword was chosen from "old iron" (1.2.101), but Shakespeare may have consulted the same histories as the revisers of the 1587 edition, perhaps *the French Chronicles* of the Burgundian historian, Monstrelet, which give a hostile, anti-French version of Joan; (b) Joan's claim to be "with child" at 5.4.74 (not in Hall): Bosewell-Stone notes that the Holinshed revisers took this suggestion of pregnancy from Polydore Virgil's account and Shakespeare could have found it there instead.

**Geoffrey of Monmouth, *Historia Regnum Britanniae*** Book VII, Ch xxi–xxiii, was used for an extended reference to "stout Pendragon" (3.2.93). The dramatist might also have used **Richard Grafton, A *Chronicle at Large*,** (1568), which is largely derived from Hall. He seems to have consulted **Robert Fabyan, *The New Chronicles of England and France*** (1516) for details involving the Lord Mayor of London (at 1.3.57ff and 3.1.76ff).

The historical Talbot died in 1453 at Bordeaux over twenty years after Joan was burnt at the stake at Rouen. The bold and anachronistic comparison between Talbot and Joan may have been suggested by a visit to Rouen, since Talbot's epitaph in the Cathedral gives a complete list of his titles. Such a visit would be consistent with the somewhat incongruous list of titles given by Sir William Lucy, in search of Talbot, who has just died on stage – a sort of unintended obsequy. Boswell-Stone compares the full text of both:

**Shakespeare *I Henry VI,* 4.7.60 [4.4.170]**

But where's the great Alcides of the field,
Valiant Lord Talbot, Earl of Shrewsbury,
Created, for his rare success in arms,
Great Earl of Washford, Waterford and Valence;
Lord Talbot of Goodrig and Urchinfield,
Lord Strange of Blackmere, Lord Verdun of Alton,
Lord Cromwell of Wingfield, Lord Furnival of Sheffield,
The thrice-victorious Lord of Falconbridge;
Knight of the noble order of Saint George,
Worthy Saint Michael and the Golden Fleece;
Great marshal to Henry the Sixth
Of all his wars within the realm of France?

**Talbot's epitaph at Rouen**

Here lieth the right noble knight Iohn Talbott Earle of Shrewsbury, Washford, Waterford and Valence, Lord Talbot of Goodrige, and Vrchenfield, Lord Strange of the blacke Meere, Lord Verdon of Alton, Lord Crumwell of Wingfield, Lord Louetoft of Worsop, Lord Furnivall of Sheffield, Lord Faulconbrige, knight of the most noble order of St George, St Michaell, and the Golden fleece, Great Marshall to king Henry the sixt of his realme of France, who died in the battell of Burdeaux in the yeare of our Lord 1453.

Boswell-Stone, followed by Tucker Brooke, asserts that the only complete list is found in Rouen; other lists are not only incomplete, but also appeared too late to be used as a source for the play, *viz.*, Roger Cotton's *Armour of Proof* (1596), Richard Crompton's *Mansion Of Magnanimity* (1599), and Ralph Brook's *Catalogue and Succession of Kings* (1619). In the absence of other written sources, it appears that the inscription in Rouen Cathedral was used as the direct source for this passage.

## Literary Allusions

There is a broad range of literary allusions in the play. Shaheen discusses Biblical references in *I Henry VI* (283–299). He argues that the author uses the Geneva Bible at 2.1.21 "God is our Fortress" (all other versions have "castel"). However, the wording of the Geneva Bible is not followed at 1.5.9 "Heavens, can you suffer hell so to prevail" which follows other versions. The author alludes to Plutarch's *Lives* (1.2.139; 1.4.25). Arthur Golding's translation of Ovid's *Metamorphosis* (1567) is echoed at 1.5.43 "Astraea's daughter". The use of Greek stichomythia (a dialogue in alternate lines) indicates classical imitation, perhaps of Seneca. Joan's desperate plea at 5.4.74–5

JOAN: It was Alençon that enjoyed my love.
YORK: Alençon! That notorious Machiavel!

York appears to echo Innocent Gentillet's attack on Machiavelli *Contre-Machiavel* (1576) which had been dedicated to the Duke of Alençon. The English translation of Gentillet did not appear until 1602. The playwright also appears to allude to William Averell's *A Mervalous Combat of Contrarietie* (1588) at 2.3.58, "How can these contrarieties agree?" and to Edmund Spenser's *The Faerie Queene* I–III (1589) at 1.1.124 "Here, there, and everywhere, enrag'd he flew" but the direction of borrowing is not fully established in either case. Other possible allusions include Agrippe, (d. 1535) *Of the Vaniety and Uncertaintie of Artes and Sciences* (translated by Sanford, 1569) at *1 Henry VI*.1.2.1–2, and Froissart (d. 1410) *Chroniques* (translated by Berner, 1523–25) at 1.2.29

## Orthodox Dating

Almost all scholars agree that *1 Henry VI* was written in the early 1590s: Chambers and Bullough proposed 1591; Cairncross and Hammond preferred 1590; more recent editors (e.g. Wells & Taylor, Knowles, Burns, Cox & Rasmussen, Jowett and Michael Taylor) follow Dover Wilson, in assigning the later date of 1592. Vickers suggests that Act 1 was written by Nashe *c.* 1592 (after *2, 3, Henry VI*) and that Shakespeare added Acts 2–5 *c.* 1594. Hattaway, however, believes the play was written just after the Armada, *c.* 1588–9. Honigmann argues that the play was composed in 1588.

## Internal Orthodox Evidence

*1 Henry VI* is one of the four Shakespeare plays to be written completely in verse (the others are *3 Henry VI, King John* and *Richard II*) and 314 lines are in pentameter rhymes, thus rhyme approximates to 10% of the lines in the play. Plays that are considered to be in the dramatist's late period contain more prose. Rhyming couplets are generally used to indicate the end of a scene and in the three scenes (4.5, 4.6 & 4.7) involving Talbot and his son John, (historically a middle-aged man). These scenes (4.5.160) are composed in rhyming couplets, and have the quality of a poem or ballad, which has been inserted into the play. Some commentators believe these speeches are not Shakespearean (or perhaps not worthy of Shakespeare).

The few speeches by lower-class characters in *1 Henry VI* are in blank verse, unlike *2 Henry VI* where there are 171 speeches in prose, especially in the Cade Rebellion scenes. In the *King Henry IV* plays, Falstaff speaks in prose; Prince Hal speaks both verse and prose; while King Henry IV, who is exalted and traditional, speaks in verse.

Lastly, *I Henry VI* has the lowest number of feminine endings in the Shakespeare canon, at 8%. Feuillerat and others have identified this versification marker as a highly predictive indicator of chronology, the lowest being the earliest. This would make *I Henry VI* Shakespeare's first play. Of course, if the play was co-authored, revised or both, then these tests have little reliability.

## External Orthodox Evidence

Opinion has been divided as to whether Shakespeare was using *I Henry VI* to refer directly to contemporary situations in Elizabeth's reign. Some believe that the situations are only general analogous to events in France or Ireland or to the person of Elizabeth herself. Other commentators have compared Henry VI's attempts (and failure) to retain his father's conquests in France with Elizabeth's attempts to hold lands in Ireland. Highley (42–3) compares Talbot's death due to factionalism within the conqueror community with the rivalry in Dublin between the New and Old English groupings, as lamented by Sir Henry Wallop in 1585.

Bullough outlines parallels between events in the play and English campaigns in France and the Netherlands 1590 – 92 (developed in detail by Leah Marcus). A small army under Willoughby was successful in Normandy in 1590. Sir John Norris was sent with another force to Brittany in 1591 and Essex left with an army to besiege Rouen 1591–2. He notes that the play depicting gallant English deeds in a divided France and featuring various sieges would have been topical until Essex's recall in partial disgrace in April 1591. A hand-written account, *Journal of the Siege of Rouen*, was quickly produced (probably by Sir Thomas Coningsby) and might have provided background details.

## Oxfordian Date

Oxfordians believe that the play dates to *c.* 1587 as one of Oxford's later history plays. It depends on the assimilation of a very wide range of sources (not necessarily including the *Journal of the Siege of Rouen*) which Oxfordians believe would have been available to Edward de Vere but not to a dramatist newly arrived in London. Similarly, the author's use of Plutarch and the Geneva Bible also link with Oxford, who bought an expensive French translation of Plutarch along with a Geneva Bible in 1569. They further argue that in *Pierce Penniless* (1592), Nashe was indicating that chronicle history plays were well established:

> First, for the subject of them, (for the most part) it is borrowed out of our English chronicles, wherein our forefathers' valiant acts (that have lain long buried in rusty brass and worm-eaten books) are revived, and they themselves raised from the grave of oblivion, and brought to plead their aged honors in open presence; than which, what can be a sharper reproof to these degenerate effeminate days of ours?

Since Nashe also seems to refer to *1 Henry VI,* Oxfordians deduce that the play was also well established by 1592 and not newly composed. Ribner believes that only a small number of history plays (none of which was Shakespeare's) had been performed on stage by 1592, the publication date of *Pierce Penniless*; however, few plays on Ribner's list were derived from the Chronicles: Legge's *Ricardius Tertius* (a play in Latin, which is only known to have been performed in Cambridge in 1579), Peele's *Jack Straw* (1587–90), the anonymous *True Tragedy of Richard the Third* (1588–90), Peele's *Edward I* (1590–1) Marlowe's *Edward II* (1591) and the anonymous *Famous Victories of Henry the Fifth* (1588) and *1, 2 Troublesome Raigne of King John* (1588–89). Therefore, Oxfordians have argued, Nashe must have been referring to Shakespeare's Henry VI plays in the above passage.

## Internal Oxfordian Evidence

Ogburn notes that York's contemptuous reference to "Alençon! That notorious Machiavel !" seems to resonate less with the character of Alençon in the play (who is simply pro-French) and more with François, Duke of Anjou and Alençon, suitor to Elizabeth (*c.* 1579–81) who was subsequently believed to be responsible for the French Fury at Antwerp in 1583. The attack on Antwerp provoked widespread condemnation and Alençon was said to have acted from selfish, cynical motives. Such a reference would have gradually lost relevance after Alençon's death in 1584.

Ogburn constructs a further argument in favour of an earlier date from insights given by J. Enoch Powell. Powell noted that, "the relish and verve with which Shakespeare's characters speak the language of ambition, intrigue and policy is not synthetic or theoretical – it could only be drawn from the experience of political struggle." Powell illustrated his points with quotations from *1 Henry VI.* Since this play is usually taken to be earlier than William Shakespeare of Stratford was ever known to have been in court, it is argued that *1 Henry VI* was the work of someone with inside knowledge of court machinations, hence Oxford.[2] Ogburn believes that play reflects the intrigues surrounding the Queen in the 1580s but, were not nearly so pressing in the 1590s.

## External Oxfordian Evidence

Oxfordians find support for a date soon after 1586, as this was the year when Edward de Vere began to receive his £1000 annuity granted him by the Queen (Nelson, 300–2). It has been proposed that this payment was for the anonymous composition and performance of patriotic drama while England prepared for the Spanish Armada. *1 Henry VI* would be particularly relevant in 1586–7, to try to unify the English against a common foreign enemy.

Eva Turner Clark agrees that the play was probably a collaboration and inclines towards 1587, linking the play both with Sir Philip Sidney and with Mary Queen of Scots. She notes that the play begins with the extended mourning for Henry V, mirroring the laments after the death of Sidney. A further parallel can be adduced from Sidney's complaint about the lack of money and supplies for his campaigns with the messenger's speech in 1.1 about the loss of Paris and Rouen. Similarly, the execution of Mary Queen of Scots (8 Feb 1587) aroused much controversy and it has been suggested that Shakespeare dramatised the execution of Joan, as both expedient and deserved, to support the judgment passed on Mary; Oxford was one of the commissioners at her trial (Nelson, 302). The analogy with Mary Queen of Scots would have been most apposite in the years leading up to her trial and execution in 1587.

Leah Marcus (not an Oxfordian) has also explored the resemblance between Joan in the play and Elizabeth as shown in her public persona. Shakespeare greatly developed Joan's historical importance, perhaps to draw comparisons with Elizabeth. Both were women in roles traditionally reserved for men; both claimed divine guidance. Both were praised excessively by their followers and vilified by their enemies. Oxfordians argue that for a dramatist to make such an obvious portrayal of the Queen would have required official authorisation and that the comparison would have been diminishing in importance by the 1590s.

## Conclusion

*1 Henry VI* (as printed in the First Folio) can be dated any time between 1577 (the publication of the first edition of Holinshed) and 1592, when Nashe mentioned in *Pierce Penniless* that Talbot's fighting prowess had been depicted on stage.

## Notes

1. Winifred Frazer (*N&Q*, 236, 1991, 34–5) noted that plays are sometimes marked "ne" twice and so could hardly be 'new' second time around. Foakes and Rickert (*Henslowe's Diary*, 2003 xxxiv, 2nd ed) have suggested that the phrase means 'newly licensed'. Neil Carson in *A Companion to Henslowe's Diary* (2004: 68) has considered the subject at length but concludes: "All such speculation is unverifiable."
2. J. E. Powell kept copious correspondence on the Shakespeare Authorship Question, which is now held at Churchill College, Cambridge. In the *Independent* newspaper of 11 February 1998, Douglas Johnson (Professor of Modern History at Birmingham University) wrote further to the obituary by Patrick Cosgrave and Professor Denis Kavanagh, 9 February:

   > Enoch Powell was still opposition spokesman on defence matters when I invited him to lecture at Birmingham University . . . . When we reached the house on Edgbaston Park Road which bore the sign "Shakespeare Institute". "What's this?" he hissed at me, with noticeable disapproval. After I had explained, he became scathing. "You don't believe in the boy from Stratford, do you?" He was transformed. There was a wild gleam in his eyes, he gesticulated, and quotations from the plays poured out, each one demonstrating that the author was a statesman with experience of power rather than "the boy from Stratford".

## Other Cited Works


Born, Hanspeter, "The date of *2, 3 Henry VI*", *SQ*, 25, 1974: 323–334

Boswell-Stone, W. G., *Shakespeare's Holinshed: The Chronicle and The Historical Plays Compared,* London: Longwell's, 1896

Bullough, Geoffrey, *Narrative and Dramatic Sources of Shakespeare,* vol. III ("Earlier English History Plays"), London: Routledge and Kegan Paul, 1960

Burns, Edward (ed.), *King Henry VI Part 1,* Arden 3, London: Arden Shakespeare, 2000

Cairncross, Andrew (ed.), *King Henry VI Part 1,* Arden 2, London: Methuen 1962

Chambers, E. K. *William Shakespeare A Study of Facts and Problems,* 2 vols, Oxford: Clarendon, 1930

Clark, Eva Turner, *Hidden Allusions in Shakespeare's Plays,* New York: Kennikat, rptd 1974

Cox, John D., & Eric Rasmussen, *King Henry VI part 3,* Arden 3, London: Arden Shakespeare, 2001
Feuillerat, Albert, *The Composition of Shakespeare's Plays: authorship, chronology*, New Haven: Yale UP, 1953
Greer, C. A., "Revision and Adaptation in *1 Henry VI*," *Studies in English,* 1942: 110–20
Greg, W. W., *The Editorial Problem in Shakespeare*, 2nd ed., Oxford: Clarendon Press, 1951
Harlow, G. C., "A source for Nashe's *Terrors of the Night* and the authorship of *1 Henry VI*", *SEL,* 5, 1965
Hattaway, Michael (ed.), *The First Part of King Henry VI,* Cambridge: CUP, 1990
Highley, Christopher, *Shakespeare, Spenser and the Crisis in Ireland*, Cambridge: CUP, 1997
Honigmann, E. A. J., *Shakespeare, the 'lost years'*, Manchester: MUP, 1985
Jowett, John (ed.), *Richard III,* Oxford: OUP, 2000
Knowles, Ronald (ed.), *King Henry VI part 2,* Arden 3, London: Arden Shakespeare, 1999
Marcus, Leah, *Puzzling Shakespeare: Local Reading and its Discontents*, Berkeley: UCP, 1988
Nelson, Alan, H., *Monstrous Adversary*, Liverpool: LUP, 2003
Ogburn, Charlton, *The Mysterious Mr Shakespeare,* Virginia: EPM, 1984
Ribner, Irving, *The English History Play in the Age of Shakespeare*, Princeton, NJ: Princeton University Press, 1957
Shaheen, Naseeb, *Biblical References in Shakespeare's Plays*, Delaware: UDP, 1999
Smallwood, Robert (ed.), *The Players of Shakespeare* 6, Cambridge: CUP, 2004
Taylor, Gary, "Shakespeare and Others: The Authorship of *Henry the Sixth, Part One*", *Medieval and Renaissance Drama in England* 7, 1993: 145–205.
Taylor, Michael (ed.), *1 Henry VI*, Oxford: OUP, 2004
Tillyard, E. M. W., *Shakespeare's History Plays*, London: Chatto and Windus, 1944
Tucker Brooke, C. F. (ed.), *1 Henry VI*, Yale Shakespeare, 1918
Vickers, Brian, *Shakespeare, Co-author,* Oxford: OUP, 2002
Vickers, Brian, "Incomplete Shakespeare: Or, Denying Co-authorship in *1 Henry VI*", *SQ*, 58.3, 2007: 311–352
Wells, Stanley & Gary Taylor (eds), *William Shakespeare: The Complete Works*. Oxford: OUP, 1986
Wells, Stanley & Gary Taylor, *William Shakespeare: A Textual Companion*, Oxford: OUP, 1987
Wilson, J. Dover (ed.), *Henry VI Parts I, II & III*, Cambridge: CUP, 1952

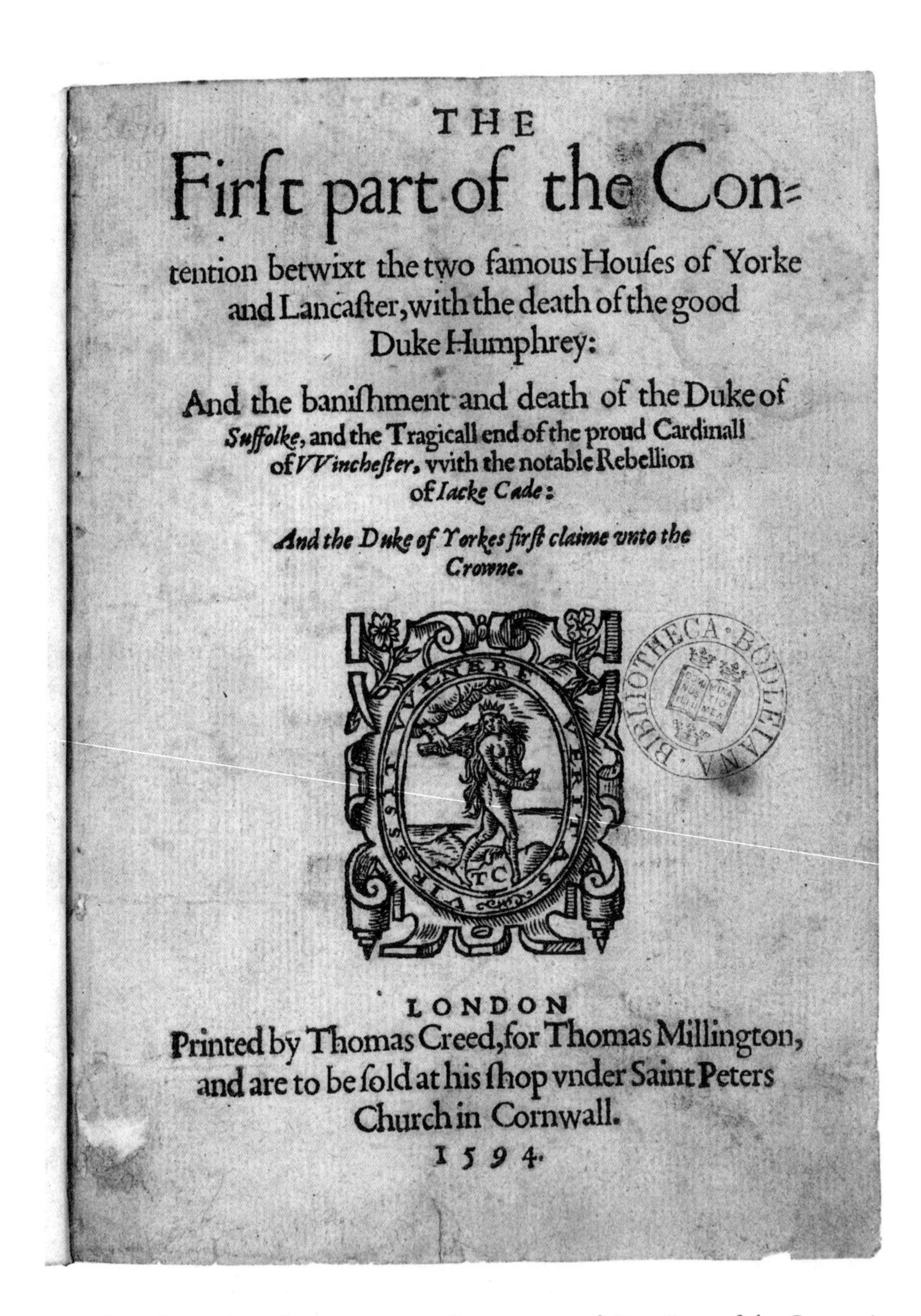

THE
First part of the Con-
tention betwixt the two famous Houses of Yorke
and Lancaster, with the death of the good
Duke Humphrey:

And the banishment and death of the Duke of
*Suffolke*, and the Tragicall end of the proud Cardinall
of *VVinchester*, vvith the notable Rebellion
of *Iacke Cade*:

*And the Duke of Yorkes first claime vnto the
Crowne.*

LONDON
Printed by Thomas Creed, for Thomas Millington,
and are to be sold at his shop vnder Saint Peters
Church in Cornwall.
1594.



15. The title page to the anonymous first quarto of *First Part of the Contention*, 1594; it has generally been believed that this version was a "Bad Quarto" derived from the Folio text. Laurie Maguire and Roger Warren, however, have argued that it was probably an early version by Shakespeare, which he later revised. By permission of Bodleian Library, University of Oxford, shelfmark Arch. G e.17 title page.

# 21

## The First Part of the Contention

# The Second Part of Henry the Sixt
## with the death of the Good Duke HVMFREY

Kevin Gilvary

The earliest date for *The First Part of the Contention* (Q1) is the first edition of Holinshed in 1577. The latest possible date would appear to be at the mention in *Groatsworth*, August 1592 (as quoted and discussed in the previous chapter). Thus *The Second Part of Henry the Sixth* can be dated anywhere between 1577 and 1592.

### Publication Date

*The First Part of the Contention (The Contention)* was registered in 1594 without attribution to a particular author. From the description it is clear that the events broadly correspond to *The Second Part of Henry the Sixth*:

> [SR 1594] xij° Marcij. Thomas Myllington. Entred for his copie vnder the handes of bothe the wardens a booke intituled, the firste parte of the Contention of the twoo famous houses of York and Lancaster with the deathe of the good Duke Humfrey and the banishement and Deathe of the Duke of Suffolk and the tragicall ende of the prowd Cardinall of Winchester, with the notable rebellion of Jack Cade and the Duke of Yorkes ffirste clayme vnto the Crowne vj$^{d}$ .

*The First Part of the Contention* was first published in quarto in 1594, again in

1600 and, for the first time with *The True Tragedy of Richard of Gloucester* (*3 Henry VI*), in 1619.

> [Q1 1594] The First part of the Contention betwixt the two famous Houses of Yorke and Lancaster, with the death of the good Duke Humphrey: And the banish-ment and death of the Duke of Suffolke, and the Tragicall end of the proud Cardinall of Winchester, with the notable rebellion of Iacke Cade: And the Duke of Yorkes first claime vnto the Crowne.
>
> [Q2 1600] The First part of the Contention betwixt the two famous houses of Yorke and Lancaster, with the death of the good Duke Humphrey: And the banishment and death of the Duke of Suffolke, and the Tragical end of the prowd Cardinall of Winchester, with the notable Rebellion of Iacke Cade: And the Duke of Yorkes first clayme to the Crowne.
>
> [Q3 1619] The Whole Contention betweene the two Famous Houses, Lancaster and Yorke. With the tragical ends of the good Duke Humfrey, Richard Duke of Yorke and King Henrie the sixt. Divided into two parts: And newly corrected and enlarged. Written by William Shakespeare, Gent.
>
> [F1 1623] The second Part of Henry the Sixt with the death of the Good Duke Hvmfrey.

*The Contention* (Q1) and *2 Henry VI* (F1) coincide scene by scene in plot but differ in a large number of readings, with Q1 only containing about two-thirds of the text of *2 Henry VI* in F1 (Chambers) or as little as half (McKerrow). Q2 and Q3 follow Q1 closely. Q3 is part of the Pavier collection of ten plays attributed to Shakespeare, printed by Jaggard and published by Pavier.

There is no contemporary evidence regarding the status of Q1 either as an early version or as a memorial reconstruction. In the nineteenth century, 'revisionists' believed that Q1 was an early version, later revised for F1 as *2 Henry VI*. Prouty argued that *The Contention* was "a source play" by another author, and Shakespeare adapted it to his play *2 Henry VI* just as he is assumed to have done with *Troublesome Raigne of King John* and *Famous Victories of Henry V* for *King John* and *Henry V* respectively.

Doran however (1928) argues that *The Contention* was a shortened version used when touring and that F1 represents the original. Cairncross believes that Q1 was a version shortened by Pembroke's Men for touring the provinces in 1592 (as he believes had happened with *The True Tragedie* (Q1 of *3 Henry VI*) and *Richard III* (Q1, 1597). Alexander (1929) argues that the Q1 was a memorial reconstruction (possibly of an abridged version) and both conclude that F1 is based on the original full version of the play, a view which is generally held (e.g. by Chambers, Hattaway and Wells & Taylor). Alexander in particular noted the illogical wording of York's claim to the Crown (2.2.9–27). In Q1, York places his ancestor, Edmund Langley, as Edward III's second son. If this was the case, then there would have been no argument over his right to the Crown. In FI, Langley is (in line with the sources) the fifth son and York has to claim the crown through matrilineal descent from the third son. Using this and other observations, Alexander claims that *The Contention* is a memorial reconstruction made by the actors. McKerrow argues against this and says that the details came from the 1577 edition of Holinshed, which were corrected in the 1587 edition.

Q1 and Q2 are anonymous. The play was not attributed to Shakespeare until Pavier's collection of 10 plays in Q3, 1619. As noted in the previous chapter, Tillyard, Cairncross, Chambers and Hattaway agreed on Shakespeare's sole authorship. However, Edmond Malone in 1790 suggested that *The Contention* was written by Greene and others, and later revised by Shakespeare into *2 Henry VI*. Dover Wilson believed that Nashe and Green contributed parts to the play, especially for the Jack Cade scenes (which are mainly in prose). Wells & Taylor, and more recently Knowles, cautiously accept the possibility of co-authorship between Shakespeare and other playwrights. Vickers has not (yet) made a special study of *2 Henry VI,* nor made any suggestion as to whether he believes the play was co-authored.

There has, however, been a general move away from rejecting early quartos as inferior texts. Laurie Maguire's detailed study of the so-called "Bad Quartos" found that very few of the criteria for naming texts as such could be detected in Q1 of The Contention. She thus rejected the theory of memorial reconstruction (and by implication abridgement). Steven Urkovitz has argued that Q1 represents a good, original acting text. Roger Warren has given a detailed account of the differences between Q1 and F, noting that there are at least ten examples of conscious revision (most notably in the Eleanor Cobham episode) and ten examples of additions. Warren accepts that there are some traces of memorial reconstruction in Q1 but of an earlier text. He believes that Shakespeare consciously revised and expanded the text. Publishing in the same year as Warren, Lukas Erne has more generally argued that Shakespeare's Folio texts were revised expanded so as to meet the demands of a reading audience. (For Randall Martin's similar arguments concerning *3 Henry VI*, see next chapter.)

## Performance Date

There is no mention of performance on the title pages of Q1, Q2 or Q3 nor are there other records of performances of *The Contention* / *2 Henry VI* until 1680. Although Henslowe might have been referring to this play when he mentioned in his diary, "Harey the vj as performed by Lord Stranges Men on 3rd March 1592", it seems almost as likely to refer to *1 Henry VI* (as suggested in the previous chapter). Since the title-page of the 1600 quarto of *True Tragedy* (*3 Henry VI*) states that the play was "sundry times acted by the Right Honourable the Earle of Pembroke his seruantes", it is assumed that *The Contention* (or *2 Henry VI*) was performed by the same players at the same time. Little is known about Pembroke's Men apart from their playing the anonymous (or early Shakespeare) *Taming of A Shrew* (SR & Q 1594). Meres does not mention any play about Henry VI (neither *The Contention* nor *True Tragedy*) possibly because he arrived in London in 1597 after its last performance (dated 1593 by Chambers) or because of multiple authorship (Wells & Taylor). Meres does, however, mention *Richard III.*

## Sources

Bullough cites the same principal historical sources for *Henry VI Part 2* as for *Parts 1* & 3:

**Edward Hall, *The Union of the Two Noble and Illustre Famelies of Lancastre and Yorke*** (1548–50). Bullough sees Hall as the primary source for the play and argues that the author began his plan for the tetralogy by studying Hall's moralising narrative of English History from Henry IV to Henry VIII. Hall provides both the details and the treatment of the quarrel between Gloucester and Winchester, with the deaths of Winchester and Suffolk in retribution for the murder of Gloucester. Bullough believes that Hall provides by far the largest amount of material but Holinshed is also significant.

Bullough describes as no more than a "probable source" **Raphael Holinshed, *The Chronicles of Englande, Scotlande, and Irelande*** (1st ed. 1577 & 2nd ed. 1587). Bullough demonstrates how Holinshed provided some of the details for the play. Shakespeare transferred many details from Holinshed's account of the Peasants' revolt in 1381 to the Jack Cade scenes. Hall had included few details of Cade's revolt. R. B. McKerrow criticises Boswell-Stone for not collating the 1577 edition with the 1587 edition when quoting passages and argues that, for the text of *First Part of the Contention*, the author used the first edition of Holinshed, e.g. in the name John Stanley at 2.3.13, which is corrected in F1 to Thomas Stanley. Lucille King has asserted that Shakespeare used the second edition of Holinshed for the text of *2 Henry VI* in F1, and argues that the text underlying F1 is the original and that Q1 is derivative (against McKerrow). However, King takes Holinshed as the principal source; her readings from Holinshed's second edition are all to be found in Hall, which Bullough had established as the main source. Therefore if the dramatist did use Holinshed for Q1, he could have consulted the earlier edition.

Shakespeare may have used **Richard Grafton, *A Chronicle at Large and Meere History of the Affayres of Englande*** (1569). Hall's and Grafton's chronicles are so alike, says Bullough, that it is "impossible to distinguish the dramatist's use of them". For the Simpcox miracle scene (2.1) he might have used

Grafton (as it is not in Hall) or John Foxe, *Actes and Monuments* (1583). Foxe may also have been used in the treatment of Duke Humphrey. The dramatist may have also used Robert Fabyan, *The New Chronicles of England and France* (1516) and the anonymous play *Life and Death of Jack Straw* (published in 1594) or its source. There is a possible echo of *The Chronicle of Iohn Hardyng* (1543) at 3.1.4–5. In the references to the Irish troubles (3.1 and 4.9), the dramatist used Richard Stanyhurst's *A Treatise containing a Plain and Perfect Description of Ireland* (1577, appended to Holinshed).

Shaheen discusses biblical references in 2 *Henry VI* . He argues that the author used the Geneva Bible when alluding to Psalms 18.18 "The Lord was my stay," which translates in the Geneva Bible at 2.3.24–25 as: "God shall be my hope, my stay, my guide." This wording contrasts with the more widely available Psalter, which reads: "The Lord was my vpholder." Plutarch's *Lives* appear to be echoed at 4.1.133–140 by Suffolk when he is about to be murdered. Shakespeare does not appear to echo Spenser's *Faerie Queene* (1589) in *Part 2.* Although *The Contention* was not published until 1594, it is possible to argue that the play was composed and acted before Spenser completed *Faerie Queene* in 1590.

## Orthodox Dating

Almost all modern commentators date the play between 1590 and 1592. Chambers proposed a date of 1590 for *The Contention,* using Greene's parody in *Groatsworth* in 1592 as a final date for the performance of both *The Contention* and *The True Tragedy* (*3 Henry VI*); many commentators (e.g. Cairncross, Hattaway & Hammond) have followed. Honigmann argued for an earlier date in 1589. Dover Wilson however suggested 1591, a date which has found adherents among most modern commentators (e.g. Wells & Taylor, Born, Knowles, Warren and Hattaway).

## Internal Evidence

Various metrical tests have placed *2 Henry VI* as the earliest play in the canon. This dating was based on a combined score derived mainly from the low incidence of open-ended (i.e. run-on) lines at 11% and mid-line speech endings at 1%. Unlike *Parts 1, 3* there are 171 speeches in prose, especially in the Cade Rebellion scenes. As an example, in the later *King Henry IV* plays, Falstaff speaks in prose; Prince Hal who is 'modern', speaks both verse and prose; while King Henry VI who is exalted and traditional speaks in verse. Plays that are considered to be in the dramatist's late period are often said to contain more prose. Wells & Taylor noted a fall in some features (e.g. amount of rhyme) after *The Contention* only to "rise again" to the later *Richard III.* Thus the stylistic analysis does not offer hard evidence of chronology, merely suggests possibilities.

Of course, such stylistic criteria would lose their value if the play were co-authored or revised as suggested by Wells & Taylor and Knowles.

## External Evidence

There have been attempts to link the portrayal of events in *2 Henry VI* with events concerning Ireland, which are freely adapted from the historical sources. Christopher Highley considers that the author developed a method of "insinuating topical meaning by manipulating chronicle sources". York, having been sent to Ireland in 3.1, announces in a soliloquy his intention to use the Irish rebels to support his bid for the crown. He is said to have returned in 4.9 and in 5.1 he openly challenges King Henry. Since neither Hall nor Holinshed represented Ireland as a threat to Henry's sovereignty, Highley believes that the author was referring to the contemporary threat of Ireland as a staging post for Spanish invasions. In particular, the Irish intrigues of York seem to evoke the case of Sir John Perrot, sent as Lord Deputy to Ireland in 1582, recalled in 1586 and arrested in 1590. Perrot's trial, where he protested his innocence, and his suspicious death in prison, are highly topical, according to Highley, and reflected in the arrest and murder of Gloucester.

Lawrence Manley (apparently unaware of the developments offered by Maguire, Urkovitz and Warren) accepted the long-standing idea that the text of F preceded the text of Q. Firstly he compares the changes between the treatment of, and charges against, Eleanor Cobham, Duchess of Gloucester in *The Contention* and *2 Henry VI*, noting various important differences. He notes the likelihood that Lord Strange's Men had played the longer Folio text and concludes that the change in the portrayal of Eleanor resulted from political pressure, especially after the trial and execution of William Hackett in 1591 for prophesying, which was deemed treasonable. Manley then compares Eleanor with Margaret Clifford (1540–96). Margaret was the grand-daughter of Henry VIII's sister and became Countess of Derby in 1554. According to Henry VIII's will, she became next in line to the throne after Lady Catherine Grey (who died in 1568); Margaret was perhaps lucky not to have lost her head. Manley observes that in 1579 the Countess of Derby had been accused of sorcery and of prophesying the Queen's death. For Manley, the death of Ferdinando, Lord Strange, meant that the text probably transferred to Pembroke's Men and that the dramatist was free to change Eleanor's joint act of prophecy in F to her sole act of treason in Q.

## Oxfordian Dating

The usual dating from an Oxfordian perspective for all the Henry VI trilogy is the period 1586 – 88, from when the Queen granted Oxford a £1000 annuity (Nelson, 300–2) until the arrival of the Spanish Armada. According to this view, Oxford was paid to write patriotic drama demonstrating the need to unite against a common enemy and the dire consequences of being divided. Eva Turner Clark, however, also argues for an earlier version of *2 Henry VI* about 1579 (unaware of the possible link with the Countess of Derby).

## Internal Evidence for Oxfordian Dating

Oxford's household links with Holinshed have been described in the Introduction to the Histories. Oxford had access in Burghley's library to the same material as the editors and contributors to Holinshed's second edition of 1587. Like Holinshed, Oxford's maternal uncle Arthur Golding was a member of Cecil's household during Oxford's wardship (Nelson, 90–2). Golding's translation of Ovid's *Metamorphosis* (1567) is echoed at 5.1.157 when Gloucester is described as 'heap of wrath, foul indigested lump'. Golding has 'chaos . . a huge, rude heap . . . a heavy lump.'

When Suffolk faces his death at 4.1.133–140, it appears that the playwright was quoting Plutarch.

> Come, soldiers, show what cruelty ye can,
> That this my death may never be forgot!
> Great men oft die by vile Bezonians:
> A Roman sworder and banditto slave
> Murder'd sweet Tully; Brutus' bastard hand
> Stabb'd Julius Caesar; savage islanders
> Pompey the Great; and Suffolk dies by pirates.

In the context, terms which could derive from either Italian or French are used ("Bezonians", i.e. beggars and "banditto slave") which suggests that the author did not use North's English translation in 1579 but perhaps an Italian version (e.g. by Jaconello, 1482) or a French version (by Amyot, 1559). The Earl of Oxford had bought a copy of Amyot's translation in 1569 (Nelson, 53).

## External Evidence for Oxfordian Dating

Eva Turner Clark also suggested an early court performance in 1579, reflecting Alençon's suitorship. The play could thus have been intended as a warning against a French marriage. According to this view, Q1 is a revision of an older play performed at court. Clark draws parallels between the Conte de Simier, and Suffolk; she cites a description of Simier's embassy to London and Suffolk's embassy to France. In addition, she sees similarities between Alençon and Margaret. Elizabeth's banishment of Lettys Knollys, Countess of Leicester (in 1578) is compared to Henry's banishment of the Duchess of Gloucester. Similarly, the news of James Fitzmaurice and Nicholas Sanders's catholic undertakings in Ireland had alarmed Elizabeth as much as York's Irish army had alarmed Henry VI.[1]

Oxford knew the Countess of Derby, Margaret Clifford, and was also sent to the Tower for a few months in 1581, at about the same time as the Countess. (Nelson, 269–271). It is possible that, at about this time, he decided to dramatise the disastrous consequences of Henry VI's foreign marriage. His players were performing at The Theatre in 1580 and at many other venues in the next few years (Nelson, 239–245). At least two of his players joined the Queen's Men in 1583 (Nelson, 245–6). It was the custom of players to take with them costumes, props and plays to their new companies. Since some of the Queen's men joined Lord Strange's Men in the late 1580s and some of these joined Pembroke's Men in the early 1590s, it is easy to see how the Henry VI plays might have been passed from one company to another. The Quarto First Part of the *Contention* would thus have been derived from Hall and from Holinshed's first edition (1577), later revised with material used in Holinshed's second edition. Oxford might have revised the Eleanor Cobham episode, presenting her in a more favourable manner in 1595 when his daughter, Lady Elizabeth Vere, was about to marry her son, William Stanley, sixth earl of Derby. The Quarto *First Part of the Contention* would thus have been derived from Hall and from Holinshed's first edition (1577), later revised with material used in Holinshed's second edition.

## Conclusion

The earliest date for Q1 is the first edition of Holinshed in 1577; the earliest date for the copy underlying the text in F1 is probably the second edition of Holinshed in 1587. The latest possible date would appear to be at the mention in *Groatsworth*, August 1592. Thus *2 Henry VI* can be dated any time between 1577 and 1592.

## Note

1. The historical details of Elizabeth's reign can be checked in the accounts of modern historians, e.g. Alison Weir, *Elizabeth the Queen* (1998): on Simier's embassy to London, "anyone observing them together might have been forgiven for concluding that she meant to marry him rather than his master" (Weir, 319); Alençon was desperate to see Elizabeth (Weir, 322); the Queen dismissed the Countess of Leicester (Weir, 323). For James Fitzmaurice's and Nicholas Sanders's attempts in Ireland (1579–81) to destablise Elizabeth's rule, see *Early Modern Ireland, 1534–1691* by Moody, Martin & Byrne (1991: 105–6).

# Other Cited Works

Alexander, Peter, *Shakespeare's 'Henry VI' and 'Richard III'*, Cambridge: CUP, 1929
Born, Hanspeter, "The date of *2, 3 Henry VI*", *SQ*, 25, 1974: 323–334
Boswell-Stone, W. G., *Shakespeare's Holinshed: The Chronicle and The Historical Plays Compared,* London: Longwell's, 1896
Bullough, Geoffrey, *Narrative and Dramatic Sources of Shakespeare*, vol. III ('Earlier English History Plays'), London: Routledge and Kegan Paul, 1960
Cairncross, Andrew (ed.), *King Henry VI parts 1 2, 3,* Arden 2 Edition: London, Methuen, 1962
Chambers, E. K., *The Elizabethan Stage,* 4 vols, Oxford: Clarendon, 1923
—, *William Shakespeare A Study of Facts and Problems*, 2 vols, Oxford: Clarendon, 1930
Clark, Eva Turner, *Hidden Allusions in Shakespeare's Plays*, New York: Kennikat, rptd 1974
Cox, John & Eric Rasmussen, *King Henry VI Part 3,* Arden 3, London: Arden Shakespeare, 2001
Doran, Madeleine, *Henry VI, Parts II and III: their Relation to the Contention and the True Tragedy*, Iowa: Iowa UP, 1928,
Erne, Lukas, *Shakespeare as a Literary Dramatist*, Cambridge: CUP, 2003
Hattaway, Michael (ed.), *The Second Part of King Henry VI*, Cambridge: CUP, 1991
Highley, Christopher, *Shakespeare, Spenser and the Crisis in Ireland*, Cambridge: CUP, 1997
Honigmann, E. A. J., *Shakespeare, the 'lost years'*, Manchester: MUP, 1985
King, Lucille, "*2* and *3 Henry VI* – Which Holinshed?" *PMLA,* 1935: 745–52
Knowles, Ronald, (ed)., *King Henry VI part 2*, Arden 3, London: Arden Shakespeare, 1999
McKerrow, R. B., "A Note on *Henry VI, Part II*, and *The Contention of York and Lancaster*", *ES*, 9, 1933: 157–169
Maguire, Laurie, *Shakespeare's Suspect Texts,* Cambridge: CUP, 1996
Malone, Edmund, *Dissertation on the Three Parts of Henry VI*, 1790
Manley, Lawrence, "From Strange's Men to Pembroke's Men*: 2 Henry VI* and *The First part of the Contention*", *SQ*, 54, 2003: 253–87
Nelson, Alan, H., *Monstrous Adversary*, Liverpool: LUP, 2003
Prouty, C. T., *"The Contention' and Shakespeare's 2 Henry VI",* Yale: YUP, 1954
Shaheen, Naseeb, *Biblical References in Shakespeare's Plays*, Delaware: UDP, 1999
Taylor, Michael (ed.), *1 Henry VI*, Oxford: OUP, 2004
Tillyard, E. M. W., *Shakespeare's History Plays*, London: Chatto and Windus, 1944
Urkovitz, Steven, "The Quarto and Folio texts of 2 Henry VI: A Reconsideration", *RES*, 51 (2000), 193–207
Vickers, Brian, *Shakespeare, Co-author*, Oxford: OUP, 2002
Warren, Roger (ed.), *Henry VI Part 2*, Oxford: OUP, 2002
Wells, Stanley & Gary Taylor (eds), *William Shakespeare: The Complete Works,* Oxford: OUP, 1987
—, *William Shakespeare: A Textual Companion*, Oxford: OUP, 1986
Wilson, J. Dover (ed.), *Henry VI Parts I, II & III,* Cambridge: CUP, 1952

p. 381. Mr. Chalmers, by obtaining this rare volume in 1796, was enabled to confirm Mr. Malone's reasoning, and to show how closely Shakspeare had copied from Marlowe's work. (See his Supplemental Apology for the Believers in the Shakspeare Papers, p. 293 - 300)



Shakespeare.

The true Tragedie of Richard Duke of Yorke, and the death of good King Henrie the Sixt,

with the whole contention betweene the two Houſes Lancaſter and Yorke, as it was ſundrie times acted by the Right Honourable the Earle of Pembrooke his ſeruants.



T M

Printed at London by P. S. for Thomas Millington, and are to be ſold at his ſhoppe vnder Saint Peters Church in Cornwal. 1595.

16. The title page to the anonymous first octavo of *True Tragedie of Richard Duke of York*, 1595. Although the narrative poems, *Venus and Adonis* and *Lucrece* were printed in octavo, this is the only Shakespeare play to appear in the smaller format. By permission of Bodleian Library, University of Oxford, shelfmark Arch. G f.1, title page.

22

# The True Tragedy of Richard Duke of York

# The third Part of King Henry the Sixt
## with the death of the Duke of YORKE

Kevin Gilvary

The earliest date for the version of this play printed in octavo format as *The True Tragedy of Richard Duke of York* is probably 1577, when the first edition of Holinshed was published. The latest possible date for the play is the allusion in *Groatsworth of Wit* in August 1592.

## Publication Date

No play was ever registered under the title *The True Tragedy of Richard Duke of York*. Some have seen this as evidence that the copy may have been obtained surreptitiously. Blayney, however, reports that, in the 1590s, about one third of published plays had not been registered.

*The True Tragedy of Richard Duke of York* was first published in 1595 and editors refer to this play as *The True Tragedy* (e.g. Cox & Rasmussen) or as *Richard Duke of York* (e.g. Wells and Taylor). The version printed in the 1623 First Folio was called *Henry VI Part 3*. Unique among the publications of Shakespeare's plays, *The True Tragedy of Richard Duke of York* was first published in 1595 in octavo (herein referred to as O1, but elsewhere called Q1):

> [O1 1595] The true Tragedie of Richard Duke of Yorke, and the death of good King Henrie Sixt, with the whole contention between the two Houses Lancaster and Yorke, as it was sundrie times acted by the Right Honour-able the Earle of Pembrooke his seruants. Printed at London by

> P[eter] S[hort] for Thomas Millington, and are to be sold at his shoppe vnder Saint Peters Church in Cornwal. 1595.

A second version appeared in quarto in 1600 (Q2) still without naming an author:

> [Q2 1600] The True Tragedie of Richarde Duke of Yorke, and the death of good King Henrie the sixt: With the whole contention betweene the two Houses, Lancaster and Yorke; as it was sundry times acted by the Right Honourable the Earle of Pembrooke his seruantes.

It is likely that the earliest entry in the Stationers' Register for this play was in 1602:

> [SR 1602] 19 Aprilis. Thomas Pavier. Entred for his copies by assignement from Thomas Millington these books following, Saluo Jure cuiuscunque viz . . the firste and Second parte of Henry the vj$^{t}$ ij bookes xij$^{d}$.

The "firste and Second parte of Henry the vj$^{t}$" is usually taken to refer to *The First Part of the Contention* and *The True Tragedy of Richard Duke of York*, (i.e. *2, 3 Henry VI*) which had already appeared in print.

The two plays *The First Part of the Contention* (*2H6*) and *The True Tragedy (3H6)* were first published together in 1619 (Q3), when they were ascribed to Shakespeare for the first time:

> [Q3 1619] The Whole Contention betweene the two Famous Houses, Lancaster and Yorke. With the tragical ends of the good Duke Humfrey, Richard Duke of Yorke and King Henrie the sixt. Divided into two parts: And newly corrected and enlarged. Written by William Shakespeare, Gent. . .the Second Part. Containing the Tragedie of Richard Duke of Yorke, and the good King Henrie the Sixt.

The Stationers' Register records another *Henry VI* in 1623, usually taken to be *I Henry VI*, which had not yet appeared in print:

> [SR 1623] The thirde parte of Henry ye Sixt.

The play was published in an expanded form in the First Folio:

> [F1 1623] The third Part of Henry the Sixt with the death of the Duke of Yorke.

*The True Tragedy* (O1) contains 2,313 lines, which amount to about two-thirds of the text of *The Third Part of King Henry the Sixt* (*3 Henry VI*) in the F1 version (3,217 lines). This proportion is similar when comparing *The Contention* with *2 Henry VI*. Q2 appears to follow O1, but with numerous corrections for mis-lineations. Q3 follows both O1 and Q2. Q3 is part of a collection of ten plays attributed to Shakespeare, printed by Jaggard and published by Pavier. Cairncross believes that O1 was a version shortened by Pembroke's Men for touring the provinces in 1592, as he believes had happened with *The First Part of the Contention* (Q1 of *2 Henry VI*) and *Richard III* (Q1, 1597).

## Performance Dates

The play seems to have been current before September 1592, as evidenced in the passing comment by Robert Greene in *Groatsworth of Wit*:

> Yet trust them not: for there is an up-start Crow, beautified with our feathers, that with his *Tygers hart wrapt in a Players hyde,* supposes he is as well able to bombast out a blanke verse as the best of you: and beeing an absolute *Johannes fac totum,* is in his owne conceit the onely Shake-scene in a countrey.

The phrase *Tygers hart wrapt in a Players hyde* appears to parody a line from *True Tragedy*: "Oh Tygers hart wrapt in a womans hide ?" [TLN 603], spoken by a very bitter Duke of York to the sadistic Queen Margaret. It appears that the author of *Groatsworth* (whether Greene or Chettle) not only knew the line from the play but also expected his audience to recognise it as well. It would thus suggest that *True Tragedy* was well known in 1592, but since the same line appears in F1 "Oh Tygers heart, wrapt in a Womans Hide," [1.4.137; TLN 603] it is unclear whether the Groatsworth-author is referring to the shorter (octavo) version or the longer (folio) version.

The play had been "sundry times acted by the Right Honourable the Earle of Pembrooke his seruantes" by 1595 as stated on the title page of O1. Chambers (*ES* ii 128) reports what little is known about Pembroke's Men, their performances of plays such as the anonymous *Taming of A Shrew* (SR/ Q 1594) and their patron, Henry Herbert, 2nd Earl of Pembroke, (*c.* 1534 – 1601). Meres does not mention any play about Henry VI (neither *The Contention* nor *True Tragedy*). It is possible that the attribution was unknown, or that the plays were thought inferior, or that Meres simply omitted them from his balanced list of six comedies and six tragedies, or perhaps, as Chambers suggests (245), possibly because he arrived in London in 1597 after its last performance (dated 1593 by Chambers) or because of multiple authorship (Wells & Taylor). Meres does, however, mention *Richard III.*

There is no evidence as to the sequence of composition. It is usually thought that the playwright made one plan for both *The First Part of the Contention* and *The True Tragedy of Richard Duke of York*, (i.e. both *2* & *3 Henry VI*), not just because of the word 'First' in the title but also because the events move across much more smoothly between *Parts 2* & *3* than between *Parts 1 & 2.*

Major discrepancies between *Part 1* and *Part 2* have strongly suggested that *Part 1* was written later as a prequel (see previous chapters). Both Chambers and Bullough (followed by many others, e.g. Tillyard, Cairncross), however, believe that the three parts of *Henry VI* and *Richard III* were planned in sequence as a tetralogy.

It is likely that Shakespeare planned at least three plays in one sweep (*2, 3 Henry VI–Richard III*) considering that Richard Duke of Gloucester plays an increasingly important part in *3 Henry VI*, clearly anticipating his machinations towards the crown, e.g. *3H6,* 3.2.168–172:

> I'll make my heaven to dream upon the crown,
> And, whiles I live, to account this world but hell,
> Until my mis-shaped trunk that bears this head
> Be round impaled with a glorious crown.
> And yet I know not how to get the crown.

Gloucester's soliloquy in *3 Henry VI* (the longest in Shakespeare and echoed in the opening of *Richard III*) would make no sense unless it were anticipating Richard's becoming king.

There is no evidence as to whether O1 represents an early version, later revised into the text underlying F1, or whether O1 is an inferior version of the play. As with *Parts 1, 2* the nineteenth-century commentators, 'revisionists', believed that O1 was an early version, later revised for F1 as *3 Henry VI.* The octavo text appears to follow Hall (e.g. 5.4–5) whereas the Folio follows Holinshed in more respects. In the twentieth century, Alexander proposed and other commentators have followed, that the O1 *True Tragedy* was a memorial reconstruction (as with *The Contention:* see previous chapter on *2 Henry VI*). Hattaway believes that *The Contention* and *The True Tragedy* were cut versions used for touring purposes, since producing three full plays about Henry VI would have been difficult.

There is, however, a growing consensus that the so-called "Bad Quartos" are in fact good versions of the play (as argued by Maguire) and that the dramatist produced a longer, more literary version of the play which appeared in the Folio (as argued by Erne). Like Roger Warren in his introduction to *2 Henry VI,* Randall Martin proposes that O is a memorial reconstruction of an earlier text and that the dramatist revised and expanded it into the longer Folio text. Similarly, the editors of the recent Arden 3 edition have developed this view: Cox & Rasmussen cautiously suggest that O1 is a full and complete play in its own right. They point out that various readings in O1 (against F1) coincide with Hall, e.g. in spellings, the number of troops and York's regency in Normandy. They tend to believe that O1 is an earlier version by Shakespeare and F1 is a later revision. They quote Blayney, who suggests that *True Tragedy* might have been a transcript made by an early actor for friends, using an authorial manuscript. However they add a caveat:

We are mindful that subjective editorial opinions about a text's origin – too often mistaken for bibliographic facts – can have a profound effect on a reader's interpretation of that text; we do not want to prejudice interpretation by pronouncing one text more authoritative than the other or even by attaching such labels as *original* and *revision*. (Cox & Rasmussen, 175–6)

## Attribution

O1 is anonymous, as is the case with quartos printed before 1598; unusually Q2 is also anonymous, despite its date in 1600, after other plays such as *Richard III*, had been ascribed to Shakespeare. In fact, the play was not attributed to Shakespeare until Pavier's collection of 10 plays in Q3, 1619. As noted in the previous chapter, Tillyard, Cairncross and Chambers agreed on Shakespeare's sole authorship of the *Henry VI* trilogy as an author promoting the 'Tudor myth'. Henry's prophecy at 4.6.68 about the future greatness of Richmond suggests some adherence on the author's part to the established view of history. Edmond Malone in 1790 suggested that *The Contention* was written by Greene and others, and later revised by Shakespeare into *3 Henry VI*. J. Dover Wilson proposed that Shakespeare revised the work of Greene, Nashe and Peele. Wells & Taylor believe Shakespeare wrote the play in collaboration with others, a view which is cautiously accepted by Cox & Rasmussen.[1]

## Sources

Bullough cites the same principal historical sources for *Henry VI Part 3* as for *Parts 1 & 2*:

**Edward Hall, *The Union of the Two Noble and Illustre Famelies of Lancastre and Yorke*** (1548–50). Bullough sees Hall as the primary source for the tetralogy as a whole and especially for this play. York's rebellion against Henry and his capture in the Battle of Wakefield (1.3) are derived from Hall. Hattaway lists other scenes 2.5, 4.1, 4.7 and 4.8 which derive from Hall.

**Raphael Holinshed, *The Chronicles of Englande, Scotlande, and Irelande*** (1st ed. 1577 & 2nd ed. 1587). Bullough demonstrates how Holinshed provided some of the details for the play, e.g. Clifford's revenge on York (1.4). Hattaway lists other scenes which seem to owe more to Holinshed (e.g. 3.2, 5.1). Boswell-Stone has demonstrated that for the text of *3 Henry VI*, Shakespeare used the second edition of Holinshed. McKerrow argues that Shakespeare used the first edition of Holinshed for *The Contention of York and Lancaster* and by implication *The True Tragedy*, which most editors believe was composed at the same time. King establishs that Shakespeare used the second edition of Holinshed for the Folio texts of Parts 2 & 3.[2]

Other chronicles which may have been consulted include Richard Grafton,

*A Chronicle at Large and Meere History of the Affayres of Englande* (1569), which is largely derivative of Hall, and Robert Fabyan *The New Chronicles of England and France* (1516), which is taken as the source at 3.3 when Queen Margaret appeals to the French King for help. At 4.6, King Henry forgives the lieutenant, who in *A Mirrour for Magistrates* had been blamed for all the official crimes under Edward IV. Michel suggests that Samuel Daniel's *Civil Wars* (1594–5) was used for material not in the chronicles, including King Henry on the molehill at Towton depicted in 2.5 and Edward's wooing of Lady Grey in 3.2.[3] These suggestions are ignored by Cairncross, Bullough and Cox & Rasmussen in their commentaries. Following Michel, who argued that the influence between Daniel and Shakespeare operated in both directions, we can suggest either that Shakespeare obtained his details elsewhere and influenced Daniel, or that these passages were later revisions before the publication of *The True Tragedy* in 1595. In general, Hall is the main source.

Shaheen discusses Biblical references in *3 Henry VI.* He shows that Shakespeare introduced his own religious references, but not as many as in other plays. He notes that when an individual version can be identified, the author appears to favour the Geneva Bible as at 1.1.42: "Henry, whose cowardice hath made us by-words to our enemies." Shaheen notes that the author retains the wording of the Geneva Bible at Ps 44.15: "Thou makest us to be a byworde among the heathen." The word "proverb" is used in other translations.

Some classical sources were used including Ovid's *Heroides,* which is quoted accurately and without a gloss at 1.3.37: "Di faciant laudis summa sit ista tuae." ('The gods grant that this may be the height of your glory') uttered by Rutland when fatally wounded by Clifford. Both Ovid's *Metamorphoses* and Golding's translation are recalled at various points, e.g. in Gloucester's soliloquy in 3.2, when he complains that he is "like to a chaos or an unlicked bear whelp, that carries no impression like the dam" (3.2.160–1); *c.f.* Golding *Met.* 15.416ff who has: "The Bear whelp . . . like an evill favoured lump of flesh alyue dooth lye. / The dam by licking shapeth out his members orderly." There are possibly other allusions, e.g. to Virgil's *Aeneid.* Further classical influence has been traced from Seneca's tragedies, especially in the violent revenge of Gloucester. Seneca's influence in the use of prophecy, dreams and premonitions has also been seen in *Part 3* and in *Richard III.* Further, the use of declamations in at least ten speeches seems particularly Senecan (as reported by Cox & Rasmussen, 96–7).

Allusions to English literary works are rare, but include Henry's description of the contending forces of Nature may be taken from *Gorboduc* (1561). Queen Margaret's attempt to rally her supporters in the face of imminent loss (5.4) appears to derive some phrases from Brooke's *Tragical History of Romeus & Juliet* (1562) lines 1359–77.

## Orthodox Date

Chambers suggested that *3 Henry VI* was composed in 1590 and in this he was followed by Honigmann. Other scholars proposed a date of 1591 (Dover Wilson, Caincross, Hammond, Born, Wells & Taylor, Hattaway, Cox & Rasmussen, Martin), with Bullough opting for a later date of 1592. Commentators are agreed that *3 Henry VI* is one of the earliest plays in the canon, immediately following *Part 2.*

## Internal Orthodox Evidence

Various metrical and other stylistic tests have placed *3 Henry VI* among the earliest plays in the canon. Like *Part 1, Part 3* is composed entirely in verse. As with *Part 2* there is a high number of feminine endings (14%), but a low incidence of open-ended (i.e. run-on) lines at 10%, and mid-line speech endings at 1%. As there is doubt about the sole authorship, tests remain unreliable

## External Orthodox Evidence

In the nineteenth century, there were attempts to link events in *3 Henry VI* with the anonymous pamphlet *Leicester's Commonwealth* (1586), e.g. the appearance of Somerville in 5.1.7 with the execution of Sir John Somerville in 1583.[4] Against this, David Bevington and Edna Boris have argued that the history plays in general refer to contemporary ideas on authority and law, rather than specific events or squabbles. More recently, however, commentators have seen Shakespeare as profoundly reflecting contemporary issues of religion and politics. Richard Dutton *et al.* state (112) that Shakespeare's portrayal of Somerville in *3 Henry VI* seems to "present a coded portrait challenging the official verdict on his contemporary namesake." Andrew Hadfield has made a case that Shakespeare did intend to relate his plays to contemporary issues of Kingship and Republicanism, dating the *Henry VI* plays to the late 1580s.

## Oxfordian Dating

The usual dating from an Oxfordian perspective for the whole *Henry VI* trilogy is the period 1586–88, from when the Queen granted Oxford a £1000 annuity (Nelson, 300–2) until the arrival of the Spanish Armada. According to this view, Oxford was paid to write patriotic drama demonstrating the need to unite against a common enemy and the dire consequences of being divided. Eva Turner Clark favours an earlier date because she sees allusions to Mary Queen of Scots and suggests that a court performance on 27 Dec 1580 by the Lord Chamberlain's Men was of an early version of this play.

## Internal Oxfordian Evidence

The earliest date is usually taken to be the publication of the second edition of Holinshed's Chronicles, but since Shakespeare independently used material from a source used by Holinshed's editors, it is possible that the earlier date of 1577 may apply. Arthur Golding's translation of Ovid's *Metamorphosis* (1567) appears to be echoed at 3.2 in Gloucester's soliloquy. Golding was Oxford's maternal uncle and a member of Cecil's household during Oxford's wardship (Nelson, 39–41). The author's use of the Geneva Bible also suggests Oxford, who had bought a copy in 1569 (Nelson, 53).

## External Oxfordian Evidence

Eva Turner Clark adduces parallels between events at court in December 1580 and *3 Henry VI*. In particular, she sees a close link between the catholic factions of Henry Howard and Charles Arundel, one time friends of Oxford, and the anti-Henry conspiracies. She notes that just as Elizabeth's detractors asserted that she had no right to the throne, so the Yorkists had railed against Henry VI. Until 1580, Elizabeth had generally shown tolerance towards the Catholics, The author in *3 Henry VI* appears to demonstrate that this policy was unwise. A performance of the play *c.* 1580 ties in with a hardening of her attitude and with the arrest of Edmund Campion.[5]

Oxford himself was arrested following accusations of treasonable catholic leanings. (Nelson, 164–73 and 203–9). Clark argues that this led him to include a favourable portrait of his forbear, John de Vere, thirteenth earl of Oxford, (1442–1513) who had been one of Henry VI's biggest supporters and a (some historians say the) key commander of Richmond's forces at the Battle of Bosworth. In *3 Henry VI* at 3.3.106–7, the character Oxford exclaims: "While life upholds this arm, This arm upholds the house of Lancaster." In their commentary, Cox & Rasmussen suggest: "Oxford would seem to be included in this fictitious scene for the sole purpose of stating his motive of personal revenge." Clark suggests that, at this point, Edward the seventeenth earl was making the character of John, the thirteenth earl, firmly promote his family's loyalty to the House of Lancaster and by implication to the Tudor dynasty.

## Conclusion

The play can only be dated between 1577 and 1592. The earliest date for the version of the play printed in octavo format as *The True Tragedy of Richard Duke of York* is probably 1577, when the first edition of Holinshed was published. The earliest date for the version printed in the First Folio as *The Third Part of King Henry the Sixt* (*3 Henry VI*) is 1587, the second edition of Holinshed.

The latest possible date for the play is the allusion in *Groatsworth of Wit* in August 1592, with a possible revision of the text underlying F1 about 1595 under the influence of Daniel.

## Notes

1. Sir Brian Vickers in *Shakespeare, Co-author* (OUP 2002) refers only briefly to the possibility that *3 Henry VI* might have been composed by two or more authors.
2. Oxford University Press has approved an ambitious project to produce *The Oxford Handbook to Holinshed's Chronicles* edited by Paulina Kewes, Felicity Heal, and Ian Archer. This handbook will relate the *Chronicles* to the historiography and literature of the medieval, early modern and subsequent periods. The parallel texts of the 1577 and 1587 editions are now available, enabling a comparison of the two versions both by regnal years and by Holinshed's original chapter structure. (http://www.cems.ox.ac.uk/holinshed/texts.shtml (accessed 22 October 2009).
3. Gillian Wiley "The Politics of Revision in Samuel Daniel's *The Civil Wars*" in *English Literary Renaissance*, 28 (2008, 461–83) has traced the change in Daniel's political priorities through the revised editions, especially evident in his treatment of Elizabeth Grey and Edward IV (1609 edition, Book VIII); at first Daniel, like Shakespeare at *3 Henry VI*, 3.2.72, showed Elizabeth's resistance in terms of her own honesty. Later Daniel "departs from the poet's sources in representing Grey's resistance to Edward's attempted seduction in explicitly politicized terms." Wiley is unsure whether Shakespeare influenced Daniel or vice versa, e.g. "Shakespeare, possibly following Daniel, similarly emphasizes Blunt's valor in *I Henry IV*."
4. Richard Simpson, "The Politics of Shakespeare's Historical Plays" in *New Shakespere Society Transactions,* 1874, 396–441, quoted by Cox and Rasmussen. For discussion on *Leicester's Commonwealth,* see the edition by D. C. Peck (Ohio University Press, 1985). Nina Green in an internet essay has noted that in *Leicester's Commonwealth*, Robert Dudley is described as a *dominus fac totum* ("a master who does everything") as a satire on his influence over the Queen. She draws the parallel with the description in *Groatsworth of Wit* of the "upstart crow" portrayed as a "*Johannes fac totum*". (htt;://www.oxford-shakespeare.com/Newsletters/Groatsworth-03.pdf, accessed on 22 October 2009).
5. These events are well documented by modern historians, e.g. Alison Weir, in *Elizabeth the Queen* (1999: 333–5). See also the discussion on equivocation in the chapter on *Macbeth* in this work (pp. 371–2).

## Other Cited Works

Alexander, Peter, *Shakespeare's 'Henry VI' and 'Richard III'*, Cambridge: CUP, 1929
Bevington, David, *Tudor Drama and Politics*, Cambridge, MA, 1968
Blayney, Peter W. M., "The publication of playbooks", in John Cox & David Kastan, (eds), *A New History of Early English Drama*, New York, 1997

Boris, Edna, *Shakespeare's English Kings, the People and the Law*, Rutherford, NJ, 1978
Born, Hanspeter, "The date of *2, 3 Henry VI*", *SQ*, 25, 1974: 323–334
Boswell-Stone, W. G., *Shakespeare's Holinshed: The Chronicle and The Historical Plays Compared,* London: Longwell's, 1896
Bullough, Geoffrey, *Narrative and Dramatic Sources of Shakespeare*, vol. III ('Earlier English History Plays'), London: Routledge and Kegan Paul, 1960
Cairncross, Andrew (ed.), *King Henry VI parts 1 2, 3,* Arden² Edition, London: Methuen 1962–3
Chambers, E. K., *William Shakespeare A Study of Facts and Problems*, 2 vols, Oxford: Clarendon, 1930
Clark, Eva Turner, *Hidden Allusions in Shakespeare's Plays,* New York: Kennikat, rptd 1974
Cox, John & Eric Rasmussen, *King Henry VI Part 3,* Arden³, London: Arden Shakespeare, 2001
Dutton, Richard, Alison Findlay & Richard Wilson, *Theatre and Religion: Lancastrian Shakespeare,* Manchester: MUP, 2003
Erne, Lukas, Shakespeare as a Literary Dramatist, Cambridge: CUP, 2003
Hadfield, Andrew, *Shakespeare and Republicanism,* Cambridge: CUP, 2005
Hammond, Antony, J. (ed.), *Richard III,* London: Arden Shakespeare, 1981
Hattaway, Michael (ed.), *The First Part of King Henry VI,* Cambridge: CUP, 1990
—, *The Second Part of King Henry VI,* Cambridge: CUP, 1991
—, *TheThird Part of King Henry VI,* Cambridge: CUP, 1993
Highley, Christopher, *Shakespeare, Spenser and the Crisis in Ireland*, Cambridge: CUP, 1997
Honigmann, E. A. J., *Shakespeare, the 'lost years'*, Manchester: MUP, 1985
King, Lucille, "*2* and *3 Henry VI* – Which Holinshed?" *PMLA,* 1935: 745–52
Knowles, Ronald (ed.), *King Henry VI part 2,* Arden³, London: Arden Shakespeare, 1999
Maguire, Laurie, Shakespeare's Suspect Texts. Cambridge: CUP, 1996
Martin, Randall (ed.), *Henry VI, Part 3,* Oxford: OUP, 2001
McKerrow, R. B., "A Note on *Henry VI, Part II,* and *The Contention of York and Lancaster*", *RES*, 9, 1933: 157–169
Michel, Laurence (ed.), *The Civil Wars by Samuel Daniel,* New haven: Yale UP, 1958
Nelson, Alan, H., *Monstrous Adversary,* Liverpool: LUP, 2003
Shaheen, Naseeb, *Biblical References in Shakespeare's Plays,* Delaware: UDP, 1999
Taylor, Michael (ed.), *1 Henry VI,* Oxford: OUP, 2004
Tillyard, E. M. W., *Shakespeare's History Plays,* London: Chatto and Windus, 1944
Wells, Stanley & Gary Taylor (eds), *William Shakespeare: The Complete Works.* Oxford: OUP, 1986
—, *William Shakespeare: A Textual Companion*, Oxford: OUP, 1987
Wilson, J. Dover (ed.), *Henry VI Parts I, II & III,* Cambridge: CUP, 1952

# 23

# The Tragedy of King Richard the Third

## with the Landing of Earle Richmond and the Battel at Bofworth Field

Kevin Gilvary

The earliest date for *The Tragedy of King Richard III* (Q1) is 1577, the first edition of Holinshed. The latest possible date is at the publication of the First Quarto in 1597.

### Publication Date

*The Tragedy of King Richard III* was registered in 1597, three years after *The Contention* (*2 Henry VI*) and three years before *The True Tragedy of Richard Duke of York* (*3 Henry VI*):

> [SR 1597] 20 Octobris. Andrewe Wise. Entred for his copie vnder thandes of master Barlowe, and master warden Man. The tragedie of kinge Richard the Third with the death of the Duke of Clarence.

The play was published anonymously:

> [Q1 1597] The Tragedy Of King Richard the third. Containing, His treacherous Plots against his brother Clarence: the pittiefull murther of his iunocent nephewes: his tyrannical! vsurpation: with the whole course of his detested life, and most deserued death. As it hath beene lately Acted by the Right honourable the Lord Chamberlaine his seruants. At London Printed by Valentine Sims, for Andrew Wise, dwelling in Paules Chuch-yard, at the Signe of the Angell. 1597.

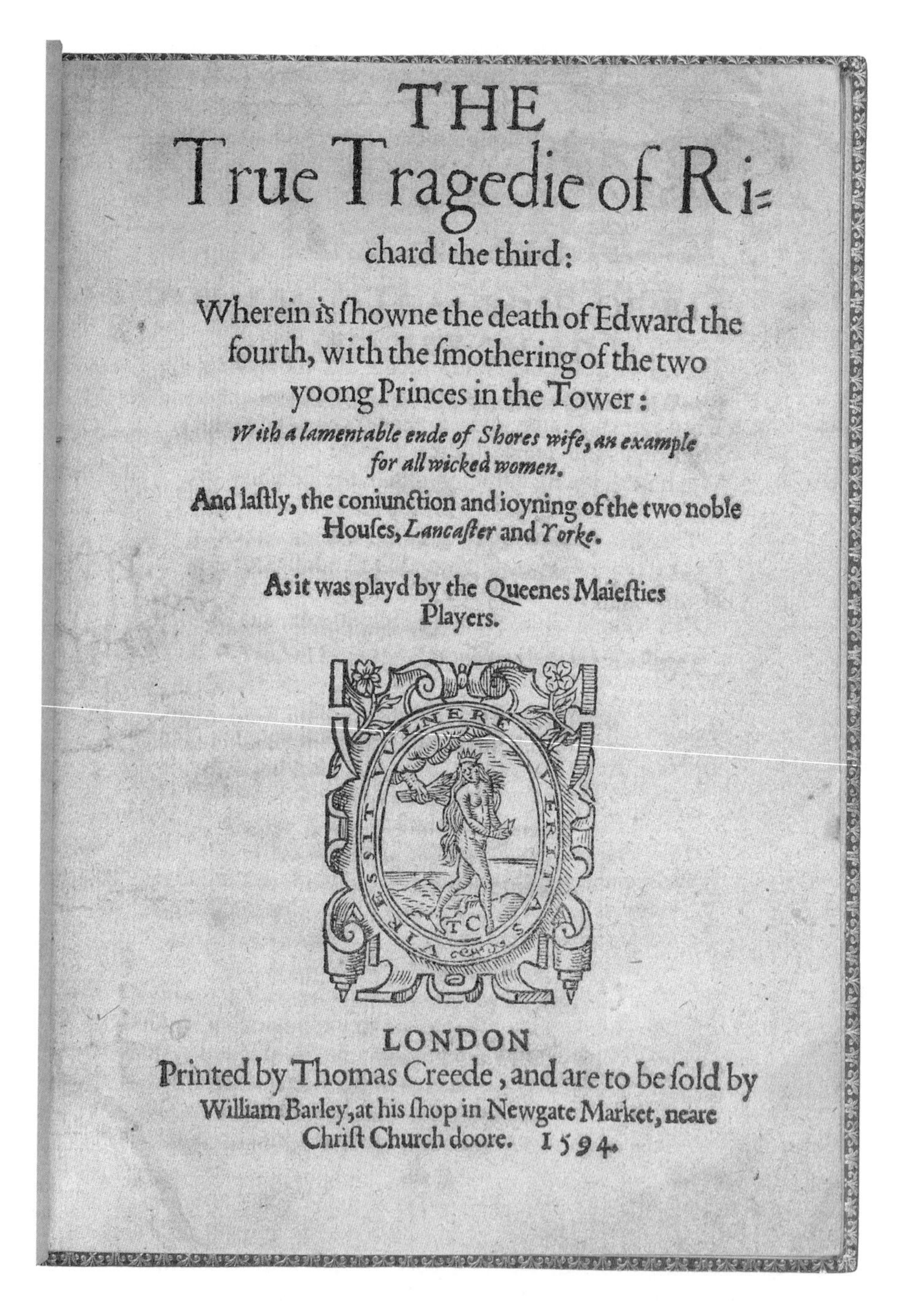

THE
True Tragedie of Ri-
chard the third:
Wherein is ſhowne the death of Edward the
fourth, with the ſmothering of the two
yoong Princes in the Tower:
*With a lamentable ende of Shores wife, an example for all wicked women.*
And laſtly, the coniunction and ioyning of the two noble
Houſes, *Lancaſter* and *Yorke.*
As it was playd by the Queenes Maieſties
Players.

LONDON
Printed by Thomas Creede, and are to be ſold by
William Barley, at his ſhop in Newgate Market, neare
Chriſt Church doore. 1594.

17. The title page to the anonymous first quarto of *True Tragedie of Richard III*, 1594; it has generally been believed that this play was not by another author but some scholars have argued that it was an early version by Shakespeare, which he later revised.
By permission of the Folger Shakespeare Library.

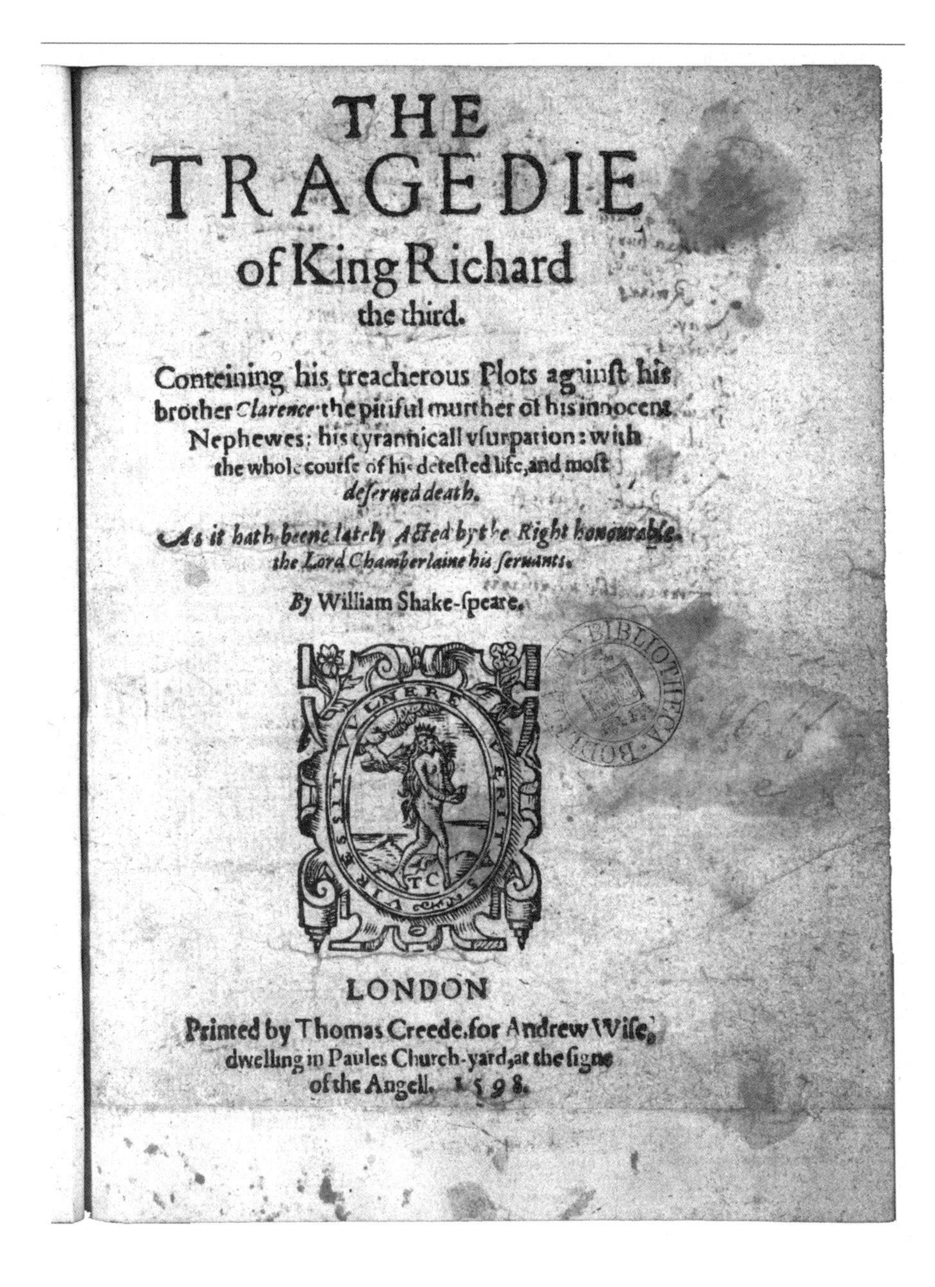

THE
TRAGEDIE
of King Richard
the third.

Conteining his treacherous Plots againſt his brother *Clarence*: the pitiful murther of his innocent Nephewes: his tyrannicall vſurpation: with the whole courſe of his deteſted life, and moſt *deſerued death.*

*As it hath beene lately Acted by the Right honourable the Lord Chamberlaine his ſeruants.*

*By* William Shake-ſpeare.

LONDON

Printed by Thomas Creede, for Andrew Wiſe, dwelling in Paules Church-yard, at the ſigne of the Angell. 1598.



18. The title page to the first quarto of *Richard III,* 1598. By permission of Bodleian Library, University of Oxford, shelfmark Arch. G e.21, title page.

The play seems to have been very successful and was quickly reprinted with attribution to William Shakespeare.

> [Q2 1598] The Tragedie of King Richard the third. Conteining his treacherous Plots against his brother Clarence: the pitiful murther of his innocent Nephewes: his tyrannicall vsurpation: with the whole course of his detested life, and most deserued death. As it hath beene lately Acted by the Right honourable the Lord Chamberlaine his seruants. By William Shake-speare. London Printed by Thomas Creede, for Andrew Wise, dwelling in Paules Churchyard, at the signe of the Angell. 1598.

The play went through four more quartos before the First Folio in 1623:

> [Q3 1602] The Tragedie of King Richard the third. Conteining his treacherous Plots against his brother Clarence: the pittifull murther of his innocent Nephewes: his tyrannical vsurpation: with the whole course of his detested life, and most deserued death. As it hath bene lately Acted by the Right Honourable the Lord Chamberlaine his seruants. Newly augmented, By William Shakespeare. London. Printed by Thomas Creede, for Andrew Wise, dwelling in Paules Church-yard, at the signe of the Angell. 1602.

The registration was transferred from Andrew Wise to Matthew Lawe in 1603:

> [SR 1603] 25. Junii Mathew Lawe. Entred for his copies in full courte Holden this Day. These ffyve copies followinge ij$^{s}$ vj$^{d}$ viz. iij enterludes or playes. The ffirst is of Richard the .3. ... all kinges . . all whiche by consent of the Company are sett ouer to him from Andrew Wyse.

> [Q4 1605] The Tragedie of King Richard the third. Containing his treacherous Plots against his brother Clarence: the pittifull murther of his innocent Nephewes: his tyrannicall vsurpation: with the whole course of his detested life, and most deserued death. As it hath bin lately Acted by the Right Honourable the Lord Chamberlaine his seruants. Newly augmented, By William Shake-speare. London, Printed by Thomas Creede, and are to be sold by Mathew Lawe, dwelling in Paules Church-yard, at the Signe of the Foxe, neare S. Austins gate, 1605.

> [Q5 1612] The Tragedie of King Richard The Third.... As it hath beene lately Acted by the Kings Maiesties seruants ... 1612. [Otherwise the same as Q4]

> [Q6 1622] The Tragedie Of King Richard The Third. Contayning his treacherous Plots against his brother Clarence: The pittifull murder of his innocent Nephewes: his tyrannicall Vsurpation: with the whole course of his detested life, and most deserued death. As it hath been lately Acted by the Kings Maiesties Seruants. Newly augmented. By William Shake-speare. [Ornament] London, Printed by Thomas Purfoot, and are to be

> sold by Mathew Law, dwelling In Pauls Church-yard, at the Signe of the Foxe, neere S. Austines gate, 1622.

Each later quarto appears to have been reprinted from its immediate predecessor, despite the claims in Q3 and successive quartos of being "newly augmented"; perhaps this was a 'publisher's lure'. Parts of Q5 seem to rely on Q3 rather than Q4. According to Chambers, the text of Q6 shows some significant differences from previous quartos, which suggests that the compositors had access to authorial papers. Some of these variations in Q6 appear in F1.

> [F1 1623] the Life & Death of Richard the Third

The status of the quartos has been the subject of debate, but is generally accepted as 'good'. The F1 version of *Richard III* is the second longest play in F1, after *Hamlet*, with about 3,600 lines. There are approximately 230 lines not in Qq and about 2,000 readings (one tenth of the text) which vary from Q1 to F1. This is less than in other quartos, allowing it to escape the label 'bad' quarto. Chambers (*WS* I, 297) asserts that the extra lines in F1 occur in long speeches or long dialogues, blending with the style and context, and smoothing over some abrupt changes which occur when they are omitted. He suggests that these extra lines in F1 were cut from the original text by the author, i.e. that F1 is derived from a copy of the original play, while Qq are cut forms of it. One passage as long as 55 lines is cut from 4.4 288–342 in what is taken as an attempt to shorten the play. Wells and Taylor concur with Chambers.

Cairncross, however, believes that Q1 was shortened by Pembroke's Men for touring the provinces in 1592, as he believes had happened with *The First Part of the Contention* (Q1 of *2 Henry VI*) and *The True Tragedie* (O1 of *3 Henry VI*). Patrick argued that Q1 was a memorial reconstruction. He cited evidence of shifting (the transposition of words and phrases, usually within a line), anticipation, recollection and synonymous substitution. Patrick also suggests that Q1 might be a deliberate simplification used for touring. One imaginative suggestion was that the text was collaboratively prepared by the company to replace a missing prompt book, perhaps during 1597 when the Lord Chamberlain's Men visited Kent and the West Country (see Hammond or Davison for more details).

Peter Davison has examined Q1 carefully and reviewed the theories explaining its origin. He argues that *The Tragedy of King Richard III* (Q1) was revised into the text underlying *Richard III* in F1. A few lines in Q1, not in F1, suggest that the Folio version was a revision.[1] One famous passage, the so-called clock dialogue (4.2.102–18) occurs in Q1 but not in F1. Furthermore, F1 seems to rely on Q3 for the passages 3.1.1–165 and 5.3.49 – end of the play. In conclusion, there is no overall agreement on the relationship between Q1 and F1.

## Performance Date

Reference to performances post-date the publication of Q1. Chambers (*WS*, I, 303) believes that the style and psychology point to an early period and he "does not think it inconceivable" that it was the *Buckingham* performed by Sussex's Men on 1 Jan 1594. Bullough rejects this on two accounts: firstly Buckingham is not the protagonist of this play (the character has 376 lines compared with Richard's 1171 lines); secondly the play *Buckingham* may refer to that Duke of Buckingham who was executed in 1521. Meres mentions the play in 1598 and it is quoted by Marston in *Scourge of Villanie* (1598) and in *2 Parnassus* (?1598–1602). Many commentators believe that *Richard III* was composed for the great actor, Richard Burbage.[2] The earliest reference to Burbage in the role is recorded by John Manningham of the Middle Temple, whose diary entry on 13 March 1601 (NS 1602), might have been referring to events some time previously:

> Vpon a tyme when Burbidge played Rich. 3. there was a citizen greue soe farr in liking with him, that before shee went from the play shee appointed him to come to her that night vnto hir by the name of Ri: the 3. Shakespeare, overhearing their conclusion, went before, was intertained and at his game ere Burbidge came. Then message being brought that Rich. The 3.[d] was at the dore, Shakespeare caused returne to be made that William the Conquerour was before Rich. The 3. Shakespeare's name William. (Chambers, *WS*, 2 212)

Burbage was a member of the Lord Chamberlain's Men, which began performing in 1594. It is assumed that the text of *Richard III* came to them along with other texts and various players including Burbage and Shakespeare. Davison argues that the play was performed by the Lord Chamberlain's Men when they toured the west, visiting Bristol and Marlborough in 1597.

There is no evidence to determine the sequence of composition of the *Henry VI* trilogy and *Richard III.* It is likely that *Richard III* was in mind when *2, 3 Henry VI* were written because events move smoothly between the plays. In particular, Gloucester's soliloquy at 3.2 in *3 Henry VI* culminating in the line: "Can I do this and cannot get the crown?" would make little sense without *Richard III* to follow. Similarly, at 5.6 in *3 Henry VI,* Gloucester begins his plots to gain the Crown and makes reference to them again in the opening soliloquy of *Richard III.* Chambers, Alexander and Bullough (among others) see this play not merely as composed immediately after the *Henry VI* trilogy but also as part of a coherent 'tetralogy'. The RSC director, Michael Boyd, (as reported frequently, e.g. in Smallwood) saw the whole sequence of eight plays from *Richard II* to *Richard III* as a coherent group, in essence 'an octology'.

While Q1 is anonymous, Q2 in 1598 and the succeeding Qq are attributed to Shakespeare. Chambers, Alexander, Tillyard and Cairncross agree on

Shakespeare's sole authorship of the play alongside the *Henry VI* trilogy. Most modern commentators (e.g. Wells & Taylor) believe that *Richard III* is solely by Shakespeare, but are less sure about various parts of the *Henry VI* trilogy.

## Relation to the anonymous *The True Tragedie of Richard the Third* (?1594)

On 19 June 1594, The Stationers' Register reports "An enterlude entituled *The True Tragedie of Richard the Third*" which was published soon afterwards:

> [Q 1594] The true tragedie of Richard the third: / wherein is showne the death of Edward the / fourth, with the smothering of the two / yoong princes in the Tower: / with a lamentable ende of Shores wife, an example / for all wicked women. / And lastly, the coniunction and ioyning of the two noble / houses, Lancaster and Yorke. / As it was playd by the Queenes Maiesties Players. Published: London : Printed by Thomas Creede, and are to be sold by / William Barley, at his shop in Newgate Market, / neare Christ Church doore, 1594.

This play opens with a Prologue spoken by the figures of Truth and Poetry, to whom the ghost of Clarence appears crying "Vindicta!" It contains the germ of a fine phrase: "A horse, a horse, a fresh horse." Logan and Smith have reviewed various interpretations of the relationship between *True Tragedie* and *Richard III.* [3]

Chambers (*ES,* vol iv, 43–4) reports that most commentators suggested that the anonymous *True Tragedie* dates to about 1586–7, when the Queen's Men were most active and when ballads on the subject apparently became popular. Chambers himself, however, dated the anonymous play to 1591, *earlier* than his dates for the *Henry VI–Richard III* tetralogy; he observes very little trace of any use by Shakespeare for his *Richard III.*

Other commentators have seen a stronger relationship between the anonymous *True Tragedie* and *Richard III,* but the perceived direction of influence reflects the assumed relative dating of the plays. Bullough, following Churchill and Wilson, sees the anonymous *True Tragedie* as the earlier play "written probably 1590–2" and exerting considerable influence on Shakespeare's play as a Senecan drama, focussing on one principal historical figure, unlike the *Henry VI* plays. Bullough accepts that some parallels may be coincidences, but he observes that the two plays depart so often from their sources and in such similar ways as to preclude coincidence. He asserts that Shakespeare took some hints from the "authentic version" of *True Tragedie* (from which, it is assumed, the version published in the 1594 quarto was debased). Maguire's analysis suggests that *True Tragedie* preceded and influenced Shakespeare's *Richard III.*

Against this, Hammond sees the anonymous *True Tragedie* as the later play, a surreptitious publication to follow on from and make capital out of the currently popular *Henry VI* plays – perhaps while Shakespeare's play was in performance but not yet published. Oxfordians such as Clark and especially Jiménez (who dates the anonymous play to the late 1560s) see *The True Tragedie of Richard the Third* as an early play by the Earl of Oxford, later expanded and revised (by him) into *Richard III.* In the early play, it is the John thirteenth earl of Oxford who proclaims:

> Henry the Seventh, by the grace of God, King of England,
> France, and Lord of Ireland, God save the King.

In Shakespeare's play, Stanley makes the announcement as he places the crown on Richmond's head. Oxfordians argue that when Oxford was paid to write history plays, (from when he began to receive his £1,000 annuity in 1586), part of the deal was to remain anonymous and to play down the historical role of his forebears (Anderson, 209–12).

## Sources

Bullough cites the same principal historical sources for *Richard III* as for *1, 2, 3 Henry VI*:

**Edward Hall, *The Union of the Two Noble and Illustre Famelies of Lancastre and Yorke*** (1548–50). Bullough sees Hall as the primary source for the tetralogy as a whole and especially for this play. The final three scenes (5.5, 5.6 & 5.7) derive from Hall. Hall's depiction of Richard as showing "courage, warlike skill and services to Edward" is followed more closely in *3 Henry VI* than through the tyrannous villainy which characterises him in *Richard III.*

**Raphael Holinshed, *The Chronicles of Englande, Scotlande, and Irelande*** (1st ed. 1577 & 2nd ed. 1587). Bullough demonstrates how the dramatist consulted Holinshed for many details, e.g. the allusion to Henry VI's wounds (1.2.55), the reference to Thomas Grey's elevation to the title of Marquis of Dorset (1.3 265–6) and Richard's dismay at the resemblance of the name Rougemont to Richmond (4.2.105). Boswell-Stone argues that the second edition of Holinshed was used because of five references, three of which are in the final scene, e.g. at 5.6.54 Richard refers to Richmond as "long kept in Bretagne at our mother's cost", a line which is in Q1; the first edition of Holinshed reads "brother's". Because the references which could derive only from Holinshed's second edition, occur in the final scene, it may be suggested that they arose from a revision of the climax.

Bullough believes that Shakespeare may have derived small details from Richard Grafton's *A Chronicle at Large and Meere History of the Affayres of Englande*, 1569, which is largely derivative from Hall, and Robert Fabyan's *The New Chronicles of England and France* (1516). The playwright certainly knew *A Mirrour for Magistrates* (1559; expanded in 1563, later editions) and may have derived some details from it, e.g. that it was Richard who ordered the murder of Clarence. There were also many ballads on the subject of Richard III including ***The Battle of Bosworth Field*** which may have contained details used by Shakespeare.[4] The playwright, thinks Bullough, does not seem to have been influenced directly by Polydore Vergil's *Historia Angliae* (published in 1534, abridged translation in 1546).

There was a Tudor literary tradition on the subject of Richard III. The possible influence (or even revision) of *The True Tragedie of Richard III* (published 1594) has been mentioned above. One major influence throughout the Tudor period was Sir Thomas More, who seems to have worked on two versions of his ***History of Richard III*** (*c.* 1513), one in Latin (published in 1557) and the other in English (published in 1543). More's *History* was used by Hall, Holinshed and Grafton. Jowett, however, believes that Shakespeare made use of More directly because of More's outright denigration of Richard's character. Another play on the same subject, ***Ricardus Tertius***, was written in Latin by Thomas Legge, master of Gonville and Caius College. It was performed at St John's College, Cambridge in 1579 and survives in nine manuscripts. Bullough believes that Legge's play did not influence Shakespeare very much. It follows Hall's *History* closely in attempting to write a Senecan narrative, emphasising the workings of Nemesis and in giving strong roles to women, including the unhistorical inclusion of Queen Margaret. Shakespeare follows Legge in all these respects as well as in some small but significant details: in both plays Norfolk obtains the postponement of the execution of Strange; in both plays, a citizen and a stranger await for Richard's coronation, discussing the sad condition of England; in both plays (and in *The True Tragedie of Richard III*) there is an important discussion between Richmond and Stanley.

Shaheen discusses Biblical references in *Richard III* (337–359). Although Hall's account, which is the principal source for the play, is very moralistic and religious in tone, there are very few actual references to the Bible in the original. Thus, according to Shaheen, Shakespeare introduced his own religious references, but not as many as in other plays. At 5.3.12 "The King's name is a tower of strength", Shakespeare seems to adopt the wording of the Geneva Bible from Proverbs 18.10 "The name of the Lorde is a strong tower" since all other versions have "strong castle".

There is strong classical influence, especially from Seneca's *Tragedies.* The combination of prologue, messenger, ghost, chorus and stichomythia seem very suggestive of Seneca. One scene in particular, Richard's wooing of Lady Anne in 1.2, seems to owe something to Lycus's attempted wooing of Megara in Seneca's *Hercules Furens.* Boyle, following Churchill, has traced the influence of Seneca through Legge's Latin play, *Richard Tertius* and the anonymous *True Tragedie of Richard III* on *Richard III.*[5] Hammond believes that Seneca's *Troades* was very influential in portraying women as victims. English translations of Seneca's plays had been assembled and published by Thomas Newton in 1581.

More classical influence has been detected in Clarence's dream at 1.4, either from Virgil's account of the death of Palinurus in *Aeneid V &VI* or a similar account of Actis's shipwreck in Ovid's *Metamorphoses* 3.792 (or both).

Allusions to other English literary works are rare, but include Richard proclaiming himself as a traditional Vice figure from English morality plays: "Thus like the formal Vice, Iniquity, / I moralize two meanings in one word," at 3.2.82–3. There also appears to be a link with Spenser's *Fairie Queene* (published in 1590, Book 2, Cave of Mammon for the connection between Hades and treasure, and the visit of Guyon to the Bower of Bliss). It is usually assumed that Shakespeare borrowed from the published work of Spenser, but the direction is not firmly established between these works. It is just about possible that Spenser was influenced by a performance of the play *c.* 1589–90. There is also a link with *The Spanish Tragedy* (usually dated *c.* 1588, published anonymously in 1592, attributed to Kyd). Hammond sees details in Clarence's Ddeam as reminiscent of Kyd's play. Jowett asserts without argument that the sequence of composition was *Spanish Tragedy* then the anonymous *True Tragedy of King Richard III* and then Shakespeare's *Richard III.*

## Orthodox Dating

Almost all commentators are agreed that *Richard III* was written *c.* 1592, very soon after the *Henry VI* plays, and thus should be dated early in Shakespeare's career, "a portrait from the artist's youth" (Alexander). Honigmann suggests a date of 1590, in line with his 'early starter' theory. Cairncross and Hammond propose a date *c.* 1591 for the final completion of the *Henry VI–Richard III* tetralogy, arguing that Marlowe's *Edward II,* which he says must have been written in 1592, was influenced by Shakespeare's 'First Tetralogy'. Jowett suggests 1592, as he believes that the play was composed and performed in the summer of that year. He observes that "nothing contradicts the assumption that the play was written in or before mid-1592," but adds, "there are many 'if's in such an account; uncertainty remains." Chambers prefers a date in 1592–93, immediately after the completion of the *Henry VI* trilogy, Wells & Taylor also date *Richard III* to the same winter; however, they believe that Shakespeare discovered Seneca after writing the *Henry VI* trilogy, which inspired first *Titus Andronicus* then *Richard III.* This line of reasoning appears to ignore the Senecan influence in *3 Henry VI* (see previous chapter). Knowles, Cox & Rasmussen, Jowett, Lull and Taylor (2008) agree with 1592–93. Bullough believes it may have been composed in 1593–94.

Vickers believes that *Richard III* was composed at about the same time as *Titus*, but believes that Act I of *Titus* was written by Peele. Jowett asserts that it is difficult to propose a date for *Titus* and therefore a "hazardous" business to then attempt to deduce the date of *Richard III.*

## Metrical Tests

Various metrical tests have placed *Richard III* among the earlier plays in the canon, but, as there is doubt about the sole authorship, metrical tests remain unreliable. There is a very high number of feminine endings (20%), a low incidence of open-ended (i.e. run-on) lines at 13% and even lower mid-line speech endings at 3%.

## External Evidence

Following Tillyard, *Richard III* is often seen as a justification of the Tudor regime in general. Randall Martin (in Dutton) has argued that *The Treatise of Treasons* (published in 1572 and probably written by John Leslie, 1527–96) was very much in the dramatist's mind during his portrayal of Gloucester's rise in *3 Henry VI* and *Richard III*, which Leslie saw as closely analogous to the rise to power of Burghley, especially in their treatment of Mary Queen of Scots. However, David Bevington, Edna Boris and to some extent Andrew Hadfield have argued that the history plays in general refer to contemporary ideas on authority and law, rather than specific events or controversies.[6]

## Oxfordian Dating

Oxfordians have in general placed *Richard III* earlier than orthodox scholars. Eva Turner Clark suggested composition in 1581 during Oxford's imprisonment in the Tower.[7] She points out that there are 26 references to the gloomy prison in the play, compared to 14 in the *Henry VI* trilogy (and just three in *Richard II*). She believes that *Richard III* shows the support which Elizabeth's grandfather, Henry VII, had received from a forebear of Edward de Vere, John thirteenth earl of Oxford. Those sent to the Tower in the play are as innocent as Oxford claimed he was in 1581. She further detects a similar alignment between characters in the play and contemporaries of Oxford. Finally, she adduces a number of verbal parallels between Oxford's letter of July 1581 (Nelson, 270–1) and *Richard III*.

Another link is that the young Oxford studied at Queens' College Cambridge and at St John's College in 1558–9 (Nelson 23–25). There appears to be a strong link between the three queens portrayed in *Richard III*. Queens' College is proudly aware of its connections with the queens who are portrayed so sympathetically in *Richard III*. The college was originally founded by Margaret of Anjou in 1448 (but without formal statutes). It was refounded by Queen Elizabeth, wife of Edward IV in 1464, who became patroness and gave the college its first statutes in 1475. There is a contemporary portrait of her in the college. Next, Richard's queen, Anne Neville, is seen as a 'patroness' as she endowed the college "magnificently" in 1484, with lands confiscated from the earldoms of Oxford and Warwick. After the accession of Henry VII, many of these lands were restored to their previous earldoms (Twigg, 1–12). The College was also at the forefront of drama in the Elizabethan period (Twigg, 106–8). Oxfordians see a link between the college and Shakespeare's dramatic representation of the arguments (in 4.4) between Queen Margaret (anachronistically alive, as she had returned to France in 1575, and died there in 1582, before events in the play began), Queen Anne and the Duchess of York.

## Conclusion

The earliest date for the known versions of the play depends on the second edition of Holinshed in 1587. The latest possible date is the publication of the First Quarto in 1597. It is possible that an earlier version was based on the first edition of Holinshed (1577). It is likely from the *Groatsworth* reference that the play was at least in mind by 1592 and possibly already composed. Existing versions of *Richard III* can be dated any time between 1587 and 1597.[8]

## Notes

1. In this respect, Davison anticipates the argument developed at length by Lukas Erne, *Shakespeare as a Literary Dramatist* (2003).
2. At the opening of *Satyr VII*, Marston parodies Richard's cry with: "A Man, a man, a kingdome for a man!" The quote in *The Return from Parnassus* at 4.3. runs as follows:

   Kemp. thou wilt do well in time, if thou wilt be ruled
   by thy betters, that is by my selfe, and such graue Aldermen
   of the playhouse as I am.
   Burbage. I like your face, and the proportion of your body
   for *Richard* the 3. I pray, M. *Phil.* let me see you act a
   little of it.
   Phil. Now is the winter of our discontent
   Made glorious summer by the sonne of Yorke.

   *The Return from Parnassus* was published in 1606. Proposed dates for its composition range between 1598 and 1602. Chambers, *ES*, 4.38, opts for 1599–1600. On Richard Burbage, see C. C. Stopes, *Burbage and Shakespeare's Stage* (1970) and Martin Holmes, *Shakespeare and Burbage* (1978).
3. The text of *The True Tragedie of Richard Duke of York* has been reprinted in 1929 (for the Malone Society by W. W. Greg) and in 2008 (under the name of Thomas Legge, but this may be a mistake). An e-text of the play is available at www. elizabethanauthors.com (accessed 31 October 2009).
4. Michael Bennett in *The Battle of Bosworth* (1985) describes the 'The Battle of Bosworth Field' as a "prose version from the late sixteenth century" and

ascribes authorship to "a member of the Stanley entourage who was probably an eyewitness".

5. Jiménez quotes Churchill, who claims that the only other chronicle play to use the Senecan revenge motif was *The Spanish Tragedy*, published anonymously in 1592, but attributed to Thomas Kyd (dated between 1582 and 1592 by J. R. Mulryne, in his 1970 edition).
6. The view expressed by Bevington is supported by John Burnett in his chapter on *Richard III* in his book *Constructing 'Monsters' in Shakespearean Drama*, MacMillan, 2002.
7. Alan Nelson (who is unsympathetic to Oxford and denies all claims for his authorship of the Shakespeare canon) sees Oxford's imprisonment as something of a just dessert (266–73).
8. After this essay was completed, the long-awaited Arden 3 edition of the play was published. The editor, James Siemon, reaches similar conclusions about the date of writing, placing it definitely between 1587 and 1597, and tending to prefer a date *c.* 1594. He sees the play as the end of a trilogy (i.e. *Contention–True Tragedy–Richard III*) with *1 Henry VI* probably a prequel. He makes some interesting points on small differences of portrayal between 'Gloucester' in *3 Henry VI* and 'Gloucester' in *Richard III*, e.g. in his theatricality and his use of humour.

## Other Cited Works

Alexander, Peter, *Shakespeare's 'Henry VI' and 'Richard III'*, Cambridge: CUP 1929

Anderson, Mark, *Shakespeare by Another Name*. New York: Gotham 2005

Bevington, David, *Tudor Drama and Politics*, Cambridge, MA, 1968

Boris, Edna, *Shakespeare's English Kings, the People and the Law*, Rutherford, NJ, 1978

Boswell-Stone, W. G., *Shakespeare's Holinshed: The Chronicle and The Historical Plays Compared,* London: Chatto & Windus, 1896

Boyle, Anthony J., *Tragic Seneca: an essay in the theatrical tradition,* London: Routledge, 1997

Bullough, Geoffrey, *Narrative and Dramatic Sources of Shakespeare*, vol. III ('Earlier English History Plays'), London: Routledge and Kegan Paul, 1960

Cairncross, Andrew (ed.), *King Henry VI parts 1 2, 3,* Arden 2 Edition, London: Methuen 1962–3.

Chambers, E. K., *The Elizabethan Stage*, 4 vols, Oxford: Clarendon, 1923

Chambers, E. K., *William Shakespeare A Study of Facts and Problems*, 2 vols, Oxford: Clarendon, 1930

Churchill, G. B., *Richard the Third up to Shakespeare*. Berlin, 1900

Clark, Eva Turner, *Hidden Allusions in Shakespeare's Plays*, New York: Kennikat, rptd 1974

Cox, John & Eric Rasmussen, *King Henry VI Part 3,* Arden 3, London: Arden Shakespeare, 2001

Davison, Peter (ed.), *The First Quarto of King Richard III*, Cambridge: CUP, 1996

Hadfield, Andrew, *Shakespeare and Republicanism,* Cambridge: CUP, 2005

Hammond, Anthony (ed.), *Richard III*, Arden 2, London: Methuen 1981

Honigmann, E. A. J., *Shakespeare, the 'lost years'*, Manchester: MUP, 1985

Jiménez, Ramón, "*The True Tragedie of Richard Duke of York*: another early history play by Edward de Vere", *The Oxfordian,* 7, 2004: 115–151
Jowett, John (ed.), *Richard III,* Oxford: OUP, 2000
King, Lucille, "*2* and *3 Henry VI* – Which Holinshed?" *PMLA,* 1935: 745–52
Knowles, Ronald (ed.), *King Henry VI part 2*, Arden 3, London: Arden Shakespeare, 1999
Legge, Thomas (ed.), *The True Tragedie of Richard Duke of York*, Bibliobazaar, rptd 2008
Logan, Terence P., and Denzell S. Smith (eds), *The Predecessors of Shakespeare: A Survey and Bibliography of Recent Studies in English Renaissance Drama*, Lincoln: University of Nebraska Press, 1973
Lull, Janis (ed.), *Richard III,* Cambridge: CUP, 1999
Maguire, Laurie, *Shakespeare's "Bad" Quartos and their Contexts*, Cambridge: CUP, 1996
Martin, Randall, "Catilines and Machiavels: reading Catholic resistance in *3 Henry VI*" in Richard Dutton, Alison Findlay & Richard Wilson, *Theatre and Religion: Lancastrian Shakespeare*, Manchester: MUP, 2003
Martin, Randall (ed.), *Henry VI, Part 3,* Oxford: OUP, 2001
McKerrow, R. B., "A Note on *Henry VI, Part II*, and *The Contention of York and Lancaster*"', *RES*, 9, 1933: 157–169
Nelson, Alan, H., *Monstrous Adversary*, Liverpool: LUP, 2003
Patrick, David L., *The Textual History of Richard III*, Stanford, 1936
Shaheen, Naseeb, *Biblical References in Shakespeare's Plays,* Delaware: UDP, 1999
Siemon, James R. (ed.), *King Richard III*, London, Arden 3, 2009
Smallwood, Robert (ed.), *Players of Shakespeare 6*, Cambridge: CUP, 2004
Tillyard, E. M. W., *Shakespeare's History Plays*, London: Chatto and Windus, 1944
Twigg, John, *A History of Queens' College, Cambridge 1448–1986,* Woodbridge, Suffolk: Boydell Press, 1987
Vickers, Sir Brian, *Shakespeare, co-author,* Oxford: OUP, 2002
Wells, Stanley & Gary Taylor (eds), *William Shakespeare: The Complete Works*. Oxford: OUP, 1986
—, *William Shakespeare: A Textual Companion*. Oxford: OUP, 1987
Wilson, J. Dover (ed.), *Richard III*, Cambridge, CUP, 1954

24

# The Life of King Henry the Eight

Kevin Gilvary and Lee Tudor-Pole

The extant *Henry VIII* can be dated to any time between 1583 (the last definite source was Foxe's *Actes and Monuments of Martyrs*) and 1613 when the play was performed.

## Publication Date

*Henry the eight* was first registered in 1623, when sixteen plays were entered in the Stationers' Register on 8 November:

> Mr Blounte Isaak Jaggard. Entered for their Copie vnder the hands of Mr Doctor Worral and Mr Cole – warden, Mr William Shakspeers Comedyes Histories, and Tragedyes soe manie of the said Copies as are not formerly entered to other men. vizt. Comedyes. The Tempest. The two gentlemen of Verona. Measure for Measure. The Comedy of Errors. As you Like it. All's well that ends well. Twelft night. The winters tale. Histories. The thirde parte of Henry the sixt. Henry the eight. Coriolanus. Timon of Athens. Julius Caesar. Tragedies. Mackbeth. Anthonie & Cleopatra. Cymbeline.

*The Life of King Henry the Eight* was first published in the First Folio:

> [F1. 1623] The Life of King Henry the Eight.

It is the last of the history plays listed in the F1 contents page, coming after *Richard III*. In the text, it is followed by *Troilus & Cressida*. The title page refers to the play as *The Famous History of the Life of King HENRY the Eight*. The running title refers to it as *The Life of King Henry the Eight*. The alternate title *All is True*, noted by many commentators in 1613, is not present in the

Folio, nor was it mentioned in the 1628 performance. Chambers says that the text is good, with elaborate stage directions. The play is somewhat episodic in nature, with the King playing a small role. Thus it resembles the *Henry VI* plays (usually dated between 1587 and 1592) in being concerned with events in the reign, more than it resembles *Richard III,* which presents the king as the protagonist.

## Performance Date

The earliest definite date for a performance of the play was on 29 June 1613, the day when the Globe caught fire and burnt down. There are various accounts of this event, with the play in performance being called *Henry VIII* or *All is True.* Chambers gives the main accounts in *ES* ii 419–23. One commentator, Edmund Howes, wrote:

> Upon S Peters Day last, the play-house or Theater called the Globe, upon Banck-side near London, by negligent discharging of a peal of ordinance, close to the south side thereof, the thatch took fire . . . the house being filled with people to behold the play, viz of Henry the Eighth.

Howe was continuing Stowe's *Annales*; this addition first appeared in 1615. Another account comes from Thomas Lorkins, who wrote to Sir Thomas Puckering on 30 June:

> No longer since than yesterday, while Burbage's company were acting at the Globe the play of Henry VIII, and there shooting off certain chambers in way of triumph, the fire catched and fastened upon the thatch of the house.

In another account, Sir Henry Wotton (sometimes spelt 'Wooton') wrote on 2 July to his nephew, Sir Edmund Bacon:

> The King's players had a new play, called *All is True*, representing some principal pieces of the reign of Henry VIII, which was set forth with many extraordinary circumstances of pomp and majesty even to the matting of the stage; the Knights of the Order with their Georges and garters, the Guards with their embroidered coats, and the like: sufficient in truth within a while to make greatness very familiar, if not ridiculous. Now, King Henry making a masque at the Cardinal Wolsey's house and certain chambers being shot off at his entry . . . did light on the thatch. . . where . . . it kindled inwardly.

Wotton's account accords with the events in Act 1 Scene 4, but there is a slight puzzle concerning the description of Knights of the Garter, for which there is no mention in the text. Another account by a young merchant, Henry Bluett, was not known to Chambers (but was reported by Cole in 1981 and is quoted by McMullan, 58). Bluett wrote:

> On Tuesday last there was acted at the Globe a new play called *All is Triewe,* which had been acted not passing 2 or 3 times before. . . . As the play was almost ended the house was fired with shooting off a chamber . . . and so burned down to the ground.

Other accounts described the fire without mentioning the title of the play. Two commentators (out of many), Wotton and Bluett, describe the play as "new", without elaborating on whether it was newly composed, new to the company or new to the general public. Given the lavish production (described by Wotton), it is possible that the play had already been performed at court or in private houses. Neither Bluett, "a young merchant", nor Wotton can be considered firm authorities on whether a play actually was "new" According to his biographer, Gerald Curzon, Wotton spent very little time in London after 1589. He was there at the time of the Essex Rebellion in February 1601 but quickly left for France and Italy, returning only in 1612. Thus it is possible that the company were able to advertise a "new play" even if it was merely a revival. Similarly, the third quarto of *Richard III* (1602, and all subsequent quartos of the play) claim it was "newly augmented" when the text remains substantially the same as in the second quarto of *Richard III.* Moreover, Samuel Pepys described *Henry VIII* as a "new play" in his diary entry of 24 December, 1663.[1]

There are, in fact, several suggestions that the life and/or reign of Henry VIII was the subject of a play (or plays) performed in the 1590s: firstly, Edward Alleyne left a list of costumes from the early part of his career including a "Harry VIII gown" and a "Cardinal's gown".[2] Because Alleyne was born in 1566, the list would seem to date from the late 1580s or early 1590s. Secondly, Henslowe in his Diary recorded an inventory on 10 March 1598, which includes a costume for the part of Will Sommers, Henry VIII's fool.[3] There were also references in 1593–4 to a play called *Buckingham* which Chambers believes may have been an early version of *Henry VIII,* as there were other Shakespeare plays performed at that time.[4] In addition, Henslowe made several payments in 1601 to Chettle for a play about Wolsey (now lost) and then to a group of authors for a 'prequel', also now lost. It is not known whether these references are to the play published in Shakespeare's Folio or to another play.

Shakespeare's play was performed again in 1628. After the Restoration, it was staged in 1663 at the Duke's House in Lincoln's Inn Fields by Sir William Davenant and starred Thomas Betteridge.

## Attribution

Some commentators, notably Alexander, Foakes, Bullough and Ribner, believe *Henry VIII* to be by Shakespeare alone, as recorded in the First Folio. Others, e.g. Chambers, Halio and McMullan, opt for co-authorship between Shakespeare and Fetcher (1579–1625). The evidence for joint authorship, mainly metrical and linguistic, has been explored in great detail by Sir Brian Vickers. In trying to date this play, however, we find that co-authorship entails serious problems:

(a) Did Shakespeare write some parts and then discard them, for Fletcher, at a later date, to expand into a five-act play (or possibly vice versa)?
(b) Did the authors agree the outline and then carve out different scenes for simultaneous, independent composition?
(c) Did the authors actively work together in composing every scene?

The following is the consensus regarding co-authorship (Vickers):

| **By Shakespeare** | **By Fletcher** |
|---|---|
| 1.1; 1.2 | 1.3; 1.4; 2.1; 2.2; 3.1 |
| 3.2a (1–202) | 3.2b (203–459); 4.1; 4.2 |
| 5.1 | 5.2; 5.3; 5.4 |

'Shakespearean' scenes tend to be fewer but longer; so the total amount attributed to Shakespeare is 1168 lines (about 42%) against 1604 lines to Fletcher (about 58%).

In his identification of who wrote which scene, Vickers appears to suggest independent working; either (a) the play was initially writtten by one author and revised by the other or (b) the authors followed an outline plan but worked independently of each other. McMullan appears to believe that the authors worked independently of each other, suggesting revision by Fletcher.

However, Vickers does not indicate whether he thinks Fletcher was a collaborator or a reviser. Shaheen (see below) believes the original play to have been by Shakespeare, later revised by Fletcher.

## Sources

Bullough favours only two definite historical sources, Holinshed and Foxe, for *Henry VIII.* However, he does accept that Hall might also have been used:

**Edward Hall, *The Union of the Two Noble and Illustre Famelies of Lancastre and Yorke*** (1548–50) covers events up until the end of Henry VIII's reign. Hall's *Chronicle* does not seem to have been used for the content or the structure of the play but may have been used for the phrasing of Wolsey's farewell speeches, e.g. at 3.2 358; these are not developed in Holinshed.

**Raphael Holinshed, *The Chronicles of Englande, Scotlande, and Irelande*** (1st ed. 1577 & 2nd ed. 1587). Bullough demonstrates how Holinshed provided most of the detailed political material for the play, e.g. in the meeting of the Kings of England and France in 1.1. McMullan points out that both Shakespeare and Fletcher appear to have read Holinshed on Henry VIII where the king finds Wolsey's private paper of the Bishop of Durham in 1508 (3.2 120–5, apparently by Shakespeare) and in Wolsey's speech bemoaning his negligence (at 3.2. 231ff, apparently by Fletcher). Fletcher must have known the earlier part of the scene anyway: he might have added to Shakespeare's section, as suggested in (a) above; or the authors might have actively collaborated, as in (b) or (c). Boswell-Stone argues that Shakespeare used the second edition of Holinshed for *Henry VIII* for details from Cavendish's *Life of Wolsey* (which was added to the second edition). However, Boswell-Stone also notes that the dramatist(s) may have used selections of Cavendish's *Wolsey* which were published in John Stow's *Chronicles of England* (1580) and again in Stow's expanded account, *The Annales* (1592).

Bullough shows how John Foxe's 1583 edition of ***Actes and Monuments of Martyrs*** was used for Cranmer's trial at 5.1 (which is ascribed to Shakespeare by all commentators, except Fleay in 1886, who ascribed it to Massinger). This is the latest definite source for the play.

Bullough believes that Samuel Rowley's play ***When You See Me, You Know Me*** (published 1605, 1613 etc) may be related to *Henry VIII.* Since the latter is usually dated *c.* 1612, then Rowley's play might have been a source. If *Henry VIII* dated from the 1590s, as suggested by the references in Alleyne and Henslowe, than the direction of influence would have been reversed. Rowley's play is very unhistorical and shows among other things Henry VIII walking the streets in disguise and fighting. There may be a reference to *When You see Me* in the prologue to *Henry VIII* when the audience are asked not to expect "a merry, bawdy play". Rowley's play covers a wider historical span (1514 – 44) than *Henry VIII* (1520 – 36). There are some broad similarities: *When You See Me* gives prominence to future greatness on the birth of a royal child; Wolsey owes his pre-eminence to his eloquence; Wolsey criticises the Queen (Katherine Parr *v.* Anne Boleyn) and the taunts against Latimer and Ridley echo similar comments against Cranmer and Cromwell. But Foakes is not persuaded that Rowley's play was a source for *Henry VIII.*

Bullough overlooks one reference which was proposed by Duncan-Jones and accepted by McMullen. This was the source of Katherine's vision in 4.2. Margaret of Navarre, Duchess of Alençon, (1492–1549) had a vision shortly before her death, as reported by Charles de Sainte Marthe in his *Tombeau de Marguerite de Valois reine de Navarre* (*ESTCS* 125774, 1551). There is a copy in the Bodleian Library at Oxford University, but the work was never translated into English. The dramatist(s) transferred this dream to Katherine at 4.2 82. It is not clear how the dramatist(s) knew this source.

Shaheen devotes more than 20 pages to discussion of Biblical allusions in *Henry VIII*. He notes that there are few biblical allusions in the sources, but plenty in the play. He sees little difference between the types of allusion in the different parts, observing that all the allusions in those scenes ascribed to Fletcher conform to Shakespeare's style of biblical allusion. He concludes that the original play was by Shakespeare, and it was later adapted by Fletcher.

Reference to other English poetical works or to classical works are very rare; the song for Katherine in 3.1 about Orpheus's music is ultimately derived from Ovid's *Metamorphoses*. Cranmer's prophecies about the Elizabeth Age (5.4 33–5) may be biblical or classical (or both):

> In her days, every man shall eat in safety,
> Under his own vine what he plants, and sing
> The Merry songs of peace to all his neighbours.

This passage seems to be reminiscent of prophecies from the Old Testament but perhaps also of Virgil's prophecies (*Eclogue IV*; *Aeneid VI*) of a Golden Age under Augustus or Ovid's similar prophecies in *Metamorphoses XV*.

## Orthodox Date – Internal Evidence

Chambers's original opinion was that the play dated from the 1590s, but he revised this to 1612–13; most commentators have agreed with his later date. This later date entails taking Wotton's mention of the play as "new" to mean 'newly composed'. Foakes agrees and sets the composition of the play in early 1613. McMullan thinks it may have been first performed soon after 1610, in the Blackfriars Theatre, since the Blackfriars Monastic Hall had been used to hear the annulment proceedings against Katherine of Aragon in 1529.

On the other hand, many leading eighteenth and nineteenth century scholars dated *Henry VIII* to 1603–4 or earlier, including Samuel Johnson, Lewis Theobald, George Steevens, Edmond Malone, Thomas Campbell, J. O. Halliwell-Phillipps (as reported and accepted by E. K. Chambers in his 1908 edition). Bullough hints at a possible early date due to the play's loose episodic structure, which recalls the *Henry VI* trilogy.

Another reason for an earlier date for the play is that the name of 'God' appears over 20 times, both in the part assigned to Shakespeare and in the part assigned to Fletcher, e.g. Wolsey's lament (at 3.2 455–7):

> Had I but served my God with half the zeal
> I served my King, he would not in mine age
> Have left me naked to mine enemies.

Similarly, Cranmer prays: “God and Your majesty / Protect mine innocence” (5.1 140–1). This strongly suggests it was composed before the Act to Restrain Abuses in 1605/6 “for the preventing and avoiding of the great abuse of the holy name of God, in stage-plays” (3 Jac. I c. 21). Tiffany Stern (53) has shown how texts composed before 1605 were revised. She scans a line from *King John* (1.1 83), proposing that the hypermetrical “heaven” was probably used to replace “God”. McMullen notes what seems to be a similar substitution at *Henry VIII* 2.4 185:

> I stood not in the smile of hea-ven, who had

Stern argues that other plays show evidence of the successful removal of swearing: *Titus, Richard III, Merry Wives, 1 Henry IV* and *Twelfth Night.* She further notes that the 1622 quarto of *Othello* is a “swearing” text, entailing the proposition that it was composed before 1605, but the Folio version of *Othello* in 1623 was not a swearing text.[5]

There are other internal reasons to suggest an early date:

- the absence of any definite source post 1583 (Rowley’s play is only vaguely related to *Henry VIII* and could have been a reaction against this play)
- range of biblical allusions being Shakespearean, suggesting a later revision by Fletcher

The metrical and linguistic analyses suggest a later date but the data is problematic when revision is suspected.

## Orthodox Date – External Evidence

Foakes has argued in detail that, since the play ends with the prediction of the future Golden Age under a baby now being baptised, it was intended to celebrate the marriage of the Princess Elizabeth to Prince Frederick, the Elector Palatine, in February 1613. He notes that the marriage had been arranged in May 1612, giving the dramatist time to prepare a new play on an old subject. He also notes that the anti-Wolsey sentiment would have been interpreted favorably in an anti-catholic atmosphere of 1612–13, just a few years after the trial of the Gunpowder plotters. Halio, Margeson and McMullen think it unlikely that the play was performed for the royal wedding[6] and accept that “new” meant “newly composed”. McMullen believes that the play may have been inspired by the sudden death, in November 1612, of Henry Prince of Wales.

Various arguments have been set against these proposals: firstly, a play dramatising the downfall of Wolsey would have pleased anti-catholic sentiment from 1580 onwards, when Pope Gregory XIII had renewed his predecessor’s excommunication of Elizabeth, with the further call to catholics to assassinate her. Secondly, a play praising the marriage of Anne Boleyn and the birth of

Elizabeth is more likely to have been written in Elizabeth's lifetime (as argued by Victorian editors such as Thomas Campbell, 1838) rather than under James I, who held Elizabeth responsible for the execution of his mother. Thirdly, *Henry VIII* involves the annulment of a foreign marriage, hardly a recommendation to the happy couple. Finally, the play ends with the promise of a golden age under the new-born princess, whereas the couple were only married and not yet parents. They would also have hoped and prayed for the birth of a son, rather than a daughter.

## Oxfordian Date

Oxfordians generally propose that Oxford wrote *Henry VIII c.* 1586, immediately after being granted the £1,000 annuity by Elizabeth. They argue that the Queen awarded him this sum to pressure him to write patriotic drama, which would be all the more effective for being anonymous (Anderson, 211). It might have been written slightly earlier than the other history plays since it lacks the "overall consistent philosophical scheme" which characterises the other history plays (Ribner). The use of an obscure French source, Charles de Saint Marthe, with connections to the Court of Navarre, suggests authorship by someone such as Oxford who travelled in France in 1575–6. Cranmer's prophecy (at 5.4, apparently by Fletcher) on the Elizabethan Golden Age also includes references to her death:

> Nor shall this peace sleep with her, but as when
> The bird of wonder dies, the maiden phoenix,
> Her ashes new create another heir
> As great in admiration as herself,
> So shall she leave her blessedness to one,
> When heaven shall call her from this cloud of darkness
> *Henry VIII* 5.4 39–44

> But she must die:
> She must, the saints must have her. Yet a virgin,
> A most unspotted lily, shall she pass to th' ground,
> And all the world shall mourn her. *Henry VIII* 5.4 59–62

Some commentators see these passages either in anticipation of Elizabeth's 70$^{th}$ birthday (she died in March 1603, less than six months before she would have completed her biblical span of three score and ten years) or as an official tribute on her death. Oxfordians argue that either scenario fits well with Oxford's authorship. The prophecy of the continued greatness under Elizabeth's successor may have contributed to James I's high opinion of Oxford. James entered London on 7 May 1603 and by 2 August he had renewed the £1,000 annuity for "Great Oxford" (Nelson, 418–423).

## Conclusion

The extant *Henry VIII* may date from any time between 1583 (the last definite source was Foxe's *Actes and Monuments of Martyrs*) and 1613 when we know the play was performed. We do not know if the text was ever revised. The play was probably co-authored by Shakespeare and Fletcher, but it is not known whether the authors wrote at the same time or whether one author revised an existing play by the other.

The timespan can probably be reduced further, from 1587 (the second edition of Holinshed until 1605/6 when Parliament passed the Act to Restrain Abuses.

## Notes

I would like to thank Dr Dan Wright of the University of Concordia, Portland, for many helpful suggestions.

1. For further entries, see *The Diary of Samuel Pepys,* vol iv, (ed.) Robert Latham & William Matthews (1971). The relevant passage on 24 December 1663 reads:

> Thence straight home, being very cold, but yet well, I thank God, and at home found my wife making mince pies, and by and by comes in Captain Ferrers to see us, and, among other talke, tells us of the goodness of the new play of "Henry VIII" which makes me think [it] long till my time is out; but I hope before I go I shall set myself such a stint as I may not forget myself as I have hitherto done till I was forced for these months last past wholly to forbid myself the seeing of one.

Samuel Pepys diary is also available on-line at www.pepysdiary.com/archive/1663/12/24/ (accessed 31.10.2009).

2. The Cardinal's gown might have been used either for Henry Beaufort, Bishop of Winchester (who appears as a character in *1, 2 Henry VI*) or Wolsey, who appears in *Henry VIII.* Historically, there were other fifteenth and sixteenth century cardinals in England, but no others were depicted by Shakespeare.
3. 'Will Sommers' is not a named character in *Henry VIII* but he might have been shown in attendance on the King. 'Sommers' appears as the title character in Thomas Nashe's *Pleesant Comedie called Summers last Will and Testament* (published in 1600, dated by Chambers, *ES,* iii, 451–2 to 1592); Sommers died in 1560. 'Sommers' is also a character in Samuel Rowley's *When You See Me, You Know Me.*
4, It is possible, though less likely, that *Buckingham* might refer to a cut version of *Richard III.* Chambers mentions (ES ii 130) that Sussex's Men performed *Buckingham* in the winter of 1593–4 together with *Titus and Vespasian*, which he takes to be *Titus Andronicus.* Chambers cites only one other play about Henry VIII, Samuel Rowley's *When You See Me, You Know Me,* which was registered and published in 1605 (*ES,* iii, 472).
5. For further discussion on blasphemy, see *Shakespeare's Religious Language: a dictionary* (London, 2007) by Rudolph Hassell, who notes the "delightful

irony" of Henry's very catholic oath "By Holy Mary, Butts", at 5.2 33 when the king fears a conspiracy from his Protestant reformer, Cranmer. For further discussion on the revision of plays, see Gary Taylor and John Jowett's *Shakespeare Reshaped: 1606–1623* (Oxford, 1993).

6. According to Chambers, *ES*, iv, 127, a large number of Shakespeare's plays were performed at Christmas time 1612–13, including *1, 2 Henry IV, J. Caesar, Much Ado, Othello, W. Tale*, and *The Tempest*. At the time of the wedding, the only entertainments recorded in the Court Calendar were a few masques.

## Other Cited Works


Alexander, Peter, *Shakespeare's Life and Art,* London: Nisbet, 1939

Anderson, Mark, *Shakespeare by Another Name*, New York: Gotham, 2005

Boswell-Stone, W. G., *Shakespeare's Holinshed: The Chronicle and The Historical Plays Compared,* London: Chatto & Windus, 1896

Bullough, Geoffrey, *Narrative and Dramatic Sources of Shakespeare*, vol. III ('Later English History Plays'), London: Routledge and Kegan Paul, 1962

Chambers E, K. (ed.), *King Henry VIII,* The Red Letter Shakespeare, 1908

—, *The Elizabethan Stage*, 4 vols, Oxford: Clarendon, 1923

—, *William Shakespeare A Study of Facts and Problems*, 2 vols, Oxford: Clarendon, 1930

Clark, Eva Turner, *Hidden Allusions in Shakespeare's Plays*, New York: Kennikat, rptd 1974

Cole, S. J., "A New Account of the Burning of the Globe", *SQ*, 32, 1981: 352

Curzon, Gerald, *Wotton And His Worlds: Spying, science and Venetian Intrigues*, Philadelphia: Xlibris Corporation, 2003

Duncan-Jones, E. E., "Queen Katherine's Vision and Queen Margaret's Dream", *N&Q*, 8, 1961: 142–3

Fleay, F. J., *A chronicle history of the life and work of William Shakespeare*, London: Nimmo, 1886

Foakes, R. A. (ed.), *King Henry VIII,* London: Arden², 1968

Halio, Jay (ed.), *King Henry VIII, or All is True.* Oxford: OUP, 1999

Honigmann, E. A. J., *Shakespeare, the 'lost years'*, Manchester: MUP, 1985

Marcus, Leah, *Puzzling Shakespeare: Local Reading and its Discontents*, Berkeley: UCP, 1988

Margeson, John (ed.), *Henry VIII,* Cambridge: CUP, 1990

McMullan, Gordon (ed.), *William Shakespeare and John Fletcher*: *King Henry VIII,* London: Arden³, 2000

Nelson, Alan, H., *Monstrous Adversary*, Liverpool: LUP, 2003

Ribner, Irving, *The English History Play in the Age of Shakespeare*, Princeton, NJ: Princeton University Press, 1957

Shaheen, Naseeb, *Biblical References in Shakespeare's Plays*, Delaware: UDP, 1999

Stern, Tiffany, *Making Shakespeare: from stage to page*, London: Routledge, 2004

Tillyard, E. M. W., *Shakespeare's History Plays*, London: Chatto and Windus, 1944

Vickers, Brian, *Shakespeare, Co-author,* Oxford: OUP, 2002

Wells, Stanley & Gary Taylor (eds), *William Shakespeare: The Complete Works.* Oxford, OUP, 1986.

—, *William Shakespeare: A Textual Companion*, Oxford: OUP, 1987

# The Tragedies

THE

# Famous Hiſtorie of

## Troylus *and* Creſſeid.

*Excellently expreſſing the beginning* of their loues, with the conceited wooing of *Pandarus* Prince of *Licia.*

*Written by* William Shakeſpeare.

LONDON
Imprinted by *G.Eld* for *R. Bonian* and *H. Walley*, and are to be ſold at the ſpred Eagle in Paules Church-yeard, ouer againſt the great North doore.
1609.

19. Title page to the first quarto of *Troilus and Cressida*, 1609. By permission of Bodleian Library, University of Oxford, shelfmark Arch. G d.43 (6), title page.

# 25

# The Tragedie of Troylus and Crefsida.

Kevin Gilvary

This play can be dated any time between Arthur Hall's translation of the first ten books of Homer's *Iliad* in 1581 and its publication in the Quarto of 1609.

## Publication

The process of publication is full of surprises, which have not been explained satisfactorily. The play was entered conditionally into the Stationers' Register in February 1603:

> [SR, 1603] 7 februarii. Master Robertes. Entred for his copie in full Court holden this day, to print when he hath gotten sufficient authority for yt. The booke of Troilus and Cresseda as yt is acted by my lord Chamberlins Men. vj$^{d}$.

It is not clear who would have provided "sufficient authority" and there is no evidence that it was published in 1603. A play of the same name was registered in January 1609 by different publishers, Richard Bonian and Henry Walley, and it was printed by George Eld:

> [SR, 1609] 28 Januarii. Richard Bonion henry Walleys. Entred for their Copy vnder thandes of mr Segar deputy to Sr geo Bucke and mr ward. Lownes a booke called The History of Troylus and Cressida.

It is always assumed that this refers to the same play mentioned in the SR in 1603, but it is possible that these entries refer to different plays or that an original version in 1603 was revised by 1609. There are only fifteen copies of the first quarto: three are known as Qa, the rest are known as Qb, with two main differences. Firstly, Qb bears a different title page:

> [Qa, 1609] THE HISTORIE OF TROYLUS / and Cresseida / As it was acted by the Kings Maiesties servants at the Globe / Written by William Shakespeare
> [Qb, 1609] THE / Famous Historie of / Troylus and Cresseid./ Excellently expressing the beginning / of their loves, with the conceited wooing of Pandarus Prince of Litia / Written by William Shakespeare / LONDON / Imprinted by G. Eld for R. Bonian and H. Walley, and / are to be sold at the spred Eagle in Paules / Church-yeard, over against the / great North-doore. / 1609

Secondly, the Preface to Qb contains the following address to the reader (omitted from Qa and from the First Folio) in which it asserts that the play had not been publicly performed:

**A neuer writer, to an euer / reader. Newes.**

> *Eternall reader, you have heere a new play, never stal'd with the Stage, never clapper-clawd with the palmes of the vulger, and yet passing full of the palme comicall; for it is a birth of your braine, that never undertooke any thing commicall, vainely: And were but the vaine names of commedies changde for the titles of Commodities, or of Playes for Pleas; you should see all those grand censors, that now stile them such vanities, flock to them for the maine grace of their gravities: especially this authors Commedies, that are so fram'd to the life, that they serve for the most common Commentaries, of all the actions of our lives, shewing such a dexteritie, and power of witte, that the most displeased with Playes, are pleasd with his Commedies. And all such dull and heavy-witted worldlings, as were never capable of the witte of a Commedie, comming by report of them to his representations, have found that witte there, that they never found in them-selves, and have parted better wittied then they came: feeling an edge of witte set upon them, more then ever they dreamd they had braine to grinde it on. So much and such savored salt of witte is in his Commedies, that they seeme (for their height of pleasure) to be borne in that sea that brought forth Venus. Amongst all there is none more witty then this: And had I time I would comment upon it, though I know it needs not, (for so much as will make you thinke your testerne well bestowd) but for so much worth, as even poore I know to be stuft in it. It deserves such a labour, as well as the best Commedy in* Terence *or* Plautus. *And beleeve this, That when hee is gone, and his Commedies out of sale, you will scramble for them, and set up a new English Inquisition. Take this for a warning, and at the perrill of your pleasures losse and Judgements, refuse not, nor like this the lesse, for not being sullied, with the smoaky breath of the multitude; but thanke fortune for the scape it hath made amongst you. Since by the grand possessors wills I beleeve you should have prayd for them rather then beene prayd. And so I leave all such to bee prayd for (for the states of their wits healths) that will not praise it.* Vale.

Alexander (among others) suggests that the play was for a private audience at one of the Inns of Court because of the claim that it had not been played publicly. He dismisses the idea of a royal performance as "the whole tone of the piece makes this impossible." (195)

The genre of the play remains obscure. The title pages of the quartos refer to it as a history but the Preface to Qb refers to it as a comedy; in the First Folio, where it is placed between the Histories and the Tragedies, it is called a tragedy. The play was omitted from the Catalogue to the First Folio (1623) but was included at the end of the Histories. The second and third page were numbered 79 and 80 (although they would have been 235 and 236 in the sequence of Histories). The next play, *Coriolanus*, is numbered 1–30 according to the pattern of separate numbering in each section. In F1, the title page and the running title give 'The Tragedie of Troylus and Cressida' despite the protagonists' separate survival at the end:

> [F1 Title Page] The Tragedie of Troylus and Cressida.

F1 seems to follow Q in general, but without the preface of Qb and with an additional prologue; there are also many verbal differences. It has been suggested that the differences arise from use of the author's foul papers (Chambers) or from a prompt book (Wells & Taylor).

## Performance Date

There is no record of any actual performance before the Restoration period, when the play was produced in 1668.

The Stationers' Register claims that the play had been acted before February 1602/3 by the Lord Chamberlain's Men. Qa states that "it was acted by the King's Majesty's servants at the Globe". Qb, however, states that the play was new and "*never stal'd with the Stage, never clapper-clawd with the palmes of the vulger*" which is usually taken to mean that it 'had never been acted before' but might just have meant that it 'had never been acted in a public theatre'. Opinions are divided as to where the author originally intended to produce the play: Peter Alexander and Gary Taylor proposed the Inns of Court as the first venue, while Ernst Honigmann considered a Cambridge college because of the reference in the *Parnassus* plays (described below). Robert Kimbrough argues for performance in the public theatre (as stated in Qa). Hotine argues for a first performance at the newly opened Blackfriars Theatre in 1608. Of course, the play might have been performed first privately and then publicly; the members of a company would have performed it at a courtly or aristocratic venue and then transferred it to a public theatre such as the Globe, rather than staging the play just once.

## Sources

Bullough cites various medieval versions of the romantic story of Troilus and Cressida (it is not found in the ancient sources):

(a) Chaucer in his longest poem *Troilus and Criseyde* (8,000 lines) provided most of the details of the romantic plot along courtly, chivalric lines and of the characters of Troilus and Pandarus. Further details seem to derive from Robert Henryson, *The Testament of Cresseid*, which continued Cressida's story and was included in the edition by Thynne in 1532 (and in later publications, e.g. by John Stow in 1561 and by Thomas Speght in 1598).
(b) Lydgate's *Troy Book*, a lengthy poem written *c.* 1420 by a monk at the request of Henry V, who wished to explore and develop notions of chivalry. This poem was published by Richard Pynson in 1513 as *The hystorye sege and dystruccyon of Troye*. It supplied the dramatist with details on the Trojan War in general and on Cressida's character.
(c) Caxton's translation of Lefèvre's *Recuyell of the Historyes of Troye* (*c.* 1475) may have been used for the scenes of military action.

Bullough also states that the dramatist might have used any of the numerous translations of Homer's *Iliad* for information about the Trojan War. Various Latin translations were published after 1474; French translations date from 1520 by Samxon and from 1545 by Salel. The earliest English translation was by Arthur Hall (London, 1581) and confined to only the first ten books (covering the events in *Troilus and Cressida*). George Chapman's *Seaven Books of the Iliades* (1598) omits some action in both the Iliad and the play, e.g. Menelaus' challenge to Paris. Bullough, however, sees no precise debt to Chapman and accepts that details used in the play had been covered in previous publications.

Ulysses' famous speeech on degree begins:

The specialty of rule hath been neglected,
And look how many Grecian tents do stand
Hollow upon this plain, so many hollow factions . . . (1.3. 78–137)

This passage, according to Bullough, influenced Chapman, who made various changes in his wording of Book III of *The Iliad* for his 1611 complete translation. There are frequent echoes of Ovid's *Metamorphoses* (Book XIII), especially in details of the quarrel between Ulysses and Achilles. Both the original Latin text and Golding's 1567 translation seem to have been consulted. The dramatist also used Virgil's *Aeneid* .[1]

There were various dramatic versions of the Trojan War in the Elizabethan Period. On 27 December 1584, a lost play called *The History of Agamemnon and Ulisses* was performed by the Earl of Oxford's Boys at court. The Admiral's Men played *Troye* at the Rose Theatre in 1596 and a lost play called *Troyeles & creasse daye*, was commissioned from Dekker and Chettle, who received various payments in April 1599. Dekker and Chettle's play is not extant but there is a fragment of an outline plot which dates *c.* 1598–1602. It has been suggested that Shakespeare was commissioned to write a rival piece. The fragmentary outline plot of Dekker and Chettle's play was published by W. W. Greg in *Dramatic Documents in Elizabethan Playhouses* (1931) and reproduced by Bullough, vol. VI, 220–1. Bullough inclines towards the idea that Shakespeare "conceived his play as a 'realistic' answer to the unsophisticated mixture of epic and didactic sentiment likely to have characterised the piece by Dekker and Chettle."

Shaheen discusses the many Biblical references in the play, e.g. at 2.3.144 "He that disciplin'd thine arms to fight." This seems to follow the Geneva Bible's translation of Psalms 144.1 "Which teacheth mine hands to fight."

There are many allusions in Shakespeare's own works to the Troilus story, including: *Much Ado* 5.2.31, *Merchant of Venice* 5.1.4, *As You Like it*, 4.1.97, *Taming of the Shrew* 4.1.153, *Merry Wives*, 1.3.83 and *Henry V* 2.1.56. Perhaps the clearest reference occurs when Feste says in *Twelfth Night* at 3.1.5:

> I would play Lord Pandarus of Phrygia, sir, to bring a Cressida to this Troilus.

Shakespeare certainly seems to have been impressed by the story. Although these references are in plays usually dated before *Troilus and Cressida*, it is possible that Shakespeare had already composed it earlier in his career.

## Orthodox Date

Chambers, following most earlier commentators, accepted a date of 1602. Most commentators link the date of the play to just before the first entry in the Stationers' Register, or to apparent allusions in plays of the period, in which the dramatists seem to be attacking one another. Some commentators place it slightly earlier in 1601. Bevington believes it possible that Jonson's *Poetaster* in 1601 was an answer to his unfavorable portrayal as Ajax in *Troilus*. Chambers accepts that the play might be as early as 1599 due to the possible allusion in Marston's *Histriomastix*.

*Troilus and Cressida* is not mentioned by Meres in 1598, and although it has occasionally been suggested that the unidentified play from Meres's list, *Love's Labour's Won,* may have been an alternative title for *Troilus & Cressida,* there is little to support this title in the text. Before Chambers, some commentators proposed an earlier date. Godshalk has argued that most suggestions for dating the play are simply conjectures.

## Internal Orthodox Evidence

Palmer notes (19) that "stylistic considerations, notoriously subjective and unreliable, have suggested both early and late dating for *Troilus*." Wells and

Taylor find plausible evidence to place *Troilus and Cressida* in 1602, after *Hamlet.*

There are a few allusions in the play which suggest a date 1601–2: some see, in the Prologue 24–25, a reference to the armed prologue of Jonson's *Poetaster, c.* 1601. There is a reference to "ten shares" at 2.3.223, which has been taken by some to refer to the ten shareholders of the Globe (from 1599 onwards). At 3.3.224, the statement, "The fool slides ore the Ice that you should brake" is sometimes taken to refer to the story of the fool and the ice in Armin's *Nest of Ninnies* (1600).

A slightly earlier date, *c.* 1599, has been proposed due to the possible allusion in Marston's *Histriomastix* (*c.* 1599), where Troilus talks to Cressida of "thy knight," who "shakes his furious speare" and then appears to parody the exchange of gifts between Troilus and Cressida at 4.4.71. Most commentators see this as an allusion to Dekker and Chettle's play.

George Saintsbury argued for an even earlier date on the grounds of poor composition:

> It is extremely difficult not to believe that [*Troilus and Cressida*] is much older than the earlier date would show. Some of the blank verse, no doubt, is fairly mature; but the author may have furbished this up, and much of it is not mature at all. Instead of transcending his materials, as Shakespeare almost invariably does, he has here failed almost entirely to bring out their possibilities; has not availed himself of Chaucer's beautiful romance so fully as he might; and has dramatised the common Troy-books with a loose yet heavy hand utterly unsuggestive of his maturer craftsmanship. If it were not for certain speeches and touches chiefly in the part of Ulysses, and in the parts of the hero and heroine, it might be called the least Shakespearean of all the plays.

This argument for early composition, based on the play's ungainly structure, might appear to be supported by the difficulty in assigning a genre to the work.

## External Orthodox Evidence

Some possible allusions seem to support a date of composition 1601–2. The Prologue seems to refer to an armed prologue, and this is taken to be a reference to Jonson's *Poetaster, c.* 1601.Honigmann, following a suggestion by Chambers, has argued that the second part of *The Retvrne from Pernassus* (a Cambridge University play, *c.* 1601) alludes to both *Poetaster* and *Troilus and Cressida*. The character Will Kemp says:

> Why heres our fellow *Shakespeare* puts them all downe, I and *Ben Ionson* too. O that *Ben Ionson* is a pestilent fellow, he brought vp *Horace* giuing

> the Poets a pill, but our fellow *Shakespeare* hath giuen him a purge that made him bewray his credit
>
> *Return from Parnassus*, 1769–1773

The allusion is often taken to refer to Shakespeare's Ajax (in *Troilus* 1.2) as a satire on Jonson. If the Cambridge playwrights were familiar with *Troilus and Cressida*, Honigmann contends, "Shakespeare's colleagues were no strangers [to the Cambridge audience] and were probably recent visitors, so they might well have put on their newest play . . . as a 'try-out,' before launching it at the Globe" (44). Honigmann's assumption that the play was recently composed is plausible, but not absolutely established. However, Palmer finds no allusion in the *Parnassus* plays to *Troilus*.

Various commentators have seen parallels between the Earl of Essex (out of favour 1599–1601) and the character of Achilles, especially as Chapman had dedicated his partial translation of Homer in 1598 to Essex as the "most honoured now living instance of the Achillean virtues". The parallels are not as strong, perhaps, as between Essex, after his fall in 1599, and Coriolanus. Hotine argued for composition in 1608, on the grounds that the play does not contain any battle scenes but criticises war and that it would have been more topical during the peace negotiations in 1608. This view has not been widely accepted.

## Oxfordian Dating

The usual dating from an Oxfordian perspective is given by Clark. She argues that, in 1584, Oxford's Boys played an early version of *Troilus* as *The History of Agamemnon and Ulisses*. She continues by suggesting that this play had been written by Oxford himself, early in his career and for a limited audience, making use of favorite texts such as the Geneva Bible and Golding's translation of the *Metamorphoses*. She thinks that the work was then revised at the time of translation by Chapman, who knew and respected Oxford. Finally she argues that Oxford's manuscript became available in 1609, five years after he died, when his widow sold their house in Hackney.[2]

## Conclusion

The play can be dated any time between Arthur Hall's translation of Homer in 1581 and the publication of the Quarto in 1609.[3]

## Notes

1 Charles and Michelle Martindale *Shakespeare and the Uses of Antiquity* (London, Routledge, 1990) review the use of various sources and conclude that only Caxton's is absolutely established. Jonathan Bate, *Shakespeare and Ovid* (Oxford, Clarendon, 1993) refers only briefly to Shakespeare's use of the Roman poet in this play. A. D. Nuttall ('Action at a distance: Shakespeare and the Greeks' pp 209–224 in *Shakespeare and the Classics* eds Charles Martindale and A. B. Taylor, Cambridge, CUP, 2004) wonders at how Shakespeare can have used Greek sources, especially *Iliad* III, so accurately.

2 In his biography of Oxford (*Monstrous Adversary*, 2003), Alan Nelson refers to the performance by "the children of Therle of Oxforde" on St John's Day, 27 December 1584 (247); his purchase of a copy of the Geneva Bible, now held by the Folger Library in Washington (53); and his widow's sale of King's Place, Hackney (431–3).

3. Godshalk reviews the proposals regarding the relationship between the different versions and similarly concludes that vital information is simply lacking "many of the accounts of its [i.e. the play's] origins are not supported by the essential data that we now possess."

## Other Works Cited

Alexander, Peter, *Shakespeare's Life and Art,* London: James Nisbet, 1939

Bevington, David (ed.), *Troilus and Cressida,* London: Arden 3, 1998

Bullough, Geoffrey, *Narrative and Dramatic Sources of Shakespeare,* vol. VI (Other 'Classical' Plays), London: Routledge and Kegan Paul, 1966

Chambers, E. K., *The Elizabethan Stage,* 4 vols, Oxford: Clarendon Press, 1923

Chambers, E. K., *William Shakespeare: A Study of Facts and Problems,* 2 vols, Oxford: Clarendon Press, 1930

Clark, Eva Turner, *Hidden Allusions in Shakespeare's Plays,* New York: Kennikat, rptd 1974

Crewe, Jonathan (ed.), *Troilus and Cressida,* Harmondsworth: Penguin, 2000

Dawson, Anthony (ed.), *Troilus and Cressida,* Cambridge: CUP, 2003

Godshalk, W. L. "The Texts of *Troilus and Cressida*", *Early Modern Literary Studies,* 1.2 (1995): 2.1–54

Honigmann, Ernest A. J., "The Date and Revision of *Troilus and Cressida,*", *Textual Criticism and Literary Interpretation*, ed. J. J. McGann, Chicago: U of Chicago P, 1985. 38–54

Hotine, Margaret, "*Troylus and Cressida*: Historical Arguments for a 1608 date", *The Bard,* 1.4, London, 1977, 153–161

Kimbrough, Robert, *Shakespeare's 'Troilus and Cressida' and Its Setting,* Cambridge MA:, Harvard UP, 1964

Muir, Kenneth (ed.), *Troilus and Cressida,* Oxford: OUP, 1982

Palmer, Kenneth (ed.), *Troilus and Cressida,* London: Methuen Arden, 1982

Saintsbury, George, "Shakespeare: The Classical Plays", *The Cambridge History of English and American Literature*: *The Drama to 1642, Part One. vol. V, ch.VIII* § 15 (1907–21)

Shaheen, Naseeb *Biblical References in Shakespeare's Plays,* Newark: UDP, 1999
Walker, Alice (ed.), *Troilus and Cressida*, Cambridge: CUP, 1952
Wells, Stanley, & Gary Taylor, *William Shakespeare: The Complete Works,* Oxford: OUP, 1986
Wells, Stanley, & Gary Taylor, *William Shakespeare: A Textual Companion,* Oxford: OUP, 1987

26

# The Tragedy of Coriolanus

## Kevin Gilvary

*Coriolanus* can be dated any time between 1579, the publication of North's *Plutarch,* and the play's publication in the First Folio, 1623.

### Publication

*Coriolanus* is one of eighteen plays in F1 which had not previously been published. It was entered into the Stationers' Register on 8 November 1623 alongside other plays as "not formerly entred to other men":

> Mr Blounte Isaak Jaggard. Entered for their Copie vunder the hands of Mr Doctor Worral and Mr Cole, warden, Mr William Shakspeers Comedyes Histories, and Tragedyes soe manie of the said Copies as are not formerly entered to other men,. vizt. Comedyes. The Tempest. The two gentlemen of Verona. Measure for Measure. The Comedy of Errors. As you Like it. All's well that ends well. Twelft night. The winters tale. Histories. The thirde parte of Henry the sixt. Henry the eight. Coriolanus. Timon of Athens. Julius Caesar. Tragedies. Mackbeth. Anthonie and Cleopatra. Cymbeline.

The play is called *The Tragedy of Coriolanus* on the title page and the running title is *The Tragedie of Coriolanus*. It occupies the first position in the tragedies, after *Troilus and Cressida* and before *Timon of Athens*.

### Performance date

There are no contemporary performances recorded. The earliest known performance was staged at at Drury Lane in 1669 by Killigrew, at which time it was listed among plays formerly acted at Blackfriars. It is assumed, e.g. by Parker,[1] that Shakespeare wrote and produced the play for the Blackfriars theatre in 1608, but other commentators have pointed out that the stage in the indoor Blackfriars theatre was much smaller than at outdoor theatres such as the Globe and would thus have presented difficulties in staging the large crowd scenes and the battle scenes.[2]

## Sources

Bullough notes that North's edition of Plutarch (1579) provides almost all the material for the play. Some material may have been taken from Livy, either from the Latin text or perhaps using Philemon Holland's translation of 1600.

Bullough notes that Menenius's Fable (1.1.95–154) on the importance of the belly was commonplace, occurring in a wide range of sources. Most notably the fable is reported in North's *Plutarch* (1579), but it also occurs in many other sources: Sidney's *Apologie for Poetrie* (composed *c.* 1581, published 1595), *Dionysius of Halicarnassus* (6, 86),[3] *Aesop's Fables* (available in Caxton's 1484 translation or through Camerarius), John of Salisbury's *Policraticon* (1159), Averill's *A Marvellous Combat of Contrarieties* (1588), Holland's *Livy* (1600) and Camden's *Remains of a Greater Worke concerning Britaine* (1605).

Camden, whose version was derived from John of Salisbury's *Policraticon* (VI, 24.) is widely cited as a source, but the echoes are slight. In fact, there are only two possible allusions to Camden, but neither reference is compelling. Firstly, we have the use of 'gulf' (95) for belly, which is paralleled elsewhere both in Shakespeare (Macbeth 4.1. 24: 'Maw and gulf of the ravin'd salt-sea shark') and in Spenser (*The Shepherdes Calender* Sept., 184: 'a wicked wolfe that with many a lambe had glutted his gulfe.'). Secondly, where Camden lists both the parts of the body and their activities, Shakespeare ignores the names of the parts of the body and simply lists their separate activities. Overall, the similarities are not close and do not require the conclusion that this passage in *Coriolanus* is dependent on Camden. It has also been suggested that Camden's *Remaines* was used for two small references in *King Lear*, but Muir rejects these.[4] As Shakespeare does not appear to allude to this text anywhere else, Gillespie is very skeptical as to whether Shakespeare ever consulted Camden's *Remaines.*

## Orthodox Date

Edmond Malone (in 1778) first suggested that *Coriolanus* should be dated to 1609. Malone quoted Camden as a source and saw references to the Great Frost, the Corn Riots, and James I's order on 19 January 1607/8 to expand the growing of mulberries at about this time. Schoenbaum (1970: 169) was very dismissive of his efforts:

> When he can find no evidence, [Malone] throws up his hands in despair and assigns a play to a year simply because that year would otherwise be blank and Shakespeare must have been continuously employed. Such is the case with *Coriolanus*.

Most commentators, however, have followed Malone's 'lucky guess' and accepted a date between 1607–09. Chambers asserts that "there is practically no concrete evidence as to date." On the grounds of style, metre and mislineations as well as of source material with those of *Antony and Cleopatra*, Chambers also accepts 1608. J. D. Wilson accepts a date *c.* 1608 based on similarity of style. Using some slight historical allusions and analysis of verse and style, Wells & Taylor opt for 1608. Brockbank, Parker and Bliss settle for 1607–9. J. Leeds Barroll argues for a later date *c.* 1610, based on the references to drought both in the play and in reports about James's Progress that year. Leeds Barroll makes it contemporaneous with *Cymbeline.*

## Style and Versification

Chambers asserts that *Coriolanus* should be placed between *Antony & Cleopatra* and *Pericles* (both entered in the Stationers' Register in 1608) on the grounds of verse. Wells and Taylor reach similar conclusions from their analyses of colloquialisms. These conclusions are questionable, as the following analyses will show. If an exception is to be made for one play on grounds other than verse, then the entire process of attempting to date this play or indeed any play in this way should be doubted.

**a) Unsplit lines with pauses:** Chambers provides relevant figures in his second volume (Table V; compare Table 6 pp. 486–7). He defines a split line of poetry as one divided between two or more speakers. Assuming the accuracy of the figures, the notion that "the evidence of the style and metre puts *Coriolanus* between *Antony and Cleopatra* and *Pericles*" is not borne out by what Chambers himself offers. The difference of seven percentage points between the incidence of unsplit lines with pauses in *Coriolanus* (37) and those in *Antony* (44) must surely indicate a different positioning.

Some very odd conclusions are drawn: for example, *Coriolanus* apparently shares more features with *Macbeth* than with *King Lear*. No clear correspondence therefore emerges between assumed dates of plays and the use of unsplit lines with pauses.

**b) Full lines split between different speakers**: the incidence of lines divided between two speakers may be significant chronologically. If so, almost every play by Shakespeare would fall between *Antony* and *Pericles*. No clear correspondence therefore emerges between assumed dates of plays and the use of split lines.

**c) Prose as a proportion of a play**: a further distinction cited as evidence of the development of Shakespeare's style lies in the increasing use of prose in his plays. However, a major difficulty exists in deciding just which scenes use prose and which are in verse, since editions vary enormously. Again, conclusions are unsatisfactory. On this basis, *Romeo and Juliet* becomes a later play than *Macbeth* and *Troilus*, while *Antony* emerges as an early play, coming, with many others, before *Pericles*. No clear correspondence is therefore demonstrated between the assumed dates of plays and the use of prose.

**d) Use of rhyme compared with use of blank verse:** another suggested dating tool is the decreasing use of rhyme. Again this is not fully conclusive, merely showing that the Roman plays use very little rhyme. By this unreliable standard, *Coriolanus* appears as the last play, having the least amount of rhyme. Only two out of 29 scenes (7%) end with a rhyming couplet, compared with six out of 38 (16%) in *Antony and Cleopatra*. It might be that this indicates that *Coriolanus* was not revised, or at least not performed in the poet's lifetime. At any rate, no clear correspondence emerges between assumed dates of plays and the decreased use of rhyme.

**e) Lines with feminine endings:** another contention is that Shakespeare increasingly allowed iambic pentameters an extra syllable: the so-called feminine ending, where the final syllable is not stressed. The outcome of this study is not very satisfactory. No commentator would place *Richard III* after *King Lear* or *Pericles*, which is supposed to be the same year as *Coriolanus* (see 1 above). No clear correspondence therefore emerges between the assumed dates of the plays and the incidence of feminine endings.

**f) Lines with light and weak endings:** lines that end with monosyllabic functional words have also been advanced as a sign of earlier or later composition. Light endings are pronouns such as 'I', 'thou', 'he', 'she' or 'them' and auxiliaries such as 'do', 'have', 'may', 'shall'. Weak endings are conjunctions ('and', 'or') or prepositions ('at', 'by', 'from'). However, *King Lear* would appear, on this basis, to be a very early play and *Julius Caesar* would come some time after *Troilus, Measure for Measure* and *Othello*. Furthermore, we can scarcely base our dating of *Coriolanus* on the difference between the 1% and 3% incidence of the combined totals of two features such as light and weak endings. There is thus no clear correspondence between assumed dates of plays and the increased incidence of light and weak endings.

**g) Changes in linguistic preference: doth/does:** Waller argues that Shakespeare's linguistic habits changed in observable patterns throughout his career. His increasing use of 'does' and 'has' (for 'doth' and 'hath') and his increasing use of contractions show that his language was becoming less formal and more colloquial. This of course does not indicate any absolute date, but that *Coriolanus* comes late in the canon. While the King James Bible in 1611 used only the archaic forms 'hath' and 'doth' (probably because the style was established in Tyndale's partial translations 1526–35), the preference for 'does' and 'has' in *Coriolanus* may simply reflect the tendencies of the compositor(s) in the printing house.

**h) Use of colloquialisms:** Wells and Taylor have argued that Shakespeare increasingly used colloquialisms in his plays and that their incidence is thus an index of relative dating. Their method was first to decide whether certain elisions were colloquial. The results gave a number of colloquialisms per 1,000 words, with *Hamlet* having only 0.5, *Pericles* 4, *The Tempest* 10, *Antony* 11, *Cymbeline* 11 and *Coriolanus* 15. The conclusion to be drawn from these figures is that *Coriolanus* was Shakespeare's last play, later than *The Tempest* and not contemporary with *Pericles.*

It is very doubtful whether such data can be relied upon. Perhaps the play was simply unrevised.

## External allusions

Some lines in *Coriolanus* which have been taken to refer to contemporary events.

**a) Corn riots:** *Coriolanus* complains that the people want "corn at their own rates" (I. 1. 187). Many commentators see the Corn Riots in Northamptonshire, Warwickshire and Leicestershire in 1607/8 (reported by Stow in Bullough, V, 559) as awakening Shakespeare's interest in the story of *Coriolanus.* But corn shortages were frequent in late Elizabethan and early Jacobean life: Chambers refers to riots in Stratford in the 1590s due to corn shortages, and "Wm Shackespere" was found guilty of hoarding 10 quarters (presumably of malt) at Stratford on 4 February 1597.[4] Thus this allusion would have been topical throughout the 1590s and 1600s.

**b) The Great Frost:** many commentators believe that Shakespeare was referring to the Great Frost of 1607, at 1.1.169:

> . . . You are no surer, no,
> Than is the coal of fire upon the ice
> Or hailstone in the sun.

However, there were other severe frosts: Stowe reports in his Annals (sig 3V3) that in December 1598 the Thames was frozen over. Nor is it necessary to accept this as a reference to a particularly severe frost, merely that the commoners are changeable. Thus it forms no basis for dating *Coriolanus.*

**c) Myddleton's project for supplying water to London (1609–12)**: We find at 3.2.82:

> To say he'll turn your current in a ditch
> And make your channel his?

G. B. Harrison believes this refers to Myddleton's project for bringing clean water into London. In fact, Myddleton took over the project to construct a 3.8-mile aqueduct from Islington, from the City of London, whose representatives had been considering doing it since 1596. The City already had 400 miles of wooden piping, with elaborate water wheels under London Bridge.[6] It is less likely that Shakespeare is referring to Myddleton's aqueducts, than to some other arrangement, possibly agricultural, since a "ditch" is referred to rather than a pipe. In a predominantly rural society, water-rights were essential for summer crops. The reference is timeless.

**d) Mulberries:** Volumnia mentions mulberries at 3.2.79 ("Now humble as the ripest mulberry / That will not hold the handling") which led Malone to wonder if there was a reference to James I's edict (January 1608/9). This is possible if we can be sure that the play was composed at this time, but mulberries were well known in Elizabethan England; Shakespeare mentions them in *Venus and Adonis* line 1103 (1593) and in *Midsummer Night's Dream* at 3.1.170 and again at 5.1.149 (Q1, 1600). Chambers observes that attempts to find such concrete evidence for dating are far-fetched.

## Oxfordian Date

Oxfordians have suggested various dates between 1581 and 1603. Clark proposes a date after 1581 and sees Drake returned from his circumnavigation of the world, as *Coriolanus*. Drake's symbol was a drum (mentioned nine times in the play, but not in Plutarch). They had similar personalities: impatient, uncooperative, faithful to friends, implacably resentful to enemies. In Plutarch there is no reference to the sea, whereas in our play there are three such references. People thronged to see Drake's procession in the streets.[7] In general, this is not very convincing. There were many street processions in Elizabethan and Jacobean times.[8] Drake never held authority such as did *Coriolanus*. We might wonder how many members of an Elizabethan audience would have compared a military hero with a naval one. The references to the sea perhaps tell us more about Shakespeare's own maritime interests than about *Coriolanus*.

Oxford may have consulted Plutarch in Amyot's French translation, an expensive copy of which he had bought in 1569.

It may be seen in MacLure (84) that William Barlow, Bishop of London, preached a sermon at St Paul's, shortly after Essex's execution in February 1601. Barlow specifically compared the Earl of Essex to Coriolanus, who might 'make a fit parallel for the late Earle, if you read his life.' Oxford had been one of the peers who tried and convicted Essex of treason.[9]

## Conclusion

At most, we can say that the play was composed between 1579 and 1623; that is, after the publication of North's translation of Plutarch's *Lives* in 1579 and before the appearance of the First Folio. There is no reference to the play before 1623. Almost all commentators are agreed that this tragedy should be ascribed to *c.* 1608, yet there is nothing that directly points to this date, and very little circumstantial evidence to support it.

Conventional attributions may well represent mis-dating. The slight references to frosts, mulberries and corn riots are not sufficient to fix any date. Arguments from style suggest that it should be associated with the later plays, but none of the criteria is very convincing for fixing an absolute date. An alternative explanation, that *Coriolanus* was never staged in the playwright's lifetime and remained unrevised at his death, must remain as a possible interpretation for the versification in the play. Barlow's sermon comparing Essex to *Coriolanus* in February 1601 appears to be the only contemporary reference to the Roman soldier and might be considered as a possible date for composition, as Jorgenson has argued.

## Notes

1. Parker (87–8) makes the following comment: "The possibility (I would even say likelihood) that *Coriolanus* was composed from the start with the newly acquired Blackfriars in mind and subsequently annotated for what would amount to a try-out in that house rather than the Globe throws certain aspects of its tone, dramatic technique, and stage directions into new relief."
2. These points have been made by Allardyce Nicholl, '"Passing over the Stage"' *Shakespeare Survey* 12, 1959, 47–55 and by Joseph Weixlmann, "How the Romans Were Beat Back to Their Trenches", *Notes & Queries*, 21, 1974, 133–4. They suggest that mass entrances were made through the theatre yard (as happened in the 2006 production at Shakespeare's Globe, London).
3. There is no specific debt to Dionysius of Halicarnassus (fl. 10 BC) whose *Roman Antiquities* was originally composed in Greek and translated into Latin in 1480 and 1549. This work was not available in English until Spelman's 1758 translation.
4. *C.f.* Muir's introduction, (page xxxvi, note) Arden 2 edition, *Macbeth* (1952).
5. Chambers, W. S., II, 99–101, Chambers describes how, after the wet summers of 1594–6, there was a dearth of corn and how the Privy Council tried to ensure that grain was not hoarded. Shakespeare breached this order.
6. See the entry for Hugh Myddleton in the DNB and A. S. Hargreaves "New River" The *Oxford Companion to British History*. Ed. John Cannon. OUP, 2009.
7. For details about Sir Francis Drake, Clark quotes Darcie's *The True and Royall History of the Famous Empress Elizabeth* (1625). Darcie's work was a translation of William Camden's *Annales* (1615). Drake's Drum has passed into folklore,

e.g. in the poem of Sir Henry Newbolt (died 1938).

8. See William Leahy, *Elizabethan Triumphal Processions* (2005) for how the common people reacted to some of Elizabeth's stately ceremonies.
9. Edward de Vere, Earl of Oxford "served as the senior of the twenty-five noblemen" as Essex and Southampton were tried for treason in February 1601: Alan Nelson, *Monstrous Adversary*, (2003: 397).

# Other Works Cited


Barroll, J. L., *Politics, Plague and Shakespeare's Theatre*, [Appendix 5 considers the date of *Coriolanus*], 1991

Bliss, L. (ed.), *Coriolanus*, New Cambridge Shakespeare, CUP, 2000

Brockbank, J. P. (ed.), *Coriolanus*, London: Methuen Arden, 1976

Bullough, G., *Narrative and Dramatic Sources of Shakespeare*, vol. V, London: Routledge, 1964

Chambers, E. K., *William Shakespeare: A Study of Facts and Problems,* 2 vols, Oxford: Clarendon Press, 1930

Clark, E. T., *Hidden Allusions in Shakespeare's Plays*, New York, 1974 edn

Gillespie, S., *Shakespeare's Books: A Dictionary of Shakespeare's Sources*, London: Athlone Press, 2001

Harrison, G. B., "A Note on *Coriolanus*" in J. G. McManaway *et al., John Quincey Adams Memorial Studies*, 1948

Jorgensen, P. A., "Shakespeare's Coriolanus: Elizabethan Soldier", *PMLA,* lxiv, 1949, 221–35

MacLure, M., *The Paul's Cross Sermons,* [contains Bishop Barlow's 1601 sermon], 1958

Muir, K. (ed.), *King Lear,* London: Methuen Arden, 1952

Parker, R. B. (ed.), *Coriolanus,* Oxford: OUP, 1994

Schoenbaum, S., *Shakespeare's Lives,* Oxford: OUP, 1970

Shaheen, Naseeb, *Biblical Allusions in Shakespeare's Plays,* Newark, University of Delaware Press, 1999

Spenser, Edmund, *The Shepheardes Calender and Colin Clout* (1579), edited by Nancy Jo Hoffman, Baltimore: Johns Hopkins University Press, 1977

Waller, F. O., "The Use of Linguistic Criteria in Determining the Copy and Dates of Shakespeare's Plays", *Pacific Coast Studies in Shakespeare,* ed. W. F. McNeir and T. N. Greenfield, 1960

Wells, S. & G. Taylor, eds, *The Complete Oxford Shakespeare*, Oxford: OUP, 1986

Wells, S. & G. Taylor, *William Shakespeare: a textual companion*, Oxford: OUP, 1987

Wilson, J. D. (ed.), *Coriolanus,* New Cambridge Shakespeare, CUP, 1960

THE
MOST LA-
mentable Romaine
Tragedie of Titus Andronicus:

As it was Plaide by the Right Ho-
nourable the Earle of *Darbie*, Earle of *Pembrooke*,
and Earle of *Suſſex* their Seruants.

LONDON,
Printed by Iohn Danter, and are
to be ſold by *Edward White & Thomas Millington*,
at the little North doore of Paules at the
ſigne of the Gunne,
1594.

20. Title page to the anonymous first quarto of *Titus Andronicus*, 1594.
By permission of the Folger Shakespeare Library.

27

# The Lamentable Tragedy of Titus Andronicus

Derran Charlton and Kevin Gilvary

*Titus Andronicus* can be dated between 1579 (the publication of North's *Plutarch*) and 1594, when it was first published.

## Publication date

The play was apparently first registered on 6 February 1594:

> [SR 1594] John Danter. Entred for his Copye vnder thandes of bothe the wardens a booke intitled A Noble Roman Historye of Tytus Andronicus. vj$^{d}$. John Danter. Entred also vnto him by warraunt from Master Woodcock the ballad thereof.

Waith has reviewed the interpretations of "a booke" cautiously accepting that the SR refers to the play. It is also possible that "a booke" refers to the prose history, whose title was transferred from Pavier's widow in 1626 to Edward Brewster and Robert Bird. It was transferred again in 1630. If Waith is correct that the SR refers to this play, then it would be the earliest reference in the SR to a play by Shakespeare (1594). It was published in the same year and its status was changed from "a noble Roman History" to "a most lamentable Roman Tragedy":

> [Q1 1594] The most lamentable Romaine tragedie of Titus Andronicus as it was plaide by the Right Honourable the Earle of Darbie, Earle of Pembrooke, and Earle of Sussex their seruants. London: printed by Iohn Danter, and are to be sold by Edward White & Thomas Millington, at the little North doore of Paules at the signe of the Gunne, 1594.

There is only one extant copy of that quarto version, discovered in Sweden in 1904, and now in the Folger Library. It is usually asserted that the play was set up from foul papers, i.e. "from Shakespeare's Working Manuscript" (Bate). Chambers suggests that Strange's Men transferred it to Pembroke's, who transferred it to Sussex's, where it was revised into its present form. However, it is not clear whether the play had been performed by the playing companies separately, as is usually thought, or once in combination, as argued by George and accepted by Bate.

The second quarto followed in 1600:

> [Q2, 1600] The most lamentable Romaine tragedie of Titus Andronicus. As it hath sundry times beene playde by the Right Honourable the Earle of Pembrooke, the Earle of Darbie, the Earle of Sussex, and the Lorde Chamberlaine theyr seruants. At London: printed by I. R. [James Roberts] for Edward White, and are to bee sold at his shoppe, at the little north doore of Paules, at the signe of the Gun, 1600.

There were very few changes from Q1 to Q2, only some corrections and some new errors. A third quarto appeared in 1611.

> [Q3, 1611] The most lamentable Romaine tragedie of Titus Andronicus. As it hath sundry times beene plaide by the Kings Maiesties seruants. London: printed [by Edward Allde] for Eedward [sic] White, and are to be solde at his shoppe, nere the little north dore of Pauls, at the signe of the Gun, 1611.

All these quarto editions were anonymous, despite Meres's attribution of the play in 1598 to Shakespeare.

The play occurs in the 1623 First Folio (F1):

> [F1, 1623] The Lamentable Tragedy of Titus Andronicus

It occupies the second position in the tragedies after *Coriolanus* and before *Romeo and Juliet.* It is usually accepted that the initial plan of the First Folio intended *Troilus and Cressida* for this position. The subsequent pagination is inconsistent, with a blank page before the next play, suggesting that there had been problems in acquiring the copyright of *Troilus.* It has also been proposed that the manuscript of *Titus* required a hasty change of plan, perhaps contributing to some of the inconsistencies. F1 gives the running title as *The Tragedy of Titus Andronicus* and the text follows Q3 with a few further corrections and errors. F1 adds more detailed stage directions and the fly-killing scene (3.2). There has been varied speculation about the time of composition of this extra scene: Waith, followed by Wells & Taylor (*TxC*), consider that it was composed at the same time as the rest of the play; Bate, however, considers it a later addition, perhaps written *c.* 1600 by another author.

# Performance dates

There are three possible references to a play about Titus in the late 1580s or early 1590s. In the induction to Jonson's *Bartholomew Fair* (1614), there is a mocking reference to a spectator who is "fixed and settled in his censure . . . He that will swear *Jeronimo* or *Andronicus* are the best plays yet, shall pass unexcepted at here as a man whose judgement shows it is constant, and hath stood still these five and twenty or thirty years." A literal reading of this would indicate that a play about Titus was being performed between 1584 and 1589 (presumably alongside Kyd's *Spanish Tragedy*).[1] Similarly, a reference in an anonymous play called *A Knack to know a Knave*, performed in 1592, contains the following allusion:

> As Titus was to the Roman Senators,
> When he had made a conquest on the Goths:
> That in requital of his seruice done,
> Did offer him the imperial Diademe,

*A Knack*, which Henslowe marked as 'ne', was published in 1594, perhaps from a memorial reconstruction, and it is possible that the reference to Titus was added after the company acquired a new play.[2] A third possible allusion occurs when Strange's Men (i.e. before they changed their title to Derby's Men on 25 September 1593) were playing at the Rose. There is an entry in Henslowe's diary on 11 April 1592 for *tittus & vespacia* which Henslowe also marks as 'ne'. It was a popular play: performances continued until January 1593. Maxwell thinks that these three allusions refer to Shakespeare's play.

Most commentators tend to believe that these are not alluding to *Titus Andronicus* but to another play which may have been Shakespeare's source. The consensus is that the earliest references to *Titus* are Henslowe's entries for January and February 1594, when Sussex's Men played:

> ne – Rd at titus & ondronicus the 23 of jeneward . . . . iij$^{li}$ viijs

Since the 23 January 1594 was a Sunday, this date is usually corrected to 24 Jan. Henslowe records two further performances in June 1594 by "my Lord Admeralle men & my Lorde Chamberlen men" although again it is not clear whether the companies had played jointly or separately.

Chambers tends to assume that Henslowe's 'ne' attached to *Titus & Ondronicus* means 'new' in the sense 'the first ever performance'. Sometimes, however, as Chambers records, it may refer to a newly revised, corrected or augmented play, or to a play new at that theatre, or even to a play given by a particular company for the first time. Honigmann points out that Henslowe was able to write "newe" on occasions and often had room for more letters than 'ne'; this consistent variation suggests that 'ne' was not intended to stand for the word 'new', and that Chambers went too far in claiming that a play marked 'ne' seems generally to have been a new play in a full sense. Frazer notes that the same play was marked as 'ne' on 11 June 1596 and again on 11 February 1597. She argues that 'ne' must be an abbreviation for the theatre at Newington Butts, which Henslowe may have owned. Thus, Henslowe might not have been recording *Titus Andronicus* as a 'new' play in 1594.

The play was soon performed at the home of Sir John Harrington in Rutland, (east Midlands) on 1 January 1596 by a London company.[3]

## The Henry Peacham Drawing & Chronogram

21. Detail of Peacham ms.

Among the papers of the Marquis of Bath (held in the library at Longleat House, Somerset) is a single sheet, folio size, with a detailed illustration of Tamora's entrance and some 40 lines of text from *Titus*. There is a signature by 'Henricus Peacham' (usually identified as Henry Peacham, born 1576 and the author of *The Compleat Gentleman,* 1620).[4] There is also a series of letters identified as a chronogram, usually explained as indicating a date of 1594 or 1595 (taking the third symbol to be a nine). David Roper has explained the system of symbols thus:

> The system used by Peacham was a medieval response to the need for abbreviation. It required that the initial letter of a word be written in the normal manner, followed by the final letter, or letters in superscript form. ... The date on the Peacham Document should therefore be a straightforward exercise in expanding these written abbreviations. Unfortunately, this has not proved to be the case. The third symbol has proved to be an insurmountable obstacle for all those who have made the attempt. Indeed, there is even uncertainty as to whether it was intended as a 'q' or a 'g'.
>
> Hence, either **Anno $m^{o}$ $q^{o}$ g $q^{to}$** or **Anno $m^{o}$ $q^{o}$ q $q^{to}$** gives the required date.
>
> Before solving this chronogram, the errors contained in previous attempts at finding a solution require attention be given to the three abbreviations carrying superscripts. These make it plain that the date has been written in the conventional form of 'thousands', 'hundreds', 'tens' and 'units'. There is no reason to doubt that $m^{o}$ = millesimo (1000); that $q^{o}$ = quingentesimo (500) and $q^{to}$ = quarto (4), although some may see $q^{to}$ as quinto (5).

David Roper then considers various interpretations of the third letter: whether it represents <g> or <q>, and argues that overall it should be dated 1575 ('g' is the seventh letter of the alphabet).

Vickers, however, accepts the 1594/5 date for both illustration and composition; he considers that the drawing illustrates a scene of English actors playing the German play *Eine sehr klägliche Tragoedia von Tito Andronico und der hoffertigen Käyserin* (printed in 1620), which was derived from Shakespeare's play. If so, this would appear to be a remarkably quick transformation of an English play from composition, to borrowing and illustration. Jonathan Bate has interpreted the chronogram as indicating 1605.

## Attribution

The play was attributed to Shakespeare by Meres in 1598 and by the editors of F1. Accordingly, Chambers accepts Shakespeare's sole authorship, as do Wells & Taylor and Hughes. For the doubters, the play "simply offended their literary taste, and they wished to absolve Shakespeare of the responsibility for perpetrating it." Similarly, Bate passes over the question of authorship very quickly and attributes the play to Shakespeare.

Some commentators, however, have taken *Titus Andronicus* to be a revision of another play. According to the 1687 testimony of Edward Ravenscroft (later supported by Malone and others), Shakespeare's contribution to this play was limited to a few master touches (Chambers, *WS,* II, 254–5):

> I have been told by some anciently conversant with the Stage, that it was not Originally his, but brought by a private Author to be Acted, and he only gave some Master-touches to one or two of the Principal Parts or Characters; this I am apt to believe, because 'tis the most incorrect and indigested piece in all his Works; It seems rather a heap of Rubbish than a Structure.

J. Dover Wilson ascribed much of Act 1 to George Peele. Brian Vickers, in a long and energetic chapter, confidently assigns co-authorship to Peele as follows:

| | |
|---|---|
| **Peele** Act 1; Act 2 Scenes 1,2 | **Shakespeare** Act 2 Scene 3; Acts 3, 4, 5. |

Vickers cites about 30 tests of co-authorship for this play. According to Vickers, editors such as Bate simply dismiss 'disintegrators' without examining their arguments in detail.

## Sources

Bullough reviewed the material used in the play and could identify no clear source for the main story, concluding that it was fictional. There is a prose version of the story, called *The Tragical History of Titus Andronicus*, printed by Cluer Dicey (1760?), now in the Folger. Bullough believed that this might be a copy of, or at least derived from, the relevant section in the now lost *Tragical Roman Historye* (printed in 1594). However, the fact that *The Tragical History* was in 1760 billed as "Newly Translated from the *Italian* Copy printed at Rome" suggests that it was not the 1594 prose history.

*The Ballad of Titus Andronicus* (printed in 1620) on the same subject, which may have been the work cited in the 1594 entry in the SR, appears to derive solely from this or from a similar prose version. There seems to be no doubt that there is a connection between prose – ballad – play, but it is not clear which came first. The prose history and the ballad are much shorter than the play. Bullough reports two similar plays, one published in German (1620) *Eine sehr klägliche Tragoedia von Tito Andronico und der hoffertigen Käyserin* and another *Aran en Titus* in Dutch (1641), which both seem to derive from Shakespeare's play.

Bullough observes that many elements of the play derive from a wide range of classical sources: Ovid's *Metamorphoses* (available in Latin or from Golding's 1567 translation into English) related the tragic tale of Philomela, who was raped and mutilated so as not to be able to incriminate the perpetrator. Seneca's *Thyestes* (available in Latin or from the collected translation into English, edited by Newton in 1581) seems to have supplied details of sons who are killed and then served as food at a feast. There are also about 15 allusions to Virgil's *Aeneid* (available in Latin or from the translation into English, by Phaer and Twyne in 1584). The punishment of a Moor by being smeared with honey and then left to be stung by insects derives from Apuleius's *Metamorphoses* (available in Latin or from the collected translation into English, edited by Adlington in 1566). The themes of the murderous Moor and of the marriage of the Moor and the white woman were common, occurring in Italian in Bandello's *Novelle* (1554) and translated into French by Belleforest in 1570.

Bullough mentions that some of the Roman history in the play, including a variety of names, derives from Plutarch (translated by North in 1579 from Amyot's French translation of 1559). Plutarch did not write about the later Roman Emperors but his "Life of Scipio" shows the ingratitude of a ruler towards a successful general. Subsequent commentators, noted by Vickers, have suggested that Plutarch was more widely used, especially for the contrast between traditional republican virtue and decadent imperial wantonness. The play also draws extensively on the Greek historian, Herodian, whose *History of the Empire after Marcus* had been translated into Latin and into English in 1550 by Nicholas Smyth. This work was known to Holinshed (*Chronicles*, 1587), who follows Herodian when referring to the Emperor Bassianus who killed his brother.

T. J. B. Spencer contrasts the various uses of Roman History in Shakespeare's plays. In *Coriolanus* and in *Julius Caesar*, Shakespeare closely follows his source; in *Titus*, the debt is wide-ranging and confused, and sometimes more of a pastiche. At times Titus's Rome is a free commonwealth with the emperor elected on merit, on other occasions Rome is a hereditary kingdom. Spencer comments, "The author seems anxious not to get it all right but to get it all in." Vickers takes this wide range of sources to support his argument for co-authorship with Peele.

There have also been various suggestions about possible influences from works in English:

> In 1570, there was a poem called *A Lamentable Ballad of the Tragical End of a Gallant Lord and of his Beautiful Lady, With the Untimely Death of Their Children, Wickedly Performed by a Heathen Blackamore, Their Servant: The Like Seldom Heard Before.* (Pepys 1.546)[5]

This is a fairly short poem and describes some events which are similar to events in *Titus*. The following works have also been suggested as possible influences on *Titus*:

> Thomas Kyd, *The Spanish Tragedy* (? 1589) may have given a model for Titus's revenge.
>
> Christopher Marlowe, *The Jew of Malta* (first performed about 1589 but not published until 1633) shows villains similar to those in *Titus Andronicus*, particularly Aaron.
>
> George Peele, *The Battell of Alcazar* (popular on stage in the early 1590s, published 1594), where the character of Muly Mahamet is similar to the character of Aaron.
>
> *The First Part of the Tragicall Raigne of Selimus, sometime Emperour of the Turkes* (perhaps performed in 1592, published 1594) showed a scene in which Titus's hand is chopped off (act 3, scene 1).
>
> In 1593, Thomas Nashe's *Christs Teares over Ierusalem* covered the conquest by Titus and Vespasian and included a consul called Saturninus and a mother eating her own child.

The possibility that these works influenced *Titus* depends on the date of its composition. If *Titus* had been composed in the 1580s or earlier, then these other works would probably be alluding to it.

## Orthodox Date

Chambers proposed a date of 1593/4, immediately prior to publication. This date has tended to gain acceptance, e.g. by Jonathan Bate.

Many commentators, however, have found *Titus Andronicus* a very crude work by Shakespearean standards, thinking it unlikely to have been composed alongside *Richard III* and *Romeo and Juliet*. Dover Wilson points out that it is a play "less homogeneous in style and more ramshackle in structure than most".

These commentators have, therefore, favoured an earlier date, saying that the play was not new in 1594, merely established by that date, and that Jonson was substantially correct in dating it to 1584–89.

Similarly, Maxwell prefers 1589–90. Eugene Waith prefers a date before 1590 with a revision *c.* 1593. Alan Hughes, more recently, prefers a crude draft *c.* 1588, citing many parallels with the portrayal of violence in plays dated to the late 1580s, e.g. *Tamburlaine* (*c.* 1587), *The Jew of Malta* (*c.* 1590) and the anonymous *Troublesome Reign of King John* (published 1591). Hughes adds that, "in the end, we can only conjecture or despair."

Wells & Taylor seem to have disagreed on dates and on attribution. Vickers notes that Stanley Wells ignores the possibility of collaboration (in his introduction to the play in *The Oxford Shakespeare*) whereas Gary Taylor, in a chapter entitled 'Works included in this Edition' in *Textual Companion*, accepts joint authorship as "plausible". Furthermore, they tend to disagree on date: Wells prefers an early date *c.* 1590-1, but Taylor prefers 1592–3. Taylor devotes more space to dating *Titus* than to any other play, asserting that the 1594 title page indicates separate performances by the three companies listed. He argues that the reference in *A Knack to know a Knave* (performed by Strange's Men in 1592 but printed in 1594) was probably added in 1594, because *Titus* had not been listed among the plays performed by Strange's Men in 1592–3. Taylor states the dilemma regarding dates: "*Titus Andronicus* must have belonged to Strange's Men either long before 1592 or not until after January 1593 [to allow its transfer between companies]."

## Oxfordian Date

Oxfordians have tended to place the play much earlier. E. T. Clark suggests that in writing *Titus Andronicus*, the Earl of Oxford undertook for the first time *c.* 1577 to serve Queen and Country by means of drama. The play was hurriedly written, contrasting the past greatness of Spain as Rome with its current decadence. He used a range of allusions found throughout his own copy of Amyot's *Plutarch,* without studying any one *Life* in particular. He had purchased a copy of Amyot's *Plutarch* in 1569 (Nelson, 53). Oxford was probably keen to depict the horrors of the Sack of Antwerp, known as the Spanish Fury.[6] This atrocity committed by Spanish Catholics against the Dutch Protestants, began on 4 November 1576. Saturninus is clearly to be identified with Philip II of Spain and Tamora as Mary Stuart. Lavinia represents both Queen Elizabeth and the city of Antwerp, ravished "within its walls and in its low-lying situation" by the Spanish Fury (Clark). Clark suggests that this may have been the play recorded as "*The historye of Titus and Gisippus* . . . showen at Whitehall on Shrovestuesdaie at night [February 19, 1577], enacted by the Children of Pawles." She proposes that '*and Gisippus*' may have been a misrepresentation of '*Andronicus*' as both have similar letters. She suggests that the play was then revised in the 1580s to include Aaron, after Oxford had been denounced by Charles Arundel.[7]

## External Oxfordian Evidence

In *Bartholomew Fair* (1614) Jonson had stated that admirers of Kyd's *The Spanish Tragedy* and *Titus Andronicus* had "stood still these five and twenty, or thirty years". This would date the two plays as having reached their peak of appeal between 1584 and 1589. Jonson gave similar figures in *Cynthia's Revels* (1600): "they say, the umbrae of ghosts of some three or four plays, departed a dozen years since, have been seen walking on your stage here." A few lines further on, there follows mention of *The Old Hieronymo* (an earlier version of *The Spanish Tragedy*), clearly one of the plays "departed" a dozen years since (i.e. *c.* 1588). Although separated by a gap of 14 years, Jonson's statements are entirely consistent. As Honigmann emphasises, Jonson clearly believed *Titus* and *The Spanish Tragedy* both to have been written and to have reached the zenith of popularity in the 1580s. Peele would have been employed at some time later, perhaps *c.* 1594, to revise the opening (Act 1 and Act 2 scenes 1 & 2).

## Conclusion

*Titus Andronicus* can be dated between 1579 (the publication of North's *Plutarch*) and 1594, when it was first published. It may refer to the Sack of Antwerp in 1576. There are various reasons to believe it was so popular in the 1580s, that it was acted by a range of companies.

## Notes

1. The quotation comes from the *Induction to Bartholomew Fair*, 107, which according to E. A. Horsman, was written and acted in 1614. He says (11) that some exaggeration of the age of Jeronimo and Andronicus "is likely in this context."
2. Chambers, *ES*, IV, 24–25, cites the play's entries in the SR and in Henslowe's *Diary*. He reports the suggestion that the play may have been revived in 1597 under the name *Osric*.
3. Mentioned by Bate, 43, the performance was described by a Frenchman, Jacques Petit, who was a tutor in the household at the time.
4. Chambers, *WS*, I, 312–22, refers to the Peacham manuscript and gives a facsimile of the illustration. This is the earliest known illustration of any play of Shakespeare.

5. This publication is held at the Pepys Library, Magdelene College, Cambridge.
6. George Gascoigne quickly published his eye-witness account of *The Spoyle of Antwerpe. Faithfully reported, by a true Englishman, who was present at the same* (1576). Gascoigne was known to Oxford at Gray's Inn during the late 1560s. Nelson (80) describes how Gascoigne and Oxford sailed together to Holland in 1572.
7. Clark in *Hidden Allusions in Shakespeare's Plays* (1931, reprinted 1974) 47–59 develops this argument in great detail. Chambers, *ES*, IV, 93, cites the performance of *Titus and Gisippus* at court on 19 February 1577. However, most Oxfordians believe that *Titus and Gisippus* is more likely to have been an early version of *Two Gentlemen of Verona*. For biographical details about Oxford's denunciation by Charles Arundel, see Nelson, (249–257).

## Other Cited Works

Bate, Jonathan (ed.), *Titus Andronicus,* London: Methuen Arden 3, 1995
Bullough, G. *Narrative and Dramatic Sources of Shakespeare,* vol. VI, London, Routledge, 1966
Chambers, E. K. *The Elizabethan Stage*, Oxford, 1923
—, *William Shakespeare: a study of facts and problems*, 2 vols, Oxford: Clarendon Press, 1930
Clark, E. T., *Hidden Allusions in Shakespeare's Plays,* 1974
Farmer, J. S. (ed.), *A Knack to know a Knave*, Kessinger Publishing, (1911) rptd 2007
Frazer, Winnifred, "Henslowe's 'ne' ", *NQ*, 236 (1991): 34-5
George, David, "Shakespeare and Pembroke's Men", *SQ*, 32 (1981): 305–23
Hess, W. R. *et al.*, "Shakespeare's dates: their Effects upon Stylistic Analysis", *The Oxfordian,* vol.II. Portland, 1999
Honigmann, E. A. J., *Shakespeare's Impact upon his Contemporaries*, 1982
Horsman, E. A. (ed.), *Bartholomew Fair: Ben Jonson*, London: Revels Plays, 1960
Hughes, Alan (ed.), *Titus Andronicus,* The New Cambridge Shakespeare: CUP, 1994
Maxwell, J. C. (ed.), *Titus Andronicus,* London: Methuen Arden 2, 1953
Nelson, Alan H, *Monstrous Adversary: The Life of Edward de Vere, 17th Earl of Oxford*, Liverpool: LUP, 2003
Roper, D., "The Henry Peacham Chronogram", *The Shakespeare Oxford Newsletter,* 37.3, Fall 2001
Spencer, T. J. B., "Shakespeare and the Elizabethan Romans", *Shakespeare Survey,* 10, 1957: 27–38
Vickers, Brian, *Shakespeare Co-Author*, Oxford: OUP, 2002
Waith, Eugene M. (ed.), *Titus Andronicus,* Oxford: OUP, 1984
Wells, S. & G. Taylor (eds), *The Complete Oxford Shakespeare*, Oxford: OUP, 1986
—, *William Shakespeare: a textual companion.* Oxford: OUP, 1987
Wilson, J. D. (ed.), *Titus Andronicus,* New Cambridge Shakespeare: CUP, 1948

28

# The Tragedie of Romeo and Juliet

Kevin Gilvary

*Romeo and Juliet* can be dated any time after 1562 (the publication of Arthur Brooke's poem *The Tragicall Historye of Romeus and Juliet*) and before 1597 when *Romeo and Juliet* appeared in print.

## Publication Date

This play was first published by John Danter in 1597 (without any corresponding entry in the Stationers' Register until 1607):

> [Q1 1597] An Excellent Conceited Tragedie of Romeo and Iuliet, As it hath been often (with great applause) plaid publiquely, by the right Honourable the L. of Hunsdon his Servants.

The author was not named. Q1 has previously been referred to as a 'bad quarto', and probably a "memorial reconstruction" which had been "pirated for publication" (Spencer). The modern approach (e.g. Erne) is to see Q1, in common with other so-called 'bad quartos', as a shorter original performance version.[1]

The play was re-published two years later by Thomas Creed:

> [Q2 1599] The Most Excellent and lamentable Tragedie of Romeo and Iuliet. Newly corrected, augmented and amended: As it hath bene sundry times publiquely acted by the right Honorable the Lord Chamberlaine his Servants.

Q2, often referred to as a 'good quarto', has about 700 more lines. It is said to have been based on Shakespeare's foul papers, apparently collating passages from Q1. The stage direction at 4.5.102 states "Enter Will Kemp", rather than Q1's "Enter Peter" perhaps showing the influence of a copy belonging to

AN
EXCELLENT
conceited Tragedie
OF
Romeo and Iuliet.

As it hath been often (with great applause)
plaid publiquely, by the right Honourable the L. of *Hunsdon*
his Seruants.

LONDON,
Printed by Iohn Danter.
1597.

22. Title page to the anonymous first quarto of *Romeo and Juliet*, 1597.
By permission of Bodleian Library, University of Oxford,
shelfmark Arch. G d.44 (2), title page.

Shakespeare's company.[2] Erne argues against the label of 'bad quarto', noting that "The first quarto has high-paced action, fuller stage directions than the second quarto, and fascinating alternatives to the famous speeches in the longer version."

The play was registered to Nicholas Ling in the Stationers' Register in 1607 and shortly afterwards transferred to John Smethwicke:

> [SR 1607] 22 Januarij Master Linge Entred for his copies by direccon of A Court and with consent of Master Bvrby under his handwrytinge these .iij copies viz. Romeo and Juliett.
> [SR 1607] 19 November John Smythick. Entred for his copies vnder thandes of the wardens, these bookes followinge Whiche dyd belonge to Nicholas Lynge viz . . . 10 Romeo and Juliett. . .

The play appeared twice more in Quarto before the First Folio (F1) in 1623:

> [Q3 1609] The Most Excellent and lamentable Tragedie of Romeo and Iuliet. As it hath bene sundry times publiquely Acted by the Kings Maiesties Servants at the Globe. Newly corrected, augmented and amended:
> [Q4 no date] The Most Excellent and lamentable Tragedie of Romeo and Iuliet. As it hath bene sundry times publiquely Acted by the Kings Maiesties Servants at the Globe. Written by W Shake-speare. Newly corrected, augmented and amended:

Some copies of Q4 do not have 'Written by W Shake-speare' on the title page. Q3, Q4 and F1 derive from Q2. Another quarto, Q5, was published in 1637 but has no independent status.

## Attribution

Meres (1598) lists *Romeo and Juliet* among Shakespeare's tragedies. Weever's sonnet, usually dated 1599 but possibly earlier, mentions Romeo among other protagonists of Shakespeare.[3] The printed text of *Romeo & Juliet*, however, remains anonymous until Q4, which is usually dated 1622.

## Performance Date

There are no surviving records of actual performances of *Romeo and Juliet* before 1660. According to the title pages of Q1 and Q2, the play was performed by the Lord Hunsden's Servants. This is usually interpreted as the Lord Chamberlain's Men, sponsored by Henry Carey, Lord Hunsdon, who was Lord Chamberlain from 1585 to 1596 (Chambers *ES* ii 192–208). However, the reference is to Lord Hunsdon's Servants, and not the Lord Chamberlain's Men. Since

Henry Hunsden had intermittently maintained a company of players from 1564, the reference may well be to pre-1594 performances, before he became patron of the Lord Chamberlain's Men, and possibly before 1586, when the Lord Chamberlain's Men are first mentioned. Alternatively, it could refer to the short period after Henry's death in 1596, and the appointment of his son George as Lord Chamberlain on 17 March 1597, which would coincide with the publication of Q1. From the title pages of Q3 and Q4, we note that the play was later performed by the King's Men (i.e. after 1603).[4]

## Sources

Bullough cites "the main and perhaps sole source" of *Romeo and Juliet* as Arthur Brooke's poem *The Tragicall Historye of Romeus and Juliet* (1562). This poem was a loose translation of Boaistuau's French version of the story (published in Belleforest's 1559 *Histoires Tragiques*). The French version was derived from Bandello's *Novelle*, (published in 1554, containing 214 stories). Shakespeare does not seem to have consulted the French or Italian versions for *Romeo and Juliet* (but he probably did for *Much Ado*). In 1567, another version of the story was published in English; William Painter's *Palace of Pleasure* may have supplied a few small details, e.g. Juliet's 42-hour sleep. But as the outline story was widely told, this detail may have been gleaned from elsewhere. There are some small similarities with Daniel's *Complaint of Rosamund* (1592) and Eliot's *Ortho-Epia* (1593). Since these are small in number, the direction of influence is by no means established.

## Orthodox Date – Internal Evidence

There is no evidence for the date of composition. The date of 1596 has been proposed to coincide with the assumed dates of composition of *Love's Labour's Lost, A Midsummer Night's Dream,* and *Richard II,* which Chambers refers to as "Shakespeare's lyrical period". Wells & Taylor prefer 1595, noting that "if *Romeo* is the last of the lyrical plays, the second half of 1596 is already rather crowded." While these plays share similarities, it is possible that Shakespeare drafted, re-worked and revised them at different times of his life.

## Orthodox Date – External Evidence

It has been suggested that the Nurse's mention of the earthquake (at 1.3.25) refers to an event in England on 6 April 1580. If so, her statement , "'Tis since the earthquake now eleven years" would give a date of composition *c.* 1591. The 1580 earthquake occurred during performances at both the Theatre and the Curtain. There were pamphlets on the subject by Thomas Churchyard and

Richard Tarleton, as well as accounts by Arthur Golding and Anthony Munday.[5] Chambers dismissed this consideration, followed by almost all commentators except Baldwin, as being too early for Shakespeare to have sufficiently developed his style by this point. There was another earthquake in France in 1584, which has been taken by some to suggest a date of 1595.

The poet, John Weever, referred to "Romeo, Richard: more whose names I know not" in his sonnet, which has usually been dated to 1599 but might (according to Chambers) have been as early as 1595.[6] It has been suggested that Richard Burbage played Romeo with the boy actor Robert Goffe as Juliet at the Theatre.

## Oxfordian Date

Oxfordians generally agree that Oxford wrote *Romeo and Juliet* soon after 1581-2, when he was involved in a series of street brawls with Thomas Knyvet, following his affair with Anne Vavasour.[7] This coincides with the eleventh anniversary of the serious earthquake which hit Verona in 1570 and destroyed the town of Ferrara. Steve Sohmer concludes that the Nurse was referring to the 1570 earthquake. Sohmer has studied the Nurse's Speech at 1.iii.18–50 and reviewed the various references to time.[8] He shows that the play was set in 1582 when the Gregorian Calendar was taking over from the Julian. Although he does not mention Oxford, his conclusion might be taken to suggest a composition date in the 1580s. Oxford would have seen the devastation for himself when he visited Italy in 1575–6. By comparison, the London earthquake of 1580 was no more than a tremor, although the writers who gave an account (Churchyard, Tarleton and especially Munday) were all theatre practitioners known to Oxford.A further coincidence is that Oxford complained about his letters having been delayed by plague in Italy; this recalls the similar delay to Friar Laurence's letter in *Romeo and Juliet.*

## Conclusion

*Romeo and Juliet* can be dated any time after 1562 (the publication of Arthur Brooke's poem *The Tragicall Historye of Romeus and Juliet*) and before 1597, when *Romeo and Juliet* appeared in print.

## Notes

1. Chambers, *WS*, 341–47 prefers the theory of a pirated copy derived from a memorial reconstruction, giving examples of many transpositions of phrases. He accepts that the play might have been shortened for performance (Q1 has 2,232 lines; F1 has 3,007) or that Shakespeare might have emended his own

play. Lukas Erne in *The First Quarto of Romeo and Juliet* (2007) surveys the idea of 'bad quartos' and compares the versions of the play.

2. Chambers shows close resemblances between Q1 and Q2 in spelling, punctuation, and the use of capitals and italics. Levenson (2000: 111) has reviewed the relationship between Q1 and Q2.
3. John Weever's poem is quoted by Chambers, *WS*, II, 199, from *Epigrammes in the oldest Cut and newest Fashion,* iv, 22, ed. R. B. McMerrow, 75.
4. For Henry Carey, Lord Hunsdon, see Chambers, *ES*, II, 191-194.
5. Alan Nelson, *Monstrous Adversary: The Life of Edward de Vere, 17th Earl of Oxford,* 2003, 241–2 gives an account of the 1580 earthquake which occurred during a performance at the Theatre. Nelson quotes from various pamphlets which described it, including two by Thomas Churchyard (STC 5259).
6. Sidney Thomas in 'The Earthquake in *Romeo and Juliet*,' MLN, 1949, 64, 417-9, quoted by Levinson, 99.
7. For Oxford's "lethal quarrel" with Knyvet, see Nelson, 280–7.
8 Steve Sohmer in "Shakespeare's Time Riddles in *Romeo and Juliet* Solved", *English Renaissance Review,* 35, 2005, 407–28.

## Other Works Cited

Baldwin, T. W., *Shakespeare's Five Act Structure*, Illinois: U. of Illinois Press, 1963
Blakemore Evans, G. (ed.), *Romeo and Juliet*, Cambridge: CUP, 2003
Bullough, G., *Narrative and Dramatic Sources of Shakespeare*, vol. I, London, 1957
Chambers, E. K., *Elizabethan Stage,* 4 vols, Oxford: Clarendon, 1923
—, *William Shakespeare: a study of facts and problems*, 2 vols, Oxford: Clarendon Press, 1930
Erne, Lukas (ed.), *The First Quarto of 'Romeo and Juliet'*, Cambridge: CUP, 2007
Evans, G. Blakemore (ed.), *Romeo and Juliet,* New Cambridge Shakespeare: CUP, 2003
Gibbons, Brian (ed.), *Romeo and Juliet,* London: Methuen Arden 2, 1980
Hunter, G. K. (ed.), *Romeo and Juliet,* London: Methuen Arden 3, 2004
Levenson, Jill (ed.), *Romeo and Juliet,* Oxford: OUP, 2000
Nelson, Alan H., *Monstrous Adversary: The Life of Edward de Vere, 17th Earl of Oxford,* Liverpool: LUP, 2003
Sohmer, Steve, "Shakespeare's Time Riddles in Romeo and Juliet Solved", *English Renaissance Review,* 35, 2005: 407–28
Spencer, T. J. B. (ed.), *Romeo and Juliet,* Harmondsworth: Penguin, 1967
Wells, S. & G. Taylor, eds, *The Complete Oxford Shakespeare,* Oxford: OUP, 1986
—, *William Shakespeare: a textual companion*, Oxford: OUP, 1987

# 29

# The Life of Timon of Athens

Kevin Gilvary

*Timon of Athens* is first mentioned in the 1623 First Folio (F1). The play can be dated any time between the latest definite source, North's translation of Plutarch in 1579, and the publication in F1 in 1623.

## Publication Date

*Timon of Athens* is one of eighteen plays in F1 which had not previously been published. *Timon* was entered into the Stationers' Register on 8 November 1623 alongside other plays as "not formerly entred to other men":

> Mr Blounte Isaak Jaggard. Entered for their Copie vnder the hands of Mr Doctor Worral and Mr Cole – warden, Mr William Shakspeers Comedyes Histories, and Tragedyes soe manie of the said Copies as are not formerly entered to other men. vizt. Comedyes. The Tempest. The two gentlemen of Verona. Measure for Measure. The Comedy of Errors. As you Like it. All's well that ends well. Twelft night. The winters tale. Histories. The thirde parte of Henry the sixt. Henry the eight. Coriolanus. Timon of Athens. Julius Caesar. Tragedies. Mackbeth. Anthonie & Cleopatra. Cymbeline.

The play is entitled THE LIFE OF TYMON OF ATHENS on the title page but the running title is simply *Timon of Athens*. Many commentators have followed Chambers who believed that the play was unfinished. The text is very poor, with "many small confusions and inconsistencies", and may have been an early draft. The verse is uneven and "cannot be the complete and jointed work of Shakespeare". Several scenes involving Alcibiades have little relevance to the main plot. Characters are inconsistent within the space of a few lines. There are two epitaphs, one of which – probably the first – Shakespeare presumably intended to omit (Oliver).[1]

## Performance Date

According to Jowett, the earliest known performance of *Timon* was in 1674 by Thomas Shadwell. His adaptation, *The Manhater*, was published in 1678. Soellner suggests that from the evidence of its academic references, the play was intended for performance at the Inns of Court.[2]

## Attribution

It is usually proposed that the play was written jointly. Some have argued that Shakespeare revised an existing play by another author (e.g. Wilkins, Chapman or Day). Others believe that Shakespeare's original play was revised by another (e.g. Heywood, Chapman, Middleton or Tourneur). In these suggestions, it is usually accepted that the play was revised (not co-authored) and also unfinished.[3] Although commentators have not consistently divided the play up between Shakespeare and the other author, the usual basis has been a literary judgment as to whether a particular passage was worthy of Shakespeare or not. Oliver (who rejected co-authorship) noted that such divisionists treated the play like a plum pudding, giving all the plums to Shakespeare. Later scholars, e.g. Nuttall and Klein, continued to argue for Shakespeare's sole authorship and an unfinished play.[4]

Vickers, in a long, vigorous chapter, has studied these arguments about the "unusual mixtures of rhyme, irregular verse, and prose in suspect scenes", concluding that *Timon* was co-authored with Thomas Middleton (1580–1627). About one third of the play is usually allocated to Middleton.[5] Dawson and Minton agree, saying: "It is certainly not impossible that they, like the two of us working on this edition, sat down together on occasion and worked through scenes that needed tinkering."[6] It remains possible that the second author revised the unfinished manuscript of the earlier author, without bringing the work to a satisfactory end.

## Sources

Bullough cites Sir Thomas North's translation of Plutarch's *Lives* (1579) as one of the principal sources for *Timon;* it was also *the* principal source for other classical plays: *Julius Caesar, Coriolanus* and *Antony and Cleopatra*. The historical Timon is mentioned in 'The Life of Antony' and referred to again in 'The Life of Alcibiades'. Unlike in the other classical plays, here Shakespeare also used a more detailed classical source, Lucian's Greek dialogue, *Timon the Misanthrope*. Lucian was not translated into English until 1634, so Shakespeare seems to have made use of a Renaissance translation, probably Thomas More's Latin text in 1506 (with subsequent reprints). Lucian was also adapted into various European versions: Boiardo wrote a play in Italian *c.* 1487; Pedro Mexia produced a Spanish story in 1542; this was translated into French by Gruget and into English by William Painter as novel 28 in his *Palace of Pleasure* (1566). Shakespeare seems to have confined his use of Lucian to *Timon*. Jonson, on the other hand, made extensive use of the Greek satirist.[7]

Most commentators now accept that Shakespeare used an anonymous play extant in manuscript and known now as *Old Timon* (Dyce MS 52, Victoria and Albert Museum). Chambers believes that Greek quotations and other pedantries suggest an academic audience for *Old Timon*, but that Shakespeare is unlikely to have seen it. Bullough notes the similarities between *Old Timon* and a play called *Pedantius* performed at Cambridge in 1580. The date of *Old Timon* is uncertain: Chambers hazards 1581–1590; Bulman (1974: 126–7) argued for a date of 1601, which the V&A accept. Since the *Old Timon* mentions a London inn called 'The Seven Stars', not known to have existed before 1602, some scholars have dated *Old Timon* post 1602. The influence of *Old Timon* on Shakespeare's play is apparent in the detailed treatment of Timon's generosity: both the *Old Timon* and Shakespeare's play give more prominence to Timon's life before he becomes bankrupt; Plutarch and Lucian only mention it in passing. Similarly two important details, the faithful steward and the mock banquet, are in the *Old Timon* but not in Lucian or Plutarch. Chambers believes that Shakespeare is unlikely to have had access to this manuscript (or its performance in academe), suggesting that both plays depended on another source, now lost. Bulman (1974), however, has argued that the *Old Timon* greatly influenced Shakespeare and most subsequent commentators have been thus persuaded.

Shaheen discusses (1999: 242) the many Biblical references in *Timon,* compared to the relatively few allusions in the sources. He notes that at 4.3.172–3, the interchange between Timon ("Yes thou spok'st well of me.") and Alcibiades ("Call'st thou that harm?") recalls the wording of the Geneva Bible at Luke 6.26: "Wo be to you when all men speake well of you." Other versions use the word "praise". Allusions to English literary works are rare, but include Lyly's *Campaspe* (1584). Shakespeare himself refers to the historical Timon in *Love's Labour's Lost* (usually dated 1590–5).[8]

## Orthodox Date

Chambers suggested 1608 since *Timon of Athens* "clearly belongs to the tragic period" which he proposes as 1605–1609. He asserts that since Shakespeare was "busy with *Lear* and *Macbeth*" in 1605–6, *Timon* can be dated in 1608, alongside *Coriolanus* and *Antony and Cleopatra,* other classical plays based on Plutarch. Bullough concurs. Oliver agrees with Chambers but observes that Shakespeare may have worked on *Timon* spasmodically and over a period of time, a theory he calls "plausible but difficult to substantiate". Soellner concurs

(1959: xlii) with 1607–8 but "would not be surprised" if it turned out to be earlier or later (1979: 201). Maxwell believes that *Timon* precedes *Lear* and prefers a date *c.* 1605, while Wells & Taylor assign 1604.

Against Chambers' assumptions, three observations may be noted:

- there is no external evidence of "a tragic period" in 1606–09;
- not all tragedies belong to this "tragic period" anyway (e.g. *Romeo, Titus* and *Richard III* are usually dated to the 1590s);
- another classical tragedy based on Plutarch, *Julius Caesar*, is usually dated *c.* 1599.

Furthermore, we could argue that although *Timon* is placed among the tragedies in F1, it does not seem to have been intended for that position, or even considered as a tragedy. Since the title page calls the play *The Life of Timon of Athens*, it might have more affinities with *Merchant of Venice* (usually dated *c.* 1596) in its concern for "affectional and monetary bonds . . . material and intangible goods" (Katherine Maus, in the introduction to the play in the Norton Shakespeare).[9] Bulman, however, argues for a date *c.* 1601, due to simularities with Jonson's 'comical satires' (1974: 126).

## Internal Orthodox Evidence

Various metrical and other stylistic tests have placed *Timon of Athens* as among the later plays in the canon. However, as there is doubt about the sole authorship, tests remain unreliable.

## External Orthodox Evidence

Bevington argued (1999) for a general comparison between James I and Timon, but this view has not attracted many adherents. Dixon Wecter attempted to link events in the play to the treatment of Essex, generous nobleman, let down by friends with a later rebellion. He suggested that the play dated from 1605. Sandra Billington argued for an earlier date about 1600, coinciding with Essex's fall from grace. She argued for allusions to *Timon* in Marston's *Jack Drum's Entertainment* (1600). The Prologue to *Jack Drum* states that the audience will have to endure "mouldy fopperies of stale Poetry, / Vnpossible drie musty Fictions", which possibly refers to a recent production of Shakespeare's play. She suggests that when Essex, under house arrest in May 1600, wrote to Elizabeth that "shortly they will play me upon the stage", he was alluding to a forthcoming production of *Timon of Athens*. She believes that this production was unsuccessful, and therefore more likely to have been in 1600 (when Middleton was untried) than 1605 when he was more successful. Bulman argues (1974) for a similar date based on similarities with *Poetaster* and other plays of Jonson around this time as well as the parallels in the legal references between *Twelfth Night* (performed at the Middle Temple in 1602) and *Timon,* as well as *Old Timon.*

## Oxfordian Dating

The usual dating from an Oxfordian perspective is between 1592 and 1604, when Oxford, the disillusioned and impoverished nobleman, withdrew from fashionable society and presumably devoted his time to embellishing his plays. He was described by Chapman as being, during his youth, as "liberal as the sun", but by 1586 he was vitually bankrupt. The later action of Timon's isolation and exile accord well with Oxford's later life. It is likely that Oxford never intended the play to be performed, perhaps to be confined to a reading group. It would thus have been left among his papers at his death, later revised to some extent by Middleton, but not even finished by the second author.

E. T. Clark proposes an earlier date because of the dramatist's use of Plutarch. Oxford had bought a copy of Amyot's French translation in 1569, ten years before North's translation. She dates an original version to 1576 when *The History of the Solitary Knight* was performed at court.[10] This play, however, may have been based on Chaucer's 'Knight's Tale'.

## Conclusion

The play can be dated anywhere between the latest source, North's translation of Plutarch in 1579 (possibly Amyot's translation of Plutarch in 1559) and the publication in the First Folio in 1623.

## Notes

1. For further discussion, see Oliver (1959: xxxiii–iv), Bulman (1976: 104). Draper notes *Timon's* inconsistencies: J. W. Draper, "The Theme of Timon of Athens", *The Modern Language Review,* Vol. 29, No. 1, Jan., 1934, 20–31.
2. Soellner (1979: 148) suggests that the appeal of *Timon* to young lawyers would have suited it to "an evening performance at one of the Inns of Court". Honigmann likewise argues that the play was intended for the Inns of Court on the basis of similarities in satirical tone of *Timon* and *Troilus and Cressida* (E.A.J. Honigmann, "Timon of Athens." *SQ* 12 (1961): 3-20).
3. See Oliver (1959: xxii). Oliver attributes the proposition of authors of an original play (which was subsequently revised by Shakespeare) to Delius, J. M. Robertson and Dugdale Sykes respectively. In respect to the revisers suggested, Oliver notes that "Verplank, for example, suggested Heywood; Fleay, Tourneur; and

Parrott, Chapman." (1959: xxiin). For a more detailed summary see Klein (2001: 62).

4. See Klein (2001: 62–66), especially the publisher's note in the title pages, which, as Vickers (2002: 288n) has observed, provides a somewhat embarrassed disclaimer of Klein's treatment, which "establishes *Timon* as one of Shakespeare's late works, arguing, contrary to recent academic views, that evidence for other author beside Shakespeare is inconclusive". Nuttall (1989: 32-4) enlists the unfinished-play theory of Chambers and Ellis-Fermor, stating assertively that this 'is widely regarded as having finally routed the disintegrators' (33) and, reiterating later, "the severest disintegrator cannot confidently banish Shakespeare from a single line or phrase" (34). Vickers (2002: 288) provides a thorough summation of relevant arguments and usefully points out that, although Nuttall concludes that "the arguments for regarding *Timon of Athens* as a collaboration are too strong to be ignored" (1989: 39), his handling nevertheless reveals the opposite tendency.
5. Vickers quotes Wells & Taylor (1987: 79) in relation to Klein's discussion of the same quotation (2001: 64).
6. Dawson and Minton discuss the question of collaboration in detail (2008: 1–9).
7. J. R. Mulryne, "Jonson's Classicism", *The Cambridge Companion to Ben Jonson*, ed. Harp and Stewart (2000: 172).
8. Biron: ... "Nestor play at pushpin with the boys,/ And critic Timon laugh at idle toys!" (*Love's Labour's Lost*, 4.3.167–8)
9. Maus goes on to discuss in her introduction to *The Life of Timon of Athens* (Norton, 1997: 2245–2251) the manner in which "love and money are here almost inextricable" (2246), monetary and intangible goods are interrelated.
10. See Clark (1974: 30–46). Nelson (2003: 53) corroborates Oxford's purchase of Plutarch's works in French in 1569.

# Other Cited Works


Bevington, David, "James I and *Timon of Athens*", *Comparative Drama,* 33.1, 1999: 56–87

Billington, Sandra, "Was Timon of Athens Performed before 1604?" *Notes and Queries,* 45 (243).3 (1998): 351–53

Bullough, G., *Narrative and Dramatic Sources of Shakespeare*, vol. I,London: Routledge, 1957

Bulman, James C., Jr., "The Date and Production of *Timon* Reconsidered", *Shakespeare Survey,* 27 1974: 111–126

Bulman, James C., Jr. "Shakespeare's Use of the *Timon* Comedy", *Shakespeare Survey* 29 (1976): 103–16

Chambers, E. K., *William Shakespeare: a study of facts and problems,* 2 vols, Oxford: Clarendon Press, 1930

Dawson, Anthony B. and Minton, G. E. (eds), *Timon of Athens,* London: Methuen Arden 3, 2008

Greenblatt, Stephen (ed.), *The Norton Shakespeare,* Norton: New York, 1997

Jowett, John (ed.), *Timon of Athens,* Oxford: OUP, 2004

Klein, Karl (ed.), *Timon of Athens*, Cambridge: CUP, 2001

Maxwell, J. C. (ed.), Introduction to *The Life of Timon of Athens,* by William Shakespeare, Cambridge: CUP, 1957
Nelson, Alan H., *Monstrous Adversary: The Life of Edward de Vere, 17th Earl of Oxford,* Liverpool: LUP, 2003
Nuttall, A. D. (ed.), *Timon of Athens,* Hemel Hempstead: Twaynes World Author Series, 1989
Oliver, H. J. (ed.), *Timon of Athens,* London, Methuen: Arden 2 Edition, 1959
Shaheen, Naseeb, *Biblical References in Shakespeare's Plays,* Newark: U. of Delaware Press, London, 1999
Soellner, Rolf (ed.), *Timon of Athens: Shakespeare's Pessimistic Tragedy,* Columbus: Ohio State UP, 1979
Vickers, B., *Shakespeare, Co-Author,* Oxford: OUP, 2002
Wecter, Dixon, "The Purpose of *Timon of Athens*", *PMLA,* 43, 1928: 701–21
Wells, S. & G. Taylor, *William Shakespeare: a textual companion,* Oxford: OUP, 1987
Wilson, J. Dover (ed.), *Timon of Athens*, Cambridge: CUP, 1961.

30

# The Life and Death of Julius Cæsar

Kevin Gilvary

*Julius Caesar* can be dated to any time between the publication of North's *Plutarch* in 1579, and a performance at the Globe in 1599 which was probably the Shakespeare play.

## Publication date

*Julius Caesar* is one of eighteen plays in the First Folio (F1) which had not previously been published. It was entered into the Stationers' Register on 8 November 1623 alongside other plays "not formerly entred to other men":

> Mr Blounte Isaak Jaggard. Entered for their Copie vnder the hands of Mr Doctor Worral and Mr Cole – warden, Mr William Shakspeers Comedyes Histories, and Tragedyes soe manie of the said Copies as are not formerly entered to other men. vizt. Comedyes. The Tempest. The two gentlemen of Verona. Measure for Measure. The Comedy of Errors. As you Like it. All's well that ends well. Twelft night. The winters tale. Histories. The thirde parte of Henry the sixt. Henry the eight. Coriolanus. Timon of Athens. Julius Caesar. Tragedies. Mackbeth. Anthonie & Cleopatra. Cymbeline.

Chambers reports that *Julius Caesar* is one of the best printed texts in F1. As it has few obvious errors, it is thought that the compositors were working from tidy papers. The punctuation is sound, there is little mislineation and there are few misattributions of speeches.

## Performance Date

The earliest definite recorded performance of the play was probably at Whitehall in 1612/13. Payment was made for fourteen plays including *Caesar's Tragedy* and four or five other plays by Shakespeare:

> Item paid to John Heminges . . . Caesars Tragedye[1]

All orthodox modern commentators, however, follow Chambers in accepting that the first performance of Shakespeare's *Julius Caesar* was at the Globe in 1599; but this is by no means established. A performance of *a* play about Julius Caesar was witnessed in London at that time by a Swiss traveller, Thomas Platter, who wrote in his diary:

> On the 21st September, after dinner, at about two o'clock, I went with my party across the water. In the straw-thatched house, we saw the tragedy of the first Emperor Julius Caesar, very pleasingly performed, with approximately fifteen characters ('*personen*'); at the end of the play they danced together admirably and exceedingly gracefully, according to their custom, two in each group, dressed in men's and two women's apparel.' (Daniell, 12)[2]

Chambers (1930, I, 397) makes three deductions about Platter's visit, all of which are plausible, but none of which has any firm supporting evidence:

> a. The "straw-thatched house" must have been the Globe Theatre, which had been rebuilt on Bankside earlier that year.
> b. "The tragedy of the first Emperor Julius Caesar" must have been Shakespeare's play.
> c. This must have been the *first* performance of Shakespeare's play, recently composed.

In addition, Sohmer has argued, from various interpretations of the text, that *Julius Caesar* was written for the opening of the Globe on 12th June 1599, which according to the Julian calendar was midsummer's day 1599.

Taking Chambers's assumptions in order: there is no other record of a Roman play performed either at the Globe or at the Rose in 1599. Against this, it should be remembered that Henslowe did not record the titles of plays after 1597. His papers and diaries for the period 1592–7 show many references to costumes and performances of 'Caesar' plays; the Admiral's Men performed "a seser & pompie" (recorded as 'ne') on sundry occasions in the 1590s. After 1597, the record consists mainly of Henslowe's payments for new plays. Thus Platter might have visited either the Globe or the Rose.

Secondly, it is supposed (by Daniell and others) that Platter's fifteen '*personen*' referred to the number of actors who performed the jig, rather than the number of characters (there are about 40 speaking parts in Shakespeare's *Julius Caesar*). Schanzer argues that Platter mentions fifteen '*personen*', which he says can refer only to *characters* in the play, not to the number of actors needed to play the parts. Schanzer concludes that Platter probably saw a different play, performed by the Admiral's Men at the Rose Theatre.

Thirdly, the suggestion that it must have been the first performance of a *recently* composed play relies on an interpretation of Francis Meres (1598), who omitted any reference to *Julius Caesar* among the twelve plays he then ascribed to Shakespeare. Because *Julius Caesar* has always proved popular, Chambers assumed that Shakespeare could not have written it by 1598.[3] However, Meres does not attribute history plays to Shakespeare, although he includes four of the histories in his list of tragedies. Furthermore, his list is not complete: he ignores the three parts of *Henry VI,* two of which had been produced and published anonymously before 1598. The quartos of *Richard II*, *Richard III* and *Love's Labour's Lost*, printed in 1598, are the first published plays to be ascribed to William Shakespeare. Meres is therefore among the first to attribute plays to Shakespeare. Since there is no reference to a play *Julius Caesar* by Shakespeare until the First Folio in 1623, it is possible that our play was famous but anonymous by 1598, when Meres wrote his list, and it may or may not have been the play witnessed by Platter at a theatre on the South Bank in 1599.[4]

## Julius Caesar in Elizabethan Drama

The story of Julius Caesar's assassination was an early and popular subject for drama in the sixteenth century. Barroll (1958) has shown that the story was well used in medieval epitomes and moralising traditions, particularly for the catastrophic consequences of Caesar's assassination. Butler has described how performances during the Elizabethan period took place at Court, at the universities, at the Inns of Court and in the houses of the nobility. Roman plays were especially popular, since education at that time concentrated on the classics.

A university performance on this theme is mentioned by Shakespeare in a dialogue between Hamlet and Polonius: (*Hamlet* 3.2.99)

| | |
|---|---|
| Hamlet | My lord, you played once i' the university, you say? |
| Polonius | That did I, my lord; and was accounted a good actor. |
| Hamlet | What did you enact? |
| Polonius | I did enact Julius Caesar: I was killed i' the Capitol; Brutus killed me. |
| Hamlet | It was a brute part of him to kill so capital a calf there. |

An actual university performance on this theme is recorded in 1592, when a Latin play, *Caesar Interfectus* (dealing with Caesar's assassination), was performed at Christ Church, Oxford. Only the highly moralistic epilogue, written by Dr Jonathan Edes (1555–1604) survives.[5] Bullough believed that the rest of the play was also by Dr Edes, but, as Edes was a theologian and there is no contemporary reference to him as a playwright, Chambers asserted that the play proper might have been by another hand.

The anonymous *Tragedy of Pompey and Caesar or Caesar's Revenge* was entered in the Stationers' Register in 1606 and published in 1607. The dedication reports it to have been privately acted by the students at Trinity College, Oxford. Schanzer has argued that it was composed in the early 1590s. This drama begins with events earlier than those which start Shakespeare's play, covering the period from Pompey's defeat at Pharsalus through his escape to Egypt and his death there, as well as Caesar's triumphant return to Rome and his murder. Almost all similarities between *Julius Caesar* and *Caesar's Revenge* can be traced to Plutarch, but there are some important differences. Both contain the following items not found in Plutarch: Caesar bombastically resolves to go to the Senate; he is offered a scroll naming all the conspirators; Anthony gives an impassioned speech about Caesar's greatness; Caesar's ghost foretells his revenge to Brutus; both Brutus and Cassius recognise Caesar's power after death. The similarities are most marked, and it is usually taken that *Julius Caesar* influenced *Caesar's Revenge*. Schanzer, however, argued that *Caesar's Revenge* was composed in the early 1590s and influenced Shakespeare's play. Bullough considers this possible.

In the Elizabethan theatre of the 1580s and 1590s, there were many plays on the late Roman Republican period. As a result, the audience might have had prior knowledge of events related in our play, so the apparently abrupt start may not have been a problem for them. Jacobean plays about Julius Caesar, however, are only recorded twice (1607 and 1613), so Shakespeare's play would seem to have been a box-office failure, if it had been composed in 1599.

Many commentators have noted that Julius Caesar is alluded to twice in *Hamlet*, (3.2.99, above, and 5.1.236: "Imperious Caesar, dead and turn'd to clay, Might stop a hole to keep the wind away.") They have drawn the conclusion that the two plays were composed at about the same time.[6] Yet there are allusions to Caesar in fifteen other plays in the canon, far more than to any other historical figure (Alexander the Great comes a poor second), including *1 Henry VI*, *Love's Labour's Lost* and *Titus Andronicus* which are usually taken to be much earlier. Since Shakespeare clearly had the greatest respect for the historical Caesar, it is not clear why he should apparently turn to writing about him half-way through his career and not at the outset.

## Allusions to Shakespeare's *Julius Caesar*

Contemporary allusions to Shakespeare's play possibly include Ben Jonson's *Every Man Out of his Humour* (1599), which quotes "*Et tu, Brute!*" This is probably a loose translation of Suetonius's phrase in Greek: *καί σύ τέκνον* (*kai su teknon – and you my son*). Bullough notes that Plutarch did not report any dying words of Caesar.[7]

## Sources

Bullough states that North's translation of Plutarch was the main source for the play, first edition 1579, second 1595. Plutarch's *Lives* had earlier been translated from Greek to French by Jacques Amyot (published in 1559 and available in England from this time). Shakespeare drew the plot from three main Lives: Julius Caesar, Marcus Brutus and Marcus Antonius. Horman sees references to other Lives of Plutarch. Shakespeare also drew on Plutarch for *Titus Andronicus*, which is usually dated in the early 1590s.

Shakespeare also drew on Golding's translation of Ovid's *Metamorphoses* (published 1567), which ends with a list of portents observed at the time of Caesar's death, used by Casca. The playwright had also read Suetonius's *Lives of the Twelve Caesars* (not translated into English until 1606, but available in Latin), Appian's *Civil Wars* (translated 1578) and perhaps Tacitus' *Annals of Roman History* (translated 1598).

A source for an incidental detail may have been an account of the fall of Caesar included in a later edition of *A Mirrour for Magistrates* (1587), in which Artemidorus reads aloud his warning (as in 2.2.1–5; Plutarch does not mention what was in the letter). Likewise, Shakespeare makes Caesar deliberately delay his reading of the letter (3.1.1-10), whereas Plutarch says that he was diverted by people thronging around him.

In *Julius Caesar* the topography of Rome is very accurately represented, and its people presented in lively fashion. The city feels alive and vibrant. The place of assassination is particularly interesting: Plutarch clearly states that Caesar was killed in the senate-house, which was located in the forum; yet in the play the senate-house is situated on the Capitoline Hill. This seems to be consistent with sixteenth century Rome, at which time Michaelangelo's Capitoline Piazza with the Palazzo Senatorio housed the seat of government.

There is also an interesting reference in Marlowe's play *Massacre at Paris* (5.2.72), when Guise says, "Yet Caesar shall go forth", which is identical to a line in *Julius Caesar* (2.2.28) His name, Guise, when pronounced in the old French manner, would have sounded very like 'Caesar'. Marlowe's play was written in 1592 and survives from an undated edition, perhaps 1593/4. Guise seems to have the same disregard for his own safety as Caesar, and with the same results. That one dramatist was influenced by the other seems very likely.

## Orthodox Date

Orthodox modern commentators are unanimous in dating *Julius Caesar* to 1599. Sohmer's contention that *Julius Caesar* was written for the opening of the Globe on midsummer's day 1599 is worthy of consideration. First, Sohmer points out that many plays seem to have been composed for special occasions, but surprisingly cites a performance of *The Merchant of Venice* for James I, whereas it was an old play from the repertoire, known to Meres in 1598. Furthermore, Sohmer fails to distinguish a royal performance from a public performance; Elizabeth is not known to have frequented the public playhouse and is unlikely to have ventured to the Globe in 1599. Next, Sohmer argues that the Globe would probably have been opened on an auspicious date such as 12th June, Julian Calendar, especially as a spring tide would have been expected at about 2pm, thus allowing the play-goers arriving by water to disembark above the usual high-water mark. Sohmer points out that there is a fixation about auspices, dates and time in the play (as will be examined later). He then links references in the play to feast days in midsummer, in particular to St Barnabas's day (11th June), St Alban's day (12th June) and St Antony of Padua's day (13th June). Such references, however, do not explain why the play should have been written in 1599.

## Oxfordian Date

The consensus is for 1582–4.[8] There is abundant evidence for plays about Caesar in the 1580s and 1590s. *Julius Caesar* is a very political play, yet the politics of 1599 are not mirrored in it. There seems to have been no motive for a new play about the disastrous consequences of political assassination. The new King of Spain, Philip III, was not seen as a threat. The Earl of Essex was in Ireland and would not invade the Queen's bedchamber until September. His rebellion in 1601 was not foreseen. The wars in the Netherlands were petering out and Elizabeth was ageing and childless.

## Oxfordian Date – Internal Evidence.

*Julius Caesar* is emphatically concerned with political assassination and with the misguided motives of the conspirators. All the conspirators are patricians; Casca is able to speak to Caesar directly, as are they all. Translated to Elizabethan life, the conspirators clearly paralleled discontented nobles, most apposite in the 1570s and 1580s but no longer a serious threat in the 1590s after the defeat of the Spanish Armada. When Messala and Brutus compare notes about the proscriptions (4.3.171), they talk only of senators – plebeians are not mentioned:

MESSALA That by proscription and bills of outlawry,
Octavius, Antony, and Lepidus,
Have put to death an hundred senators.
BRUTUS Therein our letters do not well agree;
Mine speak of seventy senators that died
By their proscriptions, Cicero being one.

Both Messala and Brutus ignore the commoners, whose response to Antony's oration determines the course of the play. The plebs are anonymous, fickle, boorish and devoid of understanding. This is hardly a flattering portrait of common people to show in a new play at a public theatre.

*Julius Caesar* is also concerned with portents, referring to the comet which appeared soon after Caesar's death (2.2.30), "When beggars die, there are no comets seen." A bright comet had appeared in 1577 and another was observed in May 1582. No further comets were observed until Halley's comet returned in 1607; and another comet appeared in 1618.[9]

Dates are vital to the plot of *Julius Caesar.* We are warned three times that the Ides of March is a special day. There are other references to actual dates or to feast days, e.g. the Lupercal (1.1.72; 3.2.100) and Cassius's birthday (5.1.72), one of only three birthdays mentioned in Shakespeare. As Pontifex Maximus, Julius Caesar had fixed the calendar in January 45BC, shortly before his assassination. The Julian calendar was subsequently used throughout Western Christendom and was important for determining Christmas and Easter. Sohmer describes further dates alluded to, both 'calendrical markers' (25–6) and 'temporal markers' (36–70). In 1582, however, Pope Gregory XIII introduced his reforms, involving the 'loss' of nine days.[10] The main idea was to bring the beginning of the year into line with the spring equinox. The Gregorian Calendar was immediately adopted in Catholic countries such as France and Spain, but was resisted in Protestant countries such as England and Holland as a devilish 'popish conspiracy'. English clergy argued that Christ had been born under the Julian Calendar. Sohmer (1999: 20) points out that for Elizabeth to adopt the Gregorian calendar would have entailed a change to the Book of Common Prayer, which could only be made by Act of Parliament.

Concern over this change of calendar was highest in 1582–4, and coincided with the Catholic plots of the 1580s, involving Mary Queen of Scots and culminating in the attack of the Spanish Armada in 1588. After that, as the foreign threats subsided, so too did concern about the calendar. By 1599, the difference in calendars was generally accepted, and the Julian Calendar remained in use in Britain until 1752. The theme was relevant during the earlier period of Elizabeth's reign, less so in 1599.[11]

Edward de Vere, Earl of Oxford may have composed the play in the 1580s. He had spent many months in Italy in 1575-6, and possibly visited Rome on his way south to Sicily. In *Julius Caesar,* the city feels alive and vibrant and its topography is accurate. In 1582 the Latin play *Caesar Interfectus* was performed at Christ Church, de Vere's college at Oxford. In 1569, he bought Amyot's translation of Plutarch, the latter being the main source for *Julius Caesar.* Many students of the play have been deeply impressed by its range of allusion to classical and European authors. Yet orthodox biographers fail to explain how Shakespeare gained this learning. Some reach astonishing conclusions: Bullough devotes over 200 pages to the sources used for *Julius Caesar* alone.

Oxford was extremely well read in French, Italian and Latin. His uncle, Arthur Golding, had translated Ovid's *Metamorphoses*, which had provided the details for Casca's list of portents.[12]

In general, *Julius Caesar* shares the aristocratic milieu of Oxford. The protagonists are all patricians, while the plebeians are depicted throughout as anonymous and fickle. Oxford was often at the hub of political developments in England. His cousins and both his sons all fought in the Netherlands. He was one of the commissioners for the trial of Mary, Queen of Scots,[13] whose exection was widely viewed by Catholics as political assassination.

## Oxfordian Date – External Evidence.

Alexander points out that no work speaks more clearly than *Julius Caesar* of the futility of honourable assassination. Traversi asserts that, for all his faults, Caesar's Rome was a better place to live than the mean, petty and dangerous Rome ruled by the Triumvirs.[14] The words of the Third Citizen, "I fear there will a worse come in his place" (3.2.112), come true with a vengeance. For an audience of 1599, this would have been exceedingly disturbing. The Queen was in her mid sixties, and in failing health. There was feverish talk over her successor, whom she refused to name.

In the 1580s, however, the Queen had been much more vigorous, and was herself the object of repeated assassination plots, many of which had noble instigators. Her excommunication had been reconfirmed by Pope Gregory (1580). Philip II of Spain had just annexed Portugal and was turning his attention to the Netherlands and to England. The Pope wrote to some unnamed English nobles in 1580 and sanctioned the murder of Elizabeth "with the pious intention of doing God service ... If these English nobles decide to undertake so glorious a work, they do not commit any sin." (Weir 335). A play about the disastrous consequences of political murder would have been most topical in this period. The Queen's death then would have been seen (by the government at least) as a terrible calamity. In the play, the main psychological interest lies in the honourable but misguided Brutus, whose actions lead to such terrible events – warning indeed for disgruntled English noblemen. So *Julius Caesar* appears more relevant as Court propaganda of the early to mid 1580s, than as a play intended for public performance in the late 1590s.

Clark offers many suggested allusions. *Julius Caesar* relates implicitly to the murder of any leader. We may consider two sixteenth-century cases. As the years of imprisonment of Mary Queen of Scots passed, she became the focus of domestic and foreign discontent. In 1586 the Babington Plot was revealed, and Elizabeth's advisers, Burghley and Walsingham, openly argued that Mary should be brought to trial and execution. However Elizabeth, concerned about taking the life of an anointed queen, was cautioned against execution by many, for fear of the consequences. Hesitation over an irrevocable act is exemplified in

Brutus's tortured soliloquy in 2.1.

The second case is that of William the Silent.[15] On 18th March 1582 the Protestant Prince of Orange was the object of an assassination attempt by a Spaniard, apparently under orders from the Spanish government, possibly even the King. William was seriously wounded and there was widespread speculation that he would die. According to a contemporary pamphlet, his would-be assassin was killed on the spot by William's bodyguard with 33 stab wounds (as in *Julius Caesar* 5.1; Plutarch has 23). A bright comet appeared in the sky in 1582 shortly after the attempted murder. The Prince of Orange had been offered the crown of the Netherlands, which he had refused. He was then offered the lesser title of Count of Holland, whose emblem is a coronet. Casca, (1.2.237) makes the special point that Caesar was offered not a crown, but a coronet. An allusion to William the Silent would clarify this otherwise inexplicable point, which is not found in the source material. William the Silent was eventually assassinated at Delft in 1584. A date of composition for the play in 1599 renders allusions to portents, assassinations and coronets almost meaningless; but a date in 1582–1584 makes them all highly topical.

## Conclusion

*Julius Caesar* can be dated any time after 1579, the publication of North's *Plutarch* (possibly after Amyot's 1559 French translation of *Plutarch*) up to 1599, when it was apparently performed at the Globe.

Orthodox modern commentators agree that Shakespeare's tragedy was written and first performed in the year 1599, yet the basis for these assertions is very fragile. Oxfordians argue that allusions in the play refer to assassination plots in England and Holland around 1582–1584, suggesting a date of composition in the mid 1580s.

## Notes

1. Chambers, *WS*, II, 343 gives date of payment as 20 May 1613 and the full list of plays:

> Item paid to John Heminges upon the Cowncells warrant dated att Whitehall xx° die Maij 1613, for presentinge before the Princes Highnes the Lady Elizabeth and the Prince Pallatyne Elector fowerteene severall playes, viz: one playe called Pilaster, One other called the Knott of Fooles, One other Much Adoe abowte Nothinge, The Mayeds Tragedy, The Merye Dyvell of Edmonton, The Tempest, A Kinge and no Kinge, The Twins Tragedie, The Winters Tale, Sir John Falstaffe, The Moore of Venice, The Nobleman, Caesars Tragedye, And one other called Love lyes a bleedinge.

Chambers does not explain, but assumes that *Caesars Tragedye* was an alternative title for Shakespeare's play, presumably because of the proximity of other Shakespearean plays. However, it also may have been the anonymous play, *Caesar's Revenge,* published in 1607, which Chambers, *ES*, IV, 4, reports as possibly dating to 1592–6. See further discussion in the section on 'Julius Caesar in Elizabethan Drama'.

Elizabeth and Frederick were married on 14 February, 1613 (see Gorst-Williams, Jessica, *Elizabeth, the Winter Queen*, 1977).

2. The original German text is reported by Chambers, *WS*, II, 322, from the account of travels of Thomas Platter, ed. G. Binz (*Anglia*, xxii. 456):

   > Den 21 Septembris nach dem Imbissessen, etwan umb zwey vhren, bin ich mitt meiner geselschaft vber daz wasser gefahren, haben in dem streiiwinen Dachhaus die Tragedy vom ersten Keyser Julio Caesare mitt ohngefahr 15 personen sehen gar artlich agieren; zu endt der Comedien dantzeten sie ihrem gebraucht nach gar vberausz zierlich, ye zwen in mannes vndt 2 in weiber kleideren angethan, wunderbahrlich mitt einanderen.

3. Dorsch (intro, page viii) is more cautious than Chambers: "Meres was not, of course, a chronicler of the stage, and did not profess to list all the works of the dramatists and poets he commended." A. R. Humphries (2) is more assertive of the value of Meres: "One would expect so noteworthy a work as Julius Caesar to be included had it already appeared." See further discussion in the Introduction, pp. 19–27.
4. There are other possibilities: the play might have been performed at court or in private houses but not on the public stage until 1599.
5. Chambers, *ES,* III, 309. Further details can be found in Frederick Boas, *University Drama in the Tudor Age,* 1914: 165, where it is stated that in *Caesar Interfectus*, the characters of Caesar and Brutus, Antonius and Cassius were much the same as "they were to play some twenty years later in Shakespeare's drama." He adds: "Nothing is more improbable than that Shakespeare should have known *Caesar Interfectus*." For a different view, see the section on 'Oxfordian Dating'.
6. E.g. Harold Jenkins, ed., *Hamlet* (1982: 1) believes the Danish play echoes the recently composed Roman play. Similarly G. R. Hibbard, ed., *Hamlet* (1987: 4). "It seems reasonable to infer that *Hamlet* was written after, but not long after, *Julius Caesar*, which can be dated with unusual accuracy as having been composed in the late summer of 1599."
7. There is an interesting reference in a poem by John Weever, published in 1601, *The Mirror for Martyrs* (Chambers, *WS*, II, 199):

   > The many-headed multitude were drawne
   > By Brutus speech, that Caesar was ambitious,
   > When eloquent Mark Antonie had showne
   > His vertues, who but Brutus then was vicious?

   As the play was not published until 1623, Hibbard (3) suggests that Weever probably saw a performance or, less likely, that he read the manuscript.
8. The following arguments were first advanced by Clark, *Hidden Allusions*, 529–534.
9. For the comets of 1577 and 1618, see David Seargeant, *The Greatest Comets in*

*History* (2009).

10. For further details about the introduction of the Gregorian Calendar, see Blackburn, B. & Holford-Strevens, L. *The Oxford Companion to the Year,* 1999.
11. For details on the Throckmorton Plot of 1582 and the Babington Plot of 1586, there are many accounts, e.g. Alison Weir, *Elizabeth the Queen* (1998).
12. See Alan Nelson, for Oxford's tour of Italy (117-156), his slight connection with Christ Church, Oxford (44-45), his 1569 purchase of expensive texts in French, Italian and Latin at the age of 19 (53) and his uncle, Arthur Golding's (90) translation of Ovid's *Metamorphoses*. For Casca's list of portents in Act 1 Scene 3 as influenced by Golding's translation of Ovid, see Humphries 119n.
13. For Oxford's cousins Francis and Horace Vere (the 'Fighting Veres') and his natural son Edward Vere in Holland see Nelson (169, 269 and notes). Among the 42 commissioners at the trial of Mary Stuart on 27 September, 1586, "Oxford was out-ranked only by the Marquess of Winchester." (Nelson, 302).

14 Alexander (148-152) argues against G. B. Shaw's suggestion that Shakespeare "had glorified a blunder of the first magnitude". Alexander states that Shakespeare's "whole treatment of Brutus comes entirely from his recognition that the assassination was a grievous political blunder". Alexander dates the play to 1599 but cites no references to the contemporary political situation. Traversi continues: "The triumvirs are already engaged in the first stages of a ruthless struggle for supremacy." Traversi shows how vividly Shakespeare portrays the chaotic consequences of a political assassination (197-8).

15. For all details about his life and assassination, see C. V. Wedgewood, *William the Silent,* 1944. She describes the 1582 assassination attempt in 229-32. Clark (531) quotes the thirty-two wounds received by the assassin from an account by Martin Hume in *The Great Lord Burghley*, (original edition 1898, page 372).

## Other Works Cited

Alexander, P., *Shakespeare's Life and Art*, London: Nisbet, 1939

Barroll, J. L., "Shakespeare and Roman History", *Modern Language Review,* 53, 1958: 327-43

Barroll, J. L., Leggatt, Hosley and Kernan (eds), *The Revels History of Drama in English*, vol. III 1576–1613, London: Methuen, 1975

Bullough, G., *Narrative and Dramatic Sources of Shakespeare*, vol. V, London: Routledge, 1964

Butler, M., "Private and Occasional Drama", *Cambridge Companion to English Renaissance Drama,* ed. E. R. Braunmuller, and M. Hathaway, 1990

Chambers, E. K. *The Elizabethan Stage* 4 vols. Oxford: Clarendon, 1923

—, *William Shakespeare: a study of facts and problems*, 2 vols, Oxford: Clarendon Press, 1930

Clark, E. T., *Hidden Allusions in Shakespeare's Plays*, Port Washington, 1974 edn

Daniell, D. (ed.), *Julius Caesar,* London: New Arden, 1998

Dorsch, T. S. (ed.), *Julius Caesar*, London: Methuen Arden, 1955

Horman, S., "Dion, Alexander and Demetrius – Plutarch's Forgotten Parallel Lives – as Mirrors for Shakespeare's *Julius Caesar*", *Shakespeare Studies,* 8, 1975:

195–210
Humphries, A. R., *Julius Caesar,* Oxford: OUP, 1984
Kernan, A., *Shakespeare, the King's Playwright*, New Haven: Yale UP, 1995
Schanzer, E., "A Neglected Source of *Julius Caesar*", *Notes and Queries,* 199, 1954: 196–7,
Schanzer, E., "Thomas Platter's Observations on the Elizabethan Stage", *Notes and Queries,* 20, 1956: 465–7
Sohmer, S., *Shakespeare's Mystery Play: the Opening of the Globe Theatre,* Manchester: MUP, 1999
Traversi, D., *Shakespeare: the Roman Plays,* London: Hollis & Carter, 1963
Weir, A., *Elizabeth the Queen*, London: Random House, 1998
Wells, S. & G. Taylor, *The Oxford Shakespeare,* Oxford: OUP, 1986
—, *William Shakespeare: a textual companion,* Oxford: OUP, 1987

31

# The Tragedie of Macbeth

Sally Hazelton

*Macbeth* can be dated between 1587 (Holinshead's *Chronicles*) and 1611 when it was witnessed by Simon Forman.

## Publication Date

*Macbeth* is one of eighteen plays in F1 which had not previously been published. It was entered into the Stationers' Register on 8 November 1623 alongside other plays as "not formerly entred to other men":

> Mr Blounte Isaak Jaggard. Entered for their Copie vnder the hands of Mr Doctor Worral and Mr Cole – warden, Mr William Shakspeers Comedyes Histories, and Tragedyes soe manie of the said Copies as are not formerly entered to other men. vizt. Comedyes. The Tempest. The two gentlemen of Verona. Measure for Measure. The Comedy of Errors. As you Like it. All's well that ends well. Twelft night. The winters tale. Histories. The thirde parte of Henry the sixt. Henry the eight. Coriolanus. Timon of Athens. Julius Caesar. Tragedies. Mackbeth. Anthonie & Cleopatra. Cymbeline.

The play is entitled *The Tragedie of Macbeth* on the title page and as the running title. It occupies the sixth position in the tragedies, coming after *Julius Caesar* and before *Hamlet.*

## Performance Date

Chambers states that the earliest recorded performance was in 1611, when Dr Simon Forman saw a performance at the Globe Theatre:

> In Mackbeth at the glob, 16jo, the 20 of Aprill, ther was to be obserued,

> firste, howe Mackbeth and Bancko, 2 noble men of Scotland, Ridinge thorowe a wod, the[r] stode before them 3 women feiries or Nimphes, And saluted Mackbeth, sayinge, 3 tyms vnto him, haille mackbeth, King of Codon ; for thon shalt be a kinge, but shalt beget No kinge, &c. then said Bancko, what all to mackbeth And nothing to me. Yes, said the nimphes, haille to thee Banko, thou shalt beget kinges, yet be no kinge. And so they departed & cam to the courte of Scotland to Dunkin king of Scotes, and yt was in the dais of Edward the Confessor. And made Mackbeth forth with Prince of Northumberland, and sent him hom to his own castell, and appointed mackbeth to prouid for him, for he wold Sup with him the next dai at night, & did soe. And mackebeth contriued to kull Dunkin, & thorowe the persuasion of his wife did that night Murder the kinge in his own castell, beinge his gueste. And ther were many prodigies seen that night & the dai before. And when Mack Beth had murdred the kinge, the blod on his handes could not be washed of by any means, nor from his wiues handes which handled the bloodi daggers in hiding them, By which means they became both much amazed & affronted. the murder being knowen, Dunkins 2 sonns fled, the on to England, the [other to] Walles, to saue them selues. They beinge fled, they were supposed guilty of the murder of their father, which was nothinge so. Then was Mackbeth crowned kinge, and then he for feare of Banko, his old companion, that he should beget kinges but be no kinge him selfe, he contriued the death of Banko, and caused him to be Murdred on the way as he Rode. The next night, being at supper with his noble men whom he had bid to a feaste to the which also Banco should haue com, he began to speak of Noble Banco, and to wish that he were ther. And as he thus did, standing vp to drincke a Carouse to him, the ghoste of Banco came and sate down in his cheier be-hind him. And he turning A-bout to sit down Again sawe the goste of banco, which fronted him so, that he fell in-to a great passion of fear and fury, Vtteringe many wordes about his murder, by which, when they hard that Banco was Murdred they Suspected Mackbet.
>
> Then Mack Dove fled to England to the kinges sonn, And soe they Raised an Army, And cam into scotland, and at dunston Anyse ouerthrue Mackbet. In the mean tyme whille macdouee was in England, Mackbet slewe Mackdoues wife & children, and after in the battelle mackdoue slewe mackbet.
>
> Obserue Also howe mackbetes quen did Rise in the night, in the night in her slepe, & walke and talked and confessed all & the doctor noted her wordes.

There are some puzzles in Forman's account:[1] the first two scenes are missing; Banquo and Macbeth open the play as at 1.3, they are on horseback riding through the wood instead of the heath and they visit Duncan's court. There is no mention of the Porter, allowing speculation that this speech was a later addition. The return of the witches (3.5) and the prophecy scene (4.1) are also absent from this account, possibly because they were added by Middleton after Forman had seen the play. For these reasons, Forman's text was dismissed as a forgery by Adams. Tannenbaum added further arguments based on handwriting, which were rejected by Wilson and Hunt.

Apart from Forman's 1611 account, Chambers accepts as possible that Macbeth may have been the theme of the tragedy of *The Kinge of Scots,* given at court 1567–8. It may also have been the theme of a show *Tres Sibyllae* given by Matthew Gwinne at Oxford to greet James on 27 August 1605. The three sibyls recall the old prophecy that Banquo's descendents, the Stuarts, would reign in perpetuity as kings of Scotland, and simultaneously remind us that James is the latest in the line. It has been suggested that Shakespeare witnessed Gwinne's show and was inspired to develop the Sybils' prophecies into *Macbeth.*[2]

## Sources

Bullough demonstrates that Shakespeare's main source was Raphael Holinshed's *Chronicle* (1587) containing chapters on the reign and murder of King Duff and the rise and fall of Macbeth, covering the years AD 1034–57. This account had been derived from Hector Boece's 1527 Latin history *Scotorum Historiae.* Holinshed probably also consulted George Buchanan's Latin History *Rerum Scoticarum Historia* (1582), but it is thought unlikely that Shakespeare had used Boece or Buchanan directly.

Beyond Holinshed, specific sources have been difficult to establish. Indeed, Nicholas Brooke is skeptical over how much further reading Shakespeare undertook for *Macbeth.* It is possible that Shakespeare used Reginald Scot's *Discoverie of Witchcraft* (1584) and King James's *Daemonologie* (1599) for background on witchcraft. He may also have used James's *Law on Free Monarchies* (1598) and *Basilicon Doron* (1599) for the divine right to kingship. It is likely that he drew on Seneca using *Medea* as the model for the description of Lady Macbeth and for details about witchcraft, as well as *Agamemnon* and *Phaedra*. Seneca's plays had appeared in a collection of translations edited by Thomas Newton in 1581.

In addition, Winstanley claims that certain details appear to have been taken from the actual depositions of the trial of the 1567 murder of Darnley (1922: 53). The Earl of Darnley was the husband of Mary, Queen of Scots; their son became James VI of Scotland and James I of England. In 1567 Mary was quick to express her horror at the murder, but it was known that she loathed Darnley, and it was widely believed that she had instigated the assassination, the assassin being her lover the Earl of Bothwell.

Winstanley also points out that the Scottish State Papers, *Proclamations and Criminal Trials,* (ch. 4) give details of how the witch scenes in *Macbeth* closely parallel details of actual Scottish witch trials. In several of these King James himself took part, and the majority of the trials were supposed to result from attempts against his life. A. M. Clark argues that *Macbeth* has a 'weaving-in of specialties from recent Scots law and procedure in relation to treason and murder under trust or *homicidium sub praetextu amicitiae*. Clark also states that *Macbeth* was based in part on *The Buick of the Chronicles of Scotland*, which was composed by William Stewart in 1535 and not published until 1858 (1981: 14). This chronicle (a rare manuscript of which is now in Cambridge University Library) has been identified with the 'Scottis Chronicle, wrettin with hand' which was in James VI's library at Holyrood House. Furthermore, Clark claims Stewart's *Buick* was the source of the characterisation of the Macbeths in Acts 1 & 2.

Various allusions in plays dated *c.* 1607 have been observed: *Lingua* features a sleep-walking scene, and both *The Puritan* and *The Knight of the Burning Pestle* contain references to a ghost like Banquo's. It is usually assumed that *Macbeth* preceded these works.

## Orthodox Date

Most scholars guardedly date *Macbeth* to mid-1606, e.g. Bradley, Chambers Wills and Leggatt. Wells & Taylor attest that "Macbeth is obviously a Jacobean play, composed probably in 1606" (*Complete Works*, 975). Gary Taylor has recently reaffirmed his date for *Macbeth* in his study on Thomas Middleton.

Braunmuller, however, is more circumspect about the allusions to the Gunpowder Plot and dates the play after James's accession in 1603 (1994: 6). J. Dover Wilson proposed an earlier date, 1601 or 1602, immediately after *Hamlet* and suggested that the play was performed in Edinburgh where he supposed Shakespeare had taken refuge after the failed Essex Rebellion (1951: xli). A. M. Clark also argues for 1601, soon after the Gowrie conspiracy.

Brooke states (59): "There is no reason to contradict 1606, but there is also very little to support it."

## Internal Orthodox Evidence

The major reference in *Macbeth* which is used to date the play concerns equivocation. Shortly after the murder of Duncan, the drunken porter imagines(2.3.9–10):

> Faith, here's an equivocator, who could swear in both the scales against either scale, who committed treason enough for God's sake, yet could not equivocate to Heaven.

Similarly, at 5.5 40–1, Macbeth states:

> I pall in resolution and begin
> To doubt [= suspect] th'equivocation of the fiend

Most editors have seen links between such references and the trials of the

Gunpowder plotters, especially that of the Jesuit, Henry Garnet in 1606. Garnet admitted his own use of equivocation as recorded in a pamphlet at the time *A true and perfect relation of the whole proceedings against the late most barbarous traitors, Garnet a Iesuite, and his confederats*, 1606.[3] Editors have therefore dated the play after May 1606.

However, Garnet himself had been encouraging the use of equivocation for at least a decade, as explained by Ceri Sullivan. Following Elizabeth's excommunication in 1570, the presence of the Jesuits in England gradually increased, resulting in an Act of Parliament in 1585 banishing all Jesuits. Jonsen & Toulimin note that 183 catholics were executed under Elizabeth, including 123 priests. Of these, the Jesuit priests, Edmund Campion (executed in 1581) and Robert Southwell (executed in 1595), were the most prominent.[4] Campion was accused of using "verbal equivocation" among other means to gain access to people all over England, as reported by the contemporary pamphleteer, Anthony Munday, in *A Discoverie of Edmund Campion, and his complices* (STC 18264, 18270).[5] Similarly, Robert Southwell used equivocation at his trial in 1595. After his execution, a pamphlet circulated anonymously, entitled *A Treatise of Equivocation* (probably written by Henry Garnet). The purpose was as follows:

> We will endeavour to prove that whosoever frameth a true proposition in his mind and uttereth some part thereof in words, which of themselves being taken several from the other part reserved were false, doth not so speak false or lie before God.

(Jonsen & Toulmin, 203). Thus, the porter's reference to equivocation in Macbeth would have been topical at the major trials of Jesuit priests in the Elizabethan period (e.g. 1581 and 1595) and does not link the play exclusively with the trials of the Gunpowder conspirators in 1606.

### (a) *Macbeth* dates to 1606, as a play about the Gunpowder Plot

Bradley strongly urged 1606 as the date of writing on the following grounds (1992: 442–64):

- At his trial in 1606, the Jesuit Garnet protested on his soul and salvation that he had not held a certain conversation, then confessed, defending equivocation at length. The porter's speech refers to the equivocator who could swear in both scales and committed treason enough for God's sake.
- The price of wheat was exceptionally low in 1606. This may be alluded to in the porter's speech (2.3): 'Here's a farmer that hang'd himself on the expectation of plenty.'
- Marston's *Sophonisba*, 1606, several times reminds Bradley of *Macbeth*. He claims that, though the echoes are slight, taken together they suggest a knowledge of *Macbeth*.

Chambers challenges Bradley. He points out that *Sophonisba* was registered on 17th March 1606, so that the equivocation passage, if it forms part of the original text, must have been written earlier than the actual trial of Garnet, which was on 28th March. He also dismisses the evidence of the farmer who "hanged himself on the expectation of plenty" because the low prices were true of many years and "in fact the suicide of a disappointed engrosser of corn was an old notion". Nevertheless, Chambers tentatively dates *Macbeth* to 1606 because in the play equivocation is associated with treason, as it was at the trial of Garnet.

Winstanley attempts to develop links between *Macbeth* and the 1605 Gunpowder Plot, which aimed to get rid of the Protestant James and the Protestantism of his newly united countries; the story of Macbeth and Banquo confirmed James's right to rule England. Winstanley also argues that the play reflects earlier political events too, pointing out that the Gunpowder Plot was compared by James himself to the very similar plot against his father, Darnley. She claims that the murder of Duff (paralleled by the murder of Duncan in *Macbeth*) is quoted by at least two contemporary historians as the nearest parallel to the Darnley murder in Scottish history. Shakespeare's version of the murder closely resembles the Darnley murder. She also points out that the Gunpowder Plot was widely compared with the French massacre of St Bartholomew (1572) and that a similar massacre of Protestants in England had been feared (1922: 116). *Macbeth* contains a number of details not found in Holinshed but which closely resemble details of St Bartholomew, especially of the Coligny murder; Shakespeare's Macbeth shares the remorse, terror and hallucinations said by contemporary French historians to have haunted Charles IX.

Paul proposes that *Macbeth* is a royal play, specially and hurriedly written in 1606 following the Gunpowder Plot, for a performance before James I the same year, during the visit of James's brother-in-law, the King of Denmark. But his suggested allusions do not amount to 'fact', despite his claims, e.g:

> Nay, had I power, I should
> Pour the sweet milk of Concord into Hell,
> Uproar the universal peace, confound
> All unity on earth. (4.3.98–101)

This does suggest the three national virtues espoused by King James. But Paul states (p. 346) that it alludes to the noisy crowd which prevented James hearing a processional pageant relaying his ideas in 1606. "The lines now seem mere rant, but Shakespeare wrote them glowing with indignation at what he had witnessed." Paul provides no supporting evidence (1950: 346).

### (b) *Macbeth* dates to 1603, as a play to impress the new king

Braunmuller, however, is more circumspect about the allusions to the Gunpowder Plot and dates the play after James's accession in 1603:

> Amidst these uncertainties, there is one highly probable claim. When Scotland's King James became England's King James in March 1603, his accession made a Shakespearean Scottish play commercially viable and creatively attractive. King James and his Scottishness created an occasion, and at some point Shakespeare and the King's Men apparently seized the popular, commercial moment, as they had less successfully done in performing *The Tragedy of Gowrie.*

Bradley argues that *Macbeth* was written after 1603, when James VI succeeded to the English throne as James I, citing these reasons (1994: 7–8):

- the style fits this phase of development of Shakespeare's writing
- the allusions to 'two-fold balls and treble sceptres' refers to the union of England and Scotland
- the emphases on the descent of Scottish kings from Banquo is relevant to a new king
- witchcraft, a key feature of the play, was a subject on which James considered himself an authority.
- the description of the English king (4.3.147) touching to cure the 'king's evil'; this was also a ceremony performed by King James.

None of these points entail that the play was written *after* 1603. The links to James were at least as apt during the 1590s, the last years of Elizabeth's reign, when attention was turned towards James as her probable successor.

Regarding the 'king's evil', the Ogburns (1952) point out that curing 'the king's evil' was an old royal practice, which went back to Macbeth's time, and continued for another century, over 700 years in total: "The King's evil [is] scrofula . . . a tuberculous swelling of the lymph glands, once popularly supposed to be curable by the touch of royalty. The custom of touching was first adopted in England by Edward the Confessor . . . [and] reached its zenith during the Restoration." (*Encyclopaedia Britannica,* 1994–2000).

### (c) *Macbeth* dates to 1601, as a play about the Gowrie Conspiracy

A. M. Clark, however, argues in favour of an earlier date for the play, *c.* 1601, suggesting the play was written to order to compliment and appeal to King James, specifically in response to the 1600 Gowrie conspiracy. The Gowrie conspiracy almost achieved James's assassination; he was lured into a small room, and knives were drawn. The suggested parallels with *Macbeth* include:

- the actual/attempted 'murder under trust' of a Scottish King
- both murders by a host in the host's own home
- both kings lured there by invitation
- both hosts rode ahead to advise their partners in crime
- both planned a single assassination in private, unlike the Gunpowder Plot

- the play's supernatural factors (much more prevalent in Shakespeare than in Holinshed), and the condemnation of the Earl of Gowrie for his occult practices
- Lennox is not mentioned in Holinshed's account, but is given dramatic prominence throughout Macbeth. He calls himself 'young' (2.2.67). The 2nd Duke of Lennox, twenty-six in 1600, was James's close friend, was present at Gowrie, and gave a long account at the trial
- Holinshed's 'There was a sparhawke also strangled by an owle' becomes in Macbeth:

  'On Tuesday last,
  A falcon, towering in her pride of place,
  Was by a mousing owl hawk'd at and kill'd'. (2.4.11 015–13)

Tuesday was the day of the attempted assassination, and James ordered that Tuesdays were to be days of regular preaching to give thanks for his deliverance. James's hawk (= falcon) figured prominently in the Gowrie account, as represented in a later engraving.

Orthodox scholars acknowledge that there are several problems with the text, exhibiting evidence of there being more than one author. Chambers claims that *Macbeth* was printed from a prompt-copy: the stage directions are fuller than usual, and the book-keeper's "ring the bell" has got into the text (2.3.85). Without the Hecate scenes, the play is very short (only *The Comedy of Errors* is shorter). Chambers and others see some of the witch scenes as interpolations. Taylor gives detailed consideration to Middleton's possible contribution. He argues (along with many others) that in 1616 or so Middleton added scene 3.5 and parts of 4.1.38–60 and 141–148, featuring Hecate: the style is conspicuously different from the rest of the play, and there are two songs from Thomas Middleton's *Witch* (a play of uncertain date, unfortunately).

## External Orthodox Evidence:

Arthur Clark supports his 1601 claim with the fact that the Gowrie conspiracy caused an international sensation. He points out that Elizabethan dramatists practically ignored Scotland prior to 1600, but the weird and dramatic Gowrie attempted regicide focused English and European interest on Scotland and her king, the man expected to succeed Elizabeth. In 1602 Charles Massey's play *Malcolm, King of Scots* (now lost), was bought for the Lord Admiral's Company, probably "cashing in on the success of Macbeth with a sequel" (1981: 13). Another lost play was *Tragedy of Gowrie*, known to have been acted to large crowds at least twice by December 1604.

## Internal Oxfordian Evidence

E. T. Clark (1931) argues that *Macbeth* was written in 1589/90, with the murder of Duncan alluding to the assassination in 1588 of Henri, Duke of Guise, by King Henri III of France. She makes three claims: (a) that Lady Macbeth was based on the character of Catherine de Medici, the mother of Henri III; (b) that the apparition of the eight kings to Macbeth (4.1) may refer to the legend of Catherine de Medici's vision of future kings of France; (c) that the 'twofold balls and treble sceptres' may refer to the union of the three kingdoms of Henri of Navarre and Bearn, who in 1589 became Henri IV of France.

D. and C. Ogburn also argue for a probable date of composition in 1589 or 1590. They point out that a martlet (1.6.4) was Mary Stuart's maternal family emblem. In this view, Lady Macbeth parallels Mary Stuart, tormented by what she had instigated and unleashed by the murder of Darnley.

Holland argues that the date of writing was 1599, supported with various quotes and suggestions. A mission was sent to Aleppo in 1599. This may be reflected in: First witch: "Her husband's to Aleppo gone, master o' th' Tiger" (1.3 6). Holland notes Lady Macbeth's comment: "Had he not resembled/ My father as he slept, I had done it." (2.2.12–13), which suggests the murder in 1598 of Francesco Cenci by his daughter Beatrice and her lover. Evidence was given that the murderers weakened at the sight of his silver hairs. Finally Holland examines the porter's description: "Here's an equivocator that could swear in both scales against either scale; who committed treason enough for God's sake, yet could not equivocate to heaven." (Porter's lines, 2.3.8–11). He suggests that this might refer to Edward Squire, hanged in 1598. Originally a Protestant, Squire pretended to convert to Catholicism in order to discover Jesuit secrets. He was told to assassinate Queen Elizabeth, and to avoid suspicion an excuse was found by the Inquisition to try him, as a Protestant. In 1598 he was arrested for high treason. First he denied all knowledge of the plot, then he confessed, then retracted this admission, then repeated his confession, and before being hanged repudiated all former confessions.

## External Oxfordian Evidence

Moore notes that pre-1606 references to equivocation can be found in Dekker's *Satiromatrix* (printed 1602): "There's no faith to be helde with Hereticks and Infidels, and therefore thou swearest anie thing" (4.2.90–1); and also in *Hamlet* – "We must speak by the card or equivocation will undo us" (5.1.133–4).

Sobran asks that since Shakespeare of Stratford was alive until 1616, why did he not revise and perfect *Macbeth*, as he apparently did with *Hamlet* and *Lear*, judging by the differences between folio and quarto texts of these? Sobran concludes that editors probably assembled *Macbeth* from fragments left by Oxford, calling in the help of Thomas Middleton (1997: 151).

## Conclusion

*Macbeth* can be dated any time between 1587 (the publication of Holinshed's *Chronicles*) and Forman's account of a performance in 1611. There is no evidence as to the date of composition. Allusions to contemporary events have been used to support widely different dates. While most scholars accept a date a year after the Gunpowder Plot, Brooke says: "There is no evidence to contradict 1606, but there is also very little to support it." Whereas Taylor believes that Middleton revised *Macbeth c.* 1616, adding the Hecate material, Brooke believes that Middleton made these additions in 1609–10 (1990: 64–66).

It seems likely, on the current evidence, that *Macbeth* was mostly written in 1601, but that some parts are earlier; that the play was probably extended using fragments of unfinished play/s; that the main inspiration for the story was the 1600 Gowrie conspiracy, with references also to the 1567 murder of Darnley; and that the vision of the future kings was possibly suggested by the legend of Catherine de Medici's vision. The theme of equivocation, which runs through the play, was a feature of all the murders and attempted murders above.

## Notes

1. Most people accept the argument, explained by Chambers, that Forman wrote 1610 in mistake for 1611, when 20 April fell on a Saturday. Forman dates his other theatre visits to 1611.
2. Further discussion on Gwinne's *Tres Sibyllae* and its relevance to Shakespeare's *Macbeth* is available in Braunmuller's edition of *Macbeth* (New Cambridge Shakespeare, *Macbeth,* 1997: 5-6). See also Hawkins, Michael, "History, politics and Macbeth", *Focus on Macbeth*, ed. John Russell Brown, Routledge (2005), Appendix 8, 185–88.
3. Garnet's trial has been described in Philip Caraman, *Henry Garnet: 1555–1606 and the Gunpowder Plot* (1964).
4. Albert Jonsen and Stephen Toulmin *The Abuse of Casuistry: a history of moral reasoning* (1988: 203).
5. Quoted by Donna Hamilton, *Anthony Munday and the Catholics, 1560–1633* (2005: 40). The earliest citation for equivocate/equivocation in the OED is from Sir Edwin Sandys in *Europae speculum* (composed *c.* 1599 and published in 1605 according to T. K. Rabb, *Jacobean Gentleman: Sir Edwin Sandys, 1561–1629,* Princeton, 1998). Hamlet refers to "equivocation" at 5 1.134 and Jenkins (in his Arden2 edition of *Hamlet*, 1982) states that the idea of equivocation dates back at least to 1584, quoting Reginald Scot's *Discoverie of Witchcraft* (1584, XIII ch., 15): "How men have been abused with words of equivocation." The word 'equivocal' is used by Brabanzio (*Othello* 1.3 216) and by the French King (*All's Well* 5.3 253). Mark Anderson in *Shakespeare by Another Name* (2005: 402-3) says that the author could have become aware of the concept of equivocation from a tract in 1583, written by William Cecil, Lord Burghley or from the work of a Spanish prelate, Martin Azpilcueta, published in Latin in 1584.

## Other Works Cited

Bradley, A. C., *Shakespearean Tragedy,* Macmillan, London, (1904), 3rd edition 1992
Braunmuller, A. R. (ed.), *Macbeth,* Cambridge: CUP, 1994
Brooke, N. (ed.), *Macbeth*, Oxford: OUP, 1990
Bullough, G., *Narrative and Dramatic Sources of Shakespeare,* vol. VII. London: Routledge, 1973
Chambers, E. K., *William Shakespeare: a study of facts and problems,* 2 vols, Oxford: Clarendon Press, 1930
Clark, A. M., *Murder Under Trust. the Topical Macbeth and Other Jacobean Matters,* Edinburgh: Scottish Academic Press, 1981
Clark, E. T., *Hidden Allusions in Shakespeare's Plays,* New York: William Farquhar Payson, 1931
Holland, H. H., *Shakespeare, Oxford and Elizabethan Times,* London: Dennis Archer, 1933
Jenkins, Harold (ed.), *Hamlet*, London: Methuen: Arden 2, 1982
Leggatt, Alexander, *William Shakespeare's 'Macbeth': A Sourcebook.* London: Routledge, 2006
Moore. P. "The Abysm of Time; the Chronology of Shakespeare's Plays", *The Elizabethan Review,* 5, 2, 1997
Muir, K. (ed.), *Macbeth,* London: Methuen Arden, 1977
Ogburn, D. & C., *This Star of England*, New York: Coward-McCann Inc., 1952
Paul, H. N., *The Royal Play of Macbeth. When, why and how it was written.* New York: Macmillan, 1950
Sobran, J., *Alias Shakespeare,* New York: The Free Press, 1997
Sullivan, Ceri, *Dismembered Rhetoric: English Recusant Writing, 1580 to 1603*, Fairleigh Dickinson Univ Press, 1995
Tannenbaum, S. A., *Shakspearian Scraps and Other Elizabethan Fragments,* New York: Columbia University Press, 1933
Taylor, Gary, & Lavagnino, John, *Thomas Middleton and early modern textual culture,* Oxford: OUP, 2007
Wells, S. and Taylor, G. (eds), *The Complete Oxford Shakespeare,* Oxford: OUP, 1986
—, *William Shakespeare: a textual companion*, Oxford: OUP, 1987
Wills, Garry, *Witches & Jesuits: Shakespeare's 'Macbeth'*, Oxford, 1995
Wilson, J. D. & R. W. Hunt, "The Authenticity of Forman's *Booke of Plaies*", *Review of English Studies*, 1947: 193–200
Wilson, J. D. (ed.), *Macbeth,* Cambridge: CUP, 1951
Winstanley, L., *Macbeth, King Lear and Contemporary History,* Cambridge: CUP, 1922

# The Tragedy of Hamlet

## Eddi Jolly

*Hamlet* can be dated between the latest source, *c.* 1586, and the entry in the Stationers' Register in 1602.[1]

### Publication Date

The play was entered in the Stationers' Register, 26th July 1602:

> [SR, 1602] xxvj[to]Julij. James Robertes. Entred for his Copie vnder the handes of master Pasfield and master Waterson warden A booke called the Revenge of Hamlett Prince Denmark as yt was latelie Acted by the Lord Chamberleyne his servantes. vj[d]

A quarto version (Ql) was published the following year in 1603:

> [Q1, 1603] The Tragicall Historie of Hamlet Prince of Denmarke by William Shake-speare. As it hath beene diuerse times acted by his Highnesse seruants in the Cittie of London: as also in the two Vniuersities of Cambridge and Oxford, and else-where At London: printed [by Valentine Simmes] for N. L. [Nicholas Ling] and Iohn Trundell, 1603.

Two examples of Q1 are known and only one (in the Huntingdon Library) preserves the title page. Q1 is usually known as the 'bad' quarto by many scholars who have taken it to be a pirated version of *Hamlet*, memorised badly, or at least incompletely.[2] A much longer version of the play (Q2) was published in 1604:

> [Q2, 1604] The tragicall historie of Hamlet, Prince of Denmarke. By William Shakespeare. Newly imprinted and enlarged to almost as much againe as it was, according to the true and perfect Coppie.

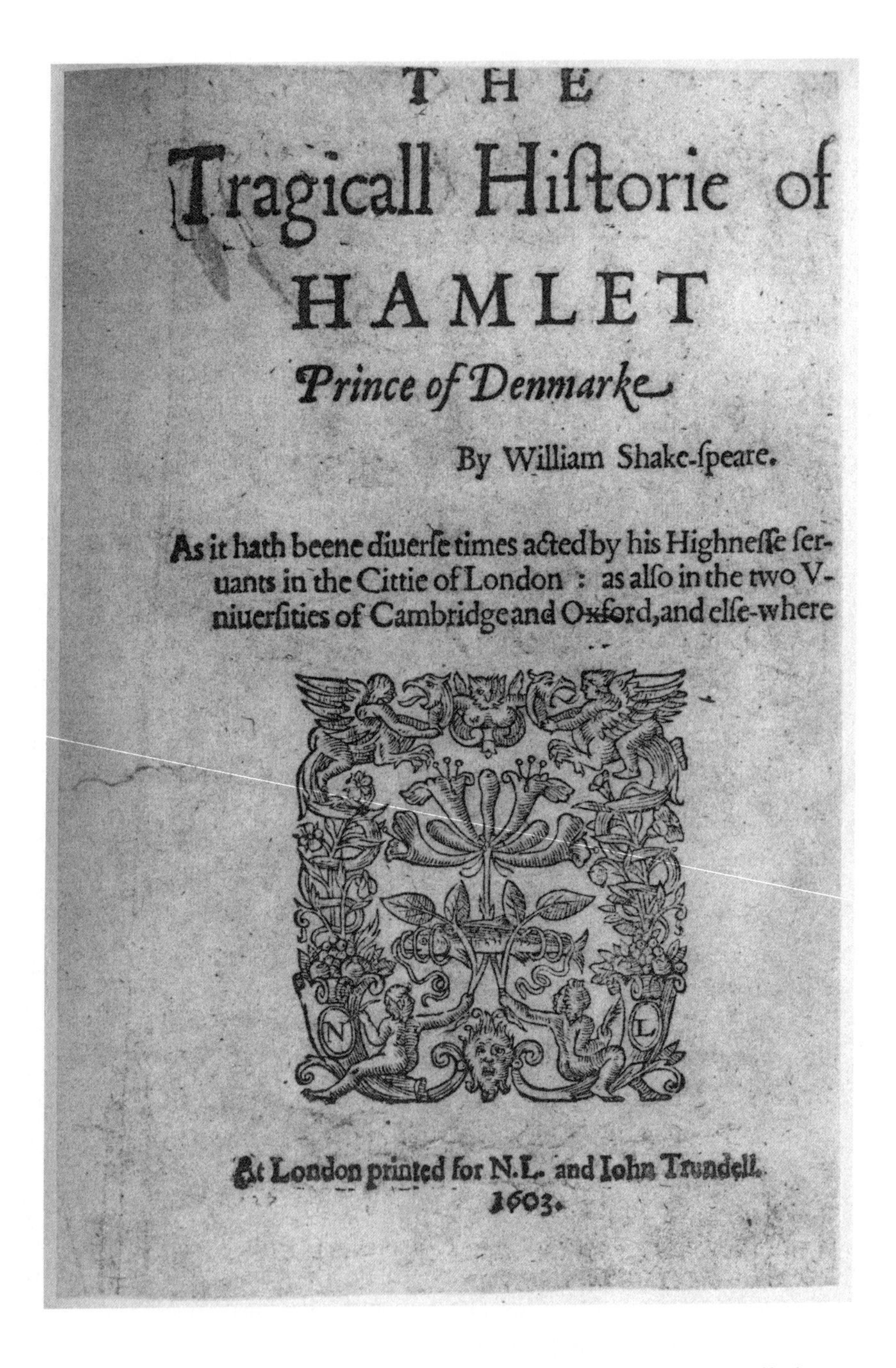

THE

Tragicall Hiſtorie of

HAMLET

*Prince of Denmarke*

By William Shake-ſpeare.

As it hath beene diuerſe times acted by his Highneſſe ſeruants in the Cittie of London : as alſo in the two V-
niuerſities of Cambridge and Oxford, and elſe-where

At London printed for N.L. and Iohn Trundell.
1603.

23. Title page to the First Quarto of *Hamlet*, 1603; it has generally been believed that this version was a 'Bad Quarto' derived from the Folio text. Some scholars, however, have argued that it was an early version by Shakespeare, which he later revised. By permission of the Huntington Library, San Marino, California.

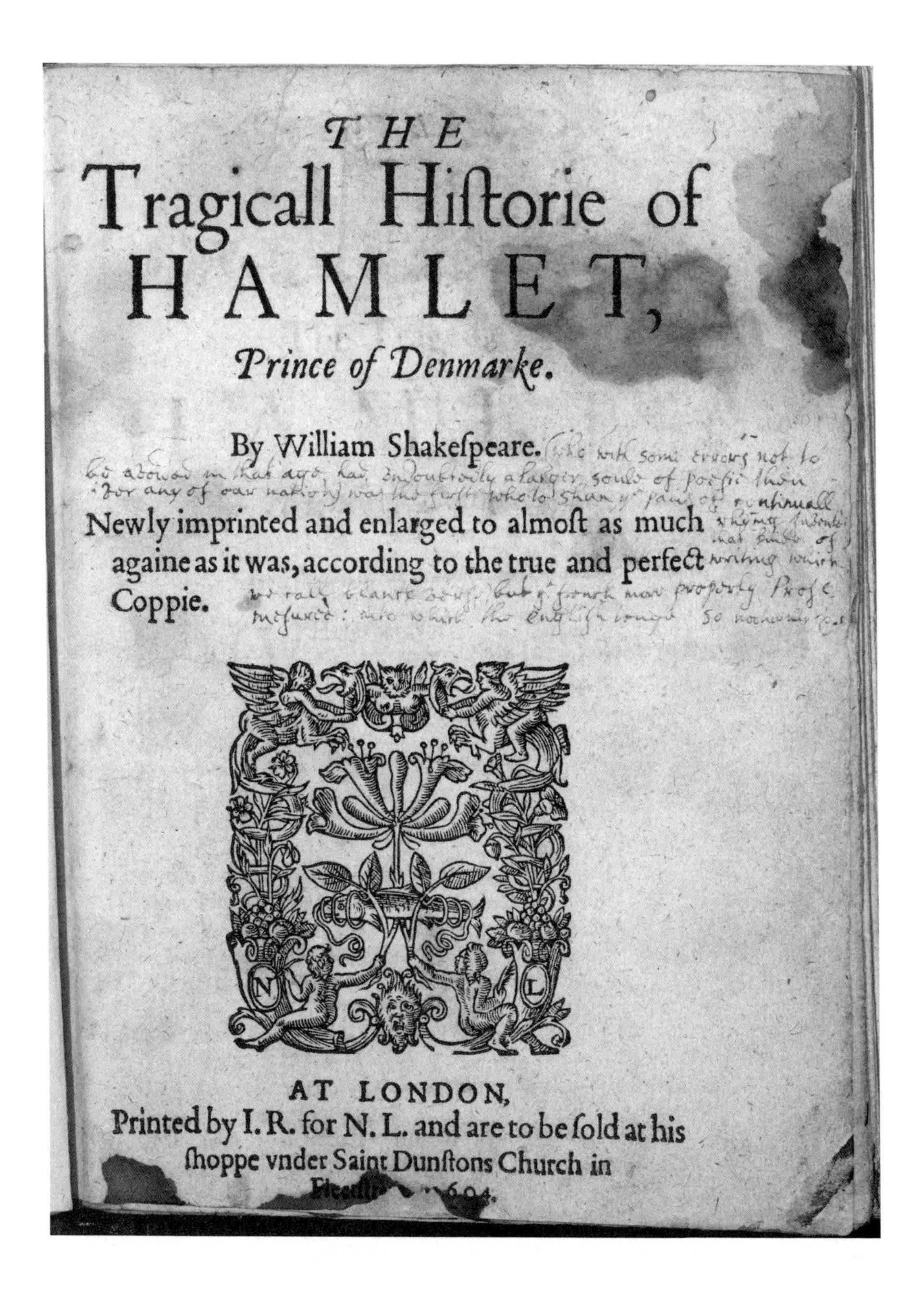

THE

Tragicall Hiſtorie of

HAMLET,

*Prince of Denmarke.*

By William Shakeſpeare.

Newly imprinted and enlarged to almoſt as much againe as it was, according to the true and perfect Coppie.

AT LONDON,

Printed by I. R. for N. L. and are to be ſold at his ſhoppe vnder Saint Dunſtons Church in Fleet[illegible]604.

24. The title page to the Second Quarto of *Hamlet*, 1604–5.
By permission of the Folger Shakespeare Library.

> At London: printed by I. R. [James Roberts] for N. L. [Nicholas Ling] and are to be sold at his shoppe vnder Saint Dunstons Church in Fleet-street, 1604.

The title page of some editions of Q2 carry the date 1605. A third quarto (Q3) followed in 1611, based on Q2, but with some variations:

> [Q3, 1611] The tragedy of Hamlet Prince of Denmarke. By William Shakespeare. Newly imprinted and enlarged to almost as much againe as it was, according to the true and perfect coppy. At London: printed [by George Eld] for Iohn Smethwicke, and are to be sold at his shoppe in Saint Dunstons Church yeard in Fleetstreet. Vnder the Diall, 1611.

A fourth quarto in 1622 showed the continuing popularity of the play:

> [Q4, 1622] The tragedy of Hamlet Prince of Denmarke. Newly imprinted and inlarged, according to the true and perfect copy lastly printed. By William Shakespeare. London: printed by W. S. [William Stansby] for Iohn Smethwicke, and are to be sold at his shop in Saint Dunstans Church-yard in Fleetstreet: vnder the Diall, [1622].

The play was printed near the end of the First Folio (F1), occupying the seventh position among the tragedies, after *Macbeth* and before *King Lear.*

## Relationship of Q1, Q2 and F1

There has been much discussion but little agreement about the relationship between these versions. According to Irace's line counts, Q1 is much the shortest edition of the play, with about 2,221 lines, compared to the longest version, Q2, which contains approx 4,056 lines. The most variation occurs in Hamlet's "To be or not to be speech ..." as it appears in Q2; originally in Q1, this speech began with the lines: 'To be or not to be; ay there's the point. / To die, to sleep: is that all? Ay all.' Overall, the speech is about ten lines shorter than in Q1. There are also changes to the names of characters: in Q1, the King's counsellor is called Corambis and his spying servant Montano, whereas in Q2 they are called Polonius and Reynaldo. The sequence of events is slightly different: in Q1, the nunnery scene is introduced immediately after Ophelia's father suggests testing Hamlet (Q1, scene 8; Act 2 Scene 2 in the longer texts), but in the following scene (3.1) in Q2. Various productions have found the Q1 sequence more logical. The question of Gertrude's complicity in murder is explicitly denied in Q1, where she promises to help Hamlet exact revenge. In Q2, however, Gertrude's conscience is not known; she makes no offer of help beyond keeping quiet. The F1 version is about 3,901 lines in total, lacking about 230 lines in Q2, but containing about 80 lines not in Q2.

In her edition of Q1, Kathleen Irace considers three possible relationships between the texts:

(a) Revision is the commonly cited reason, arguing that the dramatist composed the longer version (Q2) and then shortened it as Q1, perhaps for playing and touring purposes; according to this view, Q1 must have been authorised, since those involved in the publication of Q1 (Nicholas Ling, John Trundell and the unacknowledged printer, Valentine Simmes) were reputable. Many commentators, e.g. Sams, believe that Shakespeare wrote Q1, then revised and expanded it as Q2.

(b) Memorial reconstruction, Irace believes, is the most reasonable explanation for the differences between the plays. Chambers states that "Q2 substantially represents the original text of the play, as written once and for all by Shakespeare." This is followed by many editors, e.g. Jenkins and Hibbard. It is further thought that the actor who played the parts of Marcellus, Lucianus and Voltemand in the longer (as yet unpublished) Q2 version helped to prepare a 'bad' quarto of the play as Q1, without the author's permission. The idea that Q1 was unauthorised is suggested on the title page of Q2, "Newly imprinted and enlarged to almost as much againe as it was, according to the true and perfect Coppie." Q2's comment may, however, have been a sales pitch.

(c) Theatrical adaptation is also possible, perhaps by actors for performance in the provinces, with Q1 an abridged version of the original Q2.

Irace makes no final judgement about the relationship between these plays. Wells & Taylor accept Q1 as a memorial reconstruction of Q2, but believe that Shakespeare himself revised the play as printed in F1. Other scholars are not so circumspect as Irace: Somogyi offers a flow diagram which has in its initial box 'Shakespeare's Manuscript 1600', and confidently asserts that Q1 is a 'memorial reconstruction' and that Q2 and F1 should be combined to form the composite *Hamlet*, on the assumption that the dramatist only produced one complete play. Since it is possible that the dramatist revised the play (perhaps twice, from Q2 to Q1 then from Q2 to F1), all three versions may have authority.

## Early References to Performances

Towards the end of Elizabeth's reign, there were certainly three, and possibly four or five, references to a play about Hamlet.[3] Firstly, Thomas Nashe wrote an address to the "Gentlemen Students of both Universities" printed as an introduction to Robert Greene's romance *Menaphon* (STC 12272, 1589); Nashe stated:

> English Seneca read by candle-light yields many good sentences, as *Blood is a beggar*, and so forth; and if you entreat him fair in a frosty morning, he will afford you whole Hamlets, I should say handfuls of tragical speeches

The second reference occurs in Henslowe's Diaries, which mention a performance of a play called *Hamlet* at Newington Butts, south of the river on 9 June 1594. The entry lies on the same page as two other plays with Shakespearean titles:

| | | |
|---|---|---|
| ye 5 of June 1594 | R/ at andronicous | xij$^{s}$ |
| ye 9 of June 1594 | R/ at hamlet | viij$^{s}$ |
| ye 10 of June 1594 | R/ at the tamynge of A shrowe | ix$^{s}$ |
| ye 12 of June1594 | R/ at andronicous | vij$^{s}$ |

The third reference occurs when Thomas Lodge in his *Wit's Misery and the World's Madness* (1596) describes a devil:

> He walks for the most part in black under colour of gravity, & looks as pale as the Visard of ye ghost which cried so miserally [*sic*] at ye Theatre, like an oisterwife, *Hamlet, revenge.*

It is thought likely that Lodge saw the play at The Theatre in Shoreditch.

A fourth allusion to a play about Hamlet occurs in a hand-written marginal comment by Gabriel Harvey in his copy of Chaucer, published in 1598 by Speght:

> The younger sort takes much delight in Shakespeares Venus, & Adonis: but his Lucrece, & his tragedie of Hamlet, Prince of Denmarke haue it in them, to please the wiser sort.

The passage is not dated but has been tentatively assigned to between 1598 and not later than February 1601 since the note mentions Essex as alive, "The Earle of Essex much commendes Albions England . . ."

A fifth possible allusion occurs in Edward Pudsey's manuscript *Book of Commonplaces* in which he quotes from *Hamlet* (apparently Q2). This book has been tentatively dated to 1600.[4]

The Stationers' Register records (on 26th July 1602) performance of The Revenge of Hamlett, Prince [of] Denmark, "as yt was latelie acted by the Lord Chamberlayne his servants". The title page of Q1 in 1603 mentions performances in London, Oxford and Cambridge. Halliday notes a further performance on 5$^{th}$ September 1607 on board Captain William Keeling's East Indiaman, *Red Dragon*, when anchored off the coast of Africa.

Known performance places, therefore, seem to be Newington Butts, the City of London, the universities of Oxford and Cambridge, and on board Captain Keeling's ship. In the late twentieth century there was an interesting plaque in the entrance to a coaching inn called The Golden Cross in Oxford stating Boas's deduction that *Hamlet* was performed in that city in 1593, but that plaque has now been removed.[5]

## Was there an *Ur-Hamlet*?

In 1877, Furness reviewed the attempts by previous editors to date Shakespeare's *Hamlet* and noted that discussion on the text and date of the play "continues to divide the Shakespearean world". Malone first suggested that all references before 1600 to a play about Hamlet were simply to another, earlier play by someone other than Shakespeare; the so-called *Ur-Hamlet*, perhaps by Thomas Kyd. When Dr. Farmer discovered Lodge's allusion in 1767, Malone proposed a date of 1596 for *Hamlet* in his chronology of the plays. However, when Nashe's 1589 reference was found, Malone hastily revised his date and dismissed the Henslowe reference on the grounds that Henslowe only received eight shillings for the play.

Most modern scholars have followed the suggestion of an *Ur-Hamlet*, some (e.g. Chambers, Jenkins and Edwards) without question, believing that this earlier version was used by Shakespeare as a source. Shakespeare is then supposed to have written his own version of *Hamlet* around the turn of the century. Wells & Taylor (following Bullough) are more cautious about the existence of an *Ur-Hamlet*, somewhat reluctantly accepting the suggestion, mainly because the phrase "Hamlet, revenge!" quoted by Lodge in 1596 does not occur in Q1 (but fail to note that neither does the phrase occur in Q2 or F1). The hypothesis of an earlier play by a different author, however, is not supported by reference to any extant manuscript or printed document. If the *Ur-Hamlet* ever existed, it is now lost.

Other scholars are doubtful about an *Ur-Hamlet*: E. A. J. Honigmann had originally accepted the idea (in "The Date of *Hamlet*", 1956) but changed his mind by 1985 (*Shakespeare: the 'lost years'*) when he argued for an early version by Shakespeare. The most recent editors of the Arden edition of *Hamlet*, Thompson & Taylor, accept that it is possible that Nashe, Henslowe and Lodge were referring to Shakespeare's play (or at least to a version of it). Cairncross, Alexander and Bloom go further and reject the entire notion of a different author, asserting that these three references are to an early version of the Shakespeare play.

## Sources

Consideration of the sources used by Shakespeare depends to a large extent on the view taken about an earlier version of *Hamlet.* While any version of such a play would have derived from Belleforest, it is impossible to know how much more of the reading listed below would have been done by the supposed other writer.

Geoffrey Bullough has surveyed the extensive sources used for *Hamlet*, many of them in Latin, French or Italian. Saxo Grammaticus's Latin text, *Danicae Historiae* (1514), was the earliest printed source for the tale of Amleth, as the Prince was originally called. It is possible that the dramatist consulted both Saxo Grammaticus and a French translation by François de Belleforest in 1576, which was included in *Les Histoires Tragiques*, volume V of which contains the story of Hamlet. Jenkins argues for use of a further source in French and since the correspondence of thought suggests that Shakespeare had read Montaigne's *Essais* (published in French in 1580–88 and in English translations which began to appear inconsistently from 1595).

From classical sources, it is also thought that Shakespeare used Seneca both for his rhetorical features (e.g. doubling devices, oppositional pairs and hendiadys, as noted by Kermode) and as a model for a revenge play: Polonius even refers to Roman playwrights: "Seneca cannot be too heavy nor Plautus too light for the law of writ and liberty." (2.2.401–2) Seneca was available in the original Latin or in various translations, e.g. Thomas Newton's of 1581. There are also internal references to Virgil's *Aeneid* in Hamlet's request for a speech, based on Aeneas's tale in Book II told to Dido (available either in the original Latin or in a translation such as Henry Howard's of the 1540s, or Marlowe's *Dido, Queen of Carthage*, published 1594). Bullough also suggests as sources works by Livy (in Latin or in Philemon Holland's translation of 1600), Plutarch (in Latin or in North's translation of 1579) and Plautus's *Menaechmi* (probably in Latin, but also available from 1594 in an English translation by Warner) and possibly Juvenal's *Tenth Satire*. He further considers it likely that *The Murder of Gonzago* and the description of the ghost is based on the story of Francesco Maria della Rovere, Duke of Urbino. The murder of this duke, who was in Venice at the time, was described in a book (published in Venice in 1546 with later reprints) by Paul Iovii, *Eulogia Virorum Bellica Virtute Illustrium*, with an engraving based on a portrait by Titian.[6] Jenkins comments that an important source for the "To be or not to be speech" was *Cardanus' Comfort* (available either in the Latin text of 1514 or in Thomas Bedingfield's English translation of 1573). Erasmus' *Moriae Encomium* (1511, translated into English as *In Praise of Folly*, 1549) has also been identified as a likely source, especially for combining serious issues with humour.

Bullough also describes Italian sources, especially as Hamlet himself comments on *The Murder of Gonzago*: "His name's Gonzago: the story is extant and writ in choice Italian" (3.2.250). Bullough mentions the influence of Baldasarre Castiglione's *Il Cortegiano*, published originally in Italian (1528), then translated into English (by Hoby in 1561) and into Latin (by Clarke, 1572). Bullough then lists a small number of possible sources or analogues from English texts: John Lyly's *Euphues: Anatomy of Wit* (1578) and *Euphues and his England* (1580); Sidney's *Arcadia* (1590); Tarlton's *Newes out of Purgatorie* (1590); *A Warning for Fair Women* (anon, published in 1599) and Marston's

*Antonio's Revenge* (1600). There is also a play in German, *Der bestrafte Brudermord* (*Fratricide Punished*) which seems to have derived from Q1. Dover Wilson adds that Shakespeare was acquainted with Timothy Bright's *A Treatise of Melancholy*, printed in 1586; Jenkins cautiously accepts some influence.

Shaheen has identified more biblical allusions in *Hamlet* than in any other Shakespeare play. These allusions often echo the specific wording of the protestant Geneva Bible (published in 1560), e.g. at 3.1.77–79:

> But that dread of something after death,
> The undiscover'd country, from whose bourn
> No traveller returns.

This reference to Job 10.21 reads "shall returne no more." Other versions read "not turne agayne." Further echoes of the Geneva Bible occur at 3.3.80, 5.1.229–30 and 5.2.219–20.

There is also intriguing legal knowledge throughout the play, especially in the interchange between the gravediggers (5.1) : "Is she to be buried in Christian burial, that willfully seeks her own salvation?" The discussion which follows is based on the case of Hales *v.* Pettit, decided in 1560 (reported in Plowden, 253). Sokol & Sokol refer to various studies of this scene and find detailed, precise legal knowledge as well as allusion to "issues carrying considerable moral and philosophical importance". Plowden's reports were written in French and were published in London in 1571 as *Les Commentaries, ou Reportes de Edmunde Plowden un Apprentice de le Comen Ley.*

The above brings together most of the large number of sources identified by major scholars. *Hamlet* ranks alongside *Richard II* as the play for which the dramatist did most research. Bright's *Treatise of Melancholy* (1586) seems to be the latest definite source for the play.

## Orthodox Dates

Chambers and Bullough date the play between 1598 and 1601. J. Dover Wilson gives a slightly wider range from 1596–1601; Jenkins, Hibbard and Edwards prefer a slightly narrower range 1599–1600. Wells & Taylor give the slightly later date 1600–01, which is accepted by Cantor (after much comment about the conjectural nature of the chronology of the plays). Many see the composition of *Hamlet* as immediately following Shakespeare's composition of *Julius Caesar*. Thompson & Taylor, however, allow that Shakespeare's play may be dated back as far as 1589:

> The argument that *Hamlet* refers back to *Julius Caesar*, while attractive, remains unproven. Once that is conceded, and once it is further conceded that we are not just looking for one precise date but a process of production which involves drafts of manuscripts, performances in

> different venues, and the publication of a number of different texts, then it becomes possible to admit that a version of *Hamlet* by Shakespeare may date back to 1589 or even earlier.

Alexander, Honigmann and Bloom argue for an original date *c.* 1589, with a revision *c.* 1600, for Shakespeare's *Hamlet.*

## Orthodox Dates – External Evidence

The proposed dates are closely related to scholars' interpretations of the external evidence provided by Nashe (1589), Henslowe (1594), Lodge (1596) and Meres (1598) in contemporary documents. Most scholars reject or ignore the possibility that Nashe, Henslowe and Lodge were referring to Shakespeare's play, postulating another play, now lost, by another author and labelled the *Ur-Hamlet,* and placing Shakespeare's play in the late 1590s.

Some support for this position is claimed from Francis Meres, who did not mention *Hamlet* in his *Palladis Tamia* (1598). Most scholars see this omission as significant, precluding any earlier date. Meres's 1598 list becomes an inflexible baseline, indicating proof of when certain plays had or had not been written. Hibbard leans towards this theory and uses Meres as '"strong presumptive evidence" that a Shakespearean *Hamlet* had not yet been staged. But examination of Meres shows that he does not give a complete list of Shakespeare's plays written by 1598, e.g. he makes no mention of the three plays about the reign of Henry VI. To use Meres thus is to overstate his value. The third Arden *Hamlet* editors, Thompson & Taylor, report:

> An accidental omission by Meres, although unlikely, is not inconceivable: he was not to know how important his list would be for future scholars.

However, there are dissenting voices against a date *c.* 1600 for Shakespeare's play. Cairncross considers *Hamlet* to have been written by 1589. The nineteenth-century German scholar, Elze, preferred an earlier date 1585–86. Alexander, Honigmann, Sams and Bloom (among others) all accept the references in Nashe, Henslowe and Lodge (possibly also Harvey) as indicating an early version of Shakespeare's *Hamlet.*

Bullough notes the topicality of a *Hamlet* at the time of Mary Queen of Scots' trial and execution (1586–87). There are parallels with the trial of Mary Queen of Scots and the dilemma of Queen Elizabeth which were both explored in detail in the eighteenth-century observations of Plumptre (reported by Furness) and much later by Winstanley. Furthermore, the idea that Polonius (named Corambis in Q1) is a caricature of Lord Burghley (whose motto was: *Cor unum via una*) is accepted by several commentators, including Simpson (a biographer),[7] Rowse (a historian)[8] and Dover Wilson (a literary critic).[9] The identification of Corambis/Polonius with Burghley was queried by Chambers and has been denied by others, including Bate, Matus and Jenkins. The caricature does become much more likely if Q1, with the counsellor called Corambis, was from the 1580s. It could then be argued that Shakespeare revised that name to Polonius in his 1604 edition of Q2, as a mark of respect for Burghley who died in 1598, and because by 1604 the caricature would have lost its contemporary relevance. Jenkins has suggested that the change in the name of the King's counsellor from 'Corambis' to Polonius may have been suggested by a treatise in Latin by a Polish writer, Wawrzyniec Goślicki *De optimo senatore libri duo* (Venice, 1568), which was translated as *The Counsellor exactly portraited in two books* (1598). Goślicki argued that rulers should be responsible for their own actions.

A further connection with Burghley is found in the range of flowers mentioned by Ophelia when mad. A significant authority on flowers and plants was John Gerard, Burghley's gardener of more than twenty years, who published *The Herbal* in 1596. The 1597 edition at least contained as part of its dedications the crest and motto of Burghley, as cited above. In this text, Gerard refers to his travels in the northern parts of Europe, including Denmark and Polonia.[10]

## Orthodox Dates – Internal Evidence

The principal internal evidence that is offered concerns the "little eyases" (2.2 336 ff), which is supposed to be a reference to the boy actors who were established at the Blackfriars theatre, from Michaelmas 1600. Jenkins is one who recognizes this is sometimes taken as a later insertion, however, and not unambiguously proof of date of composition. Chambers raises a query about "a falling out of tennis" (2.1. 59), wondering whether there was an allusion here to the famous quarrel in a tennis court between Sir Philip Sidney and the Earl of Oxford in 1579.

The only agreement is that there is much uncertainty about the date at which Shakespeare's *Hamlet* was written, and that the relationships between Q1 and Q2 "are complicated and controversial", as Hibbard writes.

## Oxfordian Dates

Those who argue that the Earl of Oxford wrote the plays of 'Shakespeare' claim that *Hamlet* was composed in the 1580s. Both Holland and Clark suggest around 1583–84, Clark stating that it would be after the trip to Denmark of Peregrine Willoughby d'Eresby (the brother-in-law of Oxford) where he dined with the great Danish families including those named Rosencrantz and Guildenstern.

## Oxfordian Date – Internal Evidence

Links with the seventeenth Earl of Oxford include allusions, names and possible biographical references. Many references can be found in *Monstrous Adversary*, Alan Nelson's biography of Oxford:

- The play has detailed, precise legal references (Sokol & Sokol); Oxford trained at Gray's Inn (Nelson 46).
- The gravedigger's puns on *felo de se* may be an allusion to Oxford killing an under-cook in Burghely's household in 1567; the verdict of the jury was that the cook committed *felo de se* (Nelson 48).
- The play alludes to *Cardanus' Comfort*. Bedingfield's 1573 translation of this work was dedicated to Oxford (Nelson 77).
- Osric parodies Lyly's *Euphues*; Oxford worked with Lyly (Nelson 183).
- There are references to young players, "eyases"; Oxford had a company of boy players (Nelson 247–8).
- There are musical images; Oxford was an accomplished composer (Nelson 382).
- The pirate scene; Oxford had been captured by pirates and set ashore in his shirt (Nelson 135).
- Hamlet's confidant in the play is Horatio, and another character is Francisco; Oxford had cousins called Horace and Francis, who were known as the Fighting Veres (Nelson 169–71).
- There is reference to "a falling out at tennis" in the play; Oxford had a tennis court quarrel with Philip Sidney (Nelson 195).

Further internal references in the play link Polonius (Corambis) to Oxford's guardian and father-in-law, William Cecil, Lord Burghley (references can be found in Conyers Read's two volume biography):

- Polonius offers precepts for the behaviour of Laertes when abroad; Burghley, Oxford's father-in-law, wrote similar precepts for his sons (Read, *Cecil*, 214; *Burghley*, 304).
- Polonius asks Reynaldo to spy on Laertes; Burghley arranged for his elder son Thomas to be spied upon in Paris (Chambers, *WS*, I, 418; Beckingsale, 92).
- Polonius is a "fishmonger"; Burghley protected the English fishing fleet by insisting on 'fish-days' (Read, *Cecil*, 272–3).

Finally, Sigmund Freud was much struck by Hamlet's predicament and Oedipus complex, which he described in *The Interpretation of Dreams* (1900), linking the play to William Shakespeare's family background in Stratford-upon-Avon (see Thompson & Taylor's introduction). However, by the time he wrote his autobiography in 1925, (translated as *Autobiographical Study*, 1927), Freud had come to the conclusion that the plays of 'Shakespeare' had been written by Edward de Vere, Earl of Oxford. Sally Hazelton reports that, like many others, Freud saw a huge correlation between the situation of Hamlet and the life of the Earl of Oxford.

## Oxfordian Date – External Evidence

Further links to Oxford include:

- Oxford knew Latin, Italian and French, the languages of the sources. (Nelson, 37; 155–7).
- *Hamlet* was played at universities; Oxford's Men had been recommended in Cambridge. (Nelson, 244).
- Oxford was known to write plays; none survive unless anonymous or under another name.
- Oxford was a commissioner at the trial of Mary Queen of Scots (Nelson 302).
- Burghley's brother-in-law, Sir Thomas Hoby, made an English translation of *The Courtier*; Oxford's friend, Bartholomew Clerke, made a Latin version. This text described a Renaissance courtier and was very influential on *Hamlet*. (Nelson, 277)
- Elizabeth's dilemma about how a prince can take the life of another ruler exactly parallels Hamlet's; Oxford was a courtier.
- Elizabeth delayed until she was certain of the threats against her own life; so does Hamlet. (Chambers sees Gertrude as "certainly not a Lady Macbeth" and guiltless of any knowledge of Claudius's crime, tending to support Plumptre's 1796 reading).
- Belleforest was a political anti-English, anti-Protestant writer and aware of Burghley and Oxford; Belleforest was a source for *Hamlet*.[12]

These points, both internally and externally referring to the play, vary in force. Some are general rather than specific to *Hamlet*, but their accumulative impact and close connection with Oxford is disconcerting at the least, and they support an earlier date.

Access to the recognised sources for the play is also disconcerting: where did the author read the vast range of texts? These sources, however, were readily available to Oxford. He purchased a copy of Plutarch's *Lives* in 1569, which was also in the library of Sir Thomas Smith (Oxford's tutor). Oxford purchased a Geneva Bible in 1569, which has been identified as the copy held by the Folger Library in Washington. The Folger copy, which has the Blue Boar and coronet of Oxford on its cover, contains about 200 underlinings and various annotations. Roger Stritmatter has demonstrated this copy to be a very significant source for Shakespearean studies. For instance, Ezekiel 16:49, the only verse marked between chapters three and sixteen, begins: "Beholde, this was the iniquite of thy sister Sodom, Pride, fulness of bread . . . ." This reference to dying in a sinful, gluttonous state is echoed in Hamlet's words at 3.3.80 about his uncle murdering his father after lunch: "A took my father grossly, full of bread." Shaheen notes that this allusion is one of the specific instances where Shakespeare used the Geneva Bible, since the Coverdale, Matthew, Tavener, Great and Bishops' Bibles all have "fulnesse of meate".

Smith's library also held Saxo's treatise (1566 edition). One of the most significant Renaissance libraries belonged to William Cecil, Lord Burghley; Oxford was a member of Burghley's household from about the age of twelve in 1562 (when Burghley became his guardian), until 1575 when Oxford went on his continental travels. We know that Belleforest's *Histoires Tragiques* (volume II; we do not know about volume V) was in Burghley's library, as was Juvenal's *Tenth Satire,* Paul Iovii's *Eulogia Virorum Bellica Virtute Illustrium* dated 1551, and Erasmus's *Moriae Encomium* (*In Praise of Folly*) in several different editions. Burghley's library also held other sources relevant to *Hamlet,* such as Seneca, Plautus, Livy, Virgil, and Baldasarre Castiglione's *Il Cortegiano* in Italian.

Even more closely linked to Oxford is the Latin version of *The Courtier* because he wrote a warm and elegant dedication to Bartholomew Clerke's translation of it. Oxford's writing here demonstrates his use of rhetorical features such as doubling devices, oppositional pairs and hendiadys, all features of the text of *Hamlet.* Thomas Bedingfield dedicated his 1573 translation of *Cardanus Comfort* to the young earl and Oxford's eloquent reply is printed in the prefatory material.

Other possible sources of knowledge to which Oxford was privy include medical studies; his tutor, Sir Thomas Smith was interested in medicine and had appropriate books. Oxford also visited Padua, the most important place in European for the study of medicine at the time. Moreover, Burghley's gardener of twenty years, John Gerard, had travelled past Denmark's coast as well as producing in 1597 his *Herbal,* a history of plants in which there are illustrations to, for instance, "long purples".

Finally, a bright star is described by Bernardo at 1.1.35:

> When yond same star that's westward from the pole
> Had made his course t'illume that part of heaven
> Where now it burns . . .

This star has been identified with a supernova, SN 1572, which was observed at Wittenberg in 1572 and described by the Danish astronomer, Tycho Brahe. Brahe was known to Oxford's brother-in-law, Peregrine Willoughby d'Evesby, who visited Denmark five times on official government business between 1582 and 1585.[11] Any reference to this unusual star was no longer topical by 1600.

## Conclusion

The play can be dated to any time between the latest source, probably Timothy Bright's *A Treatise of Melancholy,* 1586, and the entry in the Stationers' Register in 1602.

An early date for composition around 1587 follows a straightforward acceptance of the allusions to the play from 1589 (Nashe), 1594 (Henslowe), 1596 (Lodge), 1598 (Henslowe), 1598–1602 (Harvey), and around 1600–02 (Pudsey). The earliest publication of the short form of the play, known as Ql, was sufficiently popular in 1603, for a revised version, Q2, to be printed in 1604. Some orthodox scholars accept an early date *c.* 1588.

Furthermore, the allusions and topicality of *Hamlet* mean that its most likely date of composition and first performance is early 1587. It could have been written as a satirical portrait of the then unpopular Lord Burghley (banned from Queen Elizabeth's presence for four months after the rapid execution of Mary Queen of Scots), and perhaps even with the distinct purpose of presenting Gertrude as innocent of the death of a sovereign, as Elizabeth wished to be innocent of the death of Mary, and with *Hamlet* reflecting the delays and dilemma of Elizabeth all those years she kept Mary prisoner. Arguably, the moment of decision for Hamlet comes when he discovers the intent of Claudius to take Hamlet's life, just as Elizabeth's moment of decision to proceed against Mary came when she was finally convinced that Mary had sought to take her (Elizabeth's) life.

Not only does an earlier date make straightforward sense of all the dates around *Hamlet*, but it also establishes Shakespeare as a great writer at about the same time as Marlowe, his contemporary, was writing. It would make Shakespeare a reviser of this play at least – and it would mean that he did not, after a good decade's experience of playwriting, suddenly write in around 1600 a play (Q2) that was too long for the theatre and had to be abridged (Q1), a rather peculiar situation that scholars have to acknowledge if Q2 really did precede Q1.

There are only two minor difficulties to prevent scholars accepting a later date. Firstly, Meres omitted to mention *Hamlet* in his *Palladis Tamia* (1598). Meres, however, was far from comprehensive: he had similarly omitted Shakespeare's three plays about the reign of Henry VI (although the reference to the "tiger's heart" seemed famous, according to its mention in *Greene's Groatsworth of Wit*); nor does he mention any play about Hamlet although the contemporary evidence shows that Hamlet's revenge was famous. Secondly, Malone originally suggested a date for *Hamlet c.* 1600 on very slender grounds and many subsequent editors have followed this 'established' date.

The evidence appears to support an early date around 1587–9.

## Notes

1. A shorter version of this chapter appeared in *Great Oxford*, ed. R Malim, 2004.
2. The label 'Bad Quarto' is examined by Irace (see 'Relationship of Q1, Q2 and F1', below) and by Lukas Erne, *Shakespeare as a Literary Dramatist*, 2003, 80–86. The term 'bad Quarto' was coined by A. W. Pollard, *Shakespeare Folios and*

*Quartos*, 1909, and has been widely accepted since, e.g. by Chambers.

3. The first four allusions are considered by Chambers, *WS*, I, 408-425 and by Thompson and Taylor, 44-48.
4. Edward Pudsey's *Book of Commonplaces* MS in the Bodleian Library contains extracts from various writers including Shakespeare. There is an abridgement, Shakespearean extracts from "Edward Pudsey's books" by Richard Savage, 1888, reprinted in1910. J. Rees offers a date for the manuscript in "Shakespeare and Edward Pudsey's *Booke*, 1600", *Notes and Queries* 237, 1992, 330–1.
5. Frederick Boas, *University Drama in the Tudor Age* (1914: 277) states that both the Queen's Men and the Lord Admiral's Men performed in Oxford between 1589 and 1591. Fuller details, taken from the audited accounts in the Oxford municipal archives, are in his article "Hamlet at Oxford" in the *Fortnightly Review* for August 1913.
6. The original portrait is in the Galleria degli Uffizi in Florence.
7. Richard Simpson, *Edmund Campion,* (1866: 145) describes the court of Elizabeth in the years after 1576, noting "the counsellors: the mysterious Burghley, in whom the world discovered a Solon, while Shakespeare more truly painted him as Polonius".
8. Rowse writes (1989): "Polonius had his worldly wise Precepts; those with which Burghley equipped his son . . . Whether Polonius was Burghley or no, Burghley was certainly a Polonius."
9. J. Dover Wilson (1934) states: "The figure of Polonius is almost without doubt intended as a caricature of Burleigh [*sic*]."
10. See Marcus Woodward (ed.),*Gerard's herbal. The history of plants* London, Senate 1994).
11. On the marriage of Lady Mary Vere to Peregrine Bertie, Lord Willoughby d' Eresby (early in 1578), see Alan Nelson, 179. For the embassies to Denmark, see Charles Henry Parry (ed.), *A Memoir of Peregrine Bertie* who states (2008: 41): "She [Elizabeth] sent the Order of the Garter to Frederick II, King of Denmark, and Peregrine, Lord Willoughby, to invest him with it. He staid some time in Denmark . . ." A personal letter of Willoughby is accompanied by a list including the names of Rosencrantz and Guildenstern (British Library: Cotton MSS Titus C VII 224–29).
12. This reference occurs in a tract published in 1572: *L'innocence de la tres illustre tres-chaste, et debonnaire Princesse, Madame Marie Royne d'Ecosse* . . . (a copy of which is held by the British Library at shelfmark 600.d.19). This book, attributed to Francois Belleforest, George Buchanan and John Leslie, Bishop of Ross, protests the innocence of Mary Queen of Scots.

## Other Cited Works


Alexander, P. (ed.), *Shakespeare: the Complete Works,* London: HarperCollins, 1983

Bate, J., *The Genius of Shakespeare*, London: Picador, 1997

Beckingsale, B. W., *Burghley: Tudor Statesman*, London: Macmillan, 1967

Bloom, Harold, *Shakespeare: The Invention of the Human*, New York: Riverhead Books 1998

Bullough, G., *Narrative and Dramatic Sources of Shakespeare,* vol. VII, London: Routledge and Kegan Paul, 1973

Cairncross, A. S., *The Problem of 'Hamlet': A Solution.* London: Macmillan and Co., 1936
Cantor, Paul A., *Shakespeare, Hamlet,* Cambridge: CUP, 2004
Chambers, E. K. (ed.), *Hamlet. The Arden Shakespeare,* Boston: Heath and Co, 1902
—, *William Shakespeare: A Study of Facts and Problems,* 2 vols, Oxford: Clarendon Press, 1930
Clark, E. T., *Hidden Allusions in Shakespeare's Plays,* New York: William Farquhar Payson, 1931
Edwards, Philip (ed.), *Hamlet,* Cambridge: CUP, 1985
Elze, K. F. (ed.), *Hamlet* (with critical notes), German ed. 1857; English trans. 1882
Furness, H. H., *A New Variorum Edition of Shakespeare: vol IV part 2 Hamlet,* London: Lippincott, 1877. Reprinted by Classic Books, 2001.
Halliday, F. E., *A Shakespeare Companion,* London: Duckworth and Co., 1955
Hazelton, Sally, "Freud and Oxford", *Great Oxford,* Malim, R. (ed.), Tunbridge Wells: Parapress, 2004
Hibbard, G. R. (ed.), *Hamlet,* The Oxford Shakespeare, Oxford: OUP, 1987
Holland, H. H., *Shakespeare, Oxford and Elizabethan Times,* London; D. Archer, 1933
Honigmann, E. A. J., "The Date of *Hamlet*", *Shakespeare Survey,* 9, 1956: 24–34
—, *Shakespeare: the 'lost years',* Manchester: MUP, 1985
Irace, Kathleen (ed.), *The First Quarto of Hamlet,* Cambridge: CUP, 1998
Jenkins, H. (ed.), *Hamlet,* London: Methuen Arden, 1982
Kermode, F., *Shakespeare's Language,* Harmondsworth: Penguin, 2001
Matus, I., *Shakespeare, IN FACT,* New York: Continuum, 1997
Nelson, Alan, *Monstrous Adversary: The Life of Edward de Vere, seventeenth earl of Oxford,* Liverpool: Liverpool University Press, 2004
Read, Conyers, *Mr Secretary Cecil and Queen Elizabeth,* London: Jonathan Cape, 1955
—, *Lord Burghley and Queen Elizabeth,* London: Jonathan Cape, 1960
Rowse, A. L., *Discovering Shakespeare,* London: Weidenfeld & Nicolson, 1989
Sams, Eric, *The Real Shakespeare,* New Haven: Yale UP, 1995
Shaheen, Naseeb, *Biblical Allusions in Shakespeare's Plays,* Newark: University of Delaware Press, 1999
Simpson, R., *Edmund Campion,* London: 1866
Sokol, B. J. & Mary Sokol, *Shakespeare's Legal Language: a dictionary,* London: Athlone Press, 2004
Somogyi de, Nick (ed.), *Hamlet: The Shakespeare Folios,* London: Nick Hern Books, 2001
Stritmatter, R., *The Marginalia of Edward de Vere's Geneva Bible,* Northhampton: Oxenford Press, 2003
Strype, J., *The Life of the Learned Sir Thomas Smith,* Oxford: Clarendon Press, 1820
Thompson Ann, and Neil Taylor (eds), *Hamlet,* London: Arden Shakespeare, 2006
Ward, B. M., *The Seventeenth Earl of Oxford,* London: John Murray, 1928
Wells, S. & Taylor, G. *The Oxford Shakespeare,* Oxford, OUP, 1986
—, *William Shakespeare: a textual companion,* Oxford: OUP, 1987
Wilson, John Dover (ed.), *Hamlet,* Cambridge: CUP, 1934
—, *What Happens in 'Hamlet',* Cambridge: CUP, 1964
Winstanley, L., *Hamlet and the Scottish Succession,* Cambridge: CUP, 1921

# 33

# The Tragedie of King Lear

## Alastair Everitt

K*ing Lear* can be dated between 1590 (the publication of Sidney's *Arcadia*) and 1606, when it was performed at court.

### Publication Date

The play was entered in the Stationers' Register on 26 November 1607 by Nathaniel Butter and John Busby:

> [SR] 26 Novembris. Nathanael Butter John Busby. Entred for their Copie under thandes of Sir George Buck knight and Thwardens A booke called. Master William Shakespeare his historye of Kinge Lear, as yt was played before the kinges maiestie at Whitehall vppon Sainct Stephans night at christmas Last, by his maiesties servantes playinge vsually at the globe on Banksyde vj$^{d}$

The first quarto was published in 1608, printed by Nicholas Okes for Butter:

> [Q1] M. William Shak-speare: HIS True Chronicle Historie of the life and death of King LEAR and his three Daughters. *With the vnfortunate* life of Edgar, *sonne* and heire to the Earle of Gloster, and his sullen and assumed humor of Tom of Bedlam: *As it was played before the Kings Maiestie at Whitehall vpon S.* Stephans *night in Christmas Hollidayes.* By his Maiesties seruants playing vsually at the Gloabe on the Bancke-side. London, Printed [by Nicholas Okes] for *Nathaniel Butter*, and are to be sold at his shop in *Pauls* Church-yard at the signe of the Pide Bull neere St. *Austins* Gate, 1608.

The second quarto is also dated 1608, although it was not printed until 1619 (one of the Pavier collection of ten plays, dated by Chambers, *WS*, I, 133, to 1619):

> [Q2] M. William Shake-speare, his true chronicle history of the life and death of King Lear, and his three daughters. With the vnfortunate life of Edgar, sonne and heire to the Earle of Glocester, and his sullen and assumed humour of Tom of Bedlam. As it was plaied before the Kings Maiesty at White-hall, vppon S. Stephens night, in Christmas hollidaies. By his Maiesties seruants, playing vsually at the Globe on the Banck-side. [London]: Printed [by William Jaggard] for Nathaniel Butter, 1608 [i.e. 1619].

Q2 was printed from the shorter Q1, but includes many changes, introduces corrections, and creates some further errors.

In the First Folio of 1623, the title is changed from "history" to "tragedy", and the folio text differs from Q1 in numerous details, some substantial. It lacks nearly 300 lines found in Q1, and has more than 100 lines not found in the quarto. Wells & Taylor in *The Oxford Shakespeare Complete Works* print both versions, arguing that Q1 and F1 were based on different copies, a decision which has subsequently been accepted by most editors, e.g. Foakes. Halio does not attempt to conflate the two texts but believes that they have equal authority, Q derived from Shakespeare's rough drafts, F derived from a manuscript used in the playhouses during the seventeenth century.[1]

## Performance Dates

There was a performance before King James on 26 December 1606 (mentioned in the Stationers' Register in the 1607 entry). There is only one other record of a performance before the Restoration: the play was performed in 1610 at Gowthwaite Hall, Nidderdale, Yorkshire.[2]

## Relationship between *Leir* and *Lear*

There has been much debate and little agreement between scholars over the relationship between an anonymous play *The Chronicle of King Leir* and Shakespeare's play in Q1 and F1 above.

Adam Islip recorded in the Stationers' Register on 14 May 1594:

> [SR 1594] The moste famous Chronicle historye of LEIRE king of England and his Three Daughters

Islip's name was subsequently crossed out and the name of Edward White, a fellow stationer, was added. The play was not published at this time and it was registered again on 8 May 1605 by Simon Stafford:

> [SR 1605] the Tragecall historie of kinge LEIR and his Three Daughters

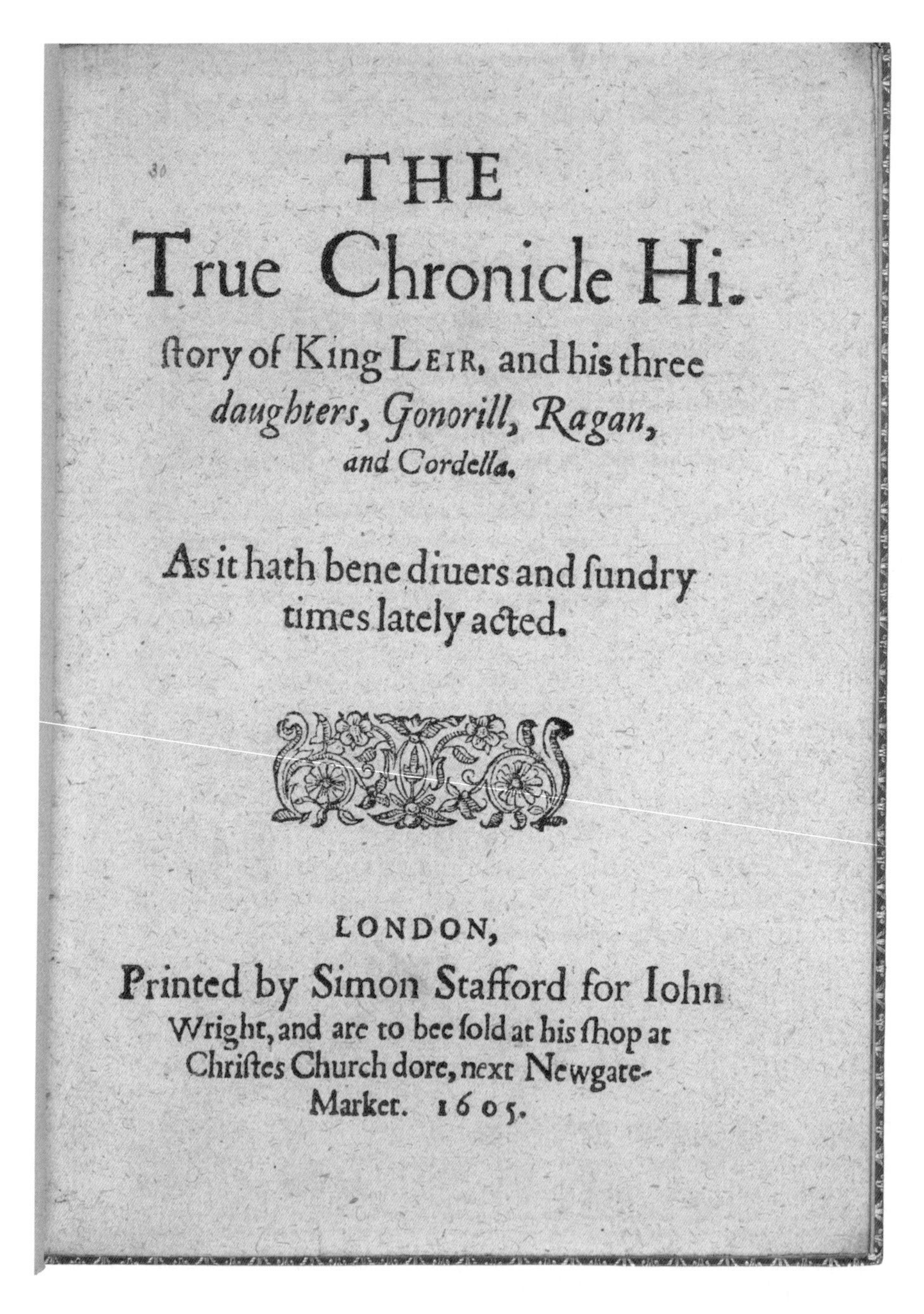

THE
True Chronicle Hi-
ſtory of King Leir, and his three
*daughters, Gonorill, Ragan,*
*and Cordella.*

As it hath bene diuers and ſundry
times lately acted.

LONDON,
Printed by Simon Stafford for Iohn
Wright, and are to bee ſold at his ſhop at
Chriſtes Church dore, next Newgate-
Market. 1605.

25. The title page to the anonymous quarto of *The True Chronicle History of King Leir*, 1605. It has generally been believed that this play was by another author but some scholars have argued that it was an early version by Shakespeare, which he later revised into *King Lear*.
By permission of the Folger Shakespeare Library.

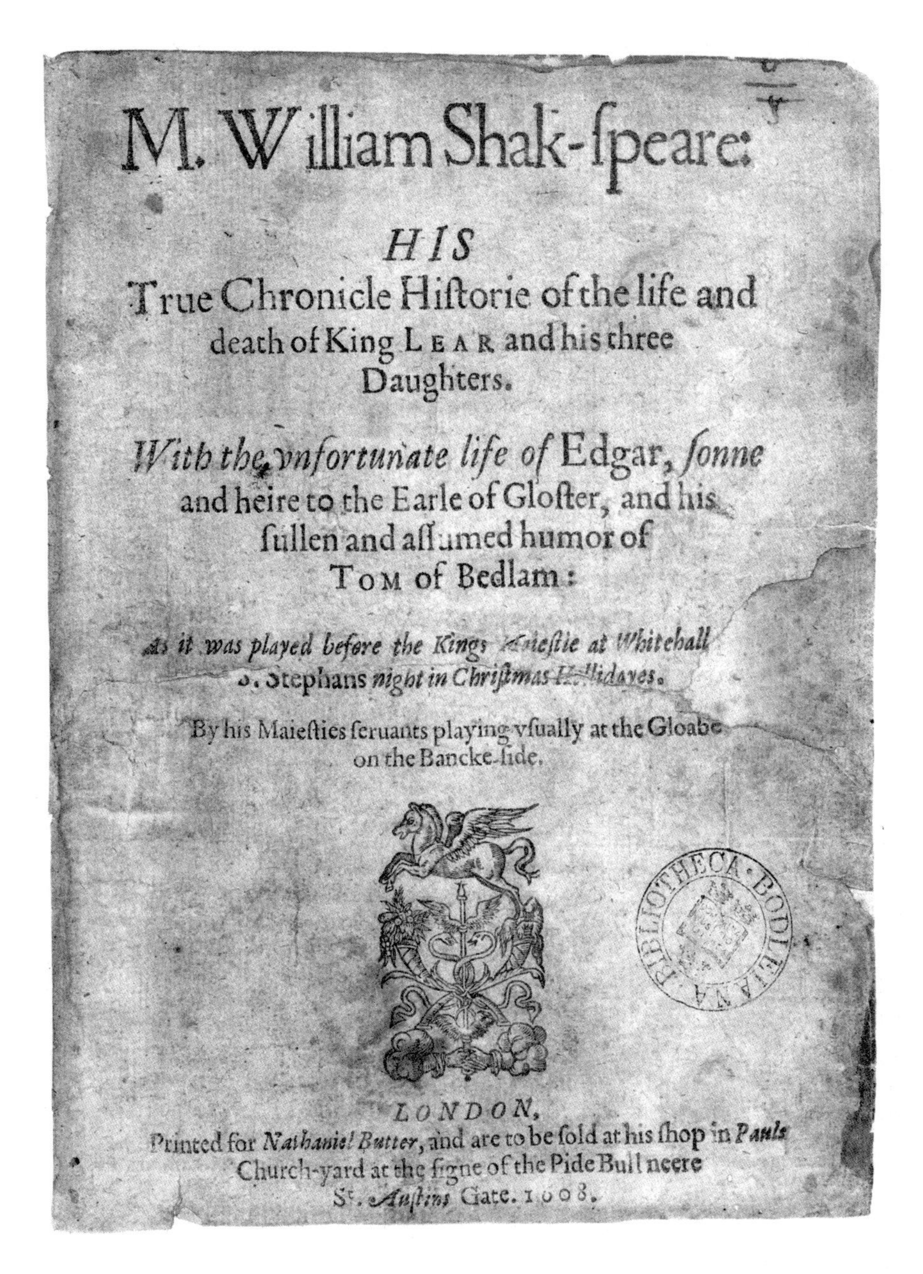

M. William Shak-ſpeare:

HIS

True Chronicle Hiſtorie of the life and death of King LEAR and his three Daughters.

*With the vnfortunate life of* Edgar, *ſonne* and heire to the Earle of Gloſter, and his ſullen and aſſumed humor of TOM of Bedlam:

*As it was played before the Kings Maieſtie at Whitehall* vpon S. Stephans *night in Chriſtmas Hollidayes.*

By his Maieſties ſeruants playing vſually at the Gloabe on the Bancke-ſide.

*LONDON,*

Printed for *Nathaniel Butter*, and are to be ſold at his ſhop in *Pauls* Church-yard at the ſigne of the Pide Bull neere St. *Auſtins* Gate. 1608.



26. The title page to the First Quarto of *Chronicle History of King Lear*, 1608. For a long time in the twentieth century, it was generally believed that this was an inferior version, derived from the Folio text. More recently, the consensus has been that this play was an early version by Shakespeare, which he later revised. By permission of Bodleian Library, University of Oxford, shelfmark Arch. G d.42 TP (6), title page.

It was printed later in the year by Simon Stafford for John Wright:

> [Q] The true Chronicle History of King Leir and his three *daughters, Gonorill, Ragan and Cordella.* As it hath bene divers and sundry times lately acted. LONDON, Printed by Simon Stafford for John Wright, and are to bee sold at his shop at Christes Church dore, next Newgate Market. 1605.

There was no further edition.

Various authors have been suggested for *The Chronicle of King Leir*, including Kyd, Greene, Peele, Lodge, Munday and Shakespeare.[3]

It is generally assumed that the ownership of *The Chronicle of King Leir* passed from the Queen's Men to the Chamberlain's Men and then to the King's Men, where it was rewritten by Shakespeare. Henslowe recorded that *Kinge Leare* was performed by a cast drawn from both the Queen's Men and the Sussex Men at the Rose Theatre on 6 and 8 April 1594. Chambers suggests that this is the anonymous *Chronicle of King Leir* and that the play was in the repertory of the Queen's Men. In May 1594, the Queen's Men gave up playing in London and sold a number of their plays to other companies. The Lord Chamberlain's Men began in 1594 with "a repertory derived from inheritance or purchase from antecedent companies" (Chambers). The Chamberlain's Men were re-formed as the King's Men in 1603.

Cairncross, however, argues that there was another play about King Lear in the 1590s, as the copyright of *King Leir* (asserted in the SR of 1594) remained with the Edward White family from 1594 until 29 June 1624 when *Leire and his daughters* was transferred from White's widow to E. Alde. Since there is no possibility of Edward White and the Lord Chamberlain's Men sharing the ownership of one single play, he argues that there must have been two separate plays in the 1590s, one of which was Shakespeare's.

## Sources

There are over forty versions of the story of King Lear, starting (as noted by Muir in 1966: xxxvi) with that of Hugh of Huntingdon in 1139. His tale is included in Holinshed's *Chronicles* (1577); Spenser's *Faerie Queene* (1596) describes how Lear gives all his land away.[4] In the *Arcadia* (1590) Philip Sidney introduces Gloucester and his sons. The anonymous play *The Chronicle of King Leir* (registered in 1594, but dated by Greg and Bullough *c.* 1590) is taken as a source by most scholars, who view it as by another hand. Some see *The Chronicle of King Leir* as an early version of Shakespeare's play.

## Orthodox Dates

Chambers proposed 1605 as the date of composition of Shakespeare's *King Lear* and the date 1605–6 has generally found acceptance. Foakes comments: "There is no direct evidence to show when it was written or first performed" (1997: 89–90). They agree that *King Lear* as we know it could not have been written before John Florio's translation of Montaigne's *Essays* (1603) and the publication of Samuel Harsnett's *A Declaration of Egregious Popish Impostures* (also 1603). The Montaigne translation is seen as important because Florio and Shakespeare sometimes use similar words and phrases and the play contains elements of Montaigne's sceptical philosophy. Harsnett is significant because the Mad Tom scenes contain references to devils such as Frateretto, Flibbertigibbet, Mahu, Modo and Smulkin, which are mentioned in the *Declaration*.

Gloucester's references to "these late eclipses of the sun and moon" (1.2.90) is usually taken to refer to the two such eclipses in September and October 1605; but such co-occurrences were also recorded in July 1590, February 1598 and November/December 1601.[5]

Cairncross defies the consensus by dating Shakespeare's play between 1590 and 1594.

## Oxfordian Dates

Clark suggests various historical parallels and writes that the "historic allusions in *King Lear* all point to 1589 or 1590" (1974: 887).

## External Oxfordian Evidence

Shakespeare is often presented as a follower rather than a leader in the cultural richness of the Elizabethan age. Foakes, puts it thus: "it often seems to be taken for granted that Shakespeare never invented when he could borrow, and searching for the 'sources' of Shakespeare's plays has long been a minor scholarly industry" (1997: 92–93). He continues: "the philosophical, religious, social and political issues can rarely be traced to a particular source; for the most part it is more helpful to think in terms of influences or contexts". However, Foakes does think (1997: 93) that perhaps the only degree of certainty in dating the composition of the play "is that Shakespeare could not have written it" before the publication of Harsnett and of Florio's translation of Montaigne, both published in 1603.

Montaigne's work was published in France in 1580, 1588, and in 1595. Oxford was an accomplished scholar, could read and speak French fluently, had easy access to libraries, and purchased important books (Nelson: 53). He could read Montaigne in the original long before Florio's 1603 translation. Montaigne would also have been read by other scholars in the original, and his ideas and philosophy would have been known by many before Florio's translation.

Harsnett offers a far more revealing and interesting challenge because of the many references and phrases found in *King Lear* that are also found in his *Declaration*. Orthodoxy has continued to take this as proof that *King Lear* was written after 1603, whereas, as long ago as 1965, Gwyneth Bowen showed that there is evidence in Harsnett that anyone could have had access to much of the information and phraseology in the *Declaration* long before 1603. How many modern Shakespearean commentators have read Harsnett?

The exorcisms exposed in the *Declaration* took place between 1585 and 1586. It was to be a busy year! From May 1586 the exorcists began to be arrested. In August 1586 the Babington Plot arrests were made. And in October 1586 Mary Queen of Scots was tried and sentenced to death by a tribunal on which the Earl of Oxford served. Oxford was therefore at the centre of events and would have been well aware of the activities and arrests of exorcists.

Harsnett's own main source was what he called the *Miracle Booke*. This turned up in 1594, when an intrepid Catholic named Robert Barnes was arrested. He was jailed and in 1598 wrote to Robert Cecil about a "book of exorcisms" found on him at his arrest and being displayed to people by his jailor. Barnes claimed he had only made a copy at the request of a friend. The book was passed on to Bishop Bancroft and Harsnett. This is the *Miracle Booke* from which Harsnett quotes so lavishly.

Harsnett wrote as follows:

> And that this declaration may be free from the carpe and cavill of ill-affected, or decomposed spirits, I have alledged nothing for materiall, or authenticall herein, but the expresse words eyther of some part of the *Miracle booke*, penned by the priests and filed upon Record, where it is publique to be seene, or els a clause of theyr confessions who were fellow actors in this impious dissimulation.

The *Miracle Booke*, along with witnesses' depositions, became part of the archives of Ecclesiastical Court of the High Commission. Alas, that archive was destroyed during the Civil War. There would have been several copies of the various parts of the work; perhaps one day another copy or version will come to light. Be that as it may, we do know that the *Miracle Booke*, in one version or another, was in circulation before 1594, that no small part of the *Declaration* was taken from it, and that Oxford (if Shakespeare) would not have had to wait until 1603 before writing his Mad Tom sequences.

Apart from Oxford's involvement in events involving Catholics in 1580, there is yet another remarkable coincidence. In the *Declaration*, Harsnett mentions eighteen times that Lord Vaux's house in Hackney, called King's Place, was one of the locations of the exorcisms. Lord Vaux was a recusant who, in 1580, had offered asylum to Edmund Campion and later sheltered many others. He was financially ruined by his recusancy and died in 1595. In 1596, King's Place was transferred to Oxford's second wife, Elizabeth Trentham, who allowed Lady Vaux to continue to live in the house. Before this, Oxford and his new wife had been living in Stoke Newington, the parish adjacent to Hackney, ever since his second marriage in 1591, and they were very possibly friendly with the Vaux, who might well have held a copy of the *Miracle Booke.*

Another possible reference concerns what is usually known as the Annesley case. Brian Annesley, an aged and long-serving court servant, made his will in 1601, giving the bulk of his property to his youngest and unmarried daughter Cordell who lived with him. The two older married sisters received considerably less. In 1603 he became senile and one of the married and less well-off sisters, Grace, attempted to have him committed. Cordell opposed the move and successfully appealed to Robert Cecil to allow a friend to take charge of her father's financial affairs.

Duncan-Jones regrets the fact that most scholars "have played down the relevance of the Annesley case". She is convinced that the Annersley case "was the immediate trigger for both the revival of the old *Leir*, on stage and in print, and for Shakespeare's radical re-writing of it on behalf of the King's Men" (2001: 187).

Duncan-Jones is mainly persuaded because of the "extraordinary coincidence" that Annesley's third daughter was called Cordell (187). It is difficult to follow her reasoning as *King Leir* has Goorill, Ragan and Cordella; Holinshed has Gonorilla, Regan and Cordeilla, and Edmund Spenser offers Gonorill, Regan and Cordeill. The argument of Duncan-Jones ignores also the probability that the *King Leir* play registered by Edward White in 1594 and the *Kinge Leare* performed by the Queen's Men in 1594 were two different plays.

## Conclusion

The early 1590s seems most likely as the date of first composition of the play. The much more generally accepted later dating depends upon the relevant works of Montaigne and Harsnett being unavailable prior to 1603; but, as we have seen above, both were, in fact, available earlier than 1603.

We have a Henslowe entry noting two performances in 1594. These are without the name of Shakespeare, but many plays began life anonymously and Henslowe never mentioned the name 'Shakespeare' or any of its variants. The Henslowe *Kinge Leare* of 1594 could well have incorporated passages based on the writings of Spenser, Sidney, Montaigne, and the passages Harsnett extracted from the *Miracle Booke.*[6]

## Notes

1. Halio (2005: 58–74) has an extended discussion on the alternative theories proffered since the dismissal of "early theories" which "held that [the Q text]... was a reported text of some kind, a version of the play taken down from memory ('memorial reconstruction') or by shorthand by someone in the theatre" (59). Halio identifies Steven Urkowitz's study, *Shakespeare's Revision of 'King Lear'*, as the first successfully to disprove theories of "memorial contamination", concluding that "Q was printed directly from Shakespeare's drafts and not from a transcript of them" (61), thereby restoring the Q text to a position of authority. Lawrie Maguire in *Shakespeare's Suspect Texts* (1996) gives a detailed argument for the same conclusion.
2. C. J. Sisson reported this performance in *Lost Plays of Shakespeare's Age* (1936: 4), having examined the records of the recusancy trials in Yorkshire. Wells and Taylor note that, as the record refers to *King Lere*, this might have been either *King Leir* or *King Lear*, since both versions were in print by 1610.
3. See Logan & Smith (1973: 219–20).
4. Foakes (1997: 95–6) suggests that it is probable that Shakespeare knew Spenser's *Faerie Queene* where in Book 2, Canto 10, "a chronicle of British kings includes a brief rehearsal of the story of Leyr and his daughters which includes two variants from the traditional narrative that had an influence on King Lear." These Foakes identifies as the revision of the name Cordeilla into Cordelia and the specificity of Spenser's version of Cordelia's death. In Spenser, Cordelia hangs herself (2006: 252) and in *King Lear*, Edmund orders that Cordelia be hanged (In the F text, 5.3.226–30; in the Q text, 5.3.248–51).
5. H. H. Furness. *Shakespeare: King Lear,* New Variorum edition 1880, p. 369.
6. Details and descriptions of Oxford's life can be found in Nelson: his knowledge of French (37), at the trial of Mary, Queen of Scots (302–3), his inclination towards Catholicism (248–59), his move to King's Place, Hackney (368) and his acquaintance with Holinshed (90–92). Stephen Greenblatt questions the direction of influence between Harsnett and *King Lear*. In "Shakespeare and the Exorcists" in J. L. Halio (ed.), *Critical Essays on Shakespeare's King Lear*. New York, 1996, Greenblatt writes "When Shakespeare borrows from Harsnett, who knows if Harsnett has not already, in a deep sense, borrowed from Shakespeare's theatre what Shakespeare borrows back?"

## Other Works Cited

Bowen, G., "Hackney, Harsnett and the Devils in King Lear", *Shakespearean Authorship Review,* 14 Autumn number, 1965

Brownlow, F. W., *Shakespeare, Harsnett and the Devils of Denham*, Newark NJ: Associated University Press, 1993

Bullough, G., *Narrative and Dramatic Sources of Shakespeare,* vol. VII. London: Routledge, 1973

Cairncross, A. S., *The Problem of Hamlet: A Solution*, London: Macmillan & Co. 1936

Chambers, E. K. *William Shakespeare: a study of facts and problems*, 2 vols, Oxford:

Clarendon Press, 1930

Clark, Eva Turner, *Hidden Allusions in Shakespeare's Plays*, New York: Kennikat, (1931) rptd 1974

Duncan-Jones, Katherine, *Ungentle Shakespeare: Scenes from his Life*, London: Arden Shakespeare, 2001

Foakes, R. A., *King Lear*, London: Methuen Arden Shakespeare, 1997

Greg, W. W., *Variants in the First Quarto of King Lear: A Bibliographial and Critical Inquiry*, Oxford: OUP, 1940

Halio, Jay (ed.), *The Tragedy of King Lear*, Cambridge: CUP, 2005

Harsnett, Samuel, *A Declaration of Egregious Popish Impostures, to with-draw the harts of her Majesties Subjects from their allegeance, and from the truth of Christian Religion professed in England, under the pretence of casting out Devils. Practised by Edmunds, Alias Weston, a Jesuit, and divers Romish Priests his wicked associates. Where-unto are annexed the Copies of the Confessions, and Examinations of the parties themselves, which were pretended to be possessed, and dispossessed, taken upon oath before her Majesties Commissioners, for Causes Ecclesiasticall,* London, 1603. (Reprinted in Brownlow, above)

Logan, Terence and Smith, Denzell, *The Predecessors of Shakespeare*, Lincoln: University of Nebraska Press, 1973

Muir, K. (ed.), *King Lear*, London: Methuen Arden Shakespeare, 1966

Muir, K., "Samuel Harsnett and *King Lear*", *Review of English Studies,* New Series 2.5, 1951

Nelson, A. H., *Monstrous Adversary*, Liverpool: LUP, 2003

Spenser, Edmund, *The Faerie Queene*, Hamilton, A. C. (ed.), Longman Annotated Editions, Pearson, 2006

Stone, P. W. K., *The Textual History of King Lear*, London: Scolar Press, 1980

Taylor, Gary and Michael Warren (eds), *The Division of the Kingdoms: Shakespeare's Two Versions of King Lear*, Oxford: OUP, 1983

Urkowitz, S., *Shakespeare's Revision of King Lear*, Guildford: Princeton University Press, 1980

Wells, Stanley (ed.), *King Lear*, Oxford: , OUP Shakespeare, 2000

Wells, S. & Taylor, G. *The Oxford Shakespeare*, Oxford: OUP, 1986

—, *William Shakespeare: a textual companion*, Oxford: OUP, 1987

THE

Tragœdy of Othello,

The Moore of Venice.

*As it hath beene diuerse times acted at the* Globe, and at the Black-Friers, by *his Maiesties Seruants.*

*Written by* VVilliam Shakespeare.

*LONDON,*

Printed by *N. O.* for *Thomas Walkley*, and are to be sold at his shop, at the Eagle and Child, in Brittans Bursse.

1622.

27. Title page to the first quarto of *Othello,* 1622
By permission of Bodleian Library, University of Oxford, shelfmark Arch. G d.43 (7), title page.

# 34

# The Tragedie of Othello, the Moore of Venice

Noemi Magri

*Othello* was composed some time between 1584 and 1604, after the publication of the French translation of Cinthio's *Hecatommithi* and before it was performed at court.

## Publication Dates

The play was entered into the Stationers' Register on 6th October 1621:

> [SR] 6° Octubris 1621. Thomas Walkley. Entred for his copie vnder the handes of Sir George Buck, and Master Swinhoe warden, the Tragedie of Othello, the moore of Venice. vj[d].

*Othello* was published in quarto (Q1) in 1622 and attributed to Shakespeare:

> [Q1] The tragœdy of Othello, the Moore of Venice. As it hath beene diuerse times acted at the Globe, and at the Black-Friers, by his Maiesties seruants. Written by William Shakespeare.
> London: printed by N. O. [Nicholas Okes] for Thomas Walkley, and are to be sold at his shop, at the Eagle and Child, in Brittans Bursse, 1622.

*Othello* was included among the tragedies of the First Folio of 1623, occupying the ninth position after *King Lear* and before *Antony & Cleopatra*, where it has the head title and running title 'The Tragedie of Othello, the Moore of Venice'. Chambers believes that Q1 and F1 are both good copies and derive from the same original. Honigmann however notes that Q1 and F1 differ in hundreds of readings and that F1 is longer by about 160 lines. He takes both to have authorial authority (1997: 2). A second quarto (Q2) appeared in 1630 and a third quarto, published 1655, was a reprint of Q2.

## Performance Date

The earliest performance of the play is usually taken as that mentioned in the Revels Accounts where "The Moor of Venis" by "Shaxberd" was recorded as being played "in the Banketinge house att Whit Hall on Hallowmas" (1 November) 1604, in the presence of the King and his wife. Hamilton has suspected the reference in the Revels Accounts to be a forgery, but most scholars accept it as authentic.[1]

It is possible that Henslowe's Diary records an earlier performance. On 14th December 1594, Henslowe entered into his diary "the mawe", a play which has not otherwise been identified, but might refer to an earlier performance of *The Mawe/Moor of Venice.* (This is discussed below, under Oxfordian dating.)

## Sources

The main source is an Italian novella, one of the stories (decade 3, story 7) from the *Hecatommithi*, by Giraldi Cinthio (1565). From this source, Shakespeare took the plot (the Moor's jealousy, the handkerchief trick, the Ensign's wickedness, the tragic death of the protagonists); the setting (Venice and Cyprus) and the main characters: Disdemona (the only named character), a Moorish captain (Capitano Moro), an ensign (alfieri) and a captain (capo di squadra). The many close linguistic parallels with the Italian source are evidence that Shakespeare had a very good knowledge of the Italian language. No English translation appeared until 1753, but a French translation by Gabriel Chappys was published in 1583/4. Neill asserts that Shakespeare almost certainly read it in the original Italian. Honigmann argues that Shakespeare knew both the Italian text (e.g. "acerb" 1.3.350, "ocular proof" 3.3.363) and the French translation (e.g. "heart-pierced" 1.3.220, "take out the work" 3.3.300).[2] Cinthio's collection of 100 tales had been inspired by Boccaccio's *Decameron* and was partly translated by William Painter in his *Palace of Pleasure* (1566–70) and in Barnaby Riche's *Farewell to Militarie Profession* (1581). Cinthio's *Hecatommithi* also provided the main plot for *Measure for Measure.* Thus, the year 1584 may be taken as the earliest time for a first version of *Othello,* assuming that the French derivations were part of the original.

It has also been suggested that Shakespeare used Sir Lewis Lewkenor's *The Commonwealth and Government of Venice* (1599). This work was a translation of a Latin treatise by Cardinal Gasparo Contarini called *De magistratibus et republicâ Venetorum*. Lewkenor's *Commonwealth* is generally considered to be the source of the dramatist's knowledge of Venetian institutions, such as the Doge's functions, the Government Boards, and the rulers of the city, but this is by no means certain. Honigmann believes that only one reference ("officers of the night" 1.1.184) in *Othello* is derived from Lewkenor, so the 1599

*Commonwealth* text is not an essential source.[3] There is no earlier description of Venetian institutions in English, so direct experience may have been the only source.

Since Shakespeare used words such as "cisterns" and "fountains", Bullough suggests that he had "almost certainly" consulted the 1600 translation by John Pory of John Leo Africanus's work, *A Geographical History of Africa*, with descriptions of cisterns and fountains in Fez. This debt does not seem very important: in almost every Italian *piazza* (square), there has been a fountain. In the middle of the 'campielli' in Venice there have always been cisterns (*cisterne*) to collect rain water. The Italian word is the same.

Another source for Shakespeare may have been Pliny's *Natural History* for the references in Othello's speech (1.3.128–169) to the Anthropophagi and to African deserts. A further reference to the flow of water from the Black Sea through the Bosphorus may have been inspired by this work:

> Like to the Pontic sea,
> Whose icy current and compulsive course
> Ne'er feels retiring ebb, but keeps due on
> To the Propontic and the Hellespont,
> Even so my bloody thoughts, with violent pace,
> Shall ne'er look back (3.3.456–61)

This striking image is thematically linked to Othello's role as a Venetian Captain. The dramatist may have derived the idea from Philemon Holland's 1601 translation of Pliny, but he could have read Pliny in the original Latin, as he had read Virgil's *Aeneid* for *The Rape of Lucrece* in 1594. It is also possible that the author picked up this piece of information from Venetian merchants who had sailed in the Sea of Marmaris (Propontis) towards Constantinople.

Direct influence of the *Aeneid* can be found in Othello's speech (1.3.128–169) where he recalls how Desdemona fell in love with him and shed tears at the narration of his past dangerous adventures by land and sea, of his deeds of courage and sorrowful misfortunes. In the same way was Dido deeply affected and moved to tears by Aeneas's pitiful story of his perilous voyage from Troy in flames to the African coast, of the Greeks' cruelties and of the Trojan defeat.

In Cinthio, there is nothing about a Turkish attack on Cyprus or Rhodes, which had taken place historically in 1570–1573. Wells & Taylor have argued that Shakespeare may have used Richard Knolles's *History of the Turks* (1603) for details of the Turkish naval movements, but this suggestion has been passed over by most commentators, e.g. Honigmann.[4] The political situation of the European States still threatened by the Turks in those years may have led the dramatist to reflect on the Venetian loss of Cyprus and its relevance to the history of the Republic. He may have wished to include the theme and to expand it into a detailed description.

## Orthodox Dates

There is very little evidence to identify a date for the play. Chambers accepts Malone's conjecture of 1604 (i.e. that the play was new when a performance at court was recorded, and says that it is "consonant with stylistic evidence". Ridley seems to accept 1604 without further argument. Wells & Taylor agree with 1603–4, citing some close verbal similarities with *Hamlet* which they date to 1601): Iago says: "I'll pour this pestilence into his ear" (2.3.347), which recalls the murder of Hamlet's father. Lodovico's closing comment in Othello, "Look on the tragic loading of this bed" (5.ii.373) echoes "looke upon this tragicke spectacle" at the end of Q1 *Hamlet* (1603). Hamlet, dying, says: "Report me and my cause aright/ To the unsatisfied" (5.2.291–2), which corresponds to Othello's final disheartened wish: "When you shall these unlucky deeds relate, Speak of me as I am" (5.2.350–1). Both characters, though admitting their faults, claim their uprightness, loyalty and honour. Wells & Taylor date *Hamlet* to 1601 and *Othello* a few years later.

Some commentators have accepted an earlier date *c.* 1601–04, most notably recent editors Norman Sanders (New Cambridge Shakespeare) and Honigmann (Arden 3 edition) who both give the range 1601–1604. J. Rees argued for an earlier date after he examined a leaf from Edward Pudsey's Booke (a manuscript commonplace book in the Bodleian Library). On one sheet is written:

> Dangerous to tell where a soldier lyes etc. yf I shold say he lodge theer I bed ther. Shee yt is free of her toung ys as frank of her lippes. An ey yt offeres parle to provocaco.

Rees observes the close connection between this entry and two passages from *Othello*: at 2.3.21-2:

> IAGO What an eye she has! Methinks it sounds a parley to provocation.

and with a second passage at 3.4.1:

> DES Do you know sirra where the lieutenant Cassio lies ?
> CLO I dare not say he lies anywhere.
> DES Why man ?
> CLO He is a soldier, and for one to say a soldier lies is stabbing.
> DES Go to, where lodges he ?

Rees notes that this sheet, conventionally marked as fo. 84, should rightfully be next to fo. 42, which is dated 1600. Rees concludes that the play had already been performed by 1600 and composed at an earlier date.[5]

## Oxfordian Dates

Oxfordians believe that the play was written before 1604 and that it refers to events in Oxford's life after his stay in Venice (1575) when he doubted his wife's fidelity (1575–81). Clark presses for 1583, which she links to Alençon and events in Antwerp at this time. Holland argues for *c.* 1588, which is accepted as the most likely Oxfordian date.

## Internal Evidence

Since *Hamlet* was already known by 1589 (as Nashe wrote in his Preface to Greene's *Menaphon*), *Othello* might have been composed in the late 1580s – a date which fits Oxfordian chronology and which is corroborated by the likely allusion to the defeat of the Spanish Armada: "The desperate tempest hath so banged the Turks" (2.2.21), an arbitrary addition of the dramatist which does not find correspondence in history. The play contains no any further internal evidence to corroborate any date. However, the many detailed historical allusions are of such accuracy and exactness that they are worth mentioning as evidence of the dramatist's direct experience of Venice. Moreover, the linguistic features of the text reflect, to the utmost degree of perfection, the influence not only of the Italian language but also of Venetian Italian.

## External Evidence

Henslowe's Diary, on 14th December 1594, records a play which has not been identified. The title he wrote is "the mawe". The word *Moor* was spelt in different ways: 'more', 'maure' and 'moore'. Henslowe's spelling probably reflects his own pronunciation. Other examples from the diary show idiosyncratic orthography: "Troyeles and Creasse daye", "The Jewe of malltuse", "warlamchester". A study of entries shows that the spelling became less strange as the theatre manager became more familiar with play titles. At least, Henslowe, as we shall see, was referring to "a black".

The play *The Mawe* is marked 'ne', which has often been read as 'new'. It could have been the first time that the play had been performed in Henslowe's theatre, or it may have been a revised play – therefore new to Henslowe and to his audience. Other plays in his diary are marked 'ne' – it has been suggested that the abbreviation stands for ' Newington '. But the long list of plays starting on 3rd June 1594 and including *The Mawe*, bears a heading which gives the name of the theatre where the plays were performed:

> ... begininge at newinton my Lord Admeralle men and my Lorde chamberlen men

As ffolowethe 1594

Thus it would have been pointless to designate the theatre by 'ne' next to the titles of some plays. Henslowe had recorded two other performances of *The Mawe* by 28th January 1595.

The element corroborating the present interpretation of *The Mawe* is given in the 'playhouse inventories', printed by Malone in 1780 from a manuscript he found at Dulwich College . This manuscript, now lost, contained (he tells us [289]) "an exact inventory of the wardrobe, playbooks, properties etc., belonging to the Lord Admiral's servants". The first lists, dated 10th March 1598, have the following entry:

Item: j mawe gowne of calleco for the queen

Calico is cotton cloth imported from the East and the word "mawe" can be interpreted as 'brown'. Throughout the inventories the word 'brown' is never used to indicate colour. Then there are the following entries:

Item: the Mores lymes
Item: Mores cotte

These may be considered one of Henslowe's variant spelling of 'moor'.

However, it is possible that Henslowe's '*mawe'* may refer not to *Othello*, but to another black man – for example the protagonist of a play written by Thomas Dekker and others: *The Spanish Moor's Tragedy*. But this, as Bullough tells us, "was commissioned for the Admiral's men in 1598/99 and the Arden edition confirms that Henslowe records making a payment for this play in February 1600. Also, in this case, his spelling is "more" (1997: 30n).[6]

## Conclusion

*Othello* was composed some time between 1584 and 1604, after the publication of the French translation of Cinthio's *Hecatommithi* and before it was performed at court. Henslowe's diary strongly suggests a performance of the play on 14 December 1594.

From an Oxfordian viewpoint, Oxford's idea of deriving this play from Cinthio came to him some time after his Italian journey, in connection with the estrangement from his wife. A first edition of *Othello* may have been written between 1584 and 1589, perhaps after the death of his wife Anne (née Cecil) in June 1588 had provoked remorse over his mistreatment of her.

It is likely that the dramatist modified his tragedy during the two-year break from 1592–94, when theatres were closed because of the plague. *The Mawe* recorded by Henslowe may be the revised play, first performed after the plague (14th December 1594), which would account for Henslowe's marking it 'new'.

## Notes

1. Most recently, Michael Neill has considered the dating of the play. Neill notes that the authenticity of the reference has been challenged by Hamilton, who remains the most recent detractor, but that "Shaxberd" is "nevertheless accepted by the majority of modern scholars, including Sanders and Honigmann" (2006: 399n).
2. Neill argues on the basis that, despite Chappys' translation in 1584, "verbal parallels overwhelmingly favour the Italian version" (2006: 22). Honigmann (1997) includes an appendix on Cinthio (368–70) and reprints a translation of the source material (370–87). Line numbers in this section are taken from the Arden 3 edition, edited by Honigmann. Honigmann's edition favours the Q text, where the *Oxford Complete Works* uses the F text (on the basis that F "seems to represent Shakespeare's second thoughts" (W&T, 819). Neill (2006: 237n) suggests "acerb is clearly preferable", a "characteristically Shakespearean coinage" which follows the Italian text. In this treatment, Neill suggests not that the substitution of "bitter" in the F text was Shakespeare's second thought, but rather that "the F reading probably indicates some editorial sophistication of Shakespeare's text, or even an unconscious substitution (perhaps prompted by the echo of *Revelations* in the phrasing of the sentence) on the part of a scribe or compositor who found the original difficult" (237n). For further general discussion, see Naseeb Shaheen, "Shakespeare's knowledge of Italian", *SS*, 47 (1994), 161–9.
3. Honigmann discusses Lewkenor in detail (1997: 5–8), referring "officers of the night" to a marginal gloss in Lewkenor, (96).
4. Wells & Taylor observe that the derivation from Knolles, "published no earlier than 30 September 1603", suggests a dating for the play "some time between that date and the summer of 1604" (819).
5. In full, Rees concludes that, given (as he asserts) that fo. 84 "should rightfully be next door to 42 in the Notebook" then "the *Othello* extracts therefore pre-date the 1622 Quarto by some twenty years" (1992: 331).
6. An account-book of Sir Thomas Egerton apparently indicates that Burbage received £10 for a performance of *Othello* in 1602 at Bridgewater House, Harefield, Middlesex. It is usually thought that John Payne Collier forged the sheet (numbered EL123) with this particular reference (Chambers, *WS*, II, 388 and Helen Hackett, *Shakespeare and Elizabeth*, 2009: 51–2). G. P. Jones, however, appears to accept the reference in "A Burbage Ballad and John Payne Collier," *RES* 40 (1989: 393–397).

*Acknowledgement*: Details of the entry about "the mawe" from Henslowe's diary, 14th December 1594, are taken by the contributor from a manuscript in the collection at Dulwich College and are reproduced here with the kind permission of the College Governors.

## Other Works Cited

Bullough, G., *Narrative and Dramatic Sources of Shakespeare,* vol. VII, London:

Routledge, 1973
Chambers, E. K., *William Shakespeare: a study of facts and problems*, 2 vols, Oxford: Clarendon Press, 1930
Clark, E. T., *Hidden Allusions in Shakespeare's Plays*, New York: William Farquhar Payson, 1931 rptd 1974
Da Mosto, A., *I Dogi di Venezia nella vita pubblica e privata*, 1977
Finlay, R., *Politics in Renaissance Venice*, London: Benn, 1980
Hamilton, Charles, *In Search of Shakespeare, A Reconnaissance Into the Poet's Life and Handwriting*, New York: Harcourt Brace Jovanovich, 1985
Hill, G., *A History of Cyprus*, 4 vols, Cambridge: CUP, 1949
Holland, H. H., *Shakespeare, Oxford and Elizabethan times*, 1933
Honigmann, E. A. J. (ed.), *Othello*, London: Arden Shakespeare, 1997
Jeffery, Violet, M., "Shakespeare's Venice", *Modern Language Review*, Jan. 1932: 24–35
Jorgensen Paul A., *Shakespeare's Military World*, Berkeley: UCP, 1956
Lane, F. C., *Venetian Ships and Shipbuilders of the Renaissance*, Johns Hopkins UP, 1966
Maranini, G., *La Costituzione di Venezia*, Firenze 1974
Neill, M. (ed.), *Othello*, Oxford: OUP, 2006
Parks, G. P. (ed.), *The History of Italy*, [a new edition of W. Thomas' 1549 book], New York: Cornell UP, 1963
Rees, J., "Shakespeare and Edward Pudsey's Booke, 1600", *Notes and Queries*, September 1992: 330–1
Ridley, M. R. (ed.), *Othello*, London: Methuen Arden Shakespeare, 1958
Sanders, N. (ed.), *Othello*, Cambridge: CUP, The New Cambridge Shakespeare, 1984
Wells, S. & Taylor, G. *The Oxford Shakespeare*, Oxford: OUP, 1986
—, *William Shakespeare: a textual companion*, Oxford: OUP, 1987

# 35

# The Tragedie of Antonie, and Cleopatra

John Rollett

*Antony and Cleopatra* was written after 1579 (the publication of North's translation of Plutarch and before 1608, when the play was registered.

## Publication Date

The play was recorded in the Stationers' Register on 20 May 1608 immediately after *Pericles*:

> [SR 1608] 20 Maij. Edward Blount. Entred for his copie vnder thandes of Sir George Buck, knight and Master Warden Seton A booke called. The booke of Pericles prynce of Tyre. vj[d].
> Edward Blount. Entred also for his copie by the like Aucthoritie. A booke Called Anthony. and Cleopatra. vj[d].

No author's name is given and there were no quarto versions of the play. *Antony & Cleopatra* was entered again in the Stationers' Register on 8 November 1623 together with other plays as "not formerly entred to other men":

> Mr Blounte Isaak Jaggard. Entered for their Copie vnder the hands of Mr Doctor Worral and Mr Cole – warden, Mr William Shakspeers Comedyes Histories, and Tragedyes soe manie of the said Copies as are not formerly entered to other men. vizt. Comedyes. The Tempest. The two gentlemen of Verona. Measure for Measure. The Comedy of Errors. As you Like it. All's well that ends well. Twelft night. The winters tale. Histories. The thirde parte of Henry the sixt. Henry the eight. Coriolanus. Timon of Athens. Julius Caesar. Tragedies. Mackbeth. Anthonie & Cleopatra. Cymbeline.

It is one of eighteen plays in the First Folio (F1) which had not previously been published and commentators generally accept that the entries in the SR in 1608 and in 1623 refer to the same play.

## Performance Dates

According to a note in the Lord Chamberlain's records for 1669, Thomas Killigrew secured the rights to the play, which had been "formerly acted at the Blackfriars". It is uncertain whether this was in Shakespeare's lifetime (before 1616), before the closing of the theatres in 1642 or after the restoration in 1660. Neill notes that the lack of allusion to any performance need not imply theatrical failure. He suggests that Fletcher and Massinger's *The False One* (1626), dramatising Caesar's affair with Cleopatra, was written as a prequel. Shakespeare's *Antony and Cleopatra* may have been performed in 1677 but the first recorded performance was David Garrick's in 1759.

## Sources

Bullough observes that the primary source was *Parallel Lives of the Greeks and Romans* by Plutarch, written in Greek in the first century AD. In 1579, Sir Thomas North's English translation appeared as *Lives of the Noble Romans and Grecians Compared Together.* It was reprinted in 1595 and the third edition of 1603 included an addition by Simon Goulart, *Life of Augustus.*

It is widely accepted that North's Plutarch was used by Shakespeare (as argued by MacCallum and Spencer) although North's English version was itself a translation of Jacques Amyot's French version of 1559. According to Bullough, Shakespeare could have developed all his plot and characterisation from the 'Life of Marcus Antonius' and the 'Comparison of Demetrius and Marcus Antonius'. The dramatist also seems to have consulted Appian's *Civil Wars* (translated in 1578 by W.B.) and Samuel Daniel's *The Tragedy of Cleopatra* (1594). Both Daniel and Shakespeare emphasise the roles of Seleucus and of Dolabella.

Goulart's *Life of Augustus* (1603) emphasises Octavius's aloof efficiency, which some have taken to be adopted by Shakespeare in *Antony* but Bullough notes that this trait is in North's Plutarch. Aloof efficiency is also in Shakespeare's own depiction of Octavius in *Julius Caesar* where he crosses Antony in taking the right wing and later gives the closing speech, making orders for the due treatment of Brutus's corpse (in contrast to Antony's extravagant praise of Brutus). Since *Julius Caesar* is usually dated to 1599, it is unlikely that Shakespeare needed to consult Goulart for his depiction of Octavius in *Antony.*

Bevington lists a wide range of 'sources' which would usually be considered allusions or analogues, including classical and Renaissance treatments of the stories of Dido and Aeneas, Mars and Venus and Hercules and Omphale. Wilders says that Shakespeare appears also to have read the Countess of Pembroke's *The Tragedy of Antony* (1592), a translation of the 1578 French play *Marc-Antoine* by Robert Garnier. However, Wilder believes the influence of Daniel or Mary Sidney was only very slight at most: "Had Shakespeare not read Daniel or the Countess of Pembroke, *Antony and Cleopatra* would probably have been much as it is." Neill sees strong echoes of Virgil's *Aeneid* and asserts (1993: 3) that the play is "an outstanding example of the Renaissance art of *paragone*, that mode of emulous imitation which sought to match or outstrip its original". Most importantly, Neill argues for a strong link between Shakespeare's *Julius Caesar* (usually dated 1599) and *Antony and Cleopatra*. The implication seems to be that Shakespeare envisaged a sequel to *Julius Caesar* even if he did not actually compose one at the same time.

Bullough further notes the popularity of classical plays in the early Jacobean period: Alexander's *Darius* (published 1603) and *Croesus* (pub. 1604), Jonson's *Sejanus* (pub. 1605), Daniel's *Philotas* (pub. 1605), Marston's *Sophonisba* (pub. 1606) and the anonymous *Caesar's Revenge* (pub. 1606). Bullough accepts the suggestion of Chambers and Ridley that Shakespeare's treatment of Cleopatra influenced Samuel Daniel, who consequently "remodelled" his tragedy *Cleopatra* (1594) in *Certain Small Works* (1607).

## Orthodox Date

Chambers accepted the date 1606–7, on the basis of the 1608 entry in the Stationers' Register and this has been followed by almost all scholars, e.g. Neill. Bevington is more circumspect, accepting a date after 1594, but tending towards 1607. Alfred Harbage prefers 1603–4.

## Internal orthodox Evidence

The only internal evidence for a date *c.* 1607 comes from verse and style. Chambers (*WS*, I, 478) states: "The metrical character of *Antony and Cleopatra* forbids us to put it before *Macbeth* or *Lear*." Yet closer examination of Chambers's own tables show that such a conclusion cannot be established: *Antony* has a relatively small amount of prose at 9%, placing it early, 12 out of 38 plays; *Antony* has the same small proportion of rhyme as *Julius Caesar* (usually dated 1599) perhaps because both are tragedies or Roman plays, but then *Merry Wives* (usually dated 1597) has the same proportion; *Antony* shares a similar proportion of feminine line endings (22%) with *Richard III* (usually dated 1594) which has (18%), unlike *Pericles* (usually dated 1607–8) which has only 8%. Wells & Taylor's study of the frequencies of 'colloquialisms' also produces unexpected results. *Antony* has 34 elisions of 'the' (as th') in 3059 lines, which is similar to *Hamlet*'s 42 in 3929 lines. *Antony* has three elisions of 'them (as 'em) apparently linking it with *Taming of the Shrew* which has two whereas *Coriolanus* has twelve. Overall, studies of metrical and linguistic preferences are not helpful in dating *Antony.*

Miola has argued for a strong link between Octavius, who sets up the Pax Romana with his defeat of Antony, and James I who was anxious to promote the idea of a Pax Britannica. Neville Davies describes James I's triumphal entry through seven arches and Ben Jonson's prophecy that the lasting glory of James would parallel that of "Augustus' state". Yachnin has drawn similar parallels with the reign of James and dates the play *c.* 1606.

## External Orthodox Evidence

The earliest possible date would appear to be set by the publication of North's *Plutarch* in 1579. If the play definitely showed strong evidence of the influence of either the Countess of Pembroke's play or Daniel's *Cleopatra*, then the earliest date would be 1592 or 1594. However, the influence of these texts is not established.

Most commentators, from Chambers to Wilders, automatically assume that the date of writing of the play was shortly before the first entry in the Stationers' Register in 1608 on the assumption that this was Shakespeare's play. Bullough comments on "verbal resemblances" in the anonymous *Nobody and Somebody* (entered 1606), and Barnabe Barnes's *The Divil's Charter*, which was first performed on 2 February 1607. Bullough therefore suggests *Antony and Cleopatra* was written in 1606. As always, the direction of influence is difficult to gauge. It is possible that *Antony* was performed in 1606, from which the authors of *Nobody and Somebody*, and *The Divil's Charter* used some lines.[1] This would not mean that *Antony* had just been composed in 1606.

## Oxfordian Date

Clark offers 1579. Mark Anderson has developed a detailed argument which would date Oxford's authorship of the play to 1588–9.

## Internal Oxfordian Evidence

In favour of the earlier dating, Clark quotes from the speech of Enobarbus (2.2):

> Age cannot wither her, nor custom stale
> Her infinite variety; other women cloy
> The appetites they feed; but she makes hungry
> Where most she satisfies; for vilest things

Become themselves in her. (2.2.241–5)

Clark argues that these lines seem "peculiarly applicable" to Queen Elizabeth in her earlier years, as are other characteristics and scenes described elsewhere in the play. Queen Elizabeth of course had a royal barge in which she travelled and which was, on occasion, used to transport herself and her important guests. For her coronation on 15 January, 1559, she was escorted from Whitehall to the Tower, and then back to Westminster by a large number of the city guilds' barges "decked and trimmed with the banners of their mysteries" which reminded a Venetian envoy of Ascension Day in Venice when the Doge and Signory were symbolically wedded to the sea.[2] It seems unlikely that a speech about age could have been recited in front of Elizabeth after 1590, when Elizabeth was in her late fifties and the effects of age could no longer be disguised.

There are also parallels with Cleopatra's questions about Octavia in Act 3.3:

| | |
|---|---|
| Cleopatra | Didst thou behold Octavia? |
| Messenger | Ay, dread queen. |
| Cleopatra | Where? |
| Messenger | Madam, in Rome;<br>I look'd her in the face, and saw her led<br>Between her brother and Mark Antony. |
| Cleopatra | Is she as tall as me? |
| Messenger | She is not, madam. |
| Cleopatra | Didst hear her speak? is she shrill-tongued or low? |
| Messenger | Madam, I heard her speak; she is low-voiced. |
| Cleopatra | That's not so good: he cannot like her long. |
| Charmian | Like her! O Isis! 'tis impossible. |
| Cleopatra | I think so, Charmian: dull of tongue, and dwarfish!<br>What majesty is in her gait? Remember,<br>If e'er thou look'dst on majesty. |

This passage recalls Elizabeth's enquiries about Mary Queen of Scots recorded in *The Memoirs of Sir James Melvil of Hal-Hill.* On a visit to England in 1564, he was questioned by Elizabeth about Mary Queen of Scots (Scott, 50–51):

> [Elizabeth] desired to know of me, what colour hair was reputed best, and whether my Queen's hair or hers was best, and which of them two was fairest. I answered the fairness of them was not their worst faults... She inquired which of them was of highest stature? I said, My Queen. Then, saith she, she is too high, for I myself am neither too high or too low...She inquired whether my Queen or she played best? In that I found myself obliged to give the praise... she inquired of me whether she or my Queen danced best? I answered, the Queen danced not so high and disposedly as she did.

It seems unlikely that an interchange expressing curiosity could have been recited in front of Elizabeth after Mary's execution in 1587. One might argue then for a date either pre 1587, or post Elizabeth's death in 1603.

Furthermore, if Cleopatra shadowed the Queen, surely Robert Dudley, Earl of Leicester, must have been shadowed in Antony, who is depicted at 1.1.13 as:

> The triple pillar of the world transformed
> Into a strumpet's fool

To utter these words in front of the court with Elizabeth and Dudley present would have been somewhat rash, and the same applies if the play was performed to entertain Alençon when the 'French marriage' was being negotiated, another suggestion Clark makes.

Against the earlier dating of the Oxfordians is the fact that this is one of the most mature of all Shakespeare's plays in terms of style and structure. To reconcile these considerations, one would have to posit an early version dating from 1579–80, which was considerably re-written late in the dramatist's career. It is quite possible, as Frances Yates remarked, that the so-called late dramas were "an archaising revival, a deliberate return to the past by an old Elizabethan living in the Jacobean age". Theodora Jankowski has investigated many similarities between Cleopatra and Elizabeth. She notes (180) that "Shakespeare's representation of Cleopatra becomes an examination of the means by which a female monarch can secure regal power." Again, this suggests composition in the Elizabethan period.

## External Oxfordian Evidence

Clark's dating of 1579 is based on a reference by Stephen Gosson in his *School of Abuse*, page 40 to a play called *Ptoleme* at the Bull (Chambers, *ES* iv, 204):

> The *Iewe* and *Ptoleme*, showne at the Bull, the one representing the greediness of worldly chusers and bloody mindes of userers; the other very liuely descrybing how seditious estates, with their own deuises, false friendes, with their own swordes, and rebellious commons in their owne snares are overthrowne.

Clark points out that Cleopatra was the 'Ptolemy' of her day, since she was the daughter of Ptolemy Auletes. The Bull was located in Bishopsgate Street, and was chosen shortly afterwards by the Queen's Men for their first winter season in 1582–3 Chambers, *ES*, ii 380–1). When the Queen's Men had formed in 1582, they had taken a leading player, John Dutton, from Oxford's Men (Nelson, 246). Clark also proposes that the record of a play at court in February 1580 called *The History of Serpedon* may have been a misreading by the clerk of the Revels of the title 'Cleopatra'.[3]

Anderson sees considerable links between events in the late 1580s and the action of the play. He sees the relationship between Cleopatra and Antony as a satire on the relationship between Elizabeth and Leicester. He sees links between the play's depiction of the Battle of Actium and the defeat of the Spanish Armada. Anderson notes that in the victory celebrations held on 24 November 1588, Oxford's boy players performed before the queen, which he hints may have included a version of *Antony and Cleopatra.*

## Conclusion

There is very little evidence to date this play. All we can say is that *Antony and Cleopatra* was written after 1579 (the publication of North's translation of Plutarch) and probably before 1608, when the play was registered by Blunt. If one accepts Daniel's *Cleopatra* as an influence on Shakespeare's play, *Antony* must be dated after 1594. Orthodox scholars date the play firmly in the seventeenth century, whereas Oxfordians see it as an Elizabethan play of the sixteenth century.

## Notes

1. The resemblances are noted by Ridley (introduction, xxvii). In *Nobody and Somebody,* King Archigallo is described in terms which resemble Antony. A longer passage in *The Divil's Charter* deals with the death of Cleopatra. *The Divil's Charter* was registered and published in 1607, but as the author, Barnabe Barnes lived *c.* 1569–1609, there have been some attempts to date it to 1604 and even 1598.
2. Widely quoted by modern historians, e.g. Alison Weir, *Elizabeth the Queen,* Pimlico, 1999 (page 34).
3. An alternative explanation of the mysterious 'Serpedon' is that it should have read 'Sarpedon', a son of Jupiter who fought with Priam in the Trojan Wars, and who was eventually slain by Patroclus (*Iliad XVI*). Although this is a possible subject for a play, there is no other reference to any play on this topic.

## Other Cited Works

Anderson, Mark, *Shakespeare by Another Name,* New York: Gotham, 2005

Bevington, David (ed.), *Antony and Cleopatra,* Cambridge: CUP The New Cambridge Shakespeare, 1990

Bullough, G. *Narrative and Dramatic Sources of Shakespeare,* vol. V., London: Routledge, 1964: 215–253

Chambers, E. K., *The Elizabethan Stage,* 4 vols, Oxford: Clarendon, 1923

—, *William Shakespeare: a Study of Facts and Problems,* 2 vols, Oxford: Clarendon, 1930

Clark, E. T., *Hidden Allusions in Shakespeare's Plays,* New York: William Farquhar Payson, 1931 rptd 1974

Davies, H. Neville, "Jacobean *Antony and Cleopatra*", *Shakespeare Studies*, 17, 1985: 123–58

Erickson, Carolly, *The First Elizabethan,* New York: MacMillan, 1983

Harbage, Alfred (ed.), *Antony and Cleopatra*, Pelican/Viking, 1969

Jankowski, Theodora, *Women in Power in the Early Modern Drama,* University of Illinois, 1992

MacCallum, M. W., *Shakespeare's Roman Plays and their Background*, London, 1910

Miola, Robert S., "Shakespeare's ancient Rome: difference and identity", Michael Hattaway (ed.), *The Cambridge Companion to Shakespeare's History Plays,* Cambridge: CUP, 2002

Neill, Michael, *Antony and Cleopatra*, Oxford: OUP, 1993

Nelson, Alan, H., *Monstrous Adversary*, Liverpool: Liverpool University Press, 2003

Ridley, M. R. (ed.), *Antony and Cleopatra*, London: The Arden Shakespeare, 1954

Scott, George (ed.), *The Memoirs of Sir James Melvil of Hal-Hil*, 1683

Spencer, T. J. B. (ed.), *Shakespeare's Plutarch*, Harmondsworth: Penguin, 1964

Wells, S. & G. Taylor (eds), *The Complete Oxford Shakespeare*, Oxford, 1986

—, *William Shakespeare: A Textual Commentary*, Oxford, 1987

Wilders, J. (ed.), *Antony and Cleopatra*, London: The Arden Shakespeare, 1995

Yachnin, Paul, "Shakespeare's Politics of Loyalty: Sovereignty and Subjectivity in *Antony and Cleopatra*", *Studies in English Literature, 1500–1900*, Vol. 33, 1993

Yates, F. A., *Shakespeare's last plays: a new approach*, London: Routledge & Kegan Paul, 1975

36

# Cymbeline, King of Britaine

Kevin Gilvary

This play can be dated any time between 1578, the latest definite source, and the first description of it in 1611.

## Publication Date

*Cymbeline, King of Britaine* is one of eighteen plays in the First Folio (F1) which had not previously been published. It was entered into the Stationers' Register on 8 November 1623 alongside other plays as "not formerly entred to other men":

> [SR]Mr Blounte Isaak Jaggard. Entered for their Copie vnder the hands of Mr Doctor Worral and Mr Cole – warden, Mr William Shakspeers Comedyes Histories, and Tragedyes soe manie of the said Copies as are not formerly entered to other men. vizt. Comedyes. The Tempest. The two gentlemen of Verona. Measure for Measure. The Comedy of Errors. As you Like it. All's well that ends well. Twelft night. The winters tale. Histories. The thirde parte of Henry the sixt. Henry the eight. Coriolanus. Timon of Athens. Julius Caesar. Tragedies. Mackbeth. Anthonie & Cleopatra. Cymbeline.

*Cymbeline* occupies the last place among the tragedies at the very end of the First Folio (F1). The Folio editors were unsure of the genre: the Catalogue to F1 refers to the play as *Cymbeline, King of Britaine* but the title page and the running title refer to the play as *The Tragedie of Cymbeline* despite the fact that the title character has a minor part and suffers no tragedy. Chambers reports that the text of *Cymbeline* is generally good with only "some room for emendation." Nosworthy reports that the text was set very neatly, probably by Compositor B, who is highly regarded.

## Performance Date

The earliest recorded performance of the play was apparently at the Globe when Simon Forman recorded in his *Bocke of Plaies* (Bodleian Ashmolean MS 208, 200-13) three accounts of Shakespeare plays: *Macbeth.* at the Globe, dated Saturday 20 April, 1610 (although this is usually corrected to 1611), *The Winter's Tale* at the Globe on 15 May 1611, and *Cymbeline* (neither date nor venue is mentioned):

> Remember also the storri of Cymbalin king of England in Lucius tyme, howe Lucius cam from octauus cesar for Tribut and being denied, after sent Lucius with a greate Arme of Souldiars who landed at milford hauen, and Affter wer vanquished by Cimbalin and Lucius taken prisoner and all by means of 3 outlawes of the w'h 2 of them were the sonns of Cimbalin stolen from him when they were but 2 yers old. by an old man whom Cymbalin banished, and he kept them as his own sonns 20 yers wt him in A cave. And howe of [sic] of them slewe Clotan that was the quens sonn goinge to milford hauen to sek the loue of Innogen kinge daughter whom he had banished also for louinge his daughter, and howe the Italian that cam from her loue convoied him selfe into A Cheste and said yt was a chest of plate sent from her loue & others to be p'sented to the kinge. And in the depest of the night she being aslepe. he opened the cheste, & cam forth of yt And vewed her in her bed and the markes of her body. & toke awai her braslet & after Accused her of adultery to her loue &c And in thend howe he came wt the Romains into England & was taken prisoner and after Reueled to Innogen. who had turned her self into man apparrell & fled to mete her loue at milford hauen, & chanchsed to fall on the Caue in the wode wher her 2 brothers were & howe by eating a sleping Dram they thought she had bin deed & laid her in the wode, & the body of cloten by her in her loues apparrell that he left behind him, & howe she was found by lucous, &c.

Forman's account clearly has in mind Shakespeare's play but there are some differences, e.g. he makes no mention of Jupiter's descent in Act 4. Forman's diary text has been suspected as a forgery by Tannenbaum, following Joseph Quincey Adams who doubted Forman's report on *Macbeth.* S. Race examined that manuscript and agreed that it was a forgery: "It would seem that the writer got tired, and lapsed unintentionally into his ordinary hand." Wilson and Hunt, however, argued that the handwriting was authentically Jacobean but did not address the discrepancies in the account of *Macbeth.* The consensus among modern scholars, e.g. Pafford, is that Forman's accounts are genuine.

## Sources

Bullough states that Shakespeare used Raphael Holinshed's *The Chronicles of Englande, Scotlande, and Irelande* (first edition, 1577; second, expanded edition, 1587), for the background, drawing on the pseudo-historical account of Cymbeline's reign, in which the British defeated the Roman forces. Since this work appears to be the major source for the play, we need to consider which edition was used. According to Boswell-Stone (6–18), the dramatist could have derived his material from either the first edition or the second edition (unlike many of the History plays, which seem to have relied on the second edition). It is only Posthumus's account of the battle (5.3 3–58) which uses some details found only in the second edition (and in widely separated parts). It is possible that Posthumus's speech (which merely reports the action which has just occurred in Act 5 Scene 2) may have been a later addition. For the story of Guiderius, Shakespeare seems to have used the 'tragedies' in *Mirror for Magistrates* (1578 edition), which had been derived from Geoffrey of Monmouth by Thomas Blenerhasset and John Higgins. This is the latest definite source used for the play.

For the wager story involving Giacomo and Imogen, the dramatist read the story of Bernabo and Ambrogiuolo in Boccaccio's *Decamaron* (day 2, novel 9). This story was only available in Italian texts or in a French translation by Le Maçon in 1545. Painter translated 16 of the novels (1566–77) but did not cover this particular story. The full translation of the *Decamaron* did not appear in English until 1620.

Bullough believes that an anonymous play published in 1589, *The Rare Triumphs of Love and Fortune* is the main literary source for *Cymbeline*. This play (which according to the title page had been played before the Queen) has been identified by Chambers (*ES*, iv, 28) with *A History of Love and Fortune* which was performed before the court at Windsor on 30 Dec 1582. In the anonymous play, Venus (love) and Fortune enter a contest with Vulcan, who is portrayed as a kind of clown. The heroine is Fidelia, daughter of the duke Phizanties; the hero is Hermione and the villain is Armenio, Fidelia's brother. Like Belarius, a banished courtier lives in a cave: his name is Bomelio. But, unlike Belarius, he is a magician, and the (unknown) father of Hermione. Unlike Cloten, Armenio is not killed, but struck dumb by Bomelio, while Hermione burns Bomelio's books of magic, which lands the latter in a desperate situation when, disguised as a French doctor, he promises duke Phizanties to cure Armenio. The play ends with the reconciliation of all foes and, in the final act, of Fortune with Love. Although the parallels between the two plays are superficial, Nosworthy concludes (introduction, xxv):

> Shakespeare's obligation, such as it was, was to *Love and Fortune* and to no other literary production of which we have knowledge, with, however, the reservation that I have applied to Holinshed and the wager sources. Precisely what led Shakespeare to this ramshackle old play [*sc. The Triumphs of Love and Fortune*] in the first place, I do not pretend to know.

*Love and Fortune* does not appear to have been such an important source for *Cymbeline* as was Holinshed's *Chronicle.*

## Influence of the Greek Romances

Carol Gesner, however, has shown that the main plot does have literary antecedents. She argues that three main elements in *Cymbeline* derive from the Greek romances:

- the wager story, Imogen's suspected infidelity and Imogen's travels;
- the loss and restoration of Cymbeline's heirs;
- Cymbeline's wars with Rome.

Gesner gives an extended comparison between *Cymbeline* and Thomas Underdowne's translation (1569) of Heliodorus' *Aethiopica,* which narrated the story of Chariclea and Theagenes. In both Shakespeare's play and the old Greek romance, these three threads are present. Gesner concludes:

> Close examination reveals that *Cymbeline* was probably influenced by the *Aethiopica* and was perhaps even a conscious imitation of that romance. If so, the idea of an imitation, of a new Heliodorean romance, could have been suggested by Sidney's imitation, *The Countess of Pembroke's Arcadia,* with which it has much in common.

Gesner then considers a second Greek Romance, which seems to have provided material for *Cymbeline*: *Achilles Tatius's romance Clitophon and Leucippe* was translated into Italian in 1550, French in 1568 and English in 1597. The passage in *Cymbeline* where Cloten's body is cast into a river and Imogen bewails her supposedly dead husband seems to be a reversal of a scene in Tatius's romance where the hero, Clitophon, thinks he has seen Leucippe beheaded and thrown into the sea. Moreover, Clitophon is required by his father to marry his half-sister, and Leucippe drinks a magic potion. Shakespeare has re-arranged these elements: it is the heroine Imogen whom King Cymbeline wants to marry to her step-brother Cloten, and she swallows the drug given her by the physician. Even more astounding are the parallels between the bedroom scene in *Cymbeline* (2.2) and another passage in the Greek romance. Just before Leucippe, through the treacherous action of a 'friend', is abducted by pirates, a portent of the disasters to come is revealed in a picture: "I did beholde a table, wherein was drawn the mishap of Progne, the violence of Tereus, the cutting out of the tongue of Philomele." In the bedroom scene in *Cymbeline,* Imogen is reading the tale of Philomele and Tereus; while the description of a painting in the room is later given as evidence for her seduction. There are references to two epic poems in the bedroom scene. The description is in the tradition of a formal *ekphrasis* of a work of art, a commonplace of the elaborate Hellenic style and frequent in Achilles Tatius, which indeed begins with an ekphrasis of painting, as does Longus's *Daphnis and Chloe* (translated into French by Amyot in 1559 and into English by Angel Day in 1587). We have of course the same ekphrasis in *The Winter's Tale, Venus and Adonis* and *The Rape of Lucrece.*

Gesner also considers other Greek Romances as providing background for *Cymbeline.* In Xenophon's *Ephesiaca* (the earliest known published text was in 1726, in Greek with a Latin translation) of which the first known edition is in Latin, the heroine Anthia is to be killed at the instigation of her jealous mistress Manto. This 'stepmother' motif, found also in *Cymbeline,* is completely absent from *Love and Fortune.* Like Pisanio in *Cymbeline,* the servant ordered to kill her spares her, but reports her death. Anthia takes a sleeping draught and awakes beside a dead body which she mistakes for her husband (4.2. 38 and 296–320). The earliest known published text of *Ephasiaca* was in 1726, in Greek with a Latin translation, but it may have proved influential through intermediate texts. In *Chaereas and Callirhoe* by Chariton, Callirhoe, like Imogen is led to believe that her husband is dead and Chaereas, like Posthumus, regrets his hasty actions, laments, and considers suicide – motifs missing from Boccaccio. The earliest text was published in Greek in 1601, and the next edition did not appear until 1640. Gesner sees not only *Cymbeline,* but also *The Winter's Tale* as much closer to the original romances than to their alleged immediate sources.

Finally, one modern editor, Martin Butler (Cambridge edition), follows Danby who argued that the philosophical narrative of Sidney's *Arcadia* (composed *c.* 1580–1, published in 1590 and again in 1593) influenced Shakespearean romance. Both *Arcadia* and *Cymbeline* contain a weak king, a power-hungry queen, a cynical villain and high-minded heroes. However, another modern editor, Roger Warren (Oxford edition) sees no influence from Sidney.

## Orthodox Date

Chambers assigns a date for the play 1609–11, shortly before Forman reported his experience. Chambers saw affinities of style with *The Winter's Tale* and *The Tempest.* Subsequent scholars follow this, e.g. Maxwell, Wells & Taylor, Butler and Warren. A more cautious note is struck by Nosworthy, who states that any attempt at dating must be "approximate and impressionistic" and proposes that *Cymbeline* falls within the range of 1606–11.

## Internal Orthodox Evidence

There is no evidence for the date of composition of *Cymbeline.* Most orthodox scholars make a comparison of style with *The Winter's Tale* and *The Tempest.* These plays, however, cannot be dated securely. The Revels Accounts indicate performances at court of *The Winter's Tale* and *The Tempest* in 1611–12 but whether the plays were newly composed at that time has been doubted. For reservations about dating plays on style alone, see the Introduction.

## External Orthodox Evidence

Warren argues for 1610, contemporary with Thomas Heywood's *The Golden Age,* in which Jupiter also descends from the heavens. Most scholars assume that Forman's account of *Cymbeline* not only dates to 1611, but also indicates that the play must have been newly composed in that year. However, in the same book he describes *Macbeth,* which most scholars date no later than 1606 and possibly as early as 1600.

## Oxfordian Date

Those who think that the Earl of Oxford wrote the plays have argued for an earlier date *c.* 1578–1582, perhaps with later revisions and a completion date in the 1590s.

## Internal Oxfordian Evidence

The argument for *Cymbeline* as an early play has been made by many commentators. Dr Johnson summed up:

> To remark the folly of the fiction, the absurdity of the conduct, the confusion of the names and manners of different times, and the impossibility of the events in any system of life, were to waste criticism upon unresisting imbecility.[1]

Similar sentiments have been expressed more moderately by Wolfgang Clemen (205):

> Almost all critics seem to agree that there are weaknesses in the play, clumsy and imperfect passages as well as structural deficiencies and inconsistencies in the plot which it is difficult to account for. There is in some passages, not only in the "archaic" soliloquies, an obvious falling back into a style that, in the great tragedies, had long been superseded by a more perfect and subtle manner.

Clemen warns against attempting to find too simplistic an explanation such as the dramatist trying to adapt to the new conditions of the Blackfriars Theatre. One example of a structural deficiency is the final scene (5.4), when over twenty-four pieces of information, already known to the audience, are revealed to all the characters on stage. G. B. Shaw called the final act "a tedious string of unsurprising dénouements sugared with insincere sentimentality."[2] Compare this scene with the more economical approach of Theseus in *A Midsummer Night's Dream*:

> Fair lovers, you are fortunately met;
> Of this discourse we more will hear anon. (*MND*, 4.1.176–7)

The play, if indeed it is early, provides what is wholly absent in traditional biographies of the Bard: evidence of youthful endeavour, the elusive juvenilia.

Oxfordians make a number of other points. Firstly, regarding sources in other languages, Oxford was competent in both French and Italian and therefore could have read Boccaccio as well as the translations of the Greek Romances before they appeared in English.[3] Secondly, they see *Cymbeline* as an attempt to answer to some of Sidney's criticisms of the stage in his *Apology for Poetry* (probably written in 1582 or 1583):

> By and by, we heare newes of a shipwracke in the same place, and then we are to blame if we accept it not for a Rock. Upon the backe of that, comes out a hidious Monster, with fire and smoke, and then the miserable beholders are bound to take it for a Cave. While in the meantime two Armies flye in, represented with foure swords and bucklers, and then what harde heart will not receive it for a pitched fielde? Now, of time they are much more liberall, for ordinary it is that two young Princes fall in love. After many traverses, she is got with childe, delivered of a faire boy; he is lost, groweth a man, falls in love, and is ready to get another child, and all this in two hours space.[4]

In answer to Sidney's criticisms, it is thought that Oxford was trying to put romance on the stage, portraying action which defied the Aristotelian unities by ranging widely in time and space. Such a riposte would be apposite in the early to mid 1580s but very out-dated by 1610. Furthermore, during the middle Elizabethan period, as shown by Carol Gesner, there was considerable interest in the Greek Romances. Thomas Underdown had dedicated his translation of Heliodorus' *Aethiopica* (STC 13041) to Oxford in 1569, when Oxford was nineteen, with a further edition appearing in 1577. This may indicate Oxford's special interest in the genre at that time, and the germ of the idea of turning the story into drama might have begun then. Moreover, Oxford and Sidney were not only rivals in the field of poetry but had also been rivals in the early 1570s for the hand of Anne Cecil.[5]

Oxfordians also believe that plays could have been used as political allegories at court. *Cymbeline* accords well with other romances that we know were performed at court before the Queen, e.g. *Delight* (1580) and *The Rare Triumphs of Love and Fortune* (1582). On 28 December, 1578, the Court Revels record *An History of The Cruelty of a Step-Mother* being played before the Queen at Richmond.[6] If this is identified with an early version of *Cymbeline*, it can be seen as a political allegory: Imogen representing the Queen; Cloten representing her inappropriate suitor, Alençon, and Imogen's step-mother, Cymbeline's queen, as the Machiavellian Catherine de Medici; the author's purpose being to argue caution towards the French connection.

## Oxford as Posthumous

Finally, many Oxfordians follow Clark (79–101) in identifying the tragic-comic story of Posthumous with Oxford's own life. *Cymbeline* describes the travels of a youth to Italy; a youth brought up by the most powerful man in the country, whose daughter he married; a youth, who while away in Italy is persuaded that his wife has been unfaithful and whom he wishes dead; a youth whose spiritual sympathies are with Rome; a youth imprisoned on his return for loyalties to Rome; a youth who later sought and received forgiveness from his maligned wife and his outraged father-in-law.

Strangely, this is not only the story of Posthumus Leonatus in *Cymbeline*, but also the contemporary tale of Edward de Vere, Earl of Oxford. In 1571, Oxford married Anne Cecil, daughter of William Cecil, Lord Burghley, but a few years later left his wife and travelled to Italy on a grand tour. While away, he heard that his wife was pregnant and that there were rumours she had been unfaithful. After Oxford returned in 1576, he refused to acknowledge his wife or his (wife's) daughter. He was sent to the Tower in 1580 after confessing his conversion to Catholicism, but was released and reconciled in 1583 with his wife and to some extent with his father-in-law.[7] Thus, a date *c.* 1583–4 would seem most likely for the composition of *Cymbeline* (perhaps revised from *An History of The Cruelty of a Step-Mother*, written in 1578).

## Conclusion

This play can be dated any time between 1578, the latest definite source, and the first description of it in 1611. It is possible that the play, or at least a version of it, was composed in the early 1580s, partly in response to Sidney's criticisms of theatrical practices and partly as a result of the contemporary vogue for Romances.

## Notes

Acknowledgement: I am indebted to Robert Detobel for many suggestions made to me privately.

1. Quoted by R. W. Desai, (ed.), (1985: 197) in *Johnson on Shakespeare*.
2. G. B. Shaw in his forward to *Cymbeline Refinished: A Variation on Shakespear's Ending* (1936).

3. See Alan Nelson (53) for his purchase in 1569 of expensive texts in French, Italian and Latin at the age of 19.
4. Sidney's criticisms come towards the end of his work (Richard Dutton, ed., *Sir Philip Sidney: Selected Writings,* 1987: 140; Elizabeth Watson, ed., *Defence of Poesie,* 1997: 120). See the chapters on *Henry V* and in *The Famous Victories of Henry V* for possible answers to other critisisms of theatre by Sidney.
5. Nelson (71–77) describes Anne Cecil's original betrothal to Philip Sidney and her subsequent marriage to Oxford.
6. Chambers, *ES*, IV, 95. Nothing further is known about this play.
7. Nelson (141–156) describes how he was 'A Stranger to his Wife'. According to Francis Osborne in *Historical Memoires on the Reigns of Queen Elizabeth and King James* (1658), Oxford was reconciled through means of a 'bed-trick' such as depicted in *Measure for Measure* and *All's Well.*

## Other Works Cited

Adams, J. Q. (ed.), *Macbeth,* Boston, 1931
Boswell-Stone, W. G. *Shakespeare's Holinshed: the Chronicle and the historical plays compared,* 1907 edn.
Bullough, G., *Narrative and Dramatic Sources of Shakespeare,* vol. VIII, London: Routledge, 1975: 3–37
Butler, M. (ed.), *Cymbeline,* Cambridge: CUP, 2005
Chambers, E. K., *The Elizabethan Stage,* 4 vols., Oxford: Clarendon, 1923
—, *William Shakespeare: a Study of Facts and Problems,* 2 vols, Oxford: Clarendon, 1930, vol I, 484–7
Clark, E. T., *Hidden Allusions in Shakespeare's Plays,* New York: William Farquhar Payson, 1931 rptd 1974
Clemen, Wolfgang, *The Development of Shakespeare's Imagery,* London: Methuen, 1966
Danby, J. F., *Elizabethan and Jacobean Poets: Studies in Sidney, Shakespeare, Beaumont and Fletcher,* London: Faber & Faber, 1965
Gesner, C., *Shakespeare and the Greek Romance: a Study of Origins,* Lexington: University of Kentucky Press, 1970
Greg, W. W., Review of Tannenbaum's 1928 work, *Review of English Studies,* 5, 1929: 349
Hess, W. R. *et al.,* "Shakespeare's dates: their effect upon stylistic analysis", *Oxfordian,* 2, Portland, 1999
Maxwell, J. C., ed. *Cymbeline,* Cambridge: CUP New Shakespeare, 1960
Nelson, Alan, H., *Monstrous Adversary,* Liverpool: Liverpool University Press, 2003
Nosworthy, J. M. (ed.), *Cymbeline,* London: Methuen Arden, 1969
Pafford, J. H. P., "Simon Forman's *Bocke of Plaies*", *Review of English Studies,* New Series, 10.39, Aug. 1959, 289–91
Race, S., "Simon Forman's *Booke of Plaies*", *Notes and Queries,* January 1958: 9–14
Tannenbaum, S. A., *Shakspearian Scraps and Other Elizabethan Fragments,* New York: Columbia University Press, 1933
Thrall, W. F., "*Cymbeline,* Boccaccio and the Wager story in England", *SP,* 28, 1931: 639–651
Warren, R. (ed.), *Cymbeline,* Oxford: OUP, 1998.

Wells, S. & G. Taylor, (eds), *The Complete Oxford Shakespeare*. Oxford: OUP, 1986
Wilson, J. D. & R. W. Hunt, "The Authenticity of Forman's *Booke of Plaies*", *Review of English Studies*, 1947

# Other Plays

THE LATE,

And much admired Play,

Called

Pericles, Prince

of Tyre.

With the true Relation of the whole Hiſtorie,
aduentures, and fortunes of the ſaid Prince:

As alſo,

The no leſſe ſtrange, and worthy accidents,
in the Birth and Life, of his Daughter
*MARIANA.*

As it hath been diuers and ſundry times acted by
his Maieſties Seruants, at the Globe on
the Banck-ſide.

By William Shakeſpeare.

Imprinted at London for *Henry Goſſon*, and are
to be ſold at the ſigne of the Sunne in
Pater-noſter row, &c.
*1609.*

28. Title page to the first quarto of *Pericles*, 1609.
By permission of Bodleian Library, University of Oxford,
shelfmark Arch. G d.41 (5), title page.

# 37

# Pericles, Prince of Tyre

Kevin Gilvary

The play can be dated any time between the publication of Laurence Twine's *Painefull Adventures* (possibly as early as 1576 but no later than 1594) and the publication of the Quarto in 1609.

## Publication

Sir Sidney Lee gave a detailed examination of the publishing history of the play, which Chambers has reviewed. The play was entered into the Stationers' Register in May 1608, on the same day as *Antony & Cleopatra* (which was not published until 1623):

> [S.R. 1608.] 20 Maij. Edward Blount. Entred for his copie vnder thandes of Sir George Buck knight and Master Warden Seton A booke called, the booke of Pericles prynce of Tyre.

Most commentators see this as a 'blocking entry', i.e. intended to prevent any other publisher from publishing the play but Chambers discounts the possibility. The play was published in the following year, but oddly not by Edward Blunt but by Henry Gosson:

> [Q1. 1609.] The Late, And much admired Play, Called Pericles, Prince of Tyre. With the true Relation of the whole Historie, aduentures, and fortunes of the said Prince: As also, The no lesse strange, and worthy accidents, in the Birth and Life, of his Daughter Mariana. As it hath been diuers and sundry times acted by his Maiesties Seruants, at the Globe on the Banck-side. By William Shakespeare. Imprinted at London (by William White) for Henry Gosson, and are to be sold at the signe of the Sunne in Pater-noster row, &c. 1609.

. The play was published again in the same year with some small differences. All subsequent publications seem to derive from Q2.

> [Q2. 1609. Title Page as in Q1]

A third version appeared two years later:

> [Q3. 1611.] The Late And much admired Play, Called Pericles, Prince of Tyre. With the true Relation of the whole History, aduentures, and fortunes of the sayd Prince: As also, The no lesse strange and worthy accidents, in the Birth and Life, of his Daughter Mariana. As it hath beene diuers and sundry times acted by his Maiestyes Seruants, at the Globe on the Banck-side. By William Shakespeare. Printed at London by S(imon) S(tafford). 1611.

A fourth version appeared some years later as part of the collection published by Thomas Pavier:

> [Q4. 1619.] The Late, And much admired Play, Called Pericles, Prince of Tyre. With the true Relation of the whole History, aduentures, and fortunes of the saide Prince. Written by W. Shakespeare.

The play did not appear in the First Folio in 1623 or in the Second Folio of 1632. The rights to the play were transferred in 1626 to Edward Brewster and Robert Birde and to Richard Cotes in 1630. Q5 appeared in 1630 and Q6 in 1635. The play was eventually included in the Third Folio of 1664:

> [F3. 1664.] . . . And unto this Impression is added seven Playes, never before Printed in Folio, viz, Pericles, Prince of Tyre . . . [six other titles[1]]
>
> The much admired Play, Called Pericles, Prince of Tyre. With the true Relation of the whole History, Adventures, and Fortunes of the saide Prince. Written by W. Shakespeare, and published in his life-time.

Suzanne Gossett has outlined three suggestions as to why such a popular play, published in quarto under the name of William Shakespeare, did not appear in the First Folio (1623):

(a) The editors of the First Folio, Heminges and Condell, were unable to obtain either a copy of the play or the rights to it or both;
(b) The editors knew the text was badly corrupted;
(c) The editors knew that the play was co-authored (which she accepts as most likely).

Editors agree that the text is very poor, believing that the copy was not authoritative. Chambers has outlined many of the problems including irregular setting of verse and prose. Edwards states that at least two different printing shops were used and at least three different compositors. Bullough points out that much of the text is unintelligible, with muddled scenes, confusions of speech and action, and omissions of necessary material.

Most editors believe that the text arises from a poor memorial reconstruction. Edwards argued that the difference in style was due to the difference in the reporting ability of two different people. Against this, some editors have argued that the text was set from a rough draft of the play.[2] Wells & Taylor create a composite text derived from Q1 and from Wilkins's novel.

## Early Performance Dates

The title page to Q1 states that the play had been acted by the King's Men at the Globe 'diuers and sundry times', without indication of when; Hoeniger assumes that the play's performances occurred in the first half of 1608, before the theatres were closed on 28 July due to plague.

The play was witnessed by the Venetian Ambassador in 1607 or 1608:

> All the ambassadors, who have come to England have gone to the play more or less. Giustinian went with the French ambassador and his wife to a play called *Pericles*, which cost Giustinian more than 20 crowns. He also took the Secretary of Florence.[3]

Another performance is recorded at Gowthwaite Hall, Nidderdale, Yorks, by a troupe of travelling actors on 2 Feb 1610. A further performance is recorded at court in 1619.[4] The play's continuing popularity is recorded with distaste by Ben Jonson in 1629 in *Ode to Myself*:

> No doubt some mouldy tale, Like Pericles ; and stale As the Shrieve's crusts, and nasty as his fish— Scraps out of every dish Throwne forth, and rak't into the common tub.

Jonson's criticism seems to be concerned with the disjointed nature of the material rather than that the play was out of date.

## Attribution

Only a few editors accept 'William Shakespeare' as sole author.[5] Eric Sams has noted that in six quartos and in F3, the attribution of the play was to Shakespeare alone; three of the quartos had been published in Wilkins's lifetime. He further notes that none of the references to the play (eg by Jonson or Dryden) ever mention another author. Sams ascribes the difference in style to Shakespeare's revision of his own earlier play. Hoeniger dismisses this as 'pure speculation' without elaboration; Wells & Taylor (1987: 130) call it an 'intrinsic improbability', again without explanation.

Most editors, however, agree that the play was co-authored by George Wilkins.[6] In 1608, Wilkins (*c.* 1576–1618) published a novel, *The Painful Adventures of Pericles, Prince of Tyre* (STC 25638). This work borrowed extensively from Laurence Twine's 1576 story, in many instances verbatim (unlike the play, which merely has similarities). The title page of Wilkins's novel presents itself as 'The true History of the Play of Pericles, as it was lately presented by the worthy and ancient Poet John Gower' which shows it to derive from the play. Wilkins makes a further mention of the play in the Argument, asking the reader:

> . . . to receiue this Historie in the same manner as it was vnder the habite of ancient *Gower* the famous English Poet by the Kings Majesties Players excellently presented.

From this, it is inferred that Wilkins's prose novel derives from the play. Thus the use of the names 'Pericles' and 'Marina' which differ from the sources would been used first in the play and then in the novel. Chambers accepted co-authorship of the play but was undecided as to whether Wilkins was the co-author. Chambers notes that 'verbally the novel is much less close to the play than one would expect' especially as Wilkins is usually taken to be paraphrasing some of his own writing. Wells & Taylor (1987: 557) suggest that Wilkins may have contributed his scenes but was left without a copy of his own writing. They refer to the Shakespearean sections as Scenes 10–22 because Q1 has no act or scene divisions.

The arguments for co-authorship have been reviewed by Vickers and examined in detail by Jackson, who concur with Wells & Taylor in assigning authorship as follows:

| by George Wilkins | by Shakespeare |
|---|---|
| Acts 1, 2 (scenes 1–9) | Acts 3, 4, 5 (Scenes 10–22) |

There are two main ways in which co-authorship may have worked:

(a) **Collaboration**. The two authors planned the work together and then wrote their parts independently.

(b) **Revision**. A shortened form of the play by one of the authors was revised and expanded by the other author. Since Wilkins was younger and his novel was published at the same time as the play, it is usually assumed that he was the reviser of a short or unfinished play by Shakespeare. According to this view, it is possible for there to be a lapse of time between the composition of the original play and its subsequent revision.

Honigmann argues (followed by Jackson) that Wilkins wrote the original play and that Shakespeare subsequently adapted it. J. C. Maxwell (introduction, xxii) doubts whether "conclusive arguments can be adduced" for deciding between collaboration and revision.

## Sources

Bullough cites various versions of the romantic story of Apollonius. For the play of *Pericles*, he identifies two major sources:

- John Gower (*c.* 1327–1408), who devoted much of Book VIII of *Confessio Amantis* to this story. Gower's work was published in 1483 and again in 1554 (STC 12144). Shakespeare also used this story for the dénouement of *Comedy of Errors.*
- Laurence Twine, whose *Patterne of Painefull Adventures* was used by Shakespeare quite extensively. Twine's prose version was registered in 1576 and an undated extant copy has been tentatively assigned to 1594 by Loomis (STC 709). Another edition is dated to 1607 (STC 710). Twine's account seems to have used a French translation (*Le Violier des histoires rornaines*, Paris, 1521), of the Latin *Gesta Romanorum.*

Opinion is divided as to whether Shakespeare consulted the Greek Romances more directly than just through the works of Gower and Twine. Gesner argues that Shakespeare was well versed in works such as those by Heliodorus, Longus and Achilles Tatius, giving him an exceptional insight into the tradition as shown in all the romances including *Pericles.*

There are also some similarities with Sidney's *Arcadia* (1590). Bullough also mentions close parallels between Marina's plight and Declamation 53 in Alexandre Silvain's *Cent Histoires* (published in 1581 and translated into English by Lazarus Piot in 1596). Hoeniger mentions some dependence on a Latin treatise by J. Falckenburgk: *Britannia, Sive de Apollonice Humilitatis, Virtutis et Honoris Porta* (STC 10674) which was dedicated to Leicester and Lord Burghley in 1578 and quotes Psalm 33: *multae sunt tribulationes iustorum, sed ex omnibus his liberat eos Dominus.* ("Many are the tribulations of the Just but the Lord delivers them from all these.") Some editors have followed Muir who proposed the notion of an intermediate, lost play on the subject. According to Shaheen, there are relatively few allusions to the Bible. The description of Antiochus' punishment for incest at Scene 8 (, i.e Act 2 Scene 1) 6–12 is derived from 2 Maccabees 9 4–10. Wood notes that the reference to Thaisa's experience in Scene 11 (, i.e. Act 3 Scene 1) lines 61–5 closely recalls Jonah's experience inside the whale (Jonas, 2.3 5), especially as explained in the accompanying notes in both the Bishop's Bible and the Geneva Bible. Wood argues for specific reference to the Geneva Bible just before this at Scene 11 (i.e. Act 3 Scene

1) line 60 in "the aye-remaining lamps" which appears to recall the chapter heading for Exodus 27.20.

## Orthodox Date

Chambers sets a date of 1607–8 to link the date of composition to just before the first entry in the Stationers' Register and contemporary allusions to the play at this time; thus also Hoeniger, Wells & Taylor, DelVecchio & Hammond, Warren and Gossett.

Chambers, however, would have preferred a date 1608–9, i.e. after its registration:

> The hypothesis here adopted [ie that Q1 of *Pericles* is a revision of an earlier play] is helpful chronologically, because it enables Shakespeare's work to be put in late 1608, instead of before Blount's entry in the previous May. It would be difficult to find room for it earlier, since it must be later than *Coriolanus* and *Timon of Athens*, for both of which we seem driven to 1607–8. On the other hand, we have nothing else for 1608–9.

Chambers's date seems to derive mainly from the assumed dates of other plays rather than the evidence for this play. Maxwell followed this slightly later date of 1608–09.

## Internal Orthodox Evidence

There are no allusions from within the play that have datable external reference. Most stylistic analysis of the play concern authorship rather than date. Wells & Taylor (1987: 130) note that "the problems of text and authorship make it impossible to use internal evidence to date *Pericles* precisely" but continue in general terms: "it is clear that Sc 10–22 [ie Acts 3–5] belong among the late plays." They say that these scenes link strongly in vocabulary with *The Tempest.* Warren develops the associations between this play and the so-called late romances which also include *The Winter's Tale* and *Cymbeline.* He observes that these plays share "a wide emotional range, focusing on extremes of love, hate, jealousy, grief, despair, even apparent death and resurrection, ultimately reunion, forgiveness and reconciliation."

## External Orthodox Evidence

Various references have been taken to suggest a Jacobean date of composition. Firstly, the play was registered in 1608 and published in 1609. Secondly, there are known performances (as stated above) from 1608. Thirdly, there is clear interest in the story with the reprinting of Twine (1607) and the publication of Wilkins's novel (1608). Finally, there are various contemporary references: one in *Pimlico*, an anonymous pamphlet circulating in 1609; another in Robert Tailor's play *The Hog hath Lost his Pearl* (1614) which both refer to the popularity of *Pericles.*

These references, however, only indicate that the play was popular – not when it had been composed. Gossett (57–60) indulges her imagination, stating: "It is not difficult to imagine Wilkins prodding Shakespeare to consider a collaboration during the slack period when the theatres were closed." Later she adds:

> The collaboration is easy to imagine: one night Shakespeare chats about travel tales with Wilkins. . . . Shakespeare had used bits of the familiar story of Apollonius of Tyre as the frame for his *Comedy of Errors*, and between then, the men sk, etc.h out a full play on the Apollonius legend. Indeed, as the play reiterates elements of Shakespeare's earlier writing, . . . Shakespeare's is the controlling hand.

The implication is that the play reflects his "earlier writing", a possibility that has been neglected in recent years.

## Oxfordian Dating

The usual dating from an Oxfordian perspective for the original play dates to the late 1570s as one of his early plays. According to this view, the play remained in a poor state either among the author's papers or among the theatre companies stock of plays, being revised c1606 by George Wilkins.

Many commentators have been surprised at the clumsy episodic structure of the play. John Dryden asserted in his Prologue to Davenant's *Circe* (1677) that *Pericles* was Shakespeare's first play:

> Shakespeare's own Muse her *Pericles* first bore,
> The Prince of Tyre was elder than the Moore:
> 'Tis miracle to see a first good Play
> All Hawthorns do not bloom on *Christmas-Day.*

Dryden of course was making his judgement on the dramatic quality of the play. Similarly, George Saintsbury believed that this was an early play, possibly later revised:

> Nothing is heard of the play till 1606, when it was licensed; and it is pretty certain that, whether the whole was written by Shakespeare or not, the whole was not written by Shakespeare at or near that time. The present writer would be prepared to take either side on the question:

> "Did Shakespeare about this time complete an early immature sk, etc.h of his own; or did he furnish, voluntarily or involuntarily, scenes to one which was vamped up and botched off by another or others?" But he rather inclines to the first alternative, because of the distinct similarity of the phenomena to those shown in others of Shakespeare's plays actually contained in the folio. That the scheme of the play is not of a mature period is shown by the fact that it has little character, and that what it has is still less concerned with the working out of the action.

Eva Turner Clark dates the play to the late 1570s after Oxford had returned from his Italian journey but was a stranger to his wife and daughter (these events are described in detail by Nelson, 141–154). She notes the aptness of Pericles' soliloquies to Oxford , e.g at Scene 5 100–1 (, i.e. Act 2 Scene 1, 58–9, Gossett):

> A man, for whom both the waters and the wind
> In that vast tennis-court had made the ball.

Oxford famously quarrelled with Sidney over use of the tennis court (Nelson, 195–200). Clark further notes Oxford's victories in the tilts, which coincides with Pericles' victory. Farina describes Oxford's links with Laurence Twine who contributed to his brother's 1573 translation of *The Breviary of Britain* (STC 16636). This work was dedicated to Oxford. Further links can be found in Oxford's Mediterranean travels, his interest in the Greek Romances (Thomas Underdown dedicated his translation of Heliodorus' *Aethiopica*, STC 13041, to Oxford in 1569) and his ownership of an expensive Geneva Bible (Nelson, 126–34; 236; and 53)[7].

## Conclusion

The play can be dated any time between the publication of Laurence Twine's *Painefull Adventures* (possibly as early as 1576 but no later than 1594) and the publication of the Quarto in 1609.

## Notes

1. The other six texts are not considered to have been composed by Shakespeare: they were *Locrine*, *The London Prodigal*, *The Puritan. Sir John Oldcastle*, *Thomas Lord Cromwell*, and *A Yorkshire Tragedy*.Three of these had been published in quarto under Shakespeare's name: *Sir John Oldcastle* in 1600, *The London Prodigal* in 1605 and *A Yorkshire Tragedy* in 1608. *Locrine* was published in 1595 by "W.S." See Wells & Taylor (1987: 134–41) for detailed discussion of the Shakespeare apocrypha.
2. H. Craig, "*Pericles* and *The Painfull Adventures*", *SPhil*, XLV, 1949 and C. J. Sisson, *New Readings in Shakespeare*, 1955.

3. This report emerges from the Venetian State Papers (*V.P.* xiv, 600) for a trial in 1617. According to Chambers, *WS*, II, 335, Guistinian was the Venetian Ambassador in England from 5 January 1606 until 23 November 1608; Antoine de la Boderie, the French Ambassador, was accompanied by his wife from April 1607; Lotto, the Duke of Tuscany's agent, was in London from May 1606 until at least March 1608.
4. Hoeniger, introduction lxvi, quoting C. J. Sisson, 'Shakespeare's Quartos as Prompt-Copies' in *RES*, XVIII, 1942, 129–143.
5. Not all editors have accepted co-authorship: F. D. Hoeniger, 'Gower and Shakespeare in *Pericles*', *ShQ* 33 (1982), 461–479 retracted the opinion of co-authorship which he had expressed in his Arden edition of 1963. DelVecchio and Hammond briefly dismiss co-authorship and accept Shakespeare as sole author.
6. Some editors have suggested other co-authors. Hoeniger, followed by Bullough, prefers John Day. David J. Lake in "The *Pericles* candidates: Heywood, Rowley and Wilkins", *NQ*, 215 (1970) 135–141, eventually opts for Wilkins, whose biography is recounted by Roger Prior, "The Life of George Wilkins", *SS* 25 (1972) 137–52.
7. Oxford's copy of the Geneva Bible is held in the Folger Shakespeare Library in Washington. It has been studied by Roger Stritmatter, *The Marginalia of Edward de Vere's Geneva Bible* (2001).

## Other Cited Works


Bullough, Geoffrey, *Narrative and Dramatic Sources of Shakespeare*, vol. VI (Other 'Classical' Plays) London, Routledge and Kegan Paul, 1966

Chambers, E. K., *The Elizabethan Stage*, 4 vols, Oxford: Clarendon, 1923

—, *William Shakespeare: A Study of Facts and Problems*. 2 vols. Oxford, Clarendon Press, 1930

Clark, Eva Turner, *Hidden Allusions in Shakespeare's Plays*. New York: Kennikat, rptd 1974

DelVecchio, D. and Hammond, A. (eds) *Pericles, Prince of Tyre*. Cambridge, CUP, 1998

Edwards, P., "An Approach to the Problem of *Pericles*", *SS*, 5, 1952, 25–49

Farina, William, *De Vere as Shakespeare: An Oxfordian Reading of the Canon*. Jefferson, NC: McFarland, 2006.

Gesner, Carol, *Shakespeare and the Greek Romance*. University Press of Kentucky, Lexington, 1970

Gossett, Suzanne, (ed.) *Pericles, Prince of Tyre*. London, Arden3, 2004

Hoeniger, F. D. (ed.) *Pericles, Prince of Tyre*. London, Arden2, 1963

Honigmann, E. A. J., *The Stability of Shakespeare's Text*. London, Edward Arnold, 1965

Jackson, MacDonald, *Defining Shakespeare: 'Pericles' as Test Case*. Oxford, OUP, 2003

Lee, Sidney, *Shakespeare's 'Pericles': Facsimile of First Edition*. Oxford, Clarendon, 1895

Loomis, Laura A., *Medieval Romance in England: A Study of the Sources and Analogues of the Non-Cyclic Metrical Romances* (1969)

Maxwell, J. C., (ed.) *Pericles, Prince of Tyre.* Cambridge, CUP, 1956
Muir, Kenneth, "The Problem of *Pericles*", *English Studies* XXX (1949): 65–83
Nelson, A. H., *Monstrous Adversary.* Manchester, MUP, 2003
Saintsbury, George, "Shakespeare: Plays omitted by Meres" in *The Cambridge History of English and American Literature*: *The Drama to 1642, Part One.* vol. V, ch. VIII § 13 (1907–21)
Sams, Eric, "The Painful Misadventures of *Pericles* I–II", *NQ*, (1991)
Shaheen, Naseeb, *Biblical References in Shakespeare's Plays,* Newark: UDP, 1999
Vickers, Brian, *Shakespeare Co-Author*, Oxford: OUP, 2002
Warren, Roger (ed.) *A Reconstructed Text of 'Pericles, Prince of Tyre' by W. Shakespeare and George Wilkins*, Oxford: OUP, 2003
Wells, Stanley, & Gary Taylor, *William Shakespeare: The Complete Works,* Oxford: OUP, 1986
—, *William Shakespeare: A Textual Companion.* Oxford: OUP,1987
Wood, James O., "Shakespeare, *Pericles* and the Genevan Bible", *Pacific Coast Philology*, 12, 1977: 82–9

38

# The Two Noble Kinsmen

Kevin Gilvary

The extant version of *The Two Noble Kinsmen* can be dated any time before Jonson's apparent reference to it in *Bartholomew Fair*, 1614. There might have been an original version as early as 1594 or even 1566.

In this chapter, line numbers are given by act and scene (according to Wells & Taylor, *The Oxford Shakespeare*).

## Publication Date

*The Two Noble Kinsmen* was entered into the Stationers' Register on 8 April 1634 to John Waterson:[1]

> [S.R. 1634] 8° Aprilis master John Waterson Entred for his Copy vnder the hands of Sir Henry Herbert and master Aspley warden a Tragi Comedy called the two noble kinsmen by John ffletcher and William Shakespeare.

*The Two Noble Kinsmen* (*TNK*) was first published in Quarto in that year. It is the only quarto to bear the name of Shakespeare alongside the name of a co-author:

> [Q1. 1634] *The Two Noble Kinsmen* presented at the Blackfriers by the Kings Maiesties servants with great applause written by the memorable worthies of their time; Mr. Iohn Fletcher, and Mr. William Shakespeare, Gent. Printed at London by Tho. [mas] Cotes for Iohn Waterson: and are to be sold at the signe of the Crowne in Pauls Church-yard. 1634

The play was not included in any of the Shakespeare Folios (F1 1623; F2 1632; F3 1663–4; F4 1685). The SR records that the play was transferred from Waterson to Moseley in 1646. It was omitted from the first folio of Beaumont

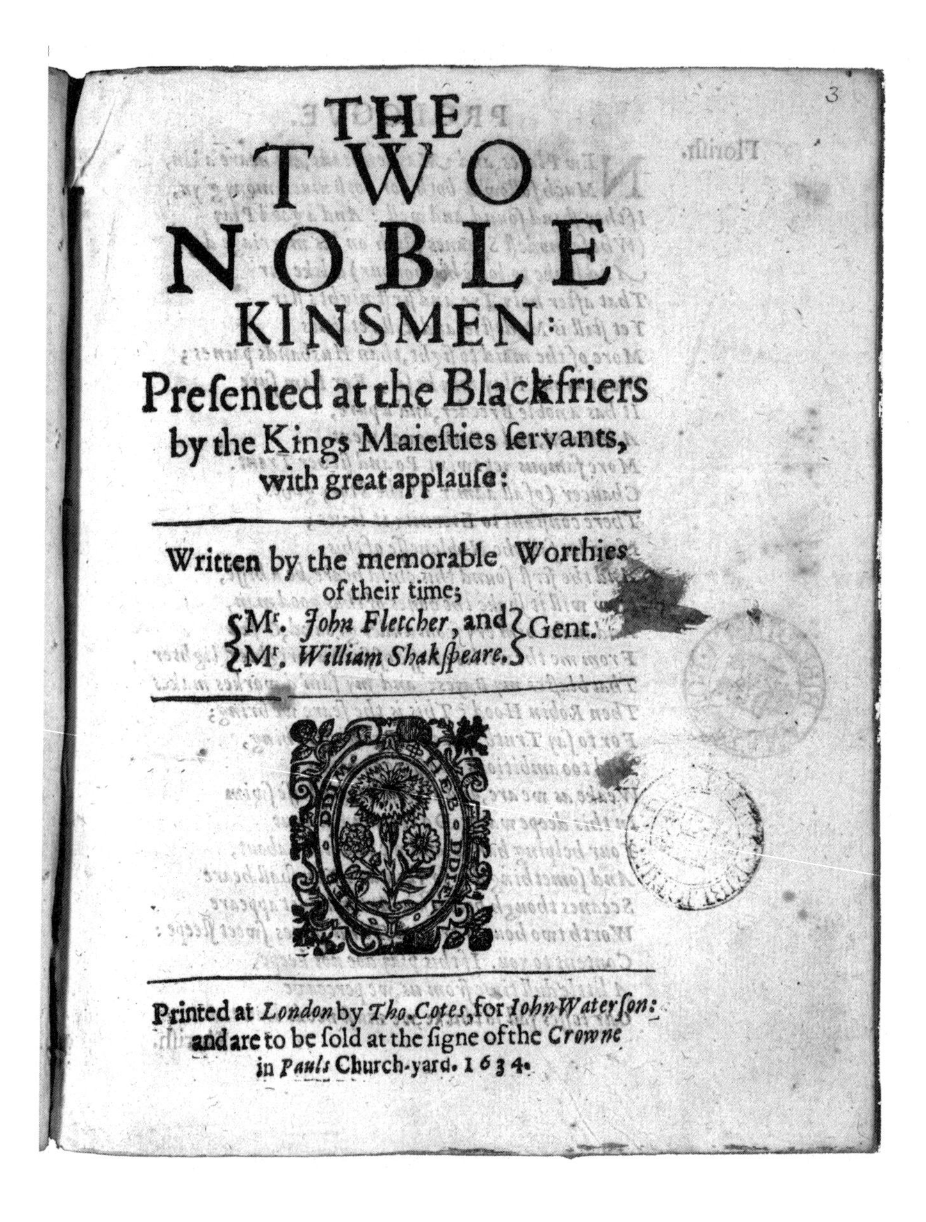

THE
TWO
NOBLE
KINSMEN:

Preſented at the Blackfriers
by the Kings Maieſties ſervants,
with great applauſe:

Written by the memorable Worthies
of their time;

Mr. *John Fletcher*, and
Mr. *William Shakſpeare*. Gent.

Printed at *London* by *Tho. Cotes*, for *Iohn Waterſon*:
and are to be ſold at the ſigne of the *Crowne*
in *Pauls* Church-yard. 1634.

29. Title page to the first quarto of *Two Noble Kinsmen,* 1634.
By permission of Bodleian Library, University of Oxford,
shelfmark Arch. G e.33 (3), title page.

and Fletcher's plays in 1647 but was later published in the second folio of 1679 (where it did not mention Shakespeare as co-author). This version seems to have derived entirely from the 1634 quarto and therefore has no independent authority (Waith, 23).

## Performance Date

Both Waith and Potter review the play's performance history. There is a vague reference in the Q1 title page of 1634 to the play's performance at the indoor Blackfriars Theatre in London, but the date is unknown. This theatre had been hosting plays from 1576. Burbage took it over in 1596 and it went over to the King's Men in 1609. There is a reference in the prologue to "our losses": (*Two Noble Kinsmen*, Prologue, 30–2).

> If this play do not keep, / A little dull time from us, we perceive /
> Our losses fall so thick, we must needs leave.

"Our losses" has been interpreted by some to mean the destruction of the Globe in 1613, but this is speculation. The phrase has also been taken to refer to financial losses, or to the death of Shakespeare in 1616 and/or the death of John Fletcher in 1625; against this, it has been pointed out that the humorous tone of the prologue would seem to militate against a reference to the death of the author(s).

In 1614, Ben Jonson seems to refer to a character in this play: firstly the character Winwife chooses the name 'Palemon' from 'The Play':

> *Grace.* Because I will bind both your Endeavours to work together friendly and jointly each to the others Fortune, and have my self fitted with some Means, to make him that is forsaken, a part of amends.
> *Quarlous.* These Conditions are very courteous. Well, my Word is out of the *Arcadia* then, *Argalus.*
> *Win-wife.* And mine out of the Play, *Palemon.*
> (*Bartholomew Fair,* 4.3.63–8)

There are further references to the character of Palemon in 5.2. Two recent editors of the play (E.A. Horsman, 1960, and Suzanne Gossett, 2000) identify the reference as alluding to *The Two Noble Kinsmen,* especially as the rivalry of Winwife and Quarlous for the love of Grace clearly parodies Palamon and Arcite, who compete for the love of Emilia in *TNK.*

The earliest reference to the play is on a fragment of paper, (Chambers, *WS*, II, 346) which suggests that it was considered for performance at court in 1619. The earliest definite reference to a performance, however, is Davenant's in 1664.

## Attribution

Because *Two Nobel Kinsmen* was omitted from Shakespeare's First Folio (and subsequent) and not published until 1634, it has remained an 'apocryphal' play. Some have claimed that Shakespeare had no hand in it and that the ascription was a publisher's lure. Brian Vickers has reviewed the tests for co-authorship in considerable detail and gives thorough support for assigning the various parts of the play as follows (Vickers, 414; as reported also by Waith, 22):

| **Shakespeare** | **Fletcher** |
|---|---|
| Act 1 Scenes 1–4 | Prologue |
| Act 2 Scene 1 | Act 2 Scenes 2–6 |
| Act 3 Scenes 1–2 | Act 3 Scenes 3–6 |
| Act 4 Scene 3 | Act 4 Scenes 1 & 2 |
| Act 5 Scene 1; Sc 3 & 4 | Act 5 Scene 2; epilogue |
| Total lines: 1,089 | Total lines: 1,458 |

There is a suggestion that 5.1.1–33 were composed by Fletcher. Potter, followed by Shaheen, thinks that the original play was written by Shakespeare and later revised by Fletcher.

## John Fletcher

John Fletcher's earliest known involvement with the theatre dates to *c.* 1606 when he wrote for the Children of the Queen's Revels. He is now believed to have co-authored (or revised) *Henry VIII* (see chapter 24) and there is a record that he co-authored with Shakespeare a lost play *Cardenio.* He is also said to have composed *The Woman's Prize or The Tamer Tamed*, as a sequel to *The Taming of the Shrew.* Fletcher is known mainly for his collaboration with Francis Beaumont, but he also worked with other playwrights.[2]

## Sources

Unfortunately for modern scholarship, Geoffrey Bullough did not consider this play in his *Narrative and Dramatic Sources of Shakespeare* (1957–74), but the sources have been reviewed by Waith, Potter and Gillespie. The principal source for *TNK* was acknowledged in the play's prologue:

> Chaucer (of all admir'd) the Story gives,
> There constant to Eternity it lives.
> (*Two Noble Kinsmen* Prologue, 13–14)

Geoffrey Chaucer's *Canterbury Tales* containing *The Knight's Tale* was available in a number of editions: Thynnes' (1532), Stow's (1561) and Speght's (1598) but there is no indication which edition was used. An error at 4.2.104 (presumably by Fletcher, as it occurs in the section attributed to him) seems to preserve a misprint from the 1598 edition (Waith, 178). The author(s) also appear to know Giovanni Boccaccio, *Teseide*, perhaps in Le Maçon's French translation of 1545 but not available in English until 1620, for some of the speeches and details concerning Arcyte's death. The author(s) made use of Plutarch's 'Life of Theseus' (available in North's Plutarch, 1579) and possibly John Lydgate's *Siege of Thebes*, included in Stow's and Speght's editions of Chaucer. Potter sees the influence in Act 1 of Euripides' *Suppliants* (possibly through Seneca's version, available in English in Newton's edition, 1581). Waith believes it likely that Ovid's *Metamorphoses* were also in mind at 1.1.78–9, in the reference to the "scythe-tusked boar" and at 1.2.85–7, in the reference to Phoebus' anger at his horses.

There are two other references to dramatic entertainment on the same subject:

> (a) a play called *Palamon and Arcyte,* probably translated by Richard Edwards from a Latin version, was performed at Christ Church, Oxford, in 1566 before the Queen; this play was not published but there are accounts of it by three observers, which are discussed below under Oxfordian Dating. Durand states that it was different from *Two Noble Kinsmen.*[3]
>
> (b) Henslowe's Diary records four performances of *Palamon and Arsett* by the Admiral's Men in 1594.

Other possible allusions occurred in Samuel Daniel's play *The Queen's Arcadia*, which features a character called Palamon. This play was performed at Christ Church, Oxford in 1605 and published in 1606. The second possible allusion occurs in Barnabe Barnes' *Four Bookes of Offices* (1606):

> [War] is the noble corrector of all prodigal states, a skillful bloodletter against all dangerous obstructions and pleurasies of peace.

This seems to echo Arcite's prayer to Mars in 5.1:

> Oh great corrector of enormous times;
> Shaker of o'er-rank states; thou grand decider
> Of dusty and old titles, that heal'st with blood
> The earth when it is sick and cur'st the world
> O'th' pleurisy of people *Two Noble Kinsmen* 5.1.62–6

According to Shaheen, *TNK* has a much lower density of biblical allusions than other plays. The reference at 1.1.158–9 "And his army full of bread and sloth" seems to echo Ezekiel, 16.49: "Pride, fulness of bread and abundance of idleness" in the wording of the 1560 Geneva Bible. Other versions read "fulness of meate".

## Orthodox Dates

Most commentators accept a date *c.* 1612–13 (e.g. Waith and Potter). Wells & Taylor propose 1613–14. They note that the morris dance (in 3.5 to entertain Theseus and his party of hunters, a scene attributed to Fletcher by them along with most commentators) was "apparently borrowed" from Francis Beaumont's *Inner Temple and Gray's Inn Masque,* performed and registered in 1613. They are of the opinion that the dance is such an integral part of the play as to confirm the suggestion that it was written and performed in 1613–4, in time for Jonson's reference in *Bartholomew Fair.*

## Oxfordian Date

Katherine Chiljan has argued that it is likely that Oxford wrote the play in his youth, perhaps in the 1560s when he was in his teens. Mark Anderson has suggested that Oxford made small additions to the play for performance in the 1590s and that Fletcher was probably invited sometime around 1612–3 to revise the play and perhaps adapt it for performance at that time.

Chiljan has also argued that Oxford probably wrote (or co-wrote with Edwards) the translation of *Palamon and Arcyte* in 1566 when it was performed before the Queen at Oxford University (see the accounts in Durand and Elliott). Richard Edwards, as Master of the Children of the Chapel, was said to have been one of the translators of the play from Latin. The sixteen-year-old Oxford was present at the performances at Christ Church and, a few days later, the Queen awarded degrees to distinguished guests, including Oxford (Nelson, 44–5). Richard Edwards was credited with the authorship of the play but (in Robinson's account) he was just one of the authors who translated it from Latin. There is no further data about this Latin play. Edwards was later associated with Oxford, for both had poems published in *The Paradies of Dainty Devices* (1576). Edwards was also named alongside Oxford as deserving of praise for Comedy and Interlude in *The Arte of English Poetrie* (by George Puttenham?) in 1589.

Chiljan adduces a number of reasons for her argument: at 5.4.44, Palamon says in disbelief: "Can that be / When, Venus, I have said, is false?" In *TNK,* Palamon does not rebuke the goddess at all, but according to Bereblock in 1566, Palamon "casts reproaches upon Venus saying that he had served her from infancy, and that now she had neither desire nor power to help him." According to Chiljan, Palamon's words at 5.4.44 are a residue from the early form of the play, while his actual rebukes had been revised. Chiljan also believes that the phrase "our losses" – usually interpreted to refer either to the destruction of the Globe or to the death of the authors in 1616 and 1625 – actually referred to the three people who were killed on the first night of the performance in 1566 when a staircase collapsed. Chiljan further notes that Richard Edwards was very busy at this time in the production of all three dramatic entertainments for the Queen and would have welcomed assistance. Finally, Chiljan sees close resemblances between Oxford's early poetry and Emily's lament, an accepted fragment from *Palamon and Arcyte*:[4]

Come follow me you nymphs,
whose eyes are never dry,
Augment your wailing number
now with me poor Emelie.

Give place ye to my plaints,
whose joys are pinched with pain:
My love, alas, through foul mishap,
most cruel death hath slain.

What wight can will, alas,
my sorrows now indict?
I wail and want my new desire,
I lack my new delight.

Gush out my trickling tears,
like mighty floods of rain:
My knight, alas, through foul mishap
most cruel death hath slain.

Oh hap, alas, most hard,
oh death why didst thou so?
Why could not I embrace my joy,
for me that bid such woe?

False fortune out, alas,
woe worth thy subtle train:
Whereby my love through foul mishap,
most cruel death hath slain.

Rock me asleep in woe,
you woeful Sisters three,
Oh cut you of my fatal thread,
dispatch poor Emelie.

Why should I live, alas,
and linger thus in pain?
Farewell my life, sith that my love
most cruel death hath slain.

After noting close similarities between the vocabulary underlined in this lament and Oxford's juvenile poetry, (published by Edwards in *Paradise of Dainty Devices*, 1576; Nelson, 150–1), Chiljan concludes that Oxford wrote the 1566 play, *Palamon and Arcyte* or possibly co-wrote with Edwards (and that the fragments that survived were taken by Fletcher decades later and incorporated into what became *Two Noble Kinsmen*)..

Further reasons for proposing Oxford's (at least part) authorship is that the author before 1620 would have needed to read Boccaccio in either Italian or French, both languages known to Oxford, but difficult to credit to William Shakespeare of Stratford. Nelson, (37), records that Oxford's educational schedule included two hours of French instruction and two hours of Latin instruction per day, and that by the age of 13 he was writing a very good letter in French to his guardian. When he was 17, his uncle, Arthur Golding, published a translation of Ovid's *Metamorphoses* (1567), which he dedicated to Oxford's guardian, William Cecil. At the age of 19, Oxford is recorded as buying expensive copies of Chaucer, Plutarch (in Amyot's French translation) and the Geneva Bible (Nelson, 53); these works were all used by the author(s) of *Two Noble Kinsmen.* At the same time, he bought other works of literature in French, Italian and Latin. While he is not known to have bought a copy of Seneca (either in Latin or in English), it is likely that he would have studied

Seneca's plays in Latin with his tutor.

Subsequent references (e.g. in Henslowe's Diary, 1594 and in Johnson's *Bartholomew Fair, c.* 1614) indicate that the play was known through performance on the public stage, rather indicating when the Shakespearean elements of the play were composed.

## Conclusion

The extant version of *The Two Noble Kinsmen* can be dated any time before Jonson's apparent reference to it in *Bartholomew Fair*, 1614. There might have been an original version as early as 1566 and/or 1594.

## Notes

1. John Waterson's father, Simon, published various literary works (but none by Shakespeare) until his death in 1634. John succeeded to the family business but is not known to have published other works of Shakespeare (see Peter Daly, et al. *The English Emblem Tradition,*1988). It has been suggested that the attribution was a publisher's lure, but Waterson does not seem to have used Shakespeare's name in this way anywhere else.
2. For details about John Fletcher, see G. E. Bentley, *The Profession of Dramatist in Shakespeare's Time, 1590–1642,* (Princeton Unversity Press, 1971). *Cardenio* was performed by the King's Men in 1613. An entry in the Stationer's Register in 1653 attributes the play to Shakespeare and Fletcher. The play may be concerned with a character called Cardenio, depicted in *Don Quixote*, which was translated into English in 1612 by Thomas Shelton.
3. W. Y. Durand came to this conclusion in his short article of 1902 (quoted by Chambers, *ES*, III, 311). Durand (1905) gave the full contemporary accounts of all three plays staged before the Queen in Oxford in 1566: principally a translation of John Bereblock's detailed Latin account, with the brief accounts of Nicholas Robinson and Richard Stephens.
4. Chiljan reports that Emily's poem survives in *Arbor of Amorous Devices*, registered Jan. 7, 1594 (unsigned), and in British Museum Additional MS 26, 737, fol. 106, signed "The song of Emelye per Edwardes".

## Other Cited Works

Anderson, Mark, *Shakespeare by Another Name*, New York: Gorham, 2005

Bowers, Fredson, *The Two Noble Kinsmen, The Dramatic Works in the Beaumont and Fletcher Canon,* vol. 7, Cambridge: CUP, 2008

Chambers, E. K., *The Elizabethan Stage*, 4 vols, Oxford: Clarendon, 1923

Chambers, E. K., *William Shakespeare A Study of Facts and Problems*, 2 vols, Oxford: Clarendon, 1930

Chiljan, Katherine, "Oxford and *Palamon and Arcite*", *Shakespeare Oxford Newsletter*, Spring 1999, available at www.shakespeare-oxford.com/?p=40 (accessed 5

November 2009)
Durand, W. Y., "Notes on Richard Edwards", *Journal of Germanic Philology*, IV, 1902
Durand, W, Y., "Palimony and Arcata, Prone, Marcus Gamins, and the Theatre in which they were acted, as described by John Bereblock (1566)", *PMLA*, 20, 1905, 502–28
Elliott, Jr., John R., "Queen Elizabeth at Oxford: New Light on the Royal Plays of 1566", *English Literary Renaissance*, 18, 1988
Gillespie, Stuart, *Shakespeare's Books,* London: Continuum Press, 2001
Nelson, Alan H., *Monstrous Adversary*, Liverpool: LUP, 2003
Potter, Lois (ed.), *The Two Noble Kinsmen*, London: Arden, 1997
Shaheen, Naseeb, *Biblical References in Shakespeare's Plays*, Delaware: UDP, 1999
Vickers, Brian, *Shakespeare Co-Author,* Oxford: OUP, 2002
Waith, Eugene M. (ed.), *The Two Noble Kinsmen*, Oxford: OUP, 1989
Wells, Stanley & Gary Taylor, *The Oxford Shakespeare: Complete Works*, Oxford: OUP, 1987
Wells, Stanley & Gary Taylor, *William Shakespeare: A Textual Companion*, Oxford: OUP, 1987

THE
RAIGNE OF
KING EDVVARD
the third:

*As it hath bin sundrie times plaied about
the Citie of London.*

LONDON,
*Printed for Cuthbert Burby.*
1596.

30. The title page to the anonymous first quarto of *Edward III*, 1596. It has generally been believed that this play was by another author but some scholars have argued that it was by Shakespeare. By permission of Bodleian Library, University of Oxford, shelfmark Mal. 209 (1), title page.

39

# Edward III

Richard Malim

The extant *Edward III* can be dated any time between 1577 and 1595 when the play was registered. An early version may well have been composed in the early 1570s.

Line numbers below are given both by act and scene (according to Melchiori's Cambridge edition) and by Through Line Numbering (TLN according to Eric Sams's Yale edition).[1]

## Publication Date

*Edward III* was first registered on 1 December 1595, a year after *Titus Andronicus* and *The First Part of the Contention* (*2 Henry VI*) were registered and published anonymously, and in the same year that *The True Tragedy* (*3 Henry VI*) was published, also anonymously:

> [S.R. 1595] primo die Decembris Cuthbert Burby Entred for his copie vnder the handes of the wardens A booke Intitled Edward the Third and the blacke prince their warres w[th] kinge Iohn of Fraunce vj[d]

*Edward III* was first published in Quarto in 1596:

> [Q1. 1596] THE RAIGNE OF KING EDVVARD the third: *As it hath bin sundrie times plaied about the Citie of London.* London. Printed for Cuthbert Burby. 1596

No (other) play by Shakespeare was registered or published in 1596. In 1597, *Richard II* and *Richard III* were registered and published anonymously and in 1598 *1 Henry IV* was registered and published also anonymously (though it was attributed to Shakespeare in Q2 in 1599). *Edward III* was published again, anonymously, three years later:

> [Q2. 1599] THE RAIGNE OF KING EDVVARD the third: As it hath bene sundry times plaied about the Citie of London. Imprinted at London by Simon Stafford for Cuthbert Burby: And are to be sold at his shop neere the Royall Exchange. 1599

The SR records that ownership of the play was transferred in 1609 to William Welby, in 1618 to Thomas Snodham,[2] in 1626 to William Stansby and finally to George Bishop in 1639. Despite these transfers, there seems to have been no further edition after 1599. The play was not included in the First Folio of 1623. Both Sams and Melchiori review possible explanations for this omission.

## Performance Date

While there are vague references to performances in London in the title pages of 1596 and 1599 quartos, there are no definite records of performances until 1911 (Melchiori). However, Sams (173–4) reports the possibility that Lord Hunsdon provided a copy of Froissart's *Chronicles* and that the play was performed under his tutelage shortly after he established the Lord Chamberlain's Men in 1594.

## Attribution

Because the play was published anonymously in the quartos of 1596 and 1599 and omitted from the First Folio (and subsequent Folios), it has remained an 'anonymous' play. Melchiori has reviewed the attributions. The consensus for Shakespearean authorship has gradually increased since Edward Capel (in 1760) first argued a serious case. Nineteenth-century German scholars were especially persuaded that Shakespeare was (at least in part) author. Chambers tentatively accepts this position as a possibility. Wells & Taylor (*Textual Companion* 136–7) exclude the play from the complete works but accept as likely that Shakespeare wrote part of it. Slater's statistical approach seemed to have established the play as by Shakespeare. The evidence for joint authorship, mainly on an analysis of strings of three words, has been explored by Brian Vickers, who sees the play as 60% by Kyd and 40% by Shakespeare.[3] Some commentators, notably Eric Sams, have envisaged the play as by Shakespeare alone.

## Sources

Unfortunately for modern scholarship, neither W. G. Boswell-Stone nor Geoffrey Bullough dealt with this play.[4] According to Melchiori, the first principal source was Holinshed's *Chronicle* (first edition 1577, second edition

1587), which supplied many details including names such as Chatillon. The usual assumption is that the dramatist(s) used the second edition, but this has not been firmly established. The second principal source was Froissart's *Chroniques* (completed in French in 1373, and translated into English as *Froissart's Chronicle* by 1525) for many important details, including the misdating of the founding of the Order of the Garter (apparently in 1344 rather than in 1348) and the knighting of the Prince (at 3.3.172–218, TLN 1494–1542). Melchiori also cites reference to William Painter's *Palace of Pleasure* (1566–75) and to some pamphlets written *c.* 1589–90, which celebrated the defeat of the Spanish Armada in 1588. These pamphlets apparently provided a few additional details for the description of the sea Battle of Sluys (at 3.1. 141–84, TLN, 1190–1231). These few details may, however, have been added in a later revision. Thus the last definite source for *Edward III* is the first edition of Holinshed, 1587.

## Orthodox Dates

Most commentators accept a date range of 1590–1595. Chambers dates the play between 1590 (after the Armada pamphlets) and before its registration in 1595, inclining towards a date of 1594 for a possible Shakespearean contribution (in *ES*, not repeated in *WS*). Wells & Taylor are also uncertain about its date, merely stating that it clearly post-dates the Armada. Slater's statistical analysis led him to the conclusion that the play was contemporary with the so-called first tetralogy, i.e *1, 2, 3 Henry VI–Richard III* which he dates to the early 1590s. In his review, Melchiori prefers 1592–3. Sams prefers a slightly earlier date, shortly after 1589 (with a possible revision *c.* 1594). Godshalk prefers a date 1589–92.

## Oxfordian Date

Oxfordians generally propose that Oxford wrote the history plays from the mid 1580s at about the time of his being granted a £1,000 annuity by Elizabeth. They argue that the Queen awarded him this sum in payment for writing patriotic drama, which would be all the more effective for being anonymous (Anderson, 211). In the case of *Edward III*, however, it is usually viewed as one of his youthful works, perhaps dating to the early 1570s, when Oxford was in his early twenties.

The naval references to the Battle of Sluys need not depend on the Armada pamphlets, being rather general in nature. They seem to point to the Battle of Lepanto on 7 October 1571, when the Christian Alliance utterly smashed a slightly larger Turkish fleet in one great clash under Don John of Austria, the leader of the Christian fleet (satirised as Don Armado, the fantastical Spaniard in *Love's Labours Lost*). The play's description is of one terrific battle taking place in one day, unlike the series of actions in 1588, while the invading English navy is described as:

> The proud Armado of King Edward's ships [3.1.64; TLN 1111]
> Majestical the order of their course [3.1.71; TLN 1119]
> Figuring the hornéd circle of the moon [3.1.72; TLN 1120]

The crescent moon formation was adopted at Lepanto by the Turks. Both the Turkish crescent at Lepanto and the Armada crescent in 1588 were mainly defensive, unlike Edward III's formation:

> The greatest before, well furnished with archers, and ever between two ships of archers, I had one ship with men-at-arms (Froissart, 50).

In *Edward III,* the French mariner reporting the battle to his King refers to a French ship:

> Much did the Nonpareille, that brave ship...[3.1 177; TLN 1225].

The ship's name was not mentioned by Holinshed. The emendation was suggested by Capell in 1760. Both Q1 and Q2 actually read "Nom per illa", which links the name with an English Nonpareil which fought successfully (but in a secondary role) against the Armada in 1588.[5]

Further suggestions that *Edward III* was an early play by Edward de Vere, Earl of Oxford, include:

(a) Nina Green, following up Slater's analysis of rare words in the play, of which he identifies about 900, notes that a high proportion (over 100) of these are found in the letters and early poems of Oxford.[6]

(b) Tillyard (111) describes the play as "one of the most academic and intellectual of the Chronicle Plays". He quotes the King's address to the Black Prince (1.1 157–9; TLN 157–9):

> And, Ned, thou must begin
> Now to forget thy study and thy book
> And use thy shoulders to an armour's weight.

This is in keeping with the age and situation of the young Earl of Oxford and the advice given to him by Gabriel Harvey (*Gratulationum Valdensis*, 1578; quoted by Nelson, 181):

> England will discover in you its hereditary Achilles. Go, Mars will see you in safety . . . Your British numbers have been widely sung, while your Epistle testifies how much you excel in letters, being more courtly than Castiglione himself. . . But, O celebrated one, put away your pen, your bloodless books, your impractical writings. Now is the need of swords. Steel must be sharpened.

(c) Although Holinshed's first edition of the *Chronicles* was not published until 1577, it is very likely that Oxford had access to the same material, as both Holinshed and Oxford were attendant at Cecil House with Lord Burghley in the late 1560s and early 1570s (Nelson, 90–2).[7]

(d) The absence of clear attributions in any publication after that date may well make this a very early play indeed. There are no Italian influences at all, which might well put the play as early as 1573–4, before Oxford went to Italy. Alan Nelson (121–154), who does not accept Oxfordian authorship, recounts Oxford's visit to Italy in 1575–6.

(f) The 1596 Quarto was apparently set in type based on a manuscript with the same characteristics as Hand D: critics agree that many of these were very old fashioned by 1590: "Current in the 15th century but antiquated in the days of Elizabeth" (Sams, 216). These characteristics are set out *in extenso* by Sams (193–7; 214–217) and logically push the writing back a decade or two. A provincial wordsmith would make sure his writing would be in fashion or have his spelling modernised by the printer. Only a powerful person not affected by such matters would have his out-of-date peculiarities preserved as in the print of the 1596 Quarto of *Edward III.*

The play was previously rejected as unworthy of Shakespeare. Now we may think of it as an apprentice effort, revised later, perhaps by or with the help of Thomas Kyd in the early 1590s.

## Conclusion

The extant *Edward III* can be dated any time between 1589 and its registration in 1595. An early version may well have been composed in the 1570s.

## Notes

1. At the time of writing (November 2009), there is no edition available either in the Oxford Shakespeare series or in the Arden Shakespeare.
2. Thomas Snodham published the sixth edition of *The Rape of Lucrece* in 1616 but is not known to have published any other work of Shakespeare. He was mainly a printer of religious texts and died *c.* 1625, after the publication of the First Folio. See Chambers, *WS,* I 513 and Sasha Roberts, *Reading Shakespeare's Poems in early modern England* (2003).
3. As reported by *The Times* of London (12 October 2009), Sir Brian Vickers is now convinced that Shakespeare was involved in the composition of the play along with Kyd in the 40–60 ratio mentioned in the text. According to this article,

Jonathan Bate gave qualified support to the attribution but Stanley Wells remained sceptical over these findings. Vickers had suggesed Shakespeare's possible contribution to *Edward III* in *Shakespeare Co-Author*, 2002.

4. Neither W. G. Boswell-Stone, *Shakespeare's Holinshed* (1896) nor Geoffrey Bullough in his *Narrative and Dramatic Sources of Shakespeare's Plays* (1957–74) considers this play.
5. As reported by Melchiori (28) and Sams (164). For further details of these sea battles, see Hugh Bicheno, *Crescent and Cross,* 2004 (for Lepanto) and Garrett Mattingly, *Defeat of the Spanish Armada*, 1972: 281.
6. Nina Green, *Edward de Vere Newsletter,* 1994, No 60 www.oxford-shakespeare.com/Newsletters, accessed 5 November, 2009)
7. For Holinshed's dedication to Cecil, see Annabel Patterson, *Reading Holinshed's Chronicles* (1994: 279). Stuart Gillespie, *Shakespeare's Books* (2002: 279–80), points out that Shakespeare had used Froissart for many details about Richard II and about John of Gaunt.

## Other Cited Works


Anderson, Mark, *Shakespeare by Another Name*, New York: Gotham, 2005

Chambers, E. K., *The Elizabethan Stage*, 4 vols, Oxford: Clarendon, 1923

Chambers, E. K., *William Shakespeare A Study of Facts and Problems*, 2 vols, Oxford: Clarendon, 1930.

Godshalk, W. L., "Shakespeare's *Edward III", West Virginia Shakespeare and Renaissance Association Selected Papers* (SRASP), 21, 1998, accessed 5 November, 2009

Melchiori, Giorgio (ed.), *Edward III,* Cambridge: New Cambridge Shakespeare, 1998

Nelson, Alan, H., *Monstrous Adversary*, Liverpool: LUP, 2003

Sams, Eric (ed.), *Shakespeare's 'Edward III': an early play restored to the canon,* New Haven: Yale UP, 1996

Slater, Eliot, *The Problem of "The Reign of King Edward III": A Statistical Approach,* Cambridge: CUP, 1988

Tillyard, E. M. W., *Shakespeare's History Plays*, London: Chatto and Windus, 1944

Wells, Stanley & Gary Taylor, *William Shakespeare: A Textual Companion*, Oxford: OUP, 1987

40

# The Famous Victories of King Henry the fift

Ramón Jiménez

In this summary article, it is proposed that four plays about Prince Hal were written by the same man – Edward de Vere, seventeenth Earl of Oxford (1550–1604); that he wrote the first, *The Famous Victories,* at a very early age, possibly in his teens [i.e. by 1570]; that he revised this early play into three plays: *Henry IV Part 1, Henry IV Part 2* and *Henry* V. Further, it is argued that in his last Prince Hal play, *Henry V,* he responded extensively, with both humour and sarcasm, to criticism of the first three by a fellow courtier-poet, Sir Philip Sidney; and that he did all this by the spring of 1584.[1]

## Publication of *Famous Victories*

*The Famous Victories of Henry the fifth* was registered in 1594 (Chambers, *ES,* IV, 17):

> [SR 1594] 14 May. A book intituled, The famous victories of Henrye the Fyft, conteyninge the honorable battell of Agincourt. *Thomas Creede*

*Famous Victories* was published anonymously four years later, in the same year as *1 Henry IV* and *Henry V*:

> [Q1 1598] The Famous Victories of Henry the fifth: Containing the Honourable Battell of Agin-court. As it was plaide by the Queenes Maiesties Players. *Thomas Creede.*

Two years later, in 1600, *Henry IV Part 2* was published, the first of the Prince Hal plays to be attributed to Shakespeare. In that same year *The Chronicle History of Henry V* (i.e. Q1 of the play known as Shakespeare's) was published anonymously.

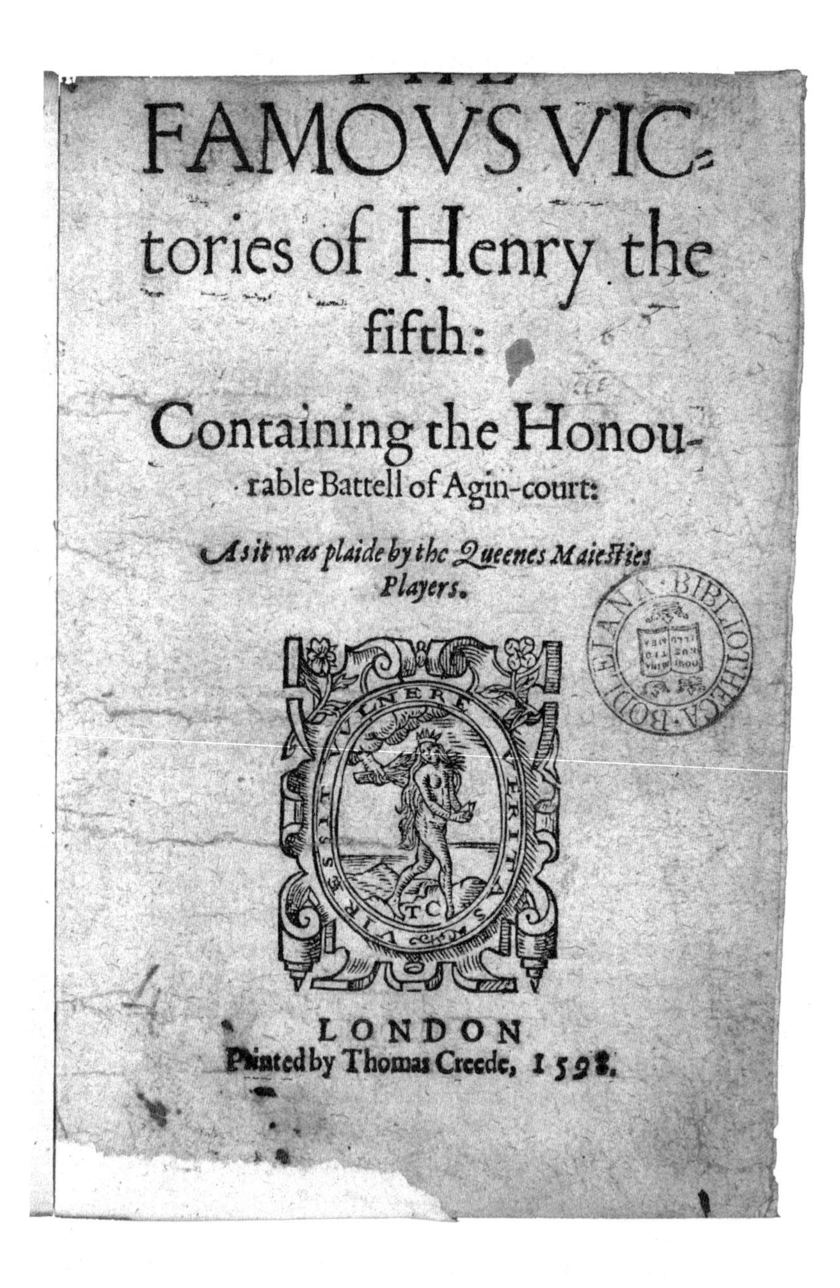

FAMOVS VIC-
tories of Henry the
fifth:

Containing the Honou-
rable Battell of Agin-court:

*As it was plaide by the Queenes Maiesties
Players.*

LONDON
Printed by Thomas Creede, 1598.



31 Title page to the anonymouse first quarto of *Famous Victories of Henry V*, 1598. It has generally been believed that this play was by another author but some scholars have argued that it was an early version by Shakespeare, later expanded into three plays: *1, 2 Henry IV* & *Henry V*. By permission of Bodleian Library, University of Oxford, shelfmark: Mal. 232 (4), title page.

*Famous Victories* was published again in Quarto in 1617:

> [Q2 1617] The Famous Victories of Henry the fifth: Containing the Honourable Battell of Agin-court. As it was acted by the Kings Maiesties Players. *Bernard Alsop.*

## Performance Date

There is no recorded performance, but the title page claims it had been played by the Queen's Men, (active in the 1580s and early 1590s). There seem to have been various plays about the reign of Henry V at this time. Richard Tarlton is recorded as performing in a Prince Hal play:

> At the [Red] Bull at Bishops-gate, was a play of Henry the fift, where in the judge was to take a box on the eare; and because he was absent that should take the blow, Tarlton himself, ever forward to please, took upon him to play the same judge, besides his owne part of the clowne: and Knell, then playing Henry the Fifth, hit Tarlton a sound box indeed, which made the people laugh the more because it was he, but anon the Judge goes in, and immediately Tarlton in his clown's clothes comes out, and asks the actors what news. "Ay," saith one, "hadst thou been here thou shouldst have seen Prince Henry hit the Judge a terrible box on the ear!" "What, man?" said Tarlton, "Strike a Judge?" "It is truth, in faith," said the other. "No other like," said Tarlton, "and it could not be but terrible to the Judge, when the report so terrifies me that methinks the blow remains still on my cheek, that it burns again." The people laughed at this mightily; and to this day I have heard it commended for rare. [2]

This performance must have preceded 3 September 1588, when Tarlton died. Since this play appears to cover the events in *FV* but which are spread across *Henry IV* and *Henry V*, it seems likely that Tarlton appeared in a version of *Famous Victories*. Another actor in this performance, William Knell, died in a duel in 1587, so *Famous Victories*, must date to 1587 at the latest.[3]

Another reference to a play about Henry V occurs in Thomas Nashe's *Piers Penniless* (1592):

> What a glorious thing it is to have Henry V represented on the stage, leading the French king prisoner and forcing both him and the Dauphin to swear fealty.[4]

Since this does not correspond precisely to the final scene in the extant versions of *Famous Victories* (or *Henry V*), Nashe's comment is taken to refer to a different play. Various commentators (e.g. Corbin & Sedge, Taylor), however, have taken the extant text of *Famous Victories* as "greatly debased" and derived "from a longer original". Thus it is possible that Nashe may have been referring in 1592 to a longer, original version of *Famous Victories* (or possibly an early version of *Henry V*). From 1595 to 1596, Henslowe's account book records 13 performances by the Admiral's Men of a 'ne' play he calls 'harey the v'. It is not clear whether 'ne' refers to a new play or if Henslowe is referring to a play already known. An inventory in 1598 of the company's apparel includes 'harye the v, velvet gowne'.

## Sources

Although most commentators assert that the author of *Famous Victories* used both Hall and Holinshed, the *FV* author could have obtained the historical knowledge mainly from Edward Hall, *The Union of the Two Noble and Illustre Famelies of Lancastre and Yorke* (1548–50) with some use of earlier chronicles. The play's title *The famous victories of Henrye the Fyft* recalls a similar chapter title in Hall: 'The victorious acts of King Henry the Fifth'.

Holinshed's *Chronicles* were first published in 1577 and then in an expanded second edition in 1587. There is an interesting connection with Ralph Holinshed: in the late 1560s, both Holinshed and Oxford were attendant at Cecil House, under the care of William Cecil. Holinshed served as a juryman on the inquest which cleared Oxford of manslaughter in 1567. He came to the help of Oxford again in 1573, when, apparently at the instigation of Cecil, he authored a pamphlet denying Oxford's complicity in a murder on Shooter's Hill, near Greenwich, in 1573 (Nelson, 48, 90–2). Thus, Oxford had a close intimacy with the author of the *Chronicles* (issued in 1577) and is likely to have had access to the same material as the historian.

## Relationship of *Famous Victories* to the *Henry IV–Henry V* trilogy.

*Famous Victories* contains about 1600 lines which modern editors have divided into 20 scenes. The *Henry IV–Henry V* trilogy contains approximately 7300 lines in 57 scenes. Each scene in *FV* corresponds to a scene in the trilogy and is used in the same sequence (see Table of Correspondences below). The relationship between the two plas may be explained in various ways:

### Table of Correspondences (after Bullough, vol IV)

| | **Scenes from *Famous Victories*** | ***1 Henry VI*** |
|---|---|---|
| i | Hal, Oldcastle & friends recount their robbery | 1.2; 2.1–3 |
| ii | Receivers search for the thieves | 2.5 |
| iii | King laments his sons antics | 1.1; 3.2 |
| iv | Trial of Gad's Hill robbers; Hal strikes LC Justice | Mock trial, 2.5 Allusion |

| | | |
|---|---|---|
| v | Oldcastle & Hal celebrate recent antics | 2.5 |
| vi | Hal is rebuked by the King | 3.2 |
| vii | Hal's friends argue at Boar's head | 3.3 |
| | | ***2 Henry IV*** |
| vii | Hal's friends argue at Boar's head | 2.4 |
| viii | Hal thinks King is dead; takes crown | 4.5 |
| ix | Hal makes LCJustice Protector; rejects old pals | 5.5 |
| | | ***Henry V*** |
| ix (contd) | Clergy explains Henry's claim; tennis balls | 1.2 |
| x | Three Army Recruits; Comic show of couple parting | 2.1; 2.3 |
| xi | French learn about their Ambassador in England | 2.4 |
| xii | Siege of Harfleur | 3.1–3 |
| xiii | French trying to learn English | 3.4 |
| xiv | Hal encourages his men & refuses to surrender | 4.3 |
| xv | Hal hears of victory; refers to Agincourt | 4.8 |
| xvi | Camp is attacked; cowards pretend to be French | 4.4 |
| xvii | Unheroic English clown brags about his own bravery | 4.4 |
| xviii | Wooing of Kate; Treaty | 5.2 |
| xix | Looting; discussion of life after war | 3.6; 5.1 |
| xx | Hal is made heir to French throne & engaged to Kate | 5.2 |

Four possible relationships between these plays have been proposed:

### (a) *Famous Victories* was derived from the Henry IV–Henry V trilogy

According to Cairncross, *FV* was a pirated copy (others have said it was a memorial reconstruction) of the *Henry IV–Henry V* trilogy, thus implying that the trilogy was written at least before 1594 (when *FV* was registered) and probably before 1588 (Tarlton's death). This would have implications in re-dating the *Henry IV–Henry V* trilogy to the mid 1580s at latest. It is very unlikely, however, that *Famous Victories* derived from the *Henry IV–Henry V* trilogy since *FV* omits some of the most memorable passages, neither developing the character of Oldcastle nor including Henry's most stirring speeches when king.

### (b) *Famous Victories* was written by another author; Shakespeare used it as a source

This is the majority view although there are variations: Chambers calls *FV* a minor source, whereas Dover Wilson, Bullough, and more recently Craik have asserted that it was a major source, as apparently does Taylor. They accept the striking similarities between the earlier play and the trilogy, following Greer who listed 15 plot elements and 42 specific details, e.g. 10 comic characters in each. Taylor notes that both plays omit Henry's second campaign (a major element in the *Chronicles*, 1417–20), but include the wooing scene between Henry and Katherine (not in the *Chronicles*).

**(c) Shakespeare wrote *Famous Victories* and later revised it**

In a full length monograph, Pitcher expanded Greer's list and argued a case for Shakespeare's authorship of *Famous Victories*, later expanded into the *Henry IV–Henry V* trilogy. He showed how many of the motifs in *FV* recur in other plays, among many others the stubborn porter (c.f. *Macbeth*) and the condescending use of the name 'Kate' (c.f. *The Taming of the Shrew*).

**(d) Oxford wrote *Famous Victories* and later revised it**

There are many connections between *Famous Victories* and the Earl of Oxford. On the title page, *FV* names the playing company as the Queen's Men, some of whom had been assembled from Oxford's own players in 1583. Secondly, both *FV* and *1 Henry IV* locate the robbery at Gad's Hill, near Rochester in Kent, although the source, the *First English Life of King Henry the Fifth* (published anonymously in 1513) did not specify a location. Oxford's own servants (and possibly himself) were involved in just such a highway robbery (which resulted in murder) in 1573 along the road to Rochester in Kent. A third argument in favour of Oxford's authorship of *FV* lies in the large and fictitious part accorded to Oxford's ancestor, Robert, eleventh earl of Oxford, who is portrayed as Henry IV's principal counsellor and as a wise, noble man.

## Orthodox Dating

The conventional dating for *Famous Victories* is usually pre 1587. McMillin and MacLean simply state that it was written before 1587; Pitcher, who argues for Shakespeare's authorship, places it *c.* 1586. Griffin says it may date back as far as 1577 (the first edition of Holinshed).[5]

## Oxfordian Dating

The usual Oxfordian position has been stated by Anderson (211): that Oxford began to write English Chronicle plays in earnest from 1586, when the Queen granted him an annuity of £1,000 for no other apparent reason. The theory is that, at a time of national crisis, Oxford was encouraged to write history plays to dramatise the dire consequences of dissension. Anderson also suggests that *Famous Victories* might well be earlier. It is likely that Oxford wrote *The Famous Victories* as a teenager, even before he began his legal studies in 1567 at Gray's Inn. This is borne out by the lack of legal references, the plain prose, flat characters, and clumsy action of the play – all reflecting the first efforts at playwriting by a very young nobleman who in the mid-1560s had only Latin classics and a few crude models in English to guide him.

By 1580, Oxford was running a playing company of men and another of boys. In 1583, leading members of the adult company, the Dutton brothers, were recruited to the newly formed Queen's Men (Nelson, 240–6). As it was usual for players to bring play-texts with them when they joined a new company, the Duttons may well have brought their text of *Famous Victories* to the Queen's Men at their formation.

The frequent appearance of the Chorus in *Henry V* to exhort the audience to use its imagination may have originated as a riposte to Philip Sidney, who in his *Defence of Poesy*, (*c.* 1581–3) had complained about the inadequacy of a theatre stage to represent grand events:

> By and by, we heare newes of a shipwracke in the same place, and then we are to blame if we accept it not for a Rock. Upon the backe of that, comes out a hidious Monster, with fire and smoke, and then the miserable beholders are bound to take it for a Cave. While in the meantime two Armies flye in, represented with foure swords and bucklers, and then what harde heart will not receive it for a pitched fielde? Now, of time they are much more liberall . . .

The demands of the Chorus in *Henry V* asking the audience to use their imagination would make little sense if the play were newly composed *c.* 1599, after so many other history plays had been written. It would be far more topical in the early 1580s when Sidney was making his critical remarks. This would appear to be the most likely time for the revision of the final section of *Famous Victories*.

## Notes

1. A detailed case for these proposals has been made in my longer article, pp 201–7 in '*The Famous Victories of Henry V* – Key to the Authorship Question?' in *Great Oxford* (ed. R. Malim, Parapress, 2004) and in an extended version at www.shakespearefellowship.org/virtualclassroom/jimenzhen5.htm, accessed 5 November, 2009.
2. *Tarlton's Jests* (from edition of 1613, Halliwell-Phillips, p24), quoted by Pitcher, 180.
3. Chambers, *ES*, II, 343, reports that Knell's widow, Rebecca was remarried on March 1588 (to John Hemming). McMillin and MacLean (89–90) report: "*Famous Victories* may be the earliest of extant English history plays among the professional companies."
4. For the quotation from *Pierce Pennilesse*, see *The Works of Thomas Nashe* (ed. R. B. McKerrow and F. P. Wilson, 1958) vol I, 123.
5. For further details, see Benjamin Griffin *Playing the Past: Approaches to English Historical Drama, 1385–1600*, (D. S. Brewer, Cambridge, 2001: 59). Griffin is not convinced by the claims for Oxfordian authorship.

## Other Cited Works

Anderson, Mark, *Shakespeare by Another Name*, New York: Gotham 2005
Cairncross, A. S., *The Problem of 'Hamlet': a solution*, London: MacMillan, 1936

Chambers, E. K. *The Elizabethan Stage*, 4 vols, Oxford: Clarendon, 1923
Chambers, E. K. *William Shakespeare: A Study of Facts and Problems*, 2 vols, Oxford: Clarendon, 1930
Corbin, Peter and Sedge, Douglas, *The Oldcastle Controversy*, Manchester: MUP, 1991
Craik, T. W. (ed.), *King Henry V*, The Arden Shakespeare, Third Series, London: Routledge, 1994
Greer, C. A., 'Shakespeare's Use of *The Famous Victories of Henry the Fifth' N&Q*, 1954; 199, 238–241
Jiménez, Ramón, "'Rebellion broachéd on his Sword': New Evidence of an Early Date for Henry V", *Shakespeare Oxford Newsletter*, V, 37, Fall 2001
McMillin, Scott, and MacLean, Sally-Beth, *The Queen's Men and their Plays*, Cambridge: CUP, 1998
Nelson, Alan, H., *Monstrous Adversary*, Liverpool: LUP, 2003
Pitcher, Seymour M., *The Case for Shakespeare's Authorship of The Famous Victories*, New York: State University of New York, 1961
Taylor, Gary, (ed.), *Henry V*, The Oxford Shakespeare, Oxford: OUP, 1982
Vickers, Brian, *Shakespeare Co-Author*, Oxford: OUP, 2002
Wilson, J. Dover (ed.), *King Henry IV Part 1, Part 2*, Cambridge: CUP, 1946
Wilson, J. Dover (ed.), *King Henry V*, Cambridge: CUP, 1947

# Conclusions and Inconclusions

## Kevin Gilvary

There is no contemporary evidence to date the composition of any play attributed to Shakespeare.

The 'scholarly consensus' about the chronology of Shakespeare's plays arose from the work of Edmund Malone in 1778 and was established by the time of Dowden in 1874. Most of this 'scholarly consensus' depended on conjecture about Shakespeare's artistic development, which cannot be sustained from the documentary record. As there is no evidence to tie any play to a particular date, every attempt to sequence the plays in order of composition is mere speculation. We do not know when the plays of Shakespeare were written, or in what order.

### Range of Dates for Each Play

Each play can only be dated within a range of years, between the source which provides the earliest possible date (the *terminus post quem*), and the latest possible date (the *terminus ante quem* or *ad quem*) established from a reference to a play (or possibly in a play). The widest date range appears to be 1579 – 1623 for *Coriolanus*, which was based on North's Plutarch (1579) but not mentioned until publication in the First Folio.

The narrowest date range seems to be for *The True Tragedy of Richard Duke of York* (*3 Henry VI*), its earliest date apparently based on Holinshed's *Chronicles* (second edition, 1587), and its latest date based on the the "Tygers hart" quotation in *Greene's Groatsworth of Wit* (1592). Even this date range is open to debate: while it has been established that the second edition of Holinshed was used for the F1 text of *3 Henry VI*, it is possible that the first edition of Holinshed (1577) might have been used for the quarto text, only to be revised. The question arises: how certain can we be that a particular text was used by Shakespeare as a source?

## Sources

Geoffrey Bullough identified Shakespeare's sources in his monumental eight-volume *Narrative and Dramatic Sources of Shakespeare* (1957–75), carefully distinguishing sources, which are texts used substantially for a play, from analogues (texts which are similar to Shakespeare's) and allusions. Since Bullough's work, a number of other sources have been identified.

One problem arises over the direction of influence. There are many cases where it is not clear whether Shakespeare's text is later than a possible source or earlier: which of them first made Richard II's queen (historically aged about 10 at the time of his deposition) into a mature and sympathetic royal consort? Shakespeare's *Richard II* or Samuel Daniel's *Civil Wars* (published 1595)? Some allusions, brief references to other texts, may have been added after the completion of a play, perhaps by an actor, e.g. the porter's reference to equivocation in *Macbeth*. There is also disagreement over whether some sources were actually used, most notably over whether Strachey's letter should definitely be considered a source for *The Tempest*.

## Allusions to the Plays

Publication gives a clear final date for a play (the only date for some plays, e.g. *Timon of Athens*, *All's Well*, which are not mentioned before their appearance in the First Folio). In 1598, Francis Meres referred to twelve plays of Shakespeare (eleven of which have been identified), but it is not clear whether he was referring to early or final versions of the plays nor, in some cases, whether he gave a complete list (as assumed by most commentators). See the Introduction for discussion on Meres.

There are doubts, moreover, concerning allusions to the plays, as to whether contemporaries are referring to works by Shakespeare or by other playwrights: a play about Hamlet was mentioned in 1589, and again in 1594, 1596 and *c.* 1599, but these references have generally been understood (on insubstantial grounds to do with the 'development' of Shakespeare's art) to refer to another work, a pre-Shakespearean play on the same subject. Similarly, Henslowe in 1594 refers to plays such as *The Mawe* and *A Wynnter Night's Pastime*, which might well be Shakespeare's *Othello* and *The Winter's Tale* (or early versions of them). Conversely, Thomas Platter describes a trip to see a play about the Emperor Julius Caesar in 1599, but it is by no means certain that he saw Shakespeare's *Julius Caesar* (nor that it had been recently finished). Similarly, there are two references to *Henry VIII* as a "new play" in 1613, but it is not clear whether these mean 'newly composed' or 'newly produced', 'newly revised' or simply that these witnesses were taken in by an impresario's lure thrown out to boost attendance: perhaps they were not experienced theatre-goers.

## Allusions to contemporary events and people

There are no named references in the plays of Shakespeare to contemporary people or events. The only reference to be taken as such occurs in the Chorus's speech before Act 5 of *Henry V* (in the Folio text; the Chorus does not feature in the quarto texts), referring to the pious hope of a triumphant return from Ireland of "the General of our gracious Empress". Neither the General nor the Empress is mentioned by name. The allusion to Queen Elizabeth seems unmistakeable but the reference to the "General", however, is not so clear; it is usually taken to refer to the Earl of Essex in 1599 but could refer to another general sent to Ireland by Elizabeth (see the chapters on *Henry V* and on *Famous Victories* for full discussion). As we are unable to give a precise date for *Henry V* or for any other play, it follows that we cannot identify for certain any allusion to contemporary people or events. All such allusions need to be proposed with caution.

## Early Plays?

As we cannot ascertain the order in which the plays were written, it is not possible to discuss the 'Development of Shakespeare's art' – except in a very speculative manner. There is no agreement over the title of Shakespeare's earliest play, nor in what genre it was likely to be classed. Various suggestions have been made: *Love's Labour's Lost* (Malone), *Comedy of Errors* (Bullough), *1 Henry VI* (Chambers, Riverside Shakespeare), *Two Gentlemen of Verona* (Wells & Taylor, Oxford Shakespeare; Greenblatt, Norton Shakespeare), *Titus Andronicus* (Hughes, New Cambridge Shakespeare). There have also been proponents of *2 Henry VI, King John* and *Taming of a Shrew* as the earliest play. Any such suggestion should be advanced as opinion (or whim).

## Late Plays?

Further consideration needs to be given to the possibility that the so-called Romances such as *Cymbeline, The Tempest* and *The Winter's Tale* might be early plays (possibly revised later). Since these plays are not apparently mentioned in any source until 1610–12, they have been assigned very late dates. Yet it is possible to argue (as implied by Carol Gesner) that they were composed at an early stage in the dramatist's career. *Cymbeline* contains a farcical scene in which every twist and turn of the plot is explained at length to a very dim-witted king, presumably for a similarly confused audience. It hardly shows the hand of an experienced playwright. *The Comedy of Errors* is taken to be an early play because it observes the classical unities of action, plot and stage. But the only other play in the Shakespeare canon to do this is *The Tempest,* which is taken to be a late play. *The Winter's Tale* contains references to the works of Greek Romance popular in the 1570s and 1580s.

## Development of Art and Style

It is not possible to trace the development of Shakespeare's dramatic art, metrical style or linguistic preferences, because none of his plays can be clearly designated early, middle or late. Thus the lofty idealism which prompted scholars such as Malone, Dowden, Chambers, Wells & Taylor to describe the "evolutionary trajectory" of Shakespeare's art, can only be described as well-intentioned speculation.

## Revision and Co-Authorship

There is no documentary evidence as to whether Shakespeare revised his own work or not, whether he worked concurrently on a number of texts, whether he left a text for a while and finished it after an intervening period, whether he worked alongside co-authors, whether he revised and expanded the works of others or whether others revised and expanded his works.

From Malone to the late twentieth century, it has often been assumed that Shakespeare produced one definitive text of a play and that variant texts (e.g. the so-called 'bad quartos') were the result of interference in the transmission of the text by the acting company and/or by other playwrights. There is no evidence of such assumptions about any play by Shakespeare. In 1986, Wells & Taylor accepted that the different texts of *King Lear* both had authorial authority. This change in attitudes towards revision has been extended to other works: in 2006, the recent Arden editors of *Hamlet* accepted that authorial revision was a possible explanation for there being three versions of the play.

Sir Brian Vickers has identified co-authorship in some works of Shakespeare by extensive comparison of stylistic preferences. Co-authorship might involve the playwrights working collaboratively or the texts might result from additional material being added to an earlier, shorter play. The evidence is insufficient to make a judgement about how co-authorship worked in practice.

## Status of Shorter Quartos

There is little original indication of the status of quartos beyond comments on the title pages, e.g. on the title page of *Romeo and Juliet* (Q2, 1599) the play is described as "newly corrected, augmented and amended". After the work of A. W. Pollard (1909), the notion of "bad" quartos was widely accepted, i.e. that the shorter versions published in quartos were the result of poor "memorial reconstruction" or touring "abridgement". However, it is now increasingly recognised as possible (or even likely) that the quartos represent earlier acting versions of the plays and that the longer versions, whether in a later quarto (e.g. Q2 *Hamlet*) or in the Folio (e.g. *Henry V*), were revised by the author and prepared for a reading audience (as argued by Lukas Erne).

## Anonymous Publications

Various plays were published anonymously in the 1590s which are not generally taken to be by Shakespeare, e.g. *Troublesome Raigne of King John, Tragedy of Richard III, Edward III, Taming of a Shrew, King Leir* as well as a play in manuscript known as the *Old Timon*. It is possible that these were Shakespeare's early acting versions of plays which were later revised.

## Authorship, Oxford & 1604

Those who believe that the plays ascribed to Shakespeare were in fact written by Edward de Vere, Earl of Oxford have provided the greatest challenge to the accepted dates of composition of the plays. These dates are considered in the individual chapters. The conclusions do not prove or disprove alternative claims to authorship. The findings merely demonstrate that each play can only be ascribed to a period within a range of dates, but that these may begin earlier than has previously been considered. No play has been found to date definitively after 1604, the year of Oxford's death.

## Final Comments

It is not wrong to hypothesise about the dates of Shakespeare's plays or to propose a possible sequence of composition. What is wrong is to advance a particular date (or sequence of composition) as established rather than conjectural. Such wild and fanciful speculation has been present from the earliest attempts to date the plays, as Samuel Schoenbaum (*Shakespeare's Lives*, 169) acknowledges, somewhat dismissively, in his comments about Malone:

> When he can find no evidence, [Malone] throws up his hands in despair and assigns a play to a year simply because that year would otherwise be blank and Shakespeare must have been continuously employed. Such is the case with *Coriolanus* (1609) and *Timon of Athens* (1610), for which objective evidence is depressingly scant.

Since the documentary evidence for dating *any* play of Shakespeare is "depressingly scant" some would claim absent, Schoenbaum's critical evaluation applies equally to many later scholars, editors, commentators and biographers.

# Appendix: Comparative Tables

# Table 1
# Date Range for Shakespeare's Plays

The earliest dates derive from identified sources used by Shakespeare. The latest dates derive from when the plays were published or allusions. The range of dates covers possible early versions.

| **Play** | **Date Range** | **Play** | **Date Range** |
|---|---|---|---|
| *Tempest* | 1580 – 1611 | *2 Henry VI* | 1587 – 1594 |
| *Two Gentlemen* | 1559 – 1598 | *3 Henry VI* | 1587 – 1592 |
| *Merry Wives* | 1558 – 1602 | *Richard III* | 1587 – 1597 |
| *Measure* | 1580 – 1604 | *Henry VIII* | 1583 – 1613 |
| *Comedy of Errors* | 1566 – 1594 | *Troilus* | 1581 – 1609 |
| *Much Ado* | 1583 – 1600 | *Coriolanus* | 1579 – 1623 |
| *Love's Labour's Lost* | 1578 – 1598 | *Titus* | 1579 – 1594 |
| *Midsummer N D* | 1585 – 1598 | *Romeo* | 1562 – 1597 |
| *Merchant* | 1558 – 1598 | *Timon* | 1579 – 1623 |
| *As You Like It* | 1590 – 1600 | *Julius Caesar* | 1579 – 1599 |
| *Taming of the Shrew* | 1579 – 1598 | *Macbeth* | 1587 – 1611 |
| *All's Well* | 1567 – 1623 | *Hamlet* | 1586 – 1602 |
| *Twelfth Night* | 1581 – 1602 | *King Lear* | 1590 – 1606 |
| *Winter's Tale* | 1588 – 1611 | *Othello* | 1584 – 1604 |
| *King John* | 1587 – 1598 | *Antony* | 1579 – 1608 |
| *Richard II* | 1587 – 1597 | *Cymbeline* | 1579 – 1611 |
| *1 Henry IV* | 1587 – 1598 | *Pericles* | 1576 – 1609 |
| *2 Henry IV* | 1587 – 1600 | *Two Noble Kinsmen* | 1566 - 1614 |
| *Henry V* | 1577 – 1600 | *Edward III* | 1577 – 1595 |
| *1 Henry VI* | 1587 – 1592 | *Famous Victories* | 1577 – 1594 |

# Table 2
# Deviation from Chambers's Proposed Dates (1930)

In 1778, Edmond Malone made the first attempt to gives dates and a chronology to the works of Shakespeare. Edward Dowden's *Critical Study* of 1875 followed Malone and incorporated some further findings. In 1930 Sir Edmund Chambers made the definitive study of the dates and chronology of Shakespeare's plays, to a large extent following Dowden. Most scholars have followed Chambers, as shown by Halliday (*Companion to Shakespeare*) and Wells & Taylor (*Oxford Shakespeare*).

## a) Comedies

| Play | Malone 1778 | Chambers 1930 | Halliday 1952 | W&T 1986 |
|---|---|---|---|---|
| *Tempest* | = | 1611–12 | = | = |
| *Two Gentlemen* | -1 | 1594–95 | = | -4 |
| *Merry Wives* | = | 1600–01 | -1 | -3 |
| *Measure* | -1 | 1604–05 | = | -1 |
| *Comedy of Errors* | +4 | 1592–93 | = | +1 |
| *Much Ado* | +1 | 1598–99 | = | = |
| *Love's Labours Lost* | -3 | 1594–95 | = | = |
| *Midsummer Night's Dream* | = | 1595–96 | = | = |
| *Merchant* | +1 | 1596–97 | = | = |
| *As You Like It* | = | 1599–1600 | = | = |
| *Taming of the Shrew* | +12 | 1593–94 | = | -3 |
| *All's Well* | -4 | 1602–03 | = | +2 |
| *Twelfth Night* | +14 | 1599–1600 | = | +1 |
| *Winter's Tale* | -16 | 1610–11 | | = |
| | Ave. 4 yrs | | | Ave. 1 yr |

## b) Histories

| Play | Malone | Chambers 1930 | Halliday 1952 | W&T 1986 |
|---|---|---|---|---|
| *King John* | = | 1596–97 | = | = |
| *Richard II* | +1 | 1595–96 | = | = |
| *1 Henry IV* | = | 1597–98 | = | -1 |
| *2 Henry IV* | = | 1597–98 | = | = |
| *Henry V* | = | 1598–99 | = | = |
| *1 Henry VI* | = | 1591–92 | = | = |
| *2 Henry VI* | = | 1590–91 | = | = |
| *3 Henry VI* | +1 | 1590–91 | = | = |
| *Richard III* | +5 | 1592–93 | = | = |
| *Henry VIII* | -11 | 1612–13 | = | = |
| | Ave. 1½ yrs | | Ave. 0 yrs | Ave. 0 yrs |

## c) Tragedies

| Play | Malone | Chambers 1930 | Halliday 1952 | W&T 1986 |
|---|---|---|---|---|
| *Troilus* | = | 1601–92 | = | = |
| *Coriolanus* | +1 | 1607–08 | = | = |
| *Titus* | -4 | 1593–94 | -1 | -1 |
| *Romeo and Juliet* | = | 1594–95 | = | = |
| *Timon* | +2 | 1607–08 | = | -2 |
| *Julius Caesar* | +4 | 1599–1600 | = | = |
| *Macbeth* | = | 1605–06 | = | = |
| *Hamlet* | -5 | 1600–01 | = | = |
| *King Lear* | = | 1605–06 | = | = |
| *Othello* | -6 | 1604–05 | = | -1 |
| *Antony and Cleopatra* | -1 | 1606–07 | = | = |
| *Cymbeline* | -6 | 1609–10 | = | = |
| | Ave. 2 yrs | | Ave. 0 yrs | Ave. 0 yrs |

# Table 3

## Materials and sources for dating the Comedies

| Play | Listed in Stationers' Register | First recorded performances at venue | | |
|---|---|---|---|---|
| | | At Court | Playhouse | Private |
| *Tempest* | 1623 | 1 Nov 1611 | | |
| *Two Gentlemen* | 1623 | | | |
| *Merry Wives* | 1602 | Whitehall 4 Nov 1604 | | |
| *Measure for Measure* | 1623 | | | |
| *Comedy of Errors* | 1623 | 1604 | | |
| *Much Ado* | 1600 | Twice 1612–1613 | *Sundrie times* publicly pre-1600 | |
| *Love's Labours Lost* | 1607 | Xmas 1597–1598 | | Between 8-15 April 1605 |
| *Midsummer Night's Dream* | 1600 | 1604 | *Sundrie times* publicly pre-1600 | |
| *Merchant of Venice* | 1598 | 10–12 Feb 1605 | | |
| *As You Like It* | 1600 | | | Wilton House 2 Dec 1603 |
| *Taming of the Shrew* | *A Shrew* 1594 | | (?) 13 Jun 1594 | |
| *All's Well* | 1623 | | | |
| *Twelfth Night* | 1623 | | | |
| *Winter's Tale* | 1623 | (Revels) 5 Nov 1611 | Globe 15 May 1611 | |

| First recorded perfs at venue | | Mentioned by | | First publication | |
|---|---|---|---|---|---|
| Inns of Court | Unknown | Records/ Individuals | Meres in 1598 | Quarto | Folio |
| | | Revels 1 Nov 1611 | | | 1623 |
| | | | yes | | 1623 |
| | *Divers times* by 1602 | Revels 4 Nov 1604 | | 1602 | |
| | In the Hall 26 Dec 1604 | | | | 1623 |
| Gray's Inn 28 Dec 1594 | | Revels 1604 | yes | | 1623 |
| | | | | 1600 | |
| | | Revels 1605 | yes | 1598 | |
| | | Dudley Carleton 15 Jan 1604 | yes | 1600 | |
| | | Revels 1605 | yes | 1600 | |
| | *Divers times* by 1602 | | | | 1623 |
| | | Henslowe 13 Jun 1594 | | ? 1594 | 1623 |
| | | | | | 1623 |
| Middle Temple 2 Feb 1602 | | Manningham 2 Feb 1602 | | | 1623 |
| | | Forman 1611 | | | 1623 |

# Table 4

## Materials and sources for dating the Histories

| Play | First recorded performances at venue | | | |
|---|---|---|---|---|
| | At Court | Playhouse | Private | Inns of Court |
| *King John* | no | no | no | no |
| *Richard II* | no | Globe 7 Feb 1601; frequently | Sir E Hoby's house Dec 1595 ? | no |
| *1 Henry IV* | The Hotspur 1612 | Frequently ? | no | no |
| *2 Henry IV* | Sir J Falstaffe 1612 | Frequently ? | no | no |
| *Henry V* | Revels 7 Jan1605 | ? Globe | no | no |
| *1 Henry VI* | no | no | no | no |
| *2 Henry VI* | no | no | no | no |
| *3 Henry VI* | no | no | no | no |
| *Richard III* | no | no | no | no |
| *Henry VIII* | no | 29 Jun 1613 | no | no |

| **First recorded performance at venue** | **Mentioned by** | | **First publication** | | |
|---|---|---|---|---|---|
| **Unknown** | **Records/ Individuals** | **Meres in 1598** | **SR** | **Quarto** | **Folio** |
| no | no | yes | no | ?1591 | 1623 |
| On ship 30 Sep 1607 | Journal of Capt W Keeling 30 Sep 1607 | yes | 1597 | 1597, 1598 | |
| 6 Mar 1600 | no | yes | 598 | 1598 | |
| *Sundrie times* Pre 1600 | no | ? | 1600 | 1600 | |
| *Sundrie times* Pre 1600 | no | no | 1600 | 1600 | |
| Nashe 3 Mar 1592 | ? Henslowe's diary 1591 | no | 1623 | 1600 | |
| no | ? Henslowe's diary 1591 | no | 1594 | 1594 | |
| *Sundrie times* Sep 1595 | Greene's parody 1592 | no | 1602 | 1595 | |
| ? 30 Dec 1593 | ? Henslowe's *Buckingham* | yes | 1597 | 1597 | |
| no | Wotton 1613 | no | 1623 | | 1623 |

# Table 5

## Materials and sources for dating the Tragedies

| Play | First recorded performance at venue | | | |
|---|---|---|---|---|
| | **Royal Court** | **Playhouse** | **Private** | **Inns of Court** |
| *Troilus* | no | no | no | no |
| *Coriolanus* | no | no | no | no |
| *Titus* | no | ? Henslowe Jun 1594 | no | no |
| *Romeo and Juliet* | no | Curtain, Globe (Q3) | no | no |
| *Timon* | no | no | no | no |
| *Julius Caesar* | *C's tragedie* 1612-1613 | ? Bankside 21 Sep 1599 | no | no |
| *Macbeth* | no | Globe 20 Apr 1611 | no | no |
| *Hamlet* | ?1619 | no | On board 1607 | no |
| *King Lear* | Whitehall Dec 1606 | no | no | no |
| *Othello* | Whitehall 1604 | Globe 30 Apr 1610 | no | no |
| *Antony and Cleopatra* | no | no | no | no |
| *Cymbeline* | no | ?Globe, 1611 | no | no |

| 1st recorded performance | Mentioned by/in | | | First Publication | |
|---|---|---|---|---|---|
| **Unknown** | **Records/ Individuals** | **Meres in 1598** | **SR** | **Quarto** | **Folio** |
| no | no | no | 1603 | 1609 | |
| no | no | no | 1623 | | 1623 |
| 11 Apr 1592 1593 1600 1611 | *A Knack*, 1592 Peacham MS; ? 1584-9 *B Fair* | yes | 1594 | 1594 | |
| *Played often* by 1597 | Marston for ref at Curtain | yes | 1607 | 1597 | |
| no | no | no | 1623 | | 1623 |
| no | no | no | 1623 | | 1623 |
| no | Forman, 1611 | no | 1623 | | 1623 |
| Oxf/Cam by 1602 | 1589, 1594 1596 | no | 1602 | 1603 | |
| no | no | no | 1607 | 1608 | |
| no | Henslowe, 1594 ? | no | 1621 | 1622 | |
| no | no | no | 1608 | | 1623 |
| no | Forman, 1611 | no | 1623 | | 1623 |

# Table 6a
# Metrical Tables (after E. K. Chambers, 1930)

Various attempts were made in the nineteenth century to use some of the following data, e.g. proportion of rhyme, to establish an order of chronology. However, such tests are largely ignored by modern scholars as unhelpful. For detailed consideration, see the Introduction

| | Line Total | prose | rhyme | blank | verse |
|---|---|---|---|---|---|
| *Tempest* | 2062 | 464 | 64 | 1445 | 1509 |
| *Two Gentlemen* | 2292 | 654 | 128 | 1510 | 1638 |
| *Merry Wives* | 3018 | 2664 | 26 | 214 | 240 |
| *Measure for Measure* | 2820 | 1154 | 89 | 1577 | 1666 |
| *Comedy of Errors* | 1777 | 244 | 378 | 1155 | 1533 |
| *Much Ado* | 2825 | 2105 | 76 | 644 | 720 |
| *Love's Labour's Lost* | 2785 | 1051 | 1150 | 584 | 1734 |
| *Midsummer N Dream* | 2174 | 470 | 798 | 746 | 1544 |
| *Merchant of Venice* | 2658 | 633 | 142 | 1883 | 2025 |
| *As You Like It* | 2856 | 1659 | 217 | 926 | 1143 |
| *Taming of the Shrew* | 1443 | 321 | 38 | 1084 | 1122 |
| *All's Well* | 2966 | 1478 | 279 | 1203 | 1482 |
| *Twelfth Night* | 2690 | 1752 | 176 | 762 | 938 |
| *Winter's Tale* | 3074 | 876 | 59 | 2107 | 2166 |
| *King John* | 2570 | 0 | 132 | 2438 | 2570 |
| *Richard II* | 2757 | 0 | 529 | 2228 | 2757 |
| *1 Henry IV* | 3116 | 1493 | 76 | 1607 | 1683 |
| *2 Henry IV* | 3446 | 1813 | 72 | 1420 | 1492 |
| *Henry V* | 3381 | 1440 | 58 | 1504 | 1562 |
| *1 Henry VI* | 2677 | 2 | 318 | 2357 | 2675 |
| *2 Henry VI* | 3162 | 551 | 96 | 2515 | 2611 |
| *3 Henry VI* | 2904 | 3 | 128 | 2773 | 2901 |
| *Richard III* | 3619 | 83 | 152 | 3384 | 3536 |
| *Henry VIII* | 2796 | 7 | 6 | 1154 | 1160 |
| *Troilus* | 3496 | 1188 | 186 | 2065 | 2251 |
| *Coriolanus* | 3406 | 829 | 28 | 2549 | 2577 |
| *Titus Andronicus* | 2523 | 41 | 130 | 2523 | 2653 |
| *Romeo and Juliet* | 3050 | 455 | 466 | 2101 | 2567 |
| *Timon of Athens* | 2374 | 701 | 64 | 1445 | 1509 |
| *Julius Caesar* | 2477 | 176 | 32 | 2269 | 2301 |
| *Macbeth* | 2106 | 158 | 108 | 1692 | 1800 |
| *Hamlet* | 3929 | 1211 | 135 | 2444 | 2579 |
| *King Lear* | 3328 | 925 | 169 | 2234 | 2403 |
| *Othello* | 3316 | 685 | 103 | 2528 | 2631 |
| *Antony and Cleopatra* | 3059 | 287 | 40 | 2732 | 2772 |
| *Cymbeline* | 3339 | 526 | 122 | 2607 | 2729 |
| *Pericles* | 2215 | 337 | 22 | 781 | 803 |
| *Two Noble Kinsmen* | 1131 | 57 | 24 | 1050 | 1074 |

# Table 6b

## Metrical Tables (after E. K. Chambers, 1930)

| | fem | light | weak | split | Unsplit + pause |
|---|---|---|---|---|---|
| *Tempest* | 334 | 16 | 5 | 227 | 481 |
| *Two Gentlemen* | 269 | 0 | 0 | 43 | 174 |
| *Merry Wives* | 54 | 1 | 0 | 9 | 41 |
| *Measure for Measure* | 377 | 7 | 0 | 148 | 398 |
| *Comedy of Errors* | 198 | 0 | 0 | 8 | 171 |
| *Much Ado* | 145 | 1 | 1 | 35 | 126 |
| *Love's Labour's Lost* | 26 | 3 | 0 | 11 | 79 |
| *Midsummer N Dream* | 59 | 0 | 1 | 28 | 131 |
| *Merchant of Venice* | 325 | 6 | 1 | 79 | 369 |
| *As You Like It* | 230 | 2 | 0 | 34 | 177 |
| *Taming of the Shrew* | 208 | 0 | 0 | 21 | 194 |
| *All's Well* | 349 | 11 | 2 | 138 | 316 |
| *Twelfth Night* | 167 | 3 | 1 | 44 | 164 |
| *Winter's Tale* | 675 | 57 | 43 | 330 | 699 |
| *King John* | 151 | 7 | 0 | 64 | 357 |
| *Richard II* | 258 | 4 | 0 | 34 | 293 |
| *1 Henry IV* | 92 | 5 | 2 | 43 | 235 |
| *2 Henry IV* | 221 | 1 | 0 | 43 | 208 |
| *Henry V* | 336 | 2 | 0 | 31 | 219 |
| *1 Henry VI* | 191 | 3 | 1 | 17 | 233 |
| *2 Henry VI* | 332 | 2 | 1 | 13 | 270 |
| *3 Henry VI* | 366 | 3 | 0 | 8 | 340 |
| *Richard III* | 638 | 4 | 0 | 66 | 423 |
| *Henry VIII* | 334 | 45 | 37 | 179 | 437 |
| *Troilus* | 463 | 6 | 0 | 133 | 439 |
| *Coriolanus* | 710 | 60 | 44 | 394 | 749 |
| *Titus Andronicus* | 200 | 5 | 0 | 17 | 303 |
| *Romeo and Juliet* | 168 | 6 | 1 | 71 | 496 |
| *Timon of Athens* | 472 | 42 | 25 | 145 | 404 |
| *Julius Caesar* | 413 | 10 | 0 | 129 | 437 |
| *Macbeth* | 420 | 21 | 2 | 246 | 494 |
| *Hamlet* | 528 | 8 | 0 | 194 | 552 |
| *King Lear* | 580 | 5 | 1 | 243 | 691 |
| *Othello* | 679 | 2 | 8 | 268 | 694 |
| *Antony and Cleopatra* | 666 | 71 | 28 | 470 | 935 |
| *Cymbeline* | 799 | 78 | 52 | 393 | 1027 |
| *Pericles* | 171 | 15 | 5 | 84 | 209 |
| *Two Noble Kinsmen* | 312 | 50 | 34 | 124 | 401 |

# Table 7a

## Colloquialisms in verse (after Wells & Taylor, 1987)

| | 't | i'th' | o'th' | th' | 'em |
|---|---|---|---|---|---|
| *Tempest* | 31 | 13 | 20 | 24 | 16 |
| *Two Gentlemen* | 5 | - | - | 3 | 11 |
| *Merry Wives* | 1 | 2 | - | 2 | - |
| *Measure for Measure* | 27 | 5 | 1 | 23 | - |
| *Comedy of Errors* | 1 | 1 | - | 3 | - |
| *Much Ado* | 2 | - | - | 1 | - |
| *Love's Labour's Lost* | 7 | 1 | - | 7 | - |
| *Midsummer N Dream* | 4 | 1 | - | 2 | - |
| *Merchant of Venice* | 3 | 1 | - | 2 | - |
| *As You Like It* | 2 | 2 | - | 5 | - |
| *Taming of the Shrew* | 15 | 1 | 1 | - | 2 |
| *All's Well* | 30 | 6 | - | 19 | - |
| *Twelfth Night* | 9 | 1 | 1 | 5 | - |
| *Winter's Tale* | 90 | 16 | 21 | 36 | 2 |
| *King John* | 7 | 1 | - | 7 | - |
| *Richard II* | 5 | - | - | 1 | - |
| *1 Henry IV* | 3 | - | - | 1 | - |
| *2 Henry IV* | 2 | - | - | 1 | - |
| *Henry V* | 3 | 2 | - | 22 | 1 |
| *1 Henry VI* | 4 | - | - | 4 | - |
| *Contention* | 25 | 1 | 1 | 5 | - |
| *Duke of York* | 7 | - | - | 3 | - |
| *Richard III* | 6 | - | - | 10 | - |
| *Henry VIII* | 47 | 18 | 24 | 45 | 57 |
| *Troilus* | 1 | 4 | - | 18 | - |
| *Coriolanus* | 56 | 31 | 13 | 103 | 12 |
| *Titus Andronicus* | 1 | - | - | 2 | - |
| *Romeo and Juliet* | 11 | - | - | 7 | - |
| *Timon of Athens* | 44 | 3 | 8 | 28 | 11 |
| *Julius Caesar* | 6 | 1 | - | 4 | 6 |
| *Macbeth* | 40 | 14 | 13 | 31 | 5 |
| *Hamlet* | 61 | 8 | 1 | 42 | - |
| *Lear (Q)* | 37 | 12 | 5 | 12 | 2 |
| *Othello* | 83 | 4 | 6 | 23 | - |
| *Antony and Cleopatra* | 76 | 24 | 18 | 34 | 3 |
| *Cymbeline* | 68 | 20 | 36 | 52 | 1 |
| *Pericles* | 28 | 3 | - | 12 | 1 |
| *Two Noble Kinsmen* | 55 | 19 | 30 | 36 | 52 |

Wells & Taylor include over 20 colloquialisms in verse which, they believe, indicates an unconscious change in the author's style over time

# Table 7b

## Colloquialisms in verse (after Wells & Taylor, 1987)

| | 'll | d/'ld | 'lt/'t | 'a'/ha' | a' |
|---|---|---|---|---|---|
| *Tempest* | 8 | 2 | | | |
| *Two Gentlemen* | - | 2 | - | - | - |
| *Merry Wives* | 9 | - | - | - | - |
| *Measure for Measure* | 9 | 5 | - | - | - |
| *Comedy of Errors* | 12 | - | - | - | 3 |
| *Much Ado* | 6 | - | - | - | - |
| *Love's Labour's Lost* | 6 | - | - | 1 | 4 |
| *Midsummer N Dream* | 11 | - | - | - | - |
| *Merchant of Venice* | 9 | - | 1 | - | - |
| *As You Like It* | 13 | - | - | - | - |
| *Taming of the Shrew* | 17 | - | - | 2 | 4 |
| *All's Well* | 11 | 2 | | | 4 |
| *Twelfth Night* | 3 | 1 | - | - | - |
| *Winter's Tale* | 20 | 12 | | 2 | |
| *King John* | 6 | 1 | - | - | - |
| *Richard II* | 7 | - | - | - | 3 |
| *1 Henry IV* | 8 | - | - | - | 1 |
| *2 Henry IV* | 1 | - | - | - | - |
| *Henry V* | 18 | - | - | - | 2 |
| *1 Henry VI* | 18 | - | - | - | 1 |
| *Contention* | 19 | - | - | - | 1 |
| *Duke of York* | 27 | 1 | - | - | 1 |
| *Richard III* | 4 | - | - | - | - |
| *Henry VIII* | 15 | 3 | | 1 | 2 |
| *Troilus* | 18 | 5 | 1 | - | 1 |
| *Coriolanus* | 34 | 10 | 1 | 1 | 24 |
| *Titus (S)* | 12 | - | 1 | - | - |
| *Romeo and Juliet* | 15 | - | - | - | 8 |
| *Timon (S)* | 9 | 7 | 3 | | 3 |
| *Julius Caesar* | 13 | - | - | 1 | - |
| *Macbeth* | 13 | 2 | 1 | | |
| *Hamlet* | 12 | - | 2 | 3 | 3 |
| *Lear (Q)* | 14 | 11 | 2 | | 1 |
| *Othello* | 15 | 7 | | | |
| *Antony and Cleopatra* | 24 | 2 | | 2 | 2 |
| *Cymbeline* | 3 1 | 8 | 2 | 1 | |
| *Pericles (S)* | 22 | 4 | | | 4 |
| *Two Noble Kinsmen* | 35 | 2 | | | 1 |

Wells & Taylor ignore differences in spelling (e.g. *o'th'*,), occurrences of *'tis, 'twas,* and *'twere,* contractions of *I'll* and of 'is' after *here, there, where, what, that, how, he, she,* and *who.*

# Table 8

## Publication of Quartos & an Octavo

| | Anonymous | Attributed to Shakespeare | Title in First Folio |
|---|---|---|---|
| 1591 | *Q1 Troublesome Raigne of King John* | | *? The Life and Death of King John* |
| 1592 | | | |
| 1593 | | | |
| 1594 | *Q1 Titus Andronicus*<br>*Q1 Contention*<br>*Q1 True Tragedie of Richard III*<br>*Q1 Taming of a Shrew* | | *Titus Andronicus*<br>*2 Henry VI*<br>*? Richard III*<br>*? Taming of the Shrew* |
| 1595 | *O1 True Tragedie of Richard Duke of York* | | *3 Henry VI* |
| 1596 | *Q1 Edward III*<br>*Q2 Taming of a Shrew* | | |
| 1597 | *Q1 Richard II,*<br>*Q1 Richard III*<br>*Q1 Romeo and Juliet* | *(? Love's Labour's Lost)* | *Richard II,*<br>*Richard III*<br>*Romeo and Juliet*<br>*Love's Labour's Lost* |
| 1598 | *Q1 Henry IV*<br>*Q1 Famous Victories of Henry V* | *Q1 Love's Labour's Lost*<br>*Q2 1 Henry IV*<br>*Q2, Q3 Richard II,*<br>*Q2 Richard III* | *Love's Labour's Lost*<br>*1 Henry IV*<br>*? Henry V* |
| 1599 | *Q2 Edward III*<br>*Q2 Romeo and Juliet* | *Q3 1 Henry IV* | |
| 1600 | *Q1 Henry V*<br>*Q2 Contention,*<br>*Q2 True Tragedie of Richard Duke of York*<br>*Q2 Titus Andronicus* | *Q1 2 Henry IV,*<br>*Q1 MND,*<br>*Q1 MV,*<br>*Q Much Ado* | *2 Henry IV*<br>*Henry V*<br>*MND*<br>*Merchant of Venice,*<br>*Much Ado* |
| 1601 | | | |
| 1602 | *Q2 Henry V* | *Q1 MWW,*<br>*Q3 Richard III* | *Merry Wives of Windsor* |
| 1603 | | *Q1 Hamlet* | *Hamlet* |
| 1604 | | *Q2 Hamlet,*<br>*Q2 1 Henry IV* | |

| | Anonymous | Attributed to Shakespeare | Title in First Folio |
|---|---|---|---|
| 1605 | *Q Chronicle History of King Leir* | *Q4 Richard III* | *? Tragedy of King Lear* |
| 1606 | | | |
| 1607 | *Q3, Q4 Taming of a Shrew* | | |
| 1608 | | *Q1 Chronicle History of King Leir*<br>*Q4 Richard II*<br>*Q5 1 Henry IV* | *Tragedy of King Lear* |
| 1609 | *Q3 Romeo and Juliet* | *Q1, Troilus*<br>*Q1, Q2 Pericles* | *Troilus & Cressida* |
| 1610 | | | |
| 1611 | *Q2 Troublesome Raigne,*<br>*Q3 Titus Andronicus* | *Q3 Hamlet*<br>*Q3 Pericles* | |
| 1612 | | *Q5 Richard III* | |
| 1613 | | *Q6 1 Henry IV* | |
| 1614 | | | |
| 1615 | | *Q5 Richard II* | |
| 1616 | | | |
| 1617 | *Q2 Famous Victories of Henry V* | | |
| 1618 | | | |
| 1619 | *Q3 Henry V (carries date 1608)* | *Pavier Quartos: Contention, True Tragedie, Pericles, Merry Wives, Merchant, Lear, MND, etc.* | |
| 1620 | | | |
| 1621 | | | |
| 1622 | | *Q1 Othello*<br>*Q6 Richard III*<br>*Q7 1 Henry IV*<br>*Q3 Troublesome Raigne*<br>*Q4 Hamlet ?*<br>*Q4 Romeo?* | *Othello* |
| 1623 | | | *First Folio (36 plays)* |
| 1634 | | *Two Noble Kinsmen* | |

# Index

Dates of plays generally refer to first publications or earliest known performances, not necessarily to the dates of composition. Page numbers in **bold** type refer to the chapter concerning the individual play.